Encompassing Gender

Encompassing Gender

Integrating International Studies and Women's Studies

Edited by Mary M. Lay, Janice Monk, and Deborah S. Rosenfelt

THE FEMINIST PRESS
AT THE CITY UNIVERSITY OF NEW YORK
NEW YORK

Published by the Feminist Press at the City University of New York
The Graduate Center, 365 Fifth Avenue, Suite 5406, New York, NY 10016
feministpress.org
First edition, 2002

Portions of this book originally appeared in *Women's Studies Quarterly*
26, nos. 3 and 4 (Fall/Winter 1998). The essay "What Counts? Critical
Analysis of Statistical Indicators" by Janice Monk originally appeared, in
slightly different form, in "Engendering a New Geographic Vision,"
Teaching Geography for a Better World, edited by John Fien and Rod
Gerber (Edinburgh: Oliver & Boyd, 1988). Also reprinted in Kathleen
Staudt, *Managing Development: State, Society, and International
Contexts* (Newbury Park, Calif.: Sage, 1991).

Encompassing gender : integrating international studies and women's
studies / edited by Mary M. Lay, Janice Monk, and Deborah S. Rosenfelt.—
1st ed.
        p. cm.
Includes bibliographical references and index.
ISBN 1-55861-269-6 (pb : alk. paper) — ISBN 1-55861-268-8 (hc : alk.
paper)
    1. Women's studies. 2. Cross-cultural studies. 3. International rela-
tions—Study and teaching. 4. Interdisciplinary approach in education. I.
Lay, Mary M. II. Monk, Janice J. III. Rosenfelt, Deborah Silverton.

HQ1180 .E53 2002
305.4'07—dc21

                                                              2002020624

This publication is made possible, in part, by a generous grant from The
Ford Foundation.

Text design and typesetting by Dayna Navaro
Printed on acid-free paper by Transcontinental Printing.
Manufactured in Canada.

09 08 07 06 05 04 03 02   6 5 4 3 2 1

The Feminist Press
dedicates this book
to the memory of
SUE ROSENBERG ZALK,
1945–2001,
psychologist, educator, scholar, activist,
member and secretary of the
Board of Directors of the Feminist Press.

This tribute is made possible
by her colleagues and friends
Mariam K. Chamberlain, Florence Howe, and Alida Brill,
who have generously supported this book
to honor her life and work.

CONTENTS

PART 3. CURRICULAR RESOURCES: STRATEGIES FOR CHANGE

PREFACE

More than ever, the world needs the voices and visions of a transnational community of feminist scholars, teachers, and activists, as they analyze the relations of power, privilege, and oppression that threaten the lives of so many; as they explore and model alternatives to violence; and as they envisage and work for social justice. This book is part of an effort to build and sustain such a community, even across the acknowledged borders—geographic, class, cultural, disciplinary—that divide it.

The feminist scholars and teachers who have contributed their ideas and documented their classroom experiences for this collection speak from various institutional, regional, and disciplinary locations, most from within the United States but many from perspectives shaped in other countries of origin. It is cumulatively rather than individually that their work "encompasses gender," a category always inflected across the many other dimensions of difference. In editing the essays, syllabi, and bibliographies included in this volume, we made no effort to standardize their styles. The syllabi in particular represent historical documents and convey a genuine sense of classroom life.

We are grateful to The Ford Foundation, which provided funding for the Women's Studies, Area and International Studies (WSAIS) Curriculum Integration Project and support for this volume. We also thank the National Council for Research on Women for facilitating productive encounters among the WSAIS project site directors.

Janice Monk extends her gratitude to Kimberly Jones and Amy Newhall, project codirectors at SIROW/University of Arizona. Deborah S. Rosenfelt gratefully acknowledges the expertise, wisdom, and labor of project codirector A. Lynn Bolles and Seung-kyung Kim, codirector of Ford's Summer Institute on Women and Gender in an Era of Global Change. She is also thankful to Claire Moses, chair of the women's studies department at the University of Maryland, for offering her support and insight.

This volume also owes much to the invaluable work of graduate research assistants in manuscript preparation and in program administration and support. We thank especially Amy Koerber and Susan Leem at the University of Minnesota; Beth Kangas, Jacquelyn E. Davoli, and Amy Schaller at the University of Arizona; and Sarah Klein, Barbara Shaw Perry, Jennifer Skulte, and Heather Rellihan at the University of Maryland.

INTRODUCTION

DEBORAH S. ROSENFELT, MARY M. LAY, AND JANICE MONK

In the past decade, a number of societal and institutional tendencies have converged to encourage the internationalization of women's studies and to advance the consideration of gender issues—informed and framed by international perspectives—across the curriculum. *Globalization* has become a household word, and its more oppressive dimensions have stirred protest from Seattle to Genoa. The processes of globalization—the restless movement of capital, technology, bodies, allegiances, and identities of individuals across national boundaries, and the accompanying reconfigurations of power and of the processes of production—have led many U.S. institutions to question whether they are adequately preparing students for life and work in the "new global order." Sometimes these concerns are narrowly vocational or nationalist, sometimes they are broadly philosophical. Although at many institutions *internationalization* has been more a buzzword than a reality (Goodman 1999), the rhetoric has supported programmatic initiatives to revise the parochialism of higher education in the United States (see, for example, Johnston and Edelstein 1993).

Women's studies has been a particularly significant site for such changes, given its sustained efforts in scholarship, theory, and the classroom to engage with difference. Some curriculum projects made efforts as early as the 1980s to internationalize women's studies, and to bring attention to women's issues and gender relations in internationally oriented fields across the disciplines, but these were relatively rare.[1] In the 1990s, as women's organizations and movements proliferated internationally and became more influential, the need to integrate international perspectives and issues into the curriculum became increasingly compelling. One important influence has been the changing tone and nature of women's engagement with the United Nations women's conferences and nongovernmental organization (NGO) forums, as they evolved from 1975 in Mexico City to 1995 in Beijing. Perhaps the 1995 Beijing Fourth World Conference on Women most dramatically expressed the emerging links among local, regional, national, and international forms of women's activism. In developing the Platform for Action, which has been described as a manifesto of global feminism (Moghadam 1998), the Beijing conference set forth a clear political and intellectual mandate for women's studies: become

1

more consistently inclusive of the experiences, voices, and strategies for change of women around the world.

Feminist research from around the world has also become more accessible in the United States since the 1980s. Exchange of feminist research across national boundaries has been enhanced through the series of International Interdisciplinary Conferences in Women's Studies, initiated in 1981 in Israel and held since then at three-year intervals in the Netherlands, Ireland, the United States, Costa Rica, Australia, Norway, and Uganda. Similarly, international networks of feminist scholars have been forged in various disciplines, such as the International Association for Feminist Economics, the Association for Women in Development, and the Commission on Gender and Geography within the International Geographical Union. The Worldwide Organization of Women's Studies (WOWS) was conceived at Beijing and launched in 1996 at the International Interdisciplinary Conference in Adelaide. By the turn of the millennium, a host of texts featuring scholarship about and often by women from around the world, as well as critiques of the parochialism of much Western feminist theory, both facilitated and demanded the transformation of women's studies curricula.[2] We agree with Patrice McDermott when she wrote that women's studies curricula "that remain exclusively oriented to U.S. content and Western feminist perspectives no longer meet the standards of scholarly rigor and political relevance that define our field" (1998, 88).

In the mid-1990s, a national initiative supported by The Ford Foundation and initially coordinated by the National Council for Research on Women began to encourage curriculum transformation efforts aimed at internationalizing the study of women in the United States. In 1995 these groups launched the Women's Studies, Area and International Studies (WSAIS) Curriculum Integration Project, designed to link programs in and insights from women's studies, area studies, and international studies, and to open curricula to materials concerning women and gender especially in the non-Western world (Chamberlain 1996). Thirteen institutions, including both campuses and consortia, received grants, and through a series of regional, national, and international conferences and various publications, these projects have had a significant impact. For this volume, we draw on our experiences as directors of three of these projects (the University of Arizona, the University of Maryland, and the University of Minnesota) and also as participants in several national WSAIS-linked conferences.

Internationalizing thinking in the U.S. academy and bringing the lens of gender to bear on international issues and global processes have entailed two related but not identical questions: How do we think and teach comparatively and relationally about women's lives and gender arrangements in locations around the world? And how do we bring international perspectives to bear on women's lives and gender arrangements in any given location, including the United States? Most of the WSAIS projects simultaneously grappled with another question essential to this historical moment: How do we think about the relation between the local and the global, both as objects of inquiry and as dimensions of subjectivity—as ways of knowing, seeing, and acting? Indeed, the local-global binary itself fails to encompass the complex intersections of identity, community, region, nation, and world. Obviously, then, internationalizing and "engendering" the curriculum is not only a daunting undertaking but also one with no clearly demarcated boundaries, geographic or substantive.

Where does one begin? This collection proffers some tentative answers—ones worked out by feminist teachers and scholars grappling with the dilemmas of internationalization, mostly at North American institutions and thus inevitably shaped by that context.[3] This volume provides three kinds of resources, corresponding to its three parts: first, broad discussions of the changing shape of knowledge and theory in women's studies in the United States as feminist scholars encounter and rework other relevant bodies of scholarship in area studies, studies in science and technology, and cultural studies to encompass the perspectives of women from around the world and the gendered and sexualized processes of social and economic change beyond and across North American borders; second, thoughtful meditations on developing, teaching, and transforming a wide range of specific courses in women's studies and in many other sites across the university, accompanied by innovative syllabi; third, specific curricular resources developed over the past decade by instructors participating in the WSAIS projects and related endeavors.

The courses and writings generated by the WSAIS initiative suggest that there are certain key issues around which much gendered, internationalized inquiry circulates. These include the changing material and economic circumstances that affect women's experiences in work and family life; questions of identity, subjectivity, cultural representation, and cultural production; issues of women's rights, citizenship, and political representation in relation to the state; historical and current forms of women's resistance and activism; questions of language and power (both the power-laden designations necessarily used in discussion—international, global, Western, non-Western, North, South, Third World, developing—and the power-fraught hierarchies that privilege some languages over others); and, crucially, underlying issues of epistemology and ethics: Who is the "we" doing the thinking, the knowing, the writing? Whose interpretive voices are heard, whose silenced? Whose interests are served in the process of producing and sharing knowledge? Who controls or mediates these processes? Not surprisingly, such questions about knowledge and power permeated the WSAIS projects. These questions, of course, are inseparable from histories of colonization, anticolonialist struggle, decolonization, and neocolonialism, and these histories themselves command the attention of those attempting to think across borders. In such histories, economic, political, and cultural issues are virtually inseparable. Most of the projects, then, also addressed issues of disciplinarity and interdisciplinarity, often requiring participants to venture into unfamiliar territories, methodological as well as geographic. Inevitably there are certain areas, geographic and substantive, that deserve better representation in this book, yet, when taken collectively, the contributions broach the range and complexity of these issues.

PART 1. THE CHANGING SHAPE OF KNOWLEDGE

In the opening part of this volume, women's studies scholars historicize, critique, and/or draw on area studies, science and technology studies, and cultural studies, suggesting how these different discursive legacies might challenge, change, and enrich one another. Barbara Burton and her colleagues, in "Cartographies of Scholarship," explore the complex history of geographically defined area studies, deftly illuminating the field's servitude to the interests of Western nation-states while simultaneously valuing its contributions to an understanding of the local and specific. Feminist and ethnic studies, the authors argue, should avoid replicating notions of globalization that, at the level of epistemology, too easily become complicit with the late capitalist agenda. Rather, women's studies should engage in ethical research through a renewed but more progressively politicized engagement with "the languages, histories, and politics of the singular." Cross-disciplinary work, they insist, is as necessary as cross-border work, but only in a way that "makes productive comparison among countries and cultures possible."

The essays by Edna Acosta-Belén and Beverly Guy-Sheftall explore the intersections of women's studies with the authors' respective areas of study: Latin American/Latino(a) studies for Acosta-Belén and African diaspora studies for Guy-Sheftall. But the fields they consider are already significantly more evolved than the traditional concentrations described by Burton and her colleagues. A Latin American studies linked with U.S. Latino(a) studies, and an African diaspora studies that views the experiences of Black people around the globe as crucially but variously linked to those of continental Africa, constitute and draw upon relatively new knowledge formations. Feminist scholars in these fields are producing new scholarship and theory on the experiences of women in migration as producers of culture, as sexual beings, as workers, as family members, and as activists in new forms of organizing. Acosta-Belén and Guy-Sheftall argue convincingly that, just as area studies must overcome an inclination to focus on masculine experience, women's studies can no longer take North America or Western Europe as an epistemological center.

Amy Koerber and Mary M. Lay offer strategies for studying women's concerns "in global and local settings through the lens of science and technology." They focus on four ways in which science and technology touch women's lives globally and locally: through the introduction of new technologies in the workplace and home, through the development of reproductive technologies, through food production and processing, and by generating forms of women's activism like the ecofeminist movement. Closing with a case study of Mexican maquiladoras, in which many of these themes converge, Koerber and Lay make an additional, vital point: the compelling importance—and possibility—of finding sources that allow those who become the objects of study in the women's studies classroom to speak about their experiences in their own voices.

Katie King's analysis of the production and distribution of two internationally popular television series, *Highlander* and *Xena*, rounds out part 1. Her discussion takes into account both global reconfigurations of capital and local processes of meaning making. Fandoms with various affiliations—identifying with and across different genders, sexualities, nations, regions, and institutions—construct stories about the social histories and erotic inclinations of characters whose fluid national and sexual identities invite such speculation. Taking account of the "ideological strategies, [both] economic and representational" in such cultural production, King explains, is central to her pedagogical practice. Her essay contributes to what Susan Friedman, in her important book *Mappings,* calls a new geography of identity, crucial to our "increasingly postmodern, migratory, syncretist, and cyberspatial global world" (1998, 33). Each of these essays contributes to shaping a transnational feminist perspective that acknowledges differences in both social and geographic location; each envisages women's studies as a site not only for producing knowledge but also for engendering social change.

PART 2. REFLECTIONS ON TEACHING: STRUGGLES, SETBACKS, SUCCESSES

The majority of essays in this collection, gathered here in the pedagogical clusters that form part 2, reflect on the creation and revision of specific courses and provide sample syllabi and course units. The authors of these essays were invited to discuss their efforts at course transformation, the obstacles they encountered as well as their achievements, and to share not only the models they developed but also the ways in which their own thinking and teaching changed in the process. The resulting accounts of struggles, setbacks, and successes are supplemented by innovative syllabi, extensive suggestions for reading, and pedagogical strategies.

Although many of the contributors were participants in the WSAIS projects, additional essays came in response to a broad call for papers. The essays and accompanying syllabi represent a variety of courses, disciplines, and institutions, including geography at Utah State University; feminist pedagogy at the University of Minnesota; Spanish and Latin American studies at the State University of New York, New Paltz; anthropology and women's studies at Monash University, Australia; sociology at Illinois State University; and Africana studies at Wellesley College.

To illuminate women's and gender issues in local, regional, national, and global contexts, and to illuminate international issues through the lens of gender, the instructors represented here often reflect on the disciplinary assumptions that must be interrogated, both within their courses and the curricula of their institutions. The experiences of women and the diversity of gender arrangements over time in different locations, they find, challenge the very structures of thought that underlie disciplines and courses—from assumptions about chronological periods and the relative importance of events and themes to understandings concerning what constitutes history, politics, and culture. They illustrate how fields both require and are enhanced by multidisciplinary and interdisciplinary approaches and how traditional curricular boundaries like those between the humanities and social sciences must necessarily blur. Those teaching in the humanities, therefore, turn to statistical compendia and atlases; while those teaching in the social sciences use humanistic methods to analyze such things as the gendered ideologies that inform policy decisions.

Helga Leitner reflects on the added work in the humanities she must do to integrate gender concerns throughout her geography course on world populations. Similarly, Geeta Chowdhry at Northern Arizona State University and Cecilia Menjívar at Arizona State University discuss incorporating fiction, life histories, and testimonies into their gender and development course. The seminar leaders of the Ways of Reading project at the University of Minnesota identify a number of crucial questions they confronted in revising Theoretical Approaches to International Relations, among them, How might studies of culture and questions of identity challenge or alter thinking about states and transnational relations? The model syllabus offered by Lay and her colleagues both draws on conventional international relations theory and utterly transforms it, not least by making central to the course the politics of knowledge making. Helen Ruth Aspaas, designing a course on women for the College of Natural Resources at Utah State University, links feminist approaches to scientific inquiry and a focus on women as environmental advocates, locally and internationally, with women's nature writing. Class projects ranged from an exploration of environmental themes in women's folk music to an analysis of farm women's perspectives on the environment.

Just as these faculty incorporated perspectives from the humanities into their social science and science courses, so faculty with humanities backgrounds found it necessary to draw on the social sciences. In

"Teaching Globalization, Gender, and Culture," Deborah S. Rosenfelt, trained in literary and textual analysis, speaks of her struggles to integrate the economic with the cultural. In exploring how the forces of globalization affect and are modified by local cultures, and how both local and global contexts construct specific texts, Rosenfelt works to turn her students' gaze away from the United States as the perceptual and geographic center of the globe. The course becomes laden with readings as Rosenfelt seeks strategies not only to avoid oversimplifying the processes of globalization but also to avoid misrepresenting or exoticizing the local cultures considered. Susanna F. Ferlito, who teaches modern Italian culture and literature, develops an innovative course on "mig-rantscapes," using "the geopolitical and cultural space of Italy" to think about "constructions of migrant identities in a globalized world." Her syllabus confronts students with questions about gender, race, and ethnicity in the processes of migration to and from Italy, and about the differing investments of disciplines like comparative literature, area studies, and anthropology in defining and representing migrant experiences. Transdisciplinary in its scope and method, the course, writes Ferlito, internationalizes the curriculum not because it adds a course on migration but because "it examines critically how people move, live, and work across spaces and places we have only recently come to assume as 'naturally' divided between nation-states: it brings under critical scrutiny the spaces between— *inter*—nations."

In representing through imaginative literature the voices of the women they study within courses that address social, geographic, political, and economic issues, instructors such as Leitner, Chowdhry, Menjívar, and Aspaas discover that they and their students must also debate "the power of authorial positions" in the production of knowledge. Questions of voice and the politics of knowledge also surface in work on internationalizing traditional courses in the humanities. Ferlito's course on Italian diasporas, for example, must deal with the issue of whose voices have been translated. Insistence on incorporating women's voices into social science courses and on exploring power-laden social contexts in humanities courses persistently challenges the disciplinary boundaries of the classroom.

The cross-disciplinary encounters demanded in so many of these courses inevitably challenge as well the assumptions of instructors' disciplinary bases. The University of Minnesota group found it necessary to pose questions about the complexity of human experience in ways other than assumed in international relations theory, raising questions that focused on the political and indeed gendered nature of the theory itself. Katherine Elaine Bliss, at the University of Massachusetts, reflects that as she revised her course in Latin American social history to discover how gender, class, race, and national identity shaped Latin American reform movements, she also had to ask hard questions about the tools and evidence historians use to understand the causes and implications of such movements. Eric Sheppard describes certain assumptions in geography that are challenged when he integrates gender issues throughout his introduction to human geography. Valentine M. Moghadam, in assessing how mainstream studies of social movements have neglected gender issues in their theoretical frameworks, suggests that instructors who wish to reverse this tradition must start with completely new questions. Similarly, Filomina Chioma Steady, in her course on environment, political ecology, and sustainable development, challenges traditional development models as fundamentally inadequate. Finally, in asking new questions about women's lives and questioning these traditional disciplinary models, as suggested by Naomi B. Scheman in her essay on revising her feminist theory and thought course, one is really challenging the nature of the "master's tool"—the university itself.

These essays also meditate on the effort to balance and connect theory and practice, or to place theory within specific contexts. Many of the instructors describe how they apply, inform, and test global models and movements within the context of local lives. For example, in the syllabus created for an international feminist theory course at the University of Minnesota, Lay and fellow faculty decided that to place theory within historical, intellectual, geographical, and social contexts, they must redefine theory as the process of reflecting upon one's situation, and include texts that would not traditionally be considered "theoretical." Theoretical approaches, they argue, are useful only when they inform and are informed by real world issues and case studies. Similarly, as Scheman reflects upon her course in feminist thought and practice, she decides she must teach "theory-laden practice" and "theorizing as a form of practice." For similar reasons, Judith McDaniel at the University of Arizona, when revising her feminist activism course to encompass international issues, draws parallels and connections between local organizations and international issues, and between activism and theory. McDaniel asks how a theoretical analysis can be informed by a grassroots activist's perspective and asks her students to explore the relations among feminist theory, local activist issues, and a larger international agenda for change.

In addition to exploring the relationship between theory and practice, many of these essays speculate on the pedagogical dilemmas of negotiating between self and other, commonality and difference. Teasing out these contradictions poses one of the central challenges in the project of internationalizing women's studies. Heather S. Dell, at the University of Delaware, explores with her students the ways in which racism and sexism in the United States operate together to reduce women in other locales to stereotypical victims. Dell challenges what she calls "dominant Western feminism's imperial legacy" by focusing on activism against dowry violence in India and by having students analyze Anita Hill's testimony during Clarence Thomas' U.S. Supreme Court confirmation hearings. In the light of these hearings, students are better able to resist casting women living outside of the United States into the role of the Other, "a foil against which a superior sense of equality is claimed." Helen Johnson, teaching a course linking anthropology and women's studies at Monash University, Australia, encourages recognition of differences among her students in gender, national origin, class, and sociocultural heritage to suggest how differences are framed within relations of power and fields of difference. For Cynthia A. Wood, teaching a course on women and development requires treading a complex path between her students' tendency to homogenize and patronize "third world women" as an alien and victimized Other, and their attempt to see all women as everywhere the same, likely to have the same hopes and aspirations if only their oppression were alleviated. Such dilemmas also become a primary focus of Amy Kaminsky's course on feminist pedagogies. In internationalizing her course, however, Kaminsky also strives to ensure that students develop a "knowledge base from which to teach," even if they cannot acquire full mastery over knowledge about the world's women. Accordingly, each student must research and present an internationalized lesson to the group, adding to the cumulative store of knowledge about at least selected areas and issues.

A central goal in many of these courses is to decenter the United States as the model of progress, prosperity, freedom, and good health. Instructors ask students to rethink their experiences in the United States on the basis of what they learn about other lives. In doing so, students question and reinterpret perceptual norms and reenvision their own cultures. Thus, one of the benefits of Doris Friedensohn and Barbara Rubin's e-mail course project linking New Jersey City University and Bilkent University in Turkey was the way in which the exchange opened space for critical reflections on Western culture. In decentering U.S. students' perceptions, instructors help them see women from other countries and cultures not as tokens, not as stereotypical victims, and not as "the Others," but as complex individuals and activists on their own behalf.

The final cluster of essays in part 2 brings gendered and international perspectives to bear on specific literatures and cultures. André Lardinois develops an advanced course for the University of Minnesota's classical and Near Eastern studies department on the voices of women in ancient Greek literature and society. Examining both the works of women and the representation of women's voices in male-authored works, Lardinois finds it useful to frame these texts not only with readings on women in antiquity but also with a contemporary debate among scholars about aspects of women's lives in modern Iran, specifically the veil, the harem, and polygamy—practices also found in ancient Greece. This curricular strategy emphasizes "the similarity between the study of women in a different geographical culture and in the historical past." Both Wilma Feliciano at SUNY, New Paltz, and Isabel Valiela at Gettysburg College discuss courses that link and compare Latin American and Latina women writers. Feliciano focuses on dramatists in a cross-cultural examination that encompasses various representations of women's lives while exploring specific regional concerns: "race, class, and historiography in Mexico, political tyranny in Argentina, political ambiguity in Puerto Rico, psychic and physical displacement among U.S. Latinas." Valiela crosses generic as well as geographic borders to consider writers as diverse as Sor Juana de la Cruz, Rigoberta Menchú, Rosario Ferré, and Gloria Anzaldúa. Her concluding remarks signify the aims and strategies of many of the faculty whose pedagogical innovations are represented in this volume:

> The entire course is organized in a transgressive way. It does not adhere to standard categories and formats. It is not a chronological survey of literature; it is multidisciplinary; it focuses on women's lives and women's actions or agency. . . . Students study jointly . . . topics that have not been studied sufficiently as a connected unit in the past. . . . [The course] is transgressive not for the sake of transgression, but for the sake of exploring other bridges, other connecting links that have been previously ignored.

PART 3. CURRICULAR RESOURCES: STRATEGIES FOR CHANGE

The final part of this collection aims to assist leaders of faculty and curriculum development efforts, though many of the contributions will also speak directly to faculty engaged in revising and creating courses. It describes some models for organizing seminars and other activities that bring together women's studies, area studies, and international studies; presents resources such as discussion scenarios, videographies, and suggestions for dealing with specific pedagogical challenges; and offers examples of exercises and assignments designed to stretch students' understanding of and thinking about women in other parts of the world, especially in comparative and relational ways.

Although institutions participating in the WSAIS project adopted a variety of approaches to instigate curriculum change, not surprisingly, given the project's goals, they commonly designed opportunities for fostering dialogue, and often collaborative work, across disciplinary, geographic, and institutional borders. The specificities of the models reflect local circumstances. Lay describes how in 1996–97, at the University of Minnesota, two interdisciplinary working groups were created to participate in a yearlong series of weekly discussions. This led not only to changes in individual faculty's departmental courses but also contributed to collective revision of two core courses, Introduction to Women's Studies and International Feminist Theory.

The Ways of Reading seminars were designed to explore the perspectives of the individual disciplines and draw on their strengths while going beyond them. Work at the University of Maryland reached across the state system, while also aiming to bring about local change at the College Park campus, the largest in the system. Rosenfelt and A. Lynn Bolles outline a model that combined a monthlong summer institute, attended by faculty from multiple campuses and some international women graduate students, with "polyseminars" at College Park during the year, small development stipends for faculty, and a concluding conference. Reporting from the University of Michigan, Abigail J. Stewart demonstrates how a local tradition of a "theme semester" was invoked to create the Genders, Bodies, Borders program. The program reached widely across geographic locations, disciplines, and genres, including not only courses but three series of "enrichment" activities, all open to the public free of charge—a film and video series, public lectures and conferences, and live performances and exhibitions.

The Southwest Institute for Research on Women (SIROW) at the University of Arizona built on its grounding in interinstitutional as well as interdisciplinary work. SIROW serves thirty campuses in several states and northern Mexico, facing distances that preclude frequent seminars. Its project operated in two phases—a preliminary summer institute to develop regional leadership among a small group of faculty, and a second summer institute that brought thirty-five faculty and graduate students for an intensive week of work, using mentors from the first summer as well as outside consultants. Kimberly Jones writes of the productive tensions that were addressed in the program's design, which attempted to balance the global and the local, gender studies and area studies, teaching and research, and various disciplinary perspectives. The Arizona project integrated the women's studies librarian into this effort, not only to help assess the needs and knowledge of the dispersed group prior to the institutes but to extend their skills in using technology to identify resources across disciplinary and regional borders. The model also incorporates outreach by the librarian to her peers and faculty on selected regional campuses during the academic year in a further effort to promote collaborative work.

Support for faculty participants—from project staff (directors, graduate assistants, and in the SIROW case, especially the librarian) and external consultants—form an important part of all these models, as does some form of institutional reward or recognition: released time from teaching, travel and lodging for out-of-town participants, and opportunities for stipends or mini-grants. Some projects included group as well as individual tasks to foster peer support while setting up challenges and stimulating the reflection that accompany the risky venture of moving into new and unfamiliar terrain. Structuring programs so that early discussions engage participants in defining collective goals and the parameters of their work, as Lay describes, contributes to a supportive model when a project seems overwhelming. A number of project directors found it helpful to provide at this stage an article by Vella Neil Evans, "Try, Try Again" (1991), which cautions against expecting a "quick fix" in integrating international perspectives into the curriculum and suggests some ways to set realistic goals.

In the course of faculty development seminars, many strategic questions recurred: How does one deal with one's own limited expertise? How does one address pedagogically "culturally challenging practices" such as veiling or arranged marriage? How does one foster empathy rather than sympathy among students? And how does one deal with languages other than English? These were as compelling as the more theoretical questions posed earlier, and indeed inextricably linked with them. The materials compiled in the cluster on faculty development both articulate such questions further and suggest ways to address them. David William Cohen and Abigail J. Stewart present an inventory of discussion points raised at the University of Michigan. They did not try to create a consensus, recognizing that challenges are contextual: Is the course being designed for graduates or undergraduates? Is the task to bring women and gender into an international course or to bring international and area studies perspectives into a women's studies course? Their discussion points are likely to arise whenever faculty attempt to bring the domains together.

Wendy Kolmar, Rosenfelt, and Janice Monk compiled a list of suggestions to address concerns about course content, syllabus structure, assignments, grading, and classroom process. In particular, they deal with the importance of problematizing the taken-for-granted, leading students to explore multiple ways of knowing and sources of information, decentering expectations about expertise, and being attentive to difference at all levels—within societies and within the classroom. Rosenfelt additionally outlines a pedagogical framework for dealing with "culturally challenging practices" so as "to negotiate between the shoals of cultural relativism on the one hand and ethnocentrism on the other."

The cluster closes with a set of "scenarios" designed by Sandra D. Shattuck, Jones, Monk, and Amy Newhall to stimulate faculty discussion on dealing with the reservations and resistances they might confront from colleagues and students, as well as within themselves. Each of the scenarios presents a hypothetical situation that faculty might face as they bring international and feminist perspectives into their teaching. Although hypothetical, the scenarios are based on experiences; they offer an opportunity to shuttle between theory and practice, to make abstractions more concrete. The problems addressed include faculty confidence and challenges to their expertise, departmental resistance to curriculum change, and linguistic concerns that arise in relation to the introduction of materials in languages other than English. The scenarios were used in a summer institute at the University of Arizona and prompted lively discussions.

As many of the contributors indicate, bringing material on women and gender issues from diverse cultures and regions into the curriculum pushes the boundaries of our knowledge of source materials and requires us to extend our capacities to access information, to question Western-centered perspectives, and to find ways to help students develop new critical awareness and ways of viewing "other" women in relation to themselves. To support faculty undertaking such work, the volume concludes with a set of resources that identify electronic, statistical, and visual materials, including related teaching exercises that engage students in working with such materials.

Ruth Dickstein contributes a guide to accessing and evaluating the diverse electronic media that have recently become available and are increasingly central in students' work. She addresses ways of learning to keep up with and discriminate among the flood of new materials, not only on the World Wide Web but also CD-ROMs, web-accessible indexes, shared cataloging information, discussion groups, electronic journals, and electronic texts. Both she and Denise Mogge, who assembled a bibliography of statistical and graphic/cartographic resources, attend to the diversity of women within the United States as well as internationally. The works included in Mogge's piece cover such topics as population, households, families, education, environment, health, and public affairs. They are useful in helping us to explore the contexts in which individual and community experience and expression are situated. In addition to the importance of access, we recognize the importance of helping students to develop critical perspectives on such sources.

Dickstein includes criteria for evaluating electronic media; Monk and Helen Henderson respectively provide teaching exercises that lead to critical thinking about what statistical data represent and how hypotheses and generalizations are derived from primary survey data. Monk's exercise juxtaposes field data on women's work in a region of Venezuela with a census typology of types of employment. Henderson's takes examples from field surveys of complex forms of households in Chad, and asks students to develop and compare possible interpretations of the raw data in order to explore relationships between household structure and women's participation in various kinds of work. Her exercise brings students closer to seeing how the generalizations and theories presented in published texts have their origins in "messy" complexities. Linda Pershing presents a collaborative, multifaceted student assignment involving "Global Research Groups" that engages students in in-depth research drawing on multiple sources of information about a specific area of the world "in which class, race, ethnicity, gender, and/or sexual identity have been pivotal aspects of contemporary social and political turmoil." She provides suggested topics (drawing on cases from Hawaii, Japan, Rwanda, Guatemala, and India), and guidelines for implementing the assignment so that students are engaged in "active learning" and can increase their sophistication in making oral and written presentations. An important goal of her work, in addition to decentering the instructor, is to help students "identify underlying assumptions about human diversity and the societal and political consequences of these assumptions."

The exercise offered by Julie K. Daniels provides yet another way of encouraging students to engage with materials while simultaneously challenging their assumptions. Like two of the scenarios offered by Shattuck and her colleagues, the exercise addresses the dilemmas of language/monolingualism. In internationalizing the curriculum (or teaching a class that includes students of diverse linguistic backgrounds), Daniels hopes to address the limitations imposed by her own and others' limited language proficiency. The task she assigns students is to write in their "second-best language." The responses highlight issues about power and language, including the privileges of (native) speakers of English, and assumptions about what constitutes "our" language (and culture). In her class, the exercise also fostered respect for international/immigrant students who were struggling with not only a second but also a third language. Daniels contrasts this response with the exoticization which might otherwise take place, and remarks that the exercise also highlights issues of access to education.

Newhall and Diane Riskedahl also take up issues of language and curriculum, though their exercise is designed for a faculty group. They pose the challenge of developing a graduate curriculum that integrates area studies (especially their emphasis on learning the specificities of culture and local language) with the contemporary focus on transnational, global, and comparative studies. Their contribution outlines an exercise assigned to a faculty group: to design a gender-sensitive graduate curriculum that addresses the global/ transnational while also retaining the grounded knowledge of area studies. Included in their piece is the model developed by one faculty group to meet this challenge. It outlines intended outcomes, proposed course descriptions, and a program for a hypothetical student.

This final group of contributions deals especially with addressing students' attitudes and values towards the "Other(s)," including issues related to teaching with visual media and the value of using role-playing strategies. To support integration of visual texts into teaching, we have provided videographies compiled for the Maryland project by Joseph Christopher Schaub, Rosenfelt, and Sujata Moorti, and for the SIROW project by Jacquelyn E. Davoli and Monk. These listings are not intended to be comprehensive nor do they include critiques of the media. Rather, the short annotations identify the geographic and cultural context and the principal subject matter, and provide information on accessing the items. Some selections were included for the information they present, others for the discussion they provoke. Many of them have been identified as high quality and/or are award-winning works. Using such films is an important strategy for bringing the voices and features of women from other countries into the classroom. Yet they carry their own dangers: Given the power of visual images, how does one teach students that any given film or video is in itself one particular construction of women's lives? How can film help to instruct our students about lives different from their own without objectifying those very lives? Instructors might note how different conventions of documentary filmmaking can shape attitudinal responses. Whose voice, whose body, is being presented? In what ways? How do filmic techniques (framing, juxtaposition of music, the spoken word, the visual image, and so on) shape our responses?

While a number of instructors have found film and video particularly useful in stimulating students' empathy for women in contexts other than their own and for helping to challenge stereotypes, the contribution by Martha E. Geores and Joseph M. Cirrincione introduces the strategy of role playing to help students understand the tensions individuals face in situations where they are caught between their cultural roots and new ways of life. They develop a case study based on Patricia Stamp's essay "Burying Otieno" (1991), which presents the perspectives of multiple actors on complex issues of gender and ethnicity in Kenya. This concrete case requires students to consider both empirical information and belief systems, and to take a position, recognizing that alternative solutions will have different and serious consequences for individuals, groups, and society. Geores and Cirrincione outline a step-by-step procedure for implementing this role-playing activity and comment on student responses.

In the five years we have been working on this book, the commitment to a women's studies that encompasses the differences among women —national, ethnic, and religious, as well as racial, class, and sexual— has become increasingly strong and widespread, as has a new willingness to seek common ground for social change. Importantly, this transformation is also marked by a new critical consciousness about power relations and knowledge production—an awareness that will help foster new forms of advocacy, agency, affiliation, and coalition. New women's studies scholars, some with Ph.D.s in women's studies itself, are now beginning to emerge from U.S. graduate schools. If the student research interests and curricula of the doctoral programs with which we are familiar are any indication, these young scholars, who themselves come from around the world, will as a matter of course engage with transnational feminisms; undertake nonexploitative, border-crossing research projects; and include the voices and perspectives of women from many countries of origin in their teaching. They will find far more resources available than was the case at the inception of the WSAIS projects. We like to think that the projects themselves have been one of the many tributaries to this progress. We hope that this volume will facilitate the continuing labor of transformation, both within women's studies programs, and—a harder task—across the disciplines throughout the university.

NOTES

Parts of this introduction draw upon previously published works; see Rosenfelt 1998 and also Monk and Rosenfelt 2000.

1. A series of three-year curriculum transformation projects on internationalizing women's studies and "engendering" international studies took place at the University of Arizona in the 1980s. For helpful discussions about this work, see *Women's Studies International Forum* 1991. Also in the 1980s, Cheryl Johnson-Odim and Margaret Strobel edited packets on women's history in Africa, Asia, Latin America and the Caribbean, and the Middle East, produced by the Organization of American Historians with support from the National Endowment for the Humanities and the Fund for the Improvement of Postsecondary Education (Johnson-Odim and Strobel 1988). These have recently been updated and published as individual texts (Berger and White, Nashat and Tucker, Navarro and Korrol, and Ramusack and Sievers; all 1999).

2. Important anthologies include Alexander and Mohanty 1997, Basu 1995, Chauduri and Strobel 1992, Chow and Berheide 1994, Chowdhury and Nelson 1994, Funk and Mueller 1993, Grewal and Kaplan 1994, Johnson-Odim and Strobel 1992, Moghadam 1994, Mohanty et al. 1991, Narayan and Harding 2000, and Shohat 1998. See also Seager 1997 for a data-rich feminist atlas.

3. Recent exchanges with women's studies faculty from around the world suggest that the dilemmas of internationalization we address in this volume are, to some extent, particular to the intellectual and social history of women's studies in the United States, and may have lesser or different salience in other locales. Thus, even as we speak of internationalizing women's studies, our discussion is situated in a particular, local context.

WORKS CITED

Alexander, M. Jacqui, and Chandra Talpade Mohanty, eds. 1997. *Feminist Genealogies, Colonial Legacies, Democratic Futures*. New York: Routledge.

Basu, Amrita, with Elizabeth McGrory, eds. 1995. *The Challenge of Local Feminisms: Women's Movements in Global Perspective*. Boulder, Colo.: Westview Press.

The Beijing Declaration and the Platform for Action. 1996. New York: United Nations Department of Public Information.

Berger, Iris, and E. Frances White. 1999. *Women in Sub-Saharan Africa*. Bloomington: Indiana University Press.

Chamberlain, Mariam K. 1996. Introduction. *Women's Studies, Area and International Studies Curriculum Project*. New York: National Council for Research on Women.

Chauduri, Nupur, and Margaret Strobel, eds. 1992. *Western Women and Imperialism: Complicity and Resistance*. Bloomington: Indiana University Press.

Chow, Esther Ngan-ling, and Catherine White Berheide, eds. 1994. *Women, the Family, and Policy: A Global Perspective*. Albany: State University of New York Press.

Chowdhury, Najma, and Barbara Nelson, eds. 1994. *Women and Politics Worldwide*. New Haven, Conn.: Yale University Press.

Evans, Vella Neil. 1991. "Try, Try Again: Incorporating International Perspectives into a Course on Sex Roles and Social Change." *Women's Studies International Forum* 14 (4): 335–343.

Friedman, Susan. 1998. *Mappings: Feminism and the Cultural Geographies of Encounter.* Princeton, N.J.: Princeton University Press.

Funk, Nanette, and Magda Mueller, eds. 1993. *Gender Politics and Post-Communism: Reflections from Eastern Europe and the Former Soviet Union.* New York: Routledge.

Goodman, Allan E. 1999. "America Is Devaluing International Exchanges for Students and Scholars." *Chronicle of Higher Education*, March 12, A56.

Grewal, Inderpal, and Caren Kaplan, eds. 1994. *Scattered Hegemonies: Postmodernity and Transnational Feminist Practices.* Minneapolis: University of Minnesota Press.

Johnson-Odim, Cheryl, and Margaret Strobel, eds. 1988. *Restoring Women to History: Teaching Packets for Integrating Women's History into Courses in Africa, Asia, Latin America, the Caribbean, and the Middle East.* Bloomington, Ind.: Organization of American Historians.

———, eds. 1992. *Expanding the Boundaries of Women's History: Essays on Women in the Third World.* Bloomington: Indiana University Press.

Johnston, Joseph S., Jr., and Richard R. Edelstein, eds. 1993. *Beyond Borders: Profiles in International Education.* Washington, D.C.: Association of American Colleges.

McDermott, Patrice. 1998. "Internationalizing the Core Curriculum." *Women's Studies Quarterly* 26 (3 & 4): 88–98.

Moghadam, Valentine M. 1998. "The Women's Movement in the Middle East and North Africa: Responding to Restructuring and Fundamentalism." *Women's Studies Quarterly* 26 (3 & 4): 57–67.

———, ed. 1994. *Identity Politics and Women: Cultural Reassertions and Feminisms in International Perspective.* Boulder, Colo.: Westview Press.

Mohanty, Chandra Talpade, Ann Russo, and Lourdes Torres, eds. 1991. *Third World Women and the Politics of Feminism.* Bloomington: Indiana University Press.

Monk, Janice, and Deborah S. Rosenfelt. 2000. *Internationalizing the Study of Women and Gender.* Towson, Md.: National Center for Curriculum Transformation Resources on Women.

Narayan, Uma, and Sandra Harding, eds. 2000. *Decentering the Center: Philosophy for a Multicultural, Postcolonial, and Feminist World.* Bloomington: Indiana University Press.

Nashat, Guity, and Judith E. Tucker. 1999. *Women in the Middle East and North Africa.* Bloomington: Indiana University Press.

Navarro, Marysa, and Virginia Sanchez Korrol. 1999. *Women in Latin America and the Caribbean.* Bloomington: Indiana University Press.

Ramusack, Barbara N., and Sharon Sievers. 1999. *Women in Asia.* Bloomington: Indiana University Press.

Rosenfelt, Deborah S. 1998. "Editorial: Crossing Boundaries—Thinking Globally and Teaching Locally about Women's Lives." *Women's Studies Quarterly* 26 (3 & 4): 4–16.

Seager, Joni. 1997. *The State of Women in the World Atlas.* 2d ed. London: Penguin.

Shohat, Ella, ed. 1998. *Talking Visions: Multicultural Feminism in a Transnational Age.* New York: New Museum of Contemporary Art; Cambridge, Mass.: MIT Press.

Stamp, Patricia. 1991. "Burying Otieno: The Politics of Gender and Ethnicity in Kenya." *Signs: Journal of Women in Culture and Society* 16 (4): 808–845.

Women's Studies International Forum. 1991. 14 (4): 285–294.

PART 1

The Changing Shape of Knowledge

CARTOGRAPHIES OF SCHOLARSHIP: THE ENDS OF NATION-STATES, INTERNATIONAL STUDIES, AND THE COLD WAR

BARBARA BURTON, NOURAY IBRYAMOVA, RANJANA KHANNA, DYAN ELLEN MAZURANA, AND S. LILY MENDOZA

Feminist scholars internationalizing women's studies or opening up area and global studies to feminist critique will recognize in our title a reference to Chandra Mohanty's (1991) "Cartographies of Struggle." By substituting "scholarship" for "struggle," we seek to shift the emphasis to a consideration of how we do international feminist work at the intersections of area studies, ethnic studies, and women's studies. We are especially interested in area studies because of their historical importance as a site of inquiry into the "international." Area studies programs in the United States were forged in the cold war era. The end of the cold war in 1990 caused a radical shift not only in the distribution of global power, but also in justifications and funding, both federal and private, for area studies programs.

Our argument constitutes a critical feminist perspective on the current transition, and on the debates over international scholarship in the post–cold war era. We argue that it is crucial to understand area studies as more than a mere extension of eighteenth- and nineteenth-century Orientalist paradigms, or as a cold war product. We engage the critique of area studies from theorists who reject the U.S.–centric structures of knowledge that emerged following the eighteenth- and nineteenth-century European Orientalisms, and from those who seek to map an alternative area-base for knowledge in the age of late capitalism and global interaction.

The histories of international research demonstrate that area studies produced knowledges that exceeded the political paradigms molding some of their research. Understanding their contributions now allows us to avoid adopting too simplistically the most current economic and political paradigm (in this case, globalization), confusing it with a disinterested critique of the one that preceded it. Simply endorsing new models of globalization for scholarly research risks catering to the logic of late capitalism, thus leaving aside the specificities of local inequities, the persistence of power of some states, and the consequent disempowerment of others. Although colonialist, nationalist, or cold war paradigms obviously require critique, the surrendering of national or areal divisions to the logic of global capital involves substituting the postmodern for the postcolonial, to the detriment of newly independent nation states of the post–World War II era.

As some recent scholarship suggests, reifying and exoticizing cultural difference has caused a blind spot concerning interrelatedness (economic and otherwise) among peoples as well as shared political concerns that affect women globally (Mohanty 1991; Said 1978). Nevertheless, we stress that our relatedness should not be emphasized at the expense of recognizing our radical differences from others, differences that must be accounted for with specific and locally informed knowledge.

Partha Chatterjee (1986) and Dipesh Chakrabarty (1992) have called for a provincialization of European master discourses in order to forge an understanding of the specific political and disciplinary frameworks that took shape during the years when concepts such as *nation-state* and its counterparts *colony* or *overseas territory* were forming. The current emphasis on globalization necessitates such a study in order to elaborate how non-European forms, disciplines, or discourses are being subsumed under the umbrella of persistent master discourses. Thus, we question what the term *globalization* means. Is it a purely economic term? Or is there an academic model that carries this term beyond an economistic one? Does the concept of the transnational offer area studies scholars a way of accounting for globalization? And what about the suggestion by Bill Readings (1996) and others that globalization is not international at all, but actually more appropriately called Americanization, and that it is structured on a kind of neocolonialism that effectively changes specific cultures into one generalized America? Provincial-izing the discourse of globalization is essential to any contemporary understanding of the effects of late capitalism on the shaping and production of knowledge. Thus, how globalization plays out within specific contexts still needs to be elaborated. This will involve more than an understanding of how global processes affect local lives (see Basu 1995).

Our focus on how scholarly paradigms emphasizing globalization often follow the logic of late capitalism stems from a concern about how the economic and the cultural are pitted against each other in the struggle to understand the international. This has been the case in context-specific studies and in more global studies that have failed to acknowledge adequately the structural differences in the ways women in different national and regional locations are placed in relation to the economic and the cultural. This, we argue, is detrimental for women and for studies of and by women whose work, and thus whose economic worth, is frequently made invisible because of a lack of cultural understanding on the part of the investigator.

Our provincialization of the histories of international scholarship is an attempt to grapple with these questions. After sketching the histories of Orientalism and area studies, we analyze the current debates over changes in area studies. Then, working comparatively, we consider developments in area studies, women's studies, ethnic studies, and global studies, suggesting how their cross-germination is beneficial for scholars conducting international research and teaching. This analysis contextualizes the issues outlined previously through a historical tracing of the philosophies and political forces that have shaped the direction of scholarship and funding priorities. We then propose alternative strategies for determining the research agenda we deem imperative, given the concerns identified. We both critique and participate in the impetus to rethink knowledge production, scholarship, and funding. Re-imagining knowledge differently in light of the changes in this period of the late twentieth and early twenty-first centuries, we propose a different cartography for scholars researching women internationally.

SITUATING THE CURRENT DEBATES IN HISTORICAL CONTEXTS

Current debates concerning appropriate models of international research economy constitute the latest form of strategizing in an ongoing battle over the relationship between scholarship and government interests. Economy-driven theoretical assertions and conflicting humanist and social science methods and ideologies have characterized debates about the "Other." For example, Edward Said (1978) has famously demonstrated how the metropolitan study of the Orient served to both create and contain the Near East and Asia with knowledge later used as the basis of colonial policy. Literature, cultural study, and knowledge production by Orientalist scholars served a direct political function. Such studies led to an idea of the West that countered that of the Orient and could stand as a justification for the civilizing mission of colonialism by creating a body of scholarship upon which colonial policy could rest. The critique of area studies can be understood in a similar light—that of scholars creating knowledge for the purpose of state politics. Thus it is worth briefly reiterating the arguments of area studies' predecessor, Orientalism.

Narrowly defined, Orientalism is a scholarly field of distinct academic lineage and tradition; specialists in this field are designated as Orientalists (see van der Veer 1993). The nineteenth- and twentieth-century form has its roots in a cultural and encyclopedist Orientalism that developed in sixteenth- and seventeenth-century Europe. Early Orientalist initiatives were shaped by political, scientific, educational, and technological developments. The paramount political development was the shift from perception of an Arab threat to its perception of threats from the rise of the Ottoman Turkish Empire. Moreover, with the Age of Reason and the Enlightenment came modern developments in science, philosophy, and education, as well as notions such as universalism, rationalism, objectivity, and citizenship. Other central developments included advances in European mapmaking and cartography, the enormous growth of printing facilities, and major advances in travel and exploration (Tolmacheva 1995). Increasingly, states, as well as some individuals, used their growing wealth from enlarged overseas trade, expansion, and colonialism to support various scientific and scholarly endeavors.

From their beginnings, it was clear that these ventures and institutions were to play a part in their countries' colonial projects. Indeed a parallel existed between the rise of nineteenth- and twentieth-century modern Orientalist scholarship and French and British colonization of expansive Eastern empires (Said 1978). Ann McClintock (1995) analyzes how fantasies of power, domination, and sexuality are cast in gendered, racial, and class terms in Orientalist ethnographic, scientific, and travel literature. In this literature, imperial domination "rightly" extended from geographical imperialism to domination of the people, particularly the native women, of the region. Indeed, the exoticization of the Orient is often played out on the bodies of women, in these narratives inaccessible, unknowable, and erotic (Said 1978; Kabbani 1986).

Early Orientalists needed to secure funding from wealthy patrons, most of whom were associated with the state through royalty or other political connection. Language study was paramount to the Orientalist, and travel and residence in the East was initially the chief means of achieving language competency and gathering information up until the time when one could study the Orient and its languages at select European universities (Tolmacheva 1995).

As a school of thought, Orientalism operated under two broad premises and two underlying strategies rooted in Enlightenment thought. In the first premise, the Orientalist ascribed a "causal primacy to language, attitude, and religious dogma" (Halliday 1993, 149). Its strategy was to characterize "orientals" as timeless, stagnant, and lacking the capacity for change (Voll 1996). The second premise held that "the study of the region requires, and can . . . be organized through, the study of its languages and writings" (Halliday 1993, 151). In confining knowledge to the realm of language and culture, it effectively denied the extent to which Orientalism was a political project (Breckenridge and van der Veer 1993). The uses of Orientalist knowledge grew far beyond the control, or even scope, of the Orientalists' political aims. Indeed, "shipments of colonial knowledge back to Britain were continuously reconstructed and re-authorized by European political discourse" (Ludden 1993, 264–265). Much empirical data was reinterpreted in parliamentary debates, scholarly and popular books, newspapers, poetry, the visual arts, and the universities, which began to constitute a static textual canon (Ludden 1993; Said 1978). But after the onset of World War II, with the rise of nationalism, the emergence of new states, and shifts in world power, it became clear that Orientalism "was not going to provide the kind of understanding that was needed for policy makers and for scholars" (Voll 1996, 5). A new model was needed.

DEVELOPING ALTERNATIVE MODELS: THE GROWTH OF AREA STUDIES

The subsequent birth of area studies coincided with several key Euro-American intellectual developments, including the waning of classical Oriental studies, the emergence of more empirically particularist social scientific methods, and the evolution of modern theories of development. Understanding contemporary debates about area studies depends upon a grasp of these tendencies in the history of area studies in the United States.

A different kind of scholarly interest in international areas was institutionally formalized during World War II. Federal funding for education, research, and travel was inextricably linked to geopolitical interests of the United States. It would be overstating the case to suggest that area studies scholarship then or now simply reflected the wishes of the state. But the dominance and strategic positioning of the U.S. government and military required regional expertise in non-Western parts of the world. There were experts on the non-Western world available among traditional Orientalists, but this scholarship rarely provided the practical and contemporary knowledge believed to be necessary for military and marketing strategy. Other emerging social science disciplines like sociology, economics, and political science were often characterized by universalist assumptions and theory that required no context-specific applications, and by a provincialism that frequently made invisible and irrelevant the world outside of the United States and Western Europe. In short, there seemed to be little space within the formal disciplines to contemplate contemporary, locally specific knowledge of many world regions. Thus, it is not surprising that the first regional experts of the sort needed were found among Office of Strategic Services (OSS) and Central Intelligence Agency (CIA) personnel.

In 1943, the Committee on World Regions of the Social Science Research Council (SSRC) wrote an internal report articulating the need for more practical knowledge about other regions of the world. The report specified the need for experts who have and use "comprehensive knowledge" that combines "linguistic and regional knowledge with technical expertise" about particular regions (in Wallerstein 1997, 196). By implication, those specialized disciplines that could not work to combine their methods and produce transdisciplinary knowledge of a given area were seen as problematic. In this way, a perceived information deficiency provided powerful fuel for new government and foundation funding initiatives for foreign language and regional area studies that would supersede former disciplinary boundaries and insularities. Furthermore, the report appeared to take political advantage of the notion of the United States as a burgeoning superpower to advocate a new form of internationalism in education that would depend upon long-term federal funding.

Throughout the early cold war period of the 1950s and early 1960s, government support of area studies research and education placed particular emphasis on regions considered to be strategically important for military and economic purposes: first Asia, then the Soviet Union. Yet area studies research was not meant only to gather valuable information with new social science methods, but also to integrate and thus improve those methods. That is, regional area information was to be the site upon and through which disciplinary integration would occur. In an apparent attempt to integrate the newest social science research methodologies, area studies centers were located at universities, not government think tanks or specialist outposts. Not surprisingly, some European scholars saw this two-sided American initiative as "less a contribution to the 'science of society' than to the pursuit of foreign policy" (Wallerstein 1997, 196–197).

This model of integrated social science drew on a specific notion of culture, broadly, that of American anthropologist Franz Boas. The Boasian concept asserted that culture was both "an accidental accretion of individual elements" and an "organizing spirit or genius continually assimilating these atomistic elements, integrating them in a spiritual totality that must be appreciated as a unique, historical whole" (Handler 1983, 209). Ethnographic researchers were to participate in and report on individual cultural elements constituting this organizing spirit or whole. The Boasian ethnographic method proliferated between the wars through the work of American anthropologists such as Ruth Benedict, Margaret Mead, and Edward Sapir. In this way, Boasian anthropology clearly became influential in conceiving the concept and mission of area studies as well.

For instance, in early initiatives, the regional area was understood as a kind of cultural whole; only by steeping oneself in the language, literature, and history of this whole could one properly understand any one component. In this way, the regional expert could both privilege local knowledge and become a kind of native informant in the ethnographic tradition. Area studies scholars had a dual role: They were informed reporters writing back to disciplinary generalists with observations about context-specific applications of disciplinary paradigms, and they were agents of the West working on the ground with other cross-disciplinary westerners to generate new questions and categories arising from local cultures. In this regard, area studies provided an important and truly innovative move to integrate disciplinary knowledges to acquire holistic regional understandings.

Paradoxically, this model apparently contributed to a further reifying of disciplinary methods and specializations. Anthropologically inflected area studies research was necessarily less systematic and descriptive than those fields less enamored of the Boasian model of culture or modeled upon a different notion of science—economics and, more recently, political science. As a result, scholars working in economics and political science were less likely to work cooperatively with area studies, because they typically viewed the outcome of their research to be scientifically important only when predictive and prescriptive. Importantly, this split helps to explain the current perceived "failure" of area studies to "move beyond the pilot project stage" (Lambert 1986). This disciplinary divergence also makes clear the heterogenous nature of work conducted under the rubric of area studies and the social science disciplines associated with it.

Another dimension of early resistance to area studies had to do with reconciling a division between the demands for a more practical knowledge and those for a more disinterested pursuit of "truth." Although new funding for non-Western study was exhilarating, it was also perceived to be dangerous. There was the danger of "being used; of subordinating knowledge to policy, rather than vice versa. And there was the subtler danger of acquiring seemingly practical knowledge that was, in fact, false" (Smith 1956, as quoted in Wallerstein 1997, 212).

Despite these tensions, scholars received more funding and support as the cold war accelerated. For example, the Rockefeller Foundation was one of the first major foundations to fund non-Western study (beginning in 1933), initiating funding for Columbia University's Russian Institute in 1945. The Carnegie Foundation boosted Harvard's Russian Research Center in 1948. The Ford Foundation, although joining relatively late in 1952, proved to be the most consistent and enduring funder of area studies research (Cumings 1997; Wallerstein 1997). In October 1957, the Soviet launching of *Sputnik* sent the Eisenhower administration into orbit with the passage of the National Defense Education Act. It was Title VI of this act, passed in 1958, that guaranteed increases in federal aid to foreign language and area studies (FLAS) centers, and, for twenty years, to the internationalization of faculties and libraries at universities throughout the United States. This initiative fit nicely with the goals of previous foreign policy initiatives for improved regional expertise while supporting the nationalist goals of the cold war. In fact, the bill was authored by liberal Democrats looking to improve federal funding for higher education, and *Sputnik* offered a much needed excuse to exploit defense and military concerns for the purposes of quite different ends. The debate in Congress was actually over the precedent of federal funding for higher education, not over its value to cold war strategy. The bill was strongly opposed by Senators Barry Goldwater and Strom Thurmond, for example, who reportedly viewed it as "opening the floodgates of federal assistance" for work that was "unbelievably remote . . . from national defense considerations" (Merkx 1995, 5).

Carl Pletsch (1981) has argued that the postwar emergence of area studies in the United States actually coevolved with the development of modernization theory and the cold war division of the globe into three conceptual worlds. In addition to guiding the political rhetoric of the post–World War II era and the processes of development essential to modernization theory, these constructions depended upon a particular intellectual division of labor. The more nomothetic and universalizing studies were applied to the First World, and, as evident in the appropriation of the Boasian culture concept, the more ideographic or particularist studies to the Third World. According to Pletsch, such divisions only reinforced and sustained previous colonial era binaries.

Interestingly, this division of scholarly labor, and the epistemological assumptions that accompanied it, also produced a variety of unintended consequences significant to the history of area studies and global studies (see Marcus and Fischer 1986; Pletsch 1981; Wallerstein 1997). First, descriptive ideographic work began to challenge the assumptions of modernization theory, as scholars began to assert that the First World should be opened up to investigation. At the same time, scholars of Third World regions began to integrate social theory from the disciplinary models created in the West and taught in the colonies with local particularisms. Such integrations produced invaluable paradigmatic shifts. In particular, scholars who asserted that the Western hegemonic disciplines themselves were ideological and framed by particular political and cultural contingencies began to challenge the division of intellectual labor and the three worlds concept, as well as the master narratives of literary and historical studies (see Chakrabarty 1992; Chatterjee 1986; Said 1978; Spivak 1985; Vishwanathan 1990) and of anthropological work and social science in general (see Visweswaran 1996; Mohamed and Lloyd 1987; Gupta and Ferguson 1992; Narayan 1993).

These epistemological struggles continue to be manifest in present discussions. The current debate surrounding area studies is clouded by a disciplinary ideological storm, this time within and around the disciplines of political science and economics in an attempt to resist many of the challenges to disciplinary paradigms from "localized" studies. Rational choice theories and methods within political science have aggressively moved to displace and devalue the culturally based challenges from area studies (Bates 1996; Shea 1997). Instead the methods appear to take the complex realities of diverse people's lives (those resident in the "areas") and attempt to use them as material for a theoretical machine that translates rich material into universalized mathematical data. For this reason, some perceive the methodological move within political science to inculcate rational choice theory as the preeminent method and theoretical paradigm as an attempt to acquire the stature and policy-relevant authority given neoclassical economics, and to apply laissez-faire market analysis to politics. Others argue that the resistance of many economics scholars to internationalizing their perspectives and contemplating critiques of their laissez-faire model has made that discipline insular and less relevant (Guyer 1996; Lie 1997). The least desirable aspects of rational choice theory and neoclassical economics include their investment in paradigms operating within Enlightenment modernism and scientific "progress." Their propensity for predictive determinations approaching "scientific" verifiability make them resistant to other recent developments in scholarship, feminist and otherwise, including examinations of identity, interrogation of concepts of culture, and emphases in many fields on contextual specificities in interpreting and determining research outcomes (Lustick 1997).

These concerns over policy-relevance, insularity, and theoretical rigor have contributed to current shifts. More recently, there has been a move among federal as well as private funding agencies within the United States to reexamine the effectiveness of traditional area studies as the primary strategy for doing international scholarship. According to SSRC president Kenneth Prewitt (1997), two major considerations compelled this move: One was changing world conditions, the other, changes in world scholarship.

Some have suggested that current dangers to U.S. supremacy and stability in the post–cold war era are the result of a failure by area studies to respond adequately to the vast changes in the international scene, specifically to the unprecedented level of interdependence among nations and the significant fragmentation within previously unified countries (Mellon Foundation 1993). Many regions of the world, such as the Middle East, are now seen as having been classified on an artificial basis that had little bearing on reality except to serve the interests of the state during the cold war (Heilbrunn 1996). Another critique, emerging from the rational choice theorists in political science, argues that area studies specialists lag behind others in terms of their familiarity with statistics and their commitment to theory, and that they practice a kind of particularist scholarship inappropriate for the more global character of today's concerns (Bates 1996). Despite decades of initiatives, some critics argue, the traditional problems within disciplines were not resolved by the creation of area studies. The resistance of certain disciplines to engage with international, context-specific work remains today a chief motivating factor for new initiatives in scholarship. Area studies, although established to address this problem, has been seen as inadequate to the task.

In keeping with these critiques, internationally oriented funders are now building their programs around transnational themes and problems associated with the presumably more salient social, economic, and political systems of the "new world order." Thus, in 1994, the SSRC concluded that the new ideological orientation of international scholarship is meant to help us "understand how the globalizing aspects of contemporary society are shaped, refracted, altered, and redefined as they encounter successions of local contexts" (Heginbotham 1994, 36–37). Within this framework, the SSRC states that area studies should focus less on gaining an in-depth understanding of the culture, history, and language of a single country and more on the ways these local elements relate to relevant international events and forces.

In this model, area studies programs would expand geographically, but areas would be demarcated by economic, trade, cultural, educational, legal, and communication links. Disciplinary programs would become more involved with international scholarship, and the topics they explore would be identified as common to many regions but shaped by local contextual specificities. Such research, the SSRC suggested, would not render area studies obsolete; rather, the need for area knowledge would increase, with "sensitivity to context" still established only through "some measure of understanding of local culture, language, and history" (Heginbotham 1994, 38).

In 1996, summarizing the new joint international research and training program of the SSRC and the American Council of Learned Societies (ACLS), the associations further reasserted the need for reorganizing scholarship along globalized lines. The new line of research would be "a scholarly enterprise that can interpret and explain the ways in which that which is global and that which is local condition each other" (Prewitt 1997, 31). The SSRC and ACLS suggested that their new model moved away from a U.S.–centric cold war rationale for area knowledge. They argued that studying the ways local and global issues interweave requires area knowledge, comparative studies, building models, and testing theories. Furthermore, while the value of American scholarly outposts seems significant in these reports, emphasis is also placed upon cooperative work with indigenous scholars and international exchanges. Building partnerships with local counterparts, according to the SSRC, would not only expand American social scientists' knowledge of local contexts, but would also allow for collaborative comparative work on a global range of thematic programs (Heginbotham 1994).

Likewise, the Ford, MacArthur, and Mellon foundations, long influential in area knowledge and policy, have made significant structural and focal changes. In 1997, the Ford Foundation abolished regional directorships, including those for Africa, Latin America, the Middle East, Asia, and the Caribbean, and collapsed its eight programs into three. According to Ford, this new structure reflects the foundation's understanding that some of the most pressing problems in the world are not local or national, but global. The three theme-based programs that emerged within the Ford Foundation are "Education, Media, Arts, and Culture" (EMAC), "Asset Building and Community Development," and "Peace and Social Justice." EMAC has announced a new grant program titled "Crossing Borders: Revitalizing Area Studies" as an effort to encourage scholarship that takes into account the fluidity of national borders. The declared purpose of the program is to develop understanding of "processes that are at once local and global, such as diaspora and migration, social movements, and new forms of culture and identity" (Mercer 1997, A29). However, the current Ford Foundation initiatives seem not as supportive of area studies as the previous programs were, nor do they provide the same boost for advancing knowledge of particular regions.

Similarly, the MacArthur Foundation has created new areas of emphasis in response to the "dynamic global environment," concentrating its funding priorities on two integrated programs: the Program on Human and Community Development and the Program on Global Security and Sustainability. The goals of the latter include educating American leaders and the public about global problems in order to improve a U.S. response, as well as influencing policy formation through public dialogue on the effects of global developments on issues of strategic importance. It also encourages international collaboration for solving global problems, building civil society, and promoting human rights (MacArthur Foundation 1998).

And, in 1993, the Andrew W. Mellon Foundation created the Seminars Program, which largely replaced funding for traditional area research and training. Instead the program encourages scholars to discuss themes relevant to regions across the globe, including nationalism and national identities, religious and ethnic conflicts, comparative urban cultures, violence, conflicting global and local cultures, and variation in the democratization process worldwide (Mellon Foundation 1993).

From this brief overview of the structural shifts that have occurred in funding priorities and knowledge organization, one thing seems clear. In each of these initiatives, there are contradictory agendas among the funding agencies and within their rationales. In spite of gestures toward an understanding of culture, history, and language, "local contexts" receive short shrift on the whole. The local is important primarily in regard to how it plays out in the international arena, where the salience of events is, more often than not, dictated by northern interests and perspectives. Such prioritizing of the international context over the local reveals an assumption that particular cultures, histories, and languages matter mostly in reference to globalization, defined in terms of dominant players' interests. The neglect of the humanities, traditionally the locus of cultural understanding, testifies to this reorientation. We should question what kind of understanding of the local can be achieved in the absence of an indepth knowledge of the cultures, histories, literatures, and languages of a single area or country.

This shift in priorities for knowledge-production has an especially detrimental effect on women. As Gayatri Spivak has shown, how value of items or people is assigned by those who have the power to do so, even in the most economistic sense, involves an understanding of the cultural context—an understanding that will continue to elude us if our assessment of globalization works only within the logic of late capitalism. Spivak suggests, in Marxist feminist terms, that scholars have been tied to the centrality of exchange value, thus failing to recognize that culture is formed on the materiality of use value. *Use value*, in Marxist terminology, bears no quantitative relation to *exchange value*. It is a back formation broadly referring to the usefulness of an object to someone prior to its entrance into a systematic arena of exchange as a commodity—in which its exchange value is established. In other words, we have mistaken labor for capital. Understanding the absolute interrelatedness between the economic and the cultural is fundamental to any study of women or of gender more broadly, as is the knowledge that the dominant model of globalization has very different influences depending on specific contexts (Spivak 1985).

THE "BOTTOM UP" MODEL AS A COUNTERMODEL: ETHNIC STUDIES AND WOMEN'S STUDIES

An unintended consequence of area studies initiatives was the ironic relationship between the history of area studies and the history of what were quite subversive curricular reforms in the 1970s, reforms that overtly inserted political movements into the university. The undermining of traditional Orientalist studies forced a disciplinary shift that involved inclusion of a larger range of data, and the questioning of formerly sacrosanct disciplinary divisions. This work in area studies paralleled the epistemological and methodological groundwork enabling the emergence of a set of secondary "area studies" within the domestic sphere: women's studies and ethnic studies (e.g., African American studies, Latino studies, Judaic studies) (Wallerstein 1997; Merkx 1995). As area studies operated from a top-down model—identifying a void and attempting to fill it—the new ethnic and women's studies programs countered this model by proceeding from the bottom up.

In the late 1960s and early 1970s, with students and supportive faculty pushing for change, new courses were instituted, and programs and departments were developed. As these changes took place, forgotten populations and histories began to emerge from silence. In this manner, ethnic and women's studies privileged "populations whose collective histories included removal, enslavement, internment, and subjugation . . . [those who have] had to fight to gain access to formal education and other benefits of citizenship" (Butler and Schmitz 1992). Although both ethnic and women's studies emerged from social movements, they were integrated differently within the academy. Departmental status was favored for ethnic studies, and women's studies developed as programs with adjunct appointments from other departments. Either way, drawbacks accompanied many of the structural benefits of the programs (see Castro 1990; Butler and Schmitz 1992; Rao 1991). As the disciplines have become established within academia, critique from within has arisen, again from the "bottom up." These have included the critique of women's studies as exclusive, essentialist, heterosexist, white, middle-class, and U.S.– and Western Eurocentric; and the critique of ethnic studies as masculinist, essentialist, and heterosexist (e.g., Anzaldúa 1987, 1990; Collins 1990; hooks 1981; Mohanty, Russo, and Torres 1991; Spivak 1985). Ethnic studies and women's studies have both grown tremendously in response to these critiques, and from cross-germination among women's studies, ethnic studies, and area studies as well (Acosta-Belén 1993).

While some programs continue to fight for space, funding, and recognition, many have flourished (Butler and Schmitz 1992; Flores 1997). As of 1996, there were over 800 programs and departments in the United States whose focus was ethnic studies. While the majority were dedicated to African American studies, there were significant numbers devoted to Chicano and Puerto Rican—increasingly Latino—studies, Asian American studies, and American Indian or Native American studies, with fewer focused on European, German, Jewish, Portuguese, and Scandinavian studies (Bataille, Carranza, and Lisa 1996; Flores 1997; Carbo 1995). And, as ethnic studies scholars and departments increasingly incorporate feminist, postcolonial, and gay and lesbian perspectives, they have begun to allow for greater complexities within their own theoretical insights. Importantly, the activism that established many of these departments twenty years ago is, in some places, still alive. For example, today, the most visible student protests "on college campuses throughout the country have been directed at securing commitments from university administrators to establish programs in Latino and Asian-American [sic] Studies" (Carbo 1995). As Juan Flores makes clear, however, the current rise of ethnic studies in private, elite universities is mirrored by its decline in (poorer) state-funded schools, thus raising the concern that only a privileged few within the university system will benefit from what these programs have to offer.

In 1996, at least two-thirds of all U.S. colleges and universities offered courses in women's studies. There were more than 600 programs of study, with several now offering certificates through the Ph.D.; 80 centers or institutes for research on women and gender; more than 40 feminist presses and journals; 100 feminist bookstores; more than 50 professional journals; and numerous professional and political associations (Chamberlain 1994). These figures reflect the growth and development of women's studies only in the United States. Women's studies, feminist studies, and gender studies scholars, courses, programs, departments, and institutes are growing throughout the world (see Basu 1995; Rao 1991).

In the last twenty years there has been "an explosion of knowledge and scholarship in these fields beyond any anticipated expectations" (Acosta-Belén 1993, 178). The breaching of specializations, disciplinary boundaries, and intellectual divisions of labor, coupled with innovative methodologies and analytical tools such as oral histories, testimonies, and participatory research, has challenged the implicit power relations within the academy, as well as patriarchal forms of knowledge.

Comparisons of area, ethnic, and women's studies reveal strong commonalities, with many of the formal features of women's studies and ethnic studies resembling those of area studies programs. These include the importance of interdisciplinary work; the idea of working in collaboration with experts in other disciplines who share commitments to given areas, regions, or peoples; and the holistic particularist method. In the contemporary U.S. academic environment, area, ethnic, and women's studies share similar philosophical mandates, including a commitment to the socially responsible production of knowledge and to strengthen the civic function "of engaging with the public on issues affecting" the regions of the world and the subjects with whom they work (Guyer 1996, 3; Acosta-Belén 1993; Flores 1997; Khalidi 1995; Martin 1996). Although at the outset the fields seemed quite separate, all are internationalizing their curricula, research, and scholarship, often with the need to respond to globalization as the rationale. Indeed, as Acosta-Belén's and Guy-Sheftall's essays in this volume suggest, the growth in ethnic studies may well come increasingly from globalized programs, such as Latino, African diaspora, or Pacific Rim studies, rather than from programs whose focus is a specific national or geographic area.

For similar reasons, women's studies scholars in the United States are seeking to internationalize their programs, as this volume demonstrates. We concur with Acosta-Belén and Guy-Sheftall that it is crucial for women's, ethnic, and area studies specialists to draw on each others' insights to develop and modify theories, methods, and perspectives for analyzing global and transnational phenomena. Ideally, such theories and methods would enable the particularities of each group's experiences to be framed "in reference to the historical analysis of gender and racial oppression and as part of a global system of social and macroeconomic relations among nations" (Acosta-Belén 1993, 176).

Merging theories and methods that illuminate local and macrostructural ties among sexism, racism, classism, and heterosexism, and that examine both the economic and cultural dimensions of human experience in late capitalism, is necessary to address multiple forms of oppression and resistance. In the United States, these three fields clearly have much to gain in their interactions with one another. The next step is to broaden the scholarly exchange among

U.S. universities and those in the global South. For feminists in particular, a two-sided exchange will be necessary. In the past, while most scholars from the global South interested in feminist and gender issues stayed abreast of the work of their northern counterparts, those in the latter group often failed to engage with the work of less privileged writers around the world and within their own countries (Acosta-Belén 1993; Johnson-Odim 1991). Work produced through North-South collaboration has already led feminists to a more critical engagement with area studies and globalization studies.

CRITIQUING AREA STUDIES: THE CHALLENGE OF GLOBALIZATION

Whether globalization is perceived as a continuation of the logic of modern capitalism or as a rupture from modernity (hence, the term *postmodernity*), analysts agree that profound changes have taken place in the world system. David Harvey (1989) analyzes this reconfigured system as a new regime of capitalist production based on flexible accumulation, characterized by a shift from the fixed factory site to flexible arrangements of the entire production process, from migrating production sites to disposable work forces. Other accompanying changes include the linking of financial markets across national borders, the increasingly monopolistic power of global corporations, and the growth of regional trading blocs. In addition, there has been a drastic speed-up of the processes of production and consumption, with resulting increase in the flow, transfer, and exchange of goods, labor, and capital investment across territorial boundaries. These new economic arrangements have greatly intensified traffic among cultures, peoples, and places worldwide, leading to the deterritorialization of spaces (Appadurai 1990). Consequently, the nation-state as the traditional regulator and lynchpin of international capital flow has been severely undermined (Hall 1997). With the collapse of the command economies in Eastern Europe and the ending of the cold war era, the world seems, in many ways, to be moving toward a one-world system.

These profound changes are matched by corresponding changes in the cultural spheres. Although colonialism long ago initiated the fracturing of local cultures through its imperialistic invasions, the increasing porousness of national borders to global capital, commodities, and cultural exchanges has further accelerated the process, leaving no ethnicity, community, or region untouched by exogenous influences.

Theorizing this new global phenomenon, with its complex cultural manifestations, poses a challenge for the work of scholarship. The uncertainty and flux in "postmodern" geographies and relations of production mark contemporary epistemologies and forms of theory. Today, notions of instability, the push toward the dissolution of master narratives, the privileging of the local, the blurring of boundaries, and the displacement of traditional notions of "authenticity" with the commodified image distinguish new ways of theorizing the material, social, political, and cultural.

Contemporary discourses seeking new ways to theorize the social include feminism, postcolonialism, poststructuralism, and cultural studies. These fields overlap complexly with one another. While having their own distinct emphases, histories, and scholarly traditions, the discourses share thematic concerns: a critique of power in all its forms and its various exclusions, the interrogation of the politics of knowledge-production, a skepticism toward totalizing narratives, the destabilization of meaning, the interrogation of positive knowledge-claims, the examination of the local and historical, and an interrogation of agency and subjectivity.

For these fields, analyzing late capitalism and the global processes to which it gives rise is a necessary step in understanding how the internal dynamic of contemporary societies is affected by external forces, often not within their immediate control (e.g., the 1997 debacle of Asia's "tiger" economies under the weight of devalued currencies, stock market plunges, and business failures). This impingement of global processes has highlighted the impossibility of "choos[ing] among economic, cultural and political concerns" because the very demand of critical practice is that we "link our understanding of postmodernity, global economic structures, problematics of nationalism, issues of race and imperialism, critiques of global feminism, and emergent patriarchies" (Kaplan and Grewal 1994, 439). The multifaceted nature of this critique has led to still another danger: masking "important political agendas in the service of reactionary interests" in not allowing its complicity with the beneficiaries of transnational circulation of capital to be perceived (Spivak, as quoted in Kaplan and Grewal 1994, 441). Those who are critical of global studies tend to be wary of its homogenizing and reductionist tendencies, and they warn of the temptation to project and universalize what may be merely a Western elitist, monocultural perspective that fails to appreciate the different outcomes of globalization processes worldwide. Such tendencies may feed back into theorizing and thus produce one-sided, globalizing discourses that valorize globalization as a monolithic process, in which the specificities of nation, region, and culture vanish, often with detrimental consequences. Some scholars, therefore, view the shifts in scholarship and funding priorities as little more than an attempt by "a triumphalist United States to write its economic and sermonic will on the global village; and [by] the U.S. academy to impose an intellectual order that prioritizes U.S. perceptions, problems, and preoccupations" (Zeleza 1997, 205).

Such distrust stems from the way that funding practices have served the hegemony and imperialism of Western scholarship. Western international scholars, for example, have had greater access to funding sources and information technology than field-based scholars. The rationale that globalization requires funding reforms might simply recognize neoclassical models of migratory corporate capital. Seen in this light, global studies is not a transnational model—with multiple locations and centers—but a highly hegemonic entity with the United States as its center, using newly constructed, transnational spaces for cheap labor and parts assembly. Scholars may be asked once again to play the compromised role of serving state or corporate interests.

Furthermore, Alexander Schenker suggests that the term *global studies,* rather than being more comprehensive, is, in fact, much narrower than area studies. Whereas area studies scholars may have counterparts in other universities and think-tanks around the world, global studies views the world from the vantage point of only one area. Problem-based scholarship developed under the new initiatives may not actually be transferable to international academic networks. Following this critique, perhaps "the problems that 'we' might call 'global' are seen in those countries [who are not central powers] as nothing more than our private concern for the well-being of our own commonwealth" (Schenker 1996, B3). Schenker describes this sense of *global* as having parallels to a *Pax Romana,* a global security and communication arrangement for a world designed to center on ancient Rome. Instead of promoting a genuinely cross-cultural or transnational scholarship, he suggests that global studies is the birth of a new parochialism and superficiality under the guise of progress.

Similarly, Stuart Hall (1997) argues that "globalization" has become a way of deferring or distracting attention from the lack of a good domestic or particularistic analysis of the local. He disagrees that globalization processes permanently alter and reconstruct localized identities and cultures by effacing the differences among them. Instead, it may very well be that globalization has the effect of shoring up distinctions, invented or resurrected, among localities, regional identities, and collectivities. Similar processes may take place, then, when disciplines are forced to collaborate by top-down initiatives. Instead of finding new commonalities, the fences and borders may become more strictly monitored and revered.

REIMAGINING SCHOLARSHIP IN THE NEW MILLENNIUM: TOWARD A FEMINIST CARTOGRAPHY OF KNOWLEDGE

Tani Barlow has recently suggested that we need not mourn the loss of regional area studies as they have been configured historically. Rather, we should remain open to the possibility that there are other ways to do good, locally attentive, counterhegemonic research about "areas" in the world, without having to conform to nationalist or market-oriented initiatives. She reminds us that area and global studies are a concern of scholars and institutions not only in the United States, but elsewhere in the world. "Maybe," she suggests, "the boundaries of area studies are not being displaced but are rather being recoded or reconfigured." Barlow insists that we pay attention to contributions outside mainstream scholarship, like the growing presence of "racialized, ethnicized minority populations within national state boundaries" who write and reside "alongside the ideological, singular national subject" (Barlow 1997). Barlow points to the importance of interrogating discourses of internationalization and the transnational by approaching the particular impacts on the lives of particular social actors involved in such processes (e.g., Alexander and Mohanty 1997; Lavie and Swendenberg 1996; Malkki 1995; Ong 1987).

Our attempt here to provincialize the discourse of area studies (and, to a lesser extent, ethnic studies and women's studies) has been a critique of areal boundaries, showing how intellectual and state histories are bound together and how the teleology of capitalism plays into this dynamic. This provincialization seems necessary to us as a first step in understanding our own scholarly stake in studies of local and global interactions. Nevertheless, the attention to the singular and specific advocated by many feminists seems pertinent to us, and seems to offer a way of constituting an ethical model of feminist research that does not simply succumb to the logic of late capitalism. The singular and the particular have been the backbone of feminist scholarship's grassroots basis.

As we suggested earlier, women's studies and ethnic studies derived their impetus from grassroots political formations that were not initially supported by the university. Women's studies, for the most part, trained its students with an interdisciplinary ideal in mind, drawing methodologies and materials from diverse disciplines and arenas. Area studies, in contrast, was not interdisciplinary but multidisciplinary in its formation, and its research commitments, far from being bottom-up, were top down—delineated both by the geographical designations of Title VI funding and by the disciplinary demands on its participants.

In spite of these differences, most faculty in area studies and women's studies are housed in and (perhaps more importantly) trained by disciplinary departments, although in the case of women's studies this situation is changing with the development of new Ph.D. programs in that field. We have no misguided nostalgia for disciplines or even areas as they were previously designated. Researchers will, however, almost certainly play into the logic of late capitalism if we abandon completely our local and collaborative knowledge in order to think outside national and disciplinary borders. In regard to late capitalism, then, these questions seem crucial to us. Is there a cartography of knowledge that allows for a critique of nationalism while simultaneously acknowledging both its persistence and its power? Does that cartography recognize the provincial nature of epistemologies without ignoring the particular and local demands that have been influential globally? Does it recognize disciplinary shortcomings without dismissing the value of disciplinary knowledge? Given the historical trajectories we have mapped, such a cartography of knowledge seems like the only ethical one for this historical moment.

The persistence of disciplines, enlightenment principles, and geographical designations must be acknowledged if we are going to engage with the present in a manner that is not simply presentist. To do so has been the challenge of late capitalist postmodernity, a challenge inspiring us to resist the idea that, in Marxist terms, we have come to the end of history. We have alluded to this notion in our title, but with irony. The end of the cold war has been detrimental to knowledge-producing undertakings like area studies, and to areas of knowledge more broadly that attracted funding and institutional support in the past but are currently being eroded by corporate requisites for sound bite information rather than in-depth knowledge. For feminist international scholarship, the end of the cold war cannot mean the end of history, the end of scholarship, or indeed, the end of the validity of a Marxist critique of late capitalist enterprise.

Interdisciplinarity has too often consisted of the adoption by one discipline of materials usually associated with another, for example, the novel that makes its way into an anthropology or geography class, or the political theory that is analyzed in a literature department. Although this form of boundary challenging may serve an important function, it often raises the ire not only of disciplinary purists, but also of those trained in the other discipline and taught to value at least some of its methodologies. In this sense, the real challenge of interdisciplinary work would be to do collaborative scholarship, bringing differing methodologies to bear on each other while still enjoying the specific disciplinary questions. Women's studies' challenge to disciplinarity raises an interesting point, however, even as it frequently seems to wish that disciplinarity would simply disappear. The study of gender has called attention to the inadequacy of disciplinary knowledge for analyzing the experience and status of women. We contend though that while disciplines have frequently been inadequate, the solution is not the dissolution of disciplines so much as an internal critique within disciplines as they converse with each other.

Similarly, the persistence of nation-states even in the age of so-called globalization calls for forms of knowledge that must be regionally located and local while incorporating an understanding of the global processes that affect local lives. But that knowledge would also have to engage with national models, because nationalism and regionalism are still alive and well and intensely meaningful in the lives of many. To doubt the power of nationalism is part of the privilege of writing from the global metropolis. It is also an inability to recognize that in some instances the call to nationalism, however reactionary, is a resistance to the hegemony of global capital and to the U.S. culture that accompanies it. An internal critique of nationalism, both internal and transnational, would allow for an understanding of its persistence, even as it radically undermines the nation as a primary category of analysis.

A theoretical and epistemological model of globalization based on the global exchange of goods and the distribution of capital is in danger of producing knowledge that is complicit with late capitalist agendas. While the global circulation of capital exists, it does not follow that other forms of globalization have occurred or will occur. We propose then that a more *ethical* and responsible form of research calls for an engagement with the languages, histories, and politics of the singular. Experience and facts in and of themselves cannot, of course, be taken at face value, given that they participate in narratives, positions, and silences. Acknowledging singularity involves not simply allowing those who are usually silenced to speak, for that assumes a clear intentionality in speech; our persistent and often useful disciplinary, context-specific interpretive methods should not simply assimilate and translate those words for our own ears. Attuning ourselves to differences and similarities among cultures involves understanding how value is assigned within a cultural context, what a practice or belief draws from a colonial legacy or from contemporary globalization, and how it departs from those international forces. We fail to understand this complicity if our assessment of globalization constantly works within a logic of late capitalism that has been presentist, homogenizing, and often mindlessly negligent of the persistence of political (and scholarly) demands.

To that end, we offer the following suggestions as a cartography for scholars engaged in feminist international scholarship. First, we advocate the practice of and respect for immersion into the contexts in which women and men actually live. Globalization does not make space or place irrelevant. Where location and place are contested in their meaning, immersion becomes even more important in understanding how place is constructed—how it is relevant to identities, economies, and cultural production. If the notion of transcultural identity has emerged to better map the experience and expression of people's actual lives, then that work needs to make this link between people's concrete experiences and the spaces they call "home." Such spaces may, of course, include transcultural locations and times; electronically produced sites; and sites in flux—such as migrations, diasporic literatures, refugee sites, and texts.

Second, we encourage the integration of diachronic knowledge, language fluency, and empirical support into theory. Any effort to universalize notions or categories, wherever they originate, must be regularly interrogated by indigenous and empirical data. Genuine comparison between contexts involves an effort to identify distinctive particulars and to note comparable categories that are not necessarily translatable across cultures.

Third, we support efforts to prevent provincialism and isolation. Isolating disciplines, problems, regions, institutes, and scholars is anathema to feminist international research and teaching. We must find ways to fund working spaces for collaborative, interdisciplinary, and cross-regional work. Funding reforms must therefore increase, not cut, opportunities for travel for regional field study, and suggest undergraduate and graduate exchange programs in languages and field research. In these efforts, we need to better understand and promote genuinely interdisciplinary collaboration. This undertaking might require establishing centers where various discipline-based regional studies are regularly interrogated by work on transnational problems and concerns; and where university-wide initiatives to facilitate cross-disciplinary conversations, research projects, and team teaching projects can be housed (see McMillen 1996 for an account of one such center).

Finally, cross-disciplinary work—like the ideal of empirically informed transnational scholarship—must occur in a setting that makes productive comparison among countries and cultures possible. The structure would need to make room for what is common without imposing or romanticizing coherence for its own sake. And, perhaps most importantly, such work cannot take place in a framework that denies or exacerbates the very real material imbalances of its participants, such as access to funding, libraries, or electronic resources. These imbalances, in fact, underscore the lie of globalized leveling.

In conclusion, the specific knowledges afforded by area, women's, and ethnic studies are essential to an adequate understanding of how women and men are affected by, as well as function within, the local and the global. Thus, analyses of the material, social, political, and cultural effects on diverse women and men of the crumbling of nation-states—presently under the weight of new regionalisms and new world orders—are necessary. And, as the metaphor of woman as the last colony makes clear (Mies, Bennhold-Thomsen, and Von Werlhof 1988), we are in need of tools and analyses that will enable the creation of "decolonizing discourses about women's conditions" (Acosta-Belén 1993, 182). Finally, we contend that understanding the interrelatedness between the economic and the cultural is fundamental to any study of women or of gender more broadly, as is the knowledge that the dominant model of globalization takes very different forms depending on one's gender, one's ethnicity, one's class, and the locale one calls "home."

NOTE

The authors would like to thank Samantha Lindsay.

WORKS CITED

Acosta-Belén, Edna. 1993. "Defining a Common Ground: The Theoretical Meeting of Women's, Ethnic, and Area Studies." In Edna Acosta-Belén and Christine E. Bose, eds., *Researching Women in Latin America and the Caribbean*, 175–186. Boulder: Westview Press.

Alexander, M. Jacqui, and Chandra T. Mohanty, eds. 1995. *Feminist Genealogies, Colonial Legacies, and Democratic Futures.* New York: Routledge.

Anzaldúa, Gloria. 1987. *Borderlands: The New Mestiza = La Frontera.* San Francisco: Aunt Lute.

———, ed. 1990. *Making Face, Making Soul / Haciendo Caras: Creative and Critical Perspectives by Feminists of Color.* San Francisco: Aunt Lute.

Appadurai, Arjun. 1990. "Disjuncture and Difference in the Global Cultural Economy." In Mike Featherstone, ed., *Global Culture, Nationalism, Globalization, and Modernity,* 293–310. London: Sage.

———. 1991. "Global Ethnoscapes: Notes and Queries for a Transnational Anthropology." In Richard Fox, ed., *Recapturing Anthropology,* 191–210. Santa Fe: School of American Research Press.

Barlow, Tani E. 1997. "The Virtue of Clarity and Bruce Cumings's Concern over Boundaries." *Bulletin of Concerned Asian Scholars* 29 (1): 43–46.

Basu, Amrita. 1995. *The Challenge of Local Feminisms: Women's Movements in Global Perspective.* Boulder: Westview Press.

Bataille, Gretchen, Miguel Carranza, and Laurie Lisa. 1996. *Ethnic Studies in the United States: A Guide to Research.* New York: Garland.

Bates, Robert. 1996. "Letter from the President: Area Studies and the Discipline." *APSACP: Newsletter of the APSA Organized Section on Comparative Politics* 7 (1): 1–2.

Boas, Franz. 1940, 1966. "The Study of Geography." In *Race, Language, and Culture,* 639–647. New York: Free Press.

Breckenridge, Carol A., and Peter van der Veer, eds. 1993. *Orientalism and the Postcolonial Predicament: Perspectives in South Asia.* Philadelphia: University of Pennsylvania Press.

Butler, Johnella, and Betty Schmitz. 1992. "Ethnic Studies, Women's Studies and Multiculturalism." *Change* (January/February): 36–41.

Carbo, Rosie. 1995. "Ethnic Studies on the Rise." *Hispanic Outlook in Higher Education* 6 (8): 11–13.

Castro, Ginette. 1990. *American Feminism: A Contemporary History.* Elizabeth Loverde-Bagwell, trans. New York: New York University Press.

Chakrabaty, Dipesh. 1992. "Postcoloniality and the Artifice of History." *Representations* 37: 1–24.

Chamberlain, Mariam. 1994. "Multicultural Women's Studies in the United States." *Women's Studies Quarterly* 22 (3–4): 215–225.

Chatterjee, Partha. 1986. *Nationalist Thought and the Colonial World: A Derivative Discourse.* London: Zed.

Collins, Patricia Hill. 1990. *Black Feminist Thought: Knowledge, Consciousness, and the Politics of Empowerment.* New York: Routledge.

Cumings, Bruce. 1997. "Boundary Displacement, Area Studies, and International Studies During and After the Cold War." *Bulletin of Concerned Asian Scholars* 29: 6–26.

Flores, Juan. 1997. "Latino Studies: New Contexts, New Concepts." *Harvard Educational Review* 67 (2): 208–221.

Gupta, Akhi, and James Ferguson. 1992. "Beyond 'Culture': Space, Identity, and the Politics of Difference." *Cultural Anthropology* 7 (1): 6–23.

Guyer, Jane I. 1996. *African Studies in the United States: A Perspective.* Atlanta: African Studies Association Press.

Hall, Stuart. 1997. "The Local and the Global: Globalization and the Condition of Postmodernity Ethnicity." In Anthony D. King, ed., *Culture, Globalization and the World System: Contemporary Conditions for the Representations of Identity,* 17–39. Minneapolis: University of Minnesota Press.

Halliday, Fred. 1993. "'Orientalism' and Its Critics." *British Journal of Middle Eastern Studies* 20 (2): 145–163.

Handler, Richard. 1983. "The Dainty and the Hungry Man: Literature and Anthropology in the Work of Edward Sapir." In George Stocking, Jr., ed., *Observers Observed: Essays on Ethnographic Fieldwork,* 208–232. Madison: University of Wisconsin Press.

Harvey, David. 1989. *The Condition of Postmodernity.* Cambridge and Oxford: Blackwell.

Heginbotham, Stanley. 1994. "Rethinking International Scholarship." *Items* 48 (2–3): 36–39.

Heilbrunn, Jacob. 1996. "The News from Everywhere." *Lingua Franca* (May/June): 54.

hooks, bell. 1981. *Ain't I a Woman? Black Women and Feminism.* Boston: South End Press.

Johnson, Chalmers. 1997. "Perception vs. Observation, or The Contributions of Rational Choice Theory and Area Studies to Contemporary Political Science." *Political Science and Politics* (June): 170–174.

Johnson-Odim, Cheryl. 1991. "Common Themes, Different Contexts: Third World Women and Feminism." In Chandra Talpade Mohanty, Ann Russo, and Lourdes Torres, eds., *Third World Women and the Politics of Feminism,* 314–327. Bloomington: Indiana University Press.

Kabbani, Rana. 1986. *Europe's Myths of the Orient.* Bloomington: Indiana University Press.

Kaplan, Caren, and Inderpal Grewal. 1994. "Transnational Feminist Cultural Studies: Beyond the Marxism/Poststructuralist/Feminism Divides." *positions: east asia cultures critique* 2 (2): 430–445.

Khalidi, Rashid. 1995. "Is There a Future for Middle East Studies?" *MESA Bulletin* 29 (July): 1–6.

Lambert, Richard D. 1986. *Points of Leverage: An Agenda for a National Foundation of International Studies.* New York: Social Science Research Council.

Lavie, Smader, and Ted Swedenberg, eds. 1996. *Displacement, Diaspora, and Geographies of Identity.* Durham, N.C.: Duke University Press.

Lie, John. 1997. "Moral Ambiguity, Disciplinary Power and Academic Freedom." *Bulletin for Concerned Asian Scholars* 29 (1): 1–6.

Ludden, David. 1993. "British Orientalism in the Eighteenth Century: The Dialectics of Knowledge and Government." In Carol A. Breckenridge and Peter van der Veer, eds., *Orientalism and the Postcolonial Predicament: Perspectives in South Asia,* 250–278. Philadelphia: University of Pennsylvania Press.

Lustick, Ian. 1997. "The Disciplines of Political Science: Studying the Culture of Rational Choice as a Case in Point." *Political Science and Politics* 2 (June): 175–180.

The John D. and Catherine T. MacArthur Foundation. 1998. *Program on Global Security and Sustainability.* Internet site (March 3). www.macfound.org.

Malkki, Lissa. 1995. *Purity and Exile: Violence, Memory, and National Cosmology Among Hutu Refugees in Tanzania.* Chicago: University of Chicago Press.

Marcus, George, and Michael Fischer. 1986. *Anthropology as Cultural Critique: An Experimental Moment in the Human Sciences.* Chicago: University of Chicago Press.

Martin, William. 1996. "After Area Studies: A Return to a Transnational Africa?" *Comparative Studies of South Asia, Africa and the Middle East* (formerly *South Asia Bulletin*) 26 (2): 53–61.

McClintock, Ann. 1995. *Imperial Leather: Race, Gender and Sexuality in the Colonial Context.* New York: Routledge.

McMillen, Liz. 1996. "A New Cadre at Chicago." *The Chronicle of Higher Education* (March 22): A10(2).

The Andrew W. Mellon Foundation. "President's Report." *Report from January 1993 Through December 31, 1993.* 13–17.

Mercer, Joye. 1997. "The Foundation Shifts Its Focus and Structure." *The Chronicle of Higher Education* (August 15): A29.

Merkx, Gilbert. 1995. "Foreign Area Studies: Back to the Future?" *LASA Forum: Latin American Studies Association Newsletter* 26 (2): 5–9.

Mies, Maria, Vernika Bennhold-Thomsen, and Claudia Von Werlhof. 1988. *Women: The Last Colony.* London: Zed.

Mohamed, Abdul Jan, and David Lloyd. 1987. "Introduction: Minority Discourse— What Is to Be Done?" *Cultural Critique* (Fall): 5–17.

Mohanty, Chandra Talpade. 1991. "Cartographies of Struggle." In Chandra Talpade Mohanty, Ann Russo, and Lourdes Torres, eds., *Third World Women and the Politics of Feminism,* 1–47. Bloomington: Indiana University Press.

Mohanty, Chandra Talpade, Ann Russo, and Lourdes Torres, eds. 1991. *Third World Women and the Politics of Feminism.* Bloomington: Indiana University Press.

Narayan, Kirin. 1993. "How Native Is a 'Native' Anthropologist?" *American Anthropo-logist* 95 (3): 671–686.

Ong, Aihwa. 1987. *Spirits of Resistance and Capitalist Discipline: Factory Women in Malaysia.* Albany: SUNY Press.

Pletsch, Carl. 1981. "The Three Worlds, or the Division of Social Scientific Labor, circa 1950–1975." *Comparative Studies in Society and History* 23 (4): 565–590.

Prewitt, Kenneth. 1997. "Presidential Items." *Items* 50 (2–3): 31.

Rao, Aruna. 1991. *Women's Studies International: Nairobi and Beyond.* New York: The Feminist Press.

Readings, Bill. 1996. *The University in Ruins.* Cambridge, Mass.: Harvard University Press.

Said, Edward. 1978. *Orientalism.* London: R.K.P.

Schenker, Alexander. 1996. "Questioning the Value of 'Global' Studies." In "Letters to the Editor." *The Chronicle of Higher Education* (November 6): B3.

Shea, Christopher. 1997. "Political Scientists Clash over Value of Area Studies." *The Chronicle of Higher Education* (January 10): A13.

Smith, Wilfrid C. 1956. "The Place of Oriental Studies in a University." *Diogenes* 16: 106–111.

Spivak, Gayatri Chakravorty. 1985. "Scattered Speculations on the Question of Value." *Diacritics* 15.4 (Winter): 73–93.

Tolmacheva, Marina. 1995. "The Medieval Arabic Geographers and the Beginnings of Modern Orientalism." *International Journal of Middle Eastern Studies* 27: 141–156.

van der Veer, Peter. 1993. "The Foreign Hand: Orientalist Discourse in Sociology and Communalism." In Carol A. Breckenridge and Peter van der Veer, eds., *Orientalism and the Postcolonial Predicament: Perspectives in South Asia,* 23–44. Philadelphia: University of Pennsylvania Press.

Vishwanathan, Gauri. 1990. *Masks of Conquest: Literary Study and British Rule in India.* London: Faber and Faber.

Visweswaran, Kamala. 1996. *Fictions of Feminist Ethnography.* Minneapolis: University of Minnesota Press.

Voll, John. 1996. *Globalization and the Study of Islam.* Unpublished Banquet Address given to ACSIS, Villanova University (May 3).

Wallerstein, Immanuel. 1997. "The Unintended Consequences of Cold War Area Studies." In Noam Chomsky et al., eds., *The Cold War and the University: Toward an Intellectual History of the Postwar Years,* 195–232. New York: New Press.

Zeleza, Paul Tiyambe. 1997. "The Perpetual Solitudes and Crises of African Studies in the United States." *Africa Today* 44 (2): 193–209.

ETHNIC AND GENDER ENCOUNTERS: A HEMISPHERIC APPROACH TO LATIN AMERICAN AND U.S. LATINO(A) STUDIES

Edna Acosta-Belén

As we are constantly reminded in academic and popular texts, we are in the midst of a postmodern era of contested boundaries, border transgressions, bridge-building, geographic remappings, and transnational interconnections. Yet while postmodernist thought claims the collapse of the totalizing grand narratives and ethnocentric representation practices of the West, the world is being subjected to an ever-expanding web of economic, commercial, and cultural networks and forces that continue to propagate homogenizing images and values, and a conception of a triumphant capitalist "new world order" still defined by the leading Western countries. Consequently, academics in Latin American and U.S. Latino(a) studies are becoming increasingly engaged in analyzing the compelling realities of hemispheric integration and globalization processes, enacted by the continuing international labor migration flows from the developing to the leading capitalist nations, by the expanding presence and projected demographic growth of the U.S. Latino(a) population into the twenty-first century, and by the complex economic, social, and cultural forms of transnationalism occurring within the Americas and on a global scale. All these processes are gendered and require the insights of a more transnational women's studies as well.

The hemispheric and gendered approach to the study of Latinos(as) in both parts of the Americas—North and South—introduced here stems from the ongoing interconnections that Latino(a) (im)migrants are developing *within* the United States and *between* the United States and their respective countries of origin.[1] Far more rapidly than ever before, the Latino(a) worlds of the North and South are transcending spurious geographic, cultural, and linguistic borders, particularly in view of current U.S. immigration patterns, demographic trends, and future projections. The U.S. census projects that, if current growth rates continue, Latinos(as) will become the largest "minority" group in U.S. society during the early decades of the new millennium. With a current population of over thirty-one million (the equivalent of the combined population of several Latin American countries), one out of every ten individuals living in the United States is of Hispanic origin. By the middle of the next century this could change to one out of five (see tables 1 and 2).[2]

HISPANIC/LATINO(A) POPULATION DISTRIBUTION BY GROUP, 1998. TABLE 1

Origin	Population in Millions
Total Hispanic Population	31.0
Mexican	19.8
Puerto Rican	3.1
Cuban	1.3
Central and South American	4.4
Other Hispanic	2.4

Note: Population figures for nondecennial U.S. census years are based on sample survey estimates or a relatively small number of cases, which often results in an undercount of particular population groups.

Source: U.S. Bureau of the Census, *Current Population Survey* (Washington, D.C.: U.S. Census Bureau, Population Division, March 1998).

HISPANIC/LATINO(A) POPULATION GROWTH, 1970–2030. TABLE 2

Year	Hispanic/Latino(a) Population in Millions	Percent Increase (%) U.S. Population (%)	Percent of Total
1970	9.1	—	4.5
1980	14.6	60.4	6.4
1990	22.4	53.4	9.0
2000	30.6	36.6	11.1
2010	39.3	28.4	13.2
2020	49.0	24.7	15.2
2030	59.2	20.8	17.2

Note: Figures for years 2000–2030 are based on U.S. Census 1992 middle series projections.

Source: U.S. Bureau of the Census, *Current Population Reports,* P23–183. *Hispanic Americans Today.* (Washington, D.C.: U.S. Government Printing Office, 1993).

(IM)MIGRATION AND TRANSNATIONALISM

According to some immigration researchers (Portes and Rumbaut 1990), a large portion of present-day international migration flows can be accounted for in the global diffusion of consumption patterns, values, lifestyles, perceived opportunities, and material aspirations within industrialized Western societies—and the unlikelihood of their fulfillment in the immigrants' respective countries of origin. Coupled with the shifting demographics of the United States, more recent international labor migration patterns between leading capitalist nations and developing nations, in particular between the United States and countries south of the U.S. border, are changing and expanding the scope of Latin American, Caribbean, and American studies and those ethnic and women's and gender studies programs that focus on U.S. Latino(a) experiences. These include Chicano(a) and Puerto Rican studies, which emerged out of the civil rights and educational opportunity struggles of the 1960s and 1970s, followed by Cuban, and more recently, Dominican studies, as well as other potential programs that may emerge focusing on individual groups or on panethnic U.S. Latino(a) issues and experiences. Without question, the incessant intersections between the local, the national, and the transnational, evident in new forms of socioeconomic relations, cultural production, and social and political movements, manifest the increasing interdependence among the nations of the hemisphere.

Continuous migrations between the two Americas and, more specifically, the irrepressible current and projected growth in the U.S. Latino(a) population, are sustaining what anthropologist Constance Sutton (1987) described as a *transnational sociocultural system* that increasingly and reciprocally influences cultural experiences in the United States *and* in the Latin American and Caribbean countries of origin. In contrast to early European immigrant waves, most of today's (im)migrants maintain multistranded relations that link their host societies (in this case, the United States) with their homelands. While (im)migrants from Latin America and the Caribbean contribute to the Latin Americanization or Caribbeanization of particular U.S. communities, their present commuter patterns and persistent interactions with their countries of origin influence the spread of U.S. values and ways of life and significantly impact the cultural, political, and socioeconomic structures of the countries of origin.

This transnationalism is leading scholars to engage in more integrated cross-border approaches to the study of the cultural and socioeconomic conditions and interconnections among the peoples and nations of the Americas. For many years the U.S. Latino(a)/Latin American (im)migrant experience remained sharply segmented in most teaching and research endeavors in both area and ethnic studies. Many U.S. scholars in these programs thought that their sphere of research began on the northern side of the Río Grande, while scholars living in Latin America often viewed their Latino(a) (im)migrants on the "other side of the Río Bravo" as an unappealing, illegitimate, and therefore rejected, representation of their nationality.[3] In turn, scholars in American studies focused on white America and for decades remained oblivious to issues of race, ethnicity, and gender as important components of the American experience, while women's and gender studies underwent their own struggles in the process of becoming more inclusive of the experiences of women of color. Thus, as Elsa Chaney pointed out in 1979 (Sutton and Chaney 1979), the study of the U.S. Latino(a) experience seemed to always belong *elsewhere,* with little attention paid to those who belonged to two societies. It is not surprising that until recently most textbooks used in introductory Latin American studies courses or U.S. history courses practically ignored the presence and contributions of U.S. Latinos(as). The same holds true for textbooks used in Latin American and Caribbean countries.

Now, the increasing presence of Latinos in the United States is making scholars more aware of the effects of contemporary globalization and transnationalism and how these influence the cultural, economic, and political interactions among the nations of the hemisphere. A stage has been reached in which the artificial boundaries traditionally separating the study of the Latin American and Caribbean regions from that of their counterpart Latino(a) populations in the United States are being transgressed, underscoring the need for wider hemispheric approaches to the study of different aspects of Latino(a) experiences on both sides of the border. For too long we have associated the U.S. immigrant experience with a permanent rupture or separation from the countries of origin, rather than looking at the multistranded social, economic, and political interactions and networks that link the sending countries with the host societies. These interactions and networks represent some of the most obvious areas of common ground for crossing the great divide that has traditionally separated Latin American studies from Latino(a)–focused ethnic studies programs, such as Chicano(a) and Puerto Rican studies, which emerged from the U.S. civil rights, antiwar, and ethnic revitalization movements of the 1960s and 1970s.

As a result of the ongoing efforts to be more inclusive and to rectify some of their initial shortcomings, in the last two decades it has become quite clear to specialists in Latin American, Caribbean, and other area, ethnic, and women's and gender studies that these fields are no longer centered in the United States. Instead, more scholars and activists from the countries and peoples studied are participating and contributing to the field. In the specific case of Latin American and Caribbean studies and U.S. Latino(a) studies, the parochialism of the early years is being replaced by an expanding sense of hemispheric community, in which we have come to rely on the scholarship, policymaking, and activism of our colleagues from these regions as much as they rely on the work being done by scholars in the United States and other parts of the world.

THE LOCAL AND THE GLOBAL IN THE NEW WORLD ORDER

Five hundred years ago, Europe ostensibly "discovered" the New World. It could be said that in the era of contemporary globalization, the world is beginning to discover itself as a more holistic system, with as many commonalities of purpose and pressing problems as there are divergent interests and solutions. New technologies are creating an increasing awareness of a global common destiny, and sustained efforts to bring down the barriers that traditionally separate peoples and nations are becoming more apparent. In the Americas, there is what Frank Bonilla (1996) calls a "lingering unease" about economic hemispheric initiatives. Among other actions and events, these are expressed by the heated debates that arose before and after NAFTA (the North American Free Trade Agreement) was approved by the U.S. Congress, by the Zapatista unrest in Mexico and its influence on other indigenous movements in the hemisphere, by the unprecedented and remarkable use of the World Wide Web by those movements in spreading their message and garnering international support, and by the subsequent Mexican economic crisis.

Such hemispheric events may also be considered within the framework of wider globalization processes that are forcing scholars in many fields to grapple with the implications of a new world order or, to be more accurate, with some of the "disorder" brought about by the disintegration of the socialist bloc and the concomitant structural adjustments in a world dominated by internationalized capital. In this brave new world, information and money can be exchanged in an instant, corporations move all over the planet seeking sources of low-wage labor, and goods can be transported more rapidly and efficiently than ever before. The processes of structural adjustment, privatization, and neoliberalization that Latin American and Caribbean countries have experienced in the last decade reflect some of the problems and inefficiencies that afflicted their dependent economies. Such processes continue to exacerbate existing social tensions and inequalities, causing major population displacements and considerable hardship for large sectors of their societies, with only limited and not so obvious prospects for recovery and long-term prosperity (Acosta-Belén and Santiago 1995).

Most of our contemporary societies are confronting mass unemployment, poverty, and increases in crime, violence, and homelessness even in the wealthiest countries. Clearly, "it is as if something has gone out of order with the new world order," to paraphrase the lyrics of Brazilian Caetano Veloso's popular song; words that poignantly capture the contradictions of a world characterized by growing inequalities and widening gaps between rich and poor, capital and labor, and between the status of men and women. In this new world order of transnational capital, women, immigrants, and developing nations continue to be the major sources of low-wage labor.

Nonetheless, to the mounting challenges implied in the homogenizing tendencies of contemporary globalization, more progressive forces continue to counterpose an array of social concerns—from human rights and environmental issues to a rejection of patriarchal, sexist, heterosexist, and racist viewpoints and practices. Slogans such as "think globally, act locally" also permeate our collective consciousness, reminding us of the potential threat of losing the subtleties, nuances, or particularities of each group or community, as well as the empowering potential of specific subaltern constituencies.

Suzanne Jonas and Edward McCaughan (1994, 2) perceptively capture some of these current dynamics when they point out that "globalization is creating new regional centers of capital accumulation, and hence new alliances across states among segments of classes, transnational and local, that will benefit from new technologies and new forms of accumulation." Within this new social map the authors stress the need for progressive *cross-border* coalitions that may include, for instance, labor, environmental, women's, and indigenous groups, particularly in Mexico, Canada, and the United States; in other words those groups representing people and areas that are usually most affected by the intemperate nature and undemocratic transgressions of transnational capital. New forms of activism grow from the convergence of views, strategies, and goals articulated by the various kinds of movements aimed at producing social and political change that have flourished in both Western and non-Western societies in recent decades. Among the most conspicuous examples are those that reflect the spread of what Cuauhtémoc Cárdenas (1993) calls "ideals without boundaries," referring primarily to those movements that promote human, women's, and ethnic rights, and environmental and health concerns. These particular movements are reflective of worldwide struggles for fundamental freedoms and rights and contribute to exposing uneven power relations and conflicts based on ethnic, racial, gender, and class differences, among other persistent inequalities.

Contemporary globalization processes are also contributing to the notion of a new global citizenship. As part of his proposals for forging and advancing a sense of global citizenship, Richard Falk (1993) points to two types of globalization. The first one, which he calls *globalization from above,* represents the interests of the industrial nations of the West. This type of globalization perpetuates an unbalanced new world order that, rather than being dominated by a single country, replaces the single country hegemons of the past with geographic hegemonic blocs (i.e., North America, European community, and the Pacific Rim) (Cárdenas 1993). This type of globalization reduces the world to "a homogenizing supermarket for those with the purchasing power" (Falk 1993, 50). The other form is globalization from below, which represents a social vision reflecting "an array of transnational social forces animated by environmental concerns, human rights, hostility to patriarchy, and a vision of community based on the unity of diverse cultures seeking an end to poverty, oppression, humiliation, and collective violence" (Falk 1993, 50). This type of globalization envisions a one-world community where human solidarity is based on democratic participation empowering ordinary individuals and enabling communities to have more control over the resources and conditions that influence human lives. It is this latter form of globalization that best challenges the homogenizing tendencies and best exploits the current contradictions in the practices of globalization from above.

In the edited volume *Global Visions: Beyond the New World Order* (1993), Jeremy Brecher, John Brown Childs, and Jill Cutler introduce what they call a "multifesto" (rather than manifesto) for promoting globalization from below, based on a vision of a world where we acknowledge our many differences but also search for a convergence of goals. Denis McShane (1993, 204) offers the key to this convergence of goals when he proposes moving toward a global solidarity by fostering and forging complementary coalitions based on what he identifies as the four Es—economy, ethnicity, equality, and ecology.

Some scholars are claiming that the transition we are experiencing in the current world economy is comparable in significance to the nineteenth-century Industrial Revolution, necessitating, by implication, the use of more global approaches in analyzing contemporary realities. There is discussion among these scholars about an emerging field of global studies in which researchers and policymakers in business and the social sciences get together to address major issues and questions raised by globalization processes. Some of these include the nature of competition among nations and corporations, global competition among different forms of capitalism, the local ramifications of the global economy, the role of the nation-state in a world where labor and capital are increasingly mobile, the relationship between interdependence and increasing social inequalities within and across nations, and the question of who can and should regulate businesses or corporations that have sites all over the world. Other obvious questions of particular relevance to Latinos(as) include ways in which U.S. employment and investment needs are linked to immigration, foreign trade, political regimes, the environment, and human rights concerns; the exacerbated social and political tensions and contradictions created by the widening cleavages between capital and labor and between highly industrialized North American nations and developing Latin American and Caribbean nations; and the influence of new information and media technologies on our consumption patterns, values, and aspirations, as well as on the contemporary construction of Latino(a) identities in our hemisphere.

I refer to these recent academic developments to underscore how globalization processes are confronting scholars with new challenges and with the need to articulate new responses. Needless to say, the voices and participation of specialists in gender, Latin American, Caribbean, and U.S. Latino(a) studies are essential in delving into some of the manifold implications of hemispheric integration and globalization.

The transnational encounters and crossovers between the North and the South are not exclusive to our hemisphere; they are occurring in other regions of the world, particularly between metropolitan countries and their former colonial territories. This means that cross-border coalitions have the potential of developing into far-reaching international movements aimed at more effectively counteracting the inequities, excesses, and undemocratic tendencies of transnational capital, as well as the alarming spread of right-wing activism. Indeed, perhaps the most threatening phenomenon of the new millennium is the renewed life of right-wing demagoguery, with all its xenophobic, homophobic, sexist, and racist implications and backlashes. Especially alarming is the fact that these backlashes and xenophobic attitudes are turning into mass ideologies that are no longer country-specific or localized, but have acquired a global dimension.

THE RESTRUCTURING OF KNOWLEDGE

The global restructuring of the economy not only requires transnational forms of resistance but also implies a concomitant restructuring of knowledge production. Immanuel Wallerstein (1995, 22) pointed to this necessity in an article about the state of African studies, noting that the field was reflecting "the uncertain path of redefinition, even of reassertion" as other constructs such as ethnic studies, cultural studies, diaspora studies, and other movements and constructs influenced by poststructuralist theories were introduced into the academic enterprise. He goes so far as to predict that "the whole disciplinary taxonomy is about to crumble" (23) as part of a more encompassing general process of restructuring knowledge production. One scholar, Nathan Glazer, recently "threw in the towel" and took a step beyond his *Beyond the Melting Pot* (which he coauthored with Daniel Moynihan in 1963) when he begrudgingly proclaimed in the title of his most recent book (1997) that "we are all multiculturalists now." Glazer's new book acknowledges that the multiculturalists have won the so-called U.S. culture wars due, to a large extent, to the country's failure to assimilate African Americans and other racial "minorities." His main conclusion is that, like it or not, multiculturalism is here to stay, and only a dramatic change in the bipolar black and white divisions of U.S. society would make it just another passing phase in the making of the nation. In an article published a few years ago, historians Michael Greyer and Charles Bright announced the revival of world history as an academic discipline, now that most Eurocentric biases and concepts are being exposed. They claim that "the reimagining of the world as history is under way" (Greyer and Bright 1995, 1037) and stress how the field, once again, is becoming one of the fastest growing areas of teaching.

Latin American and other area studies fields such as African studies, and for that matter, American studies, were initially influenced by cold war and other U.S. foreign policy imperatives. There was a parallel push by the U.S. government to "modernize" developing regions and to increase its knowledge and policymaking base regarding what were considered the extremely poor, undeveloped, and politically unstable peripheral regions of the world. They were fields primarily represented by North American white male academics with scant involvement of scholars from the targeted regions and little interest in gender issues or in the presence of groups of Latin American or African origin in the United States. This situation has changed significantly, particularly in the last two and a half decades, due in part to the efforts of professional area studies associations, major foundations, and research centers and programs to be more inclusive of the work of Latin American and Caribbean scholars and to provide travel and other collaborative opportunities and exchanges for scholars from these regions.

In my opinion, another development forcing the current reconceptualization of area studies is the increased academic legitimacy and institutionalization of women's and U.S. Latino(a) ethnic studies (Chicano(a), Puerto Rican, Cuban, and more recently, Dominican) and the scholarship that has come out of these fields, as well as the affinities and alliances that U.S. Latinas and other feminist scholars have begun to forge with their Latin American and Caribbean counterparts. Without the infusion of gender perspectives into area and ethnic studies by some of the feminist scholar pioneers, we probably would not have fully understood how the lives of women were affected by modernization, development, (im)migration, and the international division of labor. Nor would we know the uncounted or discounted hidden aspects of their labor, their significant role in the 1980s democratization process, their articulation and advancement of social and human rights in various countries, or their role in increasing international awareness about environmental and health concerns.

GENDER AND FEMINIST THOUGHT

Most scholars of the Latin American–U.S. Latino(a) experience who specialize in gender or feminist research would agree that the U.N. Decade for Women (1975–85) served as an important catalyst in creating awareness of women's conditions in different parts of the world, and in generating research, scholarship, and activism of a magnitude that was then hard to imagine. The 1975 International Women's Year Conference in Mexico City, followed by several other international conferences and *encuentros* (meeting of minds), underscored the diverse viewpoints, needs, and concerns of women in the developing nations from different classes and races when compared to women in the highly industrialized nations.[4] Since then gender-focused research has gradually moved from an initial concern about overcoming the absence or the invisibility to which women had been relegated within the traditional disciplines, through efforts for appropriate inclusion and representation, to a critique of their faulty assumptions and paradigms, and, finally, to the production of new knowledge. Scholarly research is now characterized by more complex analyses regarding the social construction of gender; its intersections with other categories of difference such as ethnicity or nationality, race, class, and sexuality; and its constitution in relation to specific geographic, historical, socioeconomic, cultural, and political relations.

Much of the gender-oriented research about Latin American and Caribbean women has tended to focus on case studies or on specific countries, issues, or events rather than on broad theoretical discussions. Applied or action-oriented research, intended to influence governments, institutions, and the formulation of public policy, has occupied center stage and is often a natural extension of the activism of individuals or nongovernmental organizations (NGOs). The bulk of this research is carried out at independent centers or organizations committed to the advancement of women and not strictly within the walls of the academy. Frequently, the individuals who produce this research play multiple roles, blurring the lines between basic and applied research or between the scholar and activist. Bolles (1993) finds this to be a pattern within the Caribbean region, where gender-focused research has been the product of women acting as concerned citizens, in political or civic activist groups, as members of government agencies or private institutions, or as scholars committed to social change.

Some groundbreaking research has documented Latin American and Caribbean women's extensive participation in social and political movements, as well as the emergence of feminist or women's movements during different historical periods. This research showed the active involvement of women from all classes and races in the struggles for social justice and in promoting social change, dispelling the widespread notion that women of color in developing countries passively accept their different forms of oppression, and bringing to light the hidden aspects of their productive roles. During different historical periods women from diverse social sectors came together around a common cause or established separate parallel movements of working class and middle or upper class women around similar issues. Some of these parallel movements include the nineteenth-century participation in independence movements against Spanish colonial rule, the battles for women's suffrage and labor unions during the early part of the twentieth century, and in more recent decades, women's organized opposition against the human rights abuses of authoritarian military regimes and promotion of government democratization.

During the last decade, there has been an overall expansion of scholarship about the many differences among women and the many forms feminism assumes within specific communities, social sectors, nations and races, or particular regions of the world. There is also widespread recognition of the need to make women's and gender studies a more inclusive space for women of color in the United States and other Western countries, and in the Third World.

In spite of continuing struggles and the high degree of consolidation and institutionalization of some programs, the field of women's and gender studies is still at a critical juncture in its development.

Economically, it is affected by the budgetary reductions and the educational and economic downsizing and restructuring going on in U.S. society and other parts of the world. Intellectually, as academic feminists confront the dramatic changes in the world scene, we are still far from developing broadly based multicultural and gender-inclusive teaching and learning about the differences and commonalities within and across feminist or women's movements in various parts of the globe. Do we have an adequate conception of the variety of Western feminisms as well as of non-Western feminist discourses? What, for instance, are some of the major differences in the development of North American and Western European women's movements, or the differences between those movements in Western and Eastern Europe, Latin America and Africa, the United States and Japan, Cuba and Puerto Rico? What are some of the issues and conditions that transcend national borders and are specific to a country or local community? Why is it that some women's movements do not regard the state as the major instrument for improving their status and others do? Why is it that in some countries women's movements are more grassroots-oriented than in others? What are some of the reasons that made women's and gender studies flourish in academic settings in the United States and other Western nations, but primarily at independent centers and institutes in most Third World countries? If we see feminism as a historically continuous and fluid movement, what are the factors that produce periods of expansion and stagnation in particular countries? If there is an international or global women's movement, what are the factors that bind it together? And if some of the present social and economic conditions are global and general, how can we bring about articulated forms of global action around specific issues? Which are the issues that could make transnational and cross-border coalitions possible?

The answers to these questions are far from obvious. They are posed to capture some of the challenges to and complexities of women's lives and women's studies. Nonetheless, we have achieved some clarity in that Western feminisms should not continue to be portrayed as one movement or as a master discourse that transcends cultures and national boundaries and that can, therefore, be exported just like a commodity or development program to modernize developing countries. This, of course, does not mean that scholars and activists should stop searching for commonalities and convergences across feminist and women's movements. On the contrary, emphasizing these commonalities and learning about the singularities and pluralistic nature of women's struggles around the world, and the theoretical frameworks that emerge from less privileged settings, increases the possibilities for building cross-border solidarities and coalitions around issues that affect large numbers of women. Promoting comparative and cross-cultural research can be quite valuable in increasing our understanding about those specific historical, socioeconomic, political, or cultural factors that inform ideological strategies, enhancing our visions of those women's and feminist movements that have been most effective in producing social change or in achieving particular goals.

MULTICULTURAL CROSSOVERS

No one can deny the increasing interdisciplinarity and cross-fertilization flourishing in the academy, particularly within the last few decades. Fields like ethnic studies, women's and gender studies, cultural studies, diaspora studies, and gay and lesbian studies are providing new locations for scholars to pursue more inclusive analyses of a rapidly changing world and the differences or particularities that shape human existence—social, racial, sexual, cultural, local, and transnational. This is being accomplished by challenging the construction of knowledge and canonical practices of the traditional disciplines within the Western intellectual tradition, by exploring the interstices among disciplines, and by revising long-standing paradigms or formulating new ones. Worthy of notice is the fact that, although these new interdisciplinary fields emerged as a critique of, and introduced significant changes into, the university curriculum in the United States and other major Western countries, they are also making significant inroads in the rest of the world, including the developing countries of Latin America and the Caribbean.

Significant cultural and linguistic transformations and exciting hybrid cultural configurations are emerging from the transnational sociocultural system that characterizes the Americas. These multicultural crossovers are forcing us to rethink, redefine, and transgress the conventional boundaries of what we do in our respective academic disciplines. These crossovers represent more than the study of provocative sociocultural phenomena. They are changing the scope of some of the traditional disciplines, transcending their rigid disciplinary demarcations, and opening their borders to those paradigms that not only favor more interconnected global approaches to our social realities, but also view our societies as complex conglomerates of hybrid cultures and contested identities with conflicting and uneven power relations. Some of the traditional disciplines are transforming themselves by exploring the interstices among disciplines, increasingly exposing their inherent biases and parochialism, and developing a better grasp of the social forces, power relations, and contradictions that shape disciplinary knowledge, both within Western and non-Western intellectual traditions.

These knowledge transformations are quite evident in the realms of cultural, historical, and literary studies, my main research interests. Here, new patterns of commuter (im)migration and the transnational interconnections, encounters, and crossovers taking place between the United States and Latin American and Caribbean countries are producing some provocative cultural configurations and discourses. One concrete example is how U.S. Latino(a) writers increasingly are being studied and incorporated into the canons of U.S., Latin American, and Caribbean literatures. Women writers such as Rosario Ferré, Judith Ortiz Cofer, Esmeralda Santiago, Sandra Cisneros, Julia Alvarez, and Cristina García are some of the figures who, along with several male Latino writers, are contributing to an expanding Spanish-English publication market where some of the largest U.S. publishing houses are releasing simultaneous editions of their works in each language.[5] Many Latino(a) writers also make use of their bilingual skills by engaging in code switching or the use of Spanglish within the same text—a reminder to readers of the multi-lingual-multicultural nature of U.S. society.

Another crossover research area that is receiving increased attention after being considered an almost taboo subject in Latin American and Caribbean intellectual discourse is gay and lesbian studies. This relatively new field has already yielded several major Latino(a)-focused studies in the last few years. The pioneering work of Gloria Anzaldúa and Cherríe Moraga in the collection *This Bridge Called My Back: Writings by Radical Women of Color* (1981) has been followed in recent years by a revised, Spanish version of the book, *Esta puente mi espalda: Voces de mujeres tercermundistas en los Estados Unidos* (1988), edited by Moraga and Ana Castillo. Since then several other anthologies have been published, intended to disseminate the work of lesbian and gay authors while introducing important theoretical discussions that challenge conventional heterosexist interpretations of social realities.[6]

AREA, ETHNIC, AND WOMEN'S AND GENDER STUDIES: CONJUNCTURES AND DISJUNCTURES

Although it is true that some of the processes already described are making the boundaries and scope of area, ethnic, and women's and gender studies fields more permeable, there are important distinctions to make and pitfalls to avoid. First, we should be mindful that the historical origins and fundamental approaches of these fields are substantially different, and we should continue to stress these differences. Ethnic studies programs were projects formulated out of oppositional social movements that challenged the longstanding discriminatory and exclusionary practices of U.S. society toward ethnoracial "minorities," as well as their invisibility within the university and its traditional disciplines. Thus, ethnic studies became a major tool in generating significant paradigm shifts within the traditional disciplines regarding the study of race, ethnicity, class, and gender. At the same time, ethnic studies programs struggled for recognition as more than just another locus for identity politics or political correctness. The major focus of these programs on social and racial inequalities and unresolved related problems that plague U.S. society must not be sacrificed to an analysis of "global" or "hemispheric" concerns.

To this day, faculty who move with relative ease between area and ethnic studies are frequently caught in the bind of being delegitimized as real scholars in either field, precisely because they venture out of the conventional demarcations of narrowly conceived disciplines and fields, exposing some of their biases and shortcomings and focusing on the intersecting nature of gender, racial, and ethnic constructs. Initially, Latin Americanists or Caribbeanists in the United States who happened to be of Latin American or Caribbean origin and were drawn into Chicano(a) and Puerto Rican studies (at a time when the pool of academics with doctoral training was much smaller than it is today) often saw their work undermined or ignored, because it was viewed as an extension of their genetic makeup rather than a reflection of their intellectual preferences and professional expertise. While it was perfectly legitimate for American studies to glorify the *e pluribus unum* or melting pot mythical view of U.S. society, ethnic studies scholars continued to have to push their way in, with some degree of persuasion, perseverance, and success, if we consider the proliferation of scholarship in recent decades. The whole process of making significant intellectual and educational inroads may be summarized, in the words of Chicano performing artist Guillermo Gómez-Peña (1993, 43), as a practice in "creative appropriation, expropriation, and subversion of dominant cultural forms."

During the early years, the field of women's studies was also dominated by the perspectives of white middle class women in the United States and in Western European nations, and there was a tendency to view women in Third World countries as the passive victims of oppression rather than as agents of change and participants in the articulation of feminist theories. While women in Latin America and the Caribbean were keeping abreast of the work of women in the Western countries, Western women knew very little about the different realities and responses articulated by less privileged women from different races, classes, and nationalities. In this regard, U.S. feminist scholars in area and ethnic studies fields have been instrumental in bringing a multicultural and international dimension into women's studies and in influencing the proliferation of women's studies academic programs in Latin American and Caribbean institutions of higher education.

Similarly, women of color in the United States also experienced an early absence from the then emerging fields of ethnic and women's studies, as most programs focused initially on the collective subordination and disenfranchisement from the Western intellectual tradition of what were commonly portrayed as undifferentiated colonized peoples or subaltern subjects. These programs began to expose either the lack of knowledge about these groups or the need to reconceptualize received knowledge about them by deconstructing the canonical practices of the disciplines. The years of precarious existence faced by many ethnic and women's studies programs and their struggles for institutional survival and intellectual legitimacy often relegated, to another day, discussions about commonalities and differences between the fields. After all, gender and racial oppression were not the great equalizers in bringing white women and people of color of all genders together or in fostering a better understanding of their particular struggles. Scholars in each field have had to venture in each other's direction, a process of mutual crossfertilization that is still evolving.

These examples illustrate that the prevalent crossfertilization among interdisciplinary fields is not only unavoidable within prevailing global or transnational contexts, but also desirable both in intellectual and practical terms. After almost three decades of existence, and even after generating some of the most provocative and influential scholarship around, women's and ethnic studies programs are still viewed in some institutions as too political and/or or as marginal to the academic enterprise. Thus the increased collaborations and alliances among the more established area studies programs and other interdisciplinary fields should be pursued. In some cases, this may be a productive way of sharing faculty and other resources and engaging in productive collaboration, rather than in competition for a shrinking pool of resources.

NEW *ENCUENTROS*

In an article published a few years ago (Acosta-Belén 1993), I began to emphasize the importance of having scholars in interdisciplinary fields such as area, ethnic, and women's and gender studies further explore their commonalities and differences by engaging in cross-cultural comparative research and approaches at both national and international levels. This process would move these fields beyond their shared purpose (to *decolonize* knowledge about women and other subaltern groups) into the potential formulation of alternative models of inquiry stemming from inter- and intracultural, racial, and gender dialogues around issues central to each field (Acosta-Belén and Bose 1993a; Butler 1991). With their guiding principles of decentering and deconstructing hegemonic models and their focus on the relations between elite and popular consciousness and practice, on transnational crossovers and changing identities, and on discourse and representation, contemporary postmodern, postcolonial, and feminist theories have proven to be quite useful in dealing with the issues of borders and bridges and the constant commuting among our intertwining Latino(a) worlds.

These ongoing dialogues, coupled with the tremendous increase in the U.S. Latino(a) population of groups other than Mexicans or Puerto

Ricans, are pushing some of the existing Chicano(a) and Puerto Rican studies programs to expand their research and teaching efforts and to incorporate comparative approaches that address a wide range of differences *within* and *among* U.S. Latino(a) groups. A similar process is beginning to take hold within Latin American and Caribbean studies programs, which, after many years of neglect and exclusion, are now paying more attention to the experiences of Latin American and Caribbean (im)migrant populations in the United States as part of a contextual continuum with their countries of origin. More surprising is the fact that institutions and faculty in Puerto Rico, Mexico, and other Latin American and Caribbean countries have finally "discovered" Puerto Rican, Chicano(a), and other U.S. Latino(a) ethnic studies, and these new *encuentros* are now leading to more meaningful reciprocal collaborations. Considering that immigration has become one of the most contested issues within the current U.S. political discourse, particularly as it affects some of the nation's most populated states—California, New York, Texas, and Florida—the immigrant experience is still an area that has not received the attention it deserves in Latin American and Caribbean area studies research and teaching.

Perhaps this benign indifference explains, at least in part, why the academic community is currently not playing a central role in shaping the ongoing public debates about immigration, and the prevalent discourses instead are dominated by a xenophobic immigrant-bashing, in which U.S. Latino(a) communities are becoming scapegoats, along with other communities of color, for the hardships and uncertainties caused by downsizing and economic restructuring. The passing of new restrictive laws to curb legal and undocumented immigration, the attempts to deny access to educational and social services to immigrant families, and the efforts to discredit and dismantle affirmative action and bilingual education programs are symptomatic of this immigration backlash. The U.S. public discourse is plagued with fears about balkanization and the breakdown of American culture. Old myths and stereotypes about Latinos(as) obfuscate the benefits and highlight the detrimental effects of immigration. It is both perplexing and ironic that as the world moves to increasing interdependence and dismantling of borders (at least for the movement of capital), there is such a concerted political effort for the United States to close its borders to immigrants.

Although the immigration debate was partly shaped by the political histrionics of most recent presidential and congressional elections, Latin Americanists, Caribbeanists, and U.S. Latino(a) studies specialists cannot help but wonder how far this immigrant backlash will go before a much needed sense of balance is inserted into the debate. We must produce well-articulated counterresponses to the widespread xenophobic and racist attitudes toward immigration that we have witnessed in recent years. In the process of defining our research, teaching, and public policy agendas, we must not sacrifice the pursuit of democratic values, social justice, and antiracist and antisexist practices. Considering all the effects of increased immigration on the continuing and projected demographic changes in the racial and ethnic composition of U.S. society, these are undoubtedly some of the most pressing topics of future research in area, ethnic, women's, and gender studies. As transnational migrants commute between the United States and their Latin American and Caribbean countries of origin, we must continue to assess the impact they are having on their homeland economies and the social structures of their communities, and how their communities are, in turn, responding to these changes.

Although it is true that Latin Americanists and Caribbeanists had paid some attention to the migratory movements within the countries of these regions, particularly population displacements from rural to urban areas, until recently, the interest in Latin American and Caribbean migrants in the United States had been less noticeable. Most U.S. immigration specialists tend to be demographers using census-generated data. Few are area studies specialists who, through fieldwork, may address those aspects of immigration that cannot be explained by census data. Former Latin American Studies Association President Wayne Cornelius (1996) noted a few years ago that it may already be too late for scholarship to catch up with the anti-immigration backlash and influence policymaking so that it is based on the true costs and benefits that Latino groups have on specific states, cities, and localities.

Major private initiatives, such as those undertaken in recent years by the Ford Foundation,[7] are providing funding that allows centers and institutes at U.S. universities to promote the study of gender in global perspective and bring together area, ethnic, and gender scholars to participate in a variety of scholarly activities and disseminate the work presented at these meetings. In contrast, the U.S. Department of Education Title VI area studies grant competition continues to operate within a narrow definition of the scope of area studies by excluding proposals that focus on issues and activities aimed at linking U.S. (im)migrant or ethnic groups to their countries of origin.

Clearly, a major challenge during the new millennium is how to continue acknowledging and incorporating the vast human diversity that surrounds us into teaching and learning experiences. Demographic projections are not only confirming that Latinos(as) will constitute the largest "minority" group in U.S. society by the early decades of the twenty-first century, but that almost half (47%) of the total population of the United States will be composed of groups of color (Latinos[as], Asian Americans, African Americans, and Native Americans). Out of that figure, Latinos(as) will constitute 40 percent of the combined population of these groups. Thus scholars and teachers share a major responsibility for preparing students to be active, informed, and productive participants in a multicultural U.S. society and interdependent world. Perhaps more than ever before, these changes will continue to keep area studies and other interdisciplinary programs in business, but they also provide us the opportunity to reassess what we do as we face this undiscovered country of the future.

I cannot conclude this essay without reiterating the centrality of Latin American, Caribbean, U.S. Latino(a), women's, and gender studies programs in the challenges of theorizing and analyzing hemispheric and global changes. Increasingly, U.S. Latinos(as) position themselves to participate in bringing about changes in the Americas from *within* the United States (Bonilla 1996), while at the same time governments from Latin American and Caribbean countries are showing increased interest in their respective U.S. Latino(a) communities. U.S. Latinos(as) are already playing a more proactive role in influencing the formulation of U.S. policy in the hemisphere and also in shaping domestic policies. Moreover, Latino(a) scholars and professionals are also facing a formidable responsibility and challenge in training students to be critically informed and engaged global citizens. Thus alternative visions and approaches must continue to be defined by all kinds of constituencies, and not only international agencies, governments, or political and cultural elites. Clearly, the ability to see these differences and commonalities comparatively and also assess them in their local, regional, and global dimensions will continue to yield fresh and provocative insights and possibilities.

NOTES

Portions of this essay also appear in "Reimagining Borders: A Hemispheric Approach to Latin American and U.S. Latino(a) Studies" in Butler (1991).

1. The term *immigrant* refers to those individuals who come to the United States from foreign countries. *Migrants* are populations that move within the same territory or have established commuter patterns between the United States and their countries of origin. Since Puerto Rico is a U.S. territory and island and Puerto Ricans are U.S. citizens by birth, they are considered migrants and not immigrants.

2. These U.S. census population figures for Hispanics do not include undocumented workers, who enter the United States at an estimated rate of 300,000 per year. The current estimated total for the undocumented immigrant population is around 4 million. Census figures also do not include the 3.8 million Puerto Ricans residing on the island. Although all U.S. government agencies use the umbrella term "Hispanic" in their official reports, the diverse groups prefer to be identified by their individual nationalities (e.g., Puerto Rican, Mexican/Chicano[a]), or prefer the term Latino(a) for collective identification purposes.

3. Each name refers to the same river—Río Grande in English, Río Bravo del Norte in Spanish.

4. For a summary account of some of the major *encuentros* of both grassroots and professional Latin American women between 1981 and 1990, see Sternbach et al. (1992, 393–434). Other major *encuentros* include the Fifth Annual Inter-disciplinary Congress in Costa Rica in 1993; those sponsored by the University at Albany, SUNY Ford Foundation projects in Costa Rica and Puerto Rico; and

those sponsored by the City University of New York–University of Puerto Rico exchange program. See some of the publications generated by these *encuentros: Seminario estudios sobre la mujer* 1987, Acosta-Belén and Bose 1993b, Colón 1994, and *Gender Studies in Global Perspective* by Acosta-Belén and Frank, in press.

5. A few major U.S. publishing houses (e.g., Vintage Books, Ballantine Books) have created a Spanish-language division. Some of the works available in English and Spanish editions include: Santiago 1996a and 1996b, García 1992 and 1994, and Díaz 1996 and 1997.

6. Among the most recent publications in Latin American–U.S. Latino(a) gay and lesbian studies are Martínez 1996, Molloy 1998, Mirandé 1997, Balderston and Guy 1997, Gutmann 1996, Lumsden 1996, Bergmann and Smith 1995, and Melhuus and Stolen 1996. See also Ramos 1987.

7. Under the auspices of the Ford Foundation, the Center for Latino, Latin American, and Caribbean Studies (CELAC), and the Institute for Research on Women (IROW) at the University at Albany, SUNY initiated the projects *Internationalizing Women's Studies: Crosscultural Approaches to Gender Research and Teaching* (1995–1998) and *Gender in Global Perspective: A Graduate Training Program* (1998–2001). The volume *Gender Studies in Global Perspective: Focus on Latin America, the Caribbean, Africa, and Eastern Europe* (Acosta-Belén and Frank in press) includes papers presented at the various *Internationalizing Women's Studies* project conferences and faculty development seminars.

WORKS CITED

Acosta-Belén, Edna. 1993. "Defining a Common Ground: The Theoretical Meeting of Women's, Ethnic, and Area Studies." In Edna Acosta-Belén and Christine E. Bose, eds., *Researching Women in Latin America and the Caribbean,* 175–186. Boulder: Westview Press.

Acosta-Belén, Edna, and Christine E. Bose. 1993a. *Integrating Latin American and Caribbean Women into the Curriculum and Research.* Albany: CELAC/IROW.

———. 1993b. "Women in the Development Process in Latin America and the Caribbean." in Edna Acosta-Belén and Christine E. Bose, eds., *Researching Women in Latin America and the Caribbean,* 55–76. Boulder: Westview Press.

Acosta-Belén, Edna, and Francine Frank, eds. In press. *Gender Studies in Global Perspective: Focus on Latin America, the Caribbean, Africa, and Eastern Europe.* Albany: CELAC/IROW.

Acosta-Belén, Edna, and Carlos E. Santiago. 1995. "Merging Borders: The Remapping of America." *The Latino Review of Books* 1 (1): 2–12.

Anzaldúa, Gloria, and Cherríe Moraga, eds. 1981. *This Bridge Called My Back: Writings by Radical Women of Color.* New York: Kitchen Table Press.

Balderston, Daniel, and Donna J. Guy, eds. 1997. *Sex and Sexuality in Latin America.* New York: New York University Press.

Bergmann, L., and Paul Julian Smith, eds. 1995. *Entiendes? Queer Readings, Hispanic Writings.* Durham, N.C.: Duke University Press.

Bolles, A. Lynn. 1993. "Doing It for Themselves: Women's Research and Action in the Commonwealth Caribbean." In Edna Acosta-Belén and Christine E. Bose, eds., *Researching Women in Latin America and the Caribbean,* 153–174. Boulder: Westview Press.

Bonilla, Frank. 1996. "Changing the Americas from Within the United States." *The Latino Review of Books* 2 (1): 2–4.

Brecher, Jeremy, John Brown Childs, and Jill Cutler, eds. 1993. *Global Visions: Beyond the New World Order.* Boston: South End Press.

Butler, Johnnella E., ed. 1991. *Transforming the Curriculum: Ethnic Studies and Women's Studies.* Albany: SUNY Press.

Cárdenas, Cuauhtémoc. 1993. "Moving Peoples and Nations." In Jeremy Brecher, John Brown Childs, and Jill Cutler, eds., *Global Visions: Beyond the New World Order,* 273–278. Boston: South End Press.

Colón, Alice, ed. 1994. *Gender and Puerto Rican Women.* Rio Piedras: CERES.

Cornelius, Wayne. 1996. "The Latin American Presence in the United States: Can Scholarship Catch Up with the Immigration Backlash?" *LASA Forum* (Winter): 4–6.

Díaz, Junot. 1996. *Drown.* New York: Riverhead Books.

———. 1997. *Negocios.* New York: Vintage Books.

Falk, Richard. 1993. "The Making of Global Citizenship." In Jeremy Brecher, John Brown Childs, and Jill Cutler, eds., *Global Visions: Beyond the New World Order,* 39–50. Boston: South End Press.

García, Cristina. 1992. *Dreaming in Cuban.* New York: A. Knopf.

———. 1994. *Soñar en Cubano.* New York: Ballantine Books.

Glazer, Nathan, and Daniel P. Moynihan. 1963. *Beyond the Melting Pot: the Negroes, Puerto Ricans, Jews, Italians, and Irish of New York City.* Cambridge, Mass.: M.I.T. Press.

Glazer, Nathan. 1997. *We Are All Multiculturalists Now.* Cambridge: Harvard University Press.

Gómez-Peña, Guillermo. 1993. *Warrior for Gringostroika.* St. Paul: Graywolf Press.

Greyer, Michael, and Charles Bright. 1995. "World History in a Global Age." *American Historical Review* 100 (4): 1034–1060.

Gutmann, Matthew C. 1996. *The Meanings of Macho.* Berkeley: University of California Press.

Jonas, Suzanne, and Edward J. McCaughan, eds. 1994. *Latin America Faces the Twenty-first Century: Reconstructing a Social Justice Agenda.* Boulder: Westview Press.

Lumsden, Ian. 1996. *Machos, Maricones, and Gays: Cuba and Homosexuality.* Philadelphia: Temple University Press.

Martínez, Elena M., ed. 1996. *Lesbian Voices from Latin America: Breaking Ground.* New York: Garland.

McShane, Denis. 1993. "Labor Standards and Double Standards in the New World Order." In Jeremy Brecher, John Brown Childs, and Jill Cutler, eds., *Global Visions: Beyond the New World Order,* 197–206. Boston: South End Press.

Melhuus, Marit, and Kristi Anne Stolen, eds. 1996. *Machos, Mistresses, Madonnas: Contesting the Power of Latin American Gender Imagery.* London: Verso.

Mirandé, Alfredo. 1997. *Hombres y Machos: Masculinity and Latino Culture.* Boulder: Westview Press.

Molloy, Sylvia, ed. 1998. *Hispanisms and Homosexualities.* Durham, N.C.: Duke University Press.

Moraga, Cherríe, and Ana Castillo, eds. 1988. *Esta puente, mi espalda: Voces de mujeres tercermundistas en los Estados Unidos.* San Francisco: ISM Press.

Portes, Alejandro, and Rubén Rumbaut. 1990. *Immigrant America: A Portrait.* Berkeley: University of California Press.

Ramos, Juanita, ed. 1987. *Compañeras: Latina Lesbians.* New York: Latina Lesbian History Project.

Santiago, Esmeralda. 1996a. *America's Dream.* New York: HarperCollins.

————. 1996b. *El sueño de América.* New York: HarperCollins.

Seminario estudios sobre la mujer. 1987. San Jose, Costa Rica: Ministerio de Cultura.

Sternbach, Nancy Saporta, Marysa Navarro Aranguren, Patricia Chuchryk, and Sonia Alvarez. 1992. "Feminisms in Latin America: From Bogota to San Bernardo." *Signs: Journal of Women in Culture and Society* 17 (2): 393–434.

Sutton, Constance. 1987. "The Caribbeanization of New York City and the Emergence of a Transnational Sociocultural System." In Constance Sutton and Elsa Chaney, eds., *Caribbean Life in New York City: Sociocultural Dimensions,* 15–30. New York: Center for Migration Studies.

Sutton, Constance, and Elsa Chaney, eds. 1987. *Caribbean Life in New York City: Sociocultural Dimensions.* New York: Center for Migration Studies.

U.S. Department of Commerce, Bureau of the Census. 1996. *Current Population Reports,* Series P–25–1130, *Population Projections by Age, Sex, Race, and Hispanic Origin: 1995–2050.* Washington, D.C.: U.S. Bureau of the Census.

————. 1998. *Current Population Survey, GPP–P1.* Washington, D.C.: U.S. Bureau of the Census, Population Division.

Wallerstein, Immanuel. 1995. "Africa in the Shuffle." *Issue* 23 (1): 22–23.

SHIFTING CONTEXTS: LESSONS FROM INTEGRATING BLACK, GENDER, AND AFRICAN DIASPORA STUDIES

BEVERLY GUY-SHEFTALL

In a special issue of *SAGE: A Scholarly Journal on Black Women* on "Africa and the Diaspora" (Fall 1996), the editors call attention to the emergence of a new field, African diaspora studies, which in many ways is the outcome of the evolution of Black studies since its beginnings in the 1960s.[1] In 1979, many of the world's leading scholars and Africanists assembled at Howard University for the first African Diaspora Studies Institute. The publication of *Global Dimensions of the African Diaspora* (Harris 1982) was one of the most important results of that historic conference, because it provided new conceptual frameworks for the study of African peoples around the globe. For purposes of the conference, the African diaspora was defined as "the voluntary and forced dispersal of Africans at different periods in history and in several directions; the emergence of a cultural identity abroad without losing the African base, either spiritually or physically; the psychological return to the homeland, Africa" (*SAGE* 1986, 2). The African diaspora includes both "continental Africans" and "descendant Africans" (Blacks dispersed in the New World). Four years after the first conference, the Association of Black Women Historians sponsored a historic research conference in 1983 at Howard University on "Women in the African Diaspora: An Interdisciplinary Perspective," because of the lack of women participants at the earlier Howard conference and inadequate attention to women's experiences in teaching and research about the African diaspora. *Women in Africa and the African Diaspora* (1987), the volume that came out of that conference, underscored the importance of the newly evolving field of women and African diaspora studies (also called Black women's studies or African diaspora women's studies) (Terborg-Penn, et al. 1987). The new scholarship aimed to foreground gender issues within the fields of Black or Africana studies, which had historically been focused on men or were insensitive to the intersection of race, class, and gender in the lives of African peoples.[2]

A keynote presenter at the Howard conference was Sierra Leone anthropologist Filomina Chioma Steady, whose groundbreaking anthology, *The Black Woman Cross-Culturally* (1981), provided a conceptual framework for comparative study of Black women in Africa, the Caribbean, South America, and the United States. Because of Steady's emphasis on their common African heritage and the impact of slavery, colonialism (including "internal colonialism" in the U.S. context), and neocolonialism, her work falls under the rubric of African diaspora studies (Steady 1981, 8). Despite her assertion about problematic relationships between women of African descent and the mainstream women's movement in the West, Steady argues that they have evolved their own brand of feminism and that, for them, the struggle against gender oppression has always been "fused with liberation from other forms of oppression, namely slavery, colonialism, neocolonialism, racism, poverty, illiteracy, and disease" (34). Steady amplified this concept of the simultaneity of oppressions in the lives of Black women during her keynote address, in which she called for a theory of African feminism in the study of women throughout the diaspora. For Steady, African feminism is more holistic and humanistic than Western feminism, because it has been nurtured in cultures that are more communal. She argues that the impact of patriarchy before colonialism was more benign in traditional sub-Saharan African societies because of women's autonomous economic roles and their centrality in the maintenance of lineage groups (Sudarkarsa 1981, 49–63 and 1987, 25–41).

Rosalyn Terborg-Penn's presentation at that conference, "African Feminism: A Theoretical Approach to the History of Women in the African Diaspora," reaffirmed Steady's thesis and called attention to two aspects of life for Black women in the New World that constitute the continuation of an African feminist tradition—the development of survival strategies and reliance on female networks. She also identified several Black women's history topics that African feminist analytic frameworks would be useful in exploring: cross-cultural studies of slavery, women's resistance to oppression, the impact of colonialism on gender constructs, and the involvement of Black women in suffrage struggles in various cultural contexts.

Despite urgent calls among Black women scholars for the cross-cultural study of women of African descent, Black studies and women's studies seemed to have had other priorities, though a small group of scholars, building on the foundational work of Steady, Terborg-Penn, and Beverly Lindsay,[3] would continue to make major contributions to the scholarship on women in the African diaspora and our understandings of global Black feminisms. In this regard, the pioneering anthologizing and theoretical work of Trinidadian feminist literary critic Carole Boyce Davies broadened our knowledge of African feminism, which she analyzed cogently in the introduction to *Ngambika*, the first collection of critical essays on women in African literature:

> African feminism . . . recognizes a common struggle with African men for the removal of the yokes of foreign domination and European/ American exploitation. It is not antagonistic to African men but challenges them to be aware of certain salient

aspects of women's subjugation which differ from the generalized oppression of all African peoples . . . it recognizes that certain inequities and limitations existed/exist in traditional societies and that colonialism reinforced them and introduced others . . . it acknowledges its affinities with international feminism, but delineates a specific African feminism with certain specific needs and goals arising out of the concrete realities of women's lives in African societies. . . . It examines African societies for institutions which are of value to women and rejects those which work to their detriment and does not simply import Western women's agendas. Thus, it respects African woman's status as mother but questions obligatory motherhood and the traditional favoring of sons . . . it respects African woman's self-reliance and the penchant to cooperative work and social organization (networking). . . . It rejects, however, the overburdening, exploitation and relegation to "muledom" that is often her lot. . . . It understands the interconnectedness of race, class, and sex oppression. (Davies and Graves 1986, 8–10)

Our Ford-funded curriculum development project at Spelman College—women and African diaspora studies—builds on the foundational work of scholars in the field, and has four major goals: reconceptualizing our women's studies program, which began in 1982, so that it will be more comparative, more global; gendering African diaspora studies, which has historically been more sensitive to race, class, and geographical region than it has been to gender and sexuality issues;[4] exploring feminisms (which includes theory and praxis) within the African diaspora; and contributing to the development of African diaspora women's studies, which has continued to evolve over the past two decades. In our curriculum development efforts, we have also found it necessary, like other scholars studying women around the globe (particularly the African diaspora), to problematize the binary of biological sex and social gender, which has been a fundamental conceptual paradigm within Western women's studies teaching and research. A basic limitation of the binary can be underscored by an analysis of the experiences of African women in particular cultural contexts and at various historical moments.

CHALLENGING GENDER AND SEXUAL BINARIES

In a ground-breaking anthropological text by Ifi Amadiume (1987b), *Male Daughters, Female Husbands: Gender and Sex in an African Society,* there is a useful analysis surrounding the situation of Igbo women in Nigeria during the precolonial era. In this text, Amadiume asserts the flexibility of gender constructs among the Igbo, where women could become husbands in woman-to-woman marriages and where as daughters within their lineage groups, their age or birth order significantly influenced their experiences of what it meant to be female. Amadiume offers evidence that the Western preoccupation with the role of wife obscures the important role of daughter among West African women. The tendency on the part of Western scholars to examine primarily the conjugal household in other cultural contexts misrepresents the complex institution of family within the sub-Saharan African context, for example, where women have multiple roles and statuses beyond that of wife.

Early on, conceptualizing the category "woman" was regarded as relatively unproblematic in Anglo-American feminist theory, based on the conceptual distinction between biological sex and social gender. It was understood that "woman" was socially constructed, but the category in early feminist thought remained monolithic precisely because the separation of sex and gender has constituted a basic conceptual framework in Western women's studies. A basic limitation of this sex-gender binary can be underscored by an analysis of the experiences of African women in a particular precolonial context, as Amadiume's anthropological work on the Igbo indicates.

My experience as a women's studies professor in graduate classes is that it has frequently been unsettling for "seasoned" women's studies students within the U.S. academy to have some of their basic conceptual frameworks challenged by moving outside Western cultural contexts. A primary example is the tendency of U.S. students to read woman-to-woman marriages as examples of lesbian partnerships on the African continent. In Amadiume's *Male Daughters, Female Husbands,* the discussion of woman-to-woman marriages is often very difficult for Western students to process (unless they've been exposed to anthropology classes), because they employ their familiar notions about marriage as they attempt to understand the institution of marriage, broadly speaking, in other parts of the world.[5] Like other aspects of African kinship structures and relations, the practice of "woman-to-woman" marriages is often misunderstood by Western students, in part because of a lack of understanding of the institution of marriage within the African context. It is important to underscore that marriage, whose primary purpose is procreation, is "essentially a relationship between lineages," and a way to formalize "the conferral of paternity rights of the lineage of the groom to the children born in the course of the marriage" (Oyewumi 1997, 51).

In various parts of Africa, woman-to-woman marriages in the precolonial context included the securing of a wife or wives by affluent females. This practice illustrates that one did not have to be a biological male to function in the role of husband within certain African kinship systems. In other words, certain women were permitted to perform male roles, including taking a wife. This practice enabled the female husband to exercise rights over another woman's labor and reproductive capacity (Sudarkarsa 1981, 32). A woman-to-woman marriage enabled the female husband to have heirs, because her wife could also be married or have sexual relationships with men for the purpose of procreation. Female husbands also could have male husbands. There were a variety of circumstances that led to women marrying other women. Wealthy women took wives in order to project power and authority. If they were married and childless, securing a wife enabled them to provide their husband with heirs for his lineage group (Amadiume 1987b, 72). Additional wives also assisted female husbands with other household responsibilities. Like Amadiume, most scholars studying African kinship systems insist that these woman-to-woman marriages were not sexual, though these assertions may not be based on empirical knowledge.

Lesbian students are frequently very disturbed by Amadiume's introduction, which they label heterosexist (and worse) because she challenges Western feminists, including Audre Lorde, who interpret woman-to-woman marriages as an illustration of lesbianism in the African context.[6] Although Amadiume explains the cultural context in which woman-to-woman marriages occurred among the Igbo, many women's studies students critique the text for its silences about, rather than a discourse on, sexuality, its refusal to acknowledge that the women in these marriages could in fact be practicing lesbian sex, and her lack of an analysis of the nature of female friendships in the polygamous cultures she studies.

In light of controversies likely to emerge in U.S. classrooms around unfamiliar cultural practices, it is helpful to employ alternative lenses for analyzing other cultural contexts. Gloria Wekker (1997, 1999), a Black Surinamese anthropologist who has written about *mati* work among working-class Creoles (descendants of slaves) in Paramaribo or Afro-Surinamese in Amsterdam,[7] suggests how scholars might better theorize (and teach about) "homoerotic" behavior (her language) cross-culturally. In her insightful analysis of a widespread institution among Creole working-class women in Surinam called the *mati* work (women who engage in sexual relationships with women and men, either simultaneously or consecutively, under a variety of circumstances), Wekker situates the practice (a dual sex system in which there is opposite-gendered and same-gendered sexual behavior) within its historical and cultural context and avoids language that would attribute a homosexual *identity* to these women, most of whom are mothers and single heads of their own households. Wekker does not, therefore, use Western labels such as heterosexual, homosexual, or bisexual in her analysis of *mati*. In her description of the sexual universe these Afro-Caribbean working class women inhabit, Wekker reveals that the women (whom she interviewed) consider this sexual activity, which is not stigmatized among the working class, to be pleasurable, but not an identity: "Sexual fulfillment per se is considered important, healthy, and joyous, while the gender of one's object choice is regarded as less important"

(Wekker 1999, 125). What Wekker's work emphasizes is that "homo-sexualities are multiple and manifold, realized in different contexts and charged with different meanings" (1999, 134), so that interpretations of same-sex bondings among persons of African descent around the globe need to take into consideration the cultural specificity of Western categories of sexual behavior and identity.

K. Limakatso Kendall (1997), a white American who taught English in Lesotho in 1992 and 1993 as a Fulbright scholar, edited the autobiography of an African woman, Mpho 'M'Atsepo Nthunya, who was a worker at the National University of Lesotho. While women in Lesotho with whom Kendall was familiar did not identify as lesbians, she argues that erotic relationships among them do exist, though they do not conceptualize these relationships as sexual. In the autobiography, Nthunya describes her affectionate marriage with her husband and her long-term intimate relationship with a woman, 'M'alineo. In Lesotho, these relationships are called *motsoalle*, which are close friendships between women that are recognized within the culture (and by husbands) with ritual feasts akin to marriage feasts. Kendall also points out that she did not encounter women in Lesotho living as couples with other women or choosing female partners exclusively. What these practices underscore is the need for U.S. students to analyze relationships among women in different cultural contexts without imposing U.S.-based sexual categories.

Prominent African feminist scholar and activist Molara Ogundipe-Leslie also identifies sexuality as one area of research that must be explored without the ethnocentric biases that have characterized analyses of African women in the past: "Some gender issues are not yet receiving the intellectual attention they should. . . . Too many silences persist in the area of human sexuality in Africa. Sexual orientation is certainly one area that has not been opened up for research or discussion. . . . The experiences of sexual orientation in traditional arrangements require discovery still" (Ogundipe-Leslie 1994, 15).[8] Clearly, it is also necessary to probe issues of sexuality in cultural contexts that constitute the African diaspora (the Americas, Latin America, the Caribbean, Europe, and Africa). Wekker's work attempts to do just this. There is considerable resistance, however, among some African feminist scholars to what they perceive to be a preoccupation with sexuality on the part of white feminists. Scholarship on sexualities in Africa and the African diaspora represents a particular challenge, because the discourse on sexuality outside the United States has been more limited than discussions about sexuality within this country. It is also the case that some cultures consider public discourse about sexuality to be inappropriate, so the issue of locating and adequately comprehending sources makes such investigations more difficult.

There are disciplinary biases as well, or rather, for women's studies students, a bias against work based in the traditional disciplines. Women's studies students who may not have had an anthropology course, for example, critique Amadiume's text because it does not employ interdisciplinary women's studies frameworks, though *Male Daughters, Female Husbands* is solid anthropological scholarship that attempts to disrupt the ethnocentrism of Western studies of African women, including that generated by white feminist scholars.

I am not suggesting that there are easy answers in classrooms that address cross-cultural issues or that there is one correct way to approach complicated questions. There are still many silences, many gaps in our knowledge about gender constructs outside the United States. There is considerable debate among scholars, for example, about the status of women in precolonial Africa and the impact of colonialism on the situation of women. The emergence of African feminist scholarship also calls into question the discourse about women within the contemporary context.[9]

MOVING BEYOND U.S. CATEGORIES OF IDENTITY AND AFFILIATION

Other contentious issues have emerged in our exploration of the implications of gendering the field of women's and African diaspora studies. It is necessary to interrogate traditional racial categories within and outside the United States. Racial categories familiar within this country have limited applicability in a consideration of what we would call racial or ethnic women outside it. For example, borrowing U.S.–based racial categories to analyze the experiences of women in the African diaspora, which includes the Caribbean, South America (especially Brazil), Canada, and the United Kingdom, would render invisible the complexity of racial constructs outside the United States. It is sometimes the case that Caribbean faculty, with intimate knowledge of the history of South Asians and their relationships with persons of African descent in many parts of the Caribbean, especially Trinidad, find it difficult to conceptualize South Asians as "black," though this racial categorization is common in the British context. Many other contentious issues arise when American students and faculty confront different discourses about race in assigned texts. For example, Ogundipe-Leslie asserts that she does not see herself as black and does not use this language to describe other African women, and reminds us that there are cultural contexts in which ethnicity, nationality, age, and class are more important categories for understanding identity formation. She, for example, refers to herself as an African, Yoruba, middle-aged, middle class woman (Ogundipe-Leslie 1994, 218). There are no references to her racial identity in these descriptors. When a few of my African American students read this particular essay, they asserted what I would call ethnocentric biases when they accused Ogundipe-Leslie of being in denial of her "blackness." In other words, it was difficult for them to transcend

African American or Pan-African political imperatives, which insist that people of African descent proudly espouse a "black identity" as one way of resisting the hegemony of a Western racial discourse associating blackness with a broad range of pejorative attributes.

Finally, there is the vexing problem of using black nationalist versus Afrocentric versus African feminist versus African American feminist versus Africana womanist frameworks in the study of women of African descent. In this regard, a number of contentious issues remain around linguistic categories, especially Third World–First World. There is some hostility among non–U.S. Black women about the use of the category *Third World,* which some perceive to be a derogatory category, even though women of color within the United States and around the world often embrace this terminology as a political category useful in a discourse on global feminisms.[10]

Nor have debates been resolved about the relevance of the term *feminism* for women who are not white and middle class. Alice Walker's counterdiscourse on *womanism* provided an alternative terminology for Black feminists in the early 1980s, when many African American women, as well as other women of color within the United States, were raising angry voices about their marginalization or erasure from mainstream white feminist discourse. Walker introduced the term *womanist* in her collection of essays, *In Search of Our Mothers' Gardens: Womanist Prose* (1984, xi–xii),[11] not as a rejection of the term *feminist*, which is often how her statement is interpreted, but as a way of broadening the concept to include a range of perspectives. In fact, she asserts that "womanist is to feminist as purple to lavender," which suggests that womanism is a deeper, more intense form of feminism.[12]

Walker's use of the term *womanist* underscores a particular, culturally specific way in which African American women conceptualize resistance to cultural norms of many kinds. Consider Walker's dismissal of normative categories: "A woman who loves other women, sexually and/or nonsexually. Appreciates and prefers women's culture, women's emotional flexibility . . . and women's strength." Womanists are not narrowly focused on women's liberation: "Committed to survival and wholeness of entire people, male *and* female. Not a separatist, except periodically, for health." Her concept of *womanism* (from the Black folk expression *womanish,* which mothers use to describe feisty or "outrageous" female children) captures the legacy of struggle that Black women collectively inherit as a result of our particular history in the United States: "Traditionally capable, as in: 'Mama, I'm walking to Canada and I'm taking you and a bunch of other slaves with me.'" Although the term *feminism* continues to be contested and controversial within many Black communities, students and some faculty are often surprised by the growing body of gender discourse generated by women on the continent and throughout the African diaspora who do employ the term *feminism* and who make an effective argument for our need to examine indigenous feminisms in many cultural contexts outside the West.[13]

This new feminist scholarship by African women, as well as women of African descent in Europe and the Americas,[14] is critically important for understanding the experiences of women in different regions of the world and in helping to dismantle the hegemony of Western (white) feminist analytical frameworks. Obioma Nnaemeka, who convened the first international conference on Women in Africa and the African Diaspora in Nsukka, Nigeria, in 1992 and is president of the Association of African Women Scholars, is comfortable analyzing the variety and complexity of feminisms in the African context and the diaspora. She believes that using the word *feminism* is not an endorsement of white, middle class feminism and that, in fact, feminism speaks different languages worldwide (Nnaemeka 1998, 32). In a keynote speech at the conference, prominent Ghanaian writer Ama Ata Aidoo engaged the debate about African women and feminism and is unequivocal in her assertion about the value of this liberatory politic for a new Africa:

> When people ask me rather bluntly every now and then whether I am a feminist, I not only answer yes, but I go on to insist that every woman and every man should be a feminist— especially if they believe that Africans should take charge of African land, African wealth, African lives, and the burden of African development. It is not possible to advocate independence for the African continent without also believing that African women must have the best that the environment can offer. For some of us, this is the crucial element in our feminism (Nnaemeka 1998, 47).

These emerging and evolving African diasporic feminist analytic frameworks have the potential for transforming African diaspora studies, African studies, and women's studies. I am also hopeful that the required feminist theory courses in most women's studies programs in the United States and the required introductory courses in African American or Africana studies will begin to take into consideration feminist discourses outside the West. This will certainly make for more contentious classrooms, but it will also surely provide a more textured, more complicated analysis of the meanings of race and gender and sexuality here and around the globe.

NOTES

1.   Black studies, also called Afro-American studies, African American studies, and Africana studies, emerged in the 1960s as a response to Black students' demands for a more inclusive and relevant curriculum within higher edu-

cation during the social upheaval of the civil rights movement. This interdisciplinary academic field called attention to Eurocentric biases in the construction of knowledge and the erasure of the histories, cultures, and experiences of African peoples within the U.S. academy.

2. A number of publications have appeared since *Women in Africa and the African Diaspora* (1987), many of which are comparative studies of women of African descent throughout the diaspora.

3. See Lindsay's edited anthology, *Comparative Perspectives of Third World Women* (1980). More recently, a substantial and influential body of work on women writers of the African diaspora has emerged. This includes Busby 1992 and Davies 1994, 1995.

4. The culminating activity of our Ford project was an invitational conference on Women and African Diaspora Studies (May 29–30, 1998), during which four commissioned papers were presented: Terborg-Penn's "The State of the Field of Women and African Diaspora Studies"; Rhoda E. Reddock's "Black Women in the Anglophone Caribbean"; Angela Gilliam's "Black Women in Brazil"; and Davies' "Claudia Jones: Anti-Imperialist, Black Feminist Politics." Because Patricia McFadden was unable to attend the conference, we commissioned Thelma Ravell-Pinto to write a paper on "Feminist Activism in Southern Africa," completed in Fall 1998.

5. For a discussion of the varieties of woman-to-woman marriages in other parts of Africa, see Carrier and Murray 1998.

6. For discussions of sexuality within the African context, see Murray and Roscoe 1998; Blackwood and Wieringa 1999; Gay 1985, 97–116; Kendall 1997; Frank and Khaxas 1996, 109–117.

7. Her 1999 essay in *Female Desires* on the same topic is also useful.

8. Ogundipe-Leslie is one of the most outspoken African feminist scholars and coined the term *stiwanism* (social transformation including women in Africa) in order to capture the meanings of feminism within the African context. As is the case among feminist intellectuals within the same geographic region in other parts of the globe, African women scholars have profound disagreements among themselves with respect to gender and other issues. Oyeronke Oyewumi (1997), also Yoruba, accuses Ogundipe-Leslie of mispresenting certain aspects of Yoruba culture and its treatment of women.

9. Recent publications, especially the scholarly work of African women, are useful in this regard: Ogundipe-Leslie 1994; Amadiume 1987 and 1997; Kolawoke 1997; Nnaemeka 1997 and 1998; Oyewumi 1997; House-Midamba and Ekechi 1995; Mikell 1997; Nfah-Abbenyi 1997; Ogunyemi 1996. See also the creative and political work of Osonye Tess Onwueme, especially her 1997 play, *Tell It to Women: An Epic Drama for Women*, which critiques Western feminism from the vantage point of rural African women and "is the first dramatic text from Africa to break the literary silence on issues of homosexuality," according to Ngũgi wa Thiong'o, in an excellent foreword to the play (9). The earlier work of Steady 1981 and African American anthropologist Niara Sudarkasa on African family structures is also useful.

10. See Mohanty et al. 1991, for a useful discussion of these issues.

11. See Charles 1997, 278–297, for a lengthy analysis and critique of Walker's

concept of womanism, from the perspective of a Black British critic. See also Hudson-Weems 1998, in which she rejects the terms *Black feminism, African feminism,* and Walker's *womanist.* Hudson-Weems, an African American professor, associates all feminist movements with white women and castigates "Black feminists" for their rejection of African-centered perspectives and embrace of the gender-only agendas of some white feminists.

12. Walker 1984, xii. See also Ogunyemi 1985, in which she indicates that she "arrived at the term 'womanism' independently" (72). There has been a range of responses to Walker. Some Black women reject the use of the term *feminist* altogether because of its exclusive association with white women and prefer the term *womanist.* This includes a group of self-defined African American womanist scholars doing pioneering work in theology such as Jacquelyn Grant. There are Black women, such as bell hooks and others, who prefer the term *feminist* though they continue to critique Western feminism. For hooks, in *Talking Back: Thinking Feminist, Thinking Black* (1989), "the term 'womanist' is not sufficiently linked to a tradition of radical political commitment to struggle and change" (182). See also Ogundipe-Leslie.

13. See Mirza 1992, 1997; Bryan et al.1994. 1985; Cobham and Collins 1987; Ifekwunigwe 1998; Brand 1994; d'Almeida 1994; Busby 1992; James and Busia 1993; Thiam 1986; Caipora Women's Group 1993; Philip 1992; Terborg-Penn, et al. 1987; Guy-Sheftall 1995.

14. There is a growing body of scholarship under the rubric Caribbean feminism, which includes a special issue of *Feminist Review* on "Rethinking Caribbean 'Difference'" (1998); a special issue of *Thamyris* on "Caribbean Women Writers: Imagining Caribbean Space," guest-edited by Davies (1998); Davies and Fido 1990; Reddock 1994; Momsen 1993; Lopez-Springfield 1997; Cooper 1993; McClaurin 1996. See also the work of the Caribbean Association for Feminist Research and Action (CAFRA), P.O. Bag 442, Tunapuna Post Office, Trinidad & Tobago, including their *Creation Fire.* (Espinet 1990).

WORKS CITED

Amadiume, Ifi. 1987. *Afrikan Matriarchal Foundations: The Igbo Case.* London: Karnak House.

———. 1987b. *Male Daughters, Female Husbands: Gender and Sex in an African Society.* London: Zed.

———. 1997. *Reinventing Africa: Matriarchy, Religion, and Culture.* London: Zed Books.

Blackwood, Evelyn, and Saskia E. Wieringa, eds. 1999. *Female Desires: Same-Sex Relations and Transgender Practices Across Cultures.* New York: Columbia University Press.

Brand, Dionne. 1994. *Bread Out of Stone.* Toronto: Coach House Press.

Bryan, Beverly, et al. 1985. *The Heart of the Race.* London: Virago.

Busby, Margaret, ed. 1992. *Daughters of Africa: An International Anthology of Words and Writings by Women of African Descent from the Ancient Egyptian to the Present.* New York: Pantheon.

Capoeira Women's Group. 1993. *Women in Brazil.* London: Latin American Bureau.

Carrier, Joseph M., and Stephen O. Murray. 1998. "Woman-Woman Marriage in Africa." In Stephen O. Murray and Will Roscoe, eds., *Boy-Wives and Female Husbands: Studies of African Homosexualities,* 253–266. New York: St. Martin's Press.

Charles, Helen. 1997. "The Language of Womanism: Re-thinking Difference." In Heidi Safia Mirza, ed., *Black British Feminism,* 278–297. London: Routledge.

Cobham, Rhonda, and Merle Collins, eds. 1987. *Watchers and Seekers: Creative Writing by Black Women in Britain.* London: Women's Press.

Cooper, Carolyn. 1993. *Noises in the Blood: Orality, Gender and "Vulgar" Body of Jamaican Popular Culture.* London: Macmillan.

d'Almeida, Irene A. 1994. *Francophone African Women Writers: Destroying the Emptiness of Silence.* Gainesville: University Press of Florida.

Davies, Carolyn Boyce. 1994. *Migrations of the Subject: Black Women, Writing and Identity.* London: Routledge.

———. 1995. *Moving Beyond Boundaries: International Dimensions of Black Women's Writing,* vols. 1 and 2. New York: New York University Press.

———, ed. 1998. "Caribbean Women Writers: Imagining Caribbean Space." *Thamyris: Journal on Mythmaking from Past to Present 2.*

Davies, Carolyn Boyce, and Elaine Savory Fido, eds. 1990. *Out of the Kumbla: Caribbean Women and Literature.* Trenton: Africa World Press.

Davies, Carolyn Boyce, and Anne Adams Graves, eds. 1986. *Ngambika: Studies of Women in African Literature.* Trenton: Africa World Press.

Espinet, Ramabai, ed. 1990. *Creation Fire: A CAFRA Anthology of Caribbean Women's Poetry.* Toronto: Sister Vision.

Frank, Liz, and Elizabeth Khaxas. 1996. "Lesbians in Namibia." In Monika Reinfelder, ed., *Amazon to Zami: Toward Global Lesbian Feminism,* 109–117. London: Cassell.

Gay, Judith. 1985. "Mummies and Babies and Friends and Lovers in Lesotho." *Journal of Homosexuality* 11 (3–4): 97–116.

Guy-Sheftall, Beverly, ed. 1995. *Words of Fire: An Anthology of African American Feminist Thought.* New York: New Press.

Harris, Joseph E., ed. 1982. *Global Dimensions of the African Diaspora.* Washington, D.C.: Howard University Press.

hooks, bell. 1989. *Talking Back: Thinking Feminist, Thinking Black.* Boston: South End Press.

House-Midamba, Bessie, and Flix K. Ekechi, eds. 1995. *African Market Women's Economic Power: The Role of Women in African Economic Development.* Westport, Conn.: Greenwood Press.

Hudson-Weems, Clenora. 1998. "Africana Womanism." In Obioma Nnaemeka, ed., *Sisterhood, Feminisms and Power,* 149–162. Trenton: Africa World Press.

Ifekwunigwe, Jayne O. 1998. *Scattered Belongings: The Cultural Paradoxes of "Race," Gender, Nation.* London: Routledge.

James, Stanlie M., and Abena P. A. Busia, eds. 1993. *Theorizing Black Feminisms: The Visionaary Pragmatism of Black Women.* London: Routledge.

Kendall, K. Limakatso, ed. 1997. *Singing Away the Hunger: The Autobiography of an African Woman, Mpho 'M'Atsepo.* Bloomington: Indiana University Press.

Kolawoke, Mary E. Modupe. 1997. *Womanism and African Consciousness.* Trenton: Africa World Press.

Lindsay, Beverly. 1980. *Comparative Perspectives of Third World Women: The Impact of Race, Sex, and Class.* New York: Praeger.

Lopez-Springfield, Consuelo. 1997. *Daughters of Caliban: Caribbean Women in the Twentieth Century.* Bloomington: Indiana University Press.

McClaurin, Irma. 1996. *Women of Belize: Gender and Change in Central America.* New Brunswick, N.J.: Rutgers University Press.

Mikell, Gwendolyn, ed. 1997. *African Feminism: The Politics of Survival in Sub-Saharan Africa.* Philadelphia: University of Pennsylvania Press.

Mirza, Heidi Safia. 1992. *Young, Female and Black.* London: Routledge.

———. 1997. *Black British Feminism: A Reader.* London: Routledge.

Mohanty, Chandra Talpade, Ann Russo, and Lourdes Torres, eds. 1991. *Third World Women and the Politics of Feminism.* Bloomington: Indiana University Press.

Momsen, Janet, ed. 1993. *Women and Change in the Caribbean: A Pan-Caribbean Perspective.* Bloomington: Indiana University Press.

Murray, Stephen O., and Will Roscoe, eds. 1998. *Boy-Wives and Female Husbands: Studies of African Homosexualities.* New York: St. Martin's Press.

Nfah-Abbenyi, Juliana Makuchi. 1997. *Gender in African Women's Writing: Identity, Sexuality, and Difference.* Bloomington: Indiana University Press.

Nnaemeka, Obioma, ed. 1997. *The Politics of (M)othering: Womanhood, Identity, and Resistance in African Literature.* New York: Routledge.

———. 1998. *Sisterhood, Feminisms and Power: From Africa to the Diaspora.* Trenton: Africa World Press.

Ogundipe-Leslie, Molara. 1994. *Re-Creating Ourselves: African Women & Critical Transformations.* Trenton: Africa World Press.

Ogunyemi, Chikwenye Okonjo. 1985. "Womanism: The Dynamics of the Contemporary Black Female Novel in English." *Signs: The Journal of Women in Culture and Society* 11 (1): 72.

———. 1996. *Africa Wo/Man Palava: The Nigerian Novel by Women.* Chicago: University of Chicago Press.

Onwueme, Osonye Tess. 1997. *Tell It to Women: An Epic Drama for Women.* Detroit: Wayne University Press.

Oyewumi, Oyeronke. 1997. *The Invention of Women: Making an African Sense of Western Gender Discourses.* Minneapolis: University of Minnesota Press.

Philip, M. Nourbese. 1992. *Frontiers: Essays and Writings on Racism and Culture.* Toronto, Ontario: Mercury Press.

Reddock, Rhoda E. 1994. *Women, Labour & Politics in Trinidad and Tobago: A History.* London: Zed Books.

SAGE. 1986. "Editorial." *SAGE: A Scholarly Journal on Black Women* 3 (2): 2.

Steady, Filomina Chioma, ed. 1981. *The Black Woman Cross-Culturally.* Cambridge: Schenkman.

Sudarkarsa, Niara. 1981. "Female Employment and Family Organization in West Africa." In Filomina Chioma Steady, ed., *The Black Woman Cross-Culturally,* 49–63. Cambridge: Schenkman.

———. 1987. "The Status of Women in Indigenous African Societies." In Rosalyn Terborg-Penn, Sharon Harley, and Andrea Benton Rushing, eds., *Women in Africa and the African Diaspora,* 25–41. Washington, D.C.: Howard University Press.

Terborg-Penn, Rosalyn, Sharon Harley, and Andrea Benton Rushing, eds. 1987. *Women in Africa and the African Diaspora.* Washington, D.C.: Howard University Press.

Thiam, Awa. 1986. *Speak Out, Black Sisters: Feminism and Oppression in Women.* London: Pluto Press.

Walker, Alice. 1984. *In Search of Our Mothers' Gardens: Womanist Prose.* San Diego: Harcourt Brace Jovanovich.

Wekker, Gloria. 1997. "One Finger Does Not Drink Okra Soup: Afro-Surinamese Women and Critical Agency." In M. Jacqui Alexander and Chandra Talpade Mohanty, eds., *Feminist Genealogies, Colonial Legacies, Democratic Futures,* 330–352. New York: Routledge.

———. 1999. "What's Identity Got to Do with It?: Rethinking Identity in Light of the Mati Work in Suriname." In Evelyn Blackwood and Saskia E. Wieringa, eds., *Female Desires: Same-Sex Relations and Transgender Practices Across Cultures,* 120–138. New York: Columbia University Press.

as based on social and political realities expressed through power relations and social hierarchy, including international relations, age, class, ethnic origin and race. We can do this by looking at each society as a microcosm and trying to understand how women experience gender power-relations. This can be in terms of oppression or of resistance and women's own power.

To bring international perspectives into our understanding of the connection between science and technology and women's lives, we recall the caution of Chandra Mohanty (1988, 61–62): Just as *woman* is a "cultural and ideological composite Other," such a term as *Third World women* is a "discursive mode of appropriation and codification" that takes as a "primary point of reference feminist interests as they have been articulated by the U.S. and western Europe." In looking at women's lives in relation to science and technology, we try to balance the uniqueness and specificity of women's lives with what Bolanle Awe et al. (1991, 648) call the "common gendered disabilities of subordination and the need to overcome them." Finally, in revising the Gender and the Rhetoric of Science and Technology course that inspired this essay, we attend to the recommendations of Vella Evans (1991, 335), who among many others found that international issues, just as with women's concerns, must "pervade" an entire course to "provide credibility and force to the perspective."

We resist compartmentalizing these readings and case studies but integrate them through our course work. We consider how science and technology affect the power relations that oppress women and how women might resist or change these relations. We listen to the voices of women within their particular settings as much as possible but also acknowledge that they create and recreate their own stories, just as we, in our role as teachers and scholars, narrate our own versions of women's stories. We try to respect the specifics of the women's lives at the same time that we identify what they share with other women. These complexities and challenges are demonstrated in two recent and highly recommended case studies. First, Leela Fernandes' (1997, 525) study of jute mills in Calcutta reveals the relationships between "discourses on the family, appropriate roles for women, and the politics of sexuality" in labor politics in contemporary India. Fernandes found that construction of a worker's public sphere in the jute mills excluded women workers and their interests and identified single, working class women as "disruptive of social order in the worker's community." Told through women's stories and interviews, Fernandes' case study demonstrates the relationship between the factory structure and politics and the social construction of the patriarchal working class family and the exclusion of women workers from participation and representation in this gendered public sphere. This case study not only captures the voices of local women affected by the industry but also invites generalization about how technology, and the industries that technology supports, may contribute to power relations that subordinate women.

Similarly, Ann Farnsworth-Alvear (1997, 73, 82) acknowledges in her study of the *reinados* or beauty pageants held in the Medellín, Colombia, mills in the 1930s and 1940s that, even as women workers participated in the "moral discourse" generated by the mill's gender ideology, they also told stories that undermined this ideology or stories that valorized their "memories of self." In the Medellín mills, women workers, and by extension beauty contestants, had to be not only childless but also unmarried to support "one of the central tenets of industrial paternalism in Medellín, that employing women would not threaten the culture's gender order" (72). In Medellín, the good woman worker was not just skilled but also chaste. In order to find work, the women whom Farnsworth-Alvear interviewed had accepted this message but had also combined it with their own understandings of motherhood and sexual independence in ways that "destabilized the factory orthodoxy" (93). Farnsworth-Alvear not only speculates about the relationship of technology and industry to women's lives and social gender codes but also problematizes women's stories as women revise, rather than simply report, their experiences within the Medellín mills. In this spirit, we offer the case study of the maquiladoras at the end of this essay—a case study that reflects not only upon oppression but resistance, upon specific experiences in particular locations but also common concerns, and upon the challenge of interpreting the narratives and testimonies that might inform such a case. First, however, we review four areas of women's lives particularly affected by science and technology, areas that can illuminate and inform courses on international women's issues and "pervade" the revised course in Gender and the Rhetoric of Science and Technology that inspired this essay.

GLOBAL AND LOCAL ASPECTS OF SCIENCE AND TECHNOLOGY

In exploring the introduction of new technologies into the workplace and the home, the development of reproductive technologies, the effect of science and technology on food production and processing, and the ecofeminist movement, we suggest the many ways that science and technology touch women's lives locally and globally.

NEW TECHNOLOGIES IN THE WORKPLACE AND HOME

Although new technologies are often thought to contribute to the modernization and progress of a society, women either accept or resist these technologies, depending on the impact on their lives and the inclusion or silencing of their experiential knowledge. For example, Mayuri Odedra-Straub (1995) asked why information technology has, as yet, played such a slight role in Africa. She discovered that lack of secondary equipment, training, and electrical power; dependency on expatriate personnel; and sociocultural conflicts all have slowed the integration of information technology there. Odedra-Straub found that women's workloads and economic capabilities have been threatened by this new technology. They are not educated to work with it because "it is largely assumed that educating women would make them too independent; in other words, they would not do what they are expected to do—look after the house, bring up children, and cater to their husband's needs" (Odedra-Straub 1995, 263). New technologies then may not only affect women's specific work, but these can also encounter, challenge, or reflect notions of so-called appropriate gender roles within particular cultures.

As Cecilia Ng Choon Sim and Carol Yong (1995, 200) comment in a similar study of information technology in Malaysia:

"The evidence in the case study runs counter to the assumptions about the consequences of computerization at the office level which underlie both the pessimistic 'capital accumulation logic' approach and the technological euphoria which equates technology with well-being. The stage of socioeconomic and political development within each society and the pre-existing division of labour are important mediators of how IT [information technology] and its different phases are implemented." Women may be entering information technology fields in Malaysia in great numbers, but they remain in low-level data entry jobs because they are considered primarily as homemakers (Sim and Yong 1995, 198).

Finally, in a study of another location and an earlier time, Arnold Bauer found that the invention of new Meso-American maize grinding technology was resisted for complex social reasons. Although a woman's work time would be cut considerably if she took her maize to a mill to be ground instead of grinding it on the metate, this choice threatened her reputation as a good homemaker in her neighbors' eyes and as a busy and therefore faithful wife in her husband's opinion (Bauer 1990, 15–16). As a result, grinding maize to produce tortillas remained a time-consuming, daily, household task for women until the 1950s. In these three studies of the introduction of new technologies into local settings, not only do we learn more about the social construction of gender by studying how technologies were welcomed or resisted but also about the specifics of women's work inside and outside the home.

Donna Haraway proposes that, to understand the impact of science and technology on women's bodies, we must study what she calls *the cyborg.* The cyborg is a "hybrid of machine and organism," a "creature of fiction and social reality" (Haraway 1991, 191). The cyborg exemplifies the restructuring of the public and the private, of nature and culture, so that "nothing really convincingly settles the separation of human and animal" (Haraway 1991, 192–193). In particular, Haraway finds that communications technologies and biotechnologies are

> crucial tools recrafting our bodies. These tools embody and enforce new social relations for women worldwide. Technologies and scientific discourses can be partially understood as formalizations, that is, as frozen moments, of the fluid social interactions constituting them, but they should also be viewed as instruments for enforcing meanings. The boundary is permeable between tool and myth, instrument and concept, historical systems of social relations and historical anatomies of possible bodies, including objects of knowledge. Indeed, myth and tool mutually constitute each other. Furthermore, communications sciences and modern biologies are constructed by a common move—the translation of the world into a problem of coding, a search for a common language in which all resistance to instrumental control disappears and all heterogeneity can be submitted to disassembly, reassembly, investment, and exchange. (Haraway 1991, 205–206)

The boundary between a woman's body and the machine that scans and interprets it disappears as the machine imposes meaning on the body and becomes an important source of knowledge about the body. According to Lisa Mitchell and Eugenia Georges (1997, 373–374), ultrasound technology has created the cyborg fetus, "the mode of knowing and feeling the fetus through the coupling of human and machine" that is "culturally configured through practice and discourse." This cyborg fetus is differently configured in Canada and Greece, the sites of Mitchell and Georges' study, but in both settings medical experts use the technology to shape a woman's experiences with her pregnancy according to specific cultural definitions of womanhood and motherhood.

Whether or not we accept Haraway's cyborg merger of body and machine as the best way to understand biomedical technologies, studying these technologies outside of North America and Europe increases our understanding of women's lives. Mitchell and Georges differentiated that impact according to the dictates of Canadian versus Greek culture; however, in many cultures, that impact is complicated by economic and political concerns about population control. For example, Betsy Hartmann first refutes the myth that so-called Third World women have so many children because they are "ignorant and irrational" and "exercise no control over their sexuality." She suggests instead that having a large family may be an "eminently rational strategy of survival" (Hartmann 1995, 6). And she proposes that women's lack of control of their own reproduction is also a matter of "the distortion of family planning programs to serve the end of population control" (Hartmann 1995, 43; see also Harcourt 1997, 15–18). Women's needs and experiences may be ignored as contraceptive devices are advocated and distributed to control population growth in a particular location.

Similarly, Anita Hardon (1992) found in the industrialized Netherlands that such contraceptive devices as Depo Provera, Norplant, the abortion pill, and the contraceptive vaccine might control women's fertility but not meet their needs. These devices, Hardon suggests, make women more dependent on medical professionals to administer and remove the devices, and the actual users "have the least power to influence the processes at stake" (Hardon 1992, 764). In fact, several studies propose that Depo Provera was distributed in seventy so-called Third World countries to control population, despite being banned in the United States for safety reasons, because it not only made a profit for U.S. drug companies but also involved less reliance on the "unreliable" user (Ehrenreich, et al. 1979, 36–37). Women's complaints about Depo Provera were dismissed as subjective, reinforcing the image of women as complaining or overanxious, proposes Phillida Bunkle. Reproductive technologies, then, are not value-free. As Bunkle (1993, 298) says, "technological knowledge is both a function and a source of power." Reproductive and contraceptive devices often support the values of their creators, and these values, along with the needs and experiences of women who are affected by reproductive technologies, must be assessed both globally and locally.

AGRICULTURE: WOMEN'S ROLES IN FOOD PRODUCTION AND PROCESSING

Studying women's roles in food production and processing locally and globally reveals both their victimization and their agency. For example, Elizabeth Eldredge's (1991, 709) study of women in nineteenth-century BaSotho society reveals that women were "the motivating force behind agricultural expansion" even though they were still "significantly subordinated." When the ox-drawn plow was introduced, women insisted that their future husbands own plows and know how to use them. Eldredge proposes that women initiated changes in food production and processing *because* of their marginal position; they suffered the most in times of food scarcity and were well aware of the benefits of having a surplus in grain.

Similarly, Judith Carney and Michael Watts (1991) studied the effects on women when the government repeatedly attempted to increase rice production in the Gambia River Basin through mechanized irrigation. Because rice production was considered women's work, in what Carney and Watts call "the entrenched sexual division of labor by crop in Mandinka society," women's labor increased greatly and exacerbated questions of domestic authority and ownership of property (Carney and Watts 1991, 652). Because women globally and locally have been assigned the responsibility for food production and processing, their work and lives are affected by the introduction of new agricultural science and technology. Whether they are empowered or victimized depends upon the cultural messages about gender and labor into which innovations in agricultural science and technology intrude.

ECOFEMINISM

Because of women's historical and current involvement in agriculture and their dependence on the land for food production, it seems appropriate that women are leading ecofeminist movements. By studying ecofeminist ideology and activity in a global and local setting, we understand more about women's needs and experiences; we listen to their own voices and acknowledge their expertise as they articulate those concerns. According to Carolyn Merchant (1995, 185), ecofeminism supports "feminine values of non-violence, cooperation, and nurturing" to prevent "ecocatastrophe." Ecofeminism proposes that nature has an ecological self, which must maintain and renew itself and is dependent on and connects with other selves to sustain species diversity. Pollution, nuclear waste, ozone depletion, and so on are "assaults of capitalist production on ecology" (Merchant 1995, 187). Moreover, Karen Warren (1997, 3) suggests that "important connections exist between the treatment of women, people of color, and the underclass on one hand and the treatment of nonhuman nature on the other." Thus, ecofeminist ideologies and activities demonstrate women's resistance to subordination and their agency in regard to scientific and technological assaults on the environment.

Perhaps the most studied and celebrated ecofeminist activity in non-Western culture is the Chipko movement in India. Vandana Shiva (1993b, 53) has warned that focusing only on global environmental problems and neglecting local problems can transform "the environmental crisis from being a reason for transformation into a reason for strengthening the status quo" because the lives of poor people around the world are not "the center of concern in international negotiations on global environmental issues." According to Shiva (1993a, 306), participation by rural Indian women in the Chipko movement has "challenged the Western concept of economics as production of profits and capital accumulation with their own concept of economics as production of sustenance and needs satisfaction." Forestry is connected to food production, and women's ways of harvesting enhance the productivity of the forest without reducing the trees to a market commodity. For example, lopping of trees makes them soft and palatable as food for cattle but still maintains the integrity of the tree (Shiva 1993a, 309). Thus, the Chipko movement, according to Deane Curtin (1997, 86), is a "distinctively feminist political act growing out of typically women's knowledge of the forest." Through their daily experiences with the forest and its connection to food production and processing, women have obtained expert ecological knowledge.

These four areas and the studies reviewed in this essay—new technologies in the home and workplace, reproductive technologies and women's bodies, women's agency and subordination in food production and processing, and women's leadership and experiential knowledge in ecofeminism—reveal how much more we can understand about women's lives on both the global and local level if we ask how science and technology affect cultural construction of gender, work, the body, and the family. We end this essay by describing a more extensive case study—one that constitutes an essential part of our revised course on "Gender and the Rhetoric of Science and Technology—to illustrate the rich complexity that the lens of science and technology brings to any study of women's lives.

GENDER, SCIENCE, AND TECHNOLOGY IN MEXICO'S MAQUILADORA INDUSTRY

Maquiladora is the Mexican word for foreign-owned factories that manufacture goods in Mexico for export to world markets. The first maquiladoras were built in 1965 when Mexico's Border Industrialization Program followed the lead of other developing nations and established an Export Processing Zone along the U.S.–Mexico border. This 12.5-mile-wide strip offered duty-free status and tax exemptions as a financial incentive to foreign corporations interested in outsourcing the labor-intensive components of their manufacturing processes (Tiano 1994, 18). Since its inception, the maquiladora industry and the border culture that has developed around it have been sites of intense scientific and technological conflict. The imposing presence of technologically sophisticated manufacturing facilities has irrevocably altered Mexico's traditional economic practices, creating thousands of jobs, but obliterating the conventional means by which Mexican citizens earned their livings.

Like other sites of scientific and technological conflict, the maquiladora industry is, at its heart, a human-centered phenomenon, and it is one in which women have been major players. In the first maquiladoras almost all employees were women (Catanzarite and

Strober 1993, 134). This has changed gradually over the years, so that by 1980, 20 percent of maquila employees were male, and by 1990, 38 percent were male, but women continue to be disproportionately represented in the lowest-paying maquiladora jobs (Peña 1997, 257–262). This gender imbalance has attracted the attention of post-colonial and feminist scholars in various disciplines, who have helped give voice to employees' perspectives on the industry. Employees have not been alone in telling the maquiladora story, however, and their stories have often been drowned out by voices much louder than their own. Listening to as many of these conflicting voices as possible was the impetus for the case study we designed as we revised our course Gender and the Rhetoric of Science and Technology. Reflecting on the dissonances among these conflicting voices is the purpose of this section of our essay. We hope that these reflections will inspire and enrich future scholarly and curricular work that looks at women's lives through the lens of science and technology.

Perhaps the voices that have told the maquiladora story most loudly are those that echo what Donna Haraway (1997, 89) calls "narratives of the Scientific Revolution and progress." The narratives to which Haraway refers originate in a desire that has motivated Western European philosophy and philosophy of science since at least the seventeenth century: the desire to perfect the world we live in by perfecting our ways of knowing this world. Francis Bacon, whose ideas have since come to be known as the basis of the Scientific Revolution, captures the almost spiritual status that Western philosophy has granted to knowledge as a means of improving human lives: "Lastly, I would like to give this general admonition to all men, namely, that they reflect on the true ends of knowledge, and that they seek it not from any intellectual satisfaction, nor for contention, nor to look down upon others, nor for reward, or fame, or power, or any of these baser things; but to direct and bring it to perfection in charity, for the benefit and use of life" (Bacon 1620, 1994, 5).

In the time that has lapsed since Bacon wrote these words, science, technology, and industrialization have replaced "pure" knowledge as the entities that Bacon would have us perfect "for the benefit and use of life," but the basic desire to use the products of intellectual efforts as a means of improving the world remains constant. Narratives deriving from this desire have been able to inform thinking about Mexico's well-being because, as many twentieth-century scholars have observed, the seemingly innocent desire of westerners to improve the human lot through scientific and technological advancement has been accompanied by not-so-innocent efforts to diminish other approaches to improving the world. (For other readings on Western narratives of progress, see Said 1993; Winner 1986; Wajcman 1991; Harding 1991, 1993a; Haraway 1989, 1991.) These simultaneous attempts to prove Western epistemological supremacy and diminish other ways of knowing have forged powerful links among Western philosophies of science, technology, and human progress. In Sandra Harding's (1993a, 7) words, this has allowed claims that "Western sciences and their technologies are the most important measures of human progress" to be applied to the world at large, rather than just to the Western cultures that first made them. The maquiladora industry and the border culture it has spawned are just one recent manifestation of Harding's observation.

To say that "narratives of the Scientific Revolution and progress" originate in Western philosophy is not to say that these narratives form a continuous story with a clear beginning and end, nor is it to say that an essentialist notion of a Western psyche unites everyone who lives in "the West." The Western narratives of progress to which Haraway refers have themselves been spoken by multiple voices, and in various ways, throughout Western history. In fact, the strength of these narratives lies in their proven ability to survive historical change and to convince citizens all over the world of their veracity. Augusta Dwyer (1994, 17) quotes Antonio Bermúdez, head of the Mexican National Border Program in 1960, who described the maquiladora program as "the logical thing to do. It made sense. American companies saved money. Mexicans got jobs. Everybody won." Early maquiladora enthusiasts on both sides of the border echoed Western narratives of progress, believing that industrialization would invigorate a languid border economy by creating jobs, giving Mexicans more money to spend, and facilitating technology transfer from the United States and other industrialized nations to Mexico. This enthusiasm has remained intact for some segments of the maquiladora industry. For instance, Devon Peña (1997, 14) quotes a 1981 interview he conducted with a maquiladora manager from the United States: "The way I figure, these plants are good for Mexico because they . . . offer the young women a chance to be something better. . . . We are proud of our technology. It provides solutions to a lot of problems and brings superior skills to Mexico's labor force. This is what progress is all about; the key is technology." Enthusiasts could not believe so strongly in the maquiladoras' potential to improve life for Mexicans if Western narratives of progress had not been persistent in their centuries-long attempts to depict Western science, technology, and industrialization as catalysts for positive change throughout the world.

A DIFFERENT STORY

In terms of expansion rate and the number of jobs created, the maquiladora industry has exceeded its creators' highest expectations. In 1965 there were only 12 maquiladoras employing 3,000 workers, but between 1975 and 1987, the industry grew at an average annual rate of 8 percent, and since 1987, the annual average growth rate has been estimated at 15 percent (Peña 1997, 279). In 1994, there were more than 2,180 maquiladoras in Mexico, employing more than one-half million workers, and these numbers continue to rise (Dwyer 1994, 5; Peña 1997, 279). Clearly, on one level, the maquiladoras have proven Western narratives of progress to be true. But realities of life on the border tell a different story. People who inhabit the U.S.–Mexico border and who work in maquiladoras today face egregious environmental, health, safety, and financial problems. In 1994 the average maquiladora wage throughout Mexico was the equivalent of $1.20 an hour, forcing maquiladora employees to live in substandard housing without money for adequate food, health care, and child care (Dwyer 1994, 4). Since 1994, real wages have actually decreased because of peso devaluation, so that in March 1996 average maquiladora wages were $.42 an hour. Substandard wages and squalid private living conditions are exacerbated by public environmental hazards, including toxic gas leaks, contaminated water supplies, illegal sewage treatment, and illegal management of toxic wastes (Dwyer 1994; Peña 1997). During NAFTA negotiations in 1993, politicians and environmentalists estimated it would cost between $6.5 and $10 billion to correct the damage maquiladoras had already done to the border region (Dwyer 1994, 55), but critics of NAFTA have estimated this figure to be as high as $18 billion (Peña 1997, 376, fn. 26). Although government officials in Mexico and the United States have acknowledged these numbers, the Environmental Protection Agency only requested $240 million from Congress in 1993, and Mexico stated $460 million as the amount its government could spend on environmental problems between 1993 and 1996 (Dwyer 1994). In addition to these massive financial and environmental problems, maquiladora management has been criticized for forcing employees to tolerate hazardous work environments and failing to respond to employees' demands.

In short, the realities of Mexico's maquiladora industry disrupt traditional Western narratives of scientific and technological progress, demanding alternative understandings of life on the border. One such alternative is found in postcolonial scholarship, an interdisciplinary body of scholarship concerned with global power relations as they have evolved since the official end of large-scale colonialism in the mid–twentieth century. Many postcolonial scholars argue that multinational and transnational corporations, like those that participate in Mexico's maquiladora program, enact neocolonialism by exploiting cheap labor, in much the same way that imperialist nations exploited native inhabitants and natural resources throughout Latin America, Africa, and Asia in the nineteenth century. These scholars see the neocolonialist trend as global, not just characteristic of U.S.–Mexico relations. Their view is certainly applicable to the Mexican situation, and is even corroborated by the etymology of the word *maquiladora*, which in Mexican colonial times referred to the portion of grain a miller would keep in return for his labor (Dwyer 1994, 6).

Feminist narratives accompany, and at times, intersect with, post-colonial narratives. Specifically, feminist scholars prevent us from adopting an overly simplistic view of relationships between nineteenth-century and twentieth-century forms of colonialism by observing that the gender dimension of the present phase makes it unique. As Susan Tiano (1994, 17) explains, from a feminist perspective, "The phase [the maquiladora industry] is novel, but the process [colonialism] is continuous." Tiano's statement reflects the fact that women's work is more central to the maquiladora industry than it was to economic production in earlier phases of colonialism.

Postcolonial and feminist narratives do not so much contradict Western narratives of progress as destabilize these narratives by revealing the dark undersides that become visible when science, technology, and industrialization are viewed in a global, rather than a strictly Western, perspective. Paying attention to this kind of destabilization by listening to the competing narratives of Western progress, postcolonialism, and feminism has been an important motivation for the case study we designed. In the words of Sandra Harding (1993b, 62), a feminist standpoint theorist, our case study attempts to start pedagogy "from the lives of marginalized peoples."

Feminist standpoint theory was first articulated by Nancy Hartsock in 1983. Based on her Marxist convictions, Hartsock argued that the marginal position of women in society affords them epistemic privilege. Because marginalized people are always forced to see from the perspectives of those in power as well as from their own perspectives, the knowledge they produce is more objective than that produced from dominant perspectives. Harding's analysis extends Hartsock's feminist standpoint theory by considering how race and class intersect with gender, and also by emphasizing the ethical, in addition to the epistemological, imperatives for starting research from marginal perspectives.

MAQUILADORA RESEARCH

Feminist standpoint theory instructs us to challenge Western narratives of science, technology, and industrialization by considering alternative ways to think about these phenomena. Starting research from the lives of the marginalized, however, also means considering who is developing these alternatives and how they are being developed. Reading postcolonial or feminist theory is obviously not the same as listening to a maquiladora worker tell the story of her experience, even if the two kinds of storytellers relate similar sequences of events. Awareness of this difference demands that teachers and researchers seek scholarly texts that document women's accounts of their own experiences, rather than texts that claim to speak on behalf of women or that speak of women's experiences in purely theoretical terms. The rest of our essay examines two of the texts we selected for our case-study unit, and illustrates how each succeeds in this regard.

Devon Peña, a sociologist, effectively relates the maquiladora story from the perspectives of employees in his book-length study of the maquiladora industry, *The Terror of the Machine: Technology, Work, Gender, and Ecology on the U.S.–Mexico Border* (1997). Peña opens his first chapter with a reference to Henry Ford's descriptions of assembly lines, and sets up Ford's words about control of workers as an ominous backdrop for his own analysis. Peña indicates that maquiladora management today exhibits the same desire for ultimate control over workers that Ford expressed in the early twentieth century. His analysis reveals the dark side of Western ideas about science and technology, by depicting the ways that these ideas are enacted by maquiladora management. Peña documents managerial attempts to scientifically control worker productivity and workers' responses to these attempts, and articulates his view of the relationships among Western reason, science, technology, domination, capitalism, and sexism: "The history of science is the story of the conquest and control of nature, women, workers, and colonies by means of a constant revolution in the tools of technological domination designed by experts" (Peña 1997, 27). Peña explains how the academic discipline of management science has contributed to the kind of technological domination described in this passage, and he illustrates how this phenomenon manifests itself in the maquiladoras. Furthermore, Peña reveals that, as is often the case with scientific methods, the supposedly neutral methods of productivity measurement that management science provides have serious political dimensions.

Peña also provides useful statistics on the gender inequality that characterizes management-employee relations in the maquiladoras, and proceeds to make an important observation: The managers, most of whom are male, do not have as much control over the workers, most of whom are female, as they believe they have. Although large-scale organized resistance has generally been unsuccessful in the maquiladoras, Peña illustrates that workers develop elaborate strategies to cope with and sometimes resist managerial attempts to control them. He provides a particularly interesting examination of the discourses that female maquila workers use to resist the gendered identities imposed on them by maquila management. Peña's accounts of interviews with managers and workers skillfully reveal the gap between management's view of the workplace and what he refers to as the "subaltern" life of the factory, where discourses of resistance emerge and sometimes thrive. Peña follows other scholars in evoking the ominous comparison between Ford's assembly line and maquiladoras, but he distinguishes himself from other scholars who have studied the maquiladoras by focusing on workers' resistance efforts, rather than perpetuating the image of maquiladora workers as passive victims of managerial domination. Peña's success in this regard makes his analysis a valuable resource for scholars and teachers interested in understanding the maquiladoras as a gendered site of scientific and technological conflict.

Another text that effectively tells the maquiladora story from the perspective of employees is Augusta Dwyer's *On the Line: Life on the US–Mexican Border* (1994). The topics Dwyer addresses include women's attempts at political organization in the maquiladoras, environmental issues, safety issues, and possibilities for future political organization in the border region. There is overlap between Dwyer's and Peña's texts, but Dwyer's journalistic analysis complements Peña's scholarly analysis in useful ways. Although Peña and Dwyer are both successful at documenting women's experiences, Dwyer devotes a larger portion of her book to relating first-hand accounts than does Peña, providing abundant anecdotal evidence to supplement Peña's scholarly analysis of women's experiences. For instance, Dwyer opens and closes almost every chapter by relating a narrative told to her by someone who works in a maquiladora or lives on the border. She opens her book by relating the story of Petra Santiago, whose life was risked in August 1991 when she suffered a miscarriage on the job and her supervisor would not let her leave to seek medical attention. Dwyer also tells the story of residents of Brownsville, Texas, who blame toxic wastes from maquiladoras for an alarming number of anencephalic babies born there in the early 1990s. Although government officials on both sides of the border denied industry responsibility for this epidemic, in 1993 four maquiladoras in Matamoros, just across the border from Brownsville, were fined for illegal management of toxic wastes (Dwyer 1994, 54; see also Peña 1997, 280). Furthermore, Dwyer explains, residents of Matamoros, Mexicali, and Juárez in the late 1980s and early 1990s endured toxic gas leaks from maquiladoras in and around their cities, and people in Tijuana, Mexicali, Nogales, and Cuidad Juárez have been forced to live with contaminated water supplies and illegal sewage treatment (Dwyer 1994, 50). Conditions like these have persisted for decades and have only been discovered by recent environmental tests (Dwyer 1994, 57–59). Dwyer's in-depth accounts of situations like these become intertwined with detailed historical and statistical information to make the reader feel very close to those who live on the U.S.–Mexico border.

As stated earlier, our decision to include Peña's and Dwyer's texts rather than other similar studies of life on the border reflects our interest in scholarship that acknowledges women's own voices. Although they accomplish it differently, both Peña and Dwyer succeed in this regard. On the other hand, scholars and teachers need to guard against the tendency to seek *authentic* experience. Peña's and Dwyer's skillful documentation of women's experiences as maquiladora workers make these experiences seem real, but if we have too much faith in the scholars' abilities to capture women's experiences just by recording their voices on paper, we risk essentializing women's lives in a way that ignores their rich and diverse experiences. As Joan Scott explains in her essay "Experience," scholars need to resist the temptation to take experience "as uncontestable evidence and as an originary point of explanation," because this "weakens the critical thrust" of feminist scholarship (Scott 1992, 24). In this essay, Scott, a feminist historian, acknowledges the importance of documenting the experiences of marginalized people, but claims that historians must always acknowledge that their use of evidence is rhetorical, that no piece of evidence proves a point by itself. Although Peña is a sociologist and Dwyer a journalist, Scott's insights about historiography certainly pertain to these two writers, and most importantly, to readers of their texts. As readers, the temptation to forget the rhetorical aspect of using evidence is great when we read scholarship that claims to document personal experience. We tend to think that first-hand accounts speak for themselves, that they are more authentic than other kinds of evidence, but Scott reminds us that this is not necessarily true. In short, Scott's essay on the limits of experience challenges the insights of feminist standpoint theorists without directly confronting these insights. In doing so, Scott advises us to listen to alternative accounts of reality, especially accounts offered by marginalized people, but to listen actively, and to always keep listening for further disruptions because no account will ever have the last word.

CONCLUSION

Studying women's lives on the local and global level through the lens of science and technology greatly enriches our understanding of the social construction of women and the specifics of women's lives. This essay has described four areas of women's lives that have been particularly touched by science and technology: the introduction of new technologies into the workplace and the home, the development of new reproductive technologies, the effect of science and technology on food production and processing, and the ecofeminist movement. The maquiladoras case study serves as an example of the problematization of Western notions about progress through scientific and technological development by looking at women's lives within a particular environment. The case also reminds us of the challenges we face as teachers and scholars when we attempt to capture women's voices and experiences or to speak for others.

WORKS CITED

Awe, Bolanle, Susan Geiger, Nina Mba, Marjorie Mbilinyi, Ruth Meena, and Margaret Strobel. 1991. "Editorial." *Signs: Journal of Women in Culture and Society* 16: 645–649.

Bacon, Francis. 1620, 1994. *Novum Organum,* trans. Peter Urbach and John Gibson. Chicago: Open Court.

Bauer, Arnold J. 1990. "Millers and Grinders: Technology and Household Economy in Meso-America." *Agricultural History* 64 (1): 1–17.

Bunkle, Phillida. 1993. "Calling the Shots? The International Politics of Depo-Provera." In Sandra Harding, ed., *The "Racial" Economy of Science: Toward a Democratic Future*, 287–302. Bloomington: Indiana University Press.

Carney, Judith, and Michael Watts. 1991. "Disciplining Women? Rice, Mechanization, and the Evolution of Mandinka Gender Relations in Senegambia." *Signs: Journal of Women in Culture and Society* 16: 651–681.

Catanzarite, Lisa M., and Myra H. Strober. 1993. "The Gender Recomposition of the Maquiladora Workforce in Cuidad Juárez." *Industrial Relations* 32 (1): 133–147.

Curtin, Deane. 1997. "Women's Knowledge as Expert Knowledge." In K. J. Warren, ed., *Ecofeminism: Women, Culture, Nature*, 82–98. Bloomington: Indiana University Press.

Dwyer, Augusta. 1994. *On the Line: Life on the US–Mexican Border*. London: Latin American Bureau.

Ehrenreich, Barbara, Mark Dowie, and Stephen Minkin 1979. "The Charge: Gynocide/The Accused: The U.S. Government." *Mother Jones* (November): 27–37.

Eldredge, Elizabeth A. 1991. "Women in Production: The Economic Role of Women in Nineteenth-Century Lesotho." *Signs: Journal of Women in Culture and Society* 16: 707–731.

Evans, Vella Neil. 1991. "Try, Try Again: Incorporating International Perspectives into a Course on Sex Roles and Social Change." *Women's Studies International Forum* 14: 335–343.

Farnsworth-Alvear, Ann. 1997. "Orthodox Virginity/Heterodox Memories: Understanding Women's Stories in Mill Discipline in Medellín, Colombia." *Signs: Journal of Women in Culture and Society* 23: 71–101.

Fernandes, Leela. 1997. "Beyond Public Spaces and Private Spheres: Gender, Family, and Working-Class Politics in India." *Feminist Studies* 23: 525–547.

Haraway, Donna. 1989. *Primate Visions: Gender, Race, and Nature in the World of Modern Science*. New York: Routledge.

———. 1991. *Simians, Cyborgs, and Women*. New York: Routledge.

———. 1997. *Modest_Witness@Second_Millennium.FemaleMan© _Meets_OncoMouse™*. New York: Routledge.

Harcourt, Wendy. 1997. "An Analysis of Reproductive Health: Myths, Resistance and New Knowledge." In Wendy Harcourt, ed., *Power, Reproduction and Gender: The Intergenerational Transfer of Knowledge*, 8–34. London: Zed Books.

Harding, Sandra. 1986. *The Science Question in Feminism*. Ithaca: Cornell University Press.

———. 1991. *Whose Science? Whose Knowledge? Thinking from Women's Lives*. Ithaca: Cornell University Press.

———. 1993a. *The "Racial" Economy of Science: Toward a Democratic Future*. Bloomington: Indiana University Press.

———. 1993b. "Rethinking Standpoint Epistemology: 'What Is Strong Objectivity'?" In Linda Alcoff and Elizabeth Potter, eds., *Feminist Epistemologies*, 49–82. New York: Routledge.

Hardon, Anita P. 1992. "The Needs of Women Versus the Interests of Family Planning Personnel, Policy-makers and Researchers: Conflicting Views on Safety and Acceptability of Contraceptives." *Social Science and Medicine* 35: 753–766.

Hartmann, Betsy. 1995. *Reproductive Rights & Wrongs: The Global Politics of Population Control*. Boston: South End Press.

Hartsock, Nancy. 1983. "The Feminist Standpoint: Developing the Ground for a Specifically Feminist Historical Materialism." In Sandra Harding and Merrill Hintikka, eds., *Discovering Reality*, 238–310. Dordrecht: Reidel.

Keller, Evelyn Fox. 1985. *Reflections on Gender and Science*. New Haven, Conn.: Yale University Press.

———. 1992. *Secrets of Life/Secrets of Death: Essays on Language, Gender and Science*. New York: Routledge.

Kirkup, G., and L. S. Keller. 1992. *Inventing Women: Science, Technology, and Gender*. Cambridge: Polity Press.

Longino, Helen. 1990. *Science as Social Knowledge: Value and Objectivity in Scientific Inquiry*. Princeton: Princeton University Press.

———. 1993. "Feminist Standpoint Theory and the Problems of Knowledge." *Signs: Journal of Women in Culture and Society* 19: 201–212.

———. 1994. "In Search of Feminist Epistemology." *The Monist* 77 (1994): 472–485.

———. 1993. "Subjects, Power and Knowledge: Description and Prescription in Feminist Philosophies of Science." In Linda Alcoff and Elizabeth Potter, eds., *Feminist Epistemologies*, 101–120. New York: Routledge.

Martin, Emily. 1992. *The Woman in the Body: A Cultural Analysis of Reproduction*. Boston: Beacon Press.

Merchant, Carolyn. 1995. *Earthcare: Women and the Environment*. New York: Routledge.

Mitchell, Lisa M., and Eugenia Georges. 1997. "Cross-Cultural Cyborgs: Greek and Canadian Women's Discourses on Fetal Ultrasound." *Feminist Studies* 23: 373–401.

Miyoshi, Masao. 1993. "A Borderless World? From Colonialism to Transnationalism and the Decline of the Nation-State." *Critical Inquiry* 19 (Summer): 726–751.

Mohanty, Chandra. 1988. "Under Western Eyes: Feminist Scholarship and Colonial Discourses." *Feminist Review* 30: 61–88.

Odedra-Straub, Mayuri. 1995. "Women and Information Technology in Sub-Saharan Africa." In Swasti Miller and Sheila Rowbotham, eds., *Women Encounter Technology: Changing Patterns of Employment in the Third World*, 256–277. London: Routledge.

Peña, Devon G. 1997. *The Terror of the Machine: Technology, Work, Gender, and Ecology on the U.S.–Mexico Border*. Austin: CMAS Books.

Rose, Hilary. 1983. "Hand, Brain and Heart: A Feminist Epistemology of the Natural Sciences." *Signs: Journal of Women in Culture and Society* 9 (1): 73–90.

Rossiter, M. W. 1995. *Women Scientists in America Before Affirmative Action: 1940–1972*. Baltimore: Johns Hopkins University Press.

Rothschild, J. 1984. *Machina Ex Dea: Feminist Perspectives on Technology*. New York: Pergamon.

———. 1992. *Women, Technology and Innovation*. Oxford: Pergamon.

Said, Edward. 1993. *Culture and Imperialism*. New York: Vintage Books.

Schiebinger, Londa. 1989. *The Mind Has No Sex? Women in the Origins of Modern Science*. Cambridge: Harvard University Press.

———. 1993. *Nature's Body: Gender in the Making of Modern Science*. Boston: Beacon Press.

Scott, Joan. 1992. "Experience." In Judith Butler and Joan Scott, eds., *Feminists Theorize the Political*, 22–40. New York: Routledge.

Shiva, Vandana. 1993a. "Colonialism and the Evolution of Masculinist Forestry." In Sandra Harding, ed., *The "Racial" Economy of Science: Toward a Democratic Future*, 303–314. Bloomington: Indiana University Press.

———. 1993b. "The Greening of the Global Reach." In Jeremy Brecher, John Brown Childs, and Jill Cutler, eds., *Global Visions: Beyond the New World Order*, 53–60. Boston: South End Press.

Sim, Cecilia Ng Choon, and Carol Yong. 1995. "Information Technology, Gender and Employment: A Case Study of the Telecommunications Industry in Malaysia." In Swasti Miller and Sheila Rowbotham, eds., *Women Encounter Technology: Changing Patterns of Employment in the Third World*, 175–204. London: Routledge.

Smith, Dorothy. 1987. *The Everyday World as Problematic: A Feminist Sociology*. Boston: Northeastern University Press.

———. 1990. *The Conceptual Practices of Power: A Feminist Sociology of Knowledge*. Boston: Northeastern University Press.

Spivak, Gayatri. 1987. *In Other Worlds: Essays in Cultural Politics*. New York: Methuen.

"Support Committee for Maquiladora Workers" home page. 1998 <http://www.pctvi.com/laamn/maquiladora.html> (February 17).

Tiano, Susan. 1994. *Patriarchy on the Line: Labor, Gender, and Ideology in the Mexican Maquila Industry*. Philadelphia: Temple University Press.

Wajcman, Judy. *Feminism Confronts Technology*. University Park: Pennsylvania State University Press, 1991.

Warren, K. J. 1997. "Taking Empirical Data Seriously: An Ecofeminist Philosophical Perspective." In K. J. Warren, ed., *Ecofeminism: Women, Culture, Nature*, 3–20. Bloomington: Indiana University Press.

Winner, Langdon. 1986. *The Whale and the Reactor*. Chicago: University of Chicago Press.

Wright, B. D., M. M. Feree, G. O. Mellow, L. H. Lewis, M-L. D. Samper, R. Asher, and K. Claspell. 1987. *Women, Work, and Technology*. Ann Arbor: University of Michigan Press.

SUGGESTIONS FOR FURTHER READING ON THE MAQUILADORAS

Cravey, Altha J. 1997. "The Politics of Reproduction: Households in the Mexican Industrial Transition." *Economic Geography* 73 (2): 166–186.

Kelly, María Patricia Fernández. 1984. "Maquiladoras: The View from the Inside." In Karen Brodkin Sacks and Dorothy Remy, eds., *My Troubles Are Going to Have Trouble with Me: Everyday Trials and Triumphs of Women Workers*, 22–46. New Brunswick, N.J.: Rutgers University Press.

Leonard, Rodney, and Eric Christensen. 1992. "Lax Enforcement of Environmental Laws in Mexico." In John Cavanagh, John Gershman, Karen Baker, and Gretchen

Helmke, eds., *Trading Freedom: How Free Trade Affects Our Lives, Work, and Environment.* San Francisco: Institute for Food and Development Policy.

Lucker, George W., and A. J. Álvarez. 1984. "Exploitation or Exaggeration? A Worker's Eye View of 'Maquiladora' Work." *Southwest Journal of Business and Economics* 1: 11–18.

———. 1985. "Controlling Maquiladora Turnover Through Personnel Selection." *Southwest Journal of Business and Economics* 2: 1–10.

Ruiz, Vicki L., and Susan Tiano, eds. 1987. *Women on the U.S.–Mexico Border: Responses to Change.* Boston: Allen & Unwin.

Salzinger, Leslie. 1997. "From High Heels to Swathed Bodies: Gendered Meanings Under Production in Mexico's Export-Processing Industry." *Feminist Studies* 23 (3): 549–574.

Sanderson, Susan. 1987. "Automated Manufacturing and Offshore Assembly in Mexico." In Cathryn Thorup, ed., *The United States and Mexico: Face to Face with the New Technology,* 23–36. New Brunswick, N.J.: Transaction Books.

Seligson, Mitchell A., and Edward J. Williams. 1981. *Maquiladoras and Migration: Workers in the Mexico–United States Border Industrialization Program.* Austin: Institute of Latin American Studies.

Sklair, Leslie. 1988. *Maquiladoras: Annotated Bibliography and Research Guide to Mexico's In-Bond Industry, 1980–1988.* La Jolla: Center for U.S.–Mexican Studies.

———. 1994. *Assembling for Development: The Maquila Industry in Mexico and the United States,* 2nd edition. London: Unwin Hyman.

South, Robert B. 1990. "Transnational 'Maquiladora' Location." *Annals of the Association of American Geographers* 80: 549–570.

Stoddard, Ellwyn R. 1987. *Maquila: Assembly Plants in Northern Mexico.* El Paso: Texas Western Press.

———. 1991. "Border Maquila Ownership and Mexican Economic Benefits: A Comparative Analysis of the 'Good,' the 'Bad,' and the 'Ugly.'" *Journal of Borderlands Studies* 6: 23–50.

———, ed. 1990. *Border Maquiladoras and Research Interpretations: An International Symposium,* special issue, *Journal of Borderlands Studies* 5.

Thorup, Cathryn, ed. 1987. *The United States and Mexico: Face to Face with the New Technology.* New Brunswick, N.J.: Transaction Books.

Tiano, Susan. 1990. "Labor Composition and Gender Stereotypes in the Maquilas." *Journal of Borderlands Studies* 5: 20–24.

Tolan, Sandy, and Jerry Kammer. 1991. "Life in the Low-Wage Boomtowns of Mexico." *Utne Reader* (November–December).

Warner, David V. 1991. "Health Issues at the U.S.–Mexican Border." *Journal of the American Medical Association* 265: 242–247.

GLOBALIZATIONS, TV TECHNOLOGIES, AND THE RE-PRODUCTION OF SEXUAL IDENTITIES: TEACHING *HIGHLANDER* AND *XENA* IN LAYERS OF LOCALS AND GLOBALS

KATIE KING

GLOBALIZATION PROCESSES

Globalization processes are pivotal in several of the courses I teach—from Introduction to Women's Studies, in which I focus on international art activism, to specialty courses, such as Nationalities, Sexualities and Global TV; to graduate courses in feminist interdisciplinary theory and methods. As a women's studies professor, I want students to be able to *locate* themselves rather than simply *focus* on themselves. I want to communicate to them ways of seeing themselves as subjects in history—located in fields of power that are gendered, raced, nationalized—seeing themselves moved and disposed by world historical forces, but always also as agents of change and of moral, political, and economic power.

It is with such concerns in mind that I teach and research in the field I call feminism and writing technologies. Literally, this field looks at histories of various writing technologies, for example, alphabet, movable type, index, pencil, typewriter, xerox machine, computer, and Internet. Feminism and writing technologies provides a complicated lens onto global and national TV and TV technologies, new arrangements of multinational capital and new European identities, and interpenetrated forms of vision and writing on the World Wide Web, the Internet, and in film, TV, video, and print media. Feminist and media scholars have investments in the politics of global TV production, in media fandoms dominated by women, in locations friendly to women on the web, and in the domestication of TV and video, computer, and satellite technologies, as well as in the global circulation of multiethnic, multisexual images.

Women's studies is one academic location in which students learn to cut through a slice of their world and analyze what appears to be obvious and transparent, situating their individual experiences within "layers of locals and globals." My work on the TV shows *Highlander* and *Xena* exemplifies these pedagogical concerns: to model a kind of analysis that is useful through a range of academic disciplines and research projects, and one that enriches an individual's social and political critical faculties, something broadly useful outside the academy. Most of my work has focused on *Highlander,* so I turn to it for rich pedagogical examples. Recently, I began to research *Xena* as well, though I refer to it less extensively.

GLOBALIZATION PROCESSES IN THE YEAR 1992: HIGHLANDER IN CONTEXT

The year 1992 began the countdown for the formation of the European single market, the regional economic entity—utopian for some, dystopian for others —intended now to recenter Europe in a global politics fragmented in the wake of the breakup of the Soviet Union. This new "European Union" would necessarily refigure what counted as Europe—that is to say, literally which countries now would be included in this redesigned entity "Europe" and which would not—but would also reconceive the meanings of nationalisms, regionalisms, and localisms. That year also marked the five hundredth anniversary of the so-called "discovery of the New World": the invasion of the Americas by European conquerors. The contest to represent that moment in the newer one was part of a "war" of "image superpowers." This "war" engaged national desires to valorize old colonialisms in the face of new ones, even as oppositional political movements attempted to address new racisms in Europe and elsewhere, racisms too often traveling as national and ethnic identities.

The year 1992 was also when the action adventure series *Highlander* first premiered—"the first European coproduced weekly hour to be sold into the U.S. syndication market" (Sherwood 1996b, S6). It is based on a fantasy world of immortal sword fighters. My own pleasure in *Highlander* began with the principal actor Adrian Paul's eroticized image. I immediately (and apparently somewhat idiosyncratically) "recognized" it as gay (the image, not necessarily the story character Duncan MacLeod, or the actor Adrian Paul). It was in this "recognition" that I discovered my pleasure in the show. Other signs heightened my pleasure in what seemed to me, a lesbian viewer, to be a circulation of gay meanings. First, I noted the use of Paris' Shakespeare and Company as a location and story site—the bookstore run by lesbian lovers Sylvia Beach and Adrienne Monnier in the Rue de l'Odéon in the 1920s, but known on the show simply as "the American bookstore." Second was the powerful emotional engagement of the show's theme music, "Princes of the Universe," composed and performed by Queen and sung by the late Freddie Mercury, who died of AIDS in November 1991 (Ressner 1992, 13; Block and Laermer 1991, 74; Clark-Meads 1991, 14).

It was not that I assumed that there was a latent homosexual sub-text, a topic repeatedly raised on the international Internet news-group *alt.tv.highlander* but usually treated with scorn by those fans; no, I assumed it was something else. I puzzled over it. On impulse at the supermarket I picked up a special issue of *Entertainment Weekly*. This issue shouted on its cover "The Gay '90s: Entertainment Comes out of the Closet." In the cover article by Jess Cagle, "America Sees Shades of Gay," I found words to describe the impression I had received from the show: "mutual inclusiveness—the *give* and *take back*—of gay and straight audiences. Its sex appeal bids for the atten-tion of all sexual persuasions; so do its jokes, and the screen winks broadly in all directions." Or, "The most striking and omnipresent outgrowth of that awakening has been in the mass marketing of erotic male images. . . . They're all things to all persuasions." Or, "Not gay per se but *something.* 'It's all become one bright pop blur.'" And finally, "In short, this revolution is the only kind Hollywood can trust—one driven by the marketplace" (Cagle 1995, 22, 24, 31).

Entertainment Weekly's politics differ markedly from the caution-ary story told by Rosemary Hennessy when she discusses "Queer visi-bility in commodity culture." She says, "capitalism's need for expanding markets has in its own way promoted the integration of art and life . . . continuously working and reworking desires by inviting them to take the forms dictated by the commodity market. . . . The aestheticization of daily life encourages the pursuit of new tastes and sensations as pleasures in themselves while concealing or back-grounding the labor that has gone into making them possible. . . . We need a way of understanding [queer] visibility that acknowledges both the local situations in which sexuality is made intelligible as well as the ties that bind knowledge and power to commodity production, consumption, and exchange" (Hennessy 1995, 164, 165, 177).

It was in 1995 that I first encountered *Highlander* and read Cagle's essay. Now I can watch reruns of the U.S. TV comedy *Ellen,* recently canceled, after being both captivated and depressed by the Ellen Watch,[1] the countdown to its coming-out episode (*Entertainment Weekly,* 1997, 130; Sanborn 1997, 24; *Time,* 1997; De Vries, 1997). I recall with a similar mixture of captivation and depression my inter-ested speculations concerning the commercial success of what I call "*Xena* feminism," and the politics of the producers of the globally suc-cessful action show *Xena.* I and others especially speculate about their playful encouragement of multiple readings of the sexual lives of the main characters Xena and Gabrielle, who adventure through a postmodern world vaguely modeled on ancient Greece (Kastor 1996, C1, C5). I consider these TV events examples, in layers of locals and globals, of what I call "global gay formations and local homosexuali-ties," and what David Morley and Kevin Robins titled their 1995 book: *Spaces of Identity: Global Media, Electronic Landscapes and Cultural Boundaries.*

I discuss these large political and ideological issues in the concrete terms of the Canadian-French TV show *Highlander,* and also with reference to *Xena,* the U.S. show shot in New Zealand. I have been studying *Xena* as a counterpoint to *Highlander,* aided in examining each one by its growing Internet media fandom (subculture of fans), a group that is largely female, a site of women's concentration on the World Wide Web. While importantly international, these media fandoms still tend to be dominated by English-speaking fans from all over the world, and by fans within the shows' principal market, the United States. Part of the point of this essay is to demonstrate the complex patternings of globals and locals in layers that constitute the processes of globalization in "spaces of identity," intersections of nationality, sexuality, and gender.

My purpose here is not to celebrate female media fandoms, TV shows, identity politics, or globalization. I am complexly critical of, though influenced by and, inevitably, structurally complicit with all. I consider them each sites of and for political contestation, and that is the contradictory act in which I engage here. I do not think a single-hearted stance of political "critique" is remotely adequate for the kinds of social and cultural analysis necessary under the regimes of globalized capital. This is how I would distinguish the politics and method I offer students from the politics offered by either *Entertainment Weekly* or Rosemary Hennessy.

RICH, CONCRETE EXAMPLES OF GLOBALIZATION PROCESSES FOR STUDENTS

Rather than approach these issues only abstractly, I want to describe concretely for students some of the ways in which globalization operates. To do so I turn to the economic arrangements surrounding the coming-into-being of the TV show *Highlander* in 1992, the year of formation of the European single market. *Highlander*'s principal production partner was the French company Gaumont, which has been called "the world's oldest film company" (Turman 1994, 22). That first year *Highlander*'s financing was a money mix from France, Germany, Italy, and Japan (*Hollywood Reporter* 1996, S20). In the second year Gaumont found another partner, Canadian Filmline International. *Highlander* thus became a coproduction filmed entirely in France and Canada and shot in English for a world market. It has been seen in seventy countries in Europe, North and South America, Asia, Africa, and Australia, where it has competed with syndicated series produced in the United States (Sherwood 1996a, S1). In distinctly French and Canadian cultural strategies *Highlander* has been another of those cultural products intended to combat U.S. media hegemony. Its quotas on European content were insured during several seasons by shooting half of each season in Vancouver and half in Paris under a

Franco-Canadian agreement in which "segments shot in Canada qualify as European, and segments shot in Europe qualify as Canadian" (Sherwood 1996b, S32). Note that the European single market has strategically shifting economic geographies!

In 1991, Gaumont had just opened its new television division. This marked a shift in economic strategies by a company that pioneered the winning strategy among global media corporations—overwhelming vertical integration. Gaumont's media empire, begun in 1895 with manufacturing and selling photographic equipment, quickly became first "the world's largest film studio" and, soon after, "the world's largest movie theater" (Turman 1994, 22, 23; Millar 1996, 229). Today media corporations are a complicated mix of parent companies and subsidiaries with international lineages. For example, the U.S. company MCA, the principal partner with Sam Raimi's Renaissance Pictures making the TV show *Xena,* is a private subsidiary of the Canadian multinational Seagram, who bought it in 1995 from the Japanese multinational Matsushita. MCA has divisions and subsidiaries involved in movies, TV, video tapes, publishing, music, concerts, audio tapes, cable TV, and so on. Vertical integration is about being altogether in control of production sites, materials, and talent; distribution, sales, and promotion; and places of exhibition and retailing or technologies of delivery (Wasko 1994, 63–65).[2] Students will already have everyday life connections with these and other multinationals, all of which can be opened to similar analysis.

As Gaumont's president Nicolas Seydoux has said, "Gaumont began life as an integrated company. . . . A screen has no reason to exist without a movie to show on it, and a movie doesn't exist without a screen to show it on" (*Variety,* 1994, 58). But although Gaumont may have pioneered integration, it had ceased being a winning player in the global market: its attempts to parlay its long management of film production, distribution, and theatrical exhibition into new chains of theaters throughout Europe in the 1980s had failed. Entering into economic retrenchment, Gaumont had become very vocal about French film culture, announced its plans to concentrate on making films in French only, and clearly intended now to take advantage of state protection of culture industries. Supporting limits on U.S. films and TV programs abroad, Seydoux insisted, "This is not a trade war. It is an identity statement. All we want is to preserve a world in which grandchildren have the same national identity as their grandparents" (Gubernick 1994, 118).

On the one hand, that is. Film would be Gaumont's site of cultural nationalism. But TV would be Gaumont's reentry into global flows of power and media. At the end of the first three years of its existence Gaumont's TV division accounted for one fifth of its profits (*Variety* 1994). Gaumont's first French production partner in this *Highlander* venture, channel TF1, had to end its partnership after the first year because it was no longer allowed to count English-language TV products, like *Highlander,* as "French." French channel M6, however, "had the right to produce non-French European programs," but was a smaller channel, with less money to invest (Sherwood 1996b, S34). So, in order to continue production on this English-language TV show, Gaumont had to find its Canadian partner, Filmline.

As a joint venture between Canada and France, *Highlander*'s production elements have been carefully quotaed. Indeed, the quotas on European content are the reason that for several seasons *Highlander* was shot on location in both Canada and France. *Highlander*'s narrative elements are a clever "recombinant subgenre" as well: part traditionally masculine martial arts action adventure, part traditionally feminine historical romance–costume melodrama.[3] These elements travel well and widely, engaging multiple global audiences. The audiences for *Highlander* are "split pretty equally between men and women, which is something kind of unique for an action show," says Ira Bernstein, head of domestic syndication for Rysher, *Highlander*'s distributor, which means that more women are viewers than is usual (Sherwood 1996b, S38). Each episode contains both highly ritualized sword fights between immortals and historical flashbacks recreating past events in their long lives and loves. Narrative action takes place in historical time and apparent contemporary time in specific spots on a clearly colonized globe; this global map has literally been drawn and chronologized by fans. Now fancily reproduced, it is sold in the United States and Canada out of the *Highlander* catalog, along with other merchandise.[4] The map (and some of the other merchandise) emerges from and is itself a resource in the production of fan writing, criticism, and culture. As are other media fandoms, *Highlander* fandom is largely female, white, and middle-aged. (The demographic research I am quoting from here has only been done within the United States; see Bacon-Smith 1992, Appendix C.)

Both *Highlander* and *Xena* depend on the wide currency of genre elements and on an appeal to gendered interests in the niche markets of media and electronic fandoms, on broad narratives that do not rely on dialogue and on complex systems of self-referentiality that layer audiences, markets, styles, and forms of viewing and consumption. Both *Highlander* and *Xena* are examples of strategies of economic response to new global conditions of accumulation. *Xena*'s executive producers, Sam Raimi and Rob Tapert, known for "chic-horror" movies like *Darkman,* or "pop-apocalyptic" westerns like *The Quick and the Dead* (Denby 1995, 108), have "off-shored" their twin TV shows *Hercules* and *Xena.* Indeed, New Zealand's film and TV resources have been preemptively mobilized into an elaborate localized "cultural industrial district." *Highlander*'s previous Canadian location, Vancouver, is also a similar cultural industrial district, where Hollywood products like *The X-Files* have been made. Speaking of the first season of *Hercules* but true of its off-shoot *Xena,* too, as reported in the Auckland *Sunday News*: "Contributing to its appeal here will be the local locations and actors. Shooting in Auckland not only kept the budget low but provided the heroics with an exotic backdrop that hasn't been seen on U.S. television." And the Wellington *Dominion* says, "The series has a distinctly New Zealand flavor with Kiwi slang creeping in to the dialogue." MCA enthusiastically boasts of the sudden spurt of international markets *Xena* was sold into for its second season, a surprise they say, having been "developed almost exclusively with the domestic market in mind." (They mean the U.S. market.[5]) *Highlander* represents European attempts to counter Hollywood in joint ventures with other beleaguered cultural sites, while *Xena* represents Hollywood's attempts to "externalize" its economic risks and to "maximize a variety of creative resources" (Morley and Robins 1995, 33, 36).

IMAGE SUPERPOWERS: ENTERPRISE CULTURE AND HERITAGE CULTURE IN LAYERS OF LOCALS AND GLOBALS

But in the movements of globals and locals among "image superpowers" (Freches 1986, quoted in Morley and Robins 1995, 34), *Highlander* and *Xena* complexly combine ideological strategies, economic and representational, that media theorists David Morley and Kevin Robins have called "enterprise culture" and "heritage culture." Used in a specifically British context, enterprise culture refers to Margaret Thatcher–like political promotions of national capital and local labor in pursuit of strategic alliances and joint ventures, the price of admission to a global club of flexible transnationals. Heritage culture refers to Prince Charles–like exploitations of nostalgia and invented traditions intended to make locations attractive for global investment and tourism. *Highlander*'s dual locations have been only too resonant with these notions: Vancouver as enterprise culture, an up-and-coming new global city recreated by shifting capital, now lampooned in economic racist terms as Hong-couver, the inheritor of fleeing capital from Hong Kong. Or Paris as heritage culture, long a global city though not a current site of great economic accumulations, but with "place-specific differences" that are, it is hoped, parleyed as "tools in competition over positional advantages" (Morley and Robins 1995, 107, 111, 119).

Students can examine such economic abstractions in concrete terms by considering location shots in *Highlander*. As a cultural industrial district for the film and TV industries, Vancouver's cityscapes are recognized all over the world as various and nonspecific "American" cities. *Highlander* fans writing stories that take off from and go beyond the TV show call the Vancouver location *Seacouver,* a combination of Seattle and Vancouver, delighting in the ambiguous national possession of the pivotal sites of *Highlander* narratives. And borrowing from such fan usages, the writers and directors of *Highlander* now also use the term Seacouver in their screenplays to refer to a fictional city in which contemporary *Highlander* stories take place. Or consider the location shots from Paris. The barge Duncan lives on when in Paris is parked conveniently along the Seine, right behind the cathedral of Notre Dame. Almost every shot of Duncan and the barge is backgrounded by a rear view of Notre Dame. When, during the fourth season, for one episode the producers were unable to rent that exact, now taken for granted site, their alternative dock for the barge was backgrounded by the Eiffel Tower instead. The place-specific is being sold as heritage culture Paris, not the place-ambiguous.

In these terms Seacouver becomes an emblem for that very U.S. cultural hegemony that the show's economic arrangements are intended to foil. Is *Highlander* really a kind of U.S. cultural economic off-shoring like *Xena,* but in disguise? Suddenly the fact that British citizen, also half-Italian, principal actor Adrian Paul has a home in Hollywood makes a particular kind of professional sense. Or rather does this mean something more complicated about the meanings of globalization? "Seacouver" mingles locales in a fictional regional entity that simultaneously crosses and repositions national, economic, and cultural boundaries. Both relational and relative, it simultaneously exploits similarities and differences.

As a pedagogical example that will help demonstrate this complexity, consider the term "American" (in quotes). In general usage all over the world, "America," which describes almost half a hemisphere, Northern and Southern continents together, is used as a synonym specifically for the United States. American-in-quotes is one of those specious generics that are emblems of unequal power relations, like the word *man* or the word *white.* In Mexico, the term "North America" might name an English-language, historically colonized but now colonizing cultural power. In that context, Canada and the United States are seen as a cultural unity, which obfuscates the "Canadian experience of subservience" to U.S. cultural interests (Collins 1988, quoted in Morley and Robins 1995, 43). Richard Collins refers to the "Canadianisation of European television," by which he means an extension Europe-wide of the experience Canada has suffered in relation to the United States. Such "Canadianisation" undergirds the economic alliance between Canada and France that *Highlander* embodies, and the fear of one kind of future in which it attempts to intervene. Yet to be "North American" or indeed "American" and be incorporated by the body of the United States is not always to Canada's disadvantage. The unity imagined from Mexico also emphasizes Canada's relative economic and cultural advantages vis-à-vis Mexico. It is important to teach students to ask the question: "From where do you see what?" Such a question is, perhaps, even more appropriate under the terms of globalized power than another question such specious generics also suggest, the question, "Am I included?"

UNDERSTANDING THE REPRODUCTION OF SEXUAL IDENTITIES AS BOTH RELATIVE AND RELATIONAL

Globalization also depends upon a new kind of horizontal integration; that is, markets identified as demographic groups beyond rather than within geographical boundaries, as Morley and Robins suggest. They emphatically emphasize that under the regime of globalization, the local is both "relational and relative" (Morley and Robins 1995, 117). One example would globalize sexuality as ethnicity, naming and exploiting an international "gay" market, especially one traveling, migrating, and moved around.

The mega-international rock group Queen, which composed and performed the music for the first *Highlander* movie, offers another concrete pedagogical example. Queen's lead singer Freddie Mercury embodies the global market's physical, cultural, and economic migrations—for some possible, for others compulsory. Born in Zanzibar of Zoroastrian parents of Persian descent, Mercury was educated in Bombay, India, from ages ten to sixteen. Following the 1964 revolution in Zanzibar he and his family fled to Great Britain, where he studied art and in 1970 hooked up with the other folks who made up the "British" group Queen, which he named. Over the twenty years of Mercury's association with Queen, his image morphed in self-consciously parodic shifts of cultural association, at times accentuating and at times deaccentuating his own multicultural travels, always parodying and exploiting contemporary images of masculinity. As he was dying of AIDS, Mercury denied that he was homosexual, although every element of Queen's self-presentation in each decade parodied the then-current subcultural image of the gay or bisexual man. Indeed, bisexuality, in both international rock image and cultural manifestations, and as a morphed and mixed global sexuality, was exploited by Queen and particularly by Mercury.

The music for the first *Highlander* movie appeared in Queen's album, "A Kind of Magic," the lead song of which was number one on the charts of thirty-five countries in 1986 (Hogan 1996, 96; EMI 1995). Mercury's song "Princes of the Universe" is heard in the opening and closing sequences of every episode of *Highlander: The TV Series*. In the music video of "Princes of the Universe" Mercury struts through the song with Christopher Lambert (star of the first *Highlander* film) on a concert stage built to echo and monumentalize the site of the climax of the movie, the final sword fight. The homoerotic energy of the rock music and the staged and parodied dance between Mercury and Lambert have explicit undercurrents in both movie and TV show. (Cuts from the movie darkly flash by in swift succession, many of them surreally "historical.") Fans pointedly pronounce the name "Lambert" as "lam-BEAR," intended as a mark of familiarity with Lambert's national origins, which are Belgian, and fans tell stories that his language coach for the film *Greystoke* attempted to create for him an accented English that would be recognized as "European" generally, but impossible to pin down as belonging to a particular European nation. The images of Lambert, Mercury, and half-British–half-Italian TV show star Adrian Paul's images can be read as multiethnic, as locally "like-us" in a large number of markets globally. They are profoundly attractive in a global market that also creates images like the Benneton ads' computer-morphed ethnics, parodied in gay political posters. Thus the generic and the particular are shifted back and forth in layers of locals and globals under globalization, as ethnic and also sexual mixtures. These images—the morphed—have special salience, necessarily both relative and relational.

Despite Seydoux's avowed desire to preserve and even generationally stabilize national identity in the era of the European Union, *Highlander* culture demonstrates "how the cultural construction of national identity, as articulated in both official policies and informal popular practices, is a precarious project that can never be isolated from the global, transnational relations in which it takes shape" (Ang 1996, 146). *Highlander* and *Xena* participate in morphed identities of various intentions and commercial realities, sometimes ambi-sexual, sometimes ambi-cultural, sometimes ambi-ethnic.

GRANULATING SEXUAL IDENTITIES ONLINE

When I first subscribed to the listserv that is one site of *Highlander* international media fandom, I found to my dismay that homosexuality was a "forbidden topic." After all, my own attraction to *Highlander* was very much founded in my "recognition" of a circulation of gay images. Indeed I had sought out *Highlander* fandom in order to make community with others I thought must have similar attractions. On the list, though, homosexuality as a topic had been forbidden as *flame-bait,* that is, as a topic that was assumed to inevitably incite *flame-wars,* or long exhausting vituperative attacks. Still, I also soon discovered that some fans occasionally made fun of and attempted to subvert the ban by posing mock questions using a blank instead of words like *gay, homosexual,* and so on. For example, someone might say, "Surely we know that Duncan isn't *BLANK.*" If reprimanded by another post, the trickster might claim, "Oh, I wasn't raising a forbidden topic, I was referring to CANADIANS." This became the joking equation—the word *Canadian* was invoked instead of the word *gay,* to the delight of some Canadians on the list and to the horror of others. Placing the word *Canadian* in this context, always cute, a bit trivializing, and always edged with connotations of abnormality or subordination, was only too close to colonializing assumptions on the parts of U.S. fans about Canada anyway, and also very close to complacencies on the part of tolerant fans in what was also a running joke about homosexuality. Many pleasures, some sadistic, some campy, some subversive, some smug, were encapsulated in this running joke, which allowed for some very limited encouragement to those of us who wanted to discuss things gay and possibly gay on *Highlander*. Here the sexual and the national stood in for each other, highlighting and trivializing the relations of power that made such a substitution possible.

Somewhat later a new character was introduced to the series, the oldest known *immie* (what fans call immortals), the five thousand-year-old Methos, who was hiding out as a watcher, one of the mortals who keeps track of immies. He was an immediate hit: list members went crazy over the character and the actor, who shortly thereafter came to the *Highlander* convention in Denver in October 1995. The actor, Peter Wingfield, told us during his question and answer session how he had heard about his success with the fans from the production people, who got reports from their creative consultants on the reactions of fans on the various Internet sites. He bubbled over with excitement about getting such immediate feedback on his performance and how it had encouraged the producers to use the new character in a series of story arcs (the term used by writers, actors, directors, and fans). It was his appearance in the next story that provoked a final refusal by list members to continue the homosexuality-as-forbidden-topic policy.

A brief on-screen exchange between Methos and Duncan, in which, while helping him renovate a house, Methos teased Duncan in a playful, flirting kind of way, and then was painted on the nose in retaliation, provoked many fans; even those who were, in principle, against changing the forbidden topics policy.[6] Many could not resist speculating about the charismatic charge generated between the two characters; was it erotic? And if so, who was doing it? Who was the object? Who was the subject? Almost no one was willing to allow the principal character to have such erotic interests, but this new character, without a series history—about him they were willing to speculate. Within about forty-eight hours the policy had become moot. The list owner did not intervene in the discussion, which was almost entirely flame-free. From then on homosexuality was no longer a forbidden topic, but it was marked: one had to include in the subject line of posts with homosexual content the header, "Same Sex Sex." This would permit those who found the topic offensive to delete these posts unread, without banning the subject altogether. Although later in the TV season Methos briefly acquired a mortal woman lover, some fans had begun to write fan fiction in which Methos and Duncan were lovers.

SAME SEX SEX AND SLASH AS SITES FOR THE PRODUCTION OF NEW BISEXUALITIES

Such fiction is known in the media fan world as *slash*. Slash has a long and varied history, originating in the female fandom surrounding the TV show *Star Trek* (Bacon-Smith 1992; Jenkins 1992; Penley et al. 1991;

Penley and Ross 1991; Penley 1997), The slash is a typographic cue to an eroticized relationship between characters of the same sex, usually men; in the original *Star Trek,* between Kirk and Spock (Kirk / Spock); in *Highlander* fandom, between, say, Methos and Duncan (Methos / Duncan). It is a kind of pornography written most often by heterosexual women. Slash is thus not equivalent to gay fiction, though as time has gone on, the two genres may be overlapping more, and writers and characters may be self-consciously bisexual, lesbian, or gay. I speculate myself that slash is a site for the production of new bisexualities, of both characters and fan writers. It is one cultural site in which the constructions that produce heterosexuality and homosexuality as mutually exclusive, are denied, eroded, refused, or simply not engaged.

Early slash explicitly depicted the eroticized relation between Kirk and Spock as situational, not homosexual, and as conflicted but romantic within narrative structures and pleasures stereotypically female. Contemporary slash is more varied, sometimes utopian, sometimes romantic, sometimes brutal—and always intended to be erotic. Slash once was privately circulated in circles of female fans who were both writers and readers of it (in the United States and probably also in Great Britain, Canada, and Australia). Today slash is shared in the fanzines (xerox anthologies) that emerged from such private circulation and are sold at cons (fan media conventions in the United States, Great Britain, Canada, and Australia), through mail order, or most recently and most widely, displayed and exchanged on the web and through e-mail.

How *Xena* fan fiction fits into the world of slash is perhaps more ambiguous; whether lesbian stories about Xena and Gabrielle are slash, enlarge the practice of slash, or are something else is, perhaps, in flux. The press has made much of the lesbian following among *Xena* fans. Lucy Lawless, the actress who plays Xena, and the producers of *Xena* have said they are "aware and not afraid of" their lesbian audience, as the *Xena: Warrior Princess FAQ* proudly proclaims in the section entitled "The Sapphic Subtext." (FAQ, pronounced FACK, stands for frequently asked questions, and this particular FAQ is a compendium of Xena information accessible on the World Wide Web.[7]) Indeed, Lucy Lawless appeared in a short film, *Peach,* in which she played the part of a bisexual woman. Current news stories make much of her public relationship and now recent marriage with producer Tapert. On the fan list called "The Xenaverse," talk about lesbian narratives concerning Xena and her sidekick Gabrielle has been a taken-for-granted thread of discussion. Both Xena and Gabrielle have had conspicuous male lovers; in the episode "Destiny," which I discuss later, Xena is famously paired with Julius Caesar, for example. The *Xena FAQ* goes on to say, "[The writers] have done a great job of making it so viewers can see whatever they want in the show. XWP is a fantasy/action series with a riveting relationship between the two main characters, and so appeals to many people in many different ways."

My impression is that the *Highlander* producers have never been at all sure exactly how they wanted to play the ambiguities possible within their own circulation of images, and questions of Adrian Paul at fan conventions suggest he is not as blasé as Lucy Lawless about such readings. Nor are questions directed at him so open, either. But fans with contacts with crew members claim that such interpretations are the stuff of jokes and talk on the *Highlander* set, and fans with contact with Peter Wingfield claim that he gets a kick out of hearing about the fan fiction that links Methos and Duncan. Fandom is filled with folks claiming insider information, and such seeming authority does subvert official and authorized readings. *Xena* producers seem to have decided to milk their ambiguities for all they are worth; and indeed, multiple, complicatedly contradictory and noncontradictory stories, associations, and allusions are the stuff out of which *Xena* is made. Such processes of storytelling also mark the pleasures of fan writing in general and of slash in particular.

Bringing fans, fan culture, and issues about fans into the classroom turns out to be very complicated. When I first started teaching this material I assumed that students would often be fans, and that if not, they would have friends who were. And, I thought they would have had experience with fandoms, even as outsiders. I found instead that my students, even those taking courses on TV, had rigid investments in high culture, were frankly frightened of fans because they had strong stereotypes about them, and were dismissive of the intellectual work and activities of fandoms. The investments of my students in university education as intellectual capital eclipsed any alternative experiences they might even have engaged in themselves, for example as fans of musical groups. When I wore fan paraphernalia and brought in objects from cons for students to examine and analyze, I found discussion paralyzed, only later to learn from evaluations that students had from that time marked me as one of *them*—a fan—a stigmatized category. As an out lesbian teaching in women's studies classes, I was astonished. In some courses I have since been able to raise issues about the class values that are mobilized in such stereotypes about fans and fandom, about the narrow constructions of intellectual activity that valorize only academic education, and about the definitions of feminism that seem to legitimize such class values. Certainly I always hoped to engage in such analysis, but I found that getting into it through the "fun" aspects of fans and fandoms was only to allow them to be dismissed. Raising these issues has continued to be more difficult than I expect, has to be postponed until later in the course, and has to be carefully prepared for beforehand. Starting off with economic and political issues, and carefully building in fandoms as subjects of clearly theoretical analysis seems to desensitize students' biases over time.

USING VARIOUS HISTORIES IN A WAR OF IMAGES

I have found that valuing alternative intellectual communities can be approached by examining various public histories—of which fan fiction is one. To do this, let me return here to Morley and Robins' notion of heritage culture. They point out that in a new economic regionalism characterized by a war of images, the question "Where will the pictures come from?" is crucial, and fuels some of the heat surrounding such issues as European content quotas on TV (Morley and Robins 1995, 34). Such concerns are seen by some as issues of national identity, as implied by Seydoux in his remarks on grandchildren having the same national identity as their grandparents. The European single market, at times called the European Community or now the European Union, can be seen both as an attempt to *conserve* such national identities and to protect European identity, and also as a *threat* to the national identities of some of the states that are located on the geographical entity, continental Europe, and within the ideological entity usually called European, or the West. This is one way for students to understand all these complex political uses of the term *European* today, both relative and relational. Heritage culture is a symptom of and exploits such anxieties, as well as being the site of new forms of pleasure and invented traditions. Historical dramas today cannot help but be coopted by the painful pleasures of heritage culture, and recuperated histories are mixes—real, hyperreal, imagined, and pastiche. Students need to understand the complexities represented in political appeals to history.

Highlander and *Xena* represent two approaches to being such mixtures: *Highlander* thinks of itself as committed to real history, that is, real history within low budgets. I think of *Highlander* history as reenactment history—the kind of history that war games folks put together in epic battle reenactments. One can distinguish it from other public histories, say, the kind of official history that Congress prefers when it castigates Smithsonian Air and Space Museum curators for their attempts to historicize the installation of the Enola Gay, the plane from which the bomb was dropped on Hiroshima. I myself come from a tradition of marxist historicizing, in which the purpose of history is to subvert such official readings and to insist upon economic and ideological underpinnings as privileged realities. None of these historical strategies today is immune from the pressures of heritage culture. In contrast, *Xena* prefers to self-consciously refer to its own mix, to make jokes about the contradictions produced, to focus on the simultaneous, the synchronic. Both *Highlander* and *Xena* take pleasure in the conflation of the mythic and the historic, the chronological and the anachronistic. The episodes of each that I now turn to are such elaborate fusions.

Historically, multiple frames in TV specifically are the legacy of product placement, as TV historian Lynn Spigel (1992) points out. In early television the stage-within-a-stage structure, a "quagmire of meta-realities," was found in domestic comedies with heritages from vaudeville, shows like *Burns & Allen* and *I Love Lucy*. The stage frame contained the domestic space. The stage space, which viewers inhabited, the strangely more real space, was also inhabited by the product being sold. Such early TV framing conventions achieved the effect of making "the advertiser's discourse appear to be in a world closer to the viewer's real life" (Spigel 1992, 18).

In *Xena* the final credits, which flash by more quickly than one can read, and which share the screen with upcoming episode trailers, are followed by disclaimers, one legal, one humorous. In the episode "Destiny," the production credits end with the following humorous disclaimer: "Julius Caesar was not harmed during the production of this motion picture. However, the Producers deny any responsibility for any unfortunate acts of betrayal causing some discomfort." Rather than the product occupying the stage-frame space, we have the campy production comments that parody the "legal" disclaimers. Unlike the early product placement, meant to be the clearest communication, if also often humorous, these comic disclaimers are so embedded as to be hidden. I cannot read them off the TV myself, and can barely see them on pause or slow with my two-headed VCR. To get the message in question, I raided the store of such carefully, even compulsively visioned sightings produced by fans at the Logomancy fan site on the web.[8] Most of these humorous disclaimers use the same format: "Something wasn't harmed in the making of this motion picture." The play between TV episode and "this motion picture" reminds us that this is *Xena* producers Raimi and Tapert's first TV venture in careers of movie production. Like the *Highlander* producers Peter Davis and William Panzer, Raimi and Tapert have moved from low budget independent movies to independent, limited budget syndicated TV at a particular economic moment. What was not harmed here was Julius Caesar, the chronologically specific character in a play of anachronism, the emblem of Western culture who parodies himself for us as he tells us that "Gaul is divided into three parts." In first season episodes other such Western authorities mocked but in disclaimer not harmed were "unrelenting or severely punishing deities," "fathers, spiritual or biological," and "males, centaurs, or amazons," each of these poking fun at the kind of feminism displayed both subversively and often commercially in *Xena*. I call this exuberantly commercial feminism *Xena feminism*.

It is not just that the producers make fun of possible objections to the violence of this episode of *Xena* when, after saying Caesar was not harmed, they also "deny any responsibility for any unfortunate acts of betrayal causing some discomfort." Here they also make fun of any fussy concerns about their recycled versions of myths, cultural traditions, and national histories. As the early TV framing devices included the advertiser's product (and thus the viewer) in the spectacle, so the humorous disclaimer on *Xena* includes as pleasures of reception the conditions of production, the credits and legalities (and also the viewer) inside the spectacle. Indeed the obvious joke of this episode's disclaimer is that Julius Caesar is never hurt in the story—only Xena is hurt. His betrayals of her are both emotional and violently physical. And Caesar's mode of killing Xena is to crucify her: the Western cultural betrayal by the producers then being to elevate Xena to Christlike status, and indeed to construct a story in which she is resurrected not just once, but twice. Note how the humorous ironies accustom and habituate viewers to casual movements from one level of abstraction to another, to sorting out easily those relative and relational shifts among levels of locals and globals involved in getting all the jokes and in playing one's proper market roles in a globalized economy.[9]

HISTORY AS MORALITY PLAY: ANTIRACISMS IN HIGHLANDER

Let me abstractly compare "Destiny" to an episode of *Highlander,* "The Valkyrie." I want to point to the multiple framings that include the flashback–story-within-a-story that structures this episode in layers of political and historical association. In the opening teaser we first see a picture of St. Basil's in the Kremlin, the architectural element that stands for *Moscow,* captioned in case we didn't get it. (*Highlander* eschews subtleties.) The scene cuts immediately to a TV picture, revealed to be so as the camera pulls back, then revealed to be a video tape as the viewer within the story reverses the tape momentarily and replays the speech we hear. The first lines of dialogue then set the terms of the narrative throughout this episode: the character Igor Stephenovitch, obviously an allusion to Vladimir Zhirinovsky, says, "Do they not love me? Of course they love me. I fill their empty bellies with something more than food. I fill them with someone to hate. Someone to blame for their wretched lives. Jews, Muslims, Chetchnians, it really doesn't matter. There are glorious days ahead, Dimitri. Lousy TV; that's the first thing we'll have to fix." (Such TV-watching allusions make the viewer complicit in the morally dangerous world depicted in the episode.)

This episode is explicitly about pan-European racism in its neo-Nazi forms, but at every point this theme becomes explicit it is quickly shifted, and then reembedded, as references to specific nationalities are raised and then delimited. It begins in Europe, or one might say, Europe's "margins," that is Russia, *not* in, say, Strasbourg, France, where shortly after this episode first aired demonstrations against the racism of Jean-Marie Le Pen's National Front occurred (Truehart 1997). Although in this highly colored and even stereotyped version the possible French allusions are displaced, it quickly moves to its "American-in-quotes" location, to focus on another rather cartoon-style racist, the figure Wilkinson, about whom we are told, "At sixteen he and his friends beat two gay men to death, at twenty burned three black churches in the south. . . . Now all he does is give a speech and other people go out and burn churches for him." Of course, within the flashback, all these allusions are grafted onto the figure of arch-evil, Hitler himself. In such cultural shifts of register and allusions to chronological event, history is left behind and reframed as morality play. Historical event, present and past, is *contained* as morality play, indeed contained, as are all episodes of *Highlander,* within battles between good and evil, battles that take place in individual psyches, then externalized in single combat. Methos and Duncan offer two versions of history in their interchanges throughout the episode, one a simplified and parodied version of Marxist determinism, as when Methos paraphrases Marx, saying, "History makes men, MacLeod, men don't make history"; and the other a simplified heroic capitalist-equals-democratic version, Duncan's emphasis on pivotal actions by specific individuals. But even these highly simplified versions of possible European political ideologies are trumped by the Interpol inspector's banal moralisms: "When I was a little boy everything was black and white, good and evil you see, then I grew up and discovered there was only gray."

From where do you see what? History become morality play is an effective method of defusing but also strangely including actual political content, through a scattered pattern of allusions relevant to multiple audiences and markets. This is similar to the commodified forms of queer visibility Hennessy talks about, or very like exuberant *Xena* feminism, already depoliticized and only democratized within encrustations of capitalist commodity formations and individualism. Yet, one cannot help but notice that the number of betrayals on the part of the producers have some, though quite limited, subversive effects. The Interpol inspector's banalities are too reminiscent of the only kinds of resistance imaginable amid the apathy and deeply paralyzing depression occasioned by economic shifts of catastrophic proportions. The inspector's references to a life in Romania are an allusion to these responses to history and politics, especially in Eastern European countries in the wake of the break-up of the Soviet Union. Nor is an explicit if rather opportunistic stance against European racism unimportant. In fact, concerns about racism infuse *Highlander* as a series, being a recurrent if also always redirected theme. Antiracisms in *Highlander* are almost always projected onto the screen of the history of slavery or segregation in the United States, and Duncan is almost always a heroic figure helping slaves to freedom in the underground railroad, or supporting African Americans in desegregation. He always exacts a price however: he lectures them on the meanings of freedom and tells them how to be good democratic citizens.[10] The propaganda value of such lectures and liberal encouragements, visions, and simplified histories are the didactic heart of *Highlander.* Creative consultant and head writer David Abramowitz refers to the show as "a kind of romantic Talmudic discussion with action" (Sherwood 1996a, S3), while principal actor Adrian Paul refuses a fan club unless it is directed toward charity and peaceful community building. In U.S. fan context and convention culture these obviously liberal American-in-quotes undertakings are substitutions for an occasionally almost-mentioned British Labour agenda.

Morley and Robins point out that heritage culture in the context of the European collectivist dreams for 1992 and the European Union has possible racist implications, that national identities may be in the process of transformation into a "white continentalism" (Morley and Robins 1995, 50). *Highlander* itself—within its recurrent interests in racism—is also conspicuously white, despite the inclusion of prominent and striking immortals of color, for example, Roland Gift of the British rock group Fine Young Cannibals. Vancouver and Paris locations are also conspicuously white, despite the multicultural complexities of those cities. Heritage culture is based on these catered to and contradictory visions, while European Union in 1992 was the result of uneasy bargains struck despite contradictory visions. One example is the bargain struck up among principals Germany and France, in which Germany pledged to eschew past imperial dreams while undergoing reunification by reinforcing commitments to a federal Europe and pushing for political integration, while France pushed for monetary union giving it some degree of control over Germany (Baun 1995, 605). Such tensions over economic and political attempts at resolution of Germany's past are another level of allusion in "The Valkyrie" episode of *Highlander* and another appropriation by heritage culture.

CONCLUSION

Nationalities, sexualities, and global TV are spaces of identity, and media and female media fandoms in their gendered electronic landscapes exploit, alter, ignore, and morph cultural boundaries. Sexual, national, and electronic behaviors are eroticized in a dance that sometimes mingles, sometimes denies, sometimes ignores identities. My reason for doing this kind of analysis of *Highlander* and *Xena* is to focus on the layers of locals and globals that are the resources and forms of consciousness both created but also made available by what Chela Sandoval (1991) has called "the democratization of oppression" that characterizes the shifting powers of multicapitalism. I believe that any new political movements, among them feminist and lesbian and gay human rights activisms, must be very sophisticated in their understandings of their own commodification within such layered global and local structures, as well as be risk-taking in their appropriations of pleasures, identities, and political strategies. It is this belief that motivates the work I continue to do in the field of feminism and writing technologies, studying what I call global gay formations and local homosexualities. These are the political complexities I try to convey to my students.

NOTES

My undying thanks to Chrys Sparks, long time friend and volunteer sabbatical research assistant, for introducing me to Trekker slash and downloading much for me from the web, for making arrangements and attending cons, for finding fanzines and stories, endlessly sifting through list posts, staging marathons of HL, and, best of all, making it all fun. I couldn't have done it without you!

1. Note *Entertainment Weekly* 1997 and Sanborn 1997 in which various lesbians urge DeGeneres to stop the teasing represented by the Ellen Watch and get to the coming-out episode. The coming-out episode aired in April 1997. The famous *Time* magazine cover, "Yep, I'm Gay," appeared April 14, 1997. See De Vries 1997 for retrospective discussion.
2. Diversification table in Wasko (1994, 43), adapted from *Standard & Poor's Industry Surveys* (March 11, 1993, L17).
3. I have borrowed the term "recombinant subgenre" from Sanjek 1995.
4. The *Highlander* catalogue is available at 1–800–959–2481.
5. All quoted in the *Xena Media Review and Archives,* http://xenafan.com/xmr/ (3/22/97): XMR #149.5 (01/28/96) the Auckland *Sunday News,* "Legendary Stuff," 31; XMR #144.5 (01/27/96) the Wellington *Dominion,* "Pilot to kick off Hercules' NZ run," 23; XMR #267 (05/12/96) *The Hollywood Reporter,* "MCA's dynamic duo goes int'l 'Hercules' and 'Xena' wrap up virtually every major market" by Steve Brennan.
6. See episode #95410_76 (tenth episode in season four 1995) "Chivalry," written by Michael O'Mahony and Sacha Reins; directed by Paolo Barzman; with Peter Wingfield as Adam Pierson/Methos.
7. The FAQ is located at http://whosh.org/fac/index.html (3/28/01).
8. Logomancy site: http://www.klio.net/XENA/index.html (3/28/01).
9. My thanks to Bill Pietz for long discussions about the psychology of reception and for making this particular point.
10. Footage edited together from several episodes in which Duncan's involvement in the Civil War and civil rights is depicted can be viewed on the video *The Life and Times of Duncan MacLeod,* written and researched by Maureen Russell; directed by David Wilson (Davis/Panzer Productions, 1995). Also see for example episode #93209 (ninth episode in season two, 1993) "Run for Your Life," written by Naomi Janzen; directed by Dennis Berry (with ER's Bruce Young as Carl Robinson); episode guide at http://www.highlander.org/FAQ/FAQ-3.html (3/28/01).

WORKS CITED

Ang, Ien. 1996. *Living Room Wars: Rethinking Media Audiences for a Postmodern World.* New York: Routledge.

Bacon-Smith, Camille. 1992. *Enterprising Women.* Philadelphia: University of Pennsyl-vania Press.

Baun, Michael J. 1995. "The Maastricht Treaty as High Politics: Germany, France, and European Integration." *Political Science Quarterly* 110 (Winter): 605–624.

Block, Adam, and Richard Laermer. 1991. "Freddie Mercury and the AIDS Closet." *Advocate*, December 31: 74–75.

Cagle, Jess. 1995. "America Sees Shades of Gay." *Entertainment Weekly*, September 8: 20–31.

Clark-Meads, Jeff. 1991. "Queen Sales Soar in Wake of Freddie Mercury Death." *Billboard*, December 21: 14.

Collins, Richard. 1988. "National Culture: A Contradiction in Terms?" Paper presented at the International Television Studies Conference, London, July 20–22, 1988. (Denby, David. 1995. "The Quick and the Dead" (movie review). *New York* February 27.

De Vries, Hilary. 1997. "Ellen Degeneres, Out & About." *TV Guide*, October 11: 20–27.

EMI. 1995. "Queen—The Ultimate Biography." Online; accessed May 2, 1996. Available http://fly.cc.fer.hr/~mvidacek/history.htm (March 28, 2001).

Entertainment Weekly. 1997. February 21–28.

Freches, Jose. 1986. *La Guerre des Images.* Paris: Denoel.

Gubernick, Lisa. 1994. "No Trade War Here." *Forbes,* February 28: 188.

Hennessy, Rosemary. 1995. "Queer Visibility in Commodity Culture." In Linda Nicholson and Steven Seidman, eds., *Social Postmodernism: Beyond Identity Politics,* 142–183. Cambridge: Cambridge University Press.

Hogan, Peter K. 1996. *The Complete Guide to the Music of Queen.* New York: Omnibus Press.

Hollywood Reporter, Highlander special issue. 1996. Interview with Peter Davis and William Panzer, producers of *Highlander: The TV Series.* December 3: S19–S24.

Jenkins, Henry. 1992. *Textual Poachers.* New York: Routledge.

Kastor, Elizabeth. 1996. "Woman of Steel: Television's Warrior Xena Is a Superheroine with Broad Appeal." *Washington Post,* September 21: C1, C5.

Millar, Michelle. 1996. "Alice Guy: A Life in Motion." *French Cultural Studies* 7 (October): 229.

Morley, David, and Kevin Robins. 1995. *Spaces of Identity: Global Media, Electronic Landscapes and Cultural Boundaries.* New York: Routledge.

Penley, Constance. 1991. "Brownian Motion: Women, Tactics, and Technology." In Constance Penley and Andrew Ross, eds., *Technoculture,* 135–161. Minneapolis: University of Minnesota Press.

———. 1997. *NASA / Trek: Popular Science and Sex in America.* New York: Verso.

Penley, Constance, Elisabeth Lyon, Lynn Spigel, and Janet Bergstrom, eds. 1991. *Close Encounters: Film, Feminism, and Science Fiction.* Minneapolis: University of Minnesota Press.

Penley, Constance, and Andrew Ross, eds. 1991. *Technoculture.* Minneapolis: University of Minnesota Press.

Ressner, Jeffrey. 1992. "Freddie Mercury: 1946–1991: Queen Singer Is Rock's First Major AIDS Casualty," *Rolling Stone,* January 9.

Sanborn, Katie. 1997. "Will the Real Ellen Please Stand Up?" *Curve* (January): 24.

Sandoval, Chela. 1991. "U.S. Third World Feminism: The Theory and Method of

Oppositional Consciousness in the Postmodern World." *Genders* 10 (Spring): 1–38.

Sanjek, David. 1995. "Home Alone: The Phenomenon of Direct-to-Video." *Cineaste* 21 (Winter–Spring 1995): 98–101.

———. 1996a. "Fantastic Voyages: As It Reaches the Century Mark 'Highlander' Looks to the Future while Embracing the Past." *The Hollywood Reporter, Highlander* special issue, December 3: S1–S4.

Sherwood, Rick. 1996b. "Historic Agreements: Like Its Mythic Hero, 'Highlander' Has a Distinctly International Flair." *The Hollywood Reporter, Highlander* special issue, December 3: S6, S30–S42.

Spigel, Lynn. 1992. "Installing the Television Set." In Lynn Spigel and Denise Mann, eds., *Private Screenings: Television and the Female Consumer,* 3–38. Minneapolis: University of Minnesota Press.

Time. 1997. "Yep, I'm Gay," cover (April 14).

Truehart, Charles. 1997."Thousands of Protestors March as French Far-right Group Meets." *Washington Post,* March 30.

Turman, Suzanna. 1994. "Gaumont: The World's First Film Company Is Gearing up for Its 100th Anniversary in 1995." *Films in Review* 45 (January–February).

Variety. 1994. "Gaumont Topper Thinks 'Upgrade.'" December 12–18: 58.

Wasko, Janet. 1994. *Hollywood in the Information Age: Beyond the Silver Screen.* Austin: University of Texas Press.

Xena Media Review and Archives, http://xenafan.com/xmr/ (March 22, 1007).

PART 2

Reflections on Teaching: Struggles, Setbacks, Successes

INSERTING WOMEN'S VOICES AND FEMINIST PERSPECTIVES INTO AN UNDERGRADUATE WORLD POPULATION COURSE

HELGA LEITNER

For the past fifteen years I have been teaching the upper-division undergraduate course Population in an Interacting World (Geography 3381). The purpose of this course, as originally designed, was to provide students with a basic understanding of and appreciation for human population phenomena and problems in an increasingly interdependent world. In the course, we investigate patterns and trends in fertility, mortality, and migration of human populations in different parts of the world. We study how these patterns are shaped by and in turn how they shape economic, political, cultural, and environmental conditions and processes. Throughout the course, I pay particular attention to contemporary population problems at the global, national, and local scales, including the world population explosion, high levels of fertility in parts of the less developed world, zero-population growth in developed countries, the AIDS epidemic, increasing levels of international migration, refugee crises, massive rural to urban migrations in the less developed world, and policies adopted to address these problems. Because the issues addressed in this course can only be studied through an interdisciplinary lens—ranging from geography to demography and economics—the course is interdisciplinary in approach. It fulfills the core social science, the international theme, and the writing intensive requirements in the University of Minnesota's liberal education curriculum.

Even though women are at the center of many of the issues and problems addressed in this course, and though there is a wealth of feminist research on population growth and development, feminist approaches to the study of population are generally absent in introductory textbooks in population geography or other introductory texts addressing population issues and problems in a comparative international perspective.

In order to overcome the limitations of these texts, I introduced additional readings, presented audio-visual material (films, slides, maps) on women's experiences and feminist scholarship, and revised my lectures to include gender. I took particular care in the selection of these materials to represent not only the diversity of women's experiences across the globe, but also to strike a balance between representations of negative and positive experiences of women. I did this to overcome stereotyping of women, particularly Third World women, as victims, and to avoid overwhelming students with the "evil in the world." To this end I also chose materials that would portray positive changes that had occurred, for example, in women's control over their reproductive lives, and those that allow students to think about opportunities for change.

Rather than adding "gender units" to the course, my goal was to integrate a gender perspective throughout the different units of the course, covering population theories, problems, and policies. In the following I provide some examples of how I have included women, women's voices, and feminist perspectives into individual units, and of specific pedagogic strategies employed to elicit active student participation.

THEORIES OF POPULATION GROWTH AND CHANGE

This unit introduces students to competing population theories and their influence on population policies. One goal is to problematize the reductionist explanations provided by dominant population theories. Most theories of population growth and change are silent on the role of women and of social movements, such as the birth control movement, in influencing changes in reproductive behavior and thus fertility levels. I use the example of the demographic transition in Europe, which formed the basis for the demographic transition theory, to demonstrate the impact of the birth control movement on changes in reproductive behavior in late nineteenth- and early twentieth-century Europe and the United States. In particular, I discuss Annie Besant's and Margaret Sanger's crusades to legalize birth control and to bring the advocacy of birth control into the open.

In order to make students aware of the influence of dominant population theories and of the activities of women's organizations and feminist scholarship on population policies, I require students to compare the action programs developed at the United Nations World Population Conferences held every decade since 1974. I ask students to answer the following questions: What difference do you see in the three action programs? What is the theoretical basis for these differences? What specifically distinguishes the 1994 Cairo action program, which for the first time officially recognizes the role of women in population growth and development, from the other action programs? Which of the different measures proposed in the action programs should, in your opinion, be promoted?

FAMILY PLANNING AND FERTILITY DECLINE IN THE LESS DEVELOPED WORLD

I redesigned this unit to show that contemporary family planning programs, adopted by some Third World states and international organizations, often compromise women's control over their reproductive decisions and their reproductive health. I use the manipulation of women in limiting childbirth, forced sterilizations, and forced implantations of contraceptives to reveal that women's control over their reproductive lives is often taken away by highly bureaucratized and oppressive population control programs. As part of this unit I show the film *Something Like a War*, which examines India's family planning program from the perspective of the women who are its primary targets. It traces the history of the family planning program and such problems as corruption in the program and brutality toward women. More importantly it chronicles the experiences of a diverse group of women openly discussing their sexuality, their value and identity as linked to the production of offspring (in particular boys), and their attitudes toward fertility control and its connection to their health and material well being. The women's discussion conveys to students a sense that women are not only victims of an oppressive population control program, but are actively reflecting on and resisting such programs. Students then discuss in small groups and answer a set of questions. Who are the different factions in this "war" over population and fertility control in India? What are the attitudes of women and men toward different means of birth control? Does the stated goal of reducing poverty through fertility control justify the means used?

FERTILITY TRENDS AND POPULATION POLICY IN EUROPE

During the past twenty-five years, faced with continuous decline in fertility levels, most European governments have enacted pronatalist policies to induce couples to have more children. These policies include a wide range of measures, from financial incentives, to measures making it easier for women to both have children and pursue employment outside the house (e.g., through extended maternity leaves, job guarantees, and day-care centers), to such oppressive actions as the cut-off of legal abortion and contraceptives in 1960s Romania. The unit concludes with a class discussion of motivations and justifications for the introduction of pronatalist policies, as well as opposing viewpoints that link pronatalist policies in Europe to forced population control policies in less developed countries. The discussion addresses such questions as: Why should women in Europe be concerned about declining birth rates, when approximately 250,000 people are added to the world population each day?

Why should women in less developed countries be forced to undergo sterilization when European women are being encouraged to have more children?

FERTILITY CHARACTERISTICS AND TRENDS IN THE UNITED STATES

I redesigned this unit to show the relationships between fertility decline and changing gender roles, such as increased women's educational attainment and labor force participation, in the United States during the last fifty years. In order to make it more accessible to students, I framed the discussion in terms of a tale of two generations: the lives of their grandmothers and mothers. This unit also includes a discussion of differences in marital and nonmarital childbearing among different social groups in the United States. The purpose is to convey the diversity of women's childbearing experiences in the United States and to show that these are not only rooted in women's own personal characteristics (race, age, etc.), but also in the specific cultural and economic context in which they live.

THE AIDS EPIDEMIC—A NEW THREAT ACROSS THE GLOBE

This unit includes evidence of the devastating impact of AIDS on women in the developing world, particularly in Africa and Asia, where women constitute nearly half of the AIDS-related deaths. A film and a newspaper article demonstrate contrasting perspectives on the spread of AIDS in the Third World. The film, *AIDS in Africa,* focuses on the individual behaviors of men and women in fueling the AIDS epidemic. The newspaper article, "India's Shame," while painting a grim picture of the AIDS epidemic in one Indian city, challenges the frequent blaming of AIDS victims in media portrayals by examining the AIDS epidemic in the context of sexual slavery, corruption, and neglect.

THE DYNAMICS OF INTERNATIONAL MIGRATION

Comparing international migrations around the globe during the last thirty to forty years, we can identify a distinct trend toward the feminization of international migration. For example, female labor migrants form the majority in movements from the Philippines to the Middle East and Europe, and from Thailand to Japan. Some refugee movements, including those from the former Yugoslavia, also are marked by a majority of women. In order to account for these changes the unit on dynamics of international migration now provides a detailed discussion of this feminization of international migrations. I use excerpts from my own personal interviews with Filipino domestic workers in Hong Kong to illustrate reasons for migration (lack of employment opportunity in the home country and the quest for a better life) and the specific challenges of female labor migrants at work and in public life. Students read these oral histories and view slides showing the Filipino women's weekly gatherings in downtown Hong Kong, where foreign female domestics have re-appropriated public space as their own space of empowerment.

CHANGES IN PEDAGOGY

One strategy I use is small-group discussions among two to three students, once or twice per week for ten minutes. In the discussion groups students are asked to respond to a set of questions posed by the instructor or to share their reactions to a video or slides. In each group one student is made responsible to record the major arguments advanced in the discussion and share them with the whole class. I attempt to ensure that each week a different group has the opportunity to present. At the end of the class I collect the written record from all discussion groups. I frequently select opposing interpretations or viewpoints and present them during the next class hour for further discussion. Students did not uniformly welcome the small-group discussions. Some expressed the view that they would rather learn from the professor than through discussion with fellow students. I persisted despite this initial discontent, and the student evaluations of small-group discussions at the end of the course were generally favorable.

The course also includes in-class group presentations of a five-week-long country project that students are required to complete. Students working on different population issues (fertility, mortality, and migration) for one particular country prepare a joint presentation.

In order to make the foreign more familiar, I took advantage of the diverse cultural backgrounds of students within the course, encouraging them to share their experiences with their fellow students either in class (which they sometimes were hesitant to do) or through discussions on the class website especially established for this course (with which some students were more comfortable). The web site was also used for posting overheads, additional readings (e.g., newspaper articles), announcements, study guides for exams, sample questions from previous exams, and includes links to population, women, and gender-related websites.

Introducing a gender perspective into the course seems to have changed the gender composition of the student body. While in the past the course enrolled approximately an equal number of male and female students, during the last three years it has become dominated by female students (during the last offering in the fall of 2000, 70 percent of the students were female). Although I am pleased to have more women in the course, I am currently trying to figure out ways of bringing men back into the course, because a gender perspective is also important for them!

SYLLABUS

The aim of this course is to provide students with a basic understanding of and appreciation for human population phenomena and problems in an increasingly interacting world. This will involve an investigation of patterns and trends in fertility, mortality, and migration of human populations in different parts of the world and an examination of how these are both shaped by and engender economic, political, cultural, and environmental change. Throughout the course particular attention is paid to (a) contemporary population problems at the global, national, and local scale, including world population explosion, high levels of fertility in parts of the less developed world, zero-population growth in developed countries, the AIDS epidemic, increasing levels of international migration, refugee crises, and massive rural to urban migrations in the less developed world; (b) policies adopted to address these problems such as family planning policies to reduce fertility levels; and (c) the gender dimension of contemporary population problems and policies. In addition, this course will introduce students to some basic sources, measures, and methods of representation for the study of population, and allow them to gain basic skills and experience in data analysis, interpretation, writing research reports, and giving oral presentations.

Topics and Readings

Week 1. Introduction to the Study of Population

Sources of information and measures for the study of population; world population distribution. Readings in Peters and Larkin.

Weeks 2 and 3. Population Growth and Change

History of world population growth; competing theories of population growth and change and its impact on development and the environment—Malthus and Neo-Malthusians, Marx, Boserup, Ehrlich, and the demographic transition model(s). Influence of population theories on population policies, the example of population policies promoted at world population conferences. Readings in Peters and Larkin, and Ashford.

Weeks 4 and 5. Fertility in the Less Developed World

Trends, variations, and explanations; the adoption and spread of family planning; impact of family planning on fertility decline; negative impacts on women's reproductive health. Readings in Peters and Larkin. Video: *Something Like a War.*

Weeks 6 and 7. Fertility in the Developed World

Fertility characteristics and trends in the United States and Europe; the changing status of women and fertility decline; fertility decline and pro-natalist population policies in Europe; women and motherhood in Europe. Readings in Peters and Larkin, in Gill et al., and Fagnani. Video: *Population Transition in Italy.*

Weeks 8 and 9. Mortality

Global patterns and trends in mortality; causes and consequences; the AIDS epidemic, a new threat across the globe; the spread of AIDS and differences in the transmission of the HIV virus; AIDS and women in the less developed world; AIDS prevention programs. Readings in Peters and Larkin, and Friedman. Videos: *AIDS in Africa* and/or *A Future with AIDS.*

Week 10. Migration

Migration processes and trends within countries of the developed and less developed world; causes and consequences; impact of migration on regional development; impact of rural to urban migration on the development of mega-cities in the less developed world—problems of housing, employment, environmental pollution, and public health in mega-cities. Readings in Peters and Larkin. Slide presentation: "The impact of rural to urban migration—the case of Jakarta, Indonesia."

Weeks 11 and 12. International Migration

The dynamics of international migration—globalization, acceleration, differentiation, and feminization; immigration and policy responses in contemporary Europe; immigration and immigration policy in the United States. Readings in Peters and Larkin, Leitner, and Calavita. Slide presentation: "Foreign female domestic workers in Hong Kong."

Weeks 13 and 14. Population, Food, and the Environment—Facts, Myths, Solutions

World population growth and food supply; the world food problem. Why do people go hungry? What can and should be done to achieve social and environmental sustainability? Readings in Peters and Larkin. Video: *Hungry for Profit.*

Week 15. Presentation and Discussion of Term Projects

Required Readings

Peters, G. L., and Larkin, R. P., 1999. *Population Geography—Problems, Concepts and Prospects.* Dubuque, Iowa: Kendall/Hunt, sixth edition.

World Population Data Sheet, 2000. Washington D.C.: Population Reference Bureau.

Ashford, L. S., 1995. *New Perspectives on Population: Lessons from Cairo.* Washington, D.C.: Population Reference Bureau.

Calavita, K., 1998. Gaps and contradictions in U.S. immigration policy: An analysis of recent reform efforts. In D. Jacobson (ed.) *The Immigration Reader: America in a Multidisciplinary Perspective.* Malden, Mass.: Blackwell, 92–112.

Fagnani, J., 1996. Family policies and working mothers: A comparison of France and West Germany. In M. D. García-Ramon and J. Monk (eds.) *Women of the European Union: The Politics of Work and Daily Life.* London and New York: Routledge, 126–37.

Gill, R. T., Glazer, N., and Thernstrom, S., 1992. *Our Changing Population.* Englewood Cliffs, N.J.: Prentice Hall, 161–77.

Friedman, R., 1996. India's shame. *The Nation,* April 9: 11–20.

Leitner, H., 1995. International migration and the politics of admission and exclusion in post-war Europe. *Political Geography* 14(3): 259–78.

(EN)GENDERING DEVELOPMENT, RACE(ING) WOMEN'S STUDIES: CORE ISSUES IN TEACHING GENDER AND DEVELOPMENT

GEETA CHOWDHRY AND CECILIA MENJÍVAR

Developing a course on gender and development raises pedagogical, theoretical, and practical challenges. Pedagogically and theoretically, instructors face the monumental task of familiarizing students with at least two separate, albeit sometimes overlapping, areas of scholarship. Thus a gender and development course requires the (en)gendering of materials and issues related to development and the race(ing) of feminist theories. Practically, the challenge lies in how to convey this knowledge without overwhelming and overburdening the students.

The framework of political economy is central to our understanding of the congruence of gender and development. Although there are many approaches for analyzing gender and development in political economy, we rely on two common suppositions for all of them. First, we assume that politics, economics, and society are dialectically interrelated, and second, we start from the notion that control of and access to resources are unequally distributed globally. Thus, from the vantage point of political economy, we can familiarize our students with global, national, and local distributions of power, thereby locating both structure and agency in the lives of Third World women. In addition, this framework helps us in locating "difference" in the global political economy. Theorizing difference in its relationship to political, economic, and cultural relations at the global, national, and local levels helps us avoid the naturalization of gender, development, and race. Gender, race, and development thus do not get characterized as moribund categories reflecting the excrescence of "traditional" societies. Rather they are positioned as relational and dynamic categories that are effected by the congruence of national, global, and local power.

We have intentionally moved away from developing a structured syllabus. Rather, we would like to suggest several units that we deem central to a course on gender and development. This provides flexibility to instructors who can then fashion their own syllabi for interdisciplinary graduate or undergraduate courses. Even though syllabi may reflect the instructors' own disciplinary background, we strongly recommend that this course remain cross-disciplinary, as it reflects the very nature of the issues facing women in the Third World.

UNIT 1. PROBLEMATIZING GENDER AND DEVELOPMENT

Our objective in problematizing gender and development is twofold. First, we seek to convey to students that these concepts involve complex and dynamic processes, where diverse peoples participate, rendering any monolithic understanding of gender, development, and race invalid. Second, we aim to sensitize our students to racialized stereotypes of both gender and development. On the first day of classes, we ask students to identify what they understand by these concepts and the characteristics associated with each. The instructor can list them on the board so that students can visualize the range of responses and their patterns. The responses have often clustered around the categories of masculinity and femininity for gender, and modern and traditional societies for development.[1] This exercise makes visually obvious the parallels between masculinity and modernity, and femininity and tradition. We suggest that instructors guide students through the historical construction of these concepts. For example, the concept of development as modernization can be discussed in at least two important ways: as an ideological construct and as a spatial construct.[2] Ideologically, the concept of modernization is understood when juxtaposed against tradition. This taxonomy establishes deeply rooted binary oppositions evoking images of progress, light, knowledge, superiority, and modernization juxtaposed against images of stagnation, darkness, ignorance, inferiority, and tradition. Spatially, modernization is located geographically and historically (with the exception of Japan and a few other countries) in Europe. The same exercise can be done for gender. Although both categories privilege European masculinity, it is also important to discuss the ways in which European femininity and European women were complicit in furthering the subjugation of Third World men and women. This can be accomplished by adding the category of race to discussions.

Instructors can use this process to help students interrogate their own conceptions of *modernity, tradition, Third World women,* and the *Other.* We have found it useful to keep returning to this exercise throughout the course, and to end the course with it, as the exercise helps to evaluate the knowledge that our students bring to the course and what they take from it.

This exercise is not only appropriate for students who come in with very limited or no knowledge of development issues, but also for those who are familiar with and may even empathize with Third World peoples, but who tend either to take a paternalistic view or to exoticize the Third World, for as Liu (1991, 266) observes, "to many students, they themselves embody the universal norm. In their hearts of hearts, they believe that white establishes not merely skin color, but the norm from which blacks, browns, yellows, and reds deviate. . . . For those who have been left out of the story of Western civilization, it is perfectly possible to be integrated and still remain marginal."

During the first week of a course, readings such as Escobar (1984–85), Esteva (1987), Portes (1973), Scott (1995), Kabeer (1994), Jaquette (1982), and Shiva (1988) can be used to aid students in questioning their own conceptions of modernity and tradition, because these authors locate these constructs geographically, historically, and ideologically. In addition, Scott (1995), Kabeer (1994), Jaquette (1982), and Shiva (1988) view these constructs through the lens of gender. Furthermore, selections from Amadiume (1987) can be used to probe and debunk students' conceptions of gender roles.

UNIT 2. HISTORICIZING GENDER AND DEVELOPMENT: LOCATING GLOBAL PROCESSES AND LOCAL LIVES

For two weeks, students should locate issues regarding gender and development in specific historical contexts. Although classical literature on modernity and modernization takes colonization as a starting point, we were wary of using colonization as a reference point for all societies, thereby once again privileging the West. Readings on precapitalist social arrangements including discussions on precapitalist patriarchal practices are useful for exposing students to the notion that Third World societies had histories even before they were "discovered." In addition, it is an excellent starting point for introducing students to the concept of patriarchy and the various forms it takes in specific geographical locations. It is through the theme of comparative patriarchy that instructors can make explicit how patriarchy functions in multiple ways across the world and how women across continents have "bargained with patriarchy" (Kandiyoti 1988).

At the same time, however, we do not wish to minimize the impact of colonialism on global arrangements. We use this section to suggest that even as capitalist interventions have engaged precapitalist social formations, they also have engaged precapitalist patriarchal formations. As Gordon (1996, 59) has suggested, "Colonial authorities working to establish the colonial capitalist economy superimpose their own patriarchal notions of appropriate roles or work for men and women. The patriarchy of the colonizer may or may not fit with that of the society colonized, but the resulting gender relations will have a profound effect on the articulation that occurs between capitalism and the familial mode of production."

In order to introduce students to feminist and nonfeminist theories of colonization, for example, we assign selections from Lenin (1989), accompanied by selections from Mies (1988). These readings illuminate the ways in which colonial encounters created new hierarchies of power, which in turn altered gender roles. Although we are careful to distinguish between patriarchy and capitalism, we discuss the ways in which patriarchy and capitalism are mutually constitutive and enabling.

In short, we use the intersections of indigenous and colonial history to understand the theory and politics of gender and development. The utilization of gender in servicing colonial projects cannot be minimized. For example, the practices of veiling, female circumcision, and sati were often the tools used to legitimize colonial rule. The politicization and continued imbrication of these issues with colonial policies have placed them at the center of identity politics today. Teasing out these connections may help students understand the positions of some Third World feminists on issues such as veiling and female circumcision.

UNIT 3. THEORIZING GENDER AND DEVELOPMENT

Theorizing gender and development in all its multiplicity is a challenging task for instructors. Because we see theory as central to developing students' understandings of women's locations as they interact with global, national, and local processes, we suggest that instructors spend two to three weeks on theories of gender and development, beginning with separate attention first to development theories and then to feminist theories.

There are several ways that instructors can proceed. Chowdhry uses the classifications of liberal feminism, Marxist feminism, postmodern feminism, and postcolonial feminism as they relate to development to expose students to the richness of the literature on gender and development.[3] By using the distinction between internal critics and external critics, Chowdhry positions the various theories in their relationship to the dominant international development discourse as well as the international development community. Thus a discussion on liberal feminist approaches to gender and development is accompanied by a discussion on modernization theory and liberal feminism. Through this discussion, it becomes clearer to students that although internal feminist critics on gender and development, like liberal feminist Boserup (1970), take development theories and development praxis to task for marginalizing women, they do not question the goals of modernization and the course it takes. Like liberal feminists they are critical of the system because it does not provide equal opportunities for women. It is important to point out that liberal feminist scholarship and activism have been influential within the international development community. It is also important to point out, however, that because their influence has been possible within the parameters of international development discourse, the liberal feminist discourse is subject to certain limitations. The strengths and limitations of liberal feminist discourse can be assessed by examining women in development, or gender and development sections in international development agencies.

External feminist critics question the goals and processes of modernization as well as its marginalization of women. In fact, they link the marginalization of women to the stated goals of modernization. Thus they see the modernization process itself as gendered. Instructors may face a dilemma when trying to pigeonhole Marxist-feminists into an external critic category. Those with more postmodernist leanings may use the criteria of modernity to place Marxist-feminists in the internal critic category. Given the dominance of capitalism in the international development discourse, others may be persuaded to place them in the external critic category. We suggest that instructors use this dilemma to draw students into the discussion on classifications, including a discussion on the strengths and drawbacks of classifying theoretical approaches. Perhaps a more useful approach may be to use the Marxist-feminist category as a genealogical, catch-all category for others such as dependency and world-systems feminists. Once again, instructors will need to discuss Marxism, Marxist-feminism, dependency approaches, and world-systems approaches before students can begin to understand scholars like Mies (1986) or Benería and Sen's (1981) classic critique of Boserup. So (1990) provides an extremely useful summary of modernization theory, dependency, and world systems theories that can be used in addition to readings on gender and development for graduate level classes. For undergraduate classes Scott's (1995) discussion of modernization and dependency theories should prove to be extremely useful. Tong (1989) can also be used to introduce students to the varieties of feminism.

Other external critics include the scholarship of postmodern feminists on gender and development. Once again it will be useful to include a discussion on postmodernism before discussing postmodern feminism. Marchand and Parpart's (1995) introduction is very useful in addressing literature on postmodernism, feminism, and development. In addition, several articles from their text can be used for engaging students in discussions on what postmodern feminism can offer development studies.

Similarly, discussions on postcolonial feminism need to be begin with a brief introduction to what postcolonial means. Because postcolonial feminists often use methodology similar to that of postmodern feminists, and because students often find it difficult to distinguish between the two theories, we suggest that instructors assist students in drawing the distinctions between postmodern feminism and postcolonial feminism. One of the distinctions is that imperialism and colonization, (and thus race) are foregrounded in postcolonial scholarship. It is also perhaps important to point out that

Gramsci as much as, if not more than, Foucault has influenced some postcolonial scholarship. Scholarship by Spivak (1987), Minh-ha (1990, 1991), Ong (1987), Mohanty (1991), Alexander and Mohanty (1997), and Mani (1996) can be used to demonstrate postcolonial feminisms. Finally, discussing the interconnections between external critics and grassroots movements is important so that their influence on praxis is made as visible as that of the liberal feminists.

Another possible way of discussing the multiple theoretical approaches to gender and development is to use the women in development (WID), women and development (WAD), or gender and development (GAD) classification that has been developed by Rathgeber (1990). WID approximates the liberal feminist theories of gender and development; WAD approximates the Marxist-feminist approaches; and GAD approximates the socialist-feminist approaches. This classification, however, does not address the new and important genre of "post-" theories. Instructors can use the WID–WAD–GAD schema in addition to scholarship on postmodern and postcolonial feminist theories to organize their courses.

Moser (1989, 1993) provides another interesting and useful classification for addressing gender and development. She uses the concepts of welfare, equity, antipoverty, efficiency, and empowerment to distinguish among different policy, rather than theoretical, approaches. Although some may argue that to teach gender and development is to bridge theory and praxis, we caution instructors against using the relevance of a theory to policy as the only criteria for evaluating theory, because the process may privilege those theories that support the dominant worldview of the international development community. An emphasis on policy, as Tinker (1990) suggests, may also indicate an instructor's unintended preference for "pragmatism," and consequently may position some theories as pragmatic and therefore nonideological and others as mainly theoretical and therefore ideological. Kabeer's comment points to the ideological nature of liberal feminism: "It is misleading, however, to characterize this agenda as non-ideological. It can be perceived as non-ideological only because it reflects a world-view which is dominant in the international development community. The hegemonic character of this world view, its taken-for-granted assumptions about the nature of social reality, renders it invisible, dispensing with the need to spell out the theoretical premises upon which it was founded" (Kabeer 1994, 12). We would suggest using Moser's piece in conjunction with another approach that highlights the various theoretical approaches to gender and development.

At the end of this unit students should be asked to write a paper that evaluates the various theoretical approaches. This forces the students to become familiar with all the theories and their strengths and weaknesses before they proceed with the rest of the course. Instructors can keep coming back to these theories as they discuss other units.

UNIT 4. (RE)PRESENTING THIRD WORLD WOMEN: RACE AND THE ORIENTALIST DISCOURSE

This unit is divided into several subthemes of methodology and representation, women and body politics, and women and work. Because this unit provides the bulk of the course we suggest spending four to six weeks on it. The readings for this unit will challenge students to think about the representation of Third World women in various settings and locations, and set the tone for ensuing discussions of women's images as they are manifested in scholarship, in the media's coverage of cultural practices, and through Third World women's participation in productive activities. Edward Said's classic *Orientalism* (1978), which analyzes Western writings on the "Orient" to expose the relations of power and dominance that they have engendered, can be used to organize these sections. Although Said's *Orientalism* does not have much to say on gender, many postcolonial feminist scholars like Ahmed (1992), Abu-Lughod (1986, 1993), Mohanty et al. (1991), Alexander and Mohanty (1997), Minh-ha (1991), and Ong (1987) have provided us with trenchant critiques of Western scholarship on Third World women as well as historically located retheorizing of culture and the politics of power and representation. Thus postcolonial scholarship raises pedagogical issues about "us" and "them" and assists students in rethinking the boundaries of the discourse on Third World women.

METHODOLOGICAL ISSUES AND REPRESENTATION

Because the knowledge we have about women's lives in Africa, Asia, and Latin America (in academic settings) is often generated by research activities, we start by examining how scholars conduct research, particularly feminist research, in and about the Third World. To this end, we suggest selections from Reinharz (1992) and Wolf (1996). These readings do not merely discuss the "right" way to do research, but take on the complexities and multiple contingencies that emerge as feminists reflect on the work they undertake and on situated knowledge. In addition, we suggest that discussions of feminist *fieldwork* be juxtaposed with discussions of what Visweswaran (1994) has called *homework*. Ethnographic homework requires, among other things, the decolonization of Western knowledge and the location of that knowledge in a whole range of practices that have legitimized many forms of intervention in the Third World. These discussions may be particularly useful and necessary for graduate students who will be engaged in the production of knowledge. Linking methodological practices to knowledge and power provides students with tools to read against the grain and suggests alternative ways of doing research.

Many disciplines ranging from anthropology to subaltern historical and literary studies have utilized testimonials, or life histories, as a legitimate basis for research. Utilizing testimonials or life-histories can, in part, mediate the politics of representation as colonial discourse. Thus the testimonies or life-histories of Aung San Suu Kyi (1991), Menchú (Menchú and Burgos-Debray 1984), Barrios de Chungara and Viezzer (1978), and Tula (1994) can be used not only to locate the struggles of these women in their historicity, but also to engage students in debates about the power of authorial positions in the production of knowledge. Another body of literature that can be used to engage students with issues regarding methodology and representation focuses on "folk" narration in the forms of songs, stories, and the like. The work of Prem Chowdhry (1990, 1994) utilizes "oral tradition" in the form of folklore, folk songs, popular beliefs, and other similar traditions to analyze alternatives to the practice of sati in India (1990) and the changing nature of gender roles in Haryana (1994). Narayan (1996) utilizes songs of Kangra women to explain the displacement of women's knowledge in the Kangra region of India.

Menjívar uses an exercise in her courses on immigration that utilizes oral history tradition and testimonials to bring students to an understanding of immigrant realities and to assist them in locating their own realities in the politics of immigration. This exercise provides students with methodological experience but also prevents them from exoticizing immigrants and representing them as categories of study, which produces a distancing between the students and the histories and lives of immigrants. This exercise can also be used in conjunction with the unit on border crossings.

Menjívar asks students to think of their own family as immigrants (except for Native Americans, everyone should consider themselves as such) and then interview a family member in a manner that will generate an oral history, placing emphasis on the ethnic identity of their families. Because most people's backgrounds include two or more ethnic groups, students may choose to focus on one of them. Second, she asks the students to read immigration histories or any studies that have been conducted about their ethnic group, and one or more pieces that have been written about an immigrant group significantly different from their own. She then asks the students to link their readings with their oral histories and answer several central questions: How typical is your family in relation to your ethnic group? How similar is your ethnic group from the one you thought varied greatly from your own? In answering these questions, she expects students to identify several factors in their own families' immigration history as well as in the comparison group. These include, but are not limited to, the events motivating migration, social networks, occupations, gender differences, patterns of (and barriers to) social mobility, stereotypes about the ethnic group and how these might have affected their overall prospects in society. Contrasts between the experiences of "old" (late nineteenth and early twentieth century) and contemporary immigrants are central, for they help students to understand the racialized nature of immigration realities as well as the changing contexts within which migration flows take place. To elucidate such contrasts, Menjívar uses the 1972 film *The Long, Long Journey,* which recounts the life of a Polish immigrant family in early twentieth-century New York and asks students to compare it to experiences of contemporary immigrants around issues of language, schooling, job opportunities, possibilities for socioeconomic mobility, gender, and intergenerational relations.

WOMEN, IDENTITY, AND BODY POLITICS

The subtheme of women and body politics can be explored through multiple issues, including population discourse, the discourses on female genital mutilation–female circumcision and veiling, the discourses on sati and dowry deaths, and the politics surrounding the Uniform Civil Code (UCC) in India. Ahmed's (1992) discussion of veiling provides insight into the significance of the veil in geopolitical discourse. Relating how veiling begins to occupy a central place in Western discourse about Islam, Ahmed links colonial occupation to the hypermasculinization of Islamic men. The idea that non-Western men oppressed non-Western women was utilized by colonizers, who were incidentally derisive of feminist expressions in their own countries, to legitimize colonial ventures. Since then, veiling and women's bodies have become the sites of battles over national identity. It is not surprising, then, that postcolonial subjectivity on veiling emerges in many tension-ridden ways between Western and Third World feminists.

In the discourses of geopolitics, the reemergent veil is an emblem of many things, prominent among which is its meaning as the rejection of the West. But when one considers why the veil has this meaning in the late twentieth and early twenty-first centuries, it becomes obvious that, ironically, it was the discourse of the West, and specifically the discourse of colonial domination, that determined the meaning of the veil in geopolitical discourses and thereby set the terms for its emergence as a symbol of resistance. In other words, the reemergent veil attests, by virtue of its very power as a symbol of resistance, to the contested hegemonic diffusion of the discourses of the West in our age (Ahmed 1992, 235).

The engendering of international human rights has been only recently accomplished. Central to this process has been the highly charged issue of female circumcision–genital mutilation. Clearly, the two terms *female genital mutilation* (fgm) and *female circumcision* (fc) represent the different positions of a variety of feminists. Utilizing both terms in syllabi is advantageous for demonstrating sensitivity to the various debates that have surrounded the issue. The issue of fc–fgm also allows a broader discussion of the postcolonial condition and the manner by which sovereignty, nationality, insider-outsider issues, and identity get implicated in struggles surrounding women's human rights. Chowdhry uses two films to bring some of these issues to light: Alice Walker and Pratibha Parmar's *Warrior Marks* (1993) and Soraya Mire's *Fire Eyes* (1994). Students then write a paper on the representation of Third World women in these films. Throughout Walker's film, women are stereotypically shown as victims while African men are shown as "hypermasculinized others." In contrast, Mire's film presents many different images of African women and men vis-à-vis fc–fgm. In addition, we provide students with other readings from popular media sources and postcolonial scholars, including Obiora (1997), Mugo (1997), Urban (1998), Brownlee et al (1994), and Howell (1995). Chowdhry has found that this issue in particular evokes very strong responses from Western students who are often hard pressed to understand the support of female circumcision by some women in these films. By guiding students through this process and providing comparisons with Western contexts, in which other body-altering practices, such as breast augmentation, occur, instructors can avoid an egregious othering of women undergoing and supporting fc–fgm.

The Uniform Civil Code (UCC) in India is a complex and currently debated issue that can be used to introduce students to many themes including nationalism and gender, cultural practices, women's rights, equality, religious fundamentalism, and the role of the state. The Constitution of India recommends a legally binding UCC for all its citizens. It also guarantees religious and ethnic minorities the right to cultural practices. These two guarantees have often clashed, particularly with regard to gender roles and practices. The Indian state has allowed minority groups to define their own cultural practices; as a result, a UCC has not yet been developed. Traditionally many feminists struggling for equal rights for women have argued for the development of a UCC, but in recent years the Hindu right has used it as a rallying point against the Muslim community in India. Since then many members of the Indian feminist community have distanced themselves from the UCC, and a working group has suggested the development of an optional civil code that would give every individual the right to choose between a UCC and the personal law of the community. This issue can be used to discuss the dilemmas faced by the state in building universal laws, the role of the colonial and postcolonial state in creating majority-minority relations, the egregious villainization of the Muslim minority by the Hindu right (you can substitute other majority-minority examples), and the centrality of gender in this villainization of Muslim men. The debates surrounding the UCC can be used to demonstrate how women's bodies become the battlefields, the sites where contests over cultural identity take place. Butalia and Sarkar (1995) and Chowdhry (2000) can be used to provide current information and a gendered analysis of the UCC.

Another area where discursive practices have influenced policy is population. The dominance of Malthusian and neo-Malthusian theories in international and national discourses on population and development have not only obfuscated how consumption and distribution influence growth and sustainable development, but have targeted women's bodies as the sites of population control. Interestingly, the field of eugenics continues to influence policy makers in finding target groups for population control practices. Thus the "forcible" sterilization of Native American women in the United States and the eugenicist population control policy of Singapore can be discussed to show the centrality of race, gender, and class in population discourse. Silliman and King (1999), Bandarage (1997), Hartmann (1995), and Correa (1994) provide useful discussions of "reproductive rights and wrongs" in the contexts of international and state policies on population.

We have often utilized novels by women writers to highlight cultural issues and have found that students find fiction much more interesting than articles. We suggest that instructors can use Emecheta (1988) to illustrate the social construction of motherhood and its impact on women, and Ba (1989) who highlights the issue of polygamy in urban and rural communities of Senegal.

WOMEN AND WORK

Instructors can begin this unit with a work-related exercise developed by Janice Monk (1983). This exercise allows instructors to discuss (1) that the definition of work is socially constructed and (2) that this definition is inherently gendered. Marilyn Waring (1989) deconstructs standard definitions of work, value, labor, production, and reproduction to demonstrate the biological determinism and economism that pervades their usage. In addition she discusses the limits of the United Nations System of National Accounting (UNSNA), which has laid the framework for national accounting within different countries and which, to date, shows a gender and class bias and remains ecologically problematic. Instructors can use the film *Who's Counting? Marilyn Waring on Sex, Lies, and Global Economics* to accompany this discussion.

During this week students could also examine the complexities involved in women's work. Continuing with the overall theme of representation, they can look at the increasing economic contributions of women and their underrepresentation in official statistics. We recommend that this include a discussion of the different kinds of work that women perform in both the formal and informal sectors, so that the class does not engage in any essentialist portrayal of Third World women. To address diversity and class differences among women, we recommend readings on women in agriculture, domestic work (house servants), factories, politics, microenterprise, and sex work. We recommend Agarwal (1994), Dixon (1985), Ong (1987), Prieto (1997), and Kempadoo (1999). Another aspect of Third World women's work is their participation in the entertainment industry. Tyner (1996) illustrates the gendered nature of this burgeoning sector, and reviews the constraints that compel women to work there. Sachs (1996) offers a useful discussion of rural work and environmental issues.

UNIT 5. GLOBALIZING THE LOCAL AND LOCALIZING THE GLOBAL

The discussion on globalization can be organized around two interrelated themes: (1) globalization as ideology and (2) the specific forms that globalization takes. We suggest that instructors use the globalization of ideology as the basis of their discussion, for it provides an epistemological base from which to discuss issues related to foreign direct investments, structural adjustments, and trade-related intellectual property rights (TRIPs). The framework of political economy is useful for initiating this discussion. Thus the privileging of markets and states under certain ideological conditions becomes the center of the discussions. It is very useful for instructors to discuss whether these concepts are really as oppositional as cold war history has made them out to be. In addition, it would be useful to identify how and why states and markets are differently positioned and what that means in terms of allocation of resources.

To initiate discussion, students can be asked to identify what they understand by globalization and how it impacts women. It is quite possible that students' views may cluster around two oppositional positions: (1) that globalization will deliver development and thus be a liberating force for women, and (2) that globalization will lead to increasing exploitation and poverty in the Third World. Instructors can assist students in questioning both of these positions by using the literature on women working for transnational corporations. The work of Tiano (1994), Fernández-Kelly (1996), Lim (1978), and Lim and Fong (1991) demonstrates that gender, or the social construction of women and men, is central to employment practices in transnational industrial employment. In addition, their work emphasizes that one cannot discuss globalization in terms of the simple dualism of exploitation or liberation. The effects of corporate investment on women are complex and simultaneously liberating and exploitative. Global corporations provide women with employment and wages that indigenous firms may not, thereby giving them the necessary economic tools for liberation. However, certain costs are incurred by women during this process. These costs include loss of family-support networks, loss of status and respect, and vulnerability to sexual attack. Also, such employment is often hazardous to the emotional and physical health of women (Chowdhry 1994: 161)

Furthermore, instructors can use the literature on structural adjustment programs (SAPs) introduced by the World Bank to analyze (a) the gendered nature of the economic concepts utilized to implement SAPs and (b) the impact the adjustment programs have on women. The scholarship of Elson (1995), Sparr (1994), and Bakker (1994) addresses the gendered nature of economic concepts utilized by SAPs quite effectively. Benería and Feldman (1992) and Gladwin (1991) provide rich documentation on the impact of structural adjustment. In addition, there is an emerging literature on the implications of the latest General Agreement on Tarriffs and Trade (GATT) and its implication for women. In particular, the impact of Trade Related Intellectual Property Rights (TRIPs) on traditional knowledge provides a fertile base from which to show how global discourse impacts local lives. Shiva (1993, 1997) offers a useful discussion on the impact of TRIPs on biodiversity and on gender and race.

UNIT 6. BORDER CROSSINGS: QUESTIONING FIRST/THIRD WORLD CATEGORIES

The task of this section is two-fold. First, we discuss what it means to be First World or Third World women focusing particularly on the sociopolitical, economic, and cultural processes through which these categories get created. Second, we focus on how minority women in industrialized societies have positioned themselves as Third World women in relation to the mostly white feminist movements. In particular, we focus on Third World women's immigration to industrialized countries to highlight the historical links that have conditioned their migration. Although we do not discuss the special case of refugee women, we mention Martin (1992) as a good resource that includes very useful didactic material about Third World refugee women. Approximately two weeks should be spent on this unit. We begin by examining the historical, economic, political, and cultural links that impinge on the size and direction of contemporary migrations from the periphery to the center, as it is no accident that some immigrant groups gravitate to some countries and others go elsewhere. We recommend especially Portes (1978) and Sassen-Koob (1984). The first essay offers a historical overview of movements on a global scale and the second situates women within the processes of capital flows and labor markets.

We continue with the theme of immigrant women and work, because opportunities for work impact their incorporation into the societies they enter. To this end, we recommend Menjívar's (1999) examination of the social aspects of immigrant women's paid work and its effects on gender relations. She questions whether paid work can automatically lead to more equity in the home. As immigration is allegedly one of the most important forces that alter gender roles, we recommend three works that focus on this aspect of immigrant women's lives: Hondagneu-Sotelo (1994), Kibria (1994), and Menjívar (2000). We also suggest Ui's (1991) work on Cambodians in California's Central Valley. We conclude this unit with two reading suggestions that will help bring students closer to the lives, tribulations, and reflections of immigrant women in their new countries: Hart (1997), who details the travel and travails of a Nicaraguan woman in Oregon and California, and Prose (1992), who writes about the life of a Haitian woman who works as a housekeeper in upstate New York.

CONCLUSION

In conclusion, we recommend that instructors return to the issues raised during the first week of classes, and once again conduct the opening exercise on gender and development. Although conducting this exercise at the end of the course initiates self reflection, it is also, in some sense, an evaluative exercise that provides students and instructors with a sense of what they have been able to accomplish, which is often a rewarding experience for all.

NOTES

1. Chowdhry uses this exercise regularly in her undergraduate and graduate classrooms.
2. Chowdhry develops this idea in her book manuscript entitled *(En)Gendering Development Discourse: International Financial Institutions, the State, and Women in the Third World* (pending). She has utilized these distinctions for discussions in her undergraduate and graduate courses on the political economy of development.
3. Chowdhry has used this classification in her course on gender and development. See also Chowdhry, "Engendering Development? Theoretical Considerations About Women in International Development," *The International Journal of Humanities and Peace* (Spring 1992): 41–44. In this article Chowdhry has used the term *Third World feminism*, which she has replaced in her course with *postcolonial feminism*.

SELECTED BIBLIOGRAPHY FOR RECOMMENDED UNITS

Unit 1

Ifa Amadiume, *Male Daughters, Female Husbands: Gender and Sex in an African Society* (London and Atlantic Highlands, N.J.: Zed Press, 1987).

Arturo Escobar, "Discourse and Power in Development: Michel Foucault and the Relevance of His Work to the Third World," *Alternatives* 10 (1984–85): 377–400.

Gustavo Esteva, "Regenerating People's Space," *Alternatives* 12 (1) (1987): 125–52.

Jane Jaquette, "Women in Modernization Theory: A Decade of Feminist Criticism," *World Politics* 34 (1982): 267–84.

Naila Kabeer, *Reversed Realities: Gender Hierarchies in Development Thought* (New Delhi: Kali for Women; Atlantic Highlands, N.J.: Zed Press, 1994), chapter 2.

Tessie Liu, "Teaching the Differences Among Women from a Historical Perspective," *Women Studies International Forum* 14 (4) (1991).

Alejandro Portes, "Modernity and Development, A Critique," *Studies in Comparative International Development* 8 (3) (1973): 247–79.

Catherine V. Scott, *Gender and Development: Rethinking Modernization and Dependency Theory* (Boulder: Lynne Reinner, 1995), chapters 2 and 3.

Vandana Shiva, *Staying Alive: Women, Ecology and Development* (London and Atlantic Highlands, N.J.: Zed Books, 1988).

Unit 2

Anthony Brewer, *Marxist Theories of Imperialism: A Critical Survey* (London: Routledge, 1990), chapters 1–6.

Bipan C. Chandra, "Reinterpretation of the Nineteenth Century Indian Economic History," *Indian Economic and Social History Review* 5 (1) (1968): 35–76.

Mona Etienne and Elanor Leacock (eds.), *Woman and Colonization* (New York: Praeger, 1980).

April Gordon, *Transforming Capitalism and Patriarchy* (Boulder: Lynne Rienner, 1996).

M. Annette Jaimes with Theresa Halsey, "American Indian Women At the Center of Indigenous Resistance in Contemporary America," in M. Annette Jaimes (ed.) *The State of Native America: Genocide, Colonization and Resistance* (Boston: South End Press, 1992).

Deniz Kandiyoti, "Bargaining with Patriarchy," *Gender and Society* 2 (3) (September 1988): 274–90.

V. I. Lenin, *Imperialism the Highest Stage of Capitalism* (New York: International, 1989), chapters 1–5, 7.

Maria Mies, *Women: The Last Colony* (London and Atlantic Highlands, N.J.: Zed Books, 1988).

Morris D. Morris, "Towards a Reinterpretation of Nineteenth Century Indian Economic History," *Indian Economic and Social History Review* 5 (1) (1968): 1–17.

Nancy Scheper-Hughes, "Sweetness and Death: The Legacy of Hunger in Northeast Brazil," in David L. L. Shields (ed.) *The Color of Hunger: Race and Hunger in National and International Perspective* (Lanham, Md.: Rowman and Littlefield, 1995).

Unit 3

M. Jaqui Alexander and Chandra Mohanty (eds.), *Feminist Genealogies, Colonial Legacies, Democratic Futures* (London: Routledge, 1997).

Asoka Bandarage, "Women in Development: Liberalism, Marxism and Marxist-feminism," *Development and Change* 15 (4) (1984): 495–516.

Lourdes Benería and Gita Sen, "Accumulation, Reproduction and Women's Role in Economic Development: Boserup Revisited," *Signs* (Winter 1981).

Ester Boserup, *Women's Role in Economic Development* (New York: St. Martin's Press, 1970).

Sarah Harasym (ed.), *The Post-Colonial Critic: Interviews, Strategies, Dialogues /
Gayatri Chakravorty Spivak* (London: Routledge, 1990).

Naila Kabeer, *Reversed Realities: Gender Hierarchies in Development Thought*
(New Delhi: Kali for Women; London and Atlantic Highlands, N.J.: Zed Press,
1994), chapter 3.

Donna Landry and Gerald MacLean (eds.), *The Spivak Reader: Selected Works of
Gayatri Chakravorty Spivak* (London: Routledge, 1996).

Lata Mani, "Crosscurrents, Crosstalk: Race, 'Postcoloniality,' and the Politics of
Location," in Smadar Lavie and Ted Swedenburg (eds.) *Displacement, Diaspora
and the Geographies of Identity* (Durham, N.C.: Duke University Press, 1996),
273–93.

Marianne Marchand and Jane Parpart (eds.), *Feminism/Postmodernism/Develop-
ment* (London: Routledge, 1995), introduction, conclusion, chapters 2, 3, 9.

Maria Mies, *Patriarchy and Accumulation on a World Scale* (London and Atlantic
Highlands, N.J.: Zed Press, 1986).

Trinh T. Minh-ha, "Not You / Like You: Post-colonial Women and the Interlocking
Question of Identity and Difference," in Gloria Anzaldúa (ed.) *Making Face,
Making Soul / Haciendo Caras: Creative and Critical Perspectives by Feminists
of Color* (San Francisco: Aunt Lute Books, 1990).

Trinh T. Minh-ha, *Woman, Native, Other* (Bloomington: Indiana University Press,
1991).

Chandra Mohanty, "Introduction" and "Under Western Eyes," in Chandra Talpade
Mohanty, Ann Russo, and Lourdes Torres (eds.) *Third World Women and the
Politics of Feminism* (Bloomington: Indiana University Press, 1991).

Caroline Moser, *Gender Planning and Development: Theory, Practice and
Training,* (London: Routledge, 1993).

Caroline Moser, "Gender Planning in the Third World: Meeting Practical and
Strategic Gender Needs," *World Development* 17 (11) (1989): 1799–1825.

Aihwa Ong, *Spirits of Resistance and Capitalist Discipline: Factory Women in
Malaysia* (Albany: State University of New York Press, 1987).

Eva Rathgeber, "WID, WAD, GAD: Trends in Research and Practice," *The Journal of
Developing Areas* 24 (July 1990): 489–502.

Catherine V. Scott, *Gender and Development: Rethinking Modernization and
Dependency Theory* (Boulder: Westview Press, 1995), chapters 5 and 6.

Alvin Y. So, *Social Change and Development: Modernization, Dependency and
World Systems Theories* (Newbury Park, Calif.: Sage, 1990).

Gayatri Chakravorty Spivak, *In Other Worlds: Essays in Cultural Politics* (London:
Metheun, 1987).

Kathleen Staudt, "Women, Development and the State: On the Theoretical
Impasse," *Development and Change* 17 (2) (1986): 325–33.

Irene Tinker, *Persistent Inequalities: Women and World Development* (Oxford:
Oxford University Press, 1990).

Rosemary Tong, *Feminist Thought: A Comprehensive Introduction* (Boulder:
Westview Press, 1989).

Unit 4

Lila Abu-Lughod, *Veiled Sentiments: Honor and Poetry in a Bedouin Society* (Oxford: Oxford University Press, 1986).

Lila Abu-Lughod, *Writing Women's World: Bedouin Stories* (Berkeley: University of California Press, 1993).

Bina Agarwal, *A Field of One's Own: Gender and Land Rights in South Asia* (Cambridge: Cambridge University Press, 1994).

Leila Ahmed, *Women and Gender in Islam* (New Haven, Conn.: Yale University Press, 1992).

M. Jaqui Alexander and Chandra Mohanty (eds.), *Feminist Genealogies, Colonial Legacies, Democratic Futures* (London: Routledge, 1997).

Mariama Ba, *So Long a Letter* (Oxford: Oxford University Press, 1989).

Asoka Bandarage, *Women, Population and Global Crisis: A Political-Economic Analysis* (London and Atlantic Highlands, N.J.: Zed Books, 1997).

Shannon Brownlee et. al., "In the Name of Ritual," *US News and World Report,* 7 February 1994, 56–58.

Urvashi Butalia and Tanika Sarkar, *Women and Right Wing Movements: Indian Experience* (London and Atlantic Highlands, N.J.: Zed Press, 1995).

Geeta Chowdhry, "Communalism, Nationalism and Gender: The Rise of the Bhartiya Janata Party (BJP) and the Hindu Right in India," in Sita Ranchard Nilsson and Mary Ann Tetreault (eds.) *Gender, Nation and Nationalism: Feminist Approaches to Contemporary Debates* (London: Routledge, 2000).

Prem Chowdhry, "An Alternative to the Sati Model: Perceptions of a Social Reality in Folklore," *Asian Folklore Studies* 49 (1990): 259–74.

Prem Chowdhry, *The Veiled Women: Shifting Gender Equations in Rural Haryana* (Oxford: Oxford University Press, 1994).

Domitilla Barrios de Chungara and Moema Viezzer, *Let Me Speak: Testimony of Domitilla, A Woman of the Bolivian Mines* (New York: Monthly Review Press, 1978).

Sonia Correa, *Population and Reproductive Rights* (London and Atlantic Highlands, N.J.: Zed Books, 1994).

Ruth Dixon, "Seeing the Invisible Women Farmers in Africa: Improving Research and Data Collection Methods," in J. Monson and M. Kalb (eds.) *Women as Food Producers in Developing Countries* (Los Angeles: UCLA African Studies Center and African Studies Association, 1985).

Buchi Emecheta, *The Joys of Motherhood* (Oxford: Heinemann International, 1988).

Betsy Hartmann, *Reproductive Rights and Wrongs* (Boston: South End Press, 1995).

Llewellyn Howell, "Culture and Women's Rights: Time to Choose," *USA Today,* January 1995, 53.

Kamala Kempadoo (ed.), *Sun, Sex, and Gold: Tourism and Sex Work in the Caribbean* (Lanhman, Md.: Rowman and Littlefield, 1999).

Aung San Suu Kyi, *Freedom from Fear and Other Writings* (New York: Penguin Books, 1991).

Rigoberta Menchú and Elizabeth Burgos-Debray (ed.), *I, Rigoberta Menchú: An Indian Woman in Guatemala* (London: Verso, 1984).

Cecilia Menjívar, *Fragmented Ties: Salvadorian Immigrant Networks in America* (Berkeley: University of California Press, 2000).

Trinh T. Minh-ha, *Woman, Native, Other* (Bloomington: Indiana University Press, 1991).

Soraya Mire, *Fire Eyes* (videorecording) (New York: Filmmakers Library, 1994).

Chandra Mohanty et. al., *Third World Women and the Politics of Feminism* (Bloomington: Indiana University Press, 1991).

Micere Githae Mugo, "Elitist Anti-Circumcision Discourse as Mutilating and Anti-Feminist," *Case Western Law Review* 47 (Winter 1997): 461–79.

Kirin Narayan, "Songs Lodged in Some Hearts: Displacement of Women's Knowledge in Kangrad," in Smadar Lavie and Ted Swedenburg (eds.), *Displacement, Diaspora and the Geographies of Identity* (Durham, N.C.: Duke University Press, 1996).

Amede L. Obiora, "Bridges and Barricades: Rethinking Polemics & Intransigence in the Campaign Against Female Circumcision," *Case Western Law Review* 47 (Winter 1997): 275–378.

Aihwa Ong, "Colonialism and Modernity: Feminist Representation of Women in Non-Western Societies," *Inscriptions* 3–4 (October 1988): 39–79.

Aihwa Ong, *Spirits of Resistance and Capitalist Discipline: Factory Women in Malaysia* (Albany: State University of New York Press, 1987).

Norma Iglesias Prieto, *Beautiful Flowers of the Maquiladora: Life Histories of Women Workers in Tijuana* (Austin: University of Texas Latin American Studies and University of Texas Press, 1997).

Shulamit Reinharz, *Feminist Methods in Social Research* (Oxford: Oxford University Press, 1992).

Carolyn Sachs, *Gendered Fields: Rural Women, Agriculture and Environment* (Boulder: Westview Press, 1996).

Edward Said, *Orientalism* (New York: Pantheon Books, 1978).

Chiara Saraceno, "Women's Paid and Unpaid Work in Times of Economic Crisis," in Lourdes Benería and Shelly Feldman (eds.), *Unequal Burden: Economic Crisis, Persistent Poverty and Women's Work* (Boulder: Westview Press, 1992).

Jael Silliman and Ynestra King, *Dangerous Intersections: Feminist Perspectives on Population, Environment and Development* (Boston: South End Press, 1999).

María Teresa Tula, *Hear My Testimony: María Teresa Tula, Human Rights Activist in El Salvador,* translated and edited by Lynn Stephen (Boston: South End Press, 1994).

James A. Tyner, "Constructions of the Filipina Migrant Entertainers," *Gender, Place and Culture* 3 (1) (1996): 77–93.

Jessica Urban, *Engendering (Hu)Man Rights: International Relations Postcolonial Feminism, Female Circumcision/Female Genital Mutilation and Veiling,* Depart-ment of Political Science, Master's thesis, Northern Arizona University, Flagstaff, 1998.

Kamala Visweswaran, *Fictions of Feminist Ethnography* (Minneapolis: University of Minnesota Press, 1994).

Alice Walker and Pratibha Parmar, *Warrior Marks* (videorecording) (New York: Women Make Movies, 1993).

Marilyn Waring, *If Women Counted: A New Feminist Economics* (San Francisco: Harper and Row, 1989).

Diane Wolf (ed.), *Feminist Dilemmas in Fieldwork* (Boulder: Westview Press, 1996).

Unit 5

Isabella Bakker, *Strategic Silence: Gender and Economic Policy* (London and Atlantic Highlands, N.J.: Zed Press, 1994).

Lourdes Benería and Shelly Feldman (eds.), *Unequal Burden: Economic Crisis, Persistent Poverty and Women's Work* (Boulder: Westview Press, 1992).

Geeta Chowdhry, "(En)gendering Development? Women in Development (WID) in International Development Regimes," in Marianne H. Parpart and Jane Marchand (eds.), *Feminism/Postmodernism/Development* (London: Routledge, 1995).

Geeta Chowdhry, "Women and the International Political Economy," in Peter R. Beckman and Franciene D'Amico (eds.) *Women, Gender and World Politics* (Westport, Conn.: Bergin and Garvey, 1994).

Diane Elson (ed.), *Male Bias in the Development Process* (New York: St. Martin's Press, 1995).

M. Patricia Fernández-Kelly, "Labor, Migrants, and Industrial Restructuring in Electronics," in Alan B. Simmons (ed.) *International Migration, Refugee Flows, and Human Rights in North America: The Impact of Trade and Restructuring* (New York: Center for Migration Studies, 1996), 174–92.

Christina Gladwin (ed.), *Structural Adjustment and African Women Farmers* (Gainesville: University of Florida Press, 1991).

Linda Y. C. Lim, *Women Workers in Multinational Corporations: The Case of the Electronics Industry in Malaysia and Singapore* (Ann Arbor: Women's Studies Program, University of Michigan, 1978).

Linda Y. C. Lim and Pang Eng Fong, *Foreign Direct Investment and Industrial-ization in Singapore, Taiwan and Thailand* (Paris: OECD Development Centre, 1991).

Caroline Moser, *Gender Planning and Development: Theory, Practice and Training* (London: Routledge, 1993).

Vandana Shiva, *Biopiracy: The Plunder of Nature and Knowledge* (Boston: South End Press, 1997).

Vandana Shiva, "Homeless in the Global Village" and "GATT, Agriculture and Third World Women," in Maria Mies and Vandana Shiva (eds.) *Ecofeminism* (London and Atlantic Highlands, N.J.: Zed Press, 1993).

Pamala Sparr, *Mortgaging Women's Lives* (London and Atlantic Highlands, N.J.: Zed Press, 1994).

Susan Tiano, *Patriarchy on the Line: Gender and Ideology in the Mexican Maquiladora Industry* (Philadelphia: Temple University Press, 1994).

Unit 6

Janet E. Bemson, "The Effects of Packinghouse Work on Southeast Asian Refugee Families," in Louise Lamphere, Alex Stepick, and Guillermo Grenier (eds.), *Newcomers in the Workplace: Immigrants and the Restructuring of the U.S. Economy* (Philadelphia: Temple University Press, 1994).

Donna Gabaccia, *From the Other Side: Women, Gender and Immigrant Life in the United States, 1820–1990* (Bloomington: Indiana University Press, 1994).

Ali Ghanem, *A Wife for My Son* (London and Atlantic Highlands, N.J.: Zed Books, 1984).

Sherri Grasmuck and Patricia Pessar, *Between Two Islands: Dominican International Migration* (Berkeley: University of California Press, 1991).

Diana Hart, *Undocumented in L.A.: An Immigrant's Story* (Wilmington, Del.: Scholarly Resources, 1997).

Pierrette Hondagneu-Sotelo, "Regulating the Unregulated? Domestic Workers' Social Networks," *Social Problems* 41 (1994): 50–64.

Pierrette Hondagneu-Sotelo (ed.), "Special Issue: Gender and Immigration," *American Behavioral Scientist* 42 (4) (1999).

Nazli Kibria, "Household Structure and Family Ideologies: The Dynamics of Immigrant Economic Adaptation Among Vietnamese Refugees," *Social Problems* 41 (1) (1994): 81–96.

Susan Forbes Martin, *Refugee Women* (Atlantic Highlands, N.J. Zed Books, 1992).

Cecilia Menjívar, *Fragmented Ties: Salvadorian Immigrant Networks in America* (Berkeley: University of California Press, 2000).

Cecilia Menjívar, "The Intersection of Work and Gender: Central American Women and Employment in California," *American Behavioral Scientist* 42 (40) (1999): 595–621.

Alejandro Portes, "Migration and Underdevelopment," *Politics and Society* 8 (1978): 1–48.

Francine Prose, *Primitive People* (New York: Farrar, Straus and Giroux, 1992).

Terry A. Repak, "Labor Market Incorporation of Central Americans in Washington D.C.," *Social Problems* 41 (1) (1994): 114–28.

Saskia Sassen-Koob, "Notes on the Incorporation of Third World Women into Wage Labor Through Immigration and Off-Shore Production," *International Migration Review* 18 (4) (1984): 1144–67.

Shiori Ui, "'Unlikely Heros': The Evolution of Female Leadership in a Cambodian Ethnic Enclave," in Michael Buroway, Alice Burton, Ann Arnett Ferguson, et al. (eds.) *Ethnography Unbound: Power and Resistance in the Modern Metropolis* (Berkeley: University of California Press, 1991).

Sydney Stahl Weinberg, "The Treatment of Women in Immigration History: A Call for Change," *Journal of American Ethnic History* 11 (1992): 25–46.

Hania Zlotnik, "The South-North Migration of Women," *International Migration Review* 29 (1) (1995): 229–54.

INTEGRATING GENDER INTO THE INTERNATIONAL RELATIONS CURRICULUM

MARY M. LAY, CAESAR FARAH, LISETTE JOSEPHIDES,
ANGELITA REYES, EILEEN B. SIVERT, CONSTANCE A. SULLIVAN,
AND MARGARET WADE

Five faculty members from Afro-American/African studies, anthropology, women's studies, French and Italian, and Spanish and Portuguese departments at the University of Minnesota revised a course called Theoretical Approaches to International Relations by asking not how gender analysis might be "imported" into international relations, but rather how a women's studies or feminist perspective might lead to posing questions about the complexity of human experience at the global level in new and different ways. After conducting a review of the course and its place in the international relation program's curriculum, the group concluded that, although the recent interest in gender issues in international relations has been encouraging, the materials and approaches used to teach about gender issues at the undergraduate level should be expanded significantly. Also, the group undertook a major reimagining of the structure of the course in order to meet curricular transformation goals.

The faculty group identified several key intellectual issues for specific course revisions and for the broader process of transforming the international curriculum to integrate women's studies, international studies, and area studies. These are (1) issues of disciplinarity and interdisciplinarity, including the need to see beyond the limitations and gaps of particular disciplinary lenses and intellectual paradigms to ask what is at stake in the way questions are framed; (2) the politics of knowledge, including the need to examine the political implications of particular interpretations of global "realities"; (3) the complexity of interactions between global processes and local communities, including the importance of themes of identity and difference; and (4) the indivisibility of gender analysis from questions of race and ethnicity, class, religion, postcolonial theory, and so on.

The next step in the process involved establishing more specific goals to be accomplished by the core course revision. These goals included

1. creating a more thoroughly interdisciplinary approach to the course by incorporating theoretical and empirical materials from a

range of social science disciplines, to better address the intellectual challenge of course revision and to better serve the diverse interests of undergraduate international relations majors;

2. integrating feminist approaches and the concept of gender into the course theoretically and through explorations of particular themes, such as the international political economy or global environmental issues;

3. considering primarily the explicit incorporation of non–U.S. and non-Western perspectives into a field that traditionally has been oriented toward an Anglo-American perspective;

4. addressing more explicitly the five major tracks within the international relations undergraduate curriculum (international political economy, international development, society and politics, international relations and the environment, and interstate relations and diplomacy);

5. addressing the diversity of students' backgrounds and topical interests, which range from international business to environmental issues to development; and

6. considering ways in which personal narratives and autobiographical texts could be used in a course taught primarily from a social science perspective at a macro-level of analysis.

KEY INTELLECTUAL ISSUES

The group identified a set of key intellectual issues for revising the core course in international relations while discussing disciplinary and interdisciplinary goals, developing a framework for the revised course, and suggesting potential reading materials.

DISCIPLINARITY AND INTERDISCIPLINARITY—THE POLITICS OF KNOWLEDGE

The first category of intellectual concerns involved questions of disciplinarity, interdisciplinarity, and the politics of knowledge. Although theory courses often are taught as a series of paradigms or theoretical approaches, the group noted that this teaching method limits students' ability to see the commonalities and differences among theoretical approaches and how they are used to research "real world" issues and case studies. For example, despite considerable intellectual and political differences, neoclassical and Marxist perspectives on international political economy both focus primarily on interstate relations. In contrast, a feminist economist might ask questions about the relationship between household economics and global economic processes, or focus on the gendered nature of the international division of labor.

The group also investigated the ways in which theoretical approaches and topical issues are viewed through specific disciplinary lenses, thus leading to certain assumptions and limitations on how questions are posed. Regardless of the discipline, there are always absences and gaps that have important implications for how the subject matter of global or international relations is understood. For instance, in political science and economics, the topics of international development and international political economy are often taught using a core-periphery model. Under this model, development primarily concerns North-South relations; international political economy often concentrates on relations between the developed countries of Europe, North America, and Japan. However, the attention paid to the concept of space by economic and political geographers calls into question the usefulness of a core-periphery model in the face of global economic changes that have created both cores and peripheries within a single economy, including the economies of developed countries. As a result, geographers have approached the study of international political economy by examining the emergence of knowledge-intensive industries such as computer software design in South and Southeast Asia or the impact of global economic restructuring on the "Rust Belt" region of the United States and on groups such as white women and all African Americans.

By including reading selections that frame theoretical questions in this very different way, the revised course would enable students to see some of the important assumptions within different disciplines and theoretical traditions and help them recognize the complexities of contemporary global economic relationships. The working group therefore decided that a primary goal of the revised course would be to help students become "theorists" in a broad sense, rather than simply be acquainted with the theoretical literature of a particular discipline (e.g., geography or political science). This is a particularly important consideration for "Theoretical Approaches in International Relations" for two reasons. First, this is a core course for an interdisciplinary program, and, second, students taking the course have a wide range of concentrations, including specific geographical areas, international politics, and anthropology.

The working group also recognized that examining the inherently political nature of theory and the "situatedness" of knowledge about the world is of crucial importance in teaching the course and helping students evaluate theory. The course needs to be organized so that students are encouraged to examine the political implications of how questions are framed, how research is conducted, and how "data" are interpreted. An example that the group used in the revised syllabus involves the politics of interpretation of the cold war and its end. Questions about the cold war in political science often are framed in terms of a debate between realist and liberal theorists over balance-of-power politics and the effects of economic competition between the United States and the former Soviet Union. A different perspective might suggest that the cold war was more about Western efforts to contain revolutionary or nationalist politics in Africa, Asia, and Latin America than it was about superpower politics. A scholar of development such as Arturo Escobar might consider the truly important questions about the post–World War II era to involve the institutionalization of internationalist perspectives and the growth of *developmentalism* as ideology and policy vis-à-vis the "developing" countries. Alternatively, Cynthia Enloe and other feminists suggest that examining the connections between gender and global militarism is essential for understanding the cold war and its aftermath.

All of these considerations led the faculty participants to recognize that the key task in revising the course was to reimagine its basic structure. The working group decided to change the course organization from one based primarily on teaching paradigms or theoretical approaches to one that contrasts texts from different disciplines and theoretical paradigms within a particular thematic area. The purpose of this reimagining was to help students understand what is at stake in framing questions and attempting to answer them from various perspectives.

GLOBAL PROCESSES AND LOCAL EXPERIENCES

A second category of intellectual concerns surrounded the relationship between global processes and local experiences. This concern led to a group discussion of the possibilities for and problems of building general or universal theory about international relations, given the need to help students understand the complexities of a simultaneously interconnected and fragmented world. The working group decided that the course should emphasize that although one can theorize about global social, political, and economic processes, these processes take different forms in different places and are viewed in different ways at the local level. To the extent possible, the revised course should also focus on the complex interaction between processes involving individuals, households, communities, regions, states, and transregional or transglobal forces rather than focusing exclusively or primarily on interstate relations. The changing global role of the state is an issue that students should examine closely. To a certain degree, this approach necessitates a shift away from traditional area or regional studies concerns. It also calls attention to questions of identity and difference that have long been the concern of scholars working on gender issues in a number of disciplines.

The faculty working group recognized that their agenda involved not only adding gender concerns or women's studies perspectives to the revised syllabus. The group also needed to include discussions of race and ethnicity, class, postcolonial perspectives, and other issues, and they needed to explore the relationships between these issues and the analytical category of gender. Faculty participants noted that in undergraduate courses questions of gender and race in particular have often been "added in" as discrete units or perspectives. Given that these questions are integral to theory-making and to understanding concrete global issues, however, the group decided to include them throughout the course and, where possible, in each thematic or topical unit. Attention to issues of gender throughout the course would complicate, challenge, and deepen students' understanding of current theoretical approaches to international relations.

LITERARY SOURCES

Finally, the group considered ways to incorporate personal narratives, autobiographical texts, and fiction into a course with a social science orientation. The group discussed how these kinds of texts might be used to complement social science approaches. For example, selections from Cherríe Moraga and Gloria Anzaldúa's edited volume of narratives, *This Bridge Called My Back,* could be used to help students understand the complexity of social identities—racial, ethnic, gender, regional, national, or transnational—in a rapidly changing world. This discussion raised important issues concerning the challenges posed by teaching narrative texts to students without an extensive background in the humanities and the problems of "appropriation" of the personal narratives of women.

PEDAGOGICAL CONCERNS

In addition to the key intellectual concerns, the faculty working group identified a number of important pedagogical issues involved in revising the international relations core course. The group's discussion of pedagogical goals stemmed from group members' knowledge of and direct experience with using feminist pedagogical approaches, as well as from the concerns that arose from the group's review of the international relations program and the needs of undergraduate international relations majors.

The first pedagogical issue concerned the need to help students adjust to a course taught around a set of questions and contrasting texts from different paradigms, while still achieving coherence and understanding. Second, the working group sought to incorporate feminist pedagogical approaches in the model syllabus, for example providing more time for discussion, independent study, and group work. Therefore, the group wanted to move the course further away from a lecture-based format toward a more participatory format in accordance with current university-wide efforts to transform the undergraduate curriculum. Third, in reviewing the international relations program, the group also asked how to provide an improved core theory course to a quite diverse group of students, some of whom are finishing course work and working on major projects, some of whom are at the introductory level.

The group discussed, at some length, the practical issues of how to teach a survey course covering a wide range of topics and incorporating materials from a number of disciplines. Some of the pedagogical techniques suggested included having students take turns leading discussions in recitation sections in order to decentralize the authority of the instructor and teaching assistants, assigning short reaction papers on readings due at the beginning of class to encourage students to think through the issues raised in reading prior to class discussion, and assigning group presentations to enable students to work collaboratively.

THE REVISION PROCESS

After considering the intellectual and pedagogical issues just detailed the faculty working group developed a more detailed framework of topics and questions for the course. In drafting a model syllabus, the group attempted to develop a course structure that would encourage students to think beyond theoretical paradigms and disciplinary lenses to consider the similarities, differences, limitations, and politics inherent in the ways theoretical and research questions are posed.

The resulting syllabus for the course is organized thematically around the five substantive concentrations or tracks of the program rather than around a series of theoretical approaches or paradigms. Individual course units are intended to address the subject matter of each track by juxtaposing contrasting theoretical perspectives and exploring the application of these perspectives to case studies. The situatedness and political nature of knowledge is introduced at the beginning of the course through basic readings on paradigms and categories of analysis, including gender. This theme is then treated in more depth at the end of the course, once students have had the opportunity to explore these analytical categories and the issue of knowledge production throughout the various units. Questions guide reading, discussions, and short thought pieces. These questions explicitly encourage students to identify why and how questions are posed and to examine the situatedness of knowledge and limitations of paradigms or theoretical traditions. Students are further encouraged to explore these themes through required presentations and research papers on suggested topics or on a well-developed topic of their own. Concerns about the diversity of students' backgrounds and levels of understanding are addressed in part by suggesting flexibility in terms of course requirements. In this course, students are able to pursue several different options for evaluation, including either a research paper as an initial exploration of a topic of interest for those new to the program or an outline for a major project for more advanced students.

QUESTIONS FOR REVISING THEORETICAL APPROACHES TO INTERNATIONAL RELATIONS

The following questions should serve as a solid starting point for instructors and program administrators who want to integrate gender concerns into the international relations curriculum. The faculty working group thinks these questions will prove more useful than a model syllabus. For a complete copy of the revised syllabus, see Lay et al., "Integrating Gender Concerns into the International Relations Curriculum," *Women's Studies Quarterly* 26 (3–4) (Fall/Winter 1998): 181–201.

1. In what ways is conventional or mainstream international relations theory gendered (particularly as it has been constituted in the discipline of political science) in terms of its philosophical underpinnings and theoretical assumptions, central categories of analysis, and substantive topics and areas for empirical research? What do these assumptions and categories marginalize or exclude in terms of understanding the role of gender and women in international relations? In general terms, how can a women's studies perspective (or work on gender in other disciplines) be used to challenge or reconceptualize these categories and topics and rethink the basic subject matter of international relations?

2. How have gender analysis and feminist theory entered the field of international relations theory? What challenges has scholarship on gender and women confronted in order to be heard by those coming from more conventional perspectives? In what ways has feminist or gender-related work adopted or been limited by common assumptions, such as the centrality of the state and state relations; the anarchic nature of international interactions; a core-periphery model that focuses on dominant, Western, or developed states; and an emphasis on formal global economic relations? What impact has feminist scholarship in the field had in terms of questioning or changing these assumptions and posing different questions?

3. How can scholarship from other disciplines and the current concerns and debates in women's studies and feminist theory be more effectively incorporated into the subject matter of international relations and into an undergraduate theory course? What kinds of resistance and limitations are teaching and research on gender likely to continue to face?

4. Feminist work in international relations has generally been categorized as a form of critical theory (broadly defined) and grouped with other critical social theories such as social constructivist work, interpretative or hermeneutic approaches,

postmodernist or poststructural theories, Marxist and neo-Marxist economic analyses, and postcolonial theory. How have different critical approaches been marginalized within the field and seen as distinct from one another? Is the relationship between gender analysis and these approaches an uneasy one? Why has much critical work in international relations theory largely ignored questions of gender and how might these approaches be brought together more effectively and creatively? Is gender analysis compatible with more conventional or mainstream approaches to studying and teaching international relations?

5. Is it possible to bridge the differences between the social sciences and the humanities in an undergraduate theory course in ways that make the course more truly interdisciplinary? Might narratives and texts used in humanities courses be juxtaposed against social science theory in ways that help students to understand the complexities of global relationships?

6. How can we teach and think about the human experience at the global level? What are the relationships between states and other transnational and international actors, and how do social, economic, and political processes involving global, national, group or community, and household levels fit together? International relations theory historically has adopted a macro-level of analysis. How would a women's studies perspective suggest new ways of understanding and theorizing the linkages between global and local, and between social processes and actors?

7. How has international relations theory traditionally conceptualized what constitutes the international or the global as opposed to the domestic? In what ways is this domestic or international distinction gendered? Does it implicitly rely upon a gendered separation of public and private spheres? Should the international and domestic realms be as sharply distinguished as they are in most analyses of international relations? How might feminist theoretical work on the relationship between gender and the public and private realms be used to reconceptualize this distinction? How might studies of global-transnational or subnational social processes in other disciplines illuminate areas of inquiry that international relations theory leaves largely untouched as a result of this distinction? For example, how do economic migration and women's participation in the "informal" economy fit in studies of the global political economy?

8. In what ways does much, if not most international relations scholarship explicitly or implicitly rely upon a core-periphery model to explain international political, economic, and social life? To what extent does it problematically reproduce categories such as West and non-West or developed and developing, and focus on the actions of dominant states while excluding or marginalizing perspectives of other actors, groups, and states? In particular, how does it reflect a U.S. viewpoint or make assumptions based on a particular location within global capitalism? Does feminist scholarship in international relations reflect these same assumptions? How might feminist work on difference as well as intersections between gender and postcolonial theory challenge or change a core-periphery model?

9. Questions concerning culture have only recently been posed by international relations scholars. Do assumptions from the cultural perspective of dominant groups within states and across international borders underpin international relations theory? Has feminist international relations scholarship seen gender as the

central category of analysis to the extent that it has ignored or dismissed issues of race and ethnicity? Understanding intersections of gender, race, ethnicity, and class have been at the forefront of feminist inquiry in other fields. How might discussions of culture and difference be brought into an undergraduate theory class?

10. Are the assumptions of "anarchy" and the dominance of conflict within international relations inherently gendered assumptions? Do feminist analyses suggest a different reading of the role of conflict and cooperation within global social, political, and economic life? How does a feminist approach to international relations understand global militarism and its impact on women?

11. Questions of identity have long been central to feminist theory but have only recently been entertained by international relations scholars; however, the emphasis on the individual or the personal in much feminist scholarship clashes with the world systems or state-centric approaches of the field of international relations. How can the concept of identity be used to think about the state or transnational relations? From a women's studies perspective, how might the relationship between the personal and the global be bridged? What are the theoretical assumptions in doing so?

12. How does feminist activism relate to a highly theoretical field? What are the opportunities for studying women's activism at the global level, such as transnational social movements? What are the opportunities for feminist advocacy, and how do these concerns motivate the posing of questions and the ways in which research and teaching are conducted in international relations?

13. How can topics that are of particular interest to women (such as reproductive health rights and public health policy, international human rights, population politics, and the linkage between economics and the global environment) be made more central to the study of international relations? These areas of research have traditionally been marginalized at the edges of a field that considers its subject matter to be the "high politics" of state relations, international conflict, and the formal political economy. How might feminist scholarship suggest questions about the core of the field that would decenter these assumptions and bring gender-related issues into focus?

WOMEN AND THE ENVIRONMENT: GLOBAL PROCESSES–LOCAL LIVES

HELEN RUTH ASPAAS

This course was designed to examine women's relationships with the natural environment and identify specific responsibilities that women can and do take on as environmental advocates. First, I reviewed the growing body of literature that focuses on feminist perspectives of scientific inquiry in order to apply these new theories to environmental themes. Then, I reviewed the work of women scientists and women nature writers who have stimulated and maintained a focus on environmental issues. Finally, I explored women's associations with the environment from perspectives inside and outside the West. The integration of themes during the last class meetings helped students to understand the relationships among various feminist environmental activists and their concerns.

Because students came from a variety of colleges within the university, I assumed that no one would have an extensive grounding in feminist theory. I did assume that students would be willing to grapple with challenging literature and ideas. I presented many dimensions of current feminist thought and theory. For obvious reasons, I designed the course to accommodate a variety of learning styles.

From the beginning, the classroom approach was one of collaboration. I tried to set the tone by emphasizing that we were a "community of learners," and for the annotations and journal assignments, I also submitted entries as a participant in the class. A binder contains all the students' contributions during the course, the annotations that students contributed during the term, copies of their book reviews, copies of their term projects, and copies of their journal entries about *Sisters of the Earth.*

The students selected their own research topics. The criteria I set were simple: The topic had to have a gender component and had to relate to the environment. Early in the course, we spent a class period discussing the topics and offering possible suggestions for resources and ways to focus on each research topic. One student with an interest in folk music examined feminist and environmental dimensions of contemporary folk music. She interviewed a local artist and completed a careful content analysis of twenty contemporary folk songs having environmental themes. During her presentation, she performed a song she had written. Another student in the Range Resources Department examined budding feminist perspectives in the range science discipline. One student who grew up in an urban area was very interested in rural women's perspectives on the environment, so she joined a farm women's chat group on the Internet to learn about their perspectives on the environment. A fourth student used some of her personal backpacking and camping experiences as a springboard for investigating gender differences in social interactions during extended outdoor recreation experiences. One student surveyed women scientists in his discipline, interviewed women graduate students and women professors, and compared their responses to those found in the literature. Lastly, a student from a large metropolitan area on the east coast who was participating in the national student exchange program used the project as an opportunity to investigate population issues as they relate to Native American women in the western regions of the United States.

The students offered both positive unsolicited feedback and positive formal end-of-course evaluations. One student commented that "New doors were opened to me that I never knew existed before." Another responded that participation in the course helped her to begin to look for "what is not there." She now sees areas of women's engagement in environmental issues and understands critically the absence of gender in the literature of mainstream natural resource thinking.

Informal comments throughout the term suggested that all of the students very much enjoyed reading the selections in the *Sisters of the Earth* anthology, especially the narratives, prose, and poetry focused on environmental issues. They responded very positively to the requirement of keeping a journal.

From an affective perspective I thought that the course allowed me to gain clearer insights into the lives and challenges faced by the women students in a college composed of disciplines that have traditionally been dominated by men and masculine perspectives. I became better able to provide appropriate mentoring as a consequence of my familiarity with women students' expressions of struggles they encountered in that college.

SYLLABUS

Objectives

Women and the Environment: Global Processes–Local Lives will examine unique aspects of women's relationships with the natural environment and will identify specific roles that women can and do play in environmental advocacy and preservation. The theme of Global Processes–Local Lives will serve as a conduit for addressing subjects relevant to women's interaction with the natural environment at different scales. By examining global processes and how they are linked with local lives and how local activities are often influential at the global scale, we can reach a better understanding of women's relationships with the natural environment.

Course Contents

The growing and often controversial body of literature that focuses on feminist perspectives of scientific inquiry will be reviewed for the purpose of applying some of these new theoretical constructs to environmental themes. Likewise, environmental and ecological philosophies that have evolved through mainstream modes of thought will be compared to these alternate and feminist perspectives in order to derive a better sense of commonalities as well as differences. Theoretical perspectives derived from Western and non-Western sources will be examined. The roles of women scientists and women nature writers in stimulating and maintaining the focus on environmental issues will be examined by reading some of the leading contributors' works including Rachel Carson, Anne Morrow Lindbergh, and Terry Tempest Williams. Using this theoretical context, then, women's associations with the natural environment will be examined from a domestic-Western and international–developing country perspective.

The final goal of the course is to identify commonalities between issues of developed and developing countries that affect women's participation in solving environmental problems as well as women's contributions to environmental stewardship. Integration of themes from various scales during the last class meetings will help to connect students to the ways that women's roles in solving environmental problems are played out at different scales.

Approaches

The focus for learning will be through a seminar strategy that encourages student participation as well as student leadership in the learning process. Lectures will be minimized and incorporated occasionally through the course only as springboards for introducing new materials and concepts. Students will be responsible for leading and contributing to class discussions based on readings drawn from the professor's and library's resources.

A term-long goal is for the class to work together as a community of learners. Consequently, I envision a binder at the end of the term composed of all annotations, book reviews, and projects so that each student leaves with a compendium of resources for use in future research and service.

Texts

Anderson, Lorraine, ed. 1991. *Sisters of the Earth.* New York: Vintage Books.
Rodda, Annabel. 1991. *Women and the Environment.* London: Zed Books.

Week 1. Introduction to the Class and Sociological Conceptualizations of Gender

Andersen, Margaret L. 1992. "Sex role socialization." In *Thinking About Women: Sociological perspectives on sex and gender,* 72–99. Boston: Allyn and Bacon.
Read *Sisters of the Earth* first section (select two of the readings, write a personal response in your journal and a brief biography about the authors). These are

the same directions for each section of *Sisters of the Earth* throughout the quarter.

Week 2.

A. Feminist Theory

Compile a list of feminist and masculine perspectives as a guide to understanding the distinction between the two.

Bondi, Liz. 1992. "Progress in geography and gender: Feminism and difference." *Progress in Human Geography* 14(3): 438–45.

Bondi, Liz. 1990. "Debates: Feminism, postmodernism, and geography: Space for women?" *Antipode* 22(2): 156–67.

Parpart, Jane L., and Marianne H. Marchand. 1995. "Exploding the canon: An intro-duction/conclusion." In *Feminism/Postmodernism/Development*, 1–22. Routledge: London.

Women and Geography Study Group of the IBG. 1984. "Feminism and geography: Theory and practice." In *Geography and Gender: An introduction to feminist geography*, 24–39. London: Hutchinson in association with the Explorations in Feminism Collective.

B. Feminist Critique of the Culture of Science

VIDEO: *"EVELYN FOX KELLER: SCIENCE AND GENDER." 1994. PRINCETON, NEW JERSEY: FILMS FOR THE HUMANITIES AND SCIENCES.*

Harding, Sandra. 1997. "Is modern science an ethnoscience? Rethinking epistemo-logical assumptions." In *Postcolonial African Philosophy: A critical reader*, Emmanuel Chukwudi Eze, ed., 45–70. Cambridge, Mass.: Blackwell.

Merchant, Carolyn. 1982. "Isis' consciousness raised." *Isis* 73(268): 398–409.

Read *Sisters of the Earth* second section.

Week 3. Global Environmental Issues and Feminist Environmental Theory

Small break-out groups to define and justify students' perceptions of global envi-ronmental issues.

Rocheleau, Dianne, Barbara Thomas-Slayter and Esther Wangari. 1996. "Gender and environment: A feminist political ecology perspective." In *Feminist Political Ecology: Global issues and local experiences*, Dianne Rocheleau, Barbara Thomas-Slayter and Esther Wangari, eds., 3–23. New York: Routledge.

Read *Women and the Environment*, chapters 1 and 2.

Week 4. Women Naturalists and Proposals for Projects

Carson, Rachel. 1950. *The Sea Around Us.* New York: A Mentor Book. (Select one chapter.)

Paul, Linda Joan. 1992. "Human encroachments on a domineering physical land-scape." In *A Few Acres of Snow,* Paul Simpson-Housley and Glen Norcliffe, eds., 86–98. Toronto: Dundurn Press.

Williams, Terry Tempest. 1995. "An erotics of place." In *Re-thinking Natural Resources,* Rosanna Mattingly, ed., 8–26. Corvallis: Oregon State University, College of Forestry.

Read *Sisters of the Earth,* third section.

Week 5. Women as Environmental Constituents in the Global North, Grassroots Efforts

Fairfax, Sally. 1991. "Environmental justice: What's in it for us?" In *Changing Values—Changing Institutions,* J. R. Bayle and S. L. Arbogast, comps., 17–33. Corvallis: Oregon State University, College of Forestry.

Miller, Vernice, Moya Hallsterin, and Susan Quass. 1996. "Feminist politics and environmental justice: Women's community activism in West Harlem, New York." In *Feminist Political Ecology: Global issues and local experiences,* Dianne Rocheleau, Barbara Thomas-Slayter, and Esther Wangari, eds., 62–85. New York: Routledge.

Wastl-Walter, Doris. 1996. "Protecting the environment against state policy in Austria." In *Feminist Political Ecology: Global issues and local experiences,* Dianne Rocheleau, Barbara Thomas-Slayter, and Esther Wangari, eds., 86–104. New York: Routledge.

Read *Sisters of the Earth,* fourth section.

Week 6. Women as Environmental Constituents and Women as Users of the Environment in the Global South; Women as Protectors of the Environment

GUEST SPEAKER: CAROLYN FINNEY, GRADUATE STUDENT WORKING ON WOMEN AND SOCIAL FORESTRY IN NEPAL.

Collaborative learning activity using Australian indigenous women news clips.

Coatney, Caryn. 1997. "Threats to sacred lake stir an Aborigine woman to action." *The Christian Science Monitor* 7 (August 27).

Jacobs, Jane M. 1994. "Earth honoring: Western desires and indigenous knowl-edges." In *Writing Women and Space: Colonial and postcolonial gGeographies,* Alison Blunt and Gillian Rose, eds., 169–96. New York: Guildford Press.

Read *Women and the Environment,* chapters 3–5.

Week 7.

A. Global Conferences, Gendered Environmental Politics and Activism at the Global Scale

Students select one of the following international conferences and analyze it for gender inclusivity and special attention given to women's roles with the environ-ment: Rio (environmental) Conference, Copenhagen (economic) Conference,

Cairo (population) Con-ference, and Kyoto (environmental) Conference. Read *Sisters of the Earth*, fifth section.

B. Investigate the Role of the World Bank by Examining World Bank Publications for Gender Inclusivity and Policies Toward the Environment

Week 8. Nongovernmental Organizations Operating at the Global Scale

Students select a nongovernmental organization operating at a global scale and identify gender and environmental dimensions, reporting back to the group. Use of home pages on the Internet is encouraged.

SPECIFIC GROUPS TO BE ADDRESSED: WOMEN'S ENVIRONMENT AND DEVELOPMENT ORGANIZATION *(WEDO)*, WORLD WIDE NETWORK.
Read *Sisters of the Earth*, sixth section.

Weeks 9 and 10. Presentations on Final Projects

Read *Sisters of the Earth*, seventh section.

TEACHING GLOBALIZATION, GENDER, AND CULTURE

Deborah S. Rosenfelt

Globalization, Gender, and Culture, a course in women's studies at the University of Maryland, was designed as an elective for both upper-division undergraduates and graduate students. Built around a public lecture series of the same name, the course was originally part of a "polyseminar" funded by The Ford Foundation as a component of a grant to the University of Maryland.[1] The origins of the course lie in the trajectory of my own research interests and commitments. My background is in American literature, with a focus on women's fictions since the 1930s and the processes of social change, especially women writers at the intersection of the American Left and the feminist movement. I have described my approach to literature and culture as materialist feminist, that is, as requiring a dual commitment to an understanding of the textual and of the contexts and conditions— economic, social, political—in which the textual is produced (Newton and Rosenfelt 1985). My special topic courses in the past have focused on my research interests and have evolved with the changing of contexts and conditions. For example, American Women's Literature and Social Change, a predecessor of this course, traced the responses of selected American women writers to historical events and ideologies and outlined their affiliations with social movements and their interventions into discourses, especially those about gender and class relations, racial hierarchies, and sexuality.

Gradually, though, developments in both cultural criticism and global economic relations (not, of course, disconnected from one another) problematized every term in the course title: *American, women, literature, writers, social change.* It seemed imperative, if my courses were not to become antiquated, to acknowledge that dramatic changes in global economic configurations had altered the material conditions of cultural production; that "American" literature was increasingly in dialogue with, as well as increasingly constituted by, a polylogue of voices of many national origins and many diasporic connections; that national, regional, and religious identities, as well as racial-ethnic, class, and sexual affiliations, complicated the continuities of experience implied by the term *woman;* that imaginative literature was in dialogue with a wide range of texts, ranging from platforms for change produced by committees to performances linked directly to social action; that an emergent global feminism—both necessitated and facilitated by transnational processes of change in the economy, communications, and political configurations—was an increasingly vital force intervening on behalf of the welfare of women and children around the world.

My first effort to integrate some of these perceptions into the curriculum was less than successful. A research seminar for women's studies majors, the course retained many of the materials I had previously used in American women's literature courses, while interjecting a few readings about globalization and one or two texts that implied a dialogue among American women writers and their counterparts elsewhere, including Paule Marshall's *Daughters,* an important novel about the consequences of neocolonialist development in the Caribbean and the resistance of African American women, and Jamaica Kincaid's *A Small Place,* a passionate polemic about tourism in the Caribbean.[2] The course never felt quite coherent; it sank under the dual weight of its obligation to acquaint students with research methodologies and skills in textual/contextual critical methodologies and my own efforts to incorporate a set of issues and a handful of readings that were new to me at the time—and for which I am still working out methodologies of analysis.

Globalization, Gender, and Culture worked better, if still imperfectly. Convening once a week for two and a half hours, the course began with a session designed to define meanings: What, exactly, did we mean by *globalization,* by *culture,* or for that matter by *gender?* We began in that session to posit connections among the world's women on issues articulated in the *Beijing Declaration and Platform for Action,* which became a touchstone in both the course and the grant-funded project as a whole. We noted also that the hierarchy of definitions of "global citizenship" articulated by political theorist Richard Falk might particularly value the agency and subjectivity of the women who produced the Platform for Action (and noted later that Falk's favorite type of global citizen had certain features in common with Gloria Anzaldúa's "new mestiza"), though neither feminist activism nor women of color's theorizing has entered the discourse of mainstream political theory. The politics of knowledge thus entered the course at its outset, and remained a theme throughout.

Our second session explored the globalization of the economy and its impact on women, particularly those women affected by structural adjustment policies, prescriptions for developing countries, which we viewed as analogous to belt-tightening measures in the United States. We discussed how "globalization" of the economy meant not only the increasing hegemony and interchangeability of multinational corporations but also a totalizing ideological discourse about "free markets." The third session examined women's experiences in work and family life, considering a range of geographic and structural locations. It became apparent to us that the dual burden of having to do most of the work within the home and simultaneously having to work for pay to financially support family members was an issue of global import, especially painful for, though not necessarily limited to, working-class women. We saw how in many regions of the world, sexist and unrealistic expectations about the ostensibly infinite elasticity of women's time and free labor undergirds the curtailment of adequate social services, to the ultimate detriment of families and communities, and we explored the role of institutions like the International Monetary Fund and the World Bank in demanding state policies based on such assumptions. But we also discussed some of the strategies for survival, family advancement, and resistance that have characterized women's responses to these pressures. Throughout these first sessions, and periodically during the course, we referred to the *State of the World Atlas,* which contains numerous graphic illustrations of the issues we confronted; mapping issues of gender, money, health, and power visually is far more effective and accessible than simply providing a set of numbers or a set of generalizations.[3]

A fourth session explored the links among the material conditions we had been studying, the formation of identity and subjectivity, and women's resistance through cultural expression. Valentine M. Moghadam's introduction to *Identity Politics and Women: Cultural Reassertions and Feminisms in International Perspective* and Inderpal Grewal and Caren Kaplan's introduction to *Scattered Hegemonies: Postmodernity and Transnational Feminist Practices* brought different disciplinary perspectives—and to some extent different political investments—to bear in theorizing the complex relations among local experiences and political formations; the unequal movements across borders of capital, technology, peoples, and culture (to borrow from Grewal and Kaplan's catalogue, derived from an essay by Arjun Appadurai); and the forms of feminism emerging both within and across borders. Moghadam works within world systems theory but she also genders it, arguing for a secular global feminist activism that addresses inequities in law and state practice and exposes those cultural manipulations of gender in the service of nationalism and religious fundamentalism. Grewal and Kaplan discard world system theory in favor of a more postmodernist cultural critique. They share a sense of the vitality of grassroots feminist organizing, one which has the potential to and actually often does transcend national borders. Barbara Harlow defines resistance literature (though without reference to gender); Anzaldúa, in an essay that has become a touchstone of multicultural and feminist cultural criticism, envisages the evolution of a new mestiza consciousness, constituted by its location in both geographic and metaphoric borderlands; while Grewal's essay posits a spectrum of political subjectivities for women locating themselves in such borderlands. The excerpts from Mary K. DeShazer's book look comparatively at women's poems of resistance and opposition in three different national locations: the United States, El Salvador, and South Africa, finding similarities among them. Finally, the story by Bharati Mukherjee delicately inscribes the diasporic consciousness of an Indian Canadian woman, who cannot or will not conform to the bureaucratic rationality of state social service agencies in the wake of a devastating airline crash, which killed her husband and sons along with hundreds of other Indians and Canadians of Indian descent. Students recognize in her rejection of the role of mediator between cultures, and her final ambiguous walk into a new, as yet undefined, future, an assertion of self that ironically contains both resistance to the needs of the Western state and perhaps, at the level of narrative, an endorsement of Western feminist conventions of individual growth and self-realization.

This section of the course was simultaneously too ambitious and too diffuse; and even for many of the graduate students, the readings, especially in Grewal and Kaplan, proved quite demanding. Yet Grewal and Kaplan also, in their unpacking of terms like *postmodernity, postcolonialism,* and *transnationalism;* in their linking of women's writings and women's organizing; and in their articulation of the complexity of postmodern geopolitics and culture provide one of the best syntheses of issues central to the course. In later versions of the course, I have restructured this unit into two different units, one focusing on manipulations of women's gender and national identities in the service of new nationalisms and rising fundamentalisms (Moghadam's central concern), and one focusing on women's agency as producers of transnational feminist cultures of resistance.

At the center of the course were the lectures or performances by visiting scholars and artists and the subsequent group discussions. The disadvantage of this structure is that each unit remained relatively disconnected from its antecedent; we were bound as well as informed by the materials consultants presented. But their presence in the classroom far outweighed problems in continuity. Ella Shohat argued that film in the Third World—a term her coauthored book endorses as implying a historical position of oppositionality to colonial and neo-colonial incursions—offers a certain coherent chronological/narrative pattern. During anticolonialist struggle, such films conclude with images of a unified people or nation, subsuming issues of gender and class difference. Subsequently, however, in postcolonial societies, films inscribe the breakdown of this cohesion, representing issues of difference within the national community. Shohat and Robert Stam's book, *Unthinking Eurocentrism: Multiculturalism and the Media,* proved very useful to students interested in cultural criticism, especially for those interested in historicizing the textual history of mainstream and oppositional cinema, but difficult for many undergraduates. It made an interesting stylistic—and to some extent theoretical—contrast with the *Beijing Platform's* section on media, which is more immediately oriented toward policy and activism, and which necessarily dehistoricizes and universalizes the issues of women's access to media production and women's images in film, even as it articulates a program of action.

We continued a discussion of the relationship among discourse, representation, and activism in two intense and difficult sessions focusing on female genital surgeries. I used clips from the West African film *Finzan* as a pivot between Shohat's discussion and Tuzyline Jita Allan's presentation on discourses of clitoridectomy. *Finzan* illustrates in its own structure the narrative pattern of community unification against colonial intervention, followed by an assertion of difference. In this case, the "difference" is the alliance between a village woman who refuses to be married off to the brother of her deceased husband and a younger woman who resists circumcision upon returning to her village from the city, both asserting their independence from traditions that have oppressed women. Conceptually, this strategy worked well, but emotionally it was problematic. The film concludes with a scene of forcible circumcision by the village women. The students were horrified, and their horror precluded the kind of careful analysis that I had hoped to encourage.

Both our classroom work and Allan's presentation also flowed around Alice Walker and Pratibha Parmar's *Warrior Marks* as a documentary film intended as an activist gesture to halt clitoridectomy. Sondra Hale's essay on clitoridectomy and the politics of knowledge offered an accessible critique of the too-ready willingness of Western feminists to make female circumcision *the* icon of patriarchal violence. Allan discussed the ambiguous nature of Walker and Parmar's intervention, applauding their engagement but querying many dimensions of its form. Isabelle R. Gunning's essay, "Arrogant Perception, World-Travelling and Multicultural Feminism: The Case of Female Genital Surgeries" is the best single piece I have read on the question of how feminists in the West can conceptualize and organize around a "culturally challenging practice" like clitoridectomy without arrogance and condescension. Ultimately Gunning's work has greatly influenced my own pedagogical method.[4]

In this class, though, I do not think we handled this issue well. We needed to spend much more time contextualizing the experience and history of women in West Africa, particularly within the contexts of colonialism and decolonization, and more time discussing the work of activists within African countries. Class discussion about the connotations of different terms for female genital surgeries (female mutilation being Walker's term of choice) and about analogous practices in the United States and the extent to which women here are driven to various violations of their bodies was productive, but while it de-exoticized women who have experienced clitoridectomies, it did not adequately explore other crucial dimensions of their lives. The question these sessions, and others, raised for us but did not answer was, To what extent can feminist activism be "global" without reinscribing the vestiges of colonial/neocolonial relations of power?

During the visit of two members of Sistren, the Jamaican activist theater group, issues of language and action became paramount, as well as questions about the relation between art and activism. Sistren performs in the Creole of working class Jamaican women, the daily language of most of its members and its audience. American ears are not attuned to its diction and rhythms, and students who had difficulty following the dramatic pieces were surprised that our visitors could also speak standard English quite eloquently. In the wake of their visit, we considered the political implications of Sistren's choice, including the issue of who chooses or is able to speak what language, when, for what reasons. Speaking a language that is difficult for the privileged to understand may mark a solidarity among the colonized, or may mark an insistence on the specificity and vitality of local cultures in the face of a cultural globalization that most typically speaks standard English. Since Sistren's presentations addressed, among other themes, the "globalization" through mass culture of Western criteria for beauty, the refusal to perform in a standard Western dialect could also be read as a resistance to a standardized aesthetics of the body.

Student research and presentations were an important part of the class; indeed, I relied on the students to help bring the specificity and richness of particular cultural settings into the classroom. One group gave an excellent presentation on women, tourism, and sex tourism in Thailand, drawing on Thai women's writings on the subject as well as secondary research. Another group, building on an earlier session featuring a set of readings from Moghadam's *Identity Politics and Women,* addressed in greater depth the vexed issue of women and the rise of new fundamentalisms, providing a theoretical framework for thinking about gender and fundamentalism across religions, and then exploring the conflict and the responses of local women activists in Pakistan, India, and the United States. A third group considered women's health and reproductive rights in India, in an uneven but interesting presentation that combined an interpretation of Mahasweta Devi's "Breast-Giver" (1987) with data on class, gender, and health in rural India.

As in many courses associated with the Women's Studies, Area and International Studies (WSAIS) projects, we struggled with only partial success to strike the right balance between an emphasis on the global and the local, the general and the specific. In an effort to cover a great deal of ground, I assigned too many readings and we spent too little time on them individually. We learned a little about women's experiences on many issues in many countries, and we learned a lot about contemporary feminist thought as it intersects with work on colonialism, decolonization, and globalization. Ironically, much of that thought originates with Western feminists or with "deterritorialized" elites. With no background in any area study other than American studies, I often felt out of my depth and unable to do more than raise questions. Still, I think our questions pushed usefully at the boundaries of women's studies, at least women's studies as I had practiced it until my involvement with the WSAIS project. Certainly I will never teach again in a way that simply assumes the United States as the center of a perceptual and geographic universe.

The most satisfying dimension of the course is the hardest to repli-cate: our time with scholars and artists (as well as a number of inter-national students in the class) from several different countries of origin, whose very voices and faces reminded us of the international diversity among women and the possibilities for exchange and action across borders. In subsequent years, though, I have taught the course without the embodied presence of more than one or two women from diverse national origins. I have relied on well-vetted videos, on per-sonal essay and memoir, and on the power of fictional representations (restoring Marshall's *Daughters,* for example) to facilitate students' encounters with the complex individuality of "Others" from different geographic sites. I have also added more recent readings about the subject that has always remained at the center of the course: the prac-tices and possibilities for transnational feminist alliances for social change.[5]

NOTES

1. See my essay written with A. Lynn Bolles, "Internationalizing and 'Engendering' the Curriculum at the University of Maryland," in part 3 of this volume.
2. Bibliographic information for most of the works used in the course can be found in the appended syllabus. For full citation information for films mentioned below, see the annotated bibliography "Women Around the World," also included in this volume.
3. I now use Seager (1997).
4. See my "Culturally Challenging Practices and Pedagogical Strategies," in part 3 of this volume.
5. Especially useful anthologies in this regard include Alexander and Mohanty (1997) and Shohat (1998).

WORKS CITED

Alexander, M. Jacqui, and Chandra Talpade Mohanty, eds. 1997. *Feminist Genealogies, Colonial Legacies, Democratic Futures.* New York: Routledge.
Devi, Mahasweta. 1987. "Breast-Giver," translated by Gayatri Chakravorty Spivak, eds. In Gayatri Chakravorty Spivak, *In Other Worlds: Essays in Cultural Politics.* New York: Methuen.
Newton, Judith, and Deborah S. Rosenfelt. 1985. "Toward a Materialist Feminist Criticism." In Judith Newton and Deborah S. Rosenfelt, eds., *Feminist Criticism and Social Change,* New York: Methuen.
Seager, Joni. 1997. *The State of Women in the World Atlas.* London: Penguin.
Shohat, Ella, ed. 1998. *Talking Visions: Multicultural Feminism in a Transnational Age.* New York: New Museum of Contemporary Art; Cambridge, Mass.: MIT Press.

GLOBALIZATION, GENDER, AND CULTURE: SYLLABUS

This course will examine the ways in which women's lives and local cultures are being affected by global processes of economic, political, and technological change; and will explore some of the issues of identity and action and some of the forms of cultural expression that have emerged as women respond politically and aesthetically to these changes.

Objectives

By the end of this course you should (1) have a better understanding of some contemporary economic, cultural, and social processes that are shaping and reshaping the contexts in which women in different geographic and structural locations live and work; (2) have some knowledge of the tensions in women's lives—and in their discourses—between the gendered expectations of "traditional" cultures and the forces of change, including economic imperatives, new political formations, and Western and indigenous feminisms; (3) become acquainted with some of the forms of cultural production—literature, the arts, media; with some of the modes of activism; and with some of the thought and vision through which women locally and internationally have defined and implemented their own priorities for change; and (4) both encounter and engage in feminist research and theory about relations among contemporary social change, women's lives, and cultural production.

Required Texts

Course pack (bibliographic information for these readings given in outline below).
Beijing Declaration and Platform for Action. New York: United Nations Department of Public Information, 1996.
Kidron, Michael, and Ronald Segal. *The State of the World Atlas.* Rev. ed. London: Penguin, 1995.
Kincaid, Jamaica. *A Small Place.* London: Virago, 1988.
Moghadam, Valentine M., ed. *Identity Politics and Women: Cultural Reassertions and Feminisms in International Perspective.* Boulder, Colo.: Westview Press, 1994.
Shohat, Ella, and Robert Stam. *Unthinking Eurocentrism: Multiculturalism and the Media.* New York: Routledge, 1994.
Walker, Alice. *Possessing the Secret of Joy.* New York: Simon and Schuster, 1992; Pocket Books, 1993. (If you have already read *Possessing,* you are advised to read Nawal El Saadawi, *Woman at Point Zero.* London: Zed Books, 1983, or Ngugi wa Thiong'o, *The River Between.* London: Heinemann, 1965.)

Requirements

Requirements include regular attendance and participation, essay summaries and discussion questions for specific classes, a midterm journal/paper, and a research project resulting in a classroom presentation and a final paper.

Research Projects

We are all engaged in a challenging undertaking: exploring new ground together and sharing what we learn across disciplinary and geographic boundaries. Your research projects are a crucial part of this process. You should begin working on your projects early in the course. Ideally, you will work together in pairs or even larger groups on these projects, so that you will have someone to talk with about ideas and problems, to share the labor of research by dividing up sections into manageable parts, to brainstorm with about the design of your teaching unit, and even to share in the final writing (though you may also choose to write separate papers on different aspects of the research). Collaboration is not required, but it is strongly encouraged.

1. Pick a particular country (not the United States, unless it is part of a group project looking at an issue across national boundaries) or possibly region to focus on, and pick one particular aspect of contemporary cultural expression in that location. (By *contemporary*, I mean approximately within the last twenty years, but that's somewhat flexible.) Your project might examine the work of a particular writer, artist, or filmmaker; the cultural productions of a group or collective; innovations in religious or spiritual practice; the publications or demonstrations of women's activist groups, etc.

2. Your project should contain information about the economic, social, and political situation in the country or area you examine, especially issues and changes that are affecting women's lives. You should ground your discussion of aesthetic, cultural, or religious practices and activism in that larger context.

3. Finally, you should connect your subject of inquiry to some of the overarching issues and global processes and connections we've discussed during the semester, using and drawing on appropriate readings from the course as part of your research.

4. Your classroom presentation should be on the same topic as your research paper, but it could differ from it substantially in emphasis and focus. For example, you might want to use film clips, an overhead projector, music, or other audiovisual aids for your class presentation, and/or you might want to make one or two points and then lead a class discussion about a text you've assigned.

Course Outline

Week 1. Defining Globalization *and an Overview—The World's Women: An Agenda for Action*

Richard Falk, "The Making of Global Citizenship," in *Global Visions: Beyond the New World Order*, ed. Jeremy Brecher, John Brown Childs, and Jill Cutler (Boston: South End, 1993).
International Women's Tribune Center, "Mapping Our Route," *Preview*, no. 4 (January 1995): 2–3.
Beijing Platform, pp. 1–34.

Week 2. Women in the Global Economy

Kidron and Segal, *World Atlas*, maps 4, 6, 9, 10, 11, 12, 14, 15, 22, 25, 26.
Richard J. Barnet and John Cavanagh, selection from *Global Dreams: Imperial Corporations and the New World Order* (New York: Simon and Schuster, 1994).
Shelley Feldman, "Crises, Poverty, and Gender Inequality: Current Themes and

Issues," in *Unequal Burden: Economic Crises, Persistent Poverty, and Women's Work*, ed. Lourdes Benería and Shelley Feldman (Boulder: Westview Press, 1992).

Pamela Sparr, selection from *Mortgaging Women's Lives: Feminist Critiques of Structural Adjustment* (London: Zed Books, 1994).

Beijing Platform, sections on women and poverty, education and training of women, women and the economy, women and health.

C. Mark Blackden and Elizabeth Morris-Hughes, "Paradigm Postponed: Gender and Economic Adjustment in Sub-Saharan Africa," World Bank paper, 1993.

Week 3. Women, Work, and Family

Kidron and Segal, *World Atlas*, maps 23–24.

Kathryn Ward, introduction, *Women Workers and Global Restructuring* (Ithaca: ILR Press, 1990).

Esther Ngan-ling Chow and Catherine White Berheide, "Studying Women, Families, and Policies Globally," in *Women, the Family, and Policy,* ed. Esther Ngan-ling Chow and Catherine White Berheide (Albany: State University of New York Press, 1994).

Joan Acker, "Women, Families, and Public Policy in Sweden," in Chow and Berheide, *Women.*

A. Lynn Bolles, "Surviving Manley and Seaga," *Review of Radical Political Economics* 23, nos. 3 & 4 (1991): 20–36.

Seung-kyung Kim, "Big Companies Don't Hire Us, Married Women: Exploitation and Empowerment Among Women Workers in Korea," *Feminist Studies* (forthcoming).

Dorinne K. Kondo, selection from *Crafting Selves: Power, Gender, and Discourses of Identity in a Japanese Workplace* (Chicago: University of Chicago Press, 1990).

Week 4. Identity, Culture, Consciousness, and Resistance

Valentine M. Moghadam, "Women and Identity Politics in Theoretical and Comparative Perspective" in Moghadam, *Identity Politics.*

Inderpal Grewal and Caren Kaplan, "Introduction: Transnational Feminist Practices and Questions of Postmodernity," in *Scattered Hegemonies: Postmodernity and Trans-national Feminist Practices,* ed. Inderpal Grewal and Caren Kaplan (Minneapolis: University of Minnesota Press, 1994).

Barbara Harlow, chap. 1 in *Resistance Literature* (New York: Methuen, 1987).

Gloria Anzaldúa, chap. 7, "La conciencia de la mestiza: Towards a New Consciousness," and "To Live in the Borderlands Means You. . . ," in *Borderlands/ La Frontera: The New Mestiza* (San Francisco: Aunt Lute Books, 1987).

Mary K. DeShazer, "We Make Freedom: Historicizing Contemporary Women's Resistance Poetry," in *A Poetics of Resistance: Women Writing in El Salvador, South Africa, and the United States* (Ann Arbor: University of Michigan Press, 1994).

Bharati Mukherjee, "The Management of Grief," in *The Middleman and Other Stories* (New York: Fawcett, 1988).

Week 5. Unthinking Eurocentrism: Gender, Culture, and the Global Media

Public Lecture and Classroom Guest: Ella Shohat.
Shohat and Stam, *Unthinking Eurocentrism,* esp. chaps. 1, 4, and 6–9.
Beijing Platform, section 4, J: Women and the Media.

Week 6. Discourses on Female Genital Surgeries

In-class film: *Warrior Marks*; clips from *Finzan.*
Selections from Alice Walker and Pratibha Parmar, *Warrior Marks: Female Genital Mutilation and the Sexual Blinding of Women* (New York: Harcourt Brace, 1993).

Week 7. Discourses on Female Genital Surgeries (cont.)

Public Lecture and Guest: Tuzyline Jita Allan.
Walker, *Possessing.*
Flora Nwapa, chap. 1 in *Efuru* (London: Heinemann, 1966).
Sondra Hale, "The 'Female Circumcision' Controversy and the Politics of Knowledge," *Ufahumu Journal of the African Activist Association* 22, no. 3 (fall 1994): 26–35.
Isabelle R. Gunning, "Arrogant Perception, World-Travelling and Multicultural Feminism: The Case of Female Genital Surgeries," *Columbia Human Rights Law Review* 23, no. 2 (summer 1992): 18–48.

Week 9. Identities, Cultures, and Rights

Kidron and Segal, *World Atlas,* map 45.
Further readings from Moghadam, *Identity Politics* (to be announced).
Beijing Platform, section 1, Human Rights of Women.

Week 10. Class and Cultural Activism

Performance by Sistren and workshop/discussion with Sistren members.
Excerpts from Honor Ford Smith, *Lionheart Gal: Life Stories of Jamaican Women* (London: Women's Press, 1968).
Scripts provided by Sistren.

Week 11. Women and Tourism

This unit is tentative. Perhaps some of you might want to work on women and tourism or women and the international sex trade for your own projects. Let's see how your research projects shape up.

Kincaid, *A Small Place.*
Cynthia Abbott Cone, "Crafting Selves: The Lives of Two Mayan Women," *Annals of Tourism Research* 22, no. 2 (1995): 314–327.

Barbara A. Babcock, "Mudwomen and Whitemen: A Meditation on Pueblo Potteries and the Politics of Representation," in *Discovered Country: Tourism and Survival in the American West*, eds. Scott Norris (Albuquerque: University of New Mexico Press, 1994) 180–195.

Week 12. Global Feminisms

I would like to see at least one group research project comparatively examining the question of what forms feminist movements/women's movements take in different locations, what their central issues are, what contradictions they confront or embody, what social and material texts they have produced.

Beijing Platform, remaining sections.
Kidron and Segal, *World Atlas,* maps 14–18.

Week 13. Sexualities and Transnational Migrations

Public Lecture and Guest: Lourdes Arguelles.
Lourdes Arguelles and Anne M. Rivero, "Gender/Sexual Orientation Violence and Transnational Migration, Conversations with Some Latinas We Think We Know" (Claremont Colleges: The Institute, 1993).
Lourdes Arguelles, "Crazy Wisdom: Memories of a Cuban Queer," in *Sisters, Sexperts, Queers,* ed. Arlene Stein (New York: Plume, 1993).
Kidron and Segal, *World Atlas,* map 49.

Weeks 14–15. Classroom Presentations

MIGRANTSCAPES: READING ITALIAN DIASPORA

Susanna F. Ferlito

In the process of developing a new course on migrant identities, my thinking about the syllabus changed substantially. I was originally interested in creating a course that would focus on Italian literary and cultural representations of migration from the late nineteenth century to the present. Because my research and teaching are primarily in modern Italian literature and culture, I felt relatively at ease in expanding my interests to include literary representations of emigration from Italy and, more recently, of immigration to Italy. The syllabus, as I envisioned it, would broach these representations of migration in a chronological fashion—moving from a study of Italy as a major European exporter nation of emigrant labor in the late nineteenth century to a view of its current status as a major European nation of immigrant labor from North Africa, Asia, and Eastern Europe. Within this framework I wanted to privilege stories told by and about migrant women as well as to include Italian feminist writings introducing students to ways of thinking about gender in Italy. In short, I thought my course would serve well to internationalize the curriculum, and, with its focus on issues of gender and women, would appeal to a wide range of students from women's studies, history, anthropology, and area studies to Italian studies and comparative literature.

In the course of preparing the syllabus, several theoretical and practical questions emerged: How was I to teach a course on migration to and from Italy if I knew little about the political and cultural backgrounds from which immigrants originated? Would extra readings increase sensitivity to the conditions and representations of the Senegalese community in Turin, for example, or to the conditions of migrant women from Sri Lanka living in Milan? How should I divide the syllabus in order to make questions of gender integral to the study? How would the course negotiate between global and local issues, between different languages and cultural scenarios? Would it be possible to embrace a global framework, and remain, at the same time, committed to promoting a culturally sensitive understanding of local knowledge, languages, and cultures? What pedagogical strategies would enable students from different disciplines and at different stages of their undergraduate and graduate studies to engage in a collaborative effort as they worked among different languages, cultures, and disciplinary perspectives?

At first, I thought I might compensate for my lack of expertise by adding more reading materials to the syllabus and inviting guest lecturers to provide their expertise about different areas of the world. But as I sought to revise the already lengthy reading list, cutting here and adding there, I realized that from a pedagogical and intellectual perspective it would be crucial to bring the question of expertise into our discussions rather than efface it or solve it by way of supplementation. Rather than trying to make up for it, the question of expertise could offer an opportunity to examine how disciplines like anthropology and comparative literature, for example, specialize in comparing cultural differences. We would explore in the course of our readings how some cultures and migrant identities are constructed as more Other than others—how, for example, countries like Italy, Spain, and Portugal have been historically represented in Europe itself as internal Others. In short, instead of presupposing essential cultural differences, we would investigate how differences are produced, sustained, and enforced in an increasingly globalized world. Our discussions would focus as much on the subject matter—migrant identities—as on disciplinary investments in defining cultural differences and representations of otherness.

Once I began to think of teaching the course from a starting point that did not presume essential differences between cultures but examined their production through topographies of power, time, and space, the organization of the syllabus began to come into focus. I designed a course in which students would explore, from a variety of disciplinary perspectives, how issues of gender, class, race, and ethnicity shape practices and experiences of migration. The geopolitical and cultural space of Italy would provide a local frame of analysis for thinking about the constructions of migrant identities in a globalized world. Instead of supplementing the syllabus with extra readings about Other cultures (reinforcing thereby a language of essentialized differences), I would place under critical scrutiny how notions of otherness, home, place, space, culture, identity, and nationhood get constructed and represented. In this frame, I would juxtapose questions of nineteenth-century nation building and migration with contemporary issues of postcolonial displacements. In this way the studies of past and present constructions of migrant identities would not follow a chronological and implicitly teleological discourse of progress, modernity, and civilization. I had presupposed that a course on migration would inherently "internationalize" the curriculum, because students would be reading and thinking about not only migrant Italian women, but about women from Senegal, Sri Lanka, China, Morocco, Albania, Hungary, the Philippines, Somalia, Eritrea, the Dominican Republic, Mauritius, Cape Verde, Salvador, and so on. But in my rethinking of the course I realized that it internationalizes the curriculum not because it adds a course on migration to the course offerings but because it examines critically how people move, live, and work across spaces and places we have only scrutinized between—inter—nations.

I have divided the syllabus into five thematic sections, each emphasizing stories and experiences of migrant women and foregrounding feminist readings of migration practices as shaped by gender, class, race, and ethnicity. Each thematic session will provide one or more readings about the Italian context, but my goal in each session is to keep the readings moving flexibly between local and global questions, past and present histories, rather than shuttling between sessions on Italy and patterns of migration elsewhere. With this in mind, the first two weeks offer students a large theoretical framework within which to raise questions of migrancy, identity. and culture—issues that are revisited throughout the course as students think about migrant identities from multiple perspectives and positions. In the introductory weeks, I explore with students their understanding of migration and experiences of displacement. In a first meeting, for example, I would ask students to think of related words and forms of migration (i.e., travel, displacement, tourism, exile, immigration, emigration, nomadism) and antonyms (rooted, sedentary). Other questions might include, What cultural values are attached to different kinds of displacements? For what reasons do people leave home (reasons of health, work, leisure, political constraints, evasion)? How are travel practices shaped by class, gender, and race? What are the more common markers or signs that one has traveled (languages, passport, borders, visas)?

These questions, raised at the beginning of the course, enable students to begin thinking critically about definitions of home, identity, and culture and to examine how their answers change and become more complex in the course of their subsequent readings. From the third to the fifth weeks, the class focuses on a variety of perspectives to explore the links between women migrants and colonial practices. In weeks six to eight, the readings and film focus on ways of thinking about home and explore notions of nostalgia, memory, and history. From the ninth to the eleventh weeks, Carlo Levi's novel *Christ Stopped at Eboli* functions as a literary text through which to explore constructions of otherness and experiences of migration. The novel, extremely captivating and easy to read both in Italian and English, introduces students to questions of political confinement and emigration during the 1930s in Italy. In the last thematic section of the course, students explore ways of knowing that are often marginalized, suppressed, or ignored and examine the links between language, culture, and identity.

From a pedagogical point of view, my challenge is to bring students from different disciplinary backgrounds and levels of preparation to work together. I expect the course to enroll somewhere between twenty to twenty-five students and for there to be an equal division between undergraduate and graduate students who might or might not be readers of Italian. In order to negotiate among different levels of preparation, I specify throughout the syllabus which readings are required for graduate students and undergraduate students; I also differentiate between graded assignments. At the end of each thematic session I include a list of suggested further readings. I want to ensure that each student has a clear sense of what will be required, but I also want to create a classroom based on a strong sense of collaboration among students so that each student might participate with an equal sense of commitment and energy.

In order to foster collaborative work I have built into the syllabus two extra sessions for readers of Italian and other languages, enabling them to work on untranslated material (literature, film, articles, interviews, etc.) that they would then present to the class. This exercise not only gives readers of Italian an opportunity to examine works that have not been translated, but is also a practical way of making visible to the class at large the problems of translation and thereby the limited accessibility of information. In a course that examines constructions of migrant identities, the fact that there are no English translations of the novels, essays, and autobiographies now being written by immigrants in Italy (often written in collaboration with an Italian) is a real problem that can be addressed only in part by these extra sessions.

By examining the construction of migrant identities in Italy through the lens of gender, I seek to question a range of assumptions about past and present histories of migration. Rather than devoting sections of the syllabus to a series of issues—gender, identity, migration, and the Italian context (sections from which students move on)—I wanted to structure my course in a way that renders questions of gender inseparable from a critical thinking about migrant identities and international migration practices.

SYLLABUS

This course explores past and contemporary theories and practices of constructing immigrant identities from a variety of interdisciplinary perspectives. Italy, with its current immigration "crisis" and its traumatic history of nineteenth-century emigrations, will provide us with a local frame of analysis for thinking about constructions of migrant identities in a globalized world. Our readings will raise a wide range of questions ranging from ways of reading global-local relations (how do we experience locality in a globalized, deterritorialized world? Who does this "we" refer to, include, exclude, forget?), to questions of how gender, class, race, and ethnicity shape practices and experiences of migration, to investigating ways of reading Italy's contemporary crisis as a major European receiver country of immigrant labor in light of its past emigrations and history of nation building.

Inseparable from these questions raised by local-global migrant practices is an analysis of changing institutional and disciplinary practices. How are disciplines like anthropology, area studies, and comparative literature—disciplines that specialize in the differences (or similarities) between cultures and their representation—rethinking their comparative readings of other cultures in today's increasingly globalized world? Our discussion will focus as much on the subject matter—migrant identities—as they will on disciplinary investments in defining cultural differences and representations of otherness. Divided into five thematic sections, the syllabus privileges stories and experiences of migrant women and foregrounds feminist readings of migration practices as shaped by gender.

Required Texts

Gisela Brinker-Gabler and Sidonie Smith, eds., *Writing New Identities: Gender, Nation and Immigration in Contemporary Europe* (Minneapolis: Minnesota University Press, 1997).

Carlo Levi, *Christ Stopped at Eboli* (London: Cassell, 1967). *Cristo s'e' fermato a Eboli* (Turin: Einaudi, 1990).

David Forgacs and Robert Lumley, eds., *Italian Cultural Studies: An Introduction* (London: Oxford University Press, 1996).

Donal Carter, *States of Grace: Senegalese in Italy and the New European Immigration* (Minneapolis: Minnesota University Press, 1997).

Tentative Schedule of Readings

Migrancy, Culture, Identities (Weeks 1 and 2)

Week 1

Arjun Appadurai, "Disjuncture and Difference in the Global Cultural Economy." *Public Culture* 2(2)(1990). Undergraduate required/graduate required.

Akhil Gupta and James Ferguson, "Beyond 'Culture': Space, Identity, and the Politics of Difference," in *Culture, Power, Place: Explorations in Critical Anthropology*, ed. Akhil Gupta and James Ferguson (Durham, N.C.: Duke University Press, 1997). Undergraduate required/graduate required.

John Agnew, "The Myth of Backward Italy in Modern Europe," in *Revisioning Italy: National Identity and Global Culture*, ed. Beverly Allen and Mary Russo (Minneapolis: Minnesota University Press, 1997). Undergraduate required/graduate required.

Janice Monk, "Place Matters: Comparative International Perspectives on Feminist Geography." *Professional Geographer* 46(3)(1994): 277–88. Graduate required.

Week 2

Geoffrey Nowell-Smith, "Italy: Tradition, Backwardness and Modernity," in *Culture and Conflict in Postwar Italy: Essays on Mass and Popular Culture*, ed. Zygmunt Baranski and Robert Lumley (New York: St. Martin's Press, 1990). Undergraduate required/graduate required.

Dipesh Chakrabarty, "Provincializing Europe: Postcoloniality and the Critique of History." *Cultural Studies* 6(3)(1992): 337–57. Undergraduate required/graduate required.

Pasquale Verdicchio, *Bound by Distance* (Madison, N.J.: Fairleigh Dickinson University Press, 1997). Undergraduate required/graduate required.

Doreen Massey, "A Place Called 'Home'?" in *Space, Place, and Gender* (Minneapolis: Minnesota University Press, 1994). Graduate required.

Suggested Readings for Weeks 1 and 2

Caren Kaplan, "The Politics of Location as Transnational Feminist Practices," in *Scattered Hegemonies: Postmodernity and Transnational Feminist Practices,* ed. Inderpal Grewal and Caren Kaplan. (Minneapolis: Minnesota University Press, 1994).

James Clifford, *Routes: Travel and Translation in the Late Twentieth Century* (Cambridge: Harvard University Press, 1997).

Gerard Delanty, *Inventing Europe: Idea, Identity, Reality* (New York: St Martin's Press, 1995).

Women, Migration, Empire (Weeks 3 Through 5)

Week 3

Donna Gabaccia, "In the Shadows of the Periphery: Italian Women in the Nineteenth-Century," in *Connecting Spheres: Women in the Western World: 1500 to the Present,* ed. Jean Quateart and Marilyn Boxer (New York: Oxford University Press, 1987), 166–76. Undergraduate required/graduate required.

Giovanna Campani, "Women Migrants: From Marginal Subjects to Social Actors," in *The Cambridge Survey of World Migration,* ed. Robin Cohen (Cambridge: Cambridge University Press, 1995), 546–50. Undergraduate required/graduate required.

"Feminism and the Critique of Colonial Discourse." Special issue of *Inscriptions* 3/4(1988). Graduate required.

Michael Kearney, "Borders and Boundaries of State and Self at the End of the Empire." *Journal of Historical Sociology* 4(1)(1991): 52–74. Undergraduate required/graduate required.

Week 4

Teresa A. Barnes, "The Fight for Control of African Women's Mobility in Colonial Zimababwe, 1900–1939." *Signs* 17(3)(1992): 586–608. Undergraduate required/graduate required.

Gisela Brinker-Gabler and Sidonie Smith, "Gender, Nation, and Immigration in the New Europe," in *Writing New Identities: Gender, Nation and Immigration in Contemporary Europe,* ed. Gisela Brinker-Gabler and Sidonie Smith (Minneapolis: Minnesota University Press, 1997).

Keya Gangulay, "Migrant Identities: Personal Memory and the Construction of Selfhood." *Cultural Studies* 6(1)(1992): 27–50. Undergraduate required/graduate required.

Chandra Mohanty, "Under Western Eyes: Feminist Scholarship and Colonial Discourse," in *Third World Women and the Politics of Feminism,* ed. Chandra Mohanty, Ann Russo, and Lourdes Torres (Bloomington: Indiana University, 1991). Undergraduate required/graduate required.

Week 5

Stephan Castles, "Italians in Australia: Building a Multicultural Society on the Pacific Rim." *Diaspora* 1(1)(Spring 1991): 45–66. Undergraduate required/graduate required.

William A. Douglas, "Migration in Italy," in *Urban Life in Mediterranean Europe: Anthropological Perspectives,* ed. Michael Kenny and David I. Kertzer (Urbana and Chicago: University of Illinois Press, 1983). Undergraduate required/ graduate required.

Suggested Readings for Weeks 3 Through 5

Robert Miles and Dietrich Thranhardt, eds., *Migration and European Integration: The Dynamics of Inclusion and Exclusion* (London: Pinter, 1995).

David Parker, *Through Different Eyes: The Cultural Identities of Young Chinese People in Britain* (Aldershot: Avebury, 1995).

A Place Called "Home?": Deterritorializations (Weeks 6 Through 8)

Week 6

Angelika Bammer, ed., "The Question of Home." *New Formations* 17 (1992): entire issue. Undergraduate required/graduate required.

George E. Bishart, "Exile to Compatriot: Transformations in the Social Identity of Palestinean Refugees in the West Bank," in *Culture, Power, Place: Explorations in Critical Anthropology,* ed. Akhil Gupta and James Ferguson (Durham, N.C.: Duke University Press, 1997). Undergraduate required/graduate required.

Marco Martiniello, "Italy: The Late Discovery," in *Europe: A New Immigration Continent: Policies and Politics in Comparative Perspective,* ed. Dietrich Thranhardt. (Munster: Lit Verlag, 1992), 195–218. Undergraduate required/graduate required.

Kathleen Stewart, "Nostalgia: A Polemic." *Cultural Anthropology* 3(3)(1988): 227–41. Graduate required.

Week 7

Vittorio and Paolo Taviani, *"L'altro Figlio" Kaos,* 1984 (film).

Italian readers: L. Pirandello, "L'altro Figlio," in *Novelle per un anno* (Firenze: Giunti, 1994). Undergraduate required/graduate required.

Giovanna Campani, "Immigration and Racism in Southern Europe: The Italian Case." *Ethnic and Racial Studies* 16(3)(1993): 507–35. Undergraduate required/graduate required.

Armando Montanari and Antonio Cortese, "Third World Immigrants in Italy," in *Mass Migration in Europe: The Legacy and the Future,* ed. Russell King (London: Belhaven Press, 1993). Undergraduate required/graduate required.

Week 8

Inderpal Grewal, "The Postcolonial, Ethnic Studies and the Diaspora: The Contexts of Ethnic Immigrant/Migrant Cultural Studies in the U.S." *Socialist Review* 94(4)(1994): 45–74. Undergraduate required/graduate required.

Aihwa Ong, "On the Edge of Empires: Flexible Citizenship Among Chinese in Diaspora." *Positions* 1(3)(1993).

Extra Meeting for Italian Readers

Tahar Ben Jelloun, "Villa Literno," in *Dove lo Stato non c'e'*, ed. Egi Volterrani (Turin: Einaudi, 1990). Undergraduate required/graduate required.

Suggested Readings for Weeks 6 Through 8

Caren Kaplan, "Becoming Nomad: Poststructuralist Deterritorializations," in *Questions of Travel: Postmodern Discourses of Displacement* (Durham, N.C.: Duke University Press, 1996), 65–100.

Gloria Anzaldúa, *Borderlands: The New Mestiza = La Frontera* (San Francisco: Spinsters/Aunt Lute, 1987).

Graziella Parati, "Strangers in Paradise: Foreigners and Shadows in Italian Literature," in *Revisioning Italy*, ed. Beverly Allen and Mary Russo (Minneapolis: University of Minnesota Press, 1997).

Global Villages–Invisible Cities (weeks 9 through 11)

Week 9

Carlo Levi, *Christ Stopped at Eboli* (London: Cassell, 1967); *Cristo s'e' fermato a Eboli* (Turin: Einaudi, 1990).

Clips from Francesco Rosi's film version of the novel.

Week 10

Donald Carter, *States of Grace: Senegalese in Italy and the New European Immigration* (Minneapolis: Minnesota University Press, 1997).

Calvanese Francesco and Enrico Pugliese, "Emigration and Immigration in Italy: Recent Trends." *Labour* 2(3) (1988): 181–99.

Laura Corradi, "When Immigration Is Seclusion. The African-Italian Labor Force." *Social Problems* (1993): 1–18.

Week 11

Lisa Lowe, "Literary Nomadics in Francophone Allegories of Postcolonialism: Pham Van Ky and Tahar Ben Jelloun." *Yale French Studies* 82(1993): 43–61.

Clara Gallini, "Dangerous Games: Racism as Practiced in Italian Popular Culture." *Cultural Studies* 6:(2)(1989): 207–17. Undergraduate required/graduate required.

Extra Meeting for Italian Readers

Nassera Chohra, *Volevo diventare bianca,* ed. Alessandra Atti di Sarro (Roma: Edizione e/o, 1993).

Suggested readings for weeks 9 through 11

J. B. Bosworth, *Italy and the Wider World: 1860–1960* (New York: Routledge, 1996).

Francoise Lionnet, "Spaces of Comparison," in *Comparative Literature in the Age of Multiculturalism,* ed. Charles Bernheimer (Baltimore: Johns Hopkins, 1995).

Mary Louise Pratt, *Imperial Eyes: Travel Writing and Transculturation* (London: Routledge, 1991).

Ways of Knowing: Stories, Gossip, Silence, Problematics of Translation (Weeks 12 through 14)

Week 12

Jennifer A. Gonzales and Michelle Habell-Pallan, "Heterotopias and Shared Methods of Resistance: Navigating Social Spaces and Spaces of Identity," *Inscriptions* 7(1994): 80–104.

Maria Crozgate and Omari Kokoli, eds., *Cultural Encounters: Gender and the Intersec-tion of the Local and the Global in Africa* (London: Routledge, 1979).

Week 13

R. D. Grillo, "The Representations of Problems and the Problems of Representation," in *Ideologies and Institutions in Urban France: The Representations of Immigrants* (Cambridge: Cambridge University Press, 1985), 259–80. Undergraduate required/ graduate required.

Catherine Boone, "The Making of a Rentier Class: Wealth Accumulation and Political Control in Senegal." *Journal of Development Studies* 22(3)(1990). Undergraduate required/graduate required.

Week 14

Vittoria A. Goddard, *Gender, Family, and Work in Naples* (Oxford: Berg, 1996).

Vittoria A. Goddard, "From the Mediterranean to Europe: Honour, Kinship and Gender," in *The Anthropology of Europe: Identity and Boundaries in Conflict,* ed. Victoria Goddard, Joseph R Llobera, and Cris Shore (Oxford: Berg, 1984).

Suggested Readings for Weeks 12 Through 14

Katy Gardner, "Global Migrants," *Global Migrants, Local Lives: Travel and Transformation in Rural Bangladesh* (Oxford: Clarendon Press, 1995).

Diana Cammack, "Development and Forced Migration: The Case of Afghan Refugee Women in Pakistan," in *The Cambridge Survey of World Migration,* ed. Robin Cohen (Cambridge: Cambridge University Press, 1995), 546–50.

DEVIANCE, DELINQUENCY, AND SOCIAL REFORM IN LATIN AMERICA, 1870–1945: A HISTORY COURSE

KATHERINE ELAINE BLISS

Broadly speaking, the purpose of this course is to introduce students to the relationship between economic development, demographic change, and social reform in Latin America over a seventy-five-year period. Like Germany, France, England, and the United States, nations in Latin America enacted legislation centered around state provision of social assistance between 1870 and 1945. Like their counterparts in Europe and North America, the primarily elite and middle class Latin American reformers were concerned with such topics as urban public health, widespread illiteracy, child abandonment, and juvenile delinquency. They worried about how the popularity of leisure activities including drinking, prostitution, and gambling hampered national industrial development. And they lamented the ways in which illegitimacy, the spread of contagious diseases, and workers' lack of vocational training stunted economic progress. Politicians in this period, as well as feminists, social workers, doctors, and lawyers, attempted to eliminate these social ills and reform city life in two ways. First, they worked to alter civil, sanitary, and penal codes with respect to family composition, marital responsibility, and sexual relations. Second, they created public beneficent institutions to aid, educate, and "re-adapt" the populace.

This course specifically works to encourage students to think about the ways in which conceptualizations of gender, class, race, and national identity shaped Latin American reform movements. Some research suggests that Latin Americans either copied European and North American progressive models or that the establishment of regional social insurance regimes represented natural steps in a logical pattern of modernization. Other work has suggested the utility of an approach that is sensitive to how welfare efforts evolve in distinct historical settings. Archival investigation on Latin American cities, for example, has highlighted the ways in which export-led growth and the establishment of commercial agricultural projects encouraged international migration, promoted population movement from the countryside to metropolitan areas, and stimulated the growth of an urban work force along lines similar to modernization in Europe and the United States. But historians who research Latin American urban social dynamics note that these patterns provoked a unique confluence of demographic, ideological, and political conditions in a context of industrial development arising less because of local demand than because of North American and European economic expansion.

Analysts of this era have noted that Latin American reformers' concerns over such issues as whether the indigenous "tropical" or "fanatical" temperaments of their cities' populations were even remotely conducive to progress suggests that regional welfare discussions had origins distinct from those of North American and European progressivism. Others have pointed to heated national debates over the "predatory" nature of the Mexican male or the "masculine" nature of the working woman in Argentina to show that concerns over inferiority and degeneration, in particular, dominated these discussions. In fact, some authors argue that in Latin America social reform became a battleground in which different groups struggled to define their nations in terms of their unusual ethnic, racial, and religious compositions. Reformers described their nations in *opposition* to what they perceived as the "homogeneous" societies with which they had increasing contact during the late nineteenth and early twentieth centuries, rather than in imitation of them.

Taking such debates over the origins and development of social reform as a point of departure, this undergraduate course works to accomplish three things. First, it introduces students to historiographical arguments over the nature and origins of reform and welfare. Readings on welfare history theory as well as brief case studies of European and North American reform movements provide students with the background to answer the following questions: Where are the economic and social conditions in which reform efforts arise? Who are the reformers? Who are they trying to reform? What are the class, gender, and racial differences between these groups? In particular, how do the gender differences between the reformers and those they hoped to reform influence welfare policies? What are the differences between reformers and "delinquents," in terms of geographic origin? What do the reformers want to change? What steps do they take to do this? How do those being reformed respond? And what tools and evidence can historians employ to understand the motivations and effects of reformism?

Second, the course introduces students to some of the most current issues in Latin American social history. Recent work that examines the cultural dimension of reform politics has highlighted the ways in which ideas about gender and race permeated all aspects of policy development and implementation. The focus of published research on regional social reform as well as the nature of the semester system makes a limited, comparative approach to this discussion the most practical. The readings center around work on Brazil, Mexico, and Argentina and are organized thematically, with an emphasis on articles, book chapters, and monographs. Students draw comparisons among the ways Latin Americans, Europeans, and North Americans dealt with common issues such as prostitution, drinking, juvenile delinquency, and child welfare, but they also explore debates over tango, cockfighting, and other bans on specific forms of entertainment and religious expression that were unique to Latin America. The twice-weekly class meetings focus on discussing the readings as well as on analyzing short pamphlets or newspaper editorials on controversial issues of the period, so as to highlight how the Latin American reform efforts reveal larger, underlying cultural concerns.

Third, this course gives students the opportunity to undertake independent research, allowing them to apply their theoretical knowledge and readings about social reform to concrete examples. In addition to having students write exams, I ask them to prepare a seven- to ten-page paper on one of several selected topics easily investigated in most university libraries. For example, some students have examined a series of bulletins regarding Pan American Sanitary conferences; the League of Nations' Traffic in Women and Children Committee's documents on efforts to eradicate white slavery; press coverage of regional conferences on child care; the Mexican constitutional debates over education and drinking; a few decades-worth of the Mexican, Argentine, or Brazilian census to learn about the social organization of cities; or the discussion regarding anti–venereal disease clinics in one of several Latin American welfare journals such as the Argentine *Asistencia* or the Mexican *Boletín Psicotecnía*. Many of these collections are located in large libraries and may be placed on reserve to facilitate their accessibility and use. Exploring documents in English, Spanish, or Portuguese permits students to adapt the course's analytical frameworks and topical information to a final project with some degree of independence.

Finally, I designed this course to be one in which a sensitivity to gender is incorporated into all aspects of the course's readings, lectures, and discussions. As an undergraduate student in the late 1980s and as a graduate student in the early 1990s, I was often frustrated by the failure of social history courses to address women's experiences or men's and women's perceptions of each other and how *masculine* or *feminine* activities allegedly shaped historical events. Often, it seemed, courses on Latin American history reserved a special week to address women's experiences. At best, this week on women showed students that there were differences in the ways men and women experienced colonialism, agrarian life, industrialization, or revolution. When I entered graduate school, even though gender as a category of analysis seemed well-entrenched in the social sciences, I still found that course sections on gender seemed to focus strictly on women and failed to consider the powerful implications of an analytical sensitivity to *male* and *female*. Fortunately, such issues have been the subject of much recent work on Latin America and have thus been incorporated into this course.

PERSPECTIVES ON SOCIAL REFORM

Most analysts who study how and when social welfare became a public concern and government responsibility cite industrialization, urbanization, and the expansion of the middle class as key factors. First, they note that industrial growth attracts rural residents to cities in search of work, bringing a greater number of people into closer and more frequent contact than before. Technological innovation and the reorganization of production stratify society—the ranks of company owners, investors, and administrators swell with the urban demand for goods even as more efficient production eliminates the need for highly paid, skilled artisans and contributes to their downward mobility. While some analysts note that it is workers and the poor, themselves, who militate for the public provision of assistance, others argue that the poverty and lifestyle of the working classes attracts the attention of professional men and educated women, who organize private charity missions and undertake reform efforts on behalf of the poor. States respond to these multi-class pressures to attend to urban social conditions by creating social welfare agencies (Gordon 1992; on the debates over the origins of welfare systems, see Gordon 1990; Skocpol 1992; Berkowitz 1991).

Much of the research treating the origins of state-provided social assistance analyzes how private reform interests shape public understandings of welfare. This view results, in part, because of the available evidence. Reformers formed clubs to combat what they perceived to be society's wrongs, publicized their associations' charters and constitutions, wrote letters to public officials, and prepared annual reports, many of which have been archived for public analysis. Reformers' activities also attracted national and international press coverage, provided subject material for travel writers, and generated debates within local and national bureaucracies, which are also relatively easy to access as data for researchers. Although some writers argue that reliance on these documents' legacies has warped historical understanding of reformism (they complain that these collections do not provide adequate information on those being reformed), the fact remains that these sources have provided the bulk of the material available for and utilized by researchers for social analysis (White 1990, 2–6). My course focuses on three lines of interpretation within that body of work.

One analytical thread understands reformism in terms of middle class efforts to enforce social control over the leisure, community, and reproductive activities of the urban lower classes. This work interprets efforts to eradicate drinking and prostitution and to provide sports clubs and vocational training for workers, for example, as evidence that the growing middle classes sought to harness the productive energy of the laboring public and channel workers' free time toward profitable ends (Boyer 1978). Second, by asking what men and women wanted to accomplish as reformers, as well as what they thought about male versus female deviance, this work elucidates the ways in which gender identities shaped reform imperatives. A shift of perspective has analyzed social reform in terms of reformers' own identity-formation. This view analyzes campaigns for free health care or women's higher wages as evidence of how the middle class, especially middle class women, make efforts to establish a bond with women of other racial and class categories, on the one hand, and to define their gendered responsibilities as guardians of domestic life and morality, on the other (see Ginzberg 1990; Walkowitz 1982; Kunzel 1988).

A third line of reasoning interprets reformism in terms of market discipline. These writers argue that capitalist development alters peoples' understandings of causation. In this theory, then, reformers feel responsible for the poverty and misery of the lower classes and work to alleviate the social problems for which they feel guilty about tolerating in the first place (Haskell 1992).

Some work on early Latin American welfare systems interpreted social reformism in terms of modernization, and investigators pointed toward politicians and bureaucrats in populist, corporatist governments in the 1920s and 1930s as the source of state-sponsored, top down reform (Hamilton 1982; Rock 1985). More recent work has centered around the activities of independent reformers themselves. This interest has encouraged researchers to expand the period under investigation and to examine the last quarter of the nineteenth century as a period during which reformism flourished alongside export-economies and early industrialization. If early research interpreted state-enacted progressive legislation in terms of government desires to pacify the lower classes and to channel their productive potential for development, analysis over the past ten years has focused on how groups out of power, such as business elites, feminists, case workers, and public health specialists interpreted social conditions in their own countries and mediated between the lower classes and the state.

Within this body of research, three lines of inquiry seemed worth pursuing to understand the dynamics of reform politics in Latin America. Some people have argued that regional elites became interested in social reform when they wanted to impress North American and European investors with the civilized nature of their countries (Needell 1987; Haber 1989). In addition to dressing like Europeans and redesigning their cities to look more like Paris, for example, Latin American elites created institutions to reduce the visibility of poverty and "backwardness" so as to convince foreign businesses of their development potential. Male reformers sought to control the sexuality of such "indecent" women as prostitutes and unmarried women with children, and female reformers sought public relief for children and poor mothers.

A second line of reasoning interprets reformism in terms of middle class efforts to distinguish themselves from the lower classes in the context of economic development (French 1992). Establishing prostitution regulations in a frontier outpost in which sexual commerce did not really proliferate, for example, allowed middle class men and women to differentiate themselves from others in terms of honor and respectability. These authors point out that this *developmentalist* ideology had deep roots in Latin America and should be understood less as a late nineteenth-century import than as an ongoing issue in post colonial class formation.

A third body of work argues that Latin American reformers were, indeed, influenced by international social reform movements. Those who have studied Brazil, Argentina, and Mexico, for example, interpret support for eugenics ideology or the work of the *Federation Abolitioniste,* which worked to eliminate white slavery, as evidence that Latin Americans believed they shared common social problems with "more developed" countries but adapted international reform ideology to their own local conditions (Guy 1991; Stepan 1991; Borges 1993). Analysts influenced by this train of thought have examined the ways in which reformers compared their efforts to the Europeans' but lamented the degeneration of their own populations by comparison. My own research has revealed that Mexican social hygienists at the turn of the century, for example, constantly lamented the fact that French prostitutes in the capital city were much more conscientious with respect to venereal disease prophylaxis than were Mexican women. And in Brazil, sexologists argued that thinking of female honor in terms of "mental virginity" was necessary because of what they considered to be a unique level of sexual violence and promiscuity among the Rio de Janeiro and São Paulo lower classes (Caulfield 2000).

CURRICULUM DEVELOPMENT

I chose to focus the readings and discussion around Brazil, Argentina, and Mexico for several reasons. Even if there were plenty of information on reform in all parts of Latin America, it would not make sense to try to cover the social history of South America, Central America, Mexico, and the Caribbean in one term. Comparing Brazil, Argentina, and Mexico has proven useful because of common temporal and thematic issues. They experienced foreign investment, expansion of commercial agriculture, and urbanization over roughly the same period and experienced reform efforts that were reported then, and which are being analyzed now.

Moreover, what is common among the three cases that makes their comparison practical also provides rich material for discussion about their differences. As a nation populated largely by Southern and Eastern European immigration, Argentina experienced discussions over deviancy and welfare that differed sharply from those in Brazil, a nation that did not abolish African slavery until the late nineteenth century, and Mexico, which had a large mestizo and indigenous population.

The course has the potential to serve undergraduate students in several ways. First, it provides students who have taken introductory courses on the region with a chance to explore issues in Latin American history more intensively than a survey course covering at least ten countries. Second, it seems clear that courses centered around specific questions and which require students to undertake some degree of independent investigation provide an excellent way to teach them to think critically about other cultures as well as to practice writing and research.

Further, focusing on a theme such as social reform provides an ideal opportunity to help students understand how gender shapes political, economic, and cultural processes. This course allows perspectives on gender relations and the ways in which men and women use gender to categorize and describe political issues to become full components of every class discussion.

Finally, because the provision of social welfare is currently a controversial issue not only in the United States but also in Latin America, it seems useful for undergraduates to examine welfare and reform in distinct historical and geographic settings, if only to gain analytical perspective on how ideas about gender, race, class, and nation subtly influence contemporary American life.

WORKS CITED

Berkowitz, Edward D. 1991. "How to Think about the Welfare State." *Labor History* 32 (4): 489–502.

Borges, Dain. 1993. "Puffy, Ugly, Slothful and Inert: Degeneration in Brazilian Social Thought, 1880–1940." *Journal of Latin American Studies* 25 (2): 235–256.

Boyer, Paul S. 1978. *Urban Masses and Moral Order in America, 1820–1920.* Cambridge, Mass., and London: Harvard University Press.

Caulfield, Sueann. 2000. *In Defense of Honor: Sexual Morality, Modernity and Nation in Early Twentieth-Century Brazil.* Durham, N.C.: Duke University Press.

French, William E. 1992. "Prostitutes and Guardian Angels: Women, Work and the Family in Porfirian Mexico." *Hispanic American Historical Review* 72 (4): 529–553.

Ginzberg, Lori D. 1990. *Women and the Work of Benevolence: Morality, Politics and Class in the Nineteenth-Century United States.* New Haven, Conn.: Yale University Press.

Gordon, Linda. 1990. "The New Feminist Scholarship on the Welfare State." In Linda Gordon, ed., *Women, the State and Welfare*, 9–35. Madison: University of Wisconsin Press.

———. 1992. "Social Insurance and Public Assistance: The Influence of Gender in Welfare Thought in the United States, 1890–1935." *The American Historical Review* 97 (6): 19–50.

Guy, Donna J. 1991. *Sex and Danger in Buenos Aires: Prostitution, Family and Nation in Argentina*. Lincoln: University of Nebraska Press.

Haber, Stephen H. 1989. *Industry and Underdevelopment: The Industrialization of Mexico, 1890–1940*. Stanford, Calif.: Stanford University Press.

Hamilton, Nora. 1982. *The Limits of State Autonomy: Post-Revolutionary Mexico*. Princeton, N.J.: Princeton University Press.

Haskell, Thomas L. 1992. "Capitalism and the Origins of the Humanitarian Sensibility, Parts I and II." In Thomas Bender, ed., *The Anti-Slavery Debate: Capitalism and Abolitionism as a Problem in Historical Interpretation*, 107–160. Berkeley: University of California Press.

Kunzel, Regina G. 1988. "The Professionalization of Benevolence: Evangelicals and Social Workers in the Florence Crittendon Homes, 1915–1945." *Journal of Social History* 22 (1): 21–43.

Needell, Jeffrey. 1987. *A Tropical Belle-Epoque: Elite Culture and Society in Turn-of-the-Century Rio de Janeiro*. Cambridge: Cambridge University Press.

Rock, David. 1985. *Argentina 1516–1987: From Spanish Colonization to Alfonsín*. Berkeley: University of California Press.

Skocpol, Theda. 1992. *Protecting Soldiers and Mothers: The Political Origins of Social Policy in the United States*. Cambridge, Mass. and London: Harvard University Press.

Stepan, Nancy. 1991. *The "Hour of Eugenics": Race, Gender and Nation in Latin America*. Ithaca: Cornell University Press.

Walkowitz, Judith R. 1982. "The Contagious Diseases Acts: Regulationists and Repealers." In *Prostitution and Victorian Society: Women, Class and the State*, 67–147. Cambridge: Cambridge University Press.

White, Luise. 1990. *The Comforts of Home: Prostitution in Colonial Nairobi*. Chicago: University of Chicago Press.

SYLLABUS: DEVIANCE, DELINQUENCY, AND SOCIAL REFORM IN LATIN AMERICA, 1870–1945

This course examines Latin American efforts to reform and control so-called deviant and delinquent elements in national populations between 1870 and 1945. Over this seventy-five-year period, public officials, medical specialists, feminists, social scientists, and criminologists worked to determine the origins of delinquency in their particular national contexts and to develop ways to combat its proliferation. Authorities and reformers alike experimented with a wide variety of methods to eliminate such cultural practices as cockfighting, prostitution, drinking, capoeira, and tango and to reform delinquent groups through correctional and educational institutions. In a period of industrialization, foreign trades and urban growth, experts' understandings of what constituted deviance were often culturally determined by their own beliefs about race, class, and gender roles in society and hinged on hopes and fears about national politics and economic potential.

Most course work will focus on case studies of moral reform movements in progressive-era Mexico, Argentina, and Brazil. Students will explore theoretical perspectives on the nature of social reform as well as case studies of Latin American efforts to control such activities as prostitution, drinking, gambling, tango-dancing, cockfighting, and crimes of passion. Readings and discussions will center around determining the political, social, and economic contexts in which reform movements arise as well as the different meanings *deviance* can assume in a particular historical environment. We will also discuss the extent to which experts' ideas about delinquency clashed with popular notions of deviance and respectability and how the men and women who were targets of reform agendas challenged them and inserted their own ideas about order and progress into public debates over the issues.

In addition to taking a map quiz and presenting a short paper, students will prepare a final project based on readings and independent research.

Readings

Arrom, Silvia. 1986. *The Women of Mexico City, 1790–1857*. Stanford, Calif.: Stanford University Press.

Bantjes, Adrian. 1984. "Burning Saints, Molding Minds: The Failed Cultural Revolution in Sonora," in William Beezley, Cheryl Martin, and William French, eds., *Rituals of Rule, Rituals of Resistance: Public Celebrations and Popular Culture in Mexico*, 261–84. Wilmington, Del.: Scholarly Resources.

Beezley, William. 1987. *Judas at the Jockey Club and Other Episodes of Porfirian Mexico*. Lincoln: University of Nebraska Press.

Beezley, William, Cheryl Martin, and William French, eds. 1994. *Rituals of Rule, Rituals of Resistance: Public Celebrations and Popular Culture in Mexico*. Wilmington, Del.: Scholarly Resources.

Besse, Susan K. 1989. "Crimes of Passion: The Campaign Against Wife-Killing in Brazil, 1910–1940." *Journal of Social History* 22(4): 653–66.

Bliss, Katherine. 1999. "The Science of Redemption: Syphilis, Sexual Promiscuity, and Reformism in Revolutionary Mexico." *Hispanic American Historical Review* 79(1): 1–40.

French, William. 1992. "Prostitutes and Guardian Angels: Women, Work, and the Family in Porfirian Mexico." *Hispanic American Historical Review* 72(4): 529–53.

French, William. 1994. "*Progreso Forzado*: Workers and the Inculcation of the Capitalist Work Ethic in the Parral Mining District," in William Beezley, Cheryl Martin, and William French, eds., *Rituals of Rule, Rituals of Resistance: Public Celebrations and Popular Culture in Mexico*, 191–212. Wilmington, Del.: Scholarly Resources.

Graham, Richard, ed. 1990. *The Idea of Race in Latin America, 1870–1940*. Austin: University of Texas Press.

Graham, Sandra Lauderdale. 1991. *House and Street: The Domestic World of Servants and Masters in Nineteenth-Century Rio de Janeiro*. Austin: University of Texas Press.

Guy, Donna J. 1991. *Sex and Danger in Buenos Aires: Prostitution, Family, and Nation in Argentina*. Lincoln: University of Nebraska Press.

Haber, Stephen. 1986. *Industry and Underdevelopment in Mexico*. Stanford, Calif: Stanford University Press.

Hale, Charles. 1988. "Political and Social Ideas in Latin America, 1870–1930," in Leslie Bethell, ed., *The Cambridge History of Latin America*, vol. 4, 367–441. Cambridge: Cambridge University Press.

Helg, Aline. 1990. "Race in Argentina and Cuba, 1880–1930: Theory, Policies, and Popular Reaction," in Richard Graham, ed., *The Idea of Race in Latin America*, 37–71. Austin: University of Texas Press.

Holloway, Thomas. 1993. *Policing Rio de Janeiro: Repression and Resistance in a Nineteenth-Century City*. Stanford, Calif.: Stanford University Press.

Johns, Michael. 1993. "The Antinomies of Ruling Class Culture: The Buenos Aires Elite, 1800–1900." *The Journal of Historical Sociology* 6(1): 74–101.

Johnson, Lyman, ed. 1990. *The Problem of Order in Changing Societies: Essays on Crime and Policing in Argentina and Uruguay*. Albuquerque: University of New Mexico Press.

Kicza, John. 1985. "The Role of the Family in Economic Development in Nineteenth-Century Latin America." *Journal of Family History* 10: 235–46.

Knight, Alan. 1990. "Racism, Revolution, and *Indigenismo:* Mexico, 1910–1940," in Richard Graham, ed., *The Idea of Race in Latin America*, 71–102. Austin: University of Texas Press.

Kuznesof, Elizabeth. 1980. "Household Composition and Headship as Related to Changes in Mode of Production: São Paulo, 1765–1836." *Comparative Studies in Society and History* 22: 78–108.

Moreno Toscano, Alejandra, and Carlos Aguirre. 1975. "Migration to Mexico City in the Nineteenth Century: Research Approaches." *Journal of Inter-American Studies and World Affairs* 17(1): 27–42.

Morgan, Tony. 1994. "Proletarians, Políticos, and Patriarchs: The Use and Abuse of Cultural Customs in the Early Industrialization of Mexico City, 1880–1910," in William Beezley, Cheryl Martin, and William French, eds., *Rituals of Rule, Rituals of Resistance: Public Celebrations and Popular Culture in Mexico*, 151–72. Wilmington, Del.: Scholarly Resources.

Morse, Richard M. 1969. "Cities and Society in XIX Century Latin America: The Illustrative Case of Brazil," in Jorge Enrique Hardoy and Richard Schaedel, eds., *El proceso de urbanización en América desde sus orígenes hasta nuestros días*, 303–22. Buenos Aires: Instituto Torcuato di Tella.

Needell, Jeffrey. 1984. "Making the Carioca *Belle Epoque* Concrete: The Urban Reforms of Rio de Janeiro Under Pereira Passos." *Journal of Urban History* 10(4): 383–421.

Needell, Jeffrey. 1996. "The *Revolta Contra Vacina* of 1904: The Revolt Against 'Modernization' in *Belle-Epoque* Rio de Janeiro," in Silvia Arrom and Servando Ortoll, eds., *Riots in the Cities: Popular Protests and the Urban Poor in Latin America, 1765–1910*, 155–94. Wilmington, Del.: Scholarly Resources.

Rafter, Nicole Hahn. 1990. "The Social Construction of Crime and Crime Control." *Journal of Research in Crime and Delinquency* 27(4): 376–89.

Ruggiero, Kristin. 1992. "Wives on Deposit: Internment and the Preservation of Husbands' Honor in Late Nineteenth-Century Buenos Aires." *Journal of Family History* 17(3): 253–70.

Salessi, Jorge. 1994. "The Argentine Dissemination of Homosexuality." *The Journal of the History of Sexuality* 4(3): 337–68.

Salvatore, Ricardo. 1992. "Criminology, Prison Reform, and the Buenos Aires Working Class." *Journal of Interdisciplinary History* 23(2): 279–99.

Skidmore, Thomas. 1990. "Racial Ideas and Social Policy in Brazil, 1870–1940," in Richard Graham, ed., *The Idea of Race in Latin America, 1870–1940*, 7–36. Austin: University of Texas Press.

Slatta, Richard W., and Karla Robinson. 1990. "Continuities in Crime and Punishment: Buenos Aires, 1820–1850," in Lyman Johnson, ed., *The Problem of Order in Changing Societies: Essays on Crime and Policing in Argentina and Uruguay, 1750–1940*, 19–47. Albuquerque: University of New Mexico Press.

Socolow, Susan Migden. 1990. "Women and Crime in Buenos Aires, 1757–1797," in Lyman Johnson, ed., *The Problem of Order in Changing Societies: Essays on Crime and Policing in Argentina and Uruguay, 1750–1940*, 1–19. Albuquerque: University of New Mexico Press.

Solberg, Carl. 1969. "Immigration and Urban Social Problems in Argentina and Chile, 1890–1914." *Hispanic American Historical Review* 49: 215–32.

Spitzer, Steven, and Andrew T. Scull. 1977. "Social Control in Historical Perspective: From Private to Public Responses to Crime," in David F. Greenberg, ed., *Corrections and Punishment*, 264–87. Beverly Hills, Calif.: Sage Publications.

Staples, Anne. 1994. "*Policía y Buen Gobierno*: Municipal Efforts to Regulate Public Behavior, 1821–1857," in William Beezley, Cheryl Martin, and William French, eds., *Rituals of Rule, Rituals of Resistance: Public Celebrations and Popular Culture in Mexico*, 115–26. Wilmington, Del.: Scholarly Resources.

Stepan, Nancy Leys. 1991. *The "Hour of Eugenics": Race, Gender, and Nation in Latin America*. Ithaca, N.Y.: Cornell University Press.

Stern, Steve J. 1995. *The Secret History of Gender: Men, Women, and Power in Late Colonial Mexico*. Chapel Hill: University of North Carolina Press.

Szuchman, Mark D. 1984. "Disorder and Social Control in Buenos Aires, 1810–1860." *Journal of Interdisciplinary History* 15: 83–110.

Szuchman, Mark D. 1988. *Order, Family and Community in Buenos Aires, 1810–1860*. Stanford, Calif.: Stanford University Press.

Tenenbaum, Barbara A. 1994. "Streetwise Mexico: The Paseo de la Reforma and the Porfirian Elite, 1876–1910," in William Beezley, Cheryl Martin, and William French, eds., *Rituals of Rule, Rituals of Resistance: Public Celebrations and Popular Culture in Mexico*, 127–50. Wilmington, Del.: Scholarly Resources.

Vaughan, Mary Kay. 1994. "Constructing the Patriotic Festival," in William Beezley, Cheryl Martin, and William French, eds., *Rituals of Rule, Rituals of Resistance: Public Celebrations and Popular Culture in Mexico*, 213–46. Wilmington, Del.: Scholarly Resources.

Weinstein, Barbara. 1990. "The State, the Industrialists and the Issue of Worker Training in Brazil, 1930–1950." *Hispanic American Historical Review* 70(3): 379–404.

Wolfe, Joel. 1992. "Anarchist Ideology, Worker Practice: The 1917 General Strike and the Formation of São Paulo's Working Class." *Hispanic American Historical Review* 71(4): 809–46.

Zimmerman, Eduardo A. 1992. "Racial Ideas and Social Reform: Argentina, 1890–1916." *Hispanic American Historical Review* 72(1): 23–46.

Requirements

1. Class attendance and participation in discussion
2. Map quiz
3. Mid-term exam
4. Final project
5. Presentation, discussion

Week 1. Introduction: Social Reform in Comparative Context

Week 2. Colonialism/Bourbon Legacy: Mexico, Argentina, and Brazil

A. Staples, "*Policía y Buen Gobierno*: Municipal Efforts to Regulate Public Behavior, 1821–1857."
B. Arrom, *The Women of Mexico City, 1790–1857*, selections.
C. Stern, *The Secret History of Gender: Men, Women, and Power in Late Colonial Mexico.*
D. Socolow, "Women and Crime in Buenos Aires, 1757–1797."
E. Slatta and Robinson, "Continuities in Crime and Punishment: Buenos Aires, 1820–1850."
F. Holloway, "Foundations, 1808–1930," in *Policing Rio de Janeiro.*

Week 3. Nineteenth-Century Urbanization: Components of Urbanization and the Formation of Urban Elites

A. Morse, "Cities and Society in XIX Century Latin America: The Illustrative Case of Brazil."
B. Arrom, chapter 3, "Demography," in *The Women of Mexico City.*
C. Szuchman, "Disorder and Social Control in Buenos Aires, 1810–1860."
D. Johns, "The Antinomies of Ruling Class Culture: The Buenos Aires Elite, 1800–1900."
E. Kicza, "The Role of the Family in Economic Development in Nineteenth-Century Latin America."

Week 4. Industrialization and Economic Development—Life in the Industrial City

A. Haber, *Industry and Underdevelopment in Mexico.*
B. Solberg, "Immigration and Urban Social Problems in Argentina and Chile, 1890–1914."
C. Kuznesof, "Household Composition and Headship as Related to Changes in Mode of Production: São Paulo, 1765–1836."
D. Arrom, "Employment," in *The Women of Mexico City.*
E. Moreno Toscano and Aguirre, "Migration to Mexico City in the Nineteenth Century: Research Approaches."
F. Map quiz.

Week 5. Social Reform—Theory and Practice

A. Mid-term exam.
B. Rafter, "The Social Construction of Crime and Crime Control."
C. Spitzer and Scull, "Social Control in Historical Perspective: From Private to Public Responses to Crime."

Week 6. Latin American Social Reform—Comparative Issues

A. Hale, "Political and Social Ideas in Latin America, 1870–1930."
B. Graham, "Introduction," in *The Idea of Race in Latin America, 1870–1940*.
C. Stepan, "Introduction," in *The "Hour of Eugenics": Race, Gender, and Nation in Latin America*.
D. Guy, "Introduction," in *Sex and Danger in Buenos Aires*.

Week 7. Research Methods

A. Library tour.
B. Discussion on methods in historical research.

Week 8. Imagining Reform—Reform Circles and Reformist Visions of the City

A. Skidmore, "Racial Ideas and Social Policy in Brazil, 1870–1940."
B. French, "Prostitutes and Guardian Angels: Women, Work, and the Family in Porfirian Mexico."
C. Needell, "Making the Carioca *Belle Epoque* Concrete: The Urban Reforms of Rio de Janeiro Under Pereira Passos."
D. Tenenbaum, "Streetwise Mexico: The Paseo de la Reforma and the Porfirian Elite, 1876–1910."

Week 9. The Politics of Modernization—Porfirian Mexico

A. Beezley, *Judas at the Jockey Club and Other Episodes of Porfirian Mexico*.
B. Morgan, "Proletarians, Políticos, and Patriarchs: The Use and Abuse of Cultural Customs in the Early Industrialization of Mexico City, 1880–1910."
C. French, *"Progreso Forzado:* Workers and the Inculcation of the Capitalist Work Ethic in the Parral Mining District."

Week 10. Modernization Through Revolution

A. Knight, "Racism, Revolution, and *Indigenismo:* Mexico, 1910–1940."
B. Bliss, "The Science of Redemption: Syphilis, Sexual Promiscuity, and Reformism in Revolutionary Mexico."
C. Bantjes, "Burning Saints, Molding Minds: The Failed Cultural Revolution in Sonora."
D. Vaughan, "Constructing the Patriotic Festival."

Week 11. Crime, Immigration, and Violence

A. Ruggiero, "Wives on Deposit: Internment and the Preservation of Husbands' Honor in Late Nineteenth-Century Buenos Aires."
B. Salvatore, "Criminology, Prison Reform, and the Buenos Aires Working Class," 279–99.
C. Paper proposal due with preliminary list of primary and secondary sources (one to two pages detailing major issues and questions to be posed); bring a document, photograph, cartoon, or other primary document to class.
D. Mid-term rewrites due.
E. Zimmerman, "Racial Ideas and Social Reform: Argentina, 1890–1916."
F. Helg, "Race in Argentina and Cuba, 1880–1930: Theory, Policies, and Popular Reaction."

Week 12. Gender and National Identity—Argentina

A. Guy, *Sex and Danger in Buenos Aires: Prostitution, Family, and Nation in Argentina.*
B. Salessi, "The Argentine Dissemination of Homosexuality."

Week 13. Writing the History of Deviance, Delinquency, and Social Reform

A. Short paper on historiography due (two to three pages on how the subject you are researching has been approached by other authors—their sources, arguments, and positions) to be discussed in class.

Week 14. Gender, Race, and Degeneration—Brazilian Reform Thought

A. Graham, *House and Street: The Domestic World of Servants and Masters in Nineteenth-Century Rio de Janeiro.*
B. Besse, "Crimes of Passion: The Campaign Against Wife-Killing in Brazil, 1910–1940."
C. Weinstein, "The State, the Industrialists and the Issue of Worker Training in Brazil, 1930–1950."
D. Wolfe, "Anarchist Ideology, Worker Practice: The 1917 General Strike and Formation of São Paulo's Working Class."
E. Needell, "The *Revolta Contra Vacina* of 1904: The Revolt Against 'Modernization in *Belle Epoque* Rio de Janeiro."
F. Short paper (three to four pages) on preliminary thesis, argument, evidence for final paper.

TODAY'S CHANGING WORLD: HUMAN GEOGRAPHY

Eric Sheppard

The University of Minnesota's large geography department offers students three kinds of introductory courses to the discipline, focusing on physical geography, computer mapping, and human geography, all taught without prerequisites. Because students have had minimal exposure to geography during their secondary education, the success of any geography department rests on its ability to attract students to, and excite them with, its general education courses. This situation is beginning to change since geography alliances of teachers in a number of states, many of them women, and a national education standards initiative have revitalized school geography. Yet the principal goals of an introductory course remain the same: providing students, who typically do not study geography in high school, with a basic geography education; teaching the fundamental concepts of the field; and getting students excited about a geographical perspective on the world.

It has never been difficult to attract women to the study of geography. Although fewer study physical than human geography, approximately half of all undergraduate majors are female, and many also go on to graduate school. But it has only been in the last fifteen years that a situated feminist approach to geography has developed, and until very recently introductory geography textbooks have paid little attention to women and ignored feminist perspectives (see Mayer 1989). In addition, American geography has attracted few students of color, men or women, with the low numbers of African Americans, Chicano/Chicana, and American Indians being particularly glaring.

I had never taught the introductory human geography course, but with many of the faculty who have taught it approaching retirement, I thought that it could be revitalized by making issues of feminist geography and feminist pedagogic methods more central to the course design. The syllabus presented here is the result of this effort.

The syllabus design is based on three learning objectives. First, students should learn some of the basic principles of a geographic approach to understanding the world. In part, geography examines how people and societies have shaped the geographical organization of the world. Geographers stress the evolving particularities of places and the differences among them; the changing interactions between places and the resulting spatial organization of human and biophysical (i.e., biological, geological, and climatological) phenomena; and

203

the different geographical scales at which social and biophysical processes operate—particularly the relationship between local events and globalizing cultures, polities, and economies. Geographers also offer a synthetic perspective on the world, examining the articulation among cultural, economic, political, and biophysical phenomena. For example, a course on human geography focuses on the interdependencies between human societies and ecological systems, and the practical and ethical issues these raise. Geographers are concerned with representations of the world: not only how maps represent the world, but also how landscapes function as (contested) representations of cultures and societies. Finally, as a discipline that seeks to integrate cultural and humanistic studies with social and earth science perspectives, geographers need to draw on the full range of epistemological approaches to making sense of the world, rather than seeking to fit all topics into a single way of knowing.

Second, students should learn about the diversity of the globe and the multiple ways of knowing and of human practice to be found among, and within, different regions. As stressed in contemporary feminism, students should learn that knowledge and action are situated—not only with respect to the social location of individuals within societies but also their geographical location—and that situated knowledge is best appreciated first hand (or, as geographers would say, through fieldwork). Thus the course should maximize students' exposure to and appreciation of different places, to the extent that this is possible when the place of learning is a North American classroom. Tradi-tionally, introductory human geography is either taught as a (typically rather mechanistic and descriptive) course in world regional geography, or as a more conceptual and systematic course with little attention to world regional differences. This syllabus attempts to integrate these systematic and regional approaches.

Third, in order to attract students to the class and hold their attention once they enroll, students will learn to apply the geographical perspective developed in the course to case studies of high-profile contemporary events that they are already exposed to and are learning to cope with in everyday life. These include events such as global change and environmental degradation, globalizing markets and cultures, the information revolution, ethnic and racial conflicts, and how global events are shaping local lives.

These three goals are interwoven throughout the course. After two weeks of setting out the bigger picture of a geographic perspective on the world and the situated nature of all understandings and representations, I focus on different substantive themes each week, presented in ways that resonate with students' concerns. No attempt will be made to teach about the entire world; indeed one of the principles of the course is that such a panoptic vision is impossible. Yet I intend to expose students to specific events in unfamiliar places, providing situations that will challenge them to rethink their own situated knowledges and assumptions, so that they will begin to appreciate the meaning of being a global citizen.

My revised syllabus differs from previous offerings of the course in several ways. It takes seriously the importance of gender in particular and difference in general, integrating these themes into the course throughout, in part through relevant case studies and active learning activities. The course explores the intersections between difference and inequality, challenging students to reflect on the complex question of how to respect difference while seeking to eliminate inequality. The course pays significant attention to political ecology: the ways in which relationships between human society and nature are shaped by biophysical, political, economic, and cultural processes. The course treats knowledge and understanding as situated, resisting the position that there is a single correct way of understanding the world. For example, I use the conventional discussions of maps as part of a more general discussion about contested representations of the world. Finally, the course challenges students to reassess critical assumptions they may hold about development, especially the assumption that all places follow a single path of progress toward Western society as the pinnacle of development.

In deciding how to make gendered geographies an explicit component of learning, in a course that is too often silent about half the world's population, I decided to integrate themes of gender and feminism throughout rather than devoting particular sections to feminist issues. Here, I provide examples from four of the fourteen weekly themes.

GEOGRAPHIC PERSPECTIVES

The first week of the course introduces students to a geographic approach to understanding the world, stressing the concepts of place, interaction, scale, and synthesis just described. In order to make these concepts more real for students and to draw them into the class, I introduce an exercise that asks them to utilize their own experiences in order to appreciate how their life-world differs from those of people in other places, and to understand how their lives are connected to other places. I ask students to identify ten places they have interacted with most in the last month, to make an inventory of the objects in their living room, and to record the places where these objects come from. Through discussion, students will compare their life-worlds (the places they interact with and the things they own) and how their lives are connected with other places, to the life-worlds of other students. In discussion, I emphasize the similarities and differences that emerge as structured by students' gender, race, age, and geographic origin. Students also read short accounts of the daily lives of young women and men, as well as descriptions of family belongings, from very different places in other parts of the world, and then discuss how and why these do or do not differ from their own lives (Massey and Jess 1995; Menzel 1994).

GEOGRAPHIC REPRESENTATIONS

The second week of the course looks at geography as a discipline concerned with representing the world through maps, photographs, and place narratives. I have designed an exercise that helps students to think critically about these representations, introducing them to feminist philosophical principles addressing the situated nature of knowledge. Students begin by making their own maps of a place familiar to them, such as Minneapolis or their home towns. They then examine published maps of their hometowns, identifying what is present and what is missing on these maps by comparison to their own, and learning how such "official" maps convey a scientific and panoptic view of the world (Wood 1992; Rose 1993). Comparing their maps to official versions, to one another's maps, and to photographs or videos of the same place, students can begin to understand that all representations are selective, reflecting the situation of the person making the representation. Of particular importance, students can also compare representations of the same place made by students of different gender, race, class, and sexual preference (Haraway 1991; Wood 1992; Rose 1993; Seager 1997).

THE EARTH SUSTAINS US

The purpose of this week is to examine one aspect of human-environment relations: agriculture, food production, and the question of whether there are limits to population growth. My lectures will stress general principles and debates about sustainable development. In the exercise, I want students to appreciate the existence of very different agricultural practices around the world; to learn how these practices are related to different environmental conditions and to local knowledge about how to utilize the natural environment; to be aware that differences in agricultural practices are disappearing as a result of the spread of agribusiness; and to develop a critical perspective on the question of whether this is a good thing. I also want students to appreciate how gender relations structure their participation in farming and their attitudes toward nature. Students can begin by reading accounts of the nature of farming in different parts of Africa before and after the coming of colonialism, paying attention to how colonialism and then capitalism have changed agricultural practices, attitudes toward nature, and the activities carried out by women (Johnson-Odim and Strobel 1988). They should note how women have been affected by but have also struggled against these changes, and they should also examine the impact of these changes on the gendered nature of familial relationships (Nagar 1997). Group discussion can focus on the ways in which women do double work, the importance of a sophisticated knowledge of local ecosystems to the success of farming practices, and how women's work as gatherers of fuel and water has become more difficult with the disappearance and commodification of forest and water resources. Students with a farming background, likely to be present in any Minnesota classroom, can contribute significantly to these discussions.

URBANIZATION

This week focuses on the increasingly urban nature of human society and the processes driving urbanization. I lecture on the growth of cities and urban systems and how these result from economic and demographic processes operating at different geographical scales. For example, I indicate how cities grow as a result of international migration (reflecting the situation of cities within global systems) and rural-urban migration (reflecting cities' relationship to surrounding rural hinterlands). A relevant exercise can focus particularly on processes of rural-urban migration and their gendered nature. In order to get students thinking about the migration process, I ask them where they would like to live after graduating from college, and the reasons for their choice. I pay particular attention to how differences among them are related to gender, life goals, wealth, and race. They then read biographical accounts or watch video clips of the experiences of women migrating from rural to urban areas in different parts of the world (e.g., Chant 1992; Momsen and Kinnaird 1993). Students can then identify and discuss differences between these and their own accounts. They are likely to be critical of some of the choices made by the migrants they have learned about, feeling they would have acted differently. Rather than leave these thoughts unexamined, I ask students to discuss what they might have done differently if they were in the same situation, and how they can make judgments about others' actions. Students and teaching assistants with direct experiences of other countries can lead discussion of how experiences of gender, class, and race can differ significantly in different geographic contexts (Mohanty 1991).

CONCLUSION

One side effect of the commodification of education in land grant universities is that success is measured by enrollment. Because effective teaching of large classes is difficult, I use a variety of feminist pedagogic techniques as well as telecommunications technologies to vary my lectures. I use visual materials (slides and video clips) to convey geographical patterns and places; I give students active learning exercises; and I organize semi-structured classroom discussions.

Lectures are complemented by weekly recitation sections run by instructors and graduate assistants. These are opportunities to pursue in depth the themes and case studies introduced in class, but they are also structured as opportunities for graduate assistants and students to explore different but related topics, consistent with the broad educational goals of the class. As appropriate, in order to attract a more diverse student body into the class, or to provide places within the class for particular forms of situated knowledge to be explored in detail, it may be productive to set aside a recitation section devoted to women's studies majors or to students of color. Wherever possible, however, students should be encouraged to interact and debate constructively across social boundaries, in classroom and recitation settings that encourage productive dialogues. Because a particular challenge is to give students as rich an experience as possible of distant places without leaving Minnesota, I seek to involve graduate assistants from other regions of the world, as well as to engage the experiences of students who were born or have lived in other countries.

Outside classroom settings, students work on small weekly projects, including movies and slide-shows to watch, Internet sites to visit, additional readings, computer-based self-learning modules, and writing assignments (informal writing reflecting on the course and a research paper). In the long term, I hope that e-mail and the Internet can be used to put students in direct contact with students elsewhere in the world, so that they can share with and learn from others' experiences. One further experience central to a geographical perspective is fieldwork. Depending on students' own needs and interests, I suggest self-guided field-trips, group outings around the metropolitan area, field-based research papers, or a service learning activity (in which students gain credit for participating in a social service or community activity). To make this experience as rich as possible, I encourage students to pursue their field experience in places and among people with whom they are not yet familiar. Many students come from suburbs, and they will be encouraged to experience the inner city.

Finally, it is important to note that this syllabus is, and should remain, a work in progress. I assume that the course will and should continue to evolve, through a systematic process of learning from the students who take it, from teaching assistants, and from changes both in the world around us and the ideas and epistemologies available to understand that world.

SELECTED WORKS

Bradshaw, Michael. 1997. *The New Global Order: A World Regional Geography,* Madison: Brown & Benchmark.

Chant, Sylvia, ed. 1992. *Gender and Migration in Developing Countries.* London: Belhaven.

Hall, Stuart. 1995. "New Cultures for Old." In Doreen Massey and Pat Jess, eds., *A Place in the World?* 175–214. Oxford: The Open University.

Haraway, D. 1991. *Simians, Cyborgs and Women: The Reinvention of Nature.* New York: Routledge.

Johnston, Ronald J., Peter J. Taylor, and Michael J. Watts, eds. 1995. *Geographies of Global Change.* Cambridge: Blackwell.

Johnson-Odim, Cheryl, and Margaret Strobel. 1988. *Restoring Women to History: Teaching Packets for Integrating Women's History into Courses on Africa, Asia, Latin America, the Caribbean, and the Middle East.* Bloomington, Ind.: Organization of American Historians.

Massey, Doreen, and Pat Jess, eds. 1995. *A Place in the World?* Oxford: The Open University.

Mayer, Tamar, 1989. "Consensus and Invisibility: The Representation of Women in Human Geography Textbooks." *The Professional Geographer* 41: 397–409.

Menzel, Peter. 1994. *Material World.* San Francisco: Sierra Club Books.

Mohanty, Chandra. 1991. "Under Western Eyes: Feminist Scholarship and Colonial Discourses." In C. Mohanty, A. Russo, and L. Torres, *Third World Women and the Politics of Feminism,* 51–80. Bloomington: Indiana University Press.

Momsen, Janet, and Vivian Kinnaird, eds. 1993. *Different Places, Different Voices: Gender and Development in Africa, Asia and Latin America.* London: Routledge.

Nagar, Richa. 1997. "The Difference That Gender Makes." In P. Porter and E. Sheppard, eds. *A World of Difference,* 50–60. New York: Guilford Press.

Porter, Philip W., and Eric Sheppard. 1998. *A World of Difference.* New York: Guilford Press.

Rand McNally. 1997. *Atlas of World Geography.* New York: Rand McNally, revised edition.

Rose, Gillian. 1993. *Feminism & Geography: The Limits of Geographical Knowledge.* Minneapolis: University of Minnesota Press.

———. 1995. "Place and Identity: A Sense of Place." In Doreen Massey and Pat Jess, eds., *A Place in the World?* 87–132. Oxford: The Open University.

Seager, Joni. 1997. *The State of Women in the World Atlas.* London: Penguin.

Wood, Denis. 1992. *The Power of Maps.* New York: Guilford Press.

SYLLABUS

Today's world is a place of profound contradictions. We seem to be more plugged in and better connected to people and places all around the world, but still know and understand little about life elsewhere. Lifestyles seem to be becoming more similar, with everyone drinking Coca-Cola, driving Toyotas, and listening to rock and classical music, but at the same time we increasingly celebrate difference—based on gender, race, place, religion, sexuality—or victimize people based on their difference. Global capitalism is growing like never before, creating seemingly new opportunities for prosperity in every country, but social and geographical inequalities are also increasing, and we worry about environmental catastrophe. Individuals spend more of their life at home—watching TV, on the Internet, or partying with friends—but at the same time our lives seem more under the influence and control of events in distant places beyond our influence and understanding.

How can we make sense of life and events in today's world? Geography offers a set of concepts and tools that can help, and the purpose of this course is to introduce students to these, and to apply them to contemporary social problems, with the goal of improving students' knowledge, appreciation, and understanding of contemporary events. It also represents a basic background course, which can form the basis for students to pursue more specialized and advanced studies of particular aspects of human geography and social phenomena in 3000- and 4000-level geography courses.

Why geography? Geography is not about memorizing place names and facts. It is a broad-ranging discipline (an interdisciplinary discipline) well-suited for the systematic study of complex problems facing society today. It is synthetic, looking at the relationship between social and environmental change as well as examining the interrelationships between economic, cultural, political, and social processes within human society. It focuses on why places, and lifestyles in those places, differ from one another, and also teaches how to understand and appreciate those differences. It examines how the places where we live are connected to and dependent on one another, through the movement of people, commodities, ideas, and information. It examines how local events are affected by global processes, but also how local initiatives can affect regional, national, and international events. Finally, it provides a set of tools, ranging from field observations to maps and geographic information systems (GIS), which if used carefully can help us make sense of, monitor, and understand all of these issues.

In order to introduce the basics of human geography as a field of study, and to show how relevant it is in making sense of today's world, this course will focus on three intersecting themes. First, what are some of the basic ideas, concepts, and tools that are central to geography in general, and human geography in particular? Second, what kinds of different lifestyles are to be found in different parts of the world, and how can they be understood? Third, how can these ideas be applied to make sense of contemporary events that concern us all?

Learning Objectives

By the time you have completed the course, I hope that you will

- understand the basic principles and methods used by geographers to make sense of the world
- have adequate background to take more specialized classes in geography
- have some familiarity with some of the different places and livelihoods around the globe
- have developed some skills for understanding complex problems facing humankind today

REQUIRED TEXT: KNOX, PAUL, AND SALLIE MARSTON. 2000. HUMAN GEOGRAPHY: PLACES AND REGIONS IN GLOBAL CONTEXT. NEW YORK: PRENTICE HALL.

Week 1. Geographic Perspectives

Topics will include definitions of place, space, and scale, and a synthesis of human-environmental and societal relations.

Exercise. Global Connections, Local Lives: Who Feeds, Clothes, and Informs Us?

Students will track the origins of their food, clothing, appliances, and knowledge of current events, and reflect on the relationship between these interdependencies and their own daily lives. Differences based on gender, sexuality, class, and ethnicity or race will be identified and discussed.

Week 2. Geographic Representations

Maps, photos, and verbal descriptions will be contrasted as ways geographers represent the world. Maps will be used to discuss questions of objectivity, situated knowledge, and grassroots versus "official" representations and knowledge.

Exercise. Whose Maps, Whose Knowledge?

A comparison of the maps of geographers, the media, and local residents will be used to discuss views from nowhere, views from somewhere, and contestations about geography as science.

Week 3. The Earth Sustains Us

Contrasting agricultural systems around the world and their geohistorical origins will be used to discuss questions of sustainability (Malthusian versus Boserupian views of population and resources) and whether differences in agricultural practices reflect a gradient of modernity or appropriate adaptations to different biophysical and societal contexts.

Exercise. The African Food Crisis

Case studies of sub-Saharan African agriculture will be used to discuss the richness of traditional agricultural practices, the gendered nature of those practices (raising issues of patriarchy vs. capitalism), and how traditional agriculture is affected by the rise of global agricultural markets.

Week 4. Diffusion, Communications, and Global Inequality

The diffusion of domestication, the long history of global trading networks, and contrasting interpretations of the origins and consequences of European colonialism will be used to discuss how spatial interdependencies structure geographical difference and inequality. This will provide a geohistorical background to understanding the shape of today's world.

Exercise. The (De)population of the New World

Case studies of the impact of European colonization of the New World will be used to discuss what happens when two geographically isolated cultures come into contact with one another.

Week 5. Culture, Place, and Identity

How identities and cultural institutions are created in place—their origins in daily life, the ties of daily life to local landscapes, and the relationship between cultural distinctiveness and sociogeographical self-sufficiency. Processes operating at different geographical scales construct representations of difference based in such characteristics as skin pigmentation, language, religion, gender, and values.

Exercise. Zones of Cultural Conflict

Geohistorical analysis will be used on a case study (Israel, Bosnia, Rwanda, Pacific Islands) to illuminate how such groups came to be located within the same territory and political space, why conflicts persist, and how geography can account for these as being much more complex than simply ethnic rivalries.

Week 6. Population Growth and Migration

Dynamics of natural increase and migration will be investigated as responses to and causes of geographical and social differences in well-being. Also explored will be the use of population policies for political empowerment or economic advancement of different groups and regions.

Exercise. The Immigration Challenge

We will examine the case of immigration to the United States and the questions of causes, challenges to American identity, economic consequences, gender and migration, and strategies for accommodation.

Week 7. Industrialization, Geopolitics, and Trade

This week will include discussions of processes of international trade, geographical economic specialization and spatial divisions of labor, multinational firms, and economic development gradients. These are conditioned by geopolitical processes, local production possibilities, and situation within the world economy. Globalization of capital markets and commodity chains will also be explored.

Exercise. Industrialization in China

This exercise will focus on a case study of rapid industrialization, highlighting possibilities for low wage countries, and job prospects for women in special economic zones. Hong Kong and the prospects for market communism will be examined.

Week 8. Urbanization

The class will focus on the growth of urban systems as an economic and demographic process, including the growth of cities based on their changing situation within global economic and geopolitical systems, and their relationship to rural economies and population change. Urban primacy, spatial polarization of development, and rural-urban migration will be examined.

Exercise. Mega-cities in Latin America and Asia

Case studies will focus on Mexico City, São Paulo, Jakarta, and Bangkok, exploring the following issues: the gendered nature of rural-urban migration, social polarization within large cities, congestion, and questions of sustainability. Solutions to these problems will be explored.

Week 9. Transformation of the Earth

Topics will include resource exploitation that supports industrial urban society, the commodification of nature, debates about environmental ethics, and First World–Third World contrasts in visions of sustainable development.

Exercise. Big Dam Projects in India and China

We will compare the causes behind, and ecological and social consequences of dam development, together with political debates, for two equally large but contrasting cases (one largely rural and successfully contested, one much more industrial and politically controlled).

Week 10. The Location of Industry and Services

The roles of resource location, transportation infrastructure, labor cost differences, local networks, and political intervention at different scales on the agglomeration of nonagricultural economic activities will be explored. Topics will include the increasing dependence of local economic dynamics, how places are situated within the global economy, and possibilities for insulation of local economic processes from the negative consequences of globalization.

Exercise. America's Rust Belt

The class will examine the evolution of the American manufacturing belt, its crisis under international competition combined with Fordism in the 1970s, rising female labor force participation, and possibilities for regeneration.

Week 11. City Spaces

The class will explore the economic, social, and political organization of urban space, including factors such as transportation, land use markets, and political fragmentation. Municipal strategies for urban development and competition between and within metropolitan areas will be examined.

Exercise. Spatial Mismatch

Discussion will center on the issue of African Americans in U.S. metropolitan areas. Topics will include ghetto formation, white flight, job flight, and response within local Black communities in the Twin Cities Metropolitan Area.

Week 12. Places of Exclusion and Empowerment

Discussion will center on the development of cores and peripheries at subnational, urban, and local scales; the cultural images associated with the cores and peripheries; and strategies that have been employed to create and overcome exclusion in those areas.

Exercise. Gendered Spaces

Discussion will focus on traditions of public (masculine) versus private (feminine) space, marginalization of feminine space and places, as well as on how places are used for empowerment and transformation, especially in an electronic age.

Week 13. Electronic Geographies

Discussion will focus on whether electronic communications means the end of geography. Topics will include virtual communities versus real places and their impact on identity formation, social change, and personal privacy.

Exercise. Home Work?

The issue of telecommuting, its impact on gendered lifestyles, prospects for the disadvantaged, and its relationship to ecological sustainability will be discussed.

Week 14. Earth Futures

Discussion will center on the shape of things to come, focusing on the dialectic of globalization and local difference and resistance. Strategies at the local and trans-local scale for reducing inequality while respecting difference will be explored.

Exercise. Global Warming

Debates over the cause(s) and consequences of global warming will be examined. Contrasting positions will be summarized, and the difficulties in managing a world whose future is uncertain will be discussed, including the consequences of making wrong choices and how to democratize technological choices for a sustainable future.

GENDERING AND GLOBALIZING
SOCIAL MOVEMENTS

VALENTINE M. MOGHADAM

The feminist intellectual revolution has had a profound impact on the discipline of sociology, but some subfields remain immune to feminist inroads (Johnson and Risman 1997). One subfield, the study of social movements, has generated considerable research and significant findings about the dynamics of social protest, political movements, and other forms of collective action. But the mainstream study of social movements—exemplified by key texts such as *Comparative Perspectives on Social Movements* (McAdam, et al. 1996)—has yet to systematically integrate women and gender issues into its theoretical frameworks. A similar problem exists in the study of revolution (Moghadam 1997). In contrast, feminist scholars have been attentive to women's movements and the gender dynamics of social movements (Basu 1995; Ferree and Hess 1994; Jaquette 1994; Mikell 1997; Moghadam 1994, 1996; Staggenborg 1998, Stienstra 1994; West and Blumberg 1990; West 1997).

Teaching social movements entails a dualistic approach. First one should utilize one or two mainstream texts so that students become knowledgeable about the theories and methods of social movement analysis. At this stage, women and gender issues figure not at all, at least in the texts. Then one shifts gears, introducing students to the idea that women and gender issues matter in social movements. Students should read works by feminist scholars on women's movements and women's involvement in various types of collective action. Students should be able to apply the theoretical framework to their research papers. But they should also consider the gender aspects of the social movements that they have chosen to write on and the ways that women participate in and are affected by those movements. In my course on contemporary social movements, I begin with theory (unit 1), move to women's movements (unit 2), and then examine another major social movement (unit 3), alternating between fundamentalist movements and the labor movement.

THE THEORETICAL FRAMEWORK

The term *social movement* refers to various forms of collective action aimed at societal reorganization. Research has been conducted on social movements such as revolutions, peasant rebellions in developing countries, poor people's movements, student protests, and the civil rights struggle in the United States. Early on, protests and rebellions were studied from a socio-psychological perspective. Neil Smelser and other leading scholars of collective behavior emphasized the importance of generalized beliefs and values in directing social movements, drawing attention to psychological, cultural, and ideological aspects of social movements. Resource mobilization theory then emerged, borrowing the concept of the rational actor from economics. Charles Tilly and others subsequently developed the political process theory of popular mobilizations, an approach that examines the political context in which protests arise.

Among the questions of interest to sociologists who study social movements are the following: What are the structural and proximate causes of social movements? How do political opportunities and constraints affect social movements? How are supporters recruited, coalitions built, and organizations formed? How is policy influenced? What are the short-term and long-term outcomes of social movements and social movement organizations (SMOs)? Another question pertains to the function of culture in social movements and in social movement analysis. How does a society's culture affect a social movement's structure, tactics, discourses, and strategy, and how does the movement itself affect culture? The question of culture has come to the fore in discussions of Islamic fundamentalism and the Iranian Revolution, but discussion has also evolved around "the culture" of the women's movement and of the gay and lesbian movements.

There is now an appreciation for the interconnection of political, organizational, and cultural processes in social movements. The current consensus is that social movements, including revolutions, require common interests and identity (the cultural and ideological aspect), mobilization of resources (including financial and human resources), and organization, in order for the movement to be successful. Hence sociologists McAdam, McCarthy, and Zald, whose text I have used in the course, examine political opportunities, mobilizing structures, and framing processes. The editors and various contributors to the volume argue that the three variables, or sets of variables, function in varying important ways over the course of a social movement. *Political opportunities* are critical to emergence. (Some key questions: How does the national political system influence movements? How do movement strategy and structure change in response to political opportunities? How do movements respond to, and help create, political opportunities?) *Mobilizing structures,* which entail organizational forms and dynamics, become more central as the movement develops. *Framing processes*—the ways in which objectives are formulated, expressed, and disseminated—are always important, but they become more self-conscious and tactical over the course of the movement.

Today, many theorists locate the roots of social protest in broad social change processes that destabilize existing power relations and increase the leverage of challenging groups. Yet in contrast to those theorists who view social movements as a collective response to deprivation or the contradictions of late capitalism, the present consensus stresses political processes while also viewing structural and cultural processes as key to understanding the cycles, strategies, and organizational forms of social protest.

In the 1980s in Europe, a parallel approach to social movements emerged, one that held that *new social movements* were a product of late capitalism or postindustrial society (e.g., Melucci 1985). Theorists argued that, in contradistinction to the old social movements (e.g., labor movements of the past, or revolutions), the new ones were not class based or focused on economic issues; nor were activists in the movements interested in taking over the state or in seizing state power. Rather, they were focused on criticizing the values of late capitalism and offering an alternative set of generalized beliefs, values, lifestyles, practices, cultural understandings, and so on. According to new social movement theory, contemporary social movements are "liberated" from class, ideology, and economic concerns; they employ new and creative forms of action; and they focus on identity concerns rather than on strategy. Such theorists argue that the peace, antinuclear, women's, gay, disability, animal rights, and environmental movements fall under the rubric of postmaterial and postindustrial new social movements.

New social movement theory has come under some criticism from various quarters. In my own view, the theory is rather West-centered and cannot account for the fact that some if not all of the new social movements may be found in developing countries, that is, in societies that are not postindustrial. Certainly we have seen the emergence of women's movements throughout the globe. Nor do all women's movements look alike.

In some writings associated with new social movement theory, women's movements are said to exemplify identity-oriented and non-economic types of new social movements (e.g., Kriesi 1996). Authors of these texts assume that feminist ideology and women's movements are focused on personal and sexual issues pertaining to women and that they do not address economic, political, or foreign policy issues. The model for this assumption may or may not be the American women's movement. My own research, however, suggests that women's movements are complex and exhibit various priorities, objectives, organizational forms, and strategies. Indeed, feminism itself comes in many varieties such as liberal feminism, Marxist feminism, socialist feminism, radical feminism, cultural feminism, and postmodernist feminism.

INTRODUCING WOMEN, GENDER, AND A GLOBAL PERSPECTIVE

As important as current theories of social movements are, they lack attention to women as principals in social movements, and to the ways that gender is built into political, organizational, and cultural processes (but see Einwohner, et al. 2000). Gender ideologies may shape social movements in profound ways, deeply affecting the discourses, objectives, tactics, and outcomes of social movements. Within the same movement, women may be organized and mobilized differently from men. Recruitment patterns, leadership roles, and management styles may exhibit gender patterning. Gender roles, relations, and ideologies may shape political opportunities—opportunities may exist for men but not for women, who may be less mobile or less able to respond to opportunities due to their greater involvement in family work. Concomitantly, constraints are gendered. Constraints faced by women may be not only political but also cultural and familial. Within the same movement, women and men may have different objectives, priorities, or modes of protest. Outcomes are also gendered—social movement effects may be different for women than for men. Moreover, it is important to recognize the extent to which women have organized and mobilized politically, and the ways they have formed their own, alternative movements and organizations.

In order to fill the gender gap in the McAdam, McCarthy, and Zald book, I assign students several books on women's movements. I think it is important that they learn about the structure and evolution of the American women's movement. In the past I assigned Ferree and Hess's very useful and well-written book *Controversy and Coalition: The New Feminist Movement Across Three Decades of Change,* which uses social movement theory to analyze and describe the U.S. women's movement, its major organizations, and the legislative and cultural impacts of American feminism. More recently we have read Staggenborg's *Gender, Family, and Social Movements.* To inform students about women's movements and women's activism from a broader conceptual perspective, I assign West and Blumberg's *Women and Social Protest.* This book identifies four types of women's protests and organizes the chapters around them: (1) protests and organizing around economic issues, (2) social-nurturing or humanistic protests and movements, (3) women's involvement in nationalist movements, and (4) women's rights movements. Examples come from the United States, Europe, China, Israel, and Latin America. Finally, to make clear that women's movements and organizations have been proliferating around the world, and that their priorities may vary by region, I assign Amrita Basu's *The Challenge of Local Feminisms: Women's Movements in Global Perspective.* This volume has chapters on women's movements in Asia, Africa, the Middle East, Latin America, Russia, Europe, and the United States. The texts by Basu and by West and Blumberg have helped students understand that women's protests, movements, and organizations are not limited to the West or to postindustrial society; nor do women's movements frame the issues in a predictable or uniform way. Economic justice, democracy and human rights, egalitarian family laws, land rights, reproductive rights and health, ending violence against women—these are among the issues around which women organize and mobilize.

Although these books view movements and SMOs in their local or national contexts, they do not address networking among women's SMOs, links between women in developing and developed countries, and the emergence of transnational feminist organizations. I raise these issues in a lecture, referring in part to my own articles, "Feminist Networks North and South" (1996) and "Transnational Feminist Networks: Collective Action in an Era of Globalization" (2000). I encourage students to think about social movements in a global context, and to reflect on the ways that political opportunities may be global and not merely local or national. I urge them to consider the ways that organizations and networks may span countries and regions, and the ways that discourses and strategies may be supranational. In one class, a student who was initially interested in female circumcision in the Sudan decided to write a research paper (and eventually her master's thesis) on the global movement against female circumcision. She decided to study this movement in terms of the formation of a global political opportunity structure, the emergence of transnational networks and organizations addressing the issue, and the distinctive ways that the issue has been framed by health organizations and women's groups.

The first time I taught social movements, I included a unit on fundamentalist movements. I started with a lecture on the factors behind the rise of fundamentalism (with a focus on religio-politics in Muslim societies, as I am most familiar with this type) and then discussed the ways that women and gender issues figure into Islamic fundamentalist movements. The main readings were from my book, *Modernizing Women: Gender and Social Change in the Middle East,* and two books that I edited, *Gender and National Identity: Women and Politics in Muslim Societies* and *Identity Politics and Women: Cultural Reassertions and Feminisms in International Perspective* (Moghadam 1993, 1994a, and 1994b). Chapters assigned and discussed in class were on Islamist movements and women's responses, women and Jewish fundamentalism in Israel, and feminism and fundamentalism in Algeria and Egypt. These readings underscore the fact that women and gender issues figure prominently in fundamentalist movements, as seen by the movements' discourses, objectives, mobilizing patterns, and outcomes. Contemporary fundamentalist movements exemplify the gendered nature of social movements.

More recently, I have devoted unit 3 to the labor movement in North America. Students read *A New Labor Movement for New Century* (Mantsios 1998) and articles by Linda Briskin and Dorothy Sue Cobble on women and unions. Students are thus able to acquire an understanding of the origins of the labor movement, its decline and recent revitalization, and the problems and prospects of women in what has been a predominantly male trade union movement.

CONCLUSIONS

Focusing on women's movements and on the gender dynamics of fundamentalism and the labor movement contributes to a more comprehensive understanding of contemporary social movements as global and gendered. The students choose to write research papers on aspects of specific social movements or SMOs, and I encourage them to examine the gender dynamics of these movements and women's participation in them, even if the movements selected are not women's movements. Topics chosen by the students have included the following: the Chiapas movement, the women's movement in the Czech Republic, the 1989 revolution in Romania, the global movement against female circumcision, the Black Panthers and the Black Muslims in the United States, the animal rights movement, the gay rights movement in the United States, the Irish Republican movement, the antiapartheid movement in South Africa, and the Algerian and Iranian women's movements.

WORKS CITED

Basu, Amrita, ed. 1995. *The Challenge of Local Feminisms: Women's Movements in Global Perspective.* Boulder: Westview Press.

Einwohner, Rachel L., Jocelyn A. Hollander, and Toska Olson. 2000. "Engendering Social Movements: Cultural Images and Movement Dynamics." *Gender and Society* 14 (5) (October): 679–699.

Ferree, Myra Marx, and Beth B. Hess. 1994. *Controversy and Coalition: The New Feminist Movement Across Three Decades of Change.* New York: Twayne.

Jaquette, Jane, ed. 1994. *The Women's Movement in Latin America: Participation and Democracy.* Second edition. Boulder: Westview Press.

Johnson, Jacqueline, and Barbara Risman. 1997. *"Sociology," Discipline Analysis, Women in the Curriculum.* Baltimore: National Center for Curriculum Transformation Resources on Women, Towson University.

Kriesi, Hanspeter. 1996. "The Organizational Structure of New Social Movements in a Political Context." In Doug McAdam, John D. McCarthy, and Mayer N. Zald, eds., *Contemporary Perspectives on Social Movements: Political Opportunities, Mobilizing Structures, and Cultural Framings,* 152–184. Cambridge: Cambridge University Press.

Mantsios, Gregory, ed. 1998. *A New Labor Movement for the New Century.* New York: Monthly Review.

McAdam, Doug, John D. McCarthy, and Mayer N. Zald, eds. 1996. *Comparative Perspectives on Social Movements: Political Opportunities, Mobilizing Structures, and Cultural Framings.* Cambridge: Cambridge University Press.

Melucci, Alberto. 1985. "The Symbolic Challenge of Contemporary Movements," *Social Research* 52 (4): 789–815.

Mikell, Gwendolyn, ed. 1997. *African Feminism: The Politics of Survival in Sub-Saharan Africa.* Philadelphia: University of Pennsylvania Press.

Moghadam, Valentine M. 1993. *Modernizing Women: Gender and Social Change in the Middle East.* Boulder: Lynne Rienner.

———, ed. 1994a. *Gender and National Identity: Women and Politics in Muslim Societies.* London: Zed Books.

———, ed. 1994b. *Identity Politics and Women: Cultural Reassertions and Feminisms in International Perspective.* Boulder: Westview Press.

———. 1996. "Feminist Networks North and South." *Journal of International Communication* 3 (1): 111–126.

———. 1997. "Gender and Revolutions." in John Foran, ed., *Theorizing Revolutions,* 137–167. New York and London: Routledge.

———. 2000. "Transnational Feminist Networks: Collective Action in an Era of Globalization." *International Sociology* 15 (1) (March): 57–85.

Staggenborg, Suzanne. 1998. *Gender, Family, and Social Movements.* Thousand Oaks, Calif.: Pine Forge Press.

Stienstra, Deborah. 1994. *Women's Movements and International Organizations.* New York: St. Martin's Press.

West, Guida, and Rhoda Blumberg, eds. 1990. *Women and Social Protest.* New York: Oxford University Press.

West, Lois, ed., 1997. *Feminist Nationalism.* New York and London: Routledge.

SYLLABUS

The term *social movement* covers various forms of collective action aimed at societal reorganization, ranging from millenarian or religious protest movements to secular movements for social change, including class-based labor movements, nationalist movements, social revolutions, and various reform movements. Sociological theories of social movements have their origins in Gustave Le Bon's theory of crowd behavior (published in 1895), which argued that in periods of social decline and disintegration, society is threatened by the rule of crowds. In the early 1960s Neil Smelser drew attention to the importance of "generalized beliefs" and values in directing social movements in periods of rapid social change and political disruption, and others have emphasized grievances in the causes and course of social movements. Charles Tilly holds that social movements, including revolutions, require common interests, organization, and mobilization for resources.

During the 1980s, Western sociologists debated the emergence of *new social movements,* ostensibly characteristic of postindustrial and postclass societies, such as the civil rights movement in the United States, the women's movement, the peace and antinuclear weapons movement, the disability movement, the environmental movement, the animal rights movement, and the gay and lesbian movement. Sociologists have also examined the rise of fundamentalism and communalism in the Middle East and South Asia. Feminists have focused on the rise and expansion of women's movements in the world-system, and they have drawn attention to gender aspects of broader social movements, such as revolutions, nationalist movements, and fundamentalist movements.

There are three objectives to this course:

1. to learn about sociological theories of social movements;
2. to learn about social movements in an international perspective;

3. to apply sociological insights to an understanding of the emergence of women's movements, and to grasp the gender dimension of social movements, including the role of women as participants, the role of gender ideologies in shaping the contours of the movements, and the postmovement effects on women and on gender relations.

Readings

Comparative Perspectives on Social Movements: Political Opportunities, Mobilizing Structures, and Cultural Framings, edited by Doug McAdam, John D. McCarthy, and Mayer N. Zald. Cambridge: Cambridge University Press, 1996 (required).

Controversy and Coalition: The New Feminist Movement Across Three Decades of Change, by Myra Marx Ferree and Beth B. Hess. New York: Twayne, 1994 (required).

Women and Social Protest, edited by Guida West and Rhoda Blumberg. Oxford: Oxford University Press, 1990 (recommended, on reserve).

The Challenge of Local Feminisms: Women's Movements in Global Perspective, edited by Amrita Basu. Boulder: Westview Press, 1995 (recommended, on reserve).

A New Labor Movement for the New Century, edited by Gregory Mantsios. New York: Monthly Review, 1998 (required).

"The Feminist Challenge to the Unions," by Linda Briskin and Patricia McDermott, in *Women Challenging Unions,* edited by Linda Briskin and Patricia McDermott. Toronto: University of Toronto Press, 1993 (on reserve).

"Introduction: Remaking Unions for the New Majority," by Dorothy Sue Cobble, in *Women and Unions: Forging a Partnership,* edited by Dorothy Sue Cobble. Ithaca, N.Y.: ILR Press, 1993 (on reserve).

Unit 1. Weeks 1–7: Theory and Research in the Sociology of Social Movements

McAdam, McCarthy, and Zald, eds., *Comparative Perspectives on Social Movements.*

Week 1: Introductions and Overview

Weeks 2 & 3: McAdam, et al., part I

Weeks 4 & 5: McAdam, et al., part II

Weeks 6 & 7: McAdam, et al., part III

Assignment 1: Book review

In five to eight double-spaced typed pages, summarize and review the text. How are social movements defined, and which ones are mentioned in the text? Discuss the three dimensions of social movement theory. Choose one chapter and explain how "political opportunities," "mobilizing structures," and "cultural framings" are used in that chapter. Refer to the book and the lectures. Due in Week 7.

Assignment 2: Research paper proposal

Due in Week 8: a two-page typed proposal for a research paper (which is due at the end of the semester). The proposal should identify a particular social movement or SMO that is of interest to you, suggest how you will use social movement theory to analyze it, and indicate how gender is involved in the movement or organization. Pose a research question, discuss your methodology and sources of data, and end with a brief bibliography. (Suggested topics: the suffrage movement; the Irish, Palestinian, or Basque nationalist movement; the U.S. labor movement; the U.S. civil rights movement; the disability movement; the anti-apartheid movement; the U.S. Christian Right; the anti-abortion movement; Islamic fundamentalism; or a women's, environmental, gay, or human rights movement or organization in a particular country.)

Unit 2. Weeks 8–11: Women in Movement

Ferree and Hess, *Controversy and Coalition*
Also read: Introductions to West and Blumberg, eds., *Women and Social Protest,* and
    Basu, ed., *The Challenge of Local Feminisms*—I will refer to these in my lecture.

Week 8: Ferree and Hess, chapters 1–2 (my lecture); Ferree and Hess, chapters 3–6 (student presentations)

Week 9: Ferree and Hess chapters 7–8 (student presentations)

Week 10: Assignment 3

Week 11: Discussion of research proposals

Assignment 3: Group papers and discussions

One student group for each of the four parts in the West and Blumberg book and the four parts in the Basu book. Each group will collectively prepare a written summary analysis of the assigned readings, five to eight pages, typed and double-spaced. Address the following questions: (1) Is feminism, local, or global, or both? (2) How, why, and with what consequences do women protest? (3) What kinds of movements and organizations do women join or form? (4) What concepts from social movement theory are helpful?

Unit 3. Weeks 12–16: The Labor Movement in North America

Student presentations of research papers-in-progress.

Week 12: The labor movement as a social movement (my lecture); Mantsios, part 1 (student presentations)

Week 13: Mantsios, parts 2, 3, 4, 5, and articles by Briskin and Cobble (student presentations)

Weeks 14–16: Student presentations of research papers-in-progress

Research papers due at the end of the term.

MAINSTREAMING WOMEN'S ECOLOGICAL CONCERNS AND FEMINIST PERSPECTIVES ON GLOBAL ENVIRONMENTAL CHALLENGES AND SUSTAINABLE DEVELOPMENT

Filomina Chioma Steady

The original course as designed brought a social dimension to the study of environmental issues by linking physical data with socioeconomic indicators. My ultimate aim was to analyze the social roots of the ecological crisis and to examine various approaches to its resolution. My emphasis was on the impact of human activity on the natural environment and on the relationship between people and nature. The approach was critical as well as constructive and focused on advancing an integrated, holistic worldview and planetary consciousness through readings on social and political ecology. I urge the exploration of alternatives that might ameliorate the dominance of the current technologically destructive and antipeople development model.

A major theme explored throughout the course, linking all its units, is sustainability as it relates to sustainable development defined by the Brundtland Commission—development that meets the needs of the present without compromising the ability of future generations to meet their own needs. This theme resonates well with students who can identify with the needs of future generations. It also brings into sharp focus the central function of women in maintaining many of the regenerative institutions and activities that promote sustainability.

My original course was divided into four main units: an overview of environmental problems; theoretical approaches; linking physical data and sociocultural indicators; and action for environmental change. My revision compressed these four units and added complementary ones. All eight units now incorporate gender and women's issues as well as opportunities for feminist analysis. The four new units examine the environmental and gender implications of poverty, population in conjunction with consumption patterns, health, and globalization. I use a multidisciplinary approach throughout.

The effort to mainstream women's and gender issues in development and ecology responds to several factors. First, undergraduates, especially those attending a women's institution like Wellesley College, want multidisciplinary courses on global issues, taught from a feminist perspective. Second, the structural linkages of women, the environment, and development have stimulated a growing body of literature. Third, an integrated, holistic worldview would be incomplete without feminist analysis. Such analysis helps to elucidate how human activity based on a gendered division of labor has served as an important organizing principle in many societies, often concentrating power and decision making in the hands of men.

UNIT 1: THE INTERNATIONAL DIVISION OF LABOR AND THE ENVIRONMENT

This is an expansion of the unit on the overview of environmental problems. It now includes a section on the gender division of labor to give a more accurate picture of global environmental problems. In the investigation of the ecological crisis in various parts of the world, I analyze the degree to which women use and manage natural resources. In many parts of the Third World, women's work brings them into direct and intense daily contact with the total ecosystem. Women perform most of the tasks related to farming, waste disposal, and household management. Yet development policies and programs often neglect women's important work. Furthermore, development has tended to impact negatively on women by destroying the environment and women's livelihood base in many countries. I examine two societies (one in Africa and one in Asia) in which women work significantly in forestry and agriculture to see how this work has been affected by the ecological crisis.

UNIT 2: THEORETICAL APPROACHES AND FEMINIST CRITIQUE

Readings in the philosophy of science, political ecology, development, and feminist critiques make up the core of this unit. This is followed by a multidisciplinary and historical analysis of the origins of the present ecological crisis. I encourage students to examine the main discourse, which has centered on whether nature is to be dominated and used for profit, or whether it should primarily serve the needs of all people for their survival. Such conflicts represent two opposing theoretical standpoints and ideologies, one stemming from the tradition of Western science and the other from indigenous knowledge systems that seek to maintain balance and harmony with nature. I assign new readings on ecofeminism and other relevant brands of feminism to explore in depth the relationship of ecology to feminism, and to strengthen the multidisciplinary and holistic framework of the course. I present feminist critiques of science, technology, development, and patriarchy from the theoretical positions of various schools of feminist thought. These include (a) ecofeminism, which views the environmental crisis as stemming from an ideology that equates women with nature as objects of domination; (b) feminist environmentalism, which argues for an explanation with a more materialistic basis determined by women's class, race, ethnicity, and access to power; and (c) the women, environment, and development (WED) position, which is a critique of the patriarchal approach to development planning. I encourage students to contemplate the the oretical implications of various disciplines such as anthropology, economics, political science, and sociology in explaining the environmental crisis. Because students are majoring in various disciplines, they may bring specific disciplinary perspectives to the discussions. They may also design their term papers to suit the theoretical and empirical traditions of their major disciplines.

Unit 3: Linking Physical Data and Social Indicators

This unit asks questions that seek to explain the various outcomes of the linkages between physical indicators of environmental degradation and socioeconomic data. Such questions lead to an examination of the impact of physically deteriorating environments on social organization. This includes the impact of development programs that can lead to environmentally unsound projects such as dams, intensive fishing technologies, nuclear testing, and so on. The differential impact of development on populations based on their class and racial affiliations is also an important topic. The unit includes readings on women and the environment in the Third World, particularly case studies developed from research activities by feminist academics in agriculture, forestry, sociology, anthropology, economics, and environmental studies.

Unit 4: Poverty and Environmental Degradation

This new unit examines the synergistic linkage between poverty and environmental degradation in terms of the impact on women of soil erosion, depletion of natural resources, and commercial and industrial activities on land use. The feminization of poverty, particularly rural poverty, is closely related to environmental degradation, which impoverishes ecosystems as well as people and can threaten the livelihood of entire communities. Students are encouraged to appreciate the various nuances of the relationship between poverty and environmental degradation that may allow poor people no other options than to further degrade the environment out of need and desperation. Export-oriented development processes may also contribute to the loss of environmental control by most rural households.

Because women's workloads often increase with environmental degradation, I include studies of women's work in countries with serious environmental problems in both rural and urban settings. Fortunately a large body of literature on rural women's work in the Third World, particularly in agriculture, is available, as are films and videos that convey the urgency of women's increasing workload and poverty. I attend also to situations in industrialized countries, to avoid perpetuating negative stereotypes about women in the Third World as victims, because poverty also exists in many industrialized countries.

Students study environmental problems resulting from the neglect of inner city environments, the location of dump sites and dirty industries in areas inhabited by poor people, especially people of color in the United States. Students also review the work of the environmental justice movement (EJM), which produces advocacy research calling attention to the racist motivations of many environmentally destructive programs and projects and their effects on racial minorities.

UNIT 5: POPULATION AND CONSUMPTION PATTERNS

In this essential new unit, I point out the importance, from an ecological point of view, of appreciating the negative impact of population increases and high consumption patterns on the natural environment. I present the population-environment nexus from a critical perspective that examines various ideological approaches ranging from Neo-Malthusianism to antiabortion positions. I approach the reproductive rights issue, usually associated with feminist thinking, as controversial and a topic to be critically assessed through reflective discussions. Understanding the importance of resource use and management requires examination of overconsumption and affluence as contributing factors to environmental degradation. The course explores the gender implications of the relationships among population, consumption patterns, and environmental degradation through comparisons of societies in the Third World of the South with those of industrialized countries of the North. I encourage students to develop responses to problems of overconsumption by designing hypothetical situations that could promote changes in values and lifestyles in their respective communities. Through this exercise I encourage students to share their experiential knowledge on the subject.

UNIT 6: HEALTH AND THE ENVIRONMENT

This additional unit provides students with a view of the ultimate effect of environmental degradation on the human organism through pollution, misuse of synthetic chemicals, emission of ozone-depleting substances, greenhouse gases, use of dirty technologies, and dumping of hazardous waste in Third World countries. In many Third World countries, the health of the majority of women remains relatively poor and is made worse by increasing degradation of their environments. Problems of malnutrition, infectious diseases, and pollution are becoming endemic in some areas. HIV/AIDS, which is increasingly viewed as a disease made worse by poverty, has environmental implications and poses particular threats to poor women.

Readings reflecting gender and health include sociocultural, economic, political, and epidemiological material. I critically assess gender-disaggregated health statistics to determine whether they sufficiently identify groups of women most at risk. I discuss natural approaches to healing in terms of their greater affinity to the natural world, in contrast to the biomedical model, which can lead to excessive interventions and medicalization. Reading assignments include studies from academe and the World Health Organization. I also assign literature generated by the Women's Health Care Movement, which generally views women as victims of the health care system. I show a number of videos for discussions.

UNIT 7: GLOBALIZATION TRENDS AND THE ENVIRONMENT

Designed to situate the issue of globalization within the environment and ecology debate, this new unit provides a unitary framework through which to understand the importance of environmental and gender issues in the global economy. I analyze elements in global development that impact directly and negatively on the environment or produce conditions that prevent people from protecting their environment. Many developing countries are experiencing economic recession, chronic debt burdens, and oppressive conditions related to structural adjustment. The relationship between debt and environmental degradation has been convincingly made in readings for discussions. The environmental implications of export processing zones (EPZs) that employ large numbers of women as cheap sources of labor provide the basis for discussions of the relationship between the international exploitation of female labor and environmental degradation.

UNIT 8: ENVIRONMENTAL MOVEMENTS AND INTERNATIONAL ACTION

A focus on social responsibility for the environment begins with reviews of international plans of action and activities of environmental, ecological, and green movements, and the environmental justice movement. Women's environmental movements are mushrooming throughout the world, their effectiveness especially notable since the 1992 Earth Summit. I examine the recommendations relevant to women, mainstreamed throughout *Agenda 21,* the program of action from the Rio Earth Summit.

During the year before the 1992 Earth Summit, several meetings were held by women to examine the gender issues in environmental degradation and the impact of environmental degradation on women. These included the Global Assembly on Women and the Environment and the World Congress of Women for a Healthy Planet, held in Miami in 1991. Students examine the published results of these meetings and others in which research data were presented. They will also review recent environmental activities by women's organizations.

SYLLABUS

This course is designed to bring a social dimension to the study of environmental issues from a gender perspective by linking physical data with socioeconomic indicators. The ultimate aim is to analyze the social roots of the ecological crisis embedded in human activity and to examine various approaches to its resolution. The emphasis is on the study of development processes on the natural environment, and on the relationship between people and nature. The course is simultaneously critical as well as constructive, focusing on advancing an integrated, holistic worldview and planetary consciousness through readings on the environment, social and political ecology, feminist critiques of science, and technology and development. It offers an alternative to the dominance of a technologically destructive and antipeople development model propelled by global capital.

Class Expectations and Format

Due to the broad range and volume of the material covered in the course and its multidisciplinary nature, class participation is essential. The class will be divided into teams responsible for reporting on particular reading assignments on the basis of rotation. This will provide an opportunity for students to learn from each other and to appreciate the various disciplinary backgrounds, perspectives, and experiences that each student brings to the class. The teams will be responsible for focusing discussion and criticism on the readings for their assigned portion of the class meetings. Each team should prepare, in advance of their presentations, a summary of their reading, and the main questions to be discussed.

Required Texts (available at the bookstore)

Colburn, T., et al. *Our Stolen Future,* New York: Dutton, 1996.
Goudie, A. *The Human Impact on the Natural Environment,* Cambridge: MIT Press, 1986.
Leiss, W. *The Domination of Nature,* New York: Braziller, 1992.
Rocheleau D., et al., eds. *Feminist Political Ecology: Global Issues and Local Experiences,* London, New York: Routledge, 1996.
Steady, F. C., ed. *Women and Children First: Environment, Poverty, and Sustainable Development*, Rochester: Schenkman Books, 1993.

Books on Reserve: Required and Recommended Readings

Anderson, W. *Green Man: The Archetype of Our Oneness with the Earth*, San Francisco: Harper, 1980.

Bandarage, A. *Women, Population, and Global Crisis*, London: Zed Books, 1997.

Bookchin, M. *Toward an Ecological Society*, Montreal: Black Rose Press, 1984.

Brown, L., and A. Durning. *State of the World*, New York: Norton, 1984.

Bullard, R., ed. *Confronting Environmental Racism*, Boston: South End Press, 1993.

Dankelman, I., and J. Davidson. *Women and the Environment in the Third World: Alliance for the Future*, London: Earthscan, 1988.

Diamond, I., and G. F. Orenstein, eds. *Reweaving the World: The Emergence of Ecofeminism*, San Francisco: Sierra Club Books, 1990.

Durning, A. *How Much Is Enough*, New York: Norton, 1992.

Faber, D. *Environment Under Fire: Imperialism and the Ecological Crisis in Central America*, New York: Monthly Review Press, 1993.

George, S. *The Debt Boomerang: How Third World Debt Affects Us All*, London: Pluto Press with the International Institute, 1992.

Griffin, K. *World Hunger, World Economy, and Other Essays in Development Economics*, London: Holms and Meier, 1987.

Harcourt, W. *Feminist Perspectives on Sustainable Development*, London: Zed Books, 1994.

James, U. *Women and Sustainable Development in Africa*, Westport, Conn.: Praeger, 1995.

Rodda, A. *Women and the Environment*, London, Atlantic Highlands, N.J.: Zed Books, 1991.

Ruether, M. *New Woman, New Earth*, New York: Seabury Press, 1975.

Shiva, V. *Staying Alive*, London: Zed Books, 1991.

UNEP, *Global Assembly on Women and the Environment Documents*, Nairobi, U.N.E.P., 1992.

United Nations, *Agenda 21*, New York: United Nations, 1993.

Women's Health Collective. *The New Our Bodies, Ourselves*, New York: Simon & Schuster, 1984.

World Health Organization. *An Anthology on Women, Health and the Environment*, compiled by J. Sims. Geneva: WHO, 1994 WHO/EHG/194.11.

———. *Health and Environment in Sustainable Development: Five Years After the Earth Summit*, Geneva: WHO, 1997.

Video Series: *Race to Save the Planet.*

Course Outline

Unit 1. The International Division of Labor and the Environment

READINGS: GOUDIE, PARTS 1, 2, AND 3; STEADY, INTRODUCTION, CHAPTERS 1, 2; RODDA, CHAPTERS 1, 2; BROWN AND DURNING (RECOMMENDED); BOOKIN (RECOMMENDED).

Unit 2. Theoretical Approaches and Feminist Critique

READINGS: LEISS, ALL; RUETHER, ALL; ROCHELEAU ET AL., INTRODUCTION, CHAPTER 1; SHIVA, CHAPTERS 1–3; DIAMOND AND ORENSTEIN, PARTS I AND II; HARCOURT, PARTS I AND II; ANDERSON, ALL.

Unit 3. Linking Physical Data and Social Indicators

READINGS: GOUDIE, PARTS 4, 5, AND 7; STEADY, CHAPTERS 6, 7, 8; DANKELMAN AND DAVIDSON, CHAPTERS 1–5; BROWN AND DURNING (RECOMMENDED); JAMES, CHAPTERS 1–4 (RECOMMENDED).

Unit 4. Poverty and Environmental Degradation

READINGS: STEADY, CHAPTERS 1, 3, 10; BANDARAGE, CHAPTER 5; BULLARD, CHAPTERS 1, 2, 7, 9, 11; ROCHELEAU ET AL., CHAPTER 3; DURING, ALL; GRIFFIN (RECOMMENDED).

Take home exam assigned.

Unit 5. Population and Consumption Patterns

READINGS: BANDARAGE, CHAPTERS 4, 5; DURNING, ALL; STEADY, CHAPTERS 5, 22.

Unit 6. Health and the Environment

READINGS: COLBURN, ALL; STEADY, CHAPTERS 11, 12; WORLD HEALTH ORGANIZATION 1997, CHAPTERS 1, 2, 5, 6, 7; WORLD HEALTH ORGANIZATION 1994, ALL (RESERVE); WOMEN'S HEALTH COLLECTIVE (RESERVE).

Unit 7. Globalization Trends and the Environment

READINGS: GEORGE, CHAPTER 1; STEADY, CHAPTER 4; GRIFFIN, CHAPTERS 1, 4; HARCOURT, PART III (RECOMMENDED); FABER, ALL (RECOMMENDED).

Unit 8. Environmental Movements and International Action

READINGS: UNITED NATIONS AGENDA 21, ALL; UNEP, GLOBAL ASSEMBLY ON WOMEN AND THE ENVIRONMENT, ALL; ROCHELEAU ET AL., CHAPTERS 2, 5, 6, 7; STEADY, CHAPTERS 20, 21.

ON SWAMPS, HELICOPTERS, CORKSCREWS, AND COOKING: REFLECTIONS ON INTERNATIONALIZING FEMINIST THOUGHT AND THEORY

Naomi B. Scheman

> *Tell me about your pain. I want to know your story. And then
> I will tell it back to you in a new way. Tell it back to you in
> such a way that it has become mine, my own. Re-writing you,
> I write myself anew. I am still author, authority. I am still the
> colonizer, the speaking subject, and you are now at the center
> of my talk.*
>
> **—bell hooks (1990)**

In urging us to recognize that "the master's tools will never dismantle the master's house," Audre Lorde was referring to the tools that enable some women to get ahead by availing themselves of the privileges of race, class, or sexuality; but she is often read as though the tools in question are those crafted and typically deployed in the academy, notably those of what is thought of there as "theory" (Lorde 1984). Although Lorde herself taught in a university and was deeply committed to opening the world of theory to those who have been shut and shamed out of it, the mistake is not, of course, wholly mistaken. Universities are places of privilege, and tools crafted there to serve the projects of the privileged cannot unquestioningly be put to other, liberatory uses. Nor can those of us who work in universities justifiably remain ignorant of the complexities, limitations, and compromises of our social locations or of the reasons why many of those whose allies we would be are suspicious of the places from which we speak. In using the tools of academic theory, even academic feminist theory, to what extent are we using the master's tools in the sense Lorde meant, tools that function, whatever else we might think we are doing with them, to reinforce inequalities of gender, race, class, sexuality, and so on—to reinforce our own privileges as academics? What might it mean to use those tools sufficiently differently, and why might it matter (to whom?) to try to do so? How are the tools changed when they are used by those who were never meant to deploy them? What are we—those of us who teach in women's studies, for example—

doing when we theorize in academically disciplined ways (more or less transformed by our feminist commitments) and teach others to do so? What sort of practice is that, what norms shape it, and to whom do those norms hold us responsible?

In asking for my help in articulating a topic for a term paper, students frequently start from a strong conviction that the perfect paper lies just out of reach, shimmering on the far side of a swamp—daunting equally for its muck and its alligators. They are convinced that I have a helicopter that can lift them over the swamp, to where the perfect paper awaits. My advice is always the same: I don't have a helicopter, and the swamp *is* the paper. The questions in the first paragraph and the anxieties behind them were for me the swamp that lay between me and the project of "internationalizing" a course in feminist theory, and I clearly had need of my own advice: Swamps *are* messy and dangerous, and the longing for helicopters is understandable. But what seems to make it impossible for us to get on with what we think we are supposed to be doing is likely to be what is most interesting and important. In this case, the questions and anxieties became the course.

Thinking of theories as tools is a useful first step, directing our attention to what we *do*: tools for what—meaning not only what do we want to do with them, but also, what were they designed to do? Whose hands and whose ways of working were they designed to fit? How are they most comfortably used, and what do they accomplish when used that way? What do we learn about them from using them against the grain?

I recently handed my friend Amy a wine bottle and a corkscrew, the sort that fits over the cork and withdraws it easily when you turn its handle continuously in one direction. But what I took to be a simple, effective tool didn't work for her: Amy is left-handed. At first I didn't get it; the corkscrew looked symmetrical to me, a truly generic tool. But she showed me the difficulty she had in turning it the right way— clockwise; it is, in fact, a right-handed tool. I've learned from Amy's experience and now understand that corkscrews are not generic but are designed for members of the dominant group to use with dexterity while making it harder for the others, who use them at best clumsily, often in situations in which not looking gauche really matters. Left-handed corkscrews would help, but then there would be two sorts, the left-handed and the normal; and politically correct right-handed people would worry that maybe they should get a left-handed corkscrew should any left-handed guests want to be helpful. Or perhaps we should switch from corkscrews to some other sort of genuinely generic device like an air pump—even though those things aren't "real" corkscrews and they require learning a whole new set of bottle-opening habits. At this point, a right-thinking, dexterous person could get very cranky: why should we have to change what we do to suit a bunch of gauche malcontents, probably with sinister designs on our way of life: corkscrews today, can-openers (Amy says) tomorrow.

But even without the crankiness the situation illustrates the virtues and the pitfalls of standpoint epistemology. Clearly Amy was in a position to know something that, because of my privilege, I could be ignorant about. As a left-handed person in a right-handed world, she has to be, conceptually, if not literally, ambidextrous, noticing how right-handed tools work even if she can't quite use them properly. But I can learn from her experience, as I did. And the important thing to notice is that, according to the dominant, scientifically centered, epistemic norms, I now count as the better knower. As a right-thinking person, I can launder her experience, removing the taint of gaucheness. As Uma Narayan has argued, the knowledge that subordinated peoples are taken to have is thought of as something that exudes from them, a sort of natural resource that the culturally privileged can gather and render into proper—disciplined—knowledge (Narayan 1997, 145). It is better—more objective—to *have* informants than to be one, to theorize the experiences of others than to have experiences yourself. The epistemic privilege of the subordinated too often turns out to be a trap. And attempts to level the discursive playing fields are bound to be awkward for those whose comfort and dexterity have been bought at the expense of those who have been forced to use tools that reinforced their own subordination. (Think about discussions about the supposedly generic masculine.)

It is this act of appropriation that bell hooks satirizes in the quotation that heads this essay, and it is a danger that attends the efforts of those of us who would revise our courses to incorporate the experiences and perspectives of various Others. The word should be a tip-off: to *incorporate* means to make part of one's (own) body; what we incorporate nourishes us and makes us larger, stronger. And we can only incorporate what we can digest, which means we have to break down what we would incorporate into its simple components, abstracting usable nutrients from the indigestible specificity of its own identity. One of the problems with "add Third World women and stir" is that it might work *too* well: among the tools of academic theory are powerful tenderizers; nearly anything is ultimately digestible, and what is not is most likely to be discarded.

The lesson that I think emerges from the metaphoric mix of swamps, helicopters, corkscrews, and cooking is that, especially in a "theory" course, the most important thing to teach is how to be critically reflective about one's own practices, including one's practices of theorizing, and how to listen to and learn from others in ways that respect their agency, including their agency as theorizers. It is this lesson that I tried to put at the center of the course as I redesigned it.

Feminist Thought and Theory is one of women's studies' core courses and has shifted from being intended for nonmajors wanting an introduction to feminist theory to relate to their work in other fields, to being required of majors, who let us know that they needed more theory and a way of learning how to read and engage with theoretical texts, which, when they did encounter them, often seemed dauntingly opaque. Our aims for the course are that students (both majors and nonmajors: students are divided in discussion sections between those with and without a significant background in women's studies) acquire a knowledge of some of the works of feminist theory that inform current debates; and that they acquire skills of engaging critically with such work and are able to connect it to issues in their own lives and in the world more generally. We want them to reflect on the practices out of which theory emerges and on the implications of the diverse social locations of those who theorize and are theorized about, including questions about the institutionalization and the usefulness of theory.

At the time I took on the project specifically of internationalizing the course, I had already revised it twice: first to add discussions of theory-in-practice to more specifically theoretical works, and second to better integrate the two and to frame the course around questions about theory *as* practice. I wanted to situate theory as emerging from and frequently embedded in practice, often articulated in forms that might not seem, in academic terms, theoretical. And, I wanted students to regard theorizing itself as a set of practices, attending especially to those practices that institutionalize and discipline theory. Speaking from within the academy, it is important to acknowledge equally that others construct theories and that what we do counts as practice.

I began by assuming that internationalizing the course involved (at least) adding material written within non–U.S. contexts, but fairly soon decided that doing so would make the course overly diffuse and superficial. As a group, we were also developing a course in international feminist theory, and I decided to frame my own course around learning how to think in ways that would be useful for that other course, as well as for bringing comparative perspectives to all one's work. I decided to focus on feminist theorizing within the United States, with attention to the placement of the United States in an international context. Thus, for example, we understand the United States to be that place in which we are all residing, at least for the duration of the course—keeping in mind that some of us are native-born, with varying family histories; some are immigrants; and some are temporarily resident here. We also attend to the reciprocal relationships between U.S.–based feminist theory and practice and feminist theory and practice elsewhere, especially as U.S. feminism has become increasingly cognizant of the complexities of those relationships and has been increasingly shaped by efforts better to understand and respond to the specificities of the positions in which those of us living here stand to women in the rest of the world.

My changes in reading assignments stemmed from the replacement of one text (Nancy Tuana and Rosemary Tong's *Feminism and Philosophy*, 1995) with another (Linda Nicholson's *The Second Wave*, 1997) and the addition of a collection of essays (Uma Narayan's *Dislocating Cultures*, 1997). The Nicholson anthology fits better with an approach to feminist theory that breaks with the problematic tax-onomizing of the 1980s and also includes more of the "classics" with which students should be familiar. Narayan writes as an Indian feminist from within the U.S. academy (she is a philosophy professor at Vassar), and her essays fit very well with a number of the thematic sections of the course, as well as providing an excellent example of feminist theorizing that places the Third World woman, whose interventions have helped (re)shape recent U.S. feminist theory, at the center of the conversation, both problematizing her construction and foregrounding her agency.

The course has four sections. The first starts from the idea that what counts as a question cannot be taken for granted, and that asking new questions, or old questions in new ways, is itself theoretically and politically loaded, and that it is important to consider who gets to define what counts as a real problem. The essays in this section, especially, range widely in terms of how academically theoretical they are, what they presume the reader already knows or cares about, and what conversations they take themselves to be parts of. Students will react differently from one another to the various essays; some will find certain essays more accessible than others, and for a range of reasons. Dealing with who feels welcomed or excluded by a text is part of what gets discussed in class.

The second section looks at theory in situ, in relation to particular sites of practice: the body, the self, and issues of identity; communities and politics; and relationships to the nonhuman world. In each case gender is shown to be complexly interwoven with other social structures. What gender means—even what it *is*—has to do with the role it plays in a particular location, where both the role and the location need to be understood in a broader, global context, not of similarities and differences, but of concrete, material interconnectedness. The emphasis in this section is on theory as locally emergent, responsive to particular, practical, experienced needs of particular, located agents who are trying to make sense of their worlds in order better to act in them. Most of the readings would be classified as theoretical, but they all take themselves to have particular audiences; they are written to address particular needs; and they are located within particular, practical discursive spaces, such as efforts at political organizing around peace or environmental issues or arguing sex equality cases in court.

The third, and longest, section has to do with the sources and shaping of (what are usually meant by) feminist theories, starting with the emergence of the second wave, and moving through Marxist-socialist feminism, radical feminism, psychoanalysis, standpoint theories, the deconstructing of identity and the theorizing of difference, and the question of essentialism. In each case, theory is set in historical context: Whose needs set the terms for the theories? Whose questions were they developed to answer? Adequate coverage on such a range of theories is, of course, impossible. The aim is to give students some sense of how to read these texts, contexts in which to understand them, and the confidence to grapple further with them. In particular, this sense of "theory," as referring to distinct and distinguishable entities, is shown to be an artifact (though not an unimportant one) of academic practice. This practice of producing, naming, claiming, and comparing theories needs to be understood in relation to the theories' emergence from and (to greater and lesser extents) continued embedding within liberatory practices outside of the academy.

The final section picks up on that recognition through a focus on theorizing as itself a form of practice, including questions about the disciplining and institutionalizing of theory. The essays are by academic theorists, all of whom are, in Patricia Hill Collins's term, "outsiders within," attentive to their own positions as fully accredited and authorized knowers who are nonetheless culturally and racially marginalized even within feminist academic settings. Attention in the essays is specifically on questions about how knowledge and knowers are constructed and authorized, especially within institutional settings structured by privilege and subordination. The focus of discussion is on how each of us, given the complexities of our relationships to diverse structures of privilege, can theorize responsibly, especially as we develop relationships to and through the particular institution within which we are working.

Rather than maintaining *theory* and *practice* as poles to be related, an aim of the course is to shift how we think about both: theory-laden practice (especially as in section II) and theorizing as a form of practice (especially as in section IV). The slogan "Think globally; act locally" encourages us to think of theory as generalizing and practice as particular. By contrast, the suggestion of the course is that we think of theory as emerging locally and becoming global not through generalization (similarities and differences between here and there) but through connections-in-practice (how what we do here, including theorize, is helped or hindered, helps or hinders, what they do there, including theorize).

The final class session is devoted to group presentations reflecting on what members of the groups have learned about theory in/and/of practice from meeting with organizations or individuals involved in feminist politics, arts, or community activism. In their final essays, students are asked to reflect on their experiences working in the class and in their groups as (what are intended to be) theoretically informed examples of feminist practice.

WORKS CITED

hooks, bell. 1990. "Choosing the Margin as a Space of Radical Openness." In *Yearning: Race, Gender, and Cultural Politics*. Boston: South End Press.

Lorde, Audre. 1984. "The Master's Tools Will Never Dismantle the Master's House." In *Sister Outsider*. Trumansburg, N.Y.: Crossing Press.

Narayan, Uma. 1997. "Through the Looking-Glass Darkly: Emissaries, Mirrors, and Authentic Insiders as Preoccupations." In *Dislocating Cultures: Identities, Traditions, and Third World Feminism*. New York: Routledge.

Nicholson, Linda, ed. 1997. *The Second Wave: A Reader in Feminist Theory*. New York: Routledge.

Tuana, Nancy, and Rosemary Tong. 1995. *Feminism and Philosophy: Essential Readings in Theory, Reinterpretation, and Application*. Boulder: Westview.

SYLLABUS

Feminism has to do with changing the world. In order to change it we need to know something about what might be wrong with the way it is now, why it is that way, how it might be different, which differences would be improvements, and how various means of effecting change work. All of these things are exceedingly difficult to figure out and are subject to debate. Feminist theories are developed in order to help both with the figuring out and with the debate. In this class we will focus on the ways in which theory emerges from and informs matters of practice—aspects of our personal, political, and cultural lives. Our focus will be on the United States, as the place where we are all living, at least for the moment, and as the context for the university in which this course is located. We will be attentive to the diversity both of social locations within the United States and of relationships between the United States and those who live here to places and people in the rest of the world. A central set of questions throughout the course will be, What counts as theory? Who does it? How is it institutionalized? Who gets to ask the questions and to provide the answers? Writing assignments and group work will emphasize critical engagement both with the texts and with our own responses to them, as well as the drawing of connections among the readings and between the readings and the worlds outside of class.

Texts

Free Spirits: Feminist Philosophers on Culture, eds. Kate Mehuron and Gary Percesepe (Upper Saddle River, N.J.: Prentice Hall, 1995).

The Second Wave: A Reader in Feminist Theory, ed. Linda Nicholson (New York: Routledge, 1997).

Dislocating Cultures: Identities, Traditions, and Third World Feminism, Uma Narayan (New York: Routledge, 1997).

Course Outline

Section I. Naming the Problems

Week 1. Finding a Voice, Asking New Questions, Making Trouble

Women of ACE (AIDS Counseling and Education), "Voices" (in *Free Spirits*).

Gloria Anzaldúa, "How to Tame a Wild Tongue" (in *Free Spirits*).

On Swamps, Helicopters, Corkscrews, and Cooking 239

Susan Bordo, "'Material Girl': The Effacements of Postmodern Culture" (in *Free Spirits*).

Cynthia Enloe, "On the Beach: Sexism and Tourism" (in *Free Spirits*).

Richard Rodriguez, "Complexion" (in *Free Spirits*).

Week 2. Defining the Issues: Who Gets to Say What the Problem Is?

Kimberlé Crenshaw & Gary Peller, "Reel Time, Real Justice" (in *Free Spirits*).

Wahneema Lubiano, "Black Ladies, Welfare Queens, and State Minstrels: Ideological War by Narrative Means" (in *Free Spirits*).

Uma Narayan, "Cross-Cultural Connections, Border-Crossings, and 'Death by Culture'" (in *Dislocating Cultures*).

Nancy Fraser, "Struggle Over Needs: Outline of a Socialist-Feminist Critical Theory of Late Capitalist Political Culture" (in *Free Spirits*).

Section II. Theorizing Practice: A Look at Some Issues

Week 3. Body/Self/Identity

Sandra Bartky, "Foucault, Femininity, and the Modernization of Patriarchal Power" (in *Free Spirits*).

Linda Singer, "Bodies—Pleasures—Powers" (in *Free Spirits*).

Patricia Hill Collins, "The Sexual Politics of Black Womanhood" (in *Free Spirits*).

John Stoltenberg, "How Men Have (a) Sex" (in *Free Spirits*).

Patrick Hopkins, "Gender Treachery: Homophobia, Masculinity, and Threatened Iden-tities" (in *Free Spirits*).

Week 4. Community/Politics

Leslie Kanes Weisman, "The Private Use of Public Space" (in *Free Spirits*).

Ann Snitow, "Holding the Line at Greenham Common: Being Joyously Political in Dangerous Times [Feb. 1985]" (in *Free Spirits*).

Wendy W. Williams, "The Equality Crisis: Some Reflections on Culture, Courts, and Feminism" (in *Second Wave*).

bell hooks & Cornell West, "Breaking Bread" (in *Free Spirits*).

Barbara Smith, "Between a Rock and a Hard Place: Relationships Between Black and Jewish Women" (in *Free Spirits*).

Uma Narayan, "Eating Cultures: Incorporation, Identity, & Indian Food" (in *Dislocating Cultures*).

Week 5. Relationships to the Nonhuman World

Starhawk, "Power, Authority, and Mystery: Ecofeminism and Earth-Based Spirituality" (in *Free Spirits*).

Carol J. Adams, "The Feminist Traffic in Animals" (in *Free Spirits*).

Ynestra King, "Healing the Wounds: Feminism, Ecology, and the Nature/Culture Dualism" (in *Free Spirits*).

Carolyn Merchant, "Ecofeminism" (in *Free Spirits*).

Section III. Shaping Theory

Weeks 6–7. Emergence of "Second Wave" Theory

Simone de Beauvoir, "Introduction" to *The Second Sex* (in *Second Wave*).
Shulamith Firestone, "The Dialectic of Sex" (in *Second Wave*).
Gayle Rubin, "The Traffic in Women: Notes on the 'Political Economy' of Sex" (in *Second Wave*).
The Combahee River Collective, "A Black Feminist Statement" (in *Second Wave*).

Week 8. Feminism and Marxism/Socialism

Heidi Hartmann, "The Unhappy Marriage of Marxism and Feminism" (in *Second Wave*).
Michèle Barrett, "Capitalism and Women's Liberation" (in *Second Wave*).
Linda Nicholson, "Feminism and Marx: Integrating Kinship with the Economic" (in *Second Wave*).

Weeks 9–10. Centering Gender

Radical Feminism: Radicalesbians, "The Woman Identified Woman" (in *Second Wave*); Catharine A. MacKinnon, "Sexuality" (in *Second Wave*).
Psychology/Psychoanalysis: Nancy Chodorow, "The Psychodynamics of the Family" (in *Second Wave*); Carol Gilligan, "Women's Place in Man's Life Cycle" (in *Second Wave*).
Standpoint Theory: Nancy C. M. Hartsock, "The Feminist Standpoint: Developing the Ground for a Specifically Feminist Historical Materialism" (in *Second Wave*); Patricia Hill Collins, "Defining Black Feminist Thought" (in *Second Wave*).

Week 11. Deconstructing Identity/Theorizing Difference

Monique Wittig, "One Is Not Born a Woman" (in *Second Wave*).
Judith Butler, "Imitation and Gender Insubordination" (in *Second Wave*).
Elsa Barkley Brown, "'What Has Happened Here?': The Politics of Difference in Women's History and Feminist Politics" (in *Second Wave*).
Norma Alarcón, "The Theoretical Subject(s) of *The Bridge Called My Back* and Anglo-American Feminism" (in *Second Wave*).
Uma Narayan, "Restoring History and Politics to 'Third-World' Traditions: Contrasting the Colonialist Stance and Contemporary Contestations of *Sati*" (in *Dislocating Cultures*).

Week 12. The Question of Essentialism

Luce Irigaray, "This Sex Which Is Not One" (in *Second Wave*).
Gayatri Spivak with Ellen Rooney, "'In a Word': Interview" (in *Second Wave*).
Linda Alcoff, "Cultural Feminism Versus Post-Structuralism: The Identity Crisis in Feminist Theory" (in *Second Wave*).

Nancy Fraser, "Structuralism or Pragmatics? On Discourse Theory and Feminist Politics" (in *Second Wave*).

Section IV. Practicing Theory

Week 13. Reflections on "Doing Theory"

Rayna Green, "Culture and Gender in Indian America" (in *Free Spirits*).
Uma Narayan, "Contesting Cultures: 'Westernization,' Respect for Cultures, and Third-World Feminists" (in *Dislocating Cultures*).
Uma Narayan, "Through the Looking-Glass Darkly: Emissaries, Mirrors, and Authentic Insiders as Preoccupations" (in *Dislocating Cultures*).
María Lugones, "Playfulness, 'World'-Traveling, and Loving Perception" (in *Free Spirits*).

Week 14. Group Presentations

Assignments

A. *Short Papers*

Three three-page (approx. 250 words per page) critical responses to anything in the readings or class discussions. A good place to start a paper is with a strong reaction: something makes you angry or makes an especially powerful kind of sense or reminds you of something else. You then need to ask yourself why you respond the way you do (e.g., are you angry because the author has gotten something you know about badly wrong, or because s/he has gotten something uncomfortably right?), and what your response helps you see about the text. State clearly the point(s) you want to make, and do your best to be persuasive: Think of writing to a sympathetic but skeptical friend. If you quote or paraphrase, be clear about your source(s). In particular, when the reading is from an anthology, note that the authors you need to credit (and with whom you are engaging) are not the editors but the authors of the particular essays: Refer to them by name (not, e.g., "on p. 57 of *Free Spirits* it says . . ."). The authors are real people— talk to them.

B. *Either 1 (a and b) or 2*

1a. A group project: Working with approximately four other people in the same discussion section, find a nearby individual or group involved in politics, the arts, or some form of community action, involving women, feminism, or gender issues. Prepare a presentation for the class in which you explore relationships between their activity and one or more of the theoretical works we are studying. Some possible lines to explore: Can you understand their practice better through the lens of one of the theories? Does something about their practice undercut the claims of one of the theories, or help decide some contested point between two or more of them? Is there something in one of the theories that would help clarify a problem they are having in their work? Is there a particular theoretical foundation to what they are doing, and if so, is it explicit? If there isn't, do you think it would help if there were?

In general, what does reflection on this individual or group tell you about the relationship between feminist theory and feminist practice?

and

1b. Write a *three-page paper* discussing the relation of theory to practice *either* by amplifying on your group's presentation *or* by addressing the practice of the group work and/or the class in general in relation to feminist theory. That is, our intention is for the group work and for the class as a whole to be examples of feminist practice: do you think they are? And what is their relation to the theories we have been studying?

2. Write a *ten-page term paper* on a topic of your own choice. A list of suggestions is attached, or you can discuss an alternative with the instructor or your teaching assistant.

Suggested Paper Topics

These are *suggested* topics for those of you who intend to write a paper instead of working on a group project. You are entirely free to modify one of them or to write on something entirely different if you choose (so long as it's relevant to the work we've done in this course).

1. What do you see as the role(s) of theory in relation to feminist movements? Do we (who?) need it? Why or why not? How do you define "theory"?
2. Choose an essay you disagree with and explain why. How might the author respond to you, and how would you reply? Or choose two essays that seem to disagree with each other and explore that disagreement. (In either case, you might want to write a dialogue.)
3. Think of an example from your own experience of discovering or creating your own sense of agency in relation to cultural constructions of your gender, race, class, sexuality (or other form of identity). How did you encounter these cultural influences? How did you internalize them? resist them? use them? subvert them?
4. Design a class syllabus for a feminist theory class, and explain why and how it differs from the syllabus for this class. Include readings, class format, assignments, and grading procedures and criteria (and anything else you think is relevant).
5. If there is a particular author or theory you think has badly misconstrued your experience, so that the theory is unhelpful or even damaging for you, explain how and why this is so. Give a fair reconstruction of the argument you object to, as well as specific arguments against it. Your paper can be a dialogue between yourself and the author(s).
6. If there is a particular author or theory that has given you a new insight into issues/practices in your own life, describe how this is so. What new things (behavior, assumptions, etc.) have you identified or been better able to understand because of the theory? Do you plan to make changes in your life? Do you plan not to? Why or why not?
7. Convert the group research assignment into an individual paper: that is, find some person or organization (the person may be yourself or one group you

belong to), and give a feminist analysis of it. Is a particular feminist theory informing their work (either explicitly or implicitly)? If there is no obvious theoretical underpinning, would one help? Is the work subject to a particular line of feminist criticism?

CREATING A COURSE IN
INTERNATIONAL FEMINIST THEORY

Mary M. Lay, Maria Brewer, André Lardinois,
William Mishler, Naomi B. Scheman, Jacquelyn N. Zita,
and Kris Misage

This essay reflects upon the activities of an interdisciplinary faculty working group consisting of Kris Misage, as research assistant, Professors Maria Brewer from the French and Italian department, André Lardinois from the Classical and Near Eastern studies department, William Mishler from the German, Scandinavian, and Dutch department, Naomi Scheman from the philosophy and women's studies departments, and Jacquelyn Zita from the women's studies department. This group, faced with the task of developing a new course for upper-level undergraduates entitled International Feminist Theory, began their work with discussions of readings by international feminists and with reflections about similar syllabi from other institutions (see references at the end of the essay). They quickly came to the conclusion that this new course should actively interrogate each of the descriptors of the course—*international, feminist,* and *theory.* After numerous discussions, the group developed a set of goals for the process:

1. to create a truly interdisciplinary course that does not privilege any one discipline;

2. to design a course that complements the standing women's studies curriculum at the University of Minnesota;

3. to challenge definitions of theoretical material by including narratives, autobiographies, and other texts that have theoretical effects;

4. to provide space in the course for both students and instructors to be reflective on the processes of theorizing and of learning about the international; and

5. to create a syllabus that is responsive to the input of instructors and students.

Group members also identified several key intellectual issues in the process of developing this new course:

1. making the course open-ended, that is, by including material and discussion questions that present important themes but do not provide a set of final answers;

2. framing the course as a dialogue across cultures that brings together material from around the world into sustained conversation, and especially involves a "moment" of Third World women "returning the gaze" onto the First World;

3. including context and the significance of location for all of the material presented in the course, to ensure that practices, theories, and ideas are seen as part of larger systems; and

4. including self-reflexivity, particularly to provide space within the course for understandings of *international, feminist*, and *theory*, and for looking at the international Other.

The model syllabus they developed is ambitious but should provide a starting point, as well as a challenge, for others involved in similar curricular and pedagogical efforts.

POSING QUESTIONS

The group decided that the primary theme of the course would be one that invites and poses questions rather than one that provides answers. Course topics would be open to many different interpretations, and the group strategized ways to motivate students to move beyond a superficial understanding of the material. The syllabus was designed to encourage students to be open to the material, aware of its intended audience and the context of its production while staying critical of its content, presentation, and focus in the course. Issues of theorizing Third World women or understanding Third World feminism are very complex. This course is intended to be only an entryway into these discussions, not a pronouncement of closure on these issues or on the syllabus itself.

DIALOGUE ACROSS CULTURES

U.S. residents are now partners in some form of global relations. The lives of undergraduates are intertwined with and have an impact on the lives of others throughout the world. Given that various connections already exist between students and the rest of the world, the key issue becomes how to deal with this connection in a responsible manner. Reading texts from the Third World is an important part of the process in finding out about the world. International Feminist Theory aims to go beyond this step, however, to one where a dialogue between First and Third Worlds may occur. This course is about how one theorizes interaction and dialogue across cultures.

The emphasis on dialogue and interaction entails three basic points. First, dialogue encourages students to go beyond simply accepting voices from the Third World as "authentic." It opens a critical space for examining and reacting to these texts. All voices—international and those from the United States—are engaged in power relations and are connected in some ways to other cultures; this course aims to interrogate and engage these connections. Second, a major part of this critical space that dialogue fosters is what the group termed a *returning the gaze moment* in the course. That is, the syllabus is open to critiques of First World practices and texts by women from the Third World; these international feminist theory texts are not simply women speaking of their own, isolated situation. Rather, these writers weigh in on how they are looked at from the First World. One example of this comes from the anthropology section. The course presents readings by Mexican anthropologists who are critical of anthropologists from the United States who study Mexicans. This return of the gaze upon university students and U.S. academia is a way to encourage students to reflect critically upon their own situation. Third, and most important, dialogue is the main theme of this course because of the group's belief that it is through dialogue that lasting change takes shape.

Although learning about the Third World Other poses many problems, the group's stance is that it is vital for students to think about the connection between local and global issues. Theorizing of international issues will then bear the traces of this interaction. Without interaction, without dialogue, theorizing will reflect only one's own ideas and situation. This course's emphasis on dialogue, then, ensures that students engage these difficulties of knowing and theorizing about the Other within a context of interaction with the Third World.

ATTENTION TO PLACE OR CONTEXT

Two visiting scholars to the group, Janice Monk and Natalie Kampen, influenced the group's thinking on the issue of context. As a geographer, Monk pushed the group to consider the difference that place makes in social life. Theory, as well as other aspects of social life, can be affected or influenced by one's geographical location. Theorists are influenced by their locale's intellectual history, and by traditional access to resources, education, and publishing institutions. Art historian Natalie Kampen provided a different way to think about the issue of context or location. Kampen suggested that the group's general question of how to theorize one's relationship to the Other should be considered first in a historical context. She suggested looking at cultures as systems that, taken as a whole, are social constructs. The system itself has many interrelated parts, which cannot simply be pulled out of historical context for analysis. Kampen's advice forces students to consider practices such as female genital mutilation in Egypt and veiling in Algeria within the system of the cultures within which these practices are present. This contextual or system-level view, then, prevents students from arriving at simplistic analyses of complex cultural practices.

Placing theory within its context—historically, intellectually, geographically, and socially—was a primary concern in designing the syllabus. The group sought to explore genealogies and hegemonies of feminism in different locations. One example is the unit on French feminism. All too often French feminism is considered high theory, with little attention given to the context within which these writers work. For example, when considering the development of feminist thought in France, one must also look at the specific influences on theorists, and on what feminist practices their theory addresses. On a related note, the group considered hegemony: Who defines the term *feminism* and feminists in this location?

SELF-REFLEXIVITY

The theme of self-reflexivity is at the core of all other themes in this course. The group members held differing conceptions of theory, but agreed that theory begins when one asks why things are as they are. In other words, theory is the process of reflecting upon one's situation. This broad understanding of theory (rather than what self-named theorists of philosophers do) opens the course to many different genres or material, from explicitly theoretical texts, to commentaries, to narratives, to autobiographies. From the beginning, discussions of self-reflexivity involved each of the signifiers of the course—international, feminist, and theory. How are each of these terms constructed in everyday understandings and how does dialogue across cultures force us to rethink these definitions? Cross cultural dialogue fosters the renegotiation of these terms. The group deliberately included narratives and other nontraditionally theoretical texts as a means to challenge definitions of theory.

In addition, this theme of context is also an important part of looking at U.S. feminist theory. How does a U.S. academic location affect theory? Also, the group consciously tried to construct a course attentive to Third World issues beyond the concerns of U.S. feminists. Similarly, the group worked to prevent focusing on any one discipline or type of writing over another. The group realized that its own ability for self-reflexivity was limited. The last section of the course is meant to open up content for criticism and comment from students and instructors alike. Are there better ways to theorize about the international Other? And are there other projects that might be more effective, more practical, or more connected to the international Other?

PEDAGOGICAL CONCERNS

A number of pedagogical issues arose during the creation of the "International Feminist Theory" course. The first pedagogical concern was to anticipate the issues, concerns, and expertise of those teaching and taking the course. In response, the group decided to construct a *mix-and-match syllabus,* which could be tailored to the particular instructor and set of students who enroll at any one time. The group consciously devised a malleable syllabus; parts can be moved around or left out, given the interests and experience of the instructor and the interests of the students. The group considered it crucial that students in the classroom have input on the course material and how it is taught because the students are the ones who must engage in the dialogue.

A second concern of the group was to ensure that context was provided for all material in the syllabus. Approaching the subject of Third World women can be difficult and potentially divisive. For example, topics such as female genital mutilation and veiling can bring heated discussions and charged emotions into the classroom. One way to deal with potential problems is to present cultures as integrated systems; no one practice or text can be understood without being seen in the context within which it is embedded.

A third concern was for the course to be balanced between comprehensive global coverage and focus. This is a fine line, but the group was concerned that the course focus on different areas of the world, with enough time on each area for more than a glimpse of a selected region. Toward this end, the group designed a number of modules on international feminist theory in different regions of the world, from which the instructor and students can choose.

A fourth concern involved the discussion of models for the course. Because the group was charged with the task of creating a new course, they did not begin with a template in hand. The group ultimately chose a dialogic model that presents First and Third World theorists in conversation. Had they chosen a model focused on different issues in the Third World, the group realized that they might be highlighting issues of concern to academics in the United States—female genital mutilation, for example—rather than women outside of the United States. The group hoped to avoid such conflicts by structuring the course around various areas of the world, and looking at the issues of concern to feminists in these areas.

DEVELOPMENT RESULTS

The final product, a syllabus meant to be adaptable, is organized into four sections. The introductory section on theory outlines the course's basic premise of questioning the terms *international, Third World, First World, feminist,* and *theory.* It ranges over these issues using readings by U.S. feminists that attempt to theorize the international, as well as readings by Third World feminists commenting on their own situations and looking back at the First World.

The second section, on how academic disciplines cross international borders, includes six units from which instructors might choose two or three: anthropology, history, geography, cultural studies, comparative literature, and economics.

The third and largest section of the course, on non–U.S. and Third World feminism, includes a case study on French feminism, as well as five other units on China, sub-Saharan Africa, Latin America, the Islamic world, and India, again allowing for choice. The group recommended inclusion of the French feminist case study along with other chosen units, because this case study illustrates the importance of location and context in theorizing and provides a counterpoint to a "United States versus the rest of the world" dichotomy.

The fourth and final section of the course is meant to generate suggestions for improvement of the course the next time it is taught, as well as provide the space for criticism and self-reflection that is structured throughout the course.

SELECTED REFERENCES

Abu-Lughod, Lila. 1986. "Modesty and the Poetry of Love." In *Veiled Sentiments: Honor and Poetry in a Bedouin Society.* Berkeley: University of California Press.

———. 1990. "Can There Be a Feminist Ethnography?" *Women & Performance* 5 (9): 7–27.

Behar, Ruth. 1993. *Translated Woman.* Boston: Beacon Press.

———. 1996. *The Vulnerable Observer.* Boston: Beacon Press.

Chow, Rey. 1991. "Violence in the Other Country: China as Crisis, Spectacle, and Woman." In Chandra Mohanty, Ann Russo, and Lourdes Torres, eds., *Third World Women and the Politics of Feminism.* Bloomington: Indiana University Press.

Djebar, Assia. 1992. "Women of Algiers in Their Apartment"; "Forbidden Gaze, Severed Sound"; and "Afterword." In *Women of Algiers in Their Apartment,* trans. Marjolijn de Jager. Charlottesville: University of Virginia Press.

Mohanty, Chandra. 1991. "Under Western Eyes: Feminist Scholarship and Colonial Discourse." In Chandra Mohanty, Ann Russo, and Lourdes Torres, eds., *Third World Women and the Politics of Feminism,* 51–80. Bloomington: Indiana University Press.

Note to the instructor: This document is a *mix-and-match syllabus* in that it is not meant to be taught in its entirety, but is designed so that the class can pick and choose segments. In particular, in parts III and IV of the syllabus we have included more units than would fit into a fourteen-week course. We suggest that the units offered at any one time reflect the interests and concerns of the students and instructor.

I. Introduction—Theory, Feminism, and International (2 weeks): Interrogating Understandings of Theory, Feminism, and International.

A. "The Theory Debate" in Contemporary Feminist Theory

This unit introduces students to contemporary feminist "theory debate" literature as it focuses on the questions of what theory is, how it is defined, how is it produced, and for whom and for what epistemic and non-epistemic uses.

1. Christianson, Barbara. "The Race for Theory." *Cultural Critique* 6 (Spring 1987): 51–63.
2. King, Katie. "Producing Sex, Theory, and Culture: Gay/Straight Remappings in Contemporary Feminism." *Conflicts in Feminism,* ed. Marianne Hirsch and Evelyn Fox Keller. New York and London: Routledge, 1990.
3. hooks, bell. "Theory as Liberatory Practice." *Teaching to Transgress: Education as the Practice of Freedom.* London. Routledge, 1994.
4. Davies, Carole Boyce. *Black Women, Writing, and Identity. Migrations of the Subject.* London: Routledge, 1994 (selections).
5. Lutz, Catherine. "The Gender of Theory." *Women Writing Culture,* ed. Ruth Behar and Deborah Gordon. Berkeley: University of California Press, 1995.

B. World Traveling as a Quest/ion of Transnational Feminist Practices

These readings introduce students to the problems involved in creating global feminist theory. Areas covered by the readings include an interrogation of the location of the knower, the intersubjective complexities and power relations between the knower and the known, the misrepresentation and ethnocentrism of Westernizing transnational feminist theory, and models for alternative theory production.

1. Rich, Adrienne. "Notes Toward a Politics of Location" (1984). *Blood, Bread, and Poetry: Selected Prose 1979–1985.* New York: W. W. Norton, 1986. Read also "North American Tunnel Vision" (1983) and "Blood, Bread, and Poetry: The Location of the Poet" (1984).
2. Mohanty, Chandra. "Under Western Eyes: Feminist Scholarship and Colonial Discourse." *Third World Women and the Politics of Feminism,* ed. Chandra Mohanty, Ann Russo, and Lourdes Torres. Bloomington: Indiana University, 1991.
3. Kaplan, Caren. "The Politics of Location as Transnational Feminist Practice." *Scattered Hegemonies: Postmodernity and Transnational Feminist Practices,* ed. Inderpal Grewal and Caren Kaplan. Minneapolis: University of Minnesota Press, 1994.

4. Lugones, Maria. "Playfulness, World Travelling and Loving Perception." *Hypatia* 2(1) (Spring 1986).

C. *Returning the Gaze*

This section introduces students to the epistemic and political questions raised when the gaze of the Other is turned back on the knower. Two artistic works are used to explore these questions: a photo exhibit of Native American subjects looking back at the camera that photographs them and the performance collaborations of Coco Fusco and Guillermo Gomez-Peña.

Video: Performance collaboration of Coco Fusco and Guillermo Gomez-Peña, *Primitivism in 20th Century Art.*
1. Lippard, Lucy R. "Introduction." *Partial Recall,* ed. Lucy Lippard. New York: New Press, 1992.
2. Seals, David. "'Wounded Knee, 1989' by Sarah Penman." *Partial Recall,* ed. Lucy Lippard. New York: New Press, 1992.
3. Fusco, Coco, and Guillermo Gómez-Peña. "The Year of the White Bear." Walker Art Center (exhibition), Sept. 13–Nov. 15, 1992.
4. Fusco, Coco. *English Is Broken Here: Notes on Cultural Fusion in the Americas.* New York: New Press, 1995.
5. Kaplan, Ann. *Looking for the Other: Feminism and the Imperial Gaze.* New York: Routledge, 1996.

D. *Documentatory/Testimonials in Transnational Feminisms*

This final theory unit introduces students to another set of questions concerning the creation of documentary as a means of "telling the truth," and the use and production of personal voice in testimonial literatures by Third World women as another semblance of telling the truth.

Video: Trinh T. Minh-ha, *Reassemblage.*
1. Minh-ha, Trinh T. "The Language of Nativism." *Woman Native Other.* Bloomington: Indiana University Press, 1989.
2. Minh-ha, Trinh T. "On the Politics of Contemporary Representations." *Discussions in Contemporary Culture,* ed. Hal Foster. Seattle: Bay Press, 1987.
3. Menchú, Rigoberta, with Elisabeth Burgos. *Me llamo Rigoberta Menchú y así me nació la conciencia.* Barcelona: Editorial Argos Vergara, 1983. In translation, Ann Wright, trans., *I, Rigoberta Menchú: An Indian Woman in Guatemala.* New York: Verso, 1984.
4. Carr, Robert. "Crossing the First World/Third World Divides: Testimonial, Transnational Feminisms, and the Postmodern Condition." *Scattered Hegemonies, Postmodernity and Transnational Feminist Practices,* ed. Inderpal Grewal and Caren Kaplan. Minne-apolis: University of Minnesota Press, 1994.
5. Kaplan, Caren. "Resisting Autobiography: Outlaw Genres and Transnational Feminist Subjects." *De-Colonizing the Subject: Politics and Gender in Women's Autobiographical Practice,* ed. Julia Watson and Sidonie Smith. Minneapolis: University of Minnesota Press, 1992.

II. Disciplines (3 weeks)

The disciplines section continues the pattern of starting from our own location in preparation for dialogue with those from different locations. This section poses the question of how U.S. academics engage with theorizing outside the United States. What can we learn from how different disciplines deal with, appropriate, exoticize, or learn from the international Other? Finally, this section is also meant to historicize and contextualize these U.S. disciplines. These are not "pure" disciplines; they are affected by political, social, and historical contexts.

Note to the instructor: You may have students read basic readings within each unit and then choose others to present to the class. The choice of disciplines to cover can also be up to the students (we figure three can be covered in a three-week period).

A. Anthropology Unit (1 week)

Anthropology has been defined by the study of other cultures, and many anthropologists have theorized issues such as crossing borders, translation, the academic gaze, and the problem of knowing the Other.

Class 1. Anthropological Border Crossings—How Anthropologists Look at the Other

These texts construct a theoretical picture of what anthropology entails, and the implications and possibilities of the anthropological project.

1. Clifford, James. "Introduction: Partial Truths." *Writing Culture: The Poetics and Politics of Ethnography,* ed. James Clifford and George E. Marcus. Berkeley: University of California Press, 1986.
2. Rosaldo, Renato. "Border Crossings." *Culture & Truth: The Remaking of Social Analysis.* Boston: Beacon Press, 1989.
3. Abu-Lughod, Lila. "Can There Be a Feminist Ethnography?" *Women & Performance* 5(9) (1990): 7–27.

Class 2. The Position of the Anthropologist in the Field—Making Sense of the Other

These readings are examples of noted anthropological work, in which we can see the anthropologist interpreting what goes on around her or him. The authors assign different importance to the position of the anthropologist in their work, which can be interrogated and critiqued with the help of the theoretical readings of the first class period.

1. Geertz, Clifford. "Deep Play: Notes on the Balinese Cockfight." *The Interpretation of Cultures: Selected Essays by Clifford Geertz.* New York: Basic Books, 1973.
2. Shostak, Marjorie. *Nisa: The Life and Words of a !Kung Woman.* Cambridge: Harvard University Press, 1981.

3. Behar, Ruth. *Translated Woman: Crossing the Border with Esperanza's Story.* Boston: Beacon Press, 1993; Introduction—"The Talking Serpent"—and chapter 15, "Translated Woman."

Class 3. Looking Back from the Border—Chicano Criticism of Anthropology

These readings open a space for criticism from outside the United States, but still within anthropology.

1. Tabuenca Cordoba, Maria-Socorro. "Viewing the Border: Perspectives from 'The Open Wound.'" *Discourse; Theoretical Studies in Media and Culture* 18 (Fall and Winter 1995–96): 146–68.
2. Calderon, Hector, and Jose David Saldivar, eds. *Criticism in the Borderlands: Studies in Chicano Literature, Culture, and Ideology.* Durham, N.C.: Duke University Press, 1991.
3. Chabram, Angie. "Chicano Studies as Oppositional Ethnography." *Cultural Studies* 4 (1990): 242.
4. Rosaldo, Renato. "Chicano Studies, 1970–1984." *Annual Review of Anthropology* 14 (1985): 405–27.

B. Geography Unit (1 week)

Geography, the study of place, space, and location, is intimately involved in the project of not only crossing borders, but literally constructing them. The geographical project is about attempting to know the Other, to map the unknown world, and to discover and categorize differences across places.

Class 1. General Introduction

The aim of this class period is to have students read and discuss major themes and common practices among geographers, and in particular, their historical treatment of the international other.

1. Monk, Janice. "Place Matters: Comparative International Perspectives on Feminist Geography." *Professional Geographer* 46(3) (1994): 277–88.
2. Rose, Gillian. "Looking at the Landscape: The Uneasy Pleasures of Power." *Feminism and Geography: The Limits of Geographical Knowledge.* Minneapolis, University of Minnesota Press, 1993.
3. Livingstone, David N. "Climate's Moral Economy: Science, Race and Place in Post–Darwinian British and American Geography." *Geography and Empire,* ed. Anne Godlewska and Neil Smith. Cambridge: Blackwell, 1994.
4. Rothenberg, Tamar Y. "Voyeurs of Imperialism: *The National Geographic Magazine* Before World War II." *Geography and Empire,* ed. Anne Godlewska and Neil Smith. Cambridge: Blackwell, 1994.

Class 2. New Directions in Geography—Challenging the Imperialist Gaze

1. McGee, Terry G. "Presidential Address: Eurocentrism in Geography—The Case of Asian Urbanization." *The Canadian Geographer* 35(4) (1991): 332–44.
2. Radcliffe, Sarah A. "(Representing) Post-Colonial Women: Authority, Difference and Feminisms." *Area* 26(1) (1994): 25–32.
3. Crush, Jonathan. "Post-colonialism, De-colonization, and Geography." *Geography and Empire,* ed. Anne Godlewska and Neil Smith. Cambridge: Blackwell, 1994.
4. Rose, Gillian. "A Politics of Paradoxical Space." *Feminism and Geography: The Limits of Geographical Knowledge.* Minneapolis, University of Minnesota Press, 1993.

C. Comparative Literature Unit (1 week)

Class 1. General Introduction

The two class periods that compose this segment are devoted to Isak Dinesen's (Karen Blixen) *Out of Africa,* a memoir written in English by a Danish writer about her experience of Africa in the early years of the twentieth century when she lived in Kenya and owned and operated a large coffee plantation. The first class period is devoted to examining selected chapters of the book, the second to critical analyses of it.

1. "Kamante and Lulu," "The Somali Women," "Kitosch's Story," in Isak Dinesen, *Out of Africa.* New York: Vintage, 1985.

Class 2. Critical Views of *Out of Africa*

In this class students will read two discussions that analyze the rhetoric of *Out of Africa* and its implicit claims. One of them, *Difficult Women, Artful Lives,* by Susan Horton contrasts the work of the South African novelist Olive Schreiner with Isak Dinesen's *Out of Africa,* revealing the strategy of refined myth-making that was crucial to both. The second reading, *Manichean Ethics,* by Abdul R. Janmohamed gives a sharply debunking view of Dinesen's memoir, placing it in historical and psychological frames that point out its strong component of wish-fulfillment. Rather than a narrative exemplifying timeless truths about Africa, Europe, and the human condition, Dinesen's work is placed in the context of colonialism and read as a work in which "Africa" becomes a screen on which Dinesen projected a vision comforting to her specific psychological needs.

1. Horton, Susan. "Mythic Times, Gothic Images and the Role of the Dice." *Difficult Women, Artful Lives: Olive Schreiner and Isak Dinesen In and Out of Africa.* Baltimore: The Johns Hopkins University Press, 1995.
2. Janmohamed, Abdul R. "Isak Dinesen: The Generation of Mythic Consciousness." *Manichean Aesthetics: The Politics of Literature in Colonial Africa.* Amherst: University of Massachusetts Press, 1983.

D. Cultural Studies Unit (1 week, 2nd week optional)

Week 1. England, the United States, and Other "Others"

The academic field known as cultural studies began in England, specifically, at the Centre for Contemporary Cultural Studies at Birmingham in the 1960s. Unlike the history of most other academic fields, this history is distinctive and recent enough to itself be the object of focused study, a study that falls within the field of cultural studies itself. It is also a history that places the United States in the position, first, as a studied Other, although increasingly since the 1970s the United States is as much the location of the gaze as it is the gazed-at. The field has also been characterized by attention to the placement of subjects and objects, including issues that arise when these placements are either unexpected or in flux. We look at this history and at some of these shifts between object and subject.

Note: Most of the readings for this section are from *Cultural Studies,* ed. Lawrence Grossman, Cary Nelson, and Paula Treichler. New York: Routledge, 1992. This 800-page volume, which grew out of a conference and includes discussions among the participants of each other's essays, as well as an extensive bibliography, contains lots of other essays that could fit elsewhere in the course, so it would make sense for students to buy it.

CLASS 1. CULTURAL STUDIES REFLECTS ON CULTURAL STUDIES
1. Hall, Stuart. "Cultural Studies and Its Theoretical Legacies."
2. Gilroy, Paul. "Cultural Studies and Ethnic Absolutism."
3. Video: Coco Fusco and Guillermo Gomez-Peña. "Guatinau" exhibit.

CLASS 2. RETURNING THE GAZE, INCLUDING DISCUSSION OF VIDEO
1. hooks, bell. "Representing Whiteness in the Black Imagination."
2. Mani, Lata. "Cultural Theory, Colonial Texts: Reading Eyewitness Accounts of Widow Burning."
3. Wallace, Michele. "Negative Images: Towards a Black Feminist Cultural Criticism."

Week 2 (optional). Other Others in Queer Theory

Queer theory refers to a set of interdisciplinary investigations into the cultural construction of normative and "deviant" sexualities. One of its central aims is to destabilize the taken-for-grantedness of heterosexuality; and its central techniques include interrogating the gaze (questioning who does the looking and whose place it is to be looked at) and shifting the gaze to reveal the contingency—and the "queerness"—of what is referred to as *heteronormativity.* There is also significant attention to how it is that, for example, racial Others are constructed by writers of gay-related issues.

CLASS 1. CONSTRUCTIONS OF QUEER SEXUALITY
1. Warner, Michael. "Introduction." *Fear of a Queer Planet,* ed. Michael Warner. Minneapolis: University of Minnesota Press, 1993.

2. Goldberg, Jonathan. "Sodomy in the New World: Anthropologies Old and New." *FQP* (adapted by the author from Jonathan Goldberg, *Sodometries*). Stanford: Stanford University Press, 1992).
3. de Lauretis, Teresa. "Sexual Indifference and Lesbian Representation." *Theatre Journal* 40 (1988).

CLASS 2. (RE)PRESENTATIONS OF OTHERNESS WITHIN QUEER THEORY
1. Gates, Jr., Henry Louis. "The Black Man's Burden." *FQP.*
2. Mercer, Kobena. "Looking for Trouble." *Transition* 51 (1991).
3. Alonso, Ana Maria, and Maria Teresa Koreck. "Silences: Hispanics, AIDS, and Sexual Practices. *"Differences: A Journal of Feminist Cultural Studies* 1(1) (Winter 1989): 101–24.
4. Patton, Cindy. "From Nation to Family: Containing African AMS." *Nationalism and Sexualities,* ed. Andrew Parker, Mary Russo, Doris Sommer, and Patricia Yaeger. New York: Routledge, 1992.

E. Economics Unit (1 week)

Economics is often considered to be the study of how people use their resources to produce, exchange and consume goods and services, although this definition is contested. We have included economics in our list of disciplines in part because of its intimate connection with the international Other. Global capitalism, IMF structural adjustment policies, state socialist intervention in the economy, and free trade zones are all economic policies that connect North and South, First World and Third.

Class 1. How Economists Think

These readings are meant to introduce students to how neoclassical and Marxist economists view the world. Wolff and Resnick provide a brief background on both neoclassical and Marxist economics, highlighting nicely the neoclassical reliance on individual action in explanation. England, in her critique, highlights some more specific assumptions of neoclassical economic theory; her article shows how feminist economists are rethinking basic categories. The Myerson piece is a brief summary of Paul Krugman's neoclassical argument in favor of sweatshops. Wolff and Resnick and England will be helpful in drawing out the assumptions within this sweatshop argument.

1. Wolff, Richard D., and Stephen A. Resnick. *Economics: Marxian Versus Neoclassical.* Baltimore: The Johns Hopkins University Press, 1987.
2. England, Paula. "The Separative Self: Androcentric Bias in Neoclassical Assumptions." *Beyond Economic Man: Feminist Theory and Economics,* ed. Marianne A. Ferber and Julie A. Nelson. Chicago: University of Chicago Press, 1993.
3. Myerson, Allen R. "In Principle, a Case for More 'Sweatshops.'" *New York Times* Section 4 (June 22, 1997): 5.

Class 2. Economics and the Rest of the World

The second part of this unit concerns the Third World directly. The first two pieces are critiques of economic policies aimed at the Third World. Wright's article highlights how discourse about "rights" effectively marginalizes Third World populations and specifically women in the economic realm. Harcourt details recent development programs and some important critiques of them before outlining a feminist perspective. These two articles then provide a good background for discussing how economics sees and analyzes the Third World, developing Other. The Nelson and Williams pieces move us back to theoretical grounds, on to the question of the viability and critical power of feminist economics. Nelson develops an engaging argument about the content of economics, and Williams is a hard-hitting critique of such feminist economics projects. Williams' attention to race, class, gender, and the social construction of all of these categories provides space for a discussion on representations and assumptions about the international Other by neoclassical, Marxist, and feminist economists alike.

1. Wright, Shelley. "Women and the Global Economic Order: A Feminist Perspective." *American University Journal of International Law and Policy* 10 (2) (1995): 861–87.
2. Harcourt, Wendy. "Negotiating Positions in the Sustainable Development Debate: Situating the Feminist Perspective." *Feminist Perspectives on Sustainable Development,* ed. Wendy Harcourt. London: Zed Books, 1994.
3. Nelson, Julie A. "The Study of Choice or the Study of Provisioning? Gender and the Definition of Economics." *Beyond Economic Man: Feminist Theory and Economics,* ed. Marianne A. Ferber and Julie A. Nelson. Chicago: University of Chicago Press, 1993.
4. Williams, Rhonda M. "Race, Deconstruction, and the Emergent Agenda of Feminist Economic Theory." *Beyond Economic Man: Feminist Theory and Economics,* ed. Marianne A. Ferber and Julie A. Nelson. Chicago: University of Chicago Press, 1993.

III. Non-U.S. and Third World Feminisms

A. *Case Study: French Feminism and Its Contexts (1 week).*

Class 1

This class period and its readings serve as an introduction to the writers and issues involved in the emergence and reception of French feminism. Background discussion will focus on the relationship of French feminism to psychoanalysis and poststructuralist and postmodern theory. Essays by Julia Kristeva and Luce Irigaray will demonstrate the importance of language and symbolic systems in their work on the concepts of gender, female identity, and otherness. The essay by Christine Delphy critiques these approaches and analyzes the ideological stakes involved in the construction of French feminism in the English-speaking world. Gayatri Spivak's essay relates French feminist theory both to French theory and to postcolonial perspectives.

1. Kristeva, Julia. "Women's Time." *Signs* 7 (1) (1981): 7–35. Rpt. in *Feminisms: An Anthology of Literary Theory and Criticism,* ed. Robyn R. Warhol and Diane Price Herndl. New Brunswick: Rutgers University Press, 1991.
2. Irigaray, Luce. "The Question of the Other," *Yale French Studies* 87 (1995): 7–19. See also selections from "Speculum of the Other Woman." and "This Sex Which Is Not One" in *Feminisms.*
3. Spivak, Gayatri. "French Feminism in an International Frame" (1981). *In Other Worlds: Essays in Cultural Politics,* ed. Gayatri Spivak. New York: Methuen, 1987.
4. Delphy, Christine. "The Invention of French Feminism: An Essential Move." *Yale French Studies* 87 (1995): 190–221.

Class 2

This class and its readings consider the significance of feminist discourses as critical, political, and historical practices of intervention. Questions addressed include the construction of otherness as it relates to historiography, immigration, national identity, and women's political agency in France and the new Europe.

1. Guillaumin, Colette. *Racism, Sexism, Power, and Ideology*. New York: Routledge, 1995 (selected chapters).
2. Mouffe, Chantal. "Feminism, Citizenship, and Radical Democratic Politics." *Feminists Theorize the Political,* ed. Judith Butler and Joan W. Scott. New York: Routledge, 1992.
3. Kristeva, Julia. "Open Letter to Harlem Désir." *Nations Without Nationalism.* New York: Columbia University Press, 1993.

B. China (1 week)

Class 1. Scholarship on Chinese Women

1. Waltner, Ann. "Recent Scholarship on Chinese Women." *Signs* 21(2) (1996): 410–28.
2. Barlow, Tani. "Theorizing Woman: Fun–fl, Guojia, Jiating." *Body, Subject, and Power in China,* ed. Angela Zito and Tani E. Barlow. Chicago: University of Chicago Press, 1994.
3. Li, Xiaojiang. "Economic Reform and the Awakening of Chinese Women's Collective Consciousness." *Engendering China: Women, Culture, and the State,* ed. Christina K. Gilmartin, Gail Hershatter, Lisa Rofel, and Tyrene White. Cambridge, Mass.: Harvard University Press, 1994 (both books are among those reviewed by Waltner).

Class 2. Women's Studies and Feminist Research in China

1. Li, Xiaojiang, and Xiaodan Zhang. "Creating a Space for Women: Women's Studies in China in the 1980s." *Signs* 20(1) (1994): 137–50.
2. Yiyun, Chen. "Out of the Traditional Halls of Academe: Exploring New Avenues

for Research on Women." *Engendering China,* ed. Christina K. Gilmartin et al. Cambridge, Mass.: Harvard University Press, 1994.

C. Sub-Saharan Africa (1 week)

The first reading discusses structures and forms of women's domination in Zimbabwe, in the period 1890 to 1939, presenting the case that it was not market conditions or requirements of the workplace that blocked women's employment during the colonial period, but a collusion between indigenous and colonial power structures. The second and third readings discuss the position of women in the ideological, religious, and literary discourses of the societies of southern Africa. The readings for the second class period present an overview of the novels of eight contemporary women novelists in Nigeria, with emphasis on the vernacular novel. If time permits students ought to be encouraged to choose one of the novels discussed and present it in class.

Class 1

1. Schmidt, E. "Patriarchy, Capitalism, and the Colonial State in Zimbabwe." *Signs* (1991): 732–56.
2. Strobel, M. "Women in Religion and Secular Ideology." *African Women South of the Sahara,* ed. M. J. Hay and S. Stichter. New York: Longman, 1995.
3. LaPin, D. "Women in African Literature." *African Women South of the Sahara,* ed. M. J. Hay and S. Stichter. New York: Longman, 1995.

Class 2

1. Ogunyemi, Chikwenye Okonjo. *Africa Wo/man Palava: The Nigerian Novel by Women.* Chicago: University of Chicago Press, 1996.

D. Latin America (2 weeks)

Class 1. General Introduction

This class hour and the readings are intended to introduce the students to the different feminist movements and theories in Latin America (Schutte, Sternbach), and to an important, formative period in recent Latin American history (Miller).

1. Miller, F.: "Revolution and Counterrevolution, 1959–1973." *Latin American Women and the Search for Social Justice.* Hanover: University Press of New England, 1991.
2. Schutte, O. "Cultural Identity, Liberation and Feminist Theory." *Cultural Identity and Social Liberation in Latin American Thought.* Albany: SUNY Press, 1993.
3. Sternbach, N. S., et al., "Feminisms in Latin America: From Bogotá to San Bernardo." *Signs* (1992), 393–434.

Class 2. Testimonial Literature

One distinctive way in which Latin American women have expressed their ideas is through so-called *testimonial literature,* writings that take the form of autobiographies. A selection of such writings can be found in Randall and Yanz. Most of these deal with the lives of poor peasant women or the heroic participation of women in grassroots movements or national liberation struggles, but the essay by Diamela Eltit, a leading feminist writer in Chile today, discusses, by contrast, two autobiographies of women who collaborated with the military police of the Chilean dictatorship.

1. Eltit, Diamela. "Nomadic Bodies." *Review: Latin American Literature and Arts* 54 (1997): 42–50.
2. Selections from *Sandino's Daughters,* ed. M. Randall and L. Yanz. Vancouver: New Star, 1981.

Classes 3 and 4. Brazil and Nicaragua

One of the dominant issues in Latin American feminism has been its relationship to the socialist movements. Traditionally in Latin America there exists a clear divide, even an antagonism, between those feminists who work from within the socialist parties, and those who work outside these movements or look at them with suspicion. The following two class hours will focus on two specific Latin American countries, Brazil, which experienced a right-wing dictatorship, and Nicaragua, which was under a communist regime. Some of the articles also pay attention to social organizations and conditions outside the political parties that have supported feminist writers (Alvarez on the People's Church, Nevez-Xavier de Brito on Brazilian women in exile).

READINGS ON BRAZIL

1. Alvarez, S. E. "Women's Movements and Gender Politics in the Brazilian Transition." *The Women's Movement in Latin America: Feminism and the Transition to Democracy,* ed. J. S. Jaquette. Boston: Unwin Hyman, 1989.
2. Alvarez, S. E. "Women's Participation in the Brazilian 'People's Church': A Critical Appraisal." *Feminist Studies* 16(2) (Summer 1990): 381–408.
3. de Brito, A. Nevez-Xavier. "Brazilian Women in Exile: The Quest for an Identity." *Latin American Perspectives* 13 (1986).
4. Sarthi, C. "The Panorama of Brazilian Feminism." *New Left Review* 173 (1989): 75–90.

READINGS ON NICARAGUA

1. Chinchilla, N. S. "Revolutionary Popular Feminism in Nicaragua: Articulating Class, Gender, and National Sovereignty." *Gender and Society* 4 (1990): 370–97.
2. Molineux, M. "Mobilization Without Emancipation? Women's Interests, State and Revolution." *Transition and Development: Problems of Third World Socialism,* ed. R. Fagen et al. New York: Monthly Review Press, 1986.
3. Molineux, M. "The Politics of Abortion in Nicaragua: Revolutionary Pragmatism or Feminism in the Realm of Necessity?" *Feminist Review* 29 (1988): 114–32.

E. Feminism and Islam: Women in the Maghreb (2 weeks)

Class 1. Introduction

Despite its title, this unit on feminism and Islam is necessarily modest in its aims. It seeks to introduce students to some of the questions pertaining to women and feminist issues in Islamic societies. The readings and discussion in this segment attempt to contextualize and place into historical perspective some of the terms of the debates that increasingly engage the relationship between non-Western feminism, Islamic culture, and politics.

1. Badran, Margot. "Competing Agendas: Feminists, Islam and the State in Nineteenth- and Twentieth-Century Egypt." *Women, Islam, and the State,* ed. Deniz Kandiyoti. Philadelphia: Temple University Press, 1991.
2. Hlie-Lucas, Marie-Aime. "Women, Nationalism, and Religion in the Algerian Liberation Struggle." *Opening the Gates: A Century of Arab Feminist Writing,* ed. Margot Badran and Miriam Cooke. Bloomington: Indiana University Press, 1990.
3. Ahmed, Leila. *Woman and Gender in Islam: Historical Roots of a Modern Debate.* New Haven, Conn.: Yale University Press, 1992 (selected chapter).

Classes 2 and 3. Women in Context: Writing, Performing, Exchanging

These classes and their readings explore particular contexts—literary, performative, economic, and personal narrative—in which Islamic women's voices may be heard.

1. Djebar, Assia. *Fantasia, An Algerian Cavalcade* (selections). New York: Quartet Books, 1989.
2. Badran, Margot, and Miriam Cooke, eds. *Opening the Gates: A Century of Arab Feminist Writing,* (selections) Bloomington: Indiana University Press, 1990.
3. Mernissi, Fatima, ed. *Doing Daily Battle: Interviews with Moroccan Women* (selections). New Brunswick, N.J.: Rutgers University Press, 1989.
4. Kapchan, Deborah. *Gender in the Market The Revoicing of Tradition in Beni Mellal, Morocco.* Philadelphia: University of Pennsylvania Press, 1996 (selections: Introduction: "The Dialogic Enterprise of Women in Changing Social Contexts;" chapter 3: "Words of Possession, Possession of Words: Ile Majduba").
5. Atiya, Nayra. *Khul-Khaal. Five Egyptian Women Tell Their Stories* (selections) Syracuse: Syracuse University Press, 1996.

Class 4. Women, Politics, Private and Public Life

Building on certain historical, social, and cultural perspectives gained in the previous classes, the readings and discussions in the final meeting will return to questions raised in the other three, extending those discussions into contemporary debates on women and politics in the private and public spheres in Islamic societies.

1. Badran, Margot. *Feminists, Islam, and Nation: Gender and the Making of Modern Egypt.* New York: Feminist Press, 1996 (selected chapter).
2. Hessini, Leila. "Wearing the Hijab in Contemporary Morocco." *Reconstructing Gender in the Middle East: Tradition, Identity, and Power.* New York: Columbia University Press, 1994.
3. Mernissi, Fatima. *Women's Rebellion and Islamic Memory.* Atlantic Highlands, N.J.: Zed Books, 1996 (selected chapter).

Also of interest,
4. Tohidi, Nayereh. "Gender and Islamic Fundamentalism: Feminist Politics in Iran." *Third World Women and the Politics of Feminism,* ed. Chandra Talpade Mohanty, Ann Russo, and Lourdes Torres. Bloomington: Indiana University Press, 1991.
5. Special issue: "Who's East? Whose East?" *Feminist Studies* 19:3 (Fall 1993) (selected article).

F. The Indian Subcontinent (2 weeks)

The objectives here include (1) familiarizing students with the historical social and political context of Indian feminism; (2) exploring the issues and concerns of Indian feminists; (3) critically analyzing the ways in which these theories construct subjects, objects, and addressees; and (4) exploring where, how, and with what effects Indian feminist theory intersects with Western feminist theory. Important texts in postcolonial history and subaltern studies from India serve to highlight the importance of India's colonial history and its nationalist movement in Indian politics and the academy. The reading by Spivak directly addresses the issue of subaltern studies and subaltern studies scholars' attempts to recover the voices of those marginalized by the colonial project.

Class 1. Women, Feminism, and History in India

1. Liddle, Joanna, and Rama Joshi. *Daughters of Independence: Gender, Caste and Class in India.* New Brunswick, N.J.: Rutgers University Press, 1986 (chapters 3 through 8).
2. Kumar, Radha. "From Chipko to Sati: The Contemporary Indian Women's Movement." *The Challenge of Local Feminisms: Women's Movements in Global Perspective,* ed. Amrita Basu. Boulder: Westview Press, 1995.

Class 2. Post-colonial Studies

1. Prakash, Gyan. "Subaltern Studies as Postcolonial Criticism." *American Historical Review* 99(5) (Dec. 1994): 1475–90.
2. Sangari, Kumkum, and Sudesh Vaid, "Recasting Women: An Introduction." *Recasting Women: Essays in Indian Colonial History,* ed. Kumkum Sangari and Sudesh Vaid. New Brunswick, N.J.: Rutgers University Press, 1990.
3. Chakravarti, Uma. "Whatever Happened to the Vedic Dasi? Orientalism, Nationalism, and a Script for the Past." *Recasting Women: Essays in Indian*

Colonial History, ed. Kumkum Sangari and Sudesh Vaid. New Brunswick, N.J.: Rutgers University Press, 1990.

Class 3. Spivak and the Recovery of Subaltern Voices

1. Spivak, Gayatri Charkravorty. "Can the Subaltern Speak?" *Marxism and the Interpretation of Culture,* ed. Cary Nelson and Lawrence Grossberg. Urbana: University of Illinois Press, 1988.

and/or

2. Spivak, Gayatri Charkravorty. "Subaltern Studies: Deconstructing Historiography." *In Other Worlds: Essays in Cultural Politics,* ed. Gayatri Spivak. New York: Methuen, 1987.
3. "Introduction" from *The Spivak Reader: Selected Works of Gayatri Chakravorty Spivak,* ed. Donna Landry and Gerald MacLean. New York: Routledge, 1996.
4. Varadharajan, Asha. *Exotic Parodies: Subjectivity in Adorno, Said and Spivak.* Minneapolis: University of Minnesota Press, 1995.

Class 4. Indian Feminists Look at the First and Third Worlds

1. Devi, Mahasweta. "Draupadi," translated with a foreword by Gayatri Chakravorty Spivak. *In Other Worlds: Essays in Cultural Politics,* ed. Gayatri Spivak. New York: Methuen, 1987.
2. Pathak, Zakia, and Rajeswari Sunder Rajan. "Shabano." *Signs* 14(3) (1989): 558–83.
3. Shiva, Vandana. "The Seed and the Spinning Wheel: The Political Ecology of Technological Change." *The Violence of the Green Revolution: Third World Agriculture, Ecology and Politics,* ed. Vandana Shiva. Atlantic Highlands, N.J.: Zed Books, 1991.

IV. Summary and Reflection (1 week)

The aim of this last week of the course is to reflect upon the approach and content of the syllabus itself, the project of integrating international issues into women's studies courses, and the broader issue of looking at—engaging in conversation with—theorizing about the international or global connections.

1. Syllabus for International Feminist Theory.
2. Kaplan, Ann. *Looking for the Other: Feminism and the Imperial Gaze.* New York: Routledge, 1996 (selections).

CREATING AN INTERNATIONAL
PERSPECTIVE ON LOCAL ACTIVISM

JUDITH MCDANIEL

The women's studies department at the University of Arizona began offering an M.A. degree in the fall of 1995. One of the courses designed for the new degree was Women's Activisms and Organizations, which is intended to give graduates (and undergraduates) an understanding of the connection between women's studies and feminist activism.

Women's Activisms and Organizations is structured so that each student will be working actively with a local women's organization or an organization that has a significant women's program. Students have volunteered in a wide range of groups including a feminist press, a rape crisis center, an interfaith action group, a women's studies class in high school for pregnant and parenting teens, a homeless shelter, and many others. Instructors attempt to be very conscious of the ideal of theory being grounded in practice and activism being informed by theory. As such, the course begs to be taught from an international perspective. And yet, when students are engaged in internships on a local level, it sometimes seems difficult to leap from the particular and local to the international perspective. I know from my own years of experience as an activist how essential it is to make this leap. I was reminded of that again at the United Nations Conference on Women in Beijing in 1995 as I listened to a Mexican American woman from central Arizona who had been trained in Western medical constructs of public health speak about her work with an urban indigenous community in which she used a concept of *health promoters*—an idea she had learned from activists who had been to Latin America. In some sense, the world is too small for all of us—teachers and students—not to be global in our thinking.

I attempted to address the necessity of understanding the international perspective with reading assignments that would remind students that not all feminisms began or reside in the United State. Three texts helped me in this regard. Penny A. Weiss and Marilyn Friedman's *Feminism and Community* (1995) looks at community from a variety of feminist perspectives and defines the idea of community in a flexible manner. Essays consider the separatist communities of Bedouin women and of North American lesbians; the community building efforts of mill workers in Shanghai and abortion providers in the United States; the definitions of community from a variety of perspectives, both international and theoretical.

Teaching from Amrita Basu's *The Challenge of Local Feminisms: Women's Movements in Global Perspective* (1995) is a challenge because of the number of countries included. I have chosen to focus on Asian feminisms for comparison in the syllabus, simply as a way of making the amount of material manageable for students. The third text, Pam McAllister's wonderful *This River of Courage* (1991), is now out of print. I will use excerpts in my packet the next time I teach the class. McAllister had collected hundreds of stories—historical and contemporary—about feminisms around the world and arranged them thematically. Students have read the entire text as though it were a novel and said their only criticism was that they wanted "more depth"—which they could easily find by doing research on their own once McAllister made the outline of events available.

I developed a series of questions, quotations, and speculations that I called *journal prompts* in order to guide students' written responses to the assigned readings. These have two purposes. The first is to help students place their activist-intern experience in a theoretical context. Part of the purpose of this class is to narrow the chasm between activist and theoretical work, and I have not found this to be an easy task. We have trained our students that to be *theoretical* means, of necessity, to be *objective*. They seem to have no way to reconcile their participation in an organization with an objective analysis of that organization. The journal prompts suggest ways for students to think about an analysis that could be informed by an "insider's perspective."

The second purpose for the journal prompts is to help students use the international material in their readings as they think about the work they are doing. Journal prompts 1, 3, and 4 take the most commonplace concerns of U.S. feminist activism and address them in an international framework.

Journal prompt 1 begins with an historical case study from U.S. women's suffrage (Emily Newell Blair) and asks students to place the organizations they are working in as separatist or not. I ask students to discuss the pros and cons of the choice their organizations have made. I then assign two relevant essays: one on the Jane Collective in Chicago and the other on the Philippine women's movement. The Gabrielas in the Philippines are attempting to maintain an autonomy apart from the nationalist movements—which promise to include women's agenda but to this date have not. We then ask what relevance this has to Pauline Bart's analysis of the successes of the Jane Collective in Chicago, which had a limited but crucial goal, providing abortions for women who needed them in a pre–*Roe* v. *Wade* era. When abortion became legal, the Jane Collective ceased to exist. We discuss what happens to women's power to organize when issues are subsumed in a larger agenda. We ask questions about a women's right to reproductive choices in the years since abortion became legal. In past classes, students have looked in depth at Southern Arizona Planned Parenthood (where one was doing a volunteer internship). Others have researched the restrictions on and parameters of legal abortions for poor women, immigrant women, and women in countries receiving U.S. aid whose right to hear about abortion as an alternative has been curtailed. Although some students may have thought that the separatist versus mainstream argument is fundamentally a U.S.–based problem (and to some a particularly lesbian-focused problem), it is hoped that by the end of this section their understanding of the range and necessity of women-only groups that focus specifically on women's issues will have changed.

Journal prompts 3 and 4 return to issues of how and when to use mainstream politics and legislation to further women's goals—and reminds students of the limitations of political and legislative systems. Prompt 5 also uses an insider's perspective on women's studies in China to suggest ways in which to evaluate the strengths and weaknesses of the U.S. women's studies movement. After reading the article on Chinese feminism, students can see fairly easily how the three *weaknesses,* defined by the authors, of Chinese women's studies (sex, class, and feminism) might be a result of cultural norms and restrictions. The challenge for U.S. scholars is to apply the same critical eye to local cultural limitations, as in women's studies. (Answers in class have been class, race, and a global perspective.)

I have found that students are generally more able to think about theory and action as a single unit (rather than irreconcilable concepts) when discussing the international material that is removed from their own lives and experiences. The journal prompts allow them to look internationally and then bring that discussion back to the organizations in which they are working.

Finally, an article by Ann Florini, "The Evolution of International Norms" (1996), which I use in the penultimate week of class, brings local activism into a global perspective. Noting the "sweeping changes in the broadly accepted standards of international behavior," Florini asks why one norm rather than another becomes "a widely accepted standard of behavior" (375). The article helps students understand that all norms change, and lets them see that they can, perhaps, help influence these changes through their activism. In fact, by the end of the semester, most students have wanted to become *norm enterpeneurs,* as defined by Florini (1996, 375): "an individual or organization that sets out to change the behavior of others." This seems a very satisfying conclusion to a class on women's activisms and organizations from a local and global perspective.

Syllabus

This class will look at women's activisms and organizations on a local and global level. Each student will be asked to volunteer (intern) four hours a week at a local feminist organization. Based on that experience, we will look closely at current feminist theory to see how and where it is useful to assist in explaining the "What happened?" of the internship. We will also use our experience to begin to extrapolate and generalize—in other words, to create theory. We must begin by looking at women's activisms in the contexts in which they have occurred; to that end, we will be reading some historical and sociological material that will help us understand some of the differences and similarities in women's responses to their lives.

Texts

Pam McAllister, *This River of Courage: Generations of Women's Resistance and Action*. Philadelphia: New Society, 1991.

Penny Weiss and Marilyn Friedman, ed. *Feminism and Community*. Philadelphia: Temple University Press, 1995.

Carol Seajay, ed. *Feminist Bookstores Newsletter* 19(1) (May/June 1996).

Packet of readings.

Required for graduate students

Amrita Basu, ed. *The Challenge of Local Feminisms: Women's Movements in Global Perspectives*. Boulder: Westview Press, 1995.

Course Requirements

1. Participate in a women's organization of your choice for a minimum of four hours a week. (With a greater time commitment, you may be able to earn additional credit for an internship.) You will receive as much help as you need to locate and begin your participation in the organization, but you are responsible for continuing that participation and conducting research on that organization. Your choice of an organization must be approved by the instructor. Credit for this class is based on the assumption that you are doing the internship. No credit is possible without it. Graduate students may do the basic four hours, may enroll for additional internship credit, or use this class to evaluate an internship you have already completed.

2. Keep an extensive journal about your participation in the organization. You will be given "prompts" to help you focus your journals (for example, a list of questions to ask to determine if an organization that says it is culturally diverse really is diverse). Journals will be the basis for at least one of your papers. I will collect and read them at least twice during the semester.

3. Write two papers:

a. One paper will place your organization in a context of feminist activist organizations historically and thematically.

b. One paper will analyze the successes and failures of your organization as you perceive them. In this paper you will begin to construct a theoretical basis for what might constitute a vital, effective feminist organization.

4. Complete a final evaluation of your organization and your participation in it.

Course Outline

Week 1

Introduction; discussion of internship process and options; discussion of kinds of activisms—politics, grassroots, print and media, academic, labor, and others.

"Who's Afraid of Feminism?" In *Women in Action* (Manila: ISIS International), 40–46. Handout.

David Barsamian, "Interview with Howard Zinn." *The Progressive* (July 1997): 37–40. Handout.

Weeks 2–5. Goals of Women's Activisms

Week 2. Civil Rights

"Invasion of the Justice Seekers," in McAllister, 97–115 (suffrage activism in U.S., U.K., France, China)

"Separatism as Strategy: Female Institution Building and American Feminism, 1870–1930," E. Friedman, 85–104, in Weiss and Friedman

"Rebirthing Babaye: The Women's Movement in the Philippines," Lilia Santiago, 110–28, in Basu.

Journal Prompt #1

Week 3. Freedom from Oppression

"Burning Incense, Pledging Sisterhood," E. Honig, 59–75, in Weiss and Friedman.

"Seizing the Means of Reproduction," P. Bart, 105–24, in Weiss and Friedman.

McAllister, 22–30 (reproductive rights in Ireland and New Brunswick, Canada).

Week 4. Diversity and Equality: Creating a Multi-Issue Politic

"Sisterhood: Political Solidarity Between Women," b. hooks, 293–316, in Weiss and Friedman.

"Definitions of Class," in packet (no copyright, approx. 1975).

McAllister, 61–63 (coalitions between black and white women in Port Alfred, South Africa)

Journal Prompt #2.

Week 5. Equal Agency

Laura Hershey, "Pursuing an Agenda Beyond Barriers: Women with Disabilities." *Women's Studies Quarterly* 1 & 2 (1996): 60–64. Packet.

Laura Hershey, "On the Margin of the Myth: Exploring the Landscape of Disabled Women's Lives." *Mainstream* (May 1997): 24–28. Packet.

Laura Hershey, "China Diary." *New Mobility* (December 1995): 40–45. Packet.

Weeks 6–10: Means by Which Women Achieve Their Goals

Week 6. Affirmative Action

Betsy Reed, "In Whose Interests? White Women and the Campaign Against Affirmative Action." *Sojourner: The Women's Forum* (August 1997): 18–19. Packet.

Bailey W. Jackson and Evangelina Holvino, "Developing Multicultural Organizations," unpublished paper. Packet.

McAllister, 57–60 (Equal Rights Amendment attempt in United States).

"From Chipko to Sati: The Contemporary Indian Women's Movement," in Basu, 58–86.

Journal Prompt #3.

Week 7. Women's Studies

Tillie Olsen, "Women Who Are Writers in Our Century: One Out of Twelve." *College English* 34(1) (October 1972): 6–17. Packet.

Adrienne Rich, "When We Dead Awaken: Writing As Revision." *College English* 34(1) (October 1972): 18–30. Packet.

"Discovering the Positive Within the Negative: The Women's Movement in a Changing China," Naihua Zhang 25–57, in Basu.

Journal Prompt # 4.

Week 8. Women in Print and the Arts

Feminist Bookstores Newsletter (entire).

Lester Olson, "On the Margins of Rhetoric: Audre Lorde." *Quarterly Journal of Speech* 83 (1997): 49–70. Packet.

David Joselit, "Exhibiting Gender." . *Art in America* (January 1997): 37–39. Packet.

"In a Protest, Poet Rejects Arts Medal." *New York Times* (July 11, 1997). Packet.

Journal Prompt #5.

Week 9. Community-Based Activism: Environment and Maquiladoras

Linda Vance, "Ecofeminism and the Politics of Reality." In *Ecofeminism: Women, Animals, and Nature*, edited by Greta Gaard, 118–45. Philadelphia: Temple University Press, 1993. Packet.

Chris Cuomo, "Toward Thoughtful Ecofeminist Activism." In *Ecological Feminist Philosophies*, edited by Karen J. Warren, 42–51. Bloomington: Indiana University Press, 1996. Packet.

Rachel Kamel, *The Global Factory: Analysis and Action for a New Economic Era*. Philadelphia: American Friends Service Committee, 1990, 35–45. Packet.

Journal Prompt #6.

Week 10. Community-Based Activism: Peace (at Home and in the World)

"A Letter from a Battered Wife." D. Martin, 45–50, in McAllister, 75–92 (histories of Mother's Day and International Women's Day in United States and Europe).

Starhawk, "Ritual as Bonding: Action as Ritual." In *Weaving the Visions: New Patterns in Feminist Spirituality*, edited by Judith Plaskow and Carol P. Christ, 326–35. Packet.

Journal Prompt #7.

Weeks 11–16. Theoretical Implications for Activism/Activist Implications for Theory

Week 11

"Women and the Holocaust: A Reconsideration of Research," Joan Ringelheim, 317–40 in Weiss and Friedman.
"A Community of Secrets: The Separate World of Bedouin Women," Lila Abu-Lughod, 21–44, in Weiss and Friedman.

Week 12

Kimberly Christensen, "'With Whom Do You Believe Your Lot Is Cast?' White Feminists and Racism." *Signs* 22(3) (Spring 1997): 617–48. Packet.
"The Tired Poem," K. Rushin, 77–81, in Weiss and Friedman.
"Sisterhood and Friendship as Feminist Models," M. Lugones, 135–46, in Weiss and Friedman.

Week 13

Marilyn Frye, "The Necessity of Differences: Constructing a Positive Category of Women." *Signs* 21(4) (Summer 1996): 991–1010. Packet.
Joreen, "Trashing: The Dark Side of Sisterhood." *Ms. Magazine* (1975) 49–53. Packet.

Week 14

"Feminism and Democratic Democracy," Jane Mansbridge, 341–66, in Weiss and Friedman.
Ann Florini, "The Evolution of International Norms." *International Studies Quarterly* 40(3) (September 1996): 363–90. Packet.

Week 15

"Feminist Communities and Moral Revolution," Ann Ferguson, 367–98, in Weiss and Friedman.
"If Not With Others, How?" Adrienne Rich, 399–405, in Weiss and Friedman.
"Principles of Unity," Berkeley-Oakland Women's Union, unpublished paper. Packet.

Week 16. Summary and Conclusions

MAKING "RACIALIZED MISOGYNY" VISIBLE: INTERNATIONALIZING WOMEN AND VIOLENCE

HEATHER S. DELL

White supremacy and patriarchy intertwine and reinforce one another. The establishment of university-level ethnic studies programs and the emphasis in women's studies programs on international women's issues represents part of the reformulation of how to teach in ways that challenge these dominant paradigms. Yet it remains difficult to articulate and sustain in the classroom an understanding of how profoundly and inextricably white supremacy and patriarchy are linked. In this essay, I propose a term—*racialized misogyny*—and a set of pedagogical strategies designed to insist on and facilitate a comprehension of their interdependency.

In my own courses on women and violence, I have noted how accustomed students have become to exploring, at least superficially, how racialization and misogyny are separately experienced in the United States. Yet, after discussing domestic violence in the United States, many students still develop amnesia about how extensive this violence is within this country when discussing domestic violence in so-called Third World countries.[1] The naming of racism and sexism as separate words have reflected and enforced tendencies: to disengage one from the other; to establish a hierarchy in which one is granted primary importance; and finally to obfuscate rather than clarify how they are or can be intimately linked in the social processes under critique. My term *racialized misogyny* emphasizes this linkage.

As Chandra Mohanty (1991, 57) has reminded us, "'third world women' as a homogenous 'powerless' group" remains a construct for many of us in the First World. It is a recurring image in the U.S. media, which continue to offer "disaster" stories and other worst-case scenarios when reporting on nations of the South. For example, one of my students brought in to class this quotation from *Good Housekeeping* magazine, with a circulation of twenty-four million readers: "Even though women in the United States have yet to achieve parity with men when it comes to paychecks or power, our circumstances are ideal when compared with women around the world" (Goodwin 1997, 102).

Although this article appears to be antisexist, it actually reduces women and their lives to stereotypes of helpless, ignorant femininity. By presenting non-Western women as caricatures of cartoonish horror, the article is misogynist and racist. The racialized misogyny of this widely circulated article is not surprising.[2] Where, then, in the curriculum can one intervene in these hegemonic depictions of the Third World woman? I suggest that women and violence classes are appropriate places to revise understandings of U.S. views of gender violence in nations of the South.

Based on my teaching, I offer three points of departure: (1) examining dominant Western feminism's imperial legacy; (2) challenging notions of social change as Western by focusing on Indian activism against dowry violence; and (3) bringing an understanding of racialized misogyny to the United States.

DOMINANT WESTERN FEMINISM'S IMPERIAL LEGACY

Internationalizing a syllabus for a women and violence course requires some informational background for students about colonialism, including current analyses that view a major strand of Western feminism as a product of global imperialism. For example, I assign Liddle and Joshi's chapter from *Daughters of Independence* (1986) called "The Main Enemy: Imperialism," which identifies how British imperialism transformed India, creating the conditions of poverty that are so often mistaken as indigenous and unchanging. These authors show how India was first deindustrialized by Britain, then unevenly developed, and finally taxed into economic devastation. The article also does a fine job of questioning the British civilizing mission supposedly committed to improving Indian women's lives. Instead, it shows that this ideology was used more to justify foreign rule than to challenge particular, localized patriarchies.

Antoinette Burton's article, "The White Woman's Burden," usefully follows this work by exploring how the first wave of British feminism was constituted within colonialism. Burton writes, "By imagining women of India as helpless colonial subjects, British feminists constructed 'the Indian woman' as a foil against which to gauge their own progress" (Burton 1992, 137). Although there are other views that could be used to counter Burton's tale of colonial complicity, her work nonetheless provides early instances of current (neo-) imperialism, some of which are reminiscent of the *Good Housekeeping* magazine passage already cited.[3] For example, Burton (1992, 144) quotes the late nineteenth-century feminist Josephine Butler: "Somewhere, halfway between the Martyr Saints and the tortured 'friend of man,' the noble dog, stand it seems to me these pitiful Indian women, girls, children, as many of them are. They have not even the small power of resistance which the western woman may have . . . who may have some clearer knowledge of a just and pitiful God to whom she may make her mute appeal."

My students enjoy reading this aloud, finding current U.S. examples in the media with similar assumptions of elitist compassion. The *Good*

Housekeeping passage comparing U.S. and Third World women's situations continues, "And increasingly we do compare—as news comes into our living rooms from the most far-flung corners of the globe. Unfortunately, much of that news has made us familiar with cultures and governments that are oppressive and even brutal to women. The often terrible lot faced by many women abroad literally hits home when families immigrate to the United States and bring their customs with them" (Goodwin 1997, 102). This passage alone, as well as its parallels with Butler's statement, are worth analyzing. They both express an anti-immigrant racism (West is best) under the sympathetic pretext of an antiegalitarian feminism (poor little sister). Antiegalitarian feminism is a contradiction in terms that is, therefore, hypocritical.

These readings, from Liddle and Joshi to Burton, will help prepare students to understand the more densely written article, "Under Western Eyes," by Chandra Mohanty, which criticizes the ways in which the Third World woman has been constructed in some recent feminist texts. These articles contribute to the realization that women's studies or feminisms are constituted within a set of historical and social relations that have engaged a critique of sexism on the one hand by reaping the privileges of racism on the other. Sharing a history with colonialism, some feminisms trafficked in racialized misogyny by constructing and reproducing a racialized hierarchy among women of different nations.

CHALLENGING AGENCY AS WESTERN: LOCAL ACTIVISM AGAINST DOWRY VIOLENCE

In teaching about women and violence, I include readings on women in India and the United States, providing parallel material on domestic violence, rape, and child abuse.[4] Here I will focus on one form of domestic violence in India, namely dowry death.

As Evelynn Hammonds (1997) has said, women of color are either hypervisible or completely invisible.[5] Certainly, the dowry deaths in India have been given a hypervisibility in the media that invites racism. The deaths have been presented as coterminous with life in India, to the point where they seem to form a kind of cultural identification: India = dowry deaths. As one of my students said, "But don't they realize there will be no women left in India if they keep burning them up like this?" Students tend to see gender violence as the exception in the United States and the rule in Third World countries like India. I find that I have to explain how violence is endemic in the United States, yet that I have to do the opposite in teaching about India. I have to explain that gender violence, while too often accepted in India, does not saturate social interaction there. Although marriages tend to be inegalitarian in India, they cannot be reductively understood as merely a form of domestic violence. Thus I spend more time localizing dowry violence, and most of all emphasizing activist campaigns against it. Learning about indigenous solutions accomplished in countries of the South works to resubjectify the problems and the peoples that have been objectified.

The import of dowry itself is in dispute. It may be understood as a premortem inheritance to the bride from her family at the time of her wedding that forecloses any claim she has on natal property at the time of the household head's death. Others may see it as a transfer of goods from the bride's to the groom's family (Waters 1997). This dispute may be investigated by looking at nonfeminist, anthropological classics (Srinivas 1984; Tambiah and Goody 1973). But within a women's studies context, Kishwar's (1989, 1993) analyses are more pertinent to trace changing feminist perspectives and are more informative about recent activism.

In teaching about dowry death and feminist activism, I have a checklist of techniques and topics that I now discuss, including assigning response cards, teaching social diversity, localizing dowry violence, examining the myth of people of color as tradition-bound, contextualing dowry death among more common forms of domestic violence, de-exoticizing burning, and emphasizing grassroots movements.

RESPONSE CARDS

Assigning written student responses to the readings for every class is a crucial way to monitor and intervene in racist gender critiques. Students write responses on large index cards quickly and privately, without editing into a politically correct version they might speak in class. Students can try out different stances on these cards, get my perspective on their underlying assumptions, and keep a record of their discoveries and realizations.

TEACHING SOCIAL DIVERSITY

Teaching social diversity entails examining the myth that it is the supposedly undifferentiated, uneducated Indian masses who practice dowry violence. In fact, dowry violence is middle class and urban, often practiced in educated, entrepreneurial families (Kishwar 1993; Kumar 1993).

LOCALIZING DOWRY VIOLENCE

The "India = dowry death" generalization can be countered by localizing dowry violence. It is practiced more in the Hindi heartland, or north-central India. Dowry deaths tend to be committed in Delhi as well as in urban areas in western and central Uttar Pradesh, Haryana, northeastern Rajastan, northern Madya Pradesh, and southern Punjab. I have students color in a map and judge the percentage of India it encompasses. Dowry death is, however, spreading to previously low-incident areas (Harvard University 1995).

THE MYTH OF TRADITION

The topic of dowry death can be used to challenge the myth of people of color as tradition-bound. It is not uncommon to have students write about dowry death as "an ancient tradition." But in India dowry death is a recent phenomenon, dating from the 1970s; it is often attributed to escalating consumerism and exoticized as Western (washers, cars, and the big ticket items demanded for dowry may be those promoted by U.S.–identified multinational corporations) (Kishwar 1993; Narayan 1997). One might ask if dowry deaths are created in part at the juncture of patriarchies of the North and South (without denying the perpetrators' responsibility) (Mani 1990). If your students have already read Mohanty, they will be able to connect this myth to what she calls the Third World difference, a "stable, ahistorical something that apparently oppresses most if not all the women in these countries" (1991, 53–54). Narayan (1997) calls this "death by culture." Death by culture explanations wrongly ground sexual violence in long past religious views or ancient values. These views or values are used effectively to dehistoricize the current social problem and constitute an entire population as indoctrinated through the centuries. Narayan offers a particularly helpful critique of Elizabeth Bumiller's chapter called "Flames" in her popular, if misguided book, *May You Be the Mother of a Hundred Sons: A Journey Among the Women of India* (1990).

CONTEXUALIZING DOMESTIC VIOLENCE

Dowry death can be contextualized among prevalent, less "exotic" forms of domestic violence. Dowry is not always a primary reason for domestic violence in India (Kishwar 1989, 5). Producing daughters rather than sons, a husband's jealousy, or his intention to remarry are more likely explanations of violence than dowry. And battering and desertion are more common than burning (Datar and Upendra 1981). But unfortunately, these do not make "good copy" because they are too familiar to a U.S. audience. As Narayan (1997, 101, original emphasis) also suggests, "Domestic violence against Indian women thus becomes most widely known in Western contexts in its most *extreme incarnation,* underlining its 'Otherness.'"

DE-EXOTICIZING BURNING

The choice of fire as a weapon in India has less to do with resurrecting ancient ritual and more to do with covering up a murder. Women cook over kerosene or gas flames and hence, dowry death can be made to look like an accidental kitchen fire. Furthermore, any sign of assault may be obscured by burns.

INDIGENOUS MOVEMENTS AND ACTIVISM

Finally, I place emphasis on agency from within India, exploring indigenous movements and activism. I use the Indian women's rights magazine, *Manushi,* and Kumar's *The History of Doing (1993)*. I ask them to read for solutions that Radha Kumar presents in her chapter "The Campaign Against Dowry." The film *No Longer Silent* features Indian activists talking about the various campaigns to stop female feticide and dowry deaths (Deschamps 1987). Through these experiences, students teach each other that agency is not inherently Western. In doing so, they have struggled to avoid reinscribing stereotypes of Third World helplessness or incompetence.

But the task is not easy. I have found that while using indigenous activist sources can be a strength, it can also present particular problems. One dilemma is that the articles often assume a knowledge of terms that students do not have. But the larger dilemma is that some articles do not cross national boundaries well. We need more texts that can address the sexist skepticism that might be the predominant reading within the particular country discussed, and yet can address the ethnocentrism, or more precisely the racialized misogyny, that may be the predominant reading outside of that country. Indigenous activist sources work to make clear how gender violence is pervasive in their society. Yet these messages may be amplified and distorted by another country's citizens as implying that gender violence is normative, perhaps even the most salient characteristic of the culture. Texts must find a difficult balance between emphasizing the oppressiveness of particular practices and yet not allowing them to be used as emblematic of an entire nation's culture. The production of such writing is critical to internationalizing women's studies curricula and to bridging the gap between the academy and grassroots activism. It is particularly critical in regions that continue to be simplistically represented and reduced to a form of violence—"forced prostitution = Thailand" and "female genital mutilation/female circumcision = Africa."

WHITE LIKE ME? BRINGING AN UNDERSTANDING OF RACIALIZED MISOGYNY BACK HOME

After challenging the class to explore violence against women in the United States and in India and to criticize the various myths which surround this, I move on to the work of understanding how gender violence has been constituted through racism in the United States. Working through U.S. racist depictions of gender violence in India provides a framework for examining similar practices directed at people of color here at home.

I have found that merely interspersing articles about women of color throughout a syllabus is insufficient to accomplish this task, because it often lets students read around their discomfort. Their response cards show that, when assigned two articles, some will write on the gender-centered article alone and ignore the feminist antiracism reading also assigned. The response cards also have shown me that some students will respond only to the one paragraph, in a Black feminist's article, that deals with white women. A few have been forthright in dismissing an antiracist feminist article. "I can't read this Ebonics. She keeps using the word 'brother' all the time," wrote one student on a bell hooks reading early in the semester. Recognizing evasion is a beginning. But it became evident from these initial experiences that it is important to design learning units that hold to the task of examining how white supremacy and patriarchy are inextricably entwined in the practice of racialized misogyny.

Two articles on critical race feminism give students more intellectual tools to recognize how, in some feminist analyses of violence, race is excised rather than included. I have chosen one article that focuses on facing discrimination as a Black woman and a second to make some of the patterns of sexist white supremacy visible. Adrien Katherine Wing's 1997 article "Brief Reflections Toward a Multiplicative Theory and Praxis of Being" speaks to the injury of Black women's spirit, the cumulative effect of discriminatory attacks that amount to "the slow death of the psyche, the soul, and the persona" (28). Grillo and Wildman, in their article "Obscuring the Importance of Race" (1997, 46), focus on white supremacy as a set of practices that include:

1. the taking back of center stage from people of color, even in discussions of racism, so that white issues remain or become central to the dialogue;

2. the fostering of essentialism, so that women and people of color are implicitly viewed as belonging to mutually exclusive categories, rendering women of color invisible; and

3. the appropriation of pain or the rejection of its existence that

results when whites who have compared other oppressions to race discriminations believe they understand the experience of racism.

A number of sources on the Anita Hill–Clarence Thomas hearings make racialized misogyny explicit (see, for example, the essays in Morrison 1992). I have found that Crenshaw's 1992 article, "Whose Story Is It, Anyway? Feminist and Antiracist Appropriations of Anita Hill," is one of the most useful. It explores, among many other ideas, how race and gender essentialism contribute to making women of color invisible. Crenshaw (1992, 403) argues that "social power is mediated in American society . . . through the contestation between many narrative structures through which reality might be perceived and talked about." Standard narratives of racial discrimination focus on the experiences of Black men. Narratives of gender discrimination, on the other hand, tend to derace women, transforming victims into women who are implicitly, but normatively, white. These two narratives cannot adequately represent the experience of an African American woman, since she is identified as Black yet female.

The representation of Anita Hill during the hearings was a clear example of this predicament of intersectionality, as Crenshaw calls it. It culminated in "a classic showdown between antiracism and feminism," as each side "told tales on Anita Hill, tales in which she was appropriated to tell everybody's story but her own" (Crenshaw 1992, 405–406). Hill's presentation as a victim of sexual harassment was represented to the American public using the rape narrative. Although rape and sexual harassment are not one and the same thing, in both "cases the inquiry tends to focus more on the woman's conduct and character rather than on the conduct and character of the defendant" (Crenshaw 1992, 408). The media often interviewed white feminists who constructed Hill's identity as gendered only. Most of these feminists correctly noted how Hill was vilified along the lines of a typical rape victim, as a female provocateur who then brought a false accusation against an innocent man. Hill's failure to leave her job with Thomas and her subsequent years of silence invited questions regarding the truth of her accusations. White feminist spokespersons tended to explain this as a steadfast commitment to her career. While the rape trope partially represented how Hill was read, it was incomplete because it was a "raceless tale of gender subordination" (Crenshaw 1992, 415).

The deracing of Hill, Crenshaw argues, contributed to allowing Clarence Thomas to "drape himself in a history of black male repression" using the lynching narrative, one of the most compelling tropes of race oppression in the African American community (Crenshaw 1992, 416). Some found this ironic for a man who had succeeded in law by deracing himself (Stansell 1992). He was a "black neoconservative individualist whose upward mobility was fueled by his unbounded willingness to stymie the advancement of other African

Americans" (Crenshaw 1992, 402). Nonetheless, he was able to name the hearing as a high-tech lynching, calling up the history of Black men lynched when wrongly accused of raping a white woman. Paula Giddings' 1984 article, "To Sell Myself as Dearly as Possible," the film *Rosewood* (Singleton 1997), and Angela Davis' 1981 article "Rape, Racism, and the Myth of the Black Rapist" can be used to address this history. Stansell's 1992 article, "White Feminists and Black Realities: The Politics of Authenticity," is particularly suited to exploring the historical divide between antiracists and feminists and critiquing Thomas' "rebirth" during the hearings as an antiracist. Yet, although each of these articles is worthy, in this teaching context they may be used by students to keep the narrative of race discrimination gendered masculine.

Thomas' mobilization of the lynching trope in front of an all-white Senate committee hearing against Hill, who had been repeatedly represented as implicitly white by some feminist spokespersons, was his call for race solidarity from the African American community. In the *Frontline* video *Clarence Thomas and Anita Hill: Public Hearing, Private Pain* (1992) Bickel interviewed a number of African American spokespersons who questioned whether Hill should have kept silent in order to avoid contributing to the ongoing stereotype of Black men as violent and hypersexual. Although this video offers criticism of how the media coverage set up a divide between white feminism and racial solidarity, it does not offer students a better understanding that circumvents this binary. Indeed, I have found that students often mistakenly viewed a racial solidarity unnuanced by understandings of gender inequalities as representative of the whole African American community. This acceptance is related to, and reinforces, their presuppositions that countries like India are tradition-bound, wedded to cultures abusive to women, and unlikely to change without intervention by whites.

Crenshaw's (1992) article is invaluable precisely because it takes a Black feminist activist stance that shows how racialized misogyny (although she does not call it that) in both white and Black communities has placed women of color in the unnecessary position of having to decide whether to identify themselves as Black or as women. This dichotomy must be challenged by inviting antiracists and antisexists to see how a combined critique of racism and sexism could be used to rewrite dominant tropes of discrimination.

Tropes of sexual discrimination should accommodate an understanding of how racist myths have combined with sexism. While Crenshaw's presentation of stereotypes of Black femininity is useful, further help may be obtained by assigning Patricia Hill Collins' 2000 article, "The Sexual Politics of Black Womanhood." Collins explores the history of the stereotypes and treatment of Black women in pornography, prostitution, and rape that form part of an American social context that interweaves racism and sexism. In addition, I have found that discussing how witness credibility is affected by race in both white and Black victim cases allows students to see that racism is part of every case, even if every participant is white. The unearned privilege of trust invested in being white contributes to how each participant, in part, in a court case will be received. The link in our society between whiteness and greater believability—whether you are an alleged perpetrator, the person who brings the charge, or a witness—contributes to how much credibility you will have upon entering the courtroom.

Tropes of race discrimination, argues Crenshaw, should represent not only the history of lynching but also the history of the rape and sexual harassment of Black women by white men. While we can learn the names of some of the Black men who have come to represent the experiences of racial injustice: "the names and faces of black women whose bodies also bore the scars of racial oppression are lost to history. To the limited extent that sexual victimization of black women is symbolically represented within our collective memory, it is as tragic characters whose vulnerability illustrates the racist emasculation of black men" (Crenshaw 1992, 418).

Even when the sexual abuse of African American women is included in history, it is often appropriated to signal an injury to African American men, placing Black masculinity back at the center of antiracist discourse. Crenshaw provides a recent example of the marginalization of Black women's experience. She points out that the dominant trope in discussions of racism and sexual assault attends to the way African American men "accused of raping white women are disproportionately punished relative to black-on-black or white-on-white rape" (Crenshaw 1992, 419). This information is used to illustrate the racist treatment of Black men in the criminal justice system, but it is just as much an example of discrimination against Black women: "Clearly, black women are victims of a racial hierarchy that subordinates their experiences of sexual abuse to those of white women" (Crenshaw 1992, 419). This is an important message for some students who may think that bringing antiracism into a women and violence class is just "playing the race card."

Some of my students saw racial solidarity as sexist because some African Americans insisted that Hill silently support Thomas' nomination. In previous semesters, when we watched *Public Performance, Private Pain* without supporting readings, at least 50 percent of the students remembered only the voices of antiracist solidarity, editing out the challenges offered by Black feminists. Dismissal of this position as sexist and representative of the whole Black community, therefore, allowed these students, under the guise of their commitment to antisexism, to dismiss all African Americans' antiracist solidarity. This is not simply an opportunity to teach about diversity within the Black community, but to identify the crucial parallels between representations of the Third World and those of U.S. communities of color.

First, students need to understand historically how sexual violence and discrimination have too easily been accepted as emblematic of communities of color within and beyond the United States. The media continue to represent crime and crisis as synonymous with Black communities, just as they do Third World countries. In coverage of these contexts, intrigue is heightened when the crime is one of sexual violence.

Second, identifying the parallels is an opportunity to grasp how African American culture has been viewed as backward and unchanging, in much the same way that Third World countries have been. A representation of sexist racial solidarity as representative of the entire Black community, set against the views of white feminist spokespersons, may imply that Blacks are "stuck in tradition." Narayan's term "death by culture" (1997) is particularly chilling here as it recalls Moynihan's classic study of Black culture as pathological (U.S. Department of Labor 1965; see hooks 1981 for a critique of this publication). Against a representation of African American "stuckness," the white feminist spokespersons may be interpreted as members of a white community that has progressed to a more "civilized" understanding of how to treat women. Not only does this juxtaposition evoke the old racist, colonial hierarchy that justified white rule in nations of color, it also evokes an imperial feminism wherein the woman of color is constructed as a foil against which white women may gauge their accomplishments. Nonetheless, a silenced woman, fearing ostracism by her community, is not uncommon among either white or Black women.

Feminist and womanist resistance has taken place in both communities, as well. Third, then, identifying parallels presents a chance to examine illustrations of women's indigenous activism abroad and activism by women of color in the United States. Black feminists have not been silent on the question of violence against women of color or race solidarity. Black feminist theory offers concrete ways in which race solidarity is being reconfigured by members of the African American community to include women of color and to challenge their malignment (Collins 2000; hooks 1981; Hull et al. 1982; Wing 1997).

CONCLUSION

In the United States today, many of the gender violence cases given wide national media coverage continue to involve a disproportionate number of people of color—think of Anita Hill, Robin Givens, and Desiree Washington. And, given that we are in the midst of a global communications revolution, more images of people of color from Third World countries are being circulated and broadcast than ever before. In these circumstances, the concept of racialized misogyny may help identify concepts of sexism and racism used by the media and in our lives. U.S. society often fails to link racism and sexism, and even sets one concept against the other. Racism and sexism, as separate concepts, have their heuristic uses. Yet racialized misogyny as a critical term names a set of social practices that immediately entails both, in a way that does not require us to disengage one from another, or allow a hierarchy to be reestablished in which one concept is granted primacy above the other.

Racialized misogyny risks setting aside antiracism in order to pursue gender justice. In the process, racialized misogyny, among some white feminists and their media representations, has offered a critique of sexism in communities of color in a manner that reinforces racism. And although it may seem that such a critique is racist but not sexist, it often traffics in both racism and sexism. The simplistic presentation of dowry death relies on a racist trope of the Third World as violent, troubled, and backward, yet it also treats the Indian women victimized as stick figures, passive and ignorant. This assumption of passive ignorance is, itself, a stereotype of femininity. Racist imagery of communities of color, combined with stereotypes of women, constitute the term racialized misogyny. Criticisms of sexism that reduce women's situations to caricature are misogynist, often racist, and should not be mistaken as feminist calls for sisterly support.

Racialized misogyny presumes that people of color are homogeneously bound by traditions of gender violence. It may also entail the assumption that social change is a practice that must always be introduced by outsiders, such as white or Western activists. By locating change outside a "tradition-bound" community, racialized misogyny ignores the fact that every culture offers not only methods for obtaining compliance from its members, but also standard tools for resistance (Scott 1985). Simplistic criticisms of non-Western sexism that call for Westernizing solutions set women up in a dilemma in which they seemingly must choose between community membership or foreign formulations of women's rights. Being asked to choose between racial, ethnic, religious, or national membership on the one hand and feminism on the other is an unnecessary burden.[6] Many racial, ethnic, and religious communities or nations have indigenous women's movements, with long histories of struggle and accomplishment, which effectively use local (as well as international) conceptions of resistance.[7] Both the Indian women's movement and Black feminist activism are cases in point. Yet when solutions are coded as white or foreign, this has served as ammunition for local critics who may wrongly brand indigenous women's movements as a betrayal of community solidarity. This is why many Third and Fourth World activists may not call themselves feminist, but rather identify in part as people committed to women's rights. They do not want to be associated with an older, unnuanced form of white feminism that insisted on centering gender above and beyond all other aspects of identity (Kishwar 1990). Finally, racialized misogyny is a process that also reinforces the use of representations of Othered peoples as a foil against which a superior sense of equality is claimed. By naming and also criticizing racialized misogyny, we can redouble our commitment to confronting a shared, global history.

NOTES

This article was part of a panel on teaching women and violence organized for the 1998 Eastern Sociological Society Meetings by Jessica Schiffman and Laura O'Toole. I thank them both. My thanks to Dan Cohen for his invaluable critical and editorial comments. I am grateful to my politically diverse students at the University of Delaware, West Chester University, and Rosemont College for their forthright feedback on a difficult challenge.

1. Jaffe et al. (1997, 353) state that in the United States, "One in ten women are abused every year by the man with whom they live. Repeated, severe violence occurs in one in fourteen marriages. Estimates have pointed to the fact that approximately 3 million to 4 million American households . . . live with violence every year. . . . More women are abused by their husbands or boyfriends than are injured in car accidents, muggings, and rapes."
2. Examples are plentiful. See Friedman 1996; Hornblower 1993; and Vollman 1993.
3. See these texts for instances of resistance to colonialism: Chaudhuri and Strobel 1992 and Jayawardena 1995. For an expanded version of Burton's argument, see her 1994 book, *Burdens of History: British Feminists, Indian Women, and Imperial Rule, 1865–1915*.
4. See Anne B. Waters' (1997) "The Status of Women in South Asia" for further preparation in current stereotypes of South Asian women.
5. I am grateful to A. Lynn Bolles who brought this to my attention in her introductory speech at the Transforming Knowledge for a Changing World: Internationalizing Gender, "Engendering" the International Conference.
6. For an Indian example, see Patak and Sunder Rajan's "Shahbano" (1989).
7. I am not suggesting that cultures should only draw on indigenous models of resistance. In any case, today and in the past, one would be hard pressed to identify a culturally "pure" and "authentic" practice.

WORKS CITED

Bickel, Ofra. 1992. *Clarence Thomas and Anita Hill: Public Hearing, Private Pain.* Produced by Ofra Bickel. 58 minutes. PBS. Videocassette.

Bumiller, Elizabeth. 1990. *May You Be the Mother of a Hundred Sons: A Journey Among the Women of India.* New York: Random House.

Burton, Antoinette M. 1992. "The White Woman's Burden: British Feminists and 'The Indian Woman,' 1865–1915." In Nupur Chaudhuri and Margaret Strobel, eds., *Western Women and Imperialism: Complicity and Resistance.* Bloomington: Indiana University Press.

Chaudhuri, Nupur, and Margaret Strobel, eds. 1992. *Western Women and Imperialism: Complicity and Resistance.* Bloomington: Indiana University Press.

Collins, Patricia Hill. 2000. "The Sexual Politics of Black Womanhood." In Patricia Hill Collins, ed., *Black Feminist Thought: Knowledge, Consciousness, and the Politics of Empowerment*, 123–148. New York: Routledge, second edition.

Crenshaw, Kimberle. 1992. "Whose Story Is It, Anyway? Feminist and Antiracist Appropriations of Anita Hill." In Toni Morrison, ed., *Race-ing Justice, En-gendering Power: Essays on Anita Hill, Clarence Thomas and the Construction of Social Reality*. New York: Pantheon.

Datar, Chhaya, and Hema Upendra. 1981. "Deserted Women Break Their Silence." In Chhaya Datar, ed., *The Struggle Against Violence*, 151–198. Calcutta: Stree.

Davis, Angela Y. 1981. *Women, Race, and Class*. New York: Random House.

Deschamps, Laurette. 1987. *No Longer Silent*. Produced by International Film Bureau. 57 minutes. Cine-Sita. Videocassette.

Friedman, Robert I. 1996. "India's Shame." *The Nation*, 8 April: 11.

Giddings, Paula. 1984. "'To Sell My Life as Dearly as Possible': Ida B. Wells and the First Anti-Lynching Campaign." In *When and Where I Enter: The Impact of Black Women on Race*. New York: William Morrow.

Goodwin, Jan. 1997. "The Brutalizing of Women." *Good Housekeeping* (March): 102.

Grillo, Trina, and Stephanie M. Wildman. 1997. "Obscuring the Importance of Race: The Implications of Making Comparisons Between Racism and Sexism (or Other Isms)." In Adrien Katherine Wing, ed., *Critical Race Feminism: A Reader*, 44–50. New York: New York University Press.

Hammonds, Evelynn M. 1997. "Toward a Genealogy of Black Female Sexuality: The Problematic of Silence." In M. Jacqui Alexander and Chandra Talpade Mohanty, eds., *Feminist Genealogies, Colonial Legacies, Democratic Futures*, 170–182. New York: Routledge.

Harvard University. 1995. *Souvenir of the First International Conference on Dowry Death and Bride-Burning*. Cambridge: Harvard University Law School.

hooks, bell. 1981. *Ain't I a Woman: Black Women and Feminism*. Boston: South End Press.

Hornblower, Margot. 1993. "The Skin Trade." *Time* (21 June): 44–51.

Hull, Gloria T., Patricia Bell Scott, and Barbara Smith, eds. 1982. *All the Women Are White, All the Blacks Are Men, But Some of Us Are Brave: Black Women's Studies*. Old Westbury, NY.: Feminist Press.

Jaffe, Peter, David Wolfe, and Susan Kaye Wilson. 1997. "Definition and Scope of the Problem." In Laura L. O'Toole and Jessica R. Schiffman, eds., *Gender Violence: Interdisciplinary Perspectives*, 352–361. New York: New York University Press.

Jayawardena, Kumari. 1995. *The White Woman's Other Burden: Western Women and South Asia During British Rule*. New York: Routledge.

Kishwar, Madhu. 1989. "Towards More Just Norms for Marriage: Continuing the Dowry Debate." *Manushi* (July–August): 2–9.

———. 1990. "Why I Do Not Call Myself a Feminist." *Manushi* (November–December): 2–8.

———. 1993. "Dowry Calculations: Daughter's Rights in Her Parental Family." *Manushi* (September–October): 8–17.

Kumar, Radha. 1993. *The History of Doing: An Illustrated Account of Movements for Women's Rights and Feminism in India, 1800–1990.* New Delhi: Kali for Women.

Liddle, Joanna, and Rama Joshi. 1986. *Daughters of Independence: Gender, Caste, and Class in India.* New Brunswick, N.J.: Rutgers University Press.

Mani, Lata. 1990. "Contentious Traditions: The Debate on Sati in Colonial India." In Kumkum Sangari and Sudesh Vaid, eds., *Recasting Women: Essays in Indian Colonial History,* 88–126. New Brunswick, N.J.: Rutgers University Press.

Mohanty, Chandra Talpade. 1991. "Under Western Eyes: Feminist Scholarship and Colonial Discourses." In Chandra Talpade Mohanty, Ann Russo, and Lourdes Torres, eds., *Third World Women and the Politics of Feminism,* 51–80. Bloomington: Indiana University Press.

Morrison, Toni, ed. 1992. *Race-ing Justice, En-gendering Power: Essays on Anita Hill, Clarence Thoma, and the Construction of Social Reality.* New York: Pantheon Books.

Narayan, Uma. 1997. *Dislocating Cultures: Identities, Traditions, and Third World Feminism.* New York: Routledge.

Patak, Zakia, and Rajeswari Sunder Rajan. 1989. "Shahbano." *Signs: Journal of Women in Culture and Society* (Spring): 558–582.

Scott, James. 1985. *Weapons of the Weak: Everyday Forms of Peasant Resistance.* New Haven, Conn.: Yale University Press.

Singleton, John. 1997. *Rosewood.* Produced by Tracy Barone. 146 minutes. Warner Home Video. Videocassette.

Srinivas, M.N. 1984. *Some Reflections on Dowry.* Delhi: Oxford University Press.

Stansell, Christine. 1992. "White Feminists and Black Realities: The Politics of Authenticity." In Toni Morrison, ed., *Race-ing Justice, En-gendering Power: Essays on Anita Hill, Clarence Thomas and the Construction of Social Reality,* 251–268. New York: Pantheon Books.

Tambiah, Stanley, and Jack Goody. 1973. *Bridewealth and Dowry.* Cambridge: Cambridge University Press.

U.S. Department of Labor, Office of Policy Planning and Research. 1965. *The Negro Family: The Case for National Action.* Washington, D.C.: U.S. Government Printing Office.

Vollman, William T. 1993. "Sex Slave." *Spin Magazine* (September): 74.

Waters, Anne B. 1997. "The Status of Women in South Asia." *Education About Asia* (Fall): 21–25.

Wing, Adrien Katherine. 1997. "Brief Reflections Toward a Multiplicative Theory and Praxis of Being." In Adrien Katherine Wing, ed., *Critical Race Feminism: A Reader.* New York: New York University Press.

FEMINISMS CROSS-CULTURALLY: EXPLORING WOMEN'S WORLDS

HELEN JOHNSON

In this article I elucidate how a course, Feminisms Cross-Culturally: Exploring Women's Worlds, has been fashioned for students. This course, offered to students from diverse class backgrounds and national heritages in their third or fourth year as part of a major in women's studies, anthropology, or comparative sociology, aims to broaden their access to reach an understanding of women's lived experience in non-Australian communities. The course provides material that examines the ways in which the contemporary evolution of capitalist relations, processes of decolonization, the rise of nationalisms, and religious beliefs and practices have shaped and reproduced forms of oppressive domination that may be termed *patriarchal*.[1] Students analyze theoretical sources written by "indigenous," postcolonial, and feminist scholars, as well as view video materials created by anthropologists and journalists. They reflect upon and learn to evaluate the ways in which women are constituted as biological reproducers of "the nation," to examine how women's corporeality is shaped by notions of "moral virtue," and to deconstruct the universalization of the term *woman*.

I am interested in how feminist and anthropological courses that explore "women" within and across cultures can be of significance in a challenging new world.[2] My feminist pedagogy argues for and from anthropological and women's studies perspectives. Having taught in universities for six years, the implicit challenge to create a new teaching style was generated by my work in 1997 with a women's studies colleague who encouraged me to think reflexively about my pedagogic practices. Following discussions with her I wanted to design new courses and refashion two existing courses including the one under discussion in ways that would enable students from diverse cultural backgrounds to learn in a more inclusive fashion.[3] I was also keen to find innovative, exciting ways of teaching that reflected my postmodern and poststructural theoretical position. This meant working to actively deconstruct the notion of a single norm of thought and experience which, as a younger woman, I had been encouraged to believe was universal. From my research background as an anthropologist and working within an institutional imperative to internationalize, I also realized that a change in pedagogic parameters would be helpful in widening students' perspectives and in enhancing a multicultural education. But in working toward a multicultural education, a new issue arose. As bell hooks (1994, 40) contends, "Accepting the decentering of the West globally, embracing multiculturalism, compels educators to focus attention on the issue of voice. Who speaks? Who listens? And why?" In refashioning the material for the course I accepted hooks' (1994, 38) astute caution that

> "all too often . . . a will to include those considered 'marginal' [is not matched by] a willingness to accord their work the same respect and consideration given other work. In Women's Studies, for example, individuals will often focus on women of color at the very end of the semester or lump everything about race and difference together in one section. This kind of tokenism is not multicultural transformation, but it is familiar . . . as the change most individuals are most likely to make."
>
> (hooks 1994, 38).

I wanted to ensure that the voices of women of color and indigenous scholars were a structuring trope of the course material, to avoid the tokenism that hooks has witnessed and also to ensure that students were aware of the richness of other ways of knowing.

My primary motivation as a feminist teacher is to enable students to feel at ease in contesting established ideas. As Vicki Kirby (1993, 32) proposes, enabling students to violate normative concepts can "turn to their advantage that which would oppress them." The use of intra- and intercultural texts exemplifies the possibilities of writing within what Mary Louise Pratt (1992, 4) calls "contact zones," those "social spaces where disparate cultures meet, clash, and grapple with each other, often in highly asymmetrical relations of domination and subordination—like colonialism, slavery, or their aftermaths as they are lived out across the globe today." Equally, my desire to nurture the creative agency of questioning students has shaped the scheduling of the course. Carolyn Shrewsbury's (1993, 11) model of engaged teaching and learning is one that has helped to shape the course restructure, to enable students to move from considering and reacting to power as domination, to considering and acting through "power as creative energy."

To enhance their expression of personal experiential knowledge I foster an environment in which students feel they can actively contribute, an approach that promotes peer group cohesion and positive psychodynamics in which more students feel at ease in expressing their views. The students are also encouraged to work in small groups to bring their own experiences to the discussion held in each weekly two-hour seminar. As my intention is also to educate in order to develop students' critical consciousness I have had to consider when and how it is appropriate to give up some of my authority as teacher, to admit the limits of my knowledge about certain issues, in order to construct an atmosphere of mutual intellectual enquiry. Equally, as classrooms in

Western academies become more culturally diverse, teachers must question how the politics of global economic, political, and sociocultural domination can often be reproduced in educational institutions. Indeed, I have noticed within seminars a timid self-presentation among certain Malaysian and Indonesian students, particularly those who have been raised within Islamic families, that restricts their opportunities to speak in public. More forthright Chinese students from Singapore and Hong Kong rarely need to overcome such cultural barriers and, despite sometimes onerous language differences, will maintain a presence and contribute their thoughts in each seminar. Because all students, from their differing gender, national, class, and sociocultural heritage, bring different perceptions to the course, and take away different ideas and attitudes, in the classroom I work toward generating an appreciation of difference within the similarity of their status as students.

The presence of differently positioned students in the classroom means that questions of culture, class, and dominant cultural values are immediately and visibly upon the agenda. As Heather Hill (1997, A60) proposes, "we should not overlook the tangible gains that come from having classes in which not everyone is the same colour. For whites, those gains include being prompted to think from a perspective not one's own—a critical skill that needs to be learned during the college years." I use Henrietta Moore's work (1994) to prompt students' reflection upon how identities are formed within relations of power and fields of cultural difference, how people think about others, and how images about others can be created and politically manipulated. This reading works to overcome the critical and logical barriers that students can raise when new information challenges their existing worldviews.

During the first class meeting, I propose to students that they consider how the future of feminist anthropology may be shaped, provoking their assessment of chosen theories, concepts, and practices in group discussion, through questions such as: What do you think feminism is? Is your idea of feminism applicable to all women, everywhere? Such questions stimulate students' understanding that there is no singular model of feminism and that women and men may contribute to a type of feminist or women's movement in their culture that has a history, a shape, and an agenda of its own. I also introduce material addressing the theoretical and political concerns of Third World women. I use an analysis of the perceived oppression of women globally and the ways in which feminists in Western countries have written about male dominance as a launching pad for debates about the production of knowledge, in which the definition of power locks all resistance into binary structures. Through a discussion of Chandra Mohanty's (1991, 71) assertion that "the crux of the problem lies in that initial assumption of women as an homogenous group or category ('the oppressed')," the students can learn that caution is required when speaking about women who do not share the same sociocultural, political, and economic structures as their own. I also stress the ways in which Western feminism can expand its critique of gender relations to include not only the oppression of women by men, but also the oppression of women by women. The students learn to critique the tendency of Western feminism to construct "the other woman" as backward. Taking up Mohanty's (1991, 52) suggestion that the first step to eliminating difficulties is to analyze "the discursive construction of Third World women in Western feminism," the students examine the process of "Othering" women of cultures who are different from one's own. Discussion and readings alert students to the tendency of Western theories to assume the West as the norm and non-Western histories and cultures as Other. They learn to struggle against this epistemological and political phenomenon to achieve a politically anchored understanding of both Western and other cultures.

Readings for the second week explore whether "we" can give a voice to "them." Particularly helpful is a BBC–Channel Four documentary *Let Her Die,* which focuses on the phenomenon of female infanticide and contains a distressing portrayal of bride-burning. The video promotes a consideration of what it means to be a woman in particular sociocultural environments where being perceived as female prior to and after birth can result in death. However, seminar activities throughout the course are designed to generate an awareness of the ways in which Western stereotypes can construct sociocultural practices as potent significations of the barbaric Other. Critical group discussion also empowers students to perceive the ways in which the didactic and totalizing presentation of European values reaffirms the authority of Western knowledge-makers to speak for others on their terms.

The following week moves students beyond the notion of tradition toward the concept of the discordant discourses that envelop and construct ideas about female circumcision, foot binding, and sati. While students debate the ways that power and the sociocultural construction of gender intersect to shape and control women's bodies and lives in material ways, they also learn that women are not only bound by ideologies within patriarchal families but, in turn, by discourse and practices that shape their bodies through nationalist debates that attempt to define what it means to be a woman. As one student shrewdly observed in her research essay,

> despite the excruciating pain that footbinding caused, parents continued to subject their daughters to this crippling custom because the smallest possible feet were considered an asset in the marriage market, a sign of gentility and beauty. Yung argues that as it was extremely difficult to walk unassisted, footbinding "kept women from 'wandering,'" thus reinforcing their cloistered existence and ensuring their chastity. (Yung 1995, 6)

Foot binding as a poignantly crippling gender and class symbol links with examinations of female circumcision in later seminars to illustrate how women's bodies become central to the notion of gendering a nation, of marking boundaries, and maintaining and reproducing identity, difference, and "the community," particularly *in contrast to* Western stereotypic constructions of the same phenomena (Pettman 1996). The Dutch video, *Act of Love: Female Circumcision in Western Europe,* as well as assorted readings provide a launching pad for discussions linking the previous week's focus on speaking for others about cultural practices that many young women find culturally offensive, politically invidious, and physically debasing. Students move toward understanding the ways that Western perceptions have constructed social and symbolic phenomena as bodily violences. They learn that particular cultural practices and symbols may exist and continue in particular historicized moments, but that the meanings of symbols and acts may be transformed within changing social, economic, and cultural contexts.

An examination of complex cultural practices enables students to perceive how both practices and ideologies are situated and constructed through an intersection of social factors. Rajeswari Sunder Rajan's classic work (1993) shows how the resistance of oppressed groups takes place on several levels of response, and that women's subjectivities, as victims of violence and agents of resistance, are constituted through their negotiations of specific situations. In proposing that they discuss their feelings with one another, I have found that students grapple with the conceptual and emotional difficulties of trying to place their reactions within the broad continuum of a cultural relativist position to that of a well-meaning and heart-felt notion of human rights. When one Australian student of Indian and Hindu heritage concentrated upon sati as her primary research topic, she first asked her female relatives for their thoughts upon the practice, and placed their reminiscences into her consideration of its history. Her paper was framed within a perception that sati, as well as other culturally contentious issues, reflected the prurient need of Eurocentric analysts for sexually and culturally titillating practices to satisfy a "voyeuristic gaze." Her consistent metacritical analysis, anchored in her different speaking positions, prompted other students to hold a reflexive discussion about how they would evaluate the structures and relations of power and domination in which they are shaped.

In addition, I provide materials examining Western cultural practices of cosmetic surgery to balance the strident political tone of much antifemale circumcision literature. The interaction of student analysis with radical academic critiques empowers students to consider why they resist and comply with certain kinds of psychosocial and physical control. This approach has led to ongoing and useful discussion about the ways in which scholarship can be politically (ir)responsible when analyzing contentious issues.

The fourth week concludes the first teaching and learning module. Using readings that explore the use of the senses in creating the embodied knowledge generated by participant observation, the students examine Judith Okely's (1994, 62) contention that "the anthropologist's long term participation encourages a grounded knowledge which is then used vicariously as a means of comprehending others' experience." It prompts an examination of the ways in which disciplinary knowledge and power in anthropology construct ethnographic descriptions, and links the notion of a grounded knowledge with Lila Abu-Lughod's (1993) concept of "writing against culture" so that students can discuss the ways in which the relations and structures of "knowing" others can be critiqued. A critical consideration of how to know and represent others is brought to the Long Bow ethnographic trilogy of videos, particularly *Small Happiness,* to stimulate discussion about whether feminist anthropology's recognition of difference may be a strategy to neutralize the other women, to better enable such women to be studied under the instrumental language of disembodied objectivity.

As a direct outcome of a teaching and learning modular approach, I schedule the fifth and sixth weeks as researching and writing periods, allocating this time for students to consult me.

Week seven prompts the students to consider the ways in which interpretations of religious tenets have protected privileges for men and have acted to deny women full participation in society. The inherently gendered and politicized debate about veiling and cloistering practices aims to create an understanding of how purdah may modify a woman's perception and control of her body. Representations of the experiential feelings of purdah such as separation, concealment, imprisonment, protection, and identity are linked with philosophical and political analyses of male power and patriarchal structures and with the ways in which women's bodies are constructed to incorporate notions of the physicality of moral virtue, as well as a consideration of the notion that Western fantasies of the spectacular and the bizarre in other cultures may be devised to score political power in the national and international arena.

Postcolonial critics have proposed that some feminist constructions of "indigenous" or "subaltern" peoples can be construed as a type of epistemic violence. Upon engaging in a close reading of Gayatri Spivak's translation of "Draupadi" (1987) during week eight, the students venture into discussions about whether the relationship of the two protagonists constitutes an adequate metaphor for the relationship between Western scholars' need to understand others. The students thereby join a philosophically centered debate that has focused on Third World women's control over their strategies of subversion and their ultimate ability to change the forces of power. Some students have felt intimidated by the complexity of Spivak's material. A linked debate about whether one can indeed know the subjective thoughts of an impoverished rural woman from a different culture can help to minimize students' concerns about doing anthropology and damaging others.

While the readings on Spivak focus on the difficulties inherent in translating the subjectivity of others, the final week of teaching in week nine explores women as "subject to desire," concentrating principally on an examination of the state's need to shape reproductive practices and women as biological reproducers of the nation. The students learn to recognize the need for greater attention to the colonized as human beings who reshape gender relations in their own sociocultural interactions with recent colonizers. Haleh Esfandiari's work (1997) elucidates the resistance women put in place in Iran to avoid being controlled and defined by the state. Students read her in conjunction with Beverley Skeggs' 1995 article "Theorising, Ethics and Representation in Feminist Ethnography," which illustrates how women perceive themselves and the ways in which Western analytical tools clarify the production of knowledge (201).

The exploration of contentious topics throughout the course suggests Kathleen Dunn's (1993, 41) observation that "Much of the new research on women in the different scholarly fields challenges existing paradigms." For the students the production of a counterintuitive knowledge may develop into a negative scenario in which, as Dunn observes (1993, 41), a student may "either stop paying attention to the class while struggling to make sense of the new material, or dismiss the new material and turn her thoughts elsewhere." A pertinent example came through spokespersons reporting on small group class discussions about the ways in which the state can intervene in women's reproductive decisions. I provide various journal articles that document, from feminist perspectives, the history of the abortion debate in Australia, and other comparative sources that analyze China's one-child policy, Singapore's eugenic favoring of tertiary-educated women as mothers, Malaysia's 120 million population target, and India's sterilization campaigns among low caste groups and untouchables. A video entitled *Poland: Cause for Alarm* examines the ways in which Poland's laws relating to abortion have changed under the new nonsocialist regime. But many Australian students did not view state intervention in procreation to be applicable to themselves, for they perceived Australia to enjoy a benign government and procreation to be a private issue. They had not previously considered the ways in which women's bodies can be patterned by cultural and political ideologies. The students slowly began to understand how women can be psychosocially shaped by government policies, and how women's lived experience may be materially formed. They also become aware of the seemingly contradictory demands of different feminists who argue across a broad spectrum of issues relating to reproductive control.

The content of week nine's seminar has had the heartening effect of enabling students to develop a more critical understanding of the role of governments in shaping women's choices about their bodies and their reproductive freedoms. While I had suggested to them at the beginning of the course that much of the material would challenge their existing ways of thinking, it was only toward the end that many students told me they were glad to have acquired the conceptual and methodological tools that enabled them to move beyond superficial acceptance that paternalistic state policy was authoritative and therefore good. This impressive insight plus other outcomes provide continuing motivation for me as a teacher and researcher.[4]

NOTES

1. Heidi Hartmann (1984, 177) has defined patriarchy as "a set of social relations between men, which have a material base, and which, though hierarchical, establish or create interdependence and solidarity among men that enable them to dominate women."
2. Australian universities are experiencing changes in their work environments such as larger lectures, increasing numbers of overseas students from neighboring nations, a student body determined to use its education materially, and a trend toward the "internationalization" of research, curriculum, the student body, and alliances between institutions. Students can bring their different lived experiences in a diverse range of cultures to an examination of the ways in which women's lives can be the same yet irreconcilably different.
3. The course was originally conceived by Iona Fett, fashioned and renamed by Lucy Healey, then extensively redeveloped by me. Maryanne Dever provided exceptional collegial support.
4. The final three weeks of the course are designed for students to prepare their second assessment task, a large research essay, and to conduct oral presentations of their work-in-progress for discussion, comment, encouragement, and reassurance from their peers.

WORKS CITED

Abu-Lughod, Lila. 1993. *Writing Women's Worlds.* Berkeley and Los Angeles: University of California Press, 1–42.

Dunn, Kathleen. 1993. "Feminist Teaching: Who Are Your Students?" *Women's Studies Quarterly* 3–4: 39–45.

Esfandiari, Haleh. 1997. *Reconstructed Lives: Women and Iran's Islamic Revolution.* Washington, D.C., and Baltimore: Woodrow Wilson Centre Press and The Johns Hopkins University Press, 133–155.

Hartmann, Heidi. 1984. "The Unhappy Marriage of Marxism and Feminism." In A. Jagger and P. Rothenburg, eds, *Feminist Frameworks,* 172–89. New York: McGraw Hill.

Hill, Heather. 1997. "The Importance of a Minority Perspective in the Classroom." *The Chronicle of Higher Education* November 7: A60.

hooks, bell. 1994. *Teaching to Transgress: Education as the Practice of Freedom.* New York and London: Routledge, 35–44.

Kirby, Vicki. 1993. "Feminisms, Reading, Postmodernisms: Rethinking Complicity." In S. Gunew and A. Yeatman, eds., *Feminism and the Politics of Difference,* 20–34. St. Leonards, Australia: Allen & Unwin.

Mohanty, Chandra. 1991. "Under Western Eyes: Feminist Scholarship and Colonial Discourses." In Chandra Talpade Mohanty, Ann Russo, and Lourdes Torres, eds., *Third World Women and the Politics of Feminism.* Bloomington: Indiana University Press, 51–80.

Moore, Henrietta. 1994. *A Passion for Difference.* Bloomington and Indianapolis: Indiana University Press, 49–70.

Okely, Judith. 1994. "Vicarious and Sensory Knowledge of Chronology and Change: Ageing in Rural France." In K. Halstrup and P. Hervik, eds., *Social Experience and Anthropological Knowledge.* London and New York: Routledge, 45–64.

Pettman, Jan Jindy. 1996. *Worlding Women.* Sydney: Allen & Unwin, 64–84.

Pratt, Mary Louise. 1992. *Imperial Eyes: Travel Writing and Transculturation.* London and New York: Routledge, 1–11.

Shrewsbury, Carolyn. 1993. "What Is Feminist Pedagogy?" *Women's Studies Quarterly* 3– 4: 8–16.

Skeggs, Beverley. 1995. "Theorising, Ethics and Representation in Feminist Ethnography." In Beverley Skeggs, ed., *Feminist Cultural Theory: Process and Production.* Manchester and New York: Manchester University Press, 190–206.

Spivak, Gayatri. 1987. *In Other Worlds: Essays in Cultural Politics.* New York: Methuen, 241–268.

Sunder Rajan, Rajeswari. 1993. *Real and Imagined Women: Gender, Culture and Postcolonialism.* London and New York: Routledge, 15–39.

Yung, Judy. 1995. *Unbound Feet: A Social History of Chinese Women in San Francisco.* Berkeley: University of California Press, 1–15.

Syllabus

The course is fashioned to examine the ways in which the evolution of capitalist relations, processes of colonization, and religious beliefs and practices have shaped and reproduced ideologies and forms of domination that are class-stratified, nationalized, sexualized, racialized, and gendered through diverse sociocultural configurations. Analyzing theoretical sources written by indigenous, postcolonial, and feminist scholars, as well as examining video material created by anthropological and journalistic endeavors, students will elucidate and evaluate the ways in which women are constituted as the biological reproducers of "the nation," examine how women's corporeality is shaped by notions of *moral virtue,* deconstruct the universalization of the term *woman,* and promote the intersection of the educational process with potentialities for intercultural understandings and social change.

Week 1. Shaping the Future of Feminist Anthropology: Theories, Concepts, Research, and Practice.

No set reading.

Week 2. Challenge and Response: Can "We" Give a Voice to "Them?"

Should prevailing ideas about global feminism be contested? In what ways can theorizations by women of color deepen an understanding of feminism(s), as well as sociopolitical theories and cultural practices? Questions are being posed as to what constitutes identity, subjectivity, and collectivity. In what ways do theoretical languages constitute who may count as "us?"

SMALL GROUP ACTIVITIES: *IS THE TERM WOMAN USEFUL? IN WHAT WAYS HAS THE UNIVERSALIZATION OF THE TERM WOMAN PROMOTED DEBATES ABOUT WOMEN'S ISSUES? WHAT KINDS OF REPRESENTA-TIONS OF WOMEN OF COLOR ARE YOU AWARE OF? TO WHAT EXTENT DO THE IMAGES YOU HAVE DIS-CUSSED SEEM TO CHALLENGE OR CONFIRM PREVIOUSLY HELD STEREOTYPES? TO WHAT EXTENT DO YOU THINK YOUR LIFE IS SHAPED BY YOUR "COLOR"? IN WHAT WAYS DO YOU THINK GENDER IS A FACTOR IN THIS?*

VIDEO: LET HER DIE

Jayawardena, Kumari. 1986. *Feminism and Nationalism in the Third World.* London: Zed Press.

Miller, Barbara. 1981. *The Endangered Sex: Neglect of Female Children in Rural North India.* Ithaca, N.Y., and London: Cornell University Press.

Ram, Kalpana. 1991. 'First' and 'Third World' feminisms: A new perspective?" *Asian Studies Review* 15(1): 91–96.

Rowbotham, Sheila. 1992. *Women in Movement: Feminism and Social Action.* New York and London: Routledge.

Stephens, Julie. 1989. "Feminist fictions: A critique of the category 'non-Western woman' in feminist writings on India," in Ranjit Guha (ed.), *Subaltern Studies VI.* Delhi: Oxford University Press.

Week 3. Beyond Traditions—Discordant Discourses: Fgm, Foot Binding, and Sati

What are some linkages between gender, identity, and acts of bodily violence? How does the construction of domestic space relate to ideas and practices of physical difference and the internalization of relations of difference?

SMALL GROUP ACTIVITIES: *HOW DO YOU EVALUATE THE STRUCTURES AND RELATIONS OF POWER AND DOMINATION IN WHICH YOU ARE SHAPED? WHY DO YOU RESIST AND COMPLY WITH CERTAIN KINDS OF SOCIAL CONTROL? CAN YOU THINK OF EXAMPLES OF FANTASIES OF POWER CREATING AND INTERACT-ING WITH FANTASIES OF IDENTITY?*

VIDEO: ACT OF LOVE: FEMALE CIRCUMCISION IN WESTERN EUROPE *(THE NETHERLANDS)*

Courtright, P. 1994. "The iconographies of sati," in J. S. Hawley (ed.), *Sati, the Burning and the Curse: The Burning of Wives in India.* New York: Oxford University Press.

Courtright, P. 1995. "Sati, sacrifice, and marriage: The modernity of tradition," in L. Harlan and P. Courtwright (eds.), *From the Margins of Hindu Marriage: Essays on Gender, Religion and Culture.* New York and Oxford: Oxford University Press.

Croll, Elisabeth. 1995. *Changing Identities of Chinese Women: Rhetoric, Experience, and Self-Perception in Twentieth-Century China.* London and Hong Kong: Zed Books and University of Hong Kong Press.

Daly, Mary. 1979. *Gyn/Ecology: The Metaethics of Radical Feminism.* London: Women's Press.

Davis, K. 1995. *Reshaping the Female Body.* London: Routledge.

Hawley, J. 1994. *Sati: The Blessing and the Curse.* Oxford: Oxford University Press.

Hosken, Fran. 1981. "Female genital mutilation and human rights." *Feminist Issues* 1(3): 3–23.

Kirby, Vicki. 1987. "On the cutting edge: Feminism and clitoridectomy." *Australian Feminist Studies* 5 (Summer): 35–55.

Lorde, Audre. 1984. "An open letter to Mary Daly," in Cherríe Moraga and Anzaldúa, Gloria (eds.), *This Bridge Called My Back: Writing by Radical Women of Color.* Second edition. New York: Kitchen Table.

Robertson, Claire. 1996. "Grassroots in Kenya: Women, Genital Mutilation, and collective action, 1920–1990." *Signs* 21: 615–47.

Stein. D. 1988. "Burning widows, burning brides: The perils of daughterhood in India." *Pacific Affairs* 61: 465–85.

Sunder Rajan, Rajeswari. 1993. *Real & Imagined Women: Gender, Culture, and Postcolonialism.* London and New York: Routledge.

Walker, Alice. 1993. *Warrior Marks: Female Genital Mutilation and the Sexual Blinding of Women.* New York: Harcourt Brace.

Week 4. Critical Thinking About Ethnographic Representation

How does disciplinary knowledge and power construct *ethnographic* description? In what ways does "writing against culture" problematize the relations and structures of "knowing" others?

SMALL GROUP ACTIVITIES: DO YOU THINK THAT THE RECOGNITION OF DIFFERENCE CAN BE SIMPLY A STRATEGY TO NEUTRALIZE AND/OR NATURALIZE THE OTHER WOMAN? IF SO, EXPLAIN YOUR REASONING. DOES RECOGNIZING THIRD WORLD WOMEN ALLOW FOR AN UNDERSTANDING OF CULTURAL DIFFERENCE, OR DO YOU THINK THAT OTHER WOMEN CONTINUE TO BE STUDIED AS SUBJECTS UNDER WESTERN EYES?

VIDEO: LONG BOW TRILOGY—SMALL HAPPINESS (CHINA)

Di Leonardo, Micaela. 1991. "Introduction. Gender, culture, and political economy: Feminist anthropology in historical perspective," in M. di Leonardo (ed.), *Gender at the Crossroads of Knowledge: Feminist Anthropology in the Postmodern Era.* Berkeley and Los Angeles: University of California Press.

Ertuck, Yakin. 1991. "Convergence and divergence in the status of Moslem women: The cases of Turkey and Saudi Arabia." *International Sociology* 6(3): 307–20.

Gottfried, Heidi (ed.). 1996. *Feminism and Social Change: Bridging Theory and Practice*. Urbana and Chicago: University of Illinois Press.

Lazreg, Marnia. 1988. "Feminism and difference: The perils of writing as a woman in Algeria." *Feminist Studies* 14(1): 81–107.

Mascia-Lees, Frances, et al. 1989. "The postmodern turn in anthropology: Cautions from a feminist perspective." *Signs* 15(1): 7–33.

Nzenza, Sekai. 1995. "Who should speak for whom? African women and western feminism," in Penny van Toorn and David English (eds.), *Speaking Positions*. Melbourne: Victoria University of Technology, 100–106.

Stacey, Judith. 1988. "Can there be a feminist ethnography?" *Women's Studies International Forum* 2(1): 21–27.

Visweswaran, Kamala. 1994. *Fictions of Feminist Ethnography*. Minneapolis and London: University of Minnesota Press.

Wheatley, Elizabeth. 1994. "How can we engender ethnography with a feminist imagination? A rejoinder to Judith Stacey." *Women's Studies International Forum* 17(4): 403–16.

Wikan, Unni. 1992. "Beyond the words: The power of resonance." *American Ethnologist* 19(3): 460–82.

Week 5. Reading and Research

Week 6. Research and Writing Week

Week 7. The Color of Fear: Religion, Race, and Gender Relations

Veiling and cloistering practices have been the focus of censorious attitudes. In what ways have interpretations of religious tenets protected privileges for men and denied women full participation in society?

SMALL GROUP ACTIVITIES: *WHY ARE THE RELATIONSHIPS BETWEEN RELIGION, THE "STATE," AND WOMEN SO FRAUGHT AND DIFFICULT? IN WHAT WAYS CAN ANALYSES OF MALE POWER AND PATRIARCHAL STRUCTURES ELUCIDATE THESE RELATIONSHIPS? IN WHAT WAYS DO WOMEN'S BODIES INCORPORATE NOTIONS OF THE PHYSICALITY OF MORAL VIRTUE? IN WHAT WAYS DO MANY OF THE WRITERS SET FOR THIS WEEK SUGGEST THAT GRASPING AT THE SPECTACULAR AND BIZARRE IN "OTHER CULTURES" IS A TACTIC DEVISED TO SCORE A POLITICAL POINT?*

VIDEO: ECLIPSE *(BANGLADESH)*

Abu-Odeh, Lama. 1996. "Crimes of honor and the construction of gender in Arab societies," in M. Yamani (ed.) *Feminism and Islam Legal and Literacy Perspectives*. London: Ithaca Press.

Ali, Zeenat Shaukat. 1993. "Women in Islam spirit and progress," in Z. A. Siddi and A. J. Zuberi (eds.), *Moslem Women Problems and Prospects*. New Delhi: MD Publications.

Badran, Margot. 1995. *Feminists, Islam and Nation: Gender and the Making of Modern Egypt*. Princeton, N.J.: Princeton University Press.

Chowdhry, Prem. 1994. *The Veiled Women: Shifting Gender Equations in Rural Haryana 1880–1990.* Delhi: Oxford University Press.

Eickelman, Dale F. 1996. *Muslim Politics.* Princeton, N.J.: Princeton University Press.

Göçek, Fatma, and Shiva Balaghi (eds.). 1994. *Reconstructing Gender in the Middle East: Tradition, Identity and Power.* New York: Columbia University Press.

Goodwin, Jan. 1994. *Price of Honor: Muslim Women Lift the Veil of Silence on the Islamic World.* London: Little, Brown.

Hamadeh, Najla. 1996. "Islamic family legislation: The authoritarian discourse on silence," in M. Yamani (ed.), *Feminism and Islam Legal and Literacy Perspectives.* London: Ithaca Press.

Marcus, Julie. 1992. *A World of Difference.* Sydney: Allen & Unwin.

Mernissi, Fatima. 1994. *Dreams of Trespass: Tales of a Harem Girlhood.* Boston: Addison-Wesley.

Waines, David. 1982. "Through a veil darkly: The study of women in Muslim societies." *Comparative Study of Society and History* 24: 642–59.

Wikan, Unni. 1982. *Behind the Veil in Arabia: Women in Oman.* Chicago and London: University of Chicago Press.

Week 8. Power and Identity in the World Community of Women.

Why have postcolonial critics such as Spivak, Mohanty, and Trinh characterized some Western feminist scholarship on indigenous peoples as a type of epistemic violence? Is the relationship between Dropdi and Senanayak an adequately complex metaphor for the evolving relationship between Western scholars' desire and need to understand "other women?"

SMALL GROUP ACTIVITIES: *EVALUATE THE KEY POINTS OF DEVI'S STORY OF DRAUPADI. EXAMINE WHY SENANAYAK IS DESCRIBED BY SPIVAK AS A* PLURALIST AESTHETE. *TO WHAT DEGREE DO YOU THINK THAT EDUCATED WESTERN RESEARCHERS CAN "KNOW" THE INTERIOR THOUGHTS OF A POOR RURAL WOMAN?*

Johns, Mary. 1989. "Postcolonial feminists in the western intellectual field: Anthropologists and native informants?" *Inscriptions* 5: 49–73.

Mani, Lata, and Ruth Frankenberg. "Crosscurrents, crosstalk: Race, 'postcoloniality' and the politics of location." *Cultural Studies* 7(2): 292–310.

Mohanty, Chandra. 1991. "Under western eyes: Feminist scholarship and colonial discourses," in Chandra Mohanty, Ann Russo, and Lourdes Torres (eds.), *Third World Women and the Politics of Feminism.* Bloomington: Indiana University Press.

Spivak, Gayatri Chakravorty. 1987. "Draupadi," by Mahasweta Devi, in *In Other Worlds: Essays in Cultural Politics.* New York: Methuen.

Tohidi, Nayereh. 1991. "Gender and Islamic fundamentalism: Feminist politics in Iran," in Chandra Mohanty, Ann Russo, and Lourdes Torres (eds.), *Third World Women and the Politics of Feminism.* Bloomington: Indiana University Press.

Week 9. Subject to Desire: Technologies and Social Control

How does the state's need to become a nation shape reproductive controls? In what ways are women constructed as biological reproducers of the "nation?"

SMALL GROUP ACTIVITIES: *DO YOU THINK THAT THE "STATE" SHAPES WOMEN'S REPRODUCTIVE CHOICES IN AUSTRALIA? IF SO, HOW? WHAT KINDS OF POLICIES HAVE STATES USED TO CONTROL WOMEN'S REPRODUCTIVE CHOICE? IN WHAT WAYS DO SUCH POLICIES RELATE TO ANALYSES OF GENDER AND POWER? IN WHAT WAYS DOES AN UNDERSTANDING OF STATE POWER CONFRONT YOUR IDEAS ABOUT THE PUBLIC AND PRIVATE SPHERE?*

Atwood, Margaret. 1996. *The Handmaid's Tale.* London: Vintage.

Barroso, Carmen, and C. Bruschini. 1991. "Building politics from personal lives: Discussions on sexuality among poor women in Brazil," in Chandra Mohanty et al. (eds.), *Third World Women and the Politics of Feminism.* Bloomington: Indiana University Press.

Chee, Heng Leng. 1989. "Babies to order: Recent population policies in Malaysia," in Bina Agarwal (ed.). *Women, State, Ideology.* London: Macmillan.

Fairweather, Eileen, et al. 1984. *Only the Rivers Run Free—Northern Ireland: The Women's War.* London: Pluto Press.

Heng, Geraldine, and Janades Devan. 1992. "State fatherhood: The politics of nationalism, sexuality and race in Singapore," in A. Parker et al. (eds.), *Nationalisms and Sexualities.* New York and London: Routledge.

Kabeer, Naila (ed.). 1994. *Reversed Realities: Gender Hierarchies in Development Thought.* New York and London: Verso.

Mittal, Mukta. 1995. *Women in India: Today and Tomorrow.* New Delhi: Anmoi.

Ong, Aihwa. 1990. "State versus Islam: Malay families, women's bodies, and the body politic in Malaysia." *American Ethnologist* 17(2): 258–76.

Patel, T. 1994. *Fertility Behaviour: Population and Society in a Rajasthan Village.* Delhi: Oxford University Press.

Quah, Stella. 1994. *Family in Singapore: Sociological Perspectives.* Singapore: Times Academic Press.

Scales, A., and W. Chavkin. 1996. "Refusing to take women seriously," in Karl Moss (ed.), *Man-Made Medicine.* Durham, N.C.: Duke University Press.

Yuval-Davis, Nira. 1996. "Women and the biological reproduction of 'the Nation.'" *Women's Studies International Forum* 19(1–2): 17–24.

Weeks 10–12. Oral Presentations of Work-in-Progress

TRANSFORMING "THEM" INTO "US": SOME DANGERS IN TEACHING WOMEN AND DEVELOPMENT

Cynthia A. Wood

Courses on women and the third world, or women and development, appear to satisfy all aspects of progressive demands for curricular reform in an era of globalization and multiculturalism.[1] Such courses are international in scope, give proper attention to a segment of the world's population that is often vulnerable and generally neglected, and are likely to address issues of class and race as well as gender. There would appear to be no better vehicle for the education of university students in the United States on issues of diversity in an international context. My experience in teaching courses on women and development suggests, however, that this education is not an inevitable outcome.

I argue in this essay that despite their content (or perhaps because of it), courses on women and development do not necessarily promote student or faculty engagement with issues of diversity, and as generally taught may do just the opposite. I pursue this argument by examining difficulties I have encountered in teaching such courses. And I discuss how I have changed my approach in response to these difficulties.

I have faced a variety of challenges in teaching courses on women and development, in a number of different contexts, but certain issues recurred in every venue.[2] Crucial to a discussion of inclusiveness in the curriculum are a core set of concerns, which have led me to every major change I made in the course over time, and these I see as the major problems in teaching women and development: ethnocentrism, essentialism, and intolerance of diversity.

These are problems that I believe arise also in the field of women and development, and in some ways the evolution of my course has mirrored that of the field itself. In the earliest women in development (WID) literature (arising in the 1970s and early 1980s),[3] and in the earliest version of my course, the central issues were posed in these terms: What are the conditions under which women in the third world live, and what can be done to improve their lives? In the field and in the literature, the answers to these questions were based on the practical experience of development practitioners, with policy uncritically posited as the solution.

Underlying all of this practical experience and advice, of course, was a theoretical perspective on what defines development, what constitutes an improvement in women's lives, and how best to achieve desired goals. This perspective was, in general, an ethnocentric one. Improvement was understood in terms of an increase in material welfare, especially as measured by rising gross domestic product (GDP), with the template for development being that which has occurred in the first world, that is, modernization. The means to achieving this goal was fairly straightforward: show people new technologies, provide them with capital and access to credit in order to increase production and income. The WID version of this was that women should be given equal or preferential access to technology, capital, and credit so that they would not be left behind in the process of development.

More recently, there has been a shift in the literature to an emphasis on gender systems, especially on how such systems result in women's disadvantage. The feminist literature on gender and development, such as Gita Sen and Caren Grown's 1987 book, *Development, Crises, and Alternative Visions,* suggests that the main concern should be women's empowerment. This does not preclude improving access to technology, capital, and credit, or an interest in improving women's material well-being, but it does argue that the transformation of gender systems to further empower women is a necessary condition of increasing their well-being.[4]

To get at these kinds of issues in class, I use material that presents the complexity of women's lives, such as *I, Rigoberta Menchú,* an autobiographical account of the Guatemalan indigenous activist (1984), or Tsitsi Dangarembga's 1988 novel *Nervous Conditions.* From works such as these, students can discuss the limitations of the modernization model's emphasis on material welfare, as well as its disregard of history, particularly that of colonialism and its legacies. Generally, my students did not have any problems understanding or accepting this perspective.

But this difference in approach did little to transform students' ethnocentric attitudes of patronage and protection. The interpretation of development resulting from such an approach (especially common among feminist students) goes something like this: "How can we help those poor third world women see their oppression so they can become free like us?"

Implicit in this statement is the tendency to essentialize third world women—to assume that the perceived status of such women as traditional, passive, closer to nature, irrational, and so on, is essential to their character as third world women, that they have these characteristics because they *are* third world women, that they are homogeneous in these essential characteristics, and that they are therefore essentially and radically different from (and inferior to) women in the first world.

The problems in teaching the course are that students come with these ideologies already in place and that the literature does not discourage (and may encourage) the students' tendency to homogenize and make Other. Chandra Mohanty argues that Western feminist discourse on women and development contributes to the production of a monolithic third world woman (Mohanty 1991b, 53). She continues,

> The assumption of women as an already constituted, coherent group with identical interests and desires, regardless of class, ethnic or racial location or contradictions, implies a notion of gender or sexual difference or even patriarchy which can be applied universally and cross-culturally. . . . The second analytical presupposition is evident . . . in the uncritical way "proof" of universality and cross-cultural validity are provided. . . . I argue that as a result . . . a homogeneous notion of the oppression of women as a group is assumed, which, in turn, produces the image of an "average third world woman." (Mohanty 1991b, 55–56)

Using case studies, as I do,[5] gives students a better understanding of particular circumstances facing women in different parts of the world, but does not necessarily challenge essentialist notions of a homogeneous third world woman. It may actually be implicit in the case study method that any third world woman, faced with similar circumstances, would behave as these women do—differing circumstances produce different behavior, but the women are the same. The character of "everywoman" (here "every-third-world-woman") is the object of analysis. Case studies only illustrate differing circumstances.

Some choices I have made in the course help on one front but contribute to the problem on another. For example, I do not incorporate case studies on women in the United States, Europe, or Canada in the course, primarily because there is little opportunity for students to study Asia, Africa, and Latin America in the typical undergraduate curriculum, much less women in those countries. Although I frequently bring in examples from the United States, the focus of the course on what is traditionally defined as the third world is such that students are not immediately challenged in their tendency to see and present third world women as homogeneous and alien or Other.

These examples illustrate one of the core questions that must be grappled with in a course on women and development. Can it be taught in such a way that it discourages both the tendency to see third world women as a homogeneous Other, and the implicit paternalism of this perspective, especially when combined with discussions of policy?

The problem is complex. On the one hand, the literature on women and development contributes to the creation of a homogeneous third world woman who is inherently alien to "us." On the other hand, one of the things that goes along with the modernization approach is the attitude that we are all the same: third world women's hopes and aspirations are limited by their oppression, but if we could show them the way (or alter the constraints they face), they would want what we want, and that is why the policies we recommend are universally applicable.

Students grasp this as a way of identifying with the women we read about in class, and in teaching the course, identification is a powerful way to challenge the idea that third world women are necessarily and inherently Other. This is another reason I use personal stories and novels, such as *I, Rigoberta Menchú* and *Nervous Conditions*. It is easy for students to see that they might act and react the way the women they read about do if they were faced with the same situations.

The problem with this approach is that it allows students to remain intolerant of difference and eliminates the need to acknowledge diversity: "They *look* different, but they aren't really (from us or from each other); they are like us, they want what we want." The students' desire to believe this is very strong. I once gave a paper assignment which required students to compare Menchú's early life in *I, Rigoberta Menchú* and that of Tambu in *Nervous Conditions*. Almost without exception, the students created a story of individual achievement in which each girl pulled herself up by her bootstraps to be successful, Menchú as an activist and Tambu as an educated woman. This story had little textual support and completely failed to acknowledge the differences in circumstance facing the two girls, or the authors' own interpretations of their lives and voices. It did serve, however, to recreate them as girls "just like us." And if they are girls like us, there is no need to acknowledge difference, much less to engage it.

So the other major challenge in teaching this material is in some ways the opposite of the problem of students defining a homogeneous third world woman as Other. How do you teach a course on women and development that recognizes diversity and promotes the acceptance, or better yet, the welcoming of difference? There is thus an ongoing tension in the course between the desire for sameness and an underlying ideology of otherness, conflated into an understanding of development as a process of transforming "them" into "us."

The way I dealt with this in the past was by highlighting differences when I saw the desire to homogenize, pointing out similarities when students fashioned the Other, and showing the actual and potential damage done by development policy based on either approach. This helps, but I have come to believe it is not enough, because the authority of the text, such as that of modernization or of case studies, is only challenged in the margins.

What I want the students to see is that, although there are certainly many similarities among women (e.g., mothers love their children everywhere), there are also many differences: Mothers love their children, but how they love, how they show their love, and what that love signifies to them and their children is likely to be very different across cultures and is historically specific. Culture matters. History matters.

To get at the problems I have posed here, both in theory and in classroom practice, I now incorporate in my course a substantial section on poststructuralist and postcolonial feminist critiques that address exactly these issues.[6] As I discussed previously, Chandra Mohanty gives an explicit analysis of how the literature on women and development produces a problematic universal third world woman. In positing social science discourse on development as a part of the larger colonial project, Mohanty allows us to raise questions about the importance of positioning. What interests are served in the creation of a third world woman who is by definition in need of being saved (especially from an equally homogeneous third world man), and incapable of saving herself? The role of savior is left to the first world.[7] Trinh Minh-ha, in her film *Reassemblage* (1982), and her book *Woman, Native, Other* (1989), addresses the power of first world narratives to define the third world, the dangers of such representations, and the losses incurred in accepting them. What happens to a theory of modernization when faced with Trinh's comment: "Scarcely twenty years were enough to make two billion people define themselves as underdeveloped?"[8] Anna Lowenhaupt Tsing's ethnography of the Maratus of Indonesia demonstrates the complexity of culture and the profound limits of traditional views of development when contrasted with this complexity. What does it mean for a universal concept of development when not only progress but also marginality are understood as socially constructed categories?

When placed in the context of the traditional literature on women and development, I hope to use such works not only to question and analyze the assumptions underlying this literature (as well as the students' understanding of the *third world* and *third world women*), but to begin to pose alternatives. What would development and development policy look like if it acknowledged diversity and empowered diverse peoples to define and enact their own idea of "development?" Would it resemble in any way our current understanding and practice? How would it differ and in what ways would this change women's lives?

This material is difficult on a number of fronts. It is hard to read, because in attempting to escape imposed ideologies and narratives of development, it must use unfamiliar language and challenge assumptions students often did not know were there. It is also difficult politically. The idea that development as traditionally understood may be part of the problem is a hard one for an undergraduate to face. And one of the dangers of attention to difference, especially in a culture generally intolerant of diversity, is that the students will shut down: "I can never understand them." These works not only acknowledge diversity but also invite engagement with it, however, and many students accept the invitation.

I do not believe that I have solved the problems I am pointing out here. The literature on women and development did not create ideologies of essentialism, ethnocentrism, or intolerance of diversity.

Students come to my classes with these ideologies in place, and I myself must struggle with them as a specialist in the field. But the course can be taught in such a way that it leaves such ideologies unchallenged, or it can challenge them by addressing their presence. This challenge cannot eliminate the problem, but it can provide an alternative framework that allows further challenges.

NOTES

1. I continue to use the highly problematic terms *third world* and *first world* in this context, in part because the oppositions they represent (and construct) make their way inevitably into courses on women and development. That these terms must be deconstructed does not obviate their power. At the same time, political resistance to first world domination has been and continues to be organized on the basis of an "imagined community" of peoples in the South, as Chandra Mohanty (1991a, 4) points out. For further discussion of the issues at stake here, see also Mohanty's essay (1991b), "Under Western Eyes: Feminist Scholarship and Colonial Discourses."

   I choose not to capitalize the terms *first world* and *third world* because I believe that capitalization transforms these terms into proper names that further rigidify highly problematic assumptions about the postcolonial world, while contributing in particular to the homogenization of the so-called *third world*.

2. My own background is in economics, with specializations in women and development as well as Latin American studies, but I also have longstanding interests in feminist and postcolonial theories. I have taught courses in women and development at two small liberal arts colleges in the Northeast and at a midsize public university in the Southeast, in departments of economics, international studies, and interdisciplinary studies. I have also taught short units on this material in courses on environment and development, farm workers in the United States, introduction to Latin American studies, and postcolonial theories of imperialism. I am thus basing this paper on what may be a unique experience of teaching women and development at the undergraduate level in a variety of institutional settings with differing disciplinary and interdisciplinary contexts.

3. For an excellent history of WID, see Irene Tinker (1990), "The Making of a Field: Advocates, Practitioners, and Scholars."

4. There has been a corresponding change in course titles across the country. I maintain the title of my course as "Women and Development" to avoid as much as possible the inevitable danger of de-emphasizing the importance of women's concerns, though I certainly incorporate a gender and development approach.

5. For example, Ann Leonard's 1989 anthology, *Seeds: Supporting Women's Work in the Third World.*

6. In addition to Mohanty's (1991b) "Under Western Eyes: Feminist Scholarship and Colonial Discourses," I also use Trinh Minh-ha's (1982) film *Reassemblage,* her books *Woman, Native, Other* (1989) and *Framer Framed* (1992), as well as Anna Lowenhaupt Tsing's (1993) *In the Realm of the Diamond Queen.*

7. Or, in Gayatri Spivak's (1988, 296–97) terms, "white men saving brown women from brown men." In this case, white women may be the operative agents.

8. This quotation is from Trinh's film *Reassemblage,* reprinted in *Framer Framed* (1992, 96).

WORKS CITED

Dangarembga, Tsitsi. 1988. *Nervous Conditions.* Seattle: Seal Press.

Leonard, Ann, ed. 1989. *Seeds: Supporting Women's Work in the Third World.* New York: Feminist Press.

Menchú, Rigoberta. 1984. *I, Rigoberta Menchú.* New York: Verso.

Mohanty, Chandra. 1991a. "Introduction—Cartographies of Struggle: Third World Women and the Politics of Feminism." In Chandra Mohanty, Ann Russo, and Lourdes Torres, eds., *Third World Women and the Politics of Feminism,* 1–47. Bloomington: Indiana University Press.

———. 1991b. "Under Western Eyes: Feminist Scholarship and Colonial Discourses." In Chandra Mohanty, Ann Russo, and Lourdes Torres, eds., *Third World Women and the Politics of Feminism,* 51–80. Bloomington: Indiana University Press.

Sen, Gita, and Caren Grown. 1987. *Development, Crises, and Alternative Visions: Third World Women's Perspectives.* New York: Monthly Review Press.

Spivak, Gayatri Chakravorty. 1988. "Can the Subaltern Speak?" In Cary Nelson and Lawrence Grossberg, eds., *Marxism and the Interpretation of Culture,* 271–313. Urbana: University of Illinois Press.

Tinker, Irene. 1990. "The Making of a Field: Advocates, Practitioners, and Scholars." In Irene Tinker, ed., *Persistent Inequalities: Women and World Development,* 27–53. New York: Oxford University Press.

Trinh T., Minh-ha, dir. 1982. *Reassemblage.* Women Make Movies, New York.

———. 1989. *Woman, Native, Other.* Bloomington: Indiana University Press.

———. 1992. *Framer Framed.* New York: Routledge.

Tsing, Anna Lowenhaupt. 1993. *In the Realm of the Diamond Queen.* Princeton, N.J.: Princeton University Press.

SYLLABUS. INTERDISCIPLINARY APPROACHES TO CONTEMPORARY ISSUES: WOMEN AND DEVELOPMENT

Women's experiences in the process of "development" in the third world have been very different from those of men. Policies that have benefited men have tended to have limited or even negative effects on women, and those that have had generally negative effects have tended to hurt women more than men. At the same time, however, women have come to be recognized as vital to the success of most development projects, even those from which they will not benefit. Beginning with fundamental questions addressing the meaning of development and the importance of perspective in defining the success of a policy, this course will analyze the lives and welfare of women in the South and consider alternative definitions and approaches to development which may take into account their perspectives. Topics to be covered will include work, income distribution, household formation, health and population, education, the environment, structural adjustment, and feminist critiques of the design, implementations and evaluation of policy. We will also consider the contribution postcolonial feminist theory can make to a discussion of the problems and possibilities of development as currently understood and practiced.

Texts

Dangarembga, Tsitsi. 1988. *Nervous Conditions*. Seattle: Seal Press.

Leonard, Ann, ed. 1989. *Seeds: Supporting Women's Work in the Third World*. New York: Feminist Press.

Minh-ha, Trinh T.. 1989. *Woman, Native, Other*. Bloomington: Indiana University Press.

Momsen, Janet Henshall. 1991. *Women and Development in the Third World*. New York: Routledge.

Sen, Gita, and Caren Grown. 1987. *Development, Crises, and Alternative Visions*. New York: Monthly Review Press.

Tsing, Anna Lowenhaupt. 1993. *In the Realm of the Diamond Queen*. Princeton, N.J.: Princeton University Press.

Other required reading will be put on reserve.

Week 1. Introduction: Women and Development?

Sen and Grown, "Introduction" and "Gender and Class in Development Experience," pp. 15–49.

Weeks 2 and 3. Women's Work

Momsen, chapter 5, "Women and Work in Urban Areas," and chapter 6, "Spatial Patterns of Women's Economic Activity," pp. 67–92.

Safa, Helen. 1997. "Where the Big Fish Eat the Little Fish: Women's Work in the Free-Trade Zones," *NACLA Report on the Americas* 30(5)(March–April): 31–36.

Momsen, chapter 3, "Reproduction," pp. 27–43.

Bunster, Ximena, and Elsa M. Chaney. 1989. *Sellers and Servants: Working Women in Lima, Peru*. Granby, Mass.: Bergin & Garvey. "María," pp. 81–131.

United Nations. 1991. *The World's Women*. New York: The United Nations. "Counting Economically Active Women," p. 85, and "Measuring Women's Economic Contribution in the United Nations System of National Accounts," p. 90.

Momsen, chapter 4, "Women and Work in Rural Areas," pp. 44–66.

Deere, Carmen Diana. 1987. "The Latin American Agrarian Reform Experience." In Carmen Diana Deer and Magdelena León, eds., *Rural Women and State Policy*, pp. 165–190. Boulder: Westview Press.

FILMS: WITH THESE HANDS, *1985*, CHRIS SHEPPARD AND CLAUDE SAUVAGEOT, THE NEW INTERNATION-ALIST; KUMEKUCHA (FROM SUNUP), *1987*, FLORA M'MUGU-SCHELLING; AND KAMALA AND RAJI, *1990*, MICHAEL CAMERINI, CHERYL GROFF, AND SHIREEN HUQ, PDR PRODUCTIONS.

Week 4. Household Organization and Distribution: Health

Young, Kate. 1992. "Household Resource Management." In Lise Østergaard, ed., *Gender and Development: A Practical Guide*, pp. 135–64. New York: Routledge.

Brown, Susan. 1975. "Love Unites Them and Hunger Separates Them: Poor Women in the Dominican Republic." In Rayna R. Reiter, ed., *Toward an Anthropology of Women*, pp. 322–32. New York: Monthly Review Press.

De los Angeles Crummet, María. 1992. "Rural Women and Migration in Latin America." In Carmen Diana Deere and Magdalena León, eds., *Rural Women and State Policy,* pp. 239–60. Boulder: Westview Press.

Østergaard, Lise. 1992. "Health." In Lise Østergaard, ed., *Gender and Development: A Practical Guide,* pp. 110–34. New York: Routledge.

Weeks 5 and 6. Population, Education, Environment

Barroso, Carmen, and Cristini Bruschini. 1991. "Building Politics from Personal Lives: Discussions on Sexuality Among Poor Women in Brazil." In Chandra Mohanty, Ann Russo, and Lourdes Torres, eds., *Third World Women and the Politics of Feminism,* pp. 153–72. Bloomington: Indiana University Press.

Deshingkar, Giri. 1991. "Population Control: Beyond State Policy." *Manushi* 67(November–December): 10–12.

Bang, Rani, and Abhay Bang. 1992. "Contraceptive Technologies: Experience of Rural Women." *Manushi* 70(May–June): 26–31.

Summers, Lawrence. 1994. *Investing in All the People: Educating Women in Developing Countries.* Washington, D.C.: World Bank.

Agarwal, Bina. 1992. "The Gender and Environment Debate: Lessons from India." *Feminist Studies* 18 (1): 119–58.

Week 7. Small Project Experiences

Kneerim, Jill. 1989. "Village Women Organize: The Mraru, Kenya Bus Service." In Leonard, ed., pp. 15–30.

Caughman, Susan, and Miriam N'diaye Thiam. 1989. "The Markala, Mali Cooperative: A New Approach to Traditional Economic Roles." In Leonard, ed., pp. 31–48.

McLeod, Ruth. 1989. "The Kingston Women's Construction Collective: Building for the Future in Jamaica." In Leonard, ed., pp. 163–87.

Chen, Marty. 1989. "The Working Women's Forum: Organizing for Credit and Change in Madras, India." In Leonard, ed., pp. 51–72.

Molnar, Augusta. 1989. "Forest Conservation in Nepal: Encouraging Women's Partici-pation." In Leonard, ed., pp. 98–119.

Week 8. Restructuring the Economy

Moser, Caroline O. N. 1992. "Adjustment from Below: Low-Income Women, Time and the Triple Role in Guayaquil, Ecuador." In Haleh Afshar and Carolyne Dennis, eds., *Women and Adjustment Policies in the Third World,* pp. 87–116. London: Macmillan.

Benería, Lourdes. 1992. "The Mexican Debt Crisis: Restructuring the Economy and the Household." In Lourdes Benería and Shelley Feldman, eds., *Unequal Burden: Economic Crises, Persistent Poverty, and Women's Work,* pp. 83–104. Boulder: Westview.

FILM: HELL TO PAY, *1988*, ALEXANDRA ANDERSON AND ANNE COTTRINGER, WOMEN MAKE MOVIES.

Weeks 9 and 10. Legacies of Colonialism

Dangarembga, *Nervous Conditions*.

Weeks 11–14. Questions of Representation

Mohanty, Chandra. 1991. "Under Western Eyes: Feminist Scholarship and Colonial Discourses." In Chandra Mohanty, Ann Russo, and Lourdes Torres, eds., *Third World Women and the Politics of Feminism,* pp. 51–80. Bloomington: Indiana University Press.

Trinh, "Reassemblage," pp. 95–105; "Film as Translation," pp. 111–33; and "Professional Censorship," pp. 213–21. In *Framer Framed,* (New York: Routledge).

Trinh, "The Language of Nativism," pp. 47–78; "Difference: 'A Special Third World Women Issue,'" pp. 79–116. In *Woman, Native, Other.*

Tsing, *In the Realm of the Diamond Queen.*

Week 15. Alternative Visions?

Sen and Grown, "Alternative Visions, Strategies, and Methods," pp. 78–96.

INTERNATIONALIZING FEMINIST PEDAGOGIES

Amy Kaminsky

The job description for a position in the department of women's studies at the University of Minnesota that I answered in 1983 called for a
feminist scholar in the humanities whose work dealt with an area of
the developing world. In other words, I was hired to bring an international humanities perspective to a women's studies department
whose small core faculty already boasted a distinguished historian of
Africa, Susan Geiger. Susan's presence and mine meant that the
department could regularly offer courses on women and world cultures, African and Latin American women writers, women's life histories in the developing world, and women in revolutionary struggles.
Nevertheless, the general courses offered in women's studies, even
when we taught them, tended to focus on domestic issues and texts.
When Geiger led a workshop to bring multiracial and international
gender perspectives to lower division courses, I participated in it,
redesigning Introduction to Women's Studies. The vagaries of curricular needs and faculty distribution in core courses were such that it
was years before I taught the course I redesigned. Yet the exercise was
far from futile, for the interaction with other faculty concerned with
broadening the scope of the institution's courses, together with the
range of new ideas, new materials, and new pedagogical methods to
which I was exposed, all have served me well in my teaching generally. Trained as a critic of Latin American literature, I learned about
communities of color in the United States as well as about issues concerning women from Asia and Africa, all of which have had an effect
on my teaching and thinking. Having the opportunity to engage with
colleagues on questions of content and pedagogy was of enormous
benefit to me. More recently, I undertook the revision of a feminist
pedagogy course.

There are five elements of an internationalized, gender-aware curriculum that an instructor needs to deal with. The first is simple information on women in different world regions. Demographic maps,
ethnographies, statistical data, histories, and women's expressions of
their own lives in their oral stories, their literary writing, and their
visual depictions are all means of gaining such information. Second is
a focus on feminist consciousness (a term I use very broadly) as it
emerges in different world regions and among differently placed
women in those regions. What traditional roles do women fulfill, and
what is the relation of those roles to relations of power? How do

indigenous, working class, and middle class women make their needs known? How and under what conditions do women come together to argue for their issues? What is the relationship between women's activism and feminist activism?

Third is the impact of globalization and industrialization, including issues of offshore production, agricultural sustainability, the international sex trade, and the audience for women's creative productions, on women throughout the world. Fourth is the question of the effect of globalization on women in the United States, including but not limited to immigrant women. Fifth is the question of theory, and the extent to which different theoretical approaches to both gender and questions of globalization and nation illuminate—or neglect to address—the conjuncture of gender and the global.

The extent to which any single course can sufficiently address these five elements is questionable. A revamped curriculum, however, would find ways to take account of them all, and any faculty member who takes on one or more of them in a single course needs to be aware of the others. Moreover, a number of critical issues arise for those attempting any form of internationalizing of feminist studies, from a single unit in a course to an entire curriculum. Primary among these is the dangers of reinscribing colonial relationships in the classroom. Scholars such as Chandra Mohanty (1991), Uma Narayan (1997), and Aihwa Ong (1988) have addressed this issue eloquently. Western scholars and students have had significant difficulty in differentiating among Third World women, whose distinct class, caste, ethnic, and kinship positions differentiate them from each other within their own cultures, and whose national histories and geographical locations distinguish among them in still other ways. In our classrooms, we must also be careful to avoid the pitfalls of trying to pin down the "authentic" South Asian woman, or the "representative" Latin American one. In the problematic quest for authenticity we not only neglect to note internal distinctions, but we also elide changes in culture occasioned, not least, by the effects of globalization.

The position of the Third World academic in the First World academy has come under scrutiny as well (Chow 1993; Abu-Lughod 1988). The need to get beyond the notion of a static Third World available for the scrutiny of a First World scholar or for the enlightenment of her students, continues to be a central issue for a scholarship whose aim is liberatory. Even the language we use to name the object and the method of study is problematic. The innocent use of a term like *geopolitics* among feminist historians comes up against an already existing precise usage of the term in international relations. *International* for some means, quite literally, *between nations,* as represented by state-authorized institutions, precluding an assessment of women's networks that ignore national boundaries and exist below the radar screen of the state.

There is, however, another critical issue for professors about to embark on internationalizing or gendering their course offerings, and that is the problem of mastery. For academics not trained in these areas, and who are very well trained indeed in our fields of specialization, the prospect of incorporating new perspectives, new methods, and new material into our work is more than daunting. It calls into question our notion that mastery is a prerequisite for honest teaching. And there is much to be said for mastery. Ann duCille (1996) argues that teaching and writing about African American women is often presumed not to require the special knowledge, developed after years of graduate training, that is considered prerequisite for engaging in scholarly discussion. On the one hand, duCille notes, anyone trained in literature at all is presumed qualified to teach the African American tradition. On the other, membership in an ethnic or national group is often considered enough to qualify one to teach about that group. The tendency to hold traditionally undervalued subject areas—and subjects—to less rigorous standards is an important concern that we need to take seriously. In departure from our training and from students' expectations, we must not set ourselves up as experts when we are not. (Certainly we would not hesitate to consult the work of experts when we undertake broadening the scope of our courses.) On the other hand, it is possible to gain enough knowledge to guide discussion and impart information to undergraduate students, to help them develop their own questions and find their own answers, to widen the horizons of our classes, without feeling the need for mastery. It requires a risky pedagogy that allows, indeed requires, the instructor to relinquish absolute authority over the dissemination of knowledge. If part of our teaching makes it necessary to fly without the net of years of training, we can take the opportunity to model intellectual inquiry for and with our students.

This is risky business. Students often demand perfect expertise from us, and they may well make their case for that demand in terms of getting their money's worth. By the same token, we owe it to them to equip ourselves with enough knowledge and information to get them started on their own intellectual journeys. It is not enough to say "we're all learning together," because as instructors we really do have an obligation to our students to lead and guide them, to give them the tools they need. Nevertheless, cooperative learning is not a paltry goal.

The units on international perspectives I have created for the revised pedagogy class address this question of mastery, as well as other pedagogical and intellectual issues. One of these is the debate around meanings of gender internationally. The very terms we use in the U.S. academy are called into question when we attempt to invoke them across cultures. Just as adding women (and thereby stirring things up) caused unforeseen, explosive reactions in traditional courses in the early days of women's studies, adding an international component to a course alters the whole mix.

The revisions I propose also address the dangers for students of either seeing women in other parts of the world as so different as to have no connection to them, or of reinforcing ethnocentric views of the world. They similarly address the apparently opposite tendency to assimilate all experience to their own, so that the specificity of a woman's life in Nigeria is lost as a student tries to identify with her counterpart, or, perhaps more commonly, to map the Nigerian woman's life experience onto her own. But there is also a section in the course that deals not only with pedagogy but with content, so that potential instructors can begin to create a knowledge base from which to teach, even if mastery is not a viable option. Part of this module consists in having students research and present an internationalized lesson to the group. This exercise has several purposes: to increase the store of knowledge in the researcher-presenter, to give the presenter experience researching an international topic so that she will be able to undertake that task more easily when she is developing an entire course, to expose the other members of the class to the information presented, and to provide model classes in which such issues as "othering" and reification can be dealt with before they arise in a real classroom situation.

WORKS CITED

Abu-Lughod, Lila. 1988. "Can There Be a Feminist Ethnography?" *Women and Performance* 5: 7–27.

Chow, Rey. 1993. "Against the Lures of Diaspora: Minority Discourse, Chinese Women, and Intellectual Hegemony." In *Writing Diaspora: Tactics of Intervention in Contemporary Cultural Studies*. Bloomington: Indiana University Press.

duCille, Ann. 1996. "The Occult of True Black Womanhood." In Ruth-Ellen B. Joeres and Barbara Laslett, eds., *The Second Signs Reader: Feminist Scholarship, 1983–1996*. Chicago: University of Chicago Press.

Mohanty, Chandra Talpade. 1991. "Cartographies of Struggle: Third World Women and the Politics of Feminism" and "Under Western Eyes: Feminist Scholarship and Colonial Discourse." In Chandra Talpede Mohanty, Ann Russo, and Lourdes Torres, eds., *Third World Women and the Politics of Feminism*. Bloomington: Indiana University Press.

Narayan, Uma. 1997. "Contesting Cultures: 'Westernization,' Respect for Cultures, and Third-World Feminists." In L. Nicholson, ed., *The Second Wave*. New York: Routledge.

Ong, Aihwa. 1988. "Colonialism and Modernity: Feminist Re-presentations of Women in Non-Western Societies." *Inscriptions* 3–4: 70–93.

SYLLABUS

We will examine feminist pedagogies by studying feminist, multicultural, and progressive theories of education. The course will look at both macro and micro issues: instructional and classroom practices, curriculum design and transformation, and material– structural institutional conditions. Our seminar will also serve as a practicum for the application of many kinds of progressive pedagogies.

This syllabus is a product of collaboration in the Department of Women's Studies. It represents the work of several faculty members over the course of a number of years. The integration of international issues is only the most recent of revisions it has undergone.

Course Objectives

1. To recognize the importance of student presence and participation in class so that students come to value the classroom learning experience and contribute to it willingly.
2. To recognize the importance of assuming leadership roles during class. Students will learn to cofacilitate seminar discussions.
3. To place a greater value on the study and practice of feminist, multicultural, and radical theories of education as a means to empower not only women, but diverse constituencies of disenfranchised students, as well as students who come from historically dominant groups. Students will develop various strategies for creating a more inclusive classroom.
4. To recognize the value of cooperative learning so that students develop an understanding of group processes, including how to collaborate on projects, build group trust, give feedback, and resolve conflicts within their learning groups.
5. To help teachers who are not necessarily experts in international fields deal with an internationalized curriculum and to share the objectives of such a curriculum, among which are
   a. to understand the specificity of women's experiences in different parts of the world. Although there may be some overarching themes that unite women in different parts of the world, those themes are differently realized in different countries. Within those countries, distinctions—especially of class and ethnicity—mean that women are differently located within their cultures and the oppression they experience or privileges they have will differ along these lines, internal to their society and in relation to other nations and trans- and international institutions.
   b. to understand that the categories of gender, class, race, and sexuality are not universal and have different meanings with different interplay among them, from culture to culture.
6. To be aware of the tendency toward exoticizing the Other woman and to work against that tendency actively in the classroom. Students will learn on the one hand how practices that seem entirely different from culture to culture may have similar functions within a broader ideological structure, e.g., the surgical alteration of women's bodies to make them acceptable on the marriage market, and on the other, that the practices of any one culture cannot be reduced to those of any other.
7. To be aware of and challenge a corresponding tendency to see the Other woman as a helpless victim of a benighted society. Students will learn about empowerment of women via grassroots organizations, international coalitions, artistic expression, etc.
8. To feel confident in teaching international material without the security of absolute mastery of the subject. Students should understand that the suggested readings

on different international sectors are just a beginning. We rely here on a basic tenet of feminist pedagogy: the instructor is human and should not pretend to omniscience. Pedagogical techniques for sharing the learning/teaching with students addressed at other moments in the course are of particular use in teaching and learning about women and gender in the international context.

9. To understand the material and structural conditions that determine what is possible for education located inside schools, colleges, and universities. Students should consider how educational and learning experiences are shaped by these conditions.

10. To demonstrate growth in the ability to understand theoretical materials and apply these materials to classroom practices and gain experience in classroom teaching. Students should reflect and act on the relationship between theory and practice.

11. To design learning activities and individualized projects germane to the particular fields of interests and inquiry of the members of the class. The final project ought to be useful to each student in the development of her/his special disciplinary and pedagogical interests.

Requirements

1. Regular attendance is essential if many of the other requirements are to be met.
2. Active class participation. This involves careful and critical reading of the assigned materials in order to engage fully in discussion. Each student is required to cofacilitate at least one class. This involves preparation of discussion questions, working in a small group, and, if needed, meeting with the instructor before class.
3. Case study. Each student will write up and present a brief case study (3–5 pp.) of a classroom incident that poses a dilemma, based on her or his own experience in the classroom as a teacher or student. The group as a whole will discuss the problem and try to come up with strategies and solutions. Case studies must be distributed one class in advance of their presentation.
4. International women's issue research presentation. Each student will choose a topic concerning women in a part of the world in which he or she has no previous exper-tise, do research on that topic, and present it to the class.
5. Final project. This project may be individual or collaborative. It should evolve out of class discussions, readings, and your own field(s) of inquiry. Possible topics:

  - Create a syllabus for a course you would like to teach.
  - Write a critique of any of the pedagogies we have discussed during the term.
  - Design an in-service workshop for your colleagues.
  - Apply the pedagogies we have studied to your own discipline.
  - Explore issues of diversity, national and/or international, in various pedagogies.
  - Explore the organization and structural constraints on the construction of educational experiences at the University of Minnesota or another educational institution with which you are familiar.
  - Explore what in the organizational structure or philosophy of an educational institution with which you are familiar enables innovation for progressive education to take place within that institution.

Required Readings

Daphne Patai and Noretta Koertge, *Professing Feminism: Cautionary Tales from the Strange World of Women's Studies* (New York: Basic Books, 1994).

Becky Thompson and Sangeeta Tyagi, eds., *Beyond a Dream Deferred: Multicultural Education and the Politics of Excellence* (Minneapolis: University of Minnesota Press, 1993).

Myles Horton and Paulo Freire, *We Make the Road by Walking: Conversations on Education and Social Change* (Philadelphia: Temple University Press, 1990).

Paulo Freire, *Pedagogy of the Oppressed* (New York: Seabury Press, 1968).

Johnella Butler and John Walter, eds., *Transforming the Curriculum: Ethnic and Women's Studies* (Albany: State University of New York Press, 1991).

bell hooks, *Teaching to Transgress: Education as the Practice of Freedom* (New York: Routledge, 1994).

Susan Hill Gross, *How to Do It: Teaching About Women in Contemporary Africa, Asia, and Latin America* (St. Paul: Upper Midwest Women's History Center).

Other readings as assigned.

Week 1. Introductions, Course Description, Classroom Procedures

VIDEO: WOMEN OF SUMMER.

Week 2

Part I—The Right Wing Attack on Women's Studies

Readings

1. *Professing Feminism*
2. Messer-Davidow, "Manufacturing the Attack on Liberalized Higher Education" case study: Extra!!! *Star Tribune* Exposes U of M Women's Studies Department!!!

Part II—What Kind of Educator Are You?

Readings

1. Gregorc, "Style Delineator: A Self-Assessment Instrument for Adults."
2. Collins, "Creating a Syllabus."
3. Freire, *Pedagogy of the Oppressed.*
4. Banks, "The Role of the Teacher in Prejudice Reduction," in Banks, *Multiethnic Education: Theory and Practice* (Boston: Allyn & Bacon, 1988).

Week 3. Feminist and Multicultural Education for Social Change

Cofacilitators_____; case study presentations_____

Readings

1. Thompson and Tyagi, "A Wider Landscape . . . Without the Mandate for Conquest" (*Beyond a Dream Deferred*).

2. Mohanty, "On Race and Voice: Challenges for Liberal Education in the 1990's" (*Beyond a Dream Deferred*).
3. Hu-DeHart, "Rethinking America: The Practice and Politics of Multiculturalism in Higher Education" (*Beyond a Dream Deferred*).
4. Omolade, "Quaking and Trembling: Institutional Change and Multicultural Curricular Development at CUNY" (*Beyond a Dream Deferred*).
5. Hall, "Compromising Positions" (*Beyond a Dream Deferred*).
6. Linton, Mello, and O'Neill, "Disability Studies: Expanding the Parameters of Diversity," *Radical Teacher* 47 (1995): 4–10.

Week 4. Classroom Practices I. Is There a Feminist Process?

Cofacilitators_____; case study presentations_____

Readings
1. Cannon, "Fostering Positive Race, Class, and Gender Dynamics in the Classroom," *Women's Studies Quarterly* 1– 2 (1990): 126–34.
2. hooks, "Introduction," Engaged Pedagogy," and "A Revolution of Values" (*Teaching to Transgress*).
3. Friedman, "Authority in the Feminist Classroom: A Contradiction in Terms?" in Culley and Portuguese, *Gendered Subjects.*
4. Geiger and Zita, "White Traders: The Caveat Emptor of Women's Studies," *Journal of Thought* 20(3) (Fall 1985): 106–21.

Week 5. Classroom Practices II. Feminist/Freirean/Multicultural Theories

Cofacilitators_____; case study presentations_____

Readings
1. Freire, "Letter to North American Educators," in Shor, ed., *Freire for the Classroom: A Sourcebook for Liberatory Teaching*, 211–14.
2. Finlay and Faith, "Illiteracy and Alienation in American Colleges: Is Paulo Freire's Pedagogy Relevant?" in Shor, 63–86.
3. Elsasser and John-Steiner, "An Interactionist Approach to Advancing Literacy," in Shor, 45–62.
4. Schneidewind, "Cooperatively Structured Learning: Implications for Feminist Pedagogy," *Journal of Thought* 20(3) (Fall 1988): 74–87.
5. hooks, "Embracing Change," "Paulo Freire," and "Theory as Liberatory Practice," (*Teaching to Transgress*).

Week 6. Transforming the Curriculum I

Cofacilitators_____; case study presentations_____

Readings
1. Wilkening, "Forward" (*Transforming the Curriculum*).

2. Butler, "Introduction" and "Part I: Ethnic Studies and Women's Studies: Interrelationships" (*Transforming the Curriculum*).
3. Butler, "The Difficult Dialogue of Curriculum Transformation: Ethnic Studies and Women's Studies" (*Transforming the Curriculum*).
4. Frankenberg, "Teaching 'White Women, Racism, and Anti-Racism' in a Women's Studies Program" (*Transforming the Curriculum*).
5. Guy-Sheftall, "A Black Feminist Perspective in the Academy" (*Transforming the Curriculum*).

Week 7. Transforming the Curriculum II

Cofacilitators_____; case study presentations_____

Readings
1. Butler, "Transforming the Curriculum: Teaching About Women of Color" (*Transform-ing the Curriculum*).
2. Colllins, Schneider, and Kroeger, "(Dis)Abling Images," *Radical Teacher* 47 (1995): 11–14.
3. Schneider and Zita, "untitled."
4. Spelman, "Gender in the Context of Race and Class" (*Transforming the Curriculum*).
5. Cole, "Black Studies in Liberal Arts Education" (*Transforming the Curriculum*).

Week 8. Transforming the Curriculum III

Cofacilitators_____; case study presentations_____

Readings
1. Beck, "The Politics of Jewish Invisibility in Women's Studies" (*Transforming the Curriculum*).
2. Butler and Walter, "Praxis and the Prospect of Curriculum Transformation."
3. Thompson and Tyagi, "The Politics of Inclusion: Reskilling the Academy" (*Beyond a Dream Deferred*).
4. Bauer, "Working Class Women and the University."
5. McNaron, "Mapping a Country: What Lesbian Students Want," in Pearson, Shavlik, and Touchton, *Educating the Majority: Women Challenge Tradition in Higher Education.*
6. Jackson, "The Responsibility of and to Differences: Theorizing Race and Ethnicity in Lesbian and Gay Studies" (*Beyond a Dream Deferred*).

Week 9. Transforming the Curriculum IV

Cofacilitators_____; case study presentations_____

Readings
1. Ong, "Colonialism and Modernity: Feminist Re-presentations of Women in Non-Western Societies," *Inscriptions* 3–4 (1988): 70–93.

2. Mohanty, "Under Western Eyes: Feminist Scholarship and Colonial Discourse," Mohanty, Russo, and Torres, eds., *Third World Women and the Politics of Feminism*.
3. Kaminsky, "Translating Gender," *Reading the Body Politic: Feminist Criticism and Latin American Women Writers*.
4. Evans, "Try, Try Again," *Women's Studies International Forum* 14(4) (1991): 335–43.

Week 10. Transforming the Curriculum V

Cofacilitators_____; case study presentations_____

Readings
1. Gross, *How to Do It*.
2. Betteridge and Monk, "Teaching Women's Studies from an International Perspective," *Women's Studies Quarterly* 1–2 (1990): 78–85.
3. Bassnett, "Crossing Cultural Boundaries—Or How I Became an Expert on East European Women Overnight," *Women's Studies International Forum* 15(1) (1992): 11–15.
4. Odim and Strobel "Introduction," *Restoring Women to History: Teaching Packets for Integrating Women's History into Courses on Africa, Asia, Latin America, the Caribbean, and the Middle East* (Bloomington, Indiana: Organization of American Historians, 1988).

Weeks 11 and 12. Transforming the Curriculum VI

Presentations both weeks consist of a teaching practicum on international women's issues. Using information gathered on the Internet, through library searches, and/or by means of readings in international feminist periodicals, each student will present a unit on some aspect of women's lives or feminist theory in an international context.

Suggested Sources
Restoring Women to History: Teaching Packets for Integrating Women's History into Courses on Africa, Asia, Latin America, the Caribbean, and the Middle East (Bloomington, Indiana: Organization of American Historians, 1988). "Introduction" by Cheryl Johnson Odim and Margaret Strobel.
Connexions, a quarterly publication on women's issues in an international perspective containing articles in translation from feminist reviews worldwide.
Women in Action, a quarterly publication of ISIS International, relying on women associates from all over the world to contribute reports on women's issues.
Mary Jacob, "Geographic Knowledge, Women and the Internet."

Week 13. Critical Teaching for Social Change I

Cofacilitators_____; case study presentations_____

Readings

1. Freire and Horton, vii–95 (*We Make the Road by Walking*).
2. hooks, "Essentialism and Experience," "Holding My Sister's Hand," "Feminist Thinking," and "Feminist Scholarship" (*Teaching to Transgress*).

Week 14. Critical Teaching for Social Change II

Cofacilitators_____; case study presentations_____

Readings

1. Freire and Horton, 97–197 (*We Make the Road by Walking*).
2. hooks, "Building a Teaching Community," "Language," "Confronting Class in the Classroom" (*Teaching to Transgress*).

Week 15. Critical Teaching for Social Change III

Cofacilitators_____
Presentations this week are of final projects.

Readings

1. Freire and Horton, 199–end (*We Make the Road by Walking*).
2. hooks, "Eros, Eroticism, and the Pedagogical Process" and "Ecstasy" (*Teaching to Transgress*).

TALKING TURKEY: CULTURAL EXCHANGES VIA E-MAIL BETWEEN STUDENTS AT NEW JERSEY CITY UNIVERSITY AND BILKENT UNIVERSITY, ANKARA, TURKEY

DORIS FRIEDENSOHN AND BARBARA RUBIN

New Jersey City University (NJCU), formerly Jersey City State College, is a multicultural, public, urban institution located directly across the Hudson River from the lower Manhattan financial district. The student body of approximately six thousand full time equivalents is predominantly commuter and working class. Most students work more than twenty hours a week while attending classes; most have weak academic skills and are the first in their families to attend college.

The women's studies program at NJCU, now in its twenty-fifth year, offers a minor as well as courses that are part of the general studies curriculum. The e-mail project was conceived as a way of adding an international dimension to several of our (introductory level) General Studies courses while maintaining a multicultural U.S. focus. We first tested the ideas spelled out here in the fall of 1997 with one section of women's studies students (approximately twenty people) at NJCU and a similar number of American history students at Tokyo Woman's Christian University (TWCU) in Japan. Our gratitude goes to Rui Kohiyama in the history department at TWCU for piloting the project with us.

In spring 1998, we enlarged the project significantly. At Bilkent University in Turkey, a team of English teachers had built electronic communications into a special first-year program for students in business administration. When we approached them, they wanted to include all of their 130 students in the project. By involving six sections of NJCU women's studies classes—some at the very last moment—we matched their numbers.

The authors wish to thank our intrepid NJCU faculty collaborators, Christa Olson and Christine Carmody-Arey, for engaging with us, and for their flexibility and fortitude in this endeavor. Special thanks also go to our five Bilkent colleagues: James Bowman, Daren Hodson, Humera Baysol, Umur Celikyay, and Zeynep Ozek. We appreciate their willingness to take on this collaboration without much advance planning, their generosity of spirit in tolerating the bumps in the road, and their inspired pedagogic interventions, which kept the lines of communication open and lively.

A final note: This essay draws upon our students' final papers and attachments, including e-mail correspondence. Their candor delighted us and energized our reporting. In the text, students' names have been changed or switched to protect their anonymity.

Talking turkey: *to talk candidly and bluntly (Webster's).*

Linda checks her watch as she dashes through the entrance to the Professional Studies building on her way to the Electronic Learning Lab. It's 4:40 P.M. on a bleak Monday—less than an hour before she is due in class. She makes a beeline for the only unoccupied computer in the lab, drops her gear, and opens her e-mail. "C'mon, Abdul, I gotta know how men treat women in Turkey for our class today." But this is not Linda's day; Abdul has not responded. Nevertheless, she sends her Turkish partner a light-hearted note, prodding him on.

An emergency room nurse, Linda schedules her days and evenings down to the last half hour. Because she has no computer at home, she worries about whether she'll be able to find one on campus, with print-out capacity, just when she needs it. Sometimes, the mere thought of the semester-long e-mail project exhausts her. Nevertheless, Linda feels lucky. Unlike many of her classmates, she has already had two friendly letters from Abdul. In his second e-mail, he asked Linda how she manages her career, school, and marriage. She told him that although some days are sheer hell, she has a supportive husband and is accustomed to juggling responsibilities.

When Linda and 125 other NJCU students signed up for women's studies classes, they had no idea that faculty members were launching them on an e-mail project with students in Turkey. The project, "Talking Gender via E-mail Across Oceans," is part of an effort to make women's studies more global in outlook and practice. Although all of our courses endeavor to make historical and theoretical concerns accessible and vivid through student-centered research and personal writing, this undertaking adds an experiential dimension to cross-cultural questions about gender. Thanks to the new technology, this goal is—or should be—within reach.

Why Turkey, our students ask. Serendipity, we reply. We put out a call at an academic conference for a project "mate." Bilkent University in Ankara responded, and so our course was set. Designed on an American model, with English as the language of instruction in all areas, Bilkent is a forward-looking, selective, private institution. English instructors in its School of Business and Management have been teaching intensive communications courses using electronic technology; when we proposed one-on-one conversations on-line between the groups, they agreed at once.

How ready are our students, we ask ourselves over wine at the local bistro, for this adventure? And how ready, really, are we? As faculty, we bring some knowledge of women's issues in the Eastern

Mediterranean and the Middle East to the table. However, our knowledge of Turkish geopolitics and culture comes mostly from the *New York Times*. Our students, we suspect, will have difficulty locating Turkey on a map of the world; few are e-mail users, and we ourselves are neophytes with technology. Many of our students are weak writers and slow learners; and many are immigrants or foreign students, still struggling with English. Almost all are mired in responsibilities, absorbed in the dailiness of their existence. Shaking our heads, we pour another glass of wine and imagine the glory that once was Constantinople.

Our goal is to challenge students to become increasingly self-conscious, transnational in outlook, and interpersonally sophisticated in an arena where insularity frequently defines comfort. Exploring differences across cultures, including the many cultures that coexist often uneasily in the United States and on our campus, is delicate, difficult work. Reaching across oceans and language barriers adds to the intellectual and social complexity of the undertaking.

The students have been to the electronic learning lab for a training session on using e-mail; they have obtained an e-mail address. They have been given a world map, and they have read several articles on Turkish culture, history, and the women's movement. In class, we talk about the complexities of this particular correspondence: how to approach a stranger, how to be culturally sensitive, how to extract information, how to invite personal revelations. The trick, we tell them, is to balance the giving and getting: if they are generous in recounting their experiences and explaining their positions, their partners will be more likely to respond in kind. Gabriela looks at the name of her partner, the three names actually, all unpronounceable, at least to her. The first question that Gabriela and most of her classmates ask concerns gender. Is my partner a male or a female? Why, we ask, does this matter? Do you want the comfort of a same-sex partner? Do you crave the excitement of a partner of the opposite sex—or the excitement of a same-sex partner? Ellen wonders as she writes for the first time, "Should I take the formal approach and be short and to the point? Should I be easy going and playful? My partner might get scared off or think I'm dumb. Or should I take the 'hey, I'm a 90s kind of woman' approach and stifle him (if it's a man) with my views of today's problems? No! Definitely not. I'll just be me—a little of all of the above."

Like Ellen, many female students are fearful that their strong voices will serve them poorly with Turkish males; but these same women are also unwilling to be muted. From the start the women are more engulfed in the nuances of creating a relationship with the men; they are seeing, to use anthropologist Catherine Bateson's term, with a lot of *peripheral vision.* This is not to suggest that the male students are insensitive to the subtleties of partnership. Many worry about how to approach without offending. They do not want to ask questions that might initially seem inappropriate. All of them feel bewildered by the "rules" of cross-cultural communication.

George has a generational issue. "How," he asks, "would a college kid in Turkey connect with a thirty-six-year-old American male with a wife and three kids? I thought about pretending to be a twenty year old. Could I pull it off? No. I can hardly remember being twenty. . . . I knew I had much to offer if given the chance. I wanted to tell my partner about how I grew up in America and how different it is today: how women today, like my wife, are taking on so many responsibilities; and how my father never changed a diaper in his life, while I have changed countless diapers."

Melina has a political concern. She's Greek. Will any Turk be willing to talk to her? Talk honestly? Can she break the ice?

"There are fifty e-mails in my box," Kiswana announces, "but none from my partner." For many it is a waiting game, dropping in and out of the lab and coming up empty. "They" are not writing, our students complain. What some are not telling is that neither are they. As teachers, we puzzle over this problem. Four weeks into the project and only a third of our students have made contact with Turkish partners. Only by policing the e-mail partnerships can we determine where connections are being made, who is failing to attempt communication and why. (The Turkish students are also reporting no contact from "them.") Students are full of excuses—computer troubles, tough work schedules, no baby sitter, and so on.

Not only are the logistics of the project demanding, but the match between our essentially working class, multiethnic students and Bilkent's largely upper middle class population is awkward. While almost all of our students work, either to support themselves or their (often one-parent) families, Bilkent students are taken care of by their families, freeing them to concentrate on their studies. Skills in English are unevenly distributed among both groups, but many Bilkent students display impressive proficiency.

Even with a more symmetrical match, communicating on e-mail in an intimate fashion and in the interests of "information gathering" is problem ridden. We bait students with the possibility of friendship while exhorting them to use this "friend" as a data bank. Inadvertently, we set up an "I/It," not "I/Thou," situation, to use Martin Buber's distinction between treating another as object and subject. As a consequence, both sets of students bombard their partners with lists of questions; a grade is at stake, they let the other know.

What are the odds that these practical, grade-driven needs will leave room for friendships to emerge? And how will language function? Will the partners seem interesting to one another? Will the Turkish students get the practice they were promised? When only a third of the Turkish students report working partnerships, their instructors improvise. They set up a listserv to keep the students writing—to one another if necessary—and to open an additional channel of communication. Two hundred and fifty students and nine faculty in all, in theory, connected.

The listserv crackles to the sounds of "culture" under fire. The Turkish students are chewing over McDonald's, having a love-hate relationship on-line with every burger. Those in the Camp of Transition hold forth about the ease and efficiency of it all: eating without ceremony in the hip Western way; those in the Camp of Tradition decry global economics, American cultural imperialism, and the demise of the Turkish way of life. On the listserv, McDonald's is metaphor for change run amok, with the United States the villain and Turkey the victim. Transitionalists also have some qualms about American hegemony, even as they are shaped by the West in their midst—by the institutions of European Turkey.

"Virginity testing" in Turkey brings a few U.S. females vehemently opposing onto the list. They have been waiting for just such an outlet. For over a month now, they've had in their folders a *New York Times* article entitled "Turks Clash Over Defense of Virginity Tests" by Stephen Kinzer (January 8, 1998). Turkish feminists, according to Kinzer's report, are demanding the resignation of the female cabinet minister in charge of women's affairs for defending the traditional practice of virginity testing. Of course, the issue isn't virginity; some of our students want to be virgins at the altar. What incenses them is the invasion of the state and male control of a woman's body. Barbaric, they inveigh. Virginity testing might have been restricted to classroom discussions had not some Turkish males launched diatribes on-line on the value of female virginity.

"McDonald's" and "Virginity testing" become rallying cries: food and sex strike primal chords, unleashing the critical question of who's in control. Each rallying cry is a defense of borders: the borders at the Turkish nation-state and the borders of the female body. Turkish culture is being invaded by all that McDonald's symbolizes; and at Bilkent, where American educational practices are modeled, the Other is already within. English, welcomed, represents an invasion. Turks note that the English of some of the NJCU students is incredibly sloppy—dare we say "junk English?"

For American women, the fear is not of actual virginity tests but of social control as invasion. Cultural tests of virginity have a lingering history, which in the lifetime of our students has been under attack. The knowledge that women elsewhere in the world have less control over their bodies than they (generally) does unsettle our female students. They are reminded of their vulnerability, and they take the vulnerability of other women to heart. There are no safe borders when it comes to the female body.

The faculty contemplate some links between these emotionally laden arenas: McDonald's, fast food, and the sexually liberated woman. Surely, for Turkish males, McDonald's telegraphs the disintegration of the family and the social order. If the "angel in the house" is in the workplace, women may soon try to wrest power from men. But not on the listserv. From the outset, the list is principally the domain of the Turkish males in an exchange with each other, on the highly charged issues of their cultural identity. Women students, Turkish and American, on the whole, hang back, except for the adventurous few. Is this another example of the difficulties women have in putting themselves forward and taking men on?

Reading the list, some U.S. students are impressed by the sophistication and intensity of the Turkish debates. Some are nonplussed; still others are put off by what they perceive as strutting. Complacent, they tend not to think about the nature and direction of American culture. Except for the immigrants and foreign students, they are not preoccupied by the "Americanness" of their lives—certainly not in the ways they are preoccupied by ethnic, racial, and even gender identities. They are proud of American power, opportunities, individualism, and popular culture. "Spoiled," as Melissa puts it, "I take my freedoms and liberties for granted. I do not know what it is like to be thought of as a second class citizen." For Melissa and her American-born classmates, the Turks' dialogue of resistance and protest is a foreign language.

Analuisa is a reticent woman, not given to bold political pronouncements. Thus, she surprises her classmates with the intensity of her disappointment in not getting a male partner. She wants to challenge a Turkish man, debate his sexual politics, tell him a thing or two about the importance of treating women as people. Turkish men, she feels certain, are like the men in her country, Colombia—certain of their superiority, focused on their needs, and indifferent to the claims of wives and girlfriends. While Analuisa has intimate knowledge of her oppression as a woman, she is, like a number of her female classmates from the Third World, a closet feminist. The label is alien to her more than it is to many U.S.–born women. Both groups are angry with men, but nervous about being perceived as unfeminine or antimale. Many are uneasy about face-to-face confrontations with men on issues of power. But virtual confrontation with a single e-mail partner is attractive to these women: It's an opportunity to vent without real-life consequences.

American-born Mindy unhesitatingly identifies as a feminist. At age twenty-one, she is not accustomed to having any male tell her what she can and cannot do, and certainly not what the length of her skirt should be. Encountering the macho sentiments of the Turkish men on the listserv, she is irate, even ideological. Where is their consciousness of women's freedom? If this is how "they" are, she could never live in Turkey, Mindy declares. In fact, conservative males, speaking with the passion of those on the defense, hold forth at length, lining up "reasonable" arguments or being adroitly dismissive. On a range of topics, including who pays on dates, the role of religion, and individualism as a concept, traditionalists are energized and bombastic in their assertions. Omer, for example, claims that men control women out of love. A husband who truly loves his wife won't want her to work. She will feel lucky to be married to him, happy to be able to be at home.

But a number of Turkish males are comfortably, even adamantly, egalitarian. Sevil argues that men who rationalize a desire to control women as a sign of love are wrongheaded. Women can control themselves, without any help from a man. He calls on men to "give up selfish behavior and become aware of the women's rights. Then everything (between the sexes) will become better." Still, ambiguities concerning the politics of gender equality abound. Romantic, nineteen-year-old Tunga, a self-confessed nonsexist, tells his partner Martha, "The word feminism doesn't sound nice to me. It reminds me of competition or a fight between two genders. I think washing the clothes or the dishes or cooking dinner shouldn't be a problem between couples. I would do it for my wife (if I'll have one). If there is enough love, there is no need for feminism."

And where are the Turkish women in this dialogue? The more liberated come out on e-mail in defiance of parental control and the dominance of male peers. Saadet tells her partner, "I don't know what my parents think about premarital sex, but if I really love someone, I'll think about what I want to do. You American people think that we are very strict. But it's not like that. We are free to decide what to do." Gonul is passionate in attacking the double standard. Turkish men, she says, can sleep around, but if you do it, you're a worthless bitch. They like their women to be under their control. They've got the power. They think, "I can do what I like, but you women must stay in your house, raise your children." Knowing her female partner's feminist views, she sums up, "I can imagine that you find this 'mentally fucked up.'"

What do you do on Saturday night? Terry asks Turker. It's the pivotal question of young adults (almost all Turkish students and 70 percent of U.S. students), more imperative than any their teachers might suggest about gender and culture. The question is both shorthand and code for a host of curiosities: about dating, having sex, and going to clubs; about experimentation and fidelity, loving and being loved. Terry knows she should approach these matters gingerly, not embarrass her partner by asking too much too fast, for once contact has been established, she doesn't want to risk losing the trust. But she is impatient, unable to shift gears. In her classically American style, Terry is direct.

The Turkish students encourage the Americans' confessions en route to making a few of their own. Turan (a woman student), asks, "What's it like when a boy and a girl are on a date? Here if you are dating, you cannot kiss each other on the street (on the lips). In fact, you can, but people respond in a bad way." Rosemary brushes off Turan's questions about kissing and gets down to basics. "It's not a big deal, if you 'do it,'" Rosemary says, "at least not for me. As a Catholic, I was taught premarital sex is a sin, but I don't agree with that. I mean, if I had some good chemistry with a guy and he's decent and sensitive, I would have sex with him, but not on the first date or the second or the third. Now, would I feel guilty about 'doing it'? I don't know because I haven't done it yet."

Adana, a Turkish rebel, confides to Debbie that while she's had many boyfriends since the age of 15, she keeps her parents in the dark. To the notion that virginity is proof of good moral character, she writes, "bullshit. Most of my friends talk about their lover boyfriends," she continues, surprised to be writing what sounds like a private letter. "However, you are always a virgin for your father. I am not, by the way."

Cyberspace is liberated space for grappling with anxieties about freedom, rebellion, and sexual development. Turkish and U.S. students each want to know how far the other is prepared to go—with sex and drugs and personal choices, in defiance of parental attitudes and social controls. Some of them surprise themselves with the intimacy of their talk. Laura pushes conversational intimacy to the far edge. She is an out lesbian planning to be "married" in July in a ceremony on the beach. In class, she announces that she has decided to reveal her homosexuality and impending marriage to her partner; she also mentions the risks: "While it could turn Fatma off, it may also encourage her to ask more questions and could actually be helpful to her. I have never experienced any prejudice, and I find myself fearing it. I mean, Turkey isn't that tolerant about homosexuality."

Laura is the only acknowledged homosexual in the project. Her confession is motivated by a compelling need for sexual authenticity, for playing it "straight." And her revelation just might convert one more person to the gay rights cause. Fatma responds with thanks for Laura's candor: "Your last e-mail really made me surprised. I did not have the opportunity to meet or talk to a lesbian or homosexual before. What I want to say is that I am not against these people. Everyone should have the right to choose their own sex. I want to be among the people who congratulate you." Fatma's e-mail continues in the excited, inquisitive tones of one who has just opened Pandora's box. How do Laura's close relatives take to her marriage, she asks. Will it lead to problems in Laura's academic life? How does society in general look upon marriage of this sort? In Turkey, she tells Laura, a marriage between lesbians would be impossible. Maybe in the future, she reassures her.

Not long after this exchange, homosexuality as topic takes center stage on the listserv and spills over into conversations between partners. Some Turkish students pick up on Fatma's open-minded stance. Others take a vituperative one, calling homosexuality one of the "worst concepts of life," and one of the "worst humiliations of men." The sex war battle lines are drawn again, on both sides, by traditionalists and transitionalists. Will liberals on both sides still get good grades for tolerance when the topic is homosexuality? Will traditionalists marshal their strongest opposition yet? Most of the Turks acknowledge that gays and lesbians are not accepted in Turkey but they, the younger generation, accept everything, almost everything. Live and let live, they say. The rights of the individual should be respected. For the Americans, if their partners are progressive about gays, then they have passed the litmus test for tolerance. The Turkish students are sounding more "American" everyday. But who can distinguish an opinion's deep structure from its surface structure? How honest are the U.S. students? Homophobia is still present in our classrooms, especially among males. So who are the *poseurs* in this round of discussions, and who are the truth-tellers?

Ludmila, who came to the United States from Albania only two years ago, worries about her success in the project. Will she be able to explain how gender works in the United States to her e-mail partner? Won't a Turkish student in this project want a "real" American and not a foreigner as a partner? Ludmila is hardly alone with her concerns: at least 25 percent of U.S. students in the project are immigrants or foreigners with student visas. Members of this group have a limited knowledge of American culture(s) and, in many cases, a limited command of English. Nevertheless, the newcomers have a fresh, raw perspective on U.S. life; they notice behavior and assumptions that natives take for granted. Moreover, their views could be especially interesting to Turkish partners who are thinking ahead about the United States as a place for advanced study or future work. These students wrestle with an uneasy biculturalism: a sense of being on the border, torn between attraction to the mainstream culture and feeling allegiances to the traditions of their families and homelands. In fact, the need to explain this struggle on-line to peers outside the United States, and thus to themselves, is the project's greatest gift to students like Ludmila. She writes, "I am picking between cultures. Trying to give my partner the concept of their American way of communication between the sexes, I am learning things for myself."

Students with backgrounds as varied as Indian, Cuban, Nigerian, Greek, Egyptian, Ecuadoran, Moroccan, and Filipino resonate, negatively and positively, to traditional Turkish culture. Some appreciate values such as respect for family elders and discretion in sexuality, which they find missing in contemporary U.S. life. Others recognize distressing similarities between Turkey and their homelands. Indira, who arrived in the United States from India only a year ago writes to her partner, "I think Turkish culture is like Indian culture in emphasis on religion and suppression of women's rights. Both cultures exploit women." For newcomers like Indira, the similarities in habits and values make for good bonding. For others, a sense of similar structures dulls their curiosity, flattens their appreciation of difference. Josephine from Nigeria yearns for woman-to-woman talk about problems of living with (traditional) husbands who have the concept of "ladies after men." Although she never connects with an e-mail partner, she concludes from the listserv, "For me there's not much that's new about Turkish culture."

For Melina, an American-born student of Greek parents, raised in Greece, who returned to the United States as a young adult, Turkey is a story of ethnic hatred, fears, and suspicions. Melina wears history like a mourning dress, clinging to the memories even as she would like to move on. She opens the conversation with her partner by identifying herself as Greek Orthodox. When there is no reply, she seems bewildered. It's because she is Greek, she assumes. We will never know. However, we do know that Helena, also of Greek heritage, establishes a bridge to Turkey. "There's a saying that Greeks and Turks hate each other," she writes. "I was not raised to think this way, but I did not know what to expect from my partner, Yelda. To my surprise, Yelda, she was not raised to think this way either." Their talk circumvents their histories.

Good form and cultural sensitivity dictated that students who had complaints not tell their partners. Only the cajoling from teachers reveals they're feeling let down. Without leave-taking rituals, many of these partners on both sides just slip away. In the process, students speculate about other reasons for their communication failures—from technology breakdowns to the experimental nature of the project. The disappointed students acknowledge that they haven't come away empty: They have new technological skills, and they have picked up "interesting information about another culture."

Students with responsive partners do not want to say goodbye. They may have had enough of the academic side of the assignment but not enough of each other. How they take leave has much of the familiar ring of friends saying farewell: the attendant anxieties, departing words and plan-making for the future, if indeed there is to be one.

"Is it a friendship?" some ask. "What have we really gone through," some students wonder as they deconstruct the term we handed them. "I wouldn't call what we had a friendship, but an acquaintanceship," Jake clarifies. "We both understood that we needed one another for a good grade." Joan reminds her teachers that perhaps they have been presumptuous and wrongheaded in their expectations: "I was not looking for a new best friend but information accompanied by reasonable pleasantries."

However, some *were* looking for a new friendship, and some found it. "We 'clicked' right away," Maya says, "and we were able to communicate openly and freely. Zeynep and I are alike in many ways: we both feel strongly about our views, and we are not afraid to express them. I was able to ask her if she was sexually active, and she actually answered me. Sometimes I feel like she is one of my American friends."

Over and over again, partners comment on the common threads that bind them. Strong individuality, as in Maya's case, or being from elsewhere, or grooving on Elton John and Madonna, or something as ubiquitous as two guys discovering that they just can't figure women out.

Jackie is grateful to her partner for serving as a mirror. She finds the friendship "enlightening, not only because I learned about someone from another country, but because I learned about myself. I never realized how judgmental I can be, and I found out some of my thoughts on subjects I never knew I cared about." Maya says, "This project was about experiencing life through the eyes of other people, especially women." Melissa speaks for Maya and Jackie and lots of others in the project when she declares that her partner "Nevra put me in place with regard to a lot of stereotypes about Turkish culture. I thought my partner would be this meek, ignorant 'girl.' I believed that my knowledge of the world would reign supreme. In fact, she matched me in knowledge of the 'real' world and then some."

Daniel sends his last e-mail to Omer on April 7th. "Hey, it's your friend from the U.S.," it begins. "I hope you did not forget me. I lost contact with you for a week. Are you ok?" Daniel tells him about a new job he's gotten. He inquires about Omer's family, his class work, how he spent his religious holiday, all the stuff that friends check out with one another. Then he makes one more gesture: "Maybe in the fall, when I come back to school, we can keep writing to each other, if that is cool with you." There is hope in his voice and vulnerability.

At the end of this project of unexpected complexity, it's time to play it again. The first round has been a jumble of lofty ambitions, wrong-headed assumptions, logistical confusions, and hasty improvisations. In academic terms, the project needs a course designed to accommodate it and an entire semester (rather than ten weeks) to evolve. It needs a syllabus that is both tighter and looser than the one we wrote. It needs to be more technologically grounded and more technologically venturesome: with better training for participants, including the use of websites and other on-line resources. It needs more support for students-as-actors in areas of self-expression, building relationships, and the fundamentals of communication. It needs more structures for all of the principals, students and faculty alike, to encounter one another on-line, explore commonalities and differences with equal verve, and not be deflected by resistance or conflict.

SYLLABUS

This project uses the new technology of e-mail to foster a comparative exploration of gender issues. It is our hope that through on-line communication, you will develop an appreciation of the diversity of gender arrangements in different cultural contexts and a clearer understanding of the ways in which gender operates (in conjunction with race, class, ethnicity, and sexual orientation) in our own local and particular situations. In addition to promoting an exchange of cultural data, viewpoints, and experiences, the project also seeks to encourage friendship across oceans, continents, and cultural barriers. Our e-mail collaborators for Spring 1998 are at Bilkent University, an English-language institution in Ankara, Turkey. The project will proceed as follows: Each NJCU student will be given the name and e-mail address of a Bilkent partner. A group training session on using e-mail will be scheduled in the

Electronic Learning Lab. Class time will be devoted to deciding upon some topics for discussion, examining ways of beginning a conversation with a partner, and getting beyond the mechanics of a question-answer format. Background information on Turkish culture, with a focus on the changing status of women in modern Turkey, will be assigned and discussed. It is the responsibility of NJCU students to initiate conversations with assigned Bilkent partners. You are expected to develop a pattern of regular communication with your partner—*minimally once a week for ten weeks.* And please note: expectations for Bilkent students are similar. Make it a point to print out your own e-mails and those you receive from your partner. You may want to refer to them in class discussions. Instructors may ask to see them from time to time. Keep a *detailed journal* (see attached guidelines) in which you will reflect upon exchanges with your partner. The journal, in turn, will provide the basis for a *polished 1,000-word essay* on your findings and experiences.

Topics for NJCU Students to Explore with Their Turkish Partners

1. GENDER EXPECTATIONS: *WHAT IS EXPECTED OF YOU AS A WOMAN OR MAN GROWING UP IN TURKEY? WOULD YOU DESCRIBE YOUR FAMILY AS "TRADITIONAL" OR "MODERN"? ARE YOUR FAMILY'S EXPECTATIONS FOR YOU THE NORM IN TURKEY? ARE THERE SOME IMPORTANT DIFFERENCES BETWEEN THEIR EXPECTATIONS AND WHAT IS GENERALLY EXPECTED OF WOMEN AND MEN? HOW DO YOU FEEL ABOUT THESE EXPECTATIONS: WHAT DO YOU LIKE? WHAT DO YOU DISLIKE? DO YOU FEEL LIMITED IN ANY ASPECT OF LIFE BECAUSE OF YOUR GENDER?*

2. EQUALITY: *HOW MUCH EQUALITY EXISTS BETWEEN WOMEN AND MEN? BETWEEN WOMEN STUDENTS AND MEN STUDENTS? HOW ARE WOMEN TREATED IN TURKEY?*

3. INTIMATE RELATIONSHIPS: *WHAT IS YOUR NOTION OF AN IDEAL INTIMATE RELATIONSHIP? DO YOU EXPECT TO HAVE SUCH A RELATIONSHIP? IF NOT, WHY NOT? DO YOU HAVE A "SIGNIFICANT OTHER"? WHAT ARE THE POSITIVES AND NEGATIVES IN YOUR RELATIONSHIP? IF YOU DON'T HAVE A PARTNER, ARE YOU HAPPY THAT WAY?*

4. DATING: *HOW DOES DATING START IN (YOUR CIRCLES IN) TURKEY? WHAT IS DATING LIKE FOR YOU? DO MEN (STUDENTS) GENERALLY PAY FOR WOMEN ON DATES? DO WOMEN (ORDINARILY) ASK MEN OUT? HOW DO YOU FEEL ABOUT MEN PAYING FOR WOMEN OR WOMEN ASKING MEN OUT?*

5. VIRGINITY: *WHAT IMPORTANCE DO TURKISH WOMEN GIVE TO BEING VIRGINS AT MARRIAGE? WHAT IMPORTANCE DOES A MAN GIVE TO HIS FUTURE WIFE'S VIRGINITY? WHAT'S YOUR VIEW OF THE SUBJECT?*

6. BIRTH CONTROL: *HOW EASY IS IT TO GET CONDOMS? ARE THEY AVAILABLE IN HIGH SCHOOLS? UNIVERSITIES? HOW DO YOU FEEL ABOUT BIRTH CONTROL? ABORTION? DO YOU WORRY ABOUT AIDS? DO MOST PEOPLE YOU KNOW PRACTICE SAFE SEX?*

7. HOMOSEXUALITY: *WHAT IS THE TURKISH VIEW OF HOMOSEXUALITY? WHAT IS YOUR VIEW? HOW EASY OR DIFFICULT IS IT FOR GAYS AND LESBIANS TO "COME OUT" AND BE "OUT" ON YOUR CAMPUS? IN YOUR SOCIAL CIRCLE?*

8. MARRIAGE: *WHAT IS YOUR VIEW OF MARRIAGE? ARE YOU INTERESTED IN MARRYING? IF NOT, WHY? WOULD YOU MARRY SOMEONE YOUR PARENTS DISAPPROVED OF? ON WHAT GROUNDS WOULD THEY BE MOST LIKELY TO DISAPPROVE? WOULD YOUR FAMILY TRY TO ARRANGE A MARRIAGE FOR YOU? HOW WOULD YOU FEEL IF THEY TRIED?*

9. CHANGE: *ARE THERE DIFFERENCES BETWEEN YOUR GRANDPARENTS' VIEWS OF WOMEN/MEN AND YOUR PARENTS' VIEWS? BETWEEN YOUR PARENTS' VIEWS AND BEHAVIOR AND YOUR OWN? WHAT CHANGES WOULD YOU LIKE TO SEE IN TURKEY IN RELATIONS BETWEEN WOMEN AND MEN? IS THERE "PROGRESS" TOWARD GREATER EQUALITY? EXPLAIN.*

Guidelines for the Journal

You are required to make at least one journal entry per week for a period of ten weeks. Your entries, over the course of the semester, should address the following topics and questions:

A. The Developing Relationship with Your Turkish Partner

How did you break the ice? How did your partner approach you? How easy or difficult is it to be in communication? Explain. Which issues are hard to talk about and why? What cultural barriers exist on your side—and on the Turkish side—that make communication difficult? How is the friendship progressing? What changes are occurring in the quality and style of your communications? What are you learning about your partner from this process? About yourself? (e.g., Is your partner/are you flexible or rigid? eager to communicate or shy? able or unable/unwilling to address sensitive issues? What surprises you in the relationship? What questions or problems emerge in e-mailing that you would like to share with the class?)

B. Knowledge (Data, Impressions, and Perceptions) About Gender Roles and Relationships Between Women and Men in Turkey

What does your partner report about her or his views of intimate relationships (bonds, romance, sexuality, sexual orientation, marriage, childbearing and rearing, etc.)? Accord-ing to your partner, to what extent are her or his views and behavior common to other Turks of her or his age and background? Can you distinguish between your Turkish partner's reports about her or his own relationships and what is "general" for educated young Turks today? What are the conflicts your partner struggles with? the social pressures? When you speak about yourself, do you find yourself generalizing about what "Americans" think and do? In what instances? What are you learning about your own views of gender roles and relationships from answering your Turkish partner: what aspects of his/her gendered situation would be most comfortable? most frustrating?

C. Using E-mail

How does e-mail facilitate communication? What are its disadvantages? In what ways, if any, has using e-mail changed your style of communicating? your attitude toward communicating? Is e-mail a good tool for developing a friendship? for learning about a foreign culture? Explain.

THE VOICES OF WOMEN IN ANCIENT GREEK LITERATURE AND SOCIETY

ANDRÉ LARDINOIS

At the request of my department, I designed The Voices of Women in Ancient Greek Literature and Society at an advanced level, so that graduate students and advanced undergraduates could take it. Designed as a discussion group or seminar, this course could very well function as a follow-up course to a more general "women in antiquity" course, or as part of a series on women's voices in literature or women in the "other" world.

There are three goals for this course. First, I wish to make students familiar with some of the classical works about women in the ancient world (Sappho, Homer's *Iliad*, Aeschylus' *Oresteia,* etc.), as well as some of the lesser known female poets, whose work has recently been translated and deserves far more attention than it has received so far (Korinna, Telesilla, Praxilla, Erinna, Anyte, Nossis, etc.). Second, I want to examine with the students how women's speeches are represented in the literature and how they relate to the (scarce) information we have about the actual speeches of women in ancient Greek society. In the first half of the course, the students read some genuine women's voices (Sappho and the other female poets) and recent, mostly feminist scholarship on their poetry. In the second half they read speeches of female characters as recorded in literature written by men (Aeschylus, Sophocles, Euripides, Aristophanes), and study the differences between these texts and those of the female poets, again using modern feminist and gender studies.

Last but not least, I wish to expose students to the thoughts and realities of women in a different society than their own. The essayist L. P. Hartley once said that "The past is a foreign country: they do things differently there." Examining the lives of women in the ancient world is, therefore, not that different from studying women's lives in China, India or Iran. There is, however, some advantage to the study of women in the past, because the subject is less controversial or politically charged. When examining the lives of women in the Third World, one is at the same time confronted with issues of race or neocolonialism, and one has to consider how our perception of their lives might influence their realities by tying into debates about foreign aid or the global market place. This complicates the discussion and very often scares students to a degree that they feel uncomfortable saying anything, positive or negative, about the lives of women in the Third World. The study of historical women is less complicated and therefore a good place to start. One need not worry about colonizing the past; if anything, the past has colonized us. It has shaped our modern society. The gender structures of our society are often said to have been inaugurated in ancient Greece. This makes the ancient Greeks both different and the same as us and a very interesting subject of study.

In order to get a better understanding of the historical background against which this material ought to be judged, I assign some of the relevant chapters of Sarah Pomeroy's book on the history of women in classical antiquity, *Goddesses, Whores, Wives, and Slaves: Women in Classical Antiquity*. A more recent textbook, Sue Blundell's *Women in Ancient Greece*, could also be used. If a general women in antiquity course is set as a prerequisite for this course it is possible to do without such a text. All primary texts are read in translation, so students from different departments can take the course. The amount of secondary readings is deliberately kept rather small, because most of this material is theoretically quite complex.

My participation in the Ways of Reading project was a great help to me in designing this particular course. Originally I wanted to start the course with the literature written by men, and then present the women's poetry as a reaction to this, but Jacquelyn Zita, head of the women's studies department at the University of Minnesota, convinced me to reverse the order and have students read the women's poetry first and then present the male adaptations of the female voice as a reaction. My main reason for the original plan was that I believed the students needed the information about the dominant culture, provided by the male texts, before being able to appreciate the women poets. But part of the cultural background is now filled in by having the students read the relevant chapters in Pomeroy's book, and part of it I could provide in class before or during the discussion. After I taught the course for the first time, I asked the students if they thought it would have been better to begin with the male texts and then to proceed to the female poets. They unanimously agreed that the women's poetry should come first. One of the students wrote in her evaluation of the course: "I would keep the reading list arranged as it was for this class: I thought that the fragmentary state of the lyric poetry and the fragmentary glimpses of real women in this poetry encouraged a kind of reading-as-cultural-detective that was also useful in approaching the dramas. We read the dramas differently, I think, than we would have if we had read them first."

I also benefited from the common readings we did with the Ways of Reading group, and I assigned several articles to my students that I first had read with the group, including the articles by Leila Ahmed and Azar Tabari. Finally, I profited from the visits by outside speakers to our group, in particular the visit by Natalie Kampen, a classical art historian and head of the women's studies program at Barnard College, who discussed with us some of the similarities between the study of historical women and women in the Third World. She also encouraged us to include a historical segment in the international feminist theory course we were designing collectively.

As a result of some of these discussions in my group, I open the first week with the usual introductory lecture, followed by a discussion of one of the first chapters of Pomeroy's book on the history of women in antiquity and two complementary articles by Ahmed and Tabari on the lives of women in Iran. Ahmed tries to explain the presence of the veil, the harem, and polygamy—three practices that are also found in ancient Greece—from an Islamic perspective and as not necessarily offensive to women. Tabari responds from a more essentialist and universalist perspective and condemns all three practices as oppressing women. I deliberately placed these two articles at the beginning of the course in order to make students aware of the similarity between the study of women in a different geographical culture and in the historical past.

The rest of the course is arranged more or less chronologically, except that the women poets of the fifth century B.C.E and the Hellenistic world (week 5) are discussed right after Sappho to create one block of original women's writings followed by another block of literature about women written by men (weeks 6 through 10). Week 2 opens with a discussion of some famous women's laments in Homer's *Iliad,* coupled again with a modern anthropological study (by J. Dubisch) and with a chapter from a book by Gail Holst-Warhaft, who compares ancient Greek with modern Greek laments. Both recognize in the lament a typical female speech genre that women could use to express their dissatisfaction with society. Some of the laments by female characters in the *Iliad* can be read in the same way, but questions arise as to the degree of social protest that could be voiced in laments, the ritual nature (and expectancy) of this protest, and the degree to which such protest was taken seriously or could change the lives of women. A discussion of the role of female lament passages in a male-authored text such as the *Iliad* may be deferred to the second half of the course.

The second part of the second week is devoted to the ubiquitous presence of women's choruses in ancient Greece together with a reading of the relevant chapters of Eva Stehle's recent book, *Performance and Gender in Ancient Greece* (1997). Stehle signals the paradoxical use of women—who otherwise lacked a public voice and were generally kept out of the public eye—in public performances, where they were meant to represent the community. This segment also raises questions as to the scripted nature of such performances (most of the songs they performed were written by men) and the genuine opportunity this afforded women to speak their mind.

The next three weeks are dedicated to the women poets, starting with Sappho. In this segment students look at the kinds of issues and ideas expressed in female-authored poetry and learn to distinguish among feminist, nonfeminist, and woman-identified writing. Sappho has been labeled the most feminist of all the female Greek poets, but can one judge her poetry independently of the time and place for which it was written? This problem is neatly brought out in two dueling articles by Judith Hallett and Eva Stehle, which are assigned for the second half of the third week. Hallett argues that Sappho's poetry is not very revolutionary if viewed in its own place and time, but Stehle accuses Hallett of being not sensitive enough to Sappho's distinctive female and lesbian voice, which she believes is transcultural and universal. Similar differences of opinion exist about the writings of the other female poets, whose poetry is discussed in the fifth week.

After this segment we turn to the male-authored texts in order to see how the voices attributed to women in this type of poetry differ from those expressed by women themselves. I have selected some of the best known Greek tragedies, which at the same have attracted the attention of feminist scholars, and one famous comedy of Aristophanes, *Lysistrata,* but I start with the slightly older *Homeric Hymn to Demeter,* which was probably composed by a male poet but has as its center a mother who grieves over the rape of her daughter. This text is now available in the excellent edition with commentary and accompanying essays by Helene Foley (1994).

In the last week (week 10) I assign three articles by Froma Zeitlin, Mark Griffith, and Amy Richlin to help close the discussion. They address the significance of female characterizations for the authors and male viewers of Greek tragedy, and the assessment of the lives of ancient Greek women in modern classical scholarship. I have designed this course for a ten-week quarter period, but it can easily be expanded to cover a full semester. In teaching the course I discovered that it would be better to devote two weeks instead of one to the women poets of fifth-century Greece and the women poets of the Hellenistic world, and it may also be advisable to add another comedy of Aristophanes, such as the *Thesmaphoriazousae* (with Froma Zeitlin's article on this play; see additional bibliography). Two interesting male-authored texts from the Hellenistic and Roman period are Theocritus' *Idyll* 15, which can be read together with Frederick T. Griffiths' article (see additional bibliography), and Alciphron, Letters 4.1 ("Phyrne to Praxiteles"), to be read with Patricia Rosenmeyer's article in *Making Silence Speak: Women's Voices in Greek Literature and Society,* eds. A. Lardinois and L. McClure (see additional bibliography). Rosenmeyer's article may be coupled with an article by Raffaella Cribiore on some genuine letters of Greek women from Roman Egypt in the same volume.

When I taught this course for the first time, it was a great success. Eleven students enrolled, about half graduate and half advanced undergraduate students, most from the classics department; two undergraduates came from comparative literature and two graduates from the master of liberal arts program at the University of Minnesota. Several students reported in an anonymous survey that it was the best course they had ever taken at the university, and a number of them said that they had never been exposed to feminist reading of women's poetry before. Clearly, such courses are needed.

Course Description

The aim of this course is to study the voices of women in ancient Greek literature and society, in particular their public voices. A central question will be how women's speeches are represented in the literature and how they relate to the information we have about the actual speeches of women in ancient Greek society. In the first half of the course we will be reading some genuine women's voices (Sappho and the other female poets) and recent, mostly feminist, scholarship on their poetry. In the second half we will be reading speeches of female characters as recorded in literature written by men (Homer, Aeschylus, Sophocles, Euripides, Aristophanes) and looking for the differences between these texts and those of the female poets, again using modern feminist and gender studies. In order to get a better understanding of the historical background against which this material ought to be judged, we will also be reading the secondary sources as indicated below. All primary texts will be read in translation.

Required Texts

Robert Fagles (tr.), *Sophocles: The Three Theban Plays*, Harmondsworth: Penguin Books, 1984.

Helene P. Foley, *The Homeric Hymn to Demeter*, Princeton, N.J.: Princeton University Press, 1994.

Jeffrey Henderson (tr.), *Aristophanes' Lysistrata*, Newburyport, Mass.: Focus, 1988.

Richmond Lattimore (tr.), *Aeschylus I: The Oresteia*, Chicago: University of Chicago Press, 1953 etc.

A. J. Podlecki (tr.), *Euripides' Medea*, Newburyport, Mass.: Focus, 1996, revised edition.

Sarah B. Pomeroy, *Goddesses, Whores, Wives and Slaves*, New York: Schocken Books, 1975.

Diane J. Rayor, *Sappho's Lyre: Archaic Lyric and Women Poets of Ancient Greece*, Berkeley: University of California Press, 1991.

Week 1

Introduction: The Past as a Foreign Country

READINGS: POMEROY, CHAPTER 2: "WOMEN IN THE BRONZE AGE AND HOMERIC EPIC"; LEILA AHMED, "WESTERN ETHNOCENTRISM AND PERCEPTIONS OF THE HAREM," FEMINIST STUDIES *8 (1982): 521–34;* AZAR TABARI, "THE WOMEN'S MOVEMENT IN IRAN: A HOPEFUL ANALYSIS," FEMINIST STUDIES *12 (1986): 343–60.*

Week 2

Keening Helen: Laments in the Iliad
READINGS: A. CARAVELI, "THE BITTER WOUNDING: THE LAMENT AS SOCIAL PROTEST IN RURAL

GREECE," IN GENDER AND POWER IN RURAL GREECE, ED. J. DUBISCH (PRINCETON, N.J.: PRINCETON UNIVERSITY PRESS, 1986), 169–94; GAIL HOLST-WARHAFT, DANGEROUS VOICES: WOMEN'S LAMENT AND GREEK LITERATURE, CHAPTER 4: "MOURNING IN A MAN'S WORLD" (LONDON AND NEW YORK: ROUTLEDGE, 1992), 98–126; HAND-OUT OF LAMENT PASSAGES IN THE ILIAD (18.35–64, 19.282–302, 22.460–515, 24.707–87).

Women's Choruses

READINGS: RAYOR, PP. 31–37 AND 150–55 (THE FRAGMENTS OF ALKMAN); POMEROY, CHAPTER 3: "THE DARK AGE AND THE ARCHAIC PERIOD," 32–48; EVA STEHLE, PERFORMANCE AND GENDER IN ANCIENT GREECE (PRINCETON, N.J.: PRINCETON UNIVERSITY PRESS, 1997), 27–39 AND 71–113.

Week 3

Sappho I: The Poems and Testimonia

READINGS: RAYOR, PP. 51–81 (THE FRAGMENTS OF SAPPHO); D. A. CAMPBELL, GREEK LYRIC, VOL. I (CAMBRIDGE, MASS.: HARVARD UNIERSITY. PRESS, 1982), 2–51.

Sappho II: Teacher or Rebel?

READINGS: JUDITH P. HALLETT, "SAPPHO AND HER SOCIAL CONTEXT," SIGNS 4 (1979):447–64; EVA STIGERS [STEHLE], "ROMANTIC SENSUALITY, POETIC SENSE: A RESPONSE TO HALLETT ON SAPPHO," SIGNS 4 (1979): 465–71.

Week 4

Sappho III: A Woman's Voice

READINGS: MARILYN B. SKINNER, "WOMAN AND LANGUAGE IN ANCIENT GREECE, OR, WHY SAPPHO IS A WOMAN," IN FEMINIST THEORY AND THE CLASSICS, EDS. NANCY SORKIN RABINOWITZ AND AMY RICHLIN (LONDON AND NEW YORK: ROUTLEDGE, 1993), 125–44; J. J. WINKLER, THE CONSTRAINTS OF DESIRE: THE ANTHROPOLOGY OF SEX AND GENDER IN ANCIENT GREECE, CHAPTER 6: "DOUBLE CONSCIOUSNESS IN SAPPHO'S LYRICS" (LONDON AND NEW YORK: ROUTLEDGE, 1990), 162–87; LILA ABU-LUGHOD, VEILED SENTIMENTS: HONOR AND POETRY IN A BEDOUIN SOCIETY, CHAPTER 7: "MODESTY AND THE POETRY OF LOVE" (BERKELEY: UNIVERSITY OF CALIFORNIA PRESS, 1986), 208–32, 294–95.

Sappho IV: Sappho and the Other

READINGS: RAYOR, PP. 15–20 AND 91–100 (SOME FRAGMENTS OF ARCHILOCHUS, IBYKOS, AND ANAKREON); EVA STIGERS [STEHLE], "SAPPHO'S PRIVATE WORLD," IN REFLECTIONS OF WOMEN IN ANTIQUITY, ED. HELENE P. FOLEY (NEW YORK: GORDON AND BREACH, 1981), 45–61.

Week 5

Women Poets of Fifth-Century Greece

READINGS: RAYOR, PP. 109–21 (KORINNA, TELESILLA, PRAXILLA); MARILYN B. SKINNER, "CORINNA OF TANAGRA AND HER AUDIENCE," TULSA STUDIES IN WOMEN'S LITERATURE 2 (1983): 9–20; D. J. RAYOR, "KORINNA: GENDER AND THE NARRATIVE TRADITION," ARETHUSA 26 (1993): 219–31.

Women Poets of the Hellenistic World

READINGS: RAYOR, PP. 121–141 (ERINNA, ANYTE, NOSSIS, MOIRO, HEDYLA, MELINNO); POMEROY, CHAPTER 7: "HELLENISTIC WOMEN"; MARILYN B. SKINNER, "NOSSIS THELYGLOSSIS: THE PRIVATE TEXT AND THE PUBLIC BOOK," IN WOMEN'S HISTORY AND ANCIENT HISTORY, ED. SARAH B. POMEROY (CHAPEL HILL: UNIVERSITY OF NORTH CAROLINA PRESS, 1991), 20–47.

Week 6

Mid-term Exam

Women and Ritual: The Homeric Hymn to Demeter, Part I

READING: FOLEY, PP. 3–75.

Week 7

Women and Ritual: The Homeric Hymn to Demeter, Part II.

READING: FOLEY, PP. 79–151.

Aeschylus' Oresteia, Part I

READINGS: LATTIMORE, PP. 1–131; POMEROY, CHAPTER 4: "WOMEN AND THE CITY OF ATHENS."

Week 8

Aeschylus' Oresteia, Part II

READINGS: LATTIMORE, PP. 135–71; FROMA I. ZEITLIN, PLAYING THE OTHER: GENDER AND SOCIETY IN CLASSICAL GREEK LITERATURE, CHAPTER 3: "THE DYNAMICS OF MISOGYNY: MYTH AND MYTHMAKING IN AESCHYLUS' ORESTEIA" (CHICAGO: UNIVERSITY OF CHICAGO PRESS, 1996), 87–119.

Sophocles' Antigone

READINGS: FAGLES, PP. 35–128; POMEROY, CHAPTER 5: "PRIVATE LIFE IN CLASSICAL ATHENS," AND CHAPTER 6: "IMAGES OF WOMEN IN THE LITERATURE OF CLASSICAL ATHENS," 93–103; CHRISTIANE

SOURVINOU-INWOOD, "ASSUMPTIONS AND THE CREATION OF MEANING: READING SOPHOCLES' ANTIGONE," JOURNAL OF HELLENIC STUDIES 109 (1989): 134–48.

Week 9

Euripides' Medea

READINGS: POMEROY, CHAPTER 6: "IMAGES OF WOMEN IN THE LITERATURE OF CLASSICAL ATHENS," 103–12; BERND SEIDENSTICKER, "WOMEN ON THE TRAGIC STAGE," IN HISTORY, TRAGEDY, THEORY: DIALOGUES ON ATHENIAN DRAMA, ED. BARBARA GOFF (AUSTIN: UNIVERSITY OF TEXAS PRESS, 1995), 151–73.

Aristophanes' Lysistrata

READINGS: POMEROY, CHAPTER 6: "IMAGES OF WOMEN IN THE LITERATURE OF CLASSICAL ATHENS," 112–19; NICOLE LORAUX, THE CHILDREN OF ATHENA, CHAPTER 4: "THE COMIC ACROPOLIS: ARISTOPHANES' LYSISTRATA" (PRINCETON, N.J.: PRINCETON UNIVERSITY PRESS, 1993), 147–83.

Week 10

Women in Drama

READING: FROMA I. ZEITLIN, PLAYING THE OTHER: GENDER AND SOCIETY IN CLASSICAL GREEK LITERATURE, CHAPTER 8: "PLAYING THE OTHER: THEATER, THEATRICALITY AND THE FEMININE IN GREEK DRAMA" (CHICAGO: UNIVERSITY OF CHICAGO PRESS, 1996), 341–74; MARK GRIFFITH, "ANTIGONE AND HER SISTER(S): EMBODYING WOMEN IN GREEK TRAGEDY," IN MAKING SILENCE SPEAK: WOMEN'S VOICES IN GREEK LITERATURE AND SOCIETY, EDS. A. LARDINOIS AND L. MCCLURE (PRINCETON, N.J.: PRINCETON UNIVERSITY PRESS, 2001), 117–36.

Final Discussion

READING: AMY RICHLIN, "THE ETHNOGRAPHER'S DILEMMA AND THE DREAM OF A LOST GOLDEN AGE," IN FEMINIST THEORY AND THE CLASSICS, EDS. NANCY SORKIN RABINOWITZ AND AMY RICHLIN (LONDON AND NEW YORK: ROUTLEDGE, 1993), 272–303.

Additional Bibliography

Sue Blundell, *Women in Ancient Greece*, Cambridge, Mass.: Harvard University Press, 1995.

Raffaella Cribiore, "Windows on a Woman's World: Some Letters from Roman Egypt," in *Making Silence Speak: Women's Voices in Greek Literature and Society*, eds. A. Lardinois and L. McClure (Princeton, N.J.: Princeton University Press, 2001), 223–39.

Frederick T. Griffiths, "Home Before Lunch: The Emancipated Woman in Theocritus," in *Reflections of Women in Antiquity*, ed. Helene P. Foley (New York: Gordon and Breach Science Publishers, 1981), 247–73.

Patricia A. Rosenmeyer, "(In-)Versions of Pygmalion: The Statue Talks Back," in *Making Silence Speak: Women's Voices in Greek Literature and Society*, eds. A.

Lardinois and L. McClure (Princeton, N.J.: Princeton University Press, 2001), 240–60.

Froma I. Zeitlin, "Travesties of Gender and Genre in Aristophanes' Thesmophoriazousae," in *Playing the Other: Gender and Society in Classical Greek Literature* (Chicago: University of Chicago Press, 1996), 375–416.

An excellent overview of available material for further reading can be found at "Diotima: Materials for the Study of Women and Gender in the Ancient World" on the World Wide Web at http://www.stoa.org./diotima/.

LATIN AMERICAN AND LATINA WOMEN DRAMATISTS

WILMA FELICIANO

The twelve plays in this course share the common goal of creating a
public space for female voices and visions. With rare exceptions, theater has been almost exclusively male dominated. Critics and impre-
sarios once believed that the discipline, rationality, and rigorous
structures required of drama were anathema to women's "innate" sensibility and emotionalism. Feminine orality and creativity were relegated to intimate genres such as letters, poems, and stories shared in
domestic spaces. Since the 1950s, however, women dramatists have
claimed their right to analyze social conflicts, to question the traditions of society and theater, and to stage their concerns in open
forums from a feminine-feminist perspective.

In Latin America, the home of *machismo*, patriarchy still prevails
and the angel-demon dichotomy summarizes the prevalent image of
womanhood. Consequently, women dramatists write to deconstruct
the myths and stereotypes that limit women's freedom of social movement and creative expression. Their plays reveal how ancestral paradigms of male superiority silence women's voices and suppress their
concerns. The twelve dramatists to be studied come from varied landscapes from Buenos Aires to Los Angeles; nine of them still participate
in their national theaters. With one exception, the plays were staged
between 1958 and 1998, and all represent multiple themes. Their dramatic structures range from classic comedy and modern realism to the
avant garde techniques of Artaudian ritualism, Brechtian alienation,
and metadramatic game-playing. Collectively, they affirm a woman's
right to define her own identity and vision of reality, to challenge the
gender assumptions that suppress women, and to defy patriarchal
authority in both familial and national domains. These playwrights
understand the power of words to redefine the terms of the battle of
the sexes, and resort to irony, parody, and humor to subvert established norms, transgress taboos, and promote social change.

PRIMARY TEXTS

In the process of developing the course Latin American and Latina
Women Dramatists, I had to determine the best mix of plays that would
expose my students to a wide range of themes, styles, structures, ideologies, geographical regions, and time periods. The selection of

Mexican, Puerto Rican, Argentine, and Latina playwrights combines my research interests and the major centers of dramatic activity. To avoid the portrayal of woman as victim, I selected plays with strong female characters, women who defy their limitations even if they are ultimately defeated.

Mexican drama was the natural point of departure. The historical drama of conquest, colonization, and *mestizaje* (racial and cultural fusion) resulted in a parallel fusion of Spanish and Native American patriarchal systems. Moreover, Mexico was the birthplace of Sor Juana Inés de la Cruz (1648?–1695), author of *Los empeños de una casa* (*The House of Trials*), a nun, and the first feminist of the Americas in all genres.[1] When she reverses the Renaissance tradition of women in trouser roles and dresses Castaño, *el gracioso* (the dark-skinned comic servant), in a noblewoman's clothes, Sor Juana mocks the pretensions of the nobility while she criticizes predatory male behavior and female passivity. Like Sor Juana, her feminist exemplar, Rosario Castellanos was mainly a poet. Her wildly absurd farce, *El eterno femenino* (*The Eternal Feminine*), uses Brechtian techniques and an episodic structure to demolish the rigid roles imposed on women under the guise of feminine ideals. Instead of an illusionist comedy that seeks to imitate reality, the situations are as foolish as the women forced to live them.

In *Los frutos caídos* (Fallen Fruit) Luisa Josefina Hernández also confronts female passivity and forces a professional, twice-divorced woman in conflict with her extended family to redirect her life. Romantic expectations would lead the protagonist toward a third marriage. Celia, however, rejects her lover, not for fear of social opprobrium, but as the less destructive of two bad choices. Elena Garro's *La dama boba* (Lady Simpleton) rewrites Lope de Vega's classic comedy of the Spanish Golden Age to criticize the double marginalization of Indian women with a subtle metadramatic structure that chides the Europeanized, urban values of modern Mexico. To undermine the popular appeal of folk heroes like Pancho Villa, Sabina Berman rewrites the history of the Mexican Revolution in *Entre Villa y una mujer desnuda* (*Between Pancho Villa and a Naked Woman*). By deriding Villa's supposed construction of nationhood and his legendary womanizing, Berman subverts historiography and *machismo*. Three centuries after Sor Juana argued for the intellectual and social liberation of women, the social construction of gender roles continues.

The burning issue of Puerto Rican identity is more political than gendered. The abrasive and unequal relationship between the island and the United States dominates the creative arts and daily life. Myrna Casas, for example, draws an analogy between the vagabond troupe of theater players and their threadbare circus to the people and their socio-political duality in *El gran circo eukraniano* (*The Great Uskrainian Circus*).[2] While feminist concerns are not highlighted,

Gabriela José, the protagonist, is an androgynous figure who prefers to mother her players than to reclaim the son she abandoned. In Teresa Marichal's *Paseo al atardecer* (*Evening Walk*), a flamboyant feminist writer debunks fairy tales and vows to rewrite the canon. Her rebellion, however, becomes rhetoric compared to the transgression of the woman rocking the baby carriage, her interlocutor on the park bench. The mother has murdered the baby son her husband forced her to bear as a condition of matrimonial harmony. As a mirror to society, these plays project twisted images of everyday life on "the Isle of Enchantment." The implication is that by abandoning their maternal Spanish heritage, Puerto Ricans have become cultural orphans.

Set during the 1840s dictatorship of Juan Manuel de Rosas, Griselda Gambaro's *La malasangre* (*Bad Blood*), a portrayal of domestic and political despotism, alludes to the tyranny of Argentina's "dirty war" against its own citizens from 1976 to 1983. Despite her ultimate defeat, the rebellion of Dolores against her father has direct political implications for the present. Also written during the dirty war, . . . *y a otra cosa mariposa* (. . . *And That's Enough of That!*), by Susana Torres Molina, uses the metatheatrical device of transvestism to turn the myth of the Argentine macho inside out. The play dramatizes how girls dressed as boys acquire the violence, discourse, and bravado of males, then become girls again, an allusion to female complicity in patriarchal oppression. The playful structure, confusion of identities, and homosexual nuances suggest that identity and gender are fluid constructs. Likewise, Diana Raznovich humorously redefines the mother-daughter relationship in *Casa Matriz* (*Dial-a-Mom*). This hilarious comedy based on the absurd premise that one may rent a mother to role-play various relationships probes the bewildering tugs of the umbilical cord. Argentine feminist drama continuously strives to shatter the pervasive icons of womanhood and to propose alternative images.

Displacement, language, ethnicity, and body image form the conflicts and conjunctions in woman's search for identity in the comedies of Latina playwrights. Suspended between the conflicting values of their homelands and those of American society, their characters struggle to emulate traditional role models without violating their individuality. As her double name demonstrates, Millie/Milagros, the Nuyorican protagonist of Dolores Prida's *Botánica*, incarnates the ambivalence of living in multiple worlds simultaneously.[3] Josefina López challenges immigration policy and Barbie-like body images from the confines of a sweatshop. The American Dream is achieved when one sister becomes an entrepreneur and the other a writer who asserts that *Real Women Have Curves*. In these comedies, laugh-a-line dialogue and popular culture (music, proverbs, ethnic foods) provide the means for cultural nourishment and personal introspection. They affirm the quest for self-definition by asserting the strength derived by individuals from their culture. No wonder these plays had long runs at the Spanish Repertory Theater in New York City.

PEDAGOGICAL ISSUES

In order to appreciate plays by contemporary Latin American women writers, students must have at least a cursory understanding of the origins of Western drama and the relationship between religion, ritual, and drama. By necessity, then, the course begins with the trajectory from Greco-Roman drama to the modern techniques introduced by Bertold Brecht and Antonin Artaud, among others. Also, unlike other literary genres composed to be read by the individual in silence, drama belongs to the performing arts, written for stage production and representation. As a result, students must understand such concepts as Aristotelian poetics, Brecht's alienation theory, metadramatic techniques, theatricality, and spectacle. Acquiring the concepts and skills of dramatic analysis, however, poses challenges beyond assimilating the lexicon of critical theory. Students must be trained to analyze both literature and theatricality: to imagine the stage, animate the characters, and visualize the action as they read the text. They must learn to "stage the play" in their imaginations, and articulate their interpretations in Spanish. Finally, before students can approach the material from a feminist perspective, they must examine their assumptions and deconstruct "man" as the measure of universal truth and aesthetic value. As much as possible, our class discussions are gender inclusive, culturally contrastive, and values neutral as we explore the socio-historical mores, philosophical concepts, and artistic merits of the plays. As a final project, students must apply the concepts and techniques learned to analyze a play not discussed in class, support their interpretations with outside sources, and present their findings in an oral presentation and a term paper. Students are encouraged to include discussions of class, ethnicity, religion, and gender in the analysis of female and male characters, and to adopt a comparative, cross-cultural perspective of the relationship of the women to their society. My goal is not to teach literary or feminist theory, but to have students appreciate how drama, the most social and accessible of all art forms, reflects our individual and social conflicts by creating images that are linguistic, dynamic, and visceral.[4]

Initially, I want my students to analyze how the women in these plays confront the universal struggle for equity, respect, and self-affirmation in culture-specific ways. Instead of purity, fidelity, humility, self-sacrifice, and patience—the feminine ideals of Latin American culture—the plays propose alternate images and lifestyles that encourage women to reinvent themselves and become agents of their circumstances. Several plays explore taboo subjects such as recasting motherhood and revising heterosexual mores. Moreover, while gender and social issues are paramount, the plays explore specific regional concerns: race, class, and historiography in Mexico; political tyranny in Argentina; political and cultural ambiguity in Puerto Rico; psychic and physical displacement among U.S. Latinas. In sum, these dramatists claim a public stage of their own to represent Latin American reality using the detailed nuances of theatricality and the flavors of dialogue first savored around the kitchen table. To articulate the discourse in a female voice, the playwrights challenge the canons of literature and history. By rewriting the socio-historical narratives imposed on women across time and geography, the dramatists dismantle the stereotypes of womanhood to create more freedom of action for contemporary women. Ultimately, my goal is to encourage students to examine their own values and lifestyles, to write their own narratives, and to construct more expansive social roles for themselves.

NOTES

1. Sor Juana's play, *Los empeños,* was first performed in the late 1600s in the viceregal court, Mexico City.
2. Italicized translations of titles are available in English; *Women Writing Women* by Cajiao Salas and Vargas includes *The Great Uskrainian Circus*, *Evening Walk*, and *Dial-a-Mom*.
3. The title *Botánica* has multiple meanings derived from its roots in Afro-Caribbean worship. Here it is a shop that dispenses medicinal and magical herbs and potions; religious figures and candles; and amorous, familial, and interpersonal advice.
4. Latin American and Latina Women Dramatists is a three credit graduate seminar. Most of the students are secondary school teachers of Spanish working on master's degrees or qualified undergraduate seniors majoring in Spanish or Latin American studies.

Syllabus for Graduate Seminar
Goals
- To analyze feminine or feminist plays written from the 1950s to the 1990s in Mexico, Puerto Rico, Argentina, and Latina United States;
- to learn how to "stage" texts in the imagination: to create mental images of the stage, envision the dress and demeanor of the actors, imagine their actions and reactions, and decode their discourses and silences critically;
- to trace the socio-historical and economic origins of the subordination of women, and examine the impact of race, class, and religion on women's behavior in both private and public domains; and
- to assimilate and utilize various analytical methods: Aristotelian, Brechtian, feminist, and metadramatic criticism.

Primary Readings
Berman, Sabina. *Entre Villa y una mujer desnuda* (1993). México: Gaceta, 1994, 15–85.

Casas, Myrna. *El gran circo eukraniano* (1985). Unpublished ms. English translation in *Women Writing Woman, Teresa* Cajiao Salas and Margarita Vargas (eds.). Albany: State University of New York Press, 1997.

Castellanos, Rosario. *El eterno femenino*. México: Fondo de Cultura Económica, 1974.

Gambaro, Griselda. *La malasangre* (1980). In *Dramaturgas latinoamericanas contemporáneas*, Elba Andrade and Hilde F. Cramsie (eds.). Madrid: Verbum, 1991, 147–97.

Garro, Elena. *La dama boba* (1958). In *Un hogar sólido y otras piezas.* Xalapa: Universidad Veracruzana, 1983, 171–246.

Hayman, Ronald. *How to Read a Play.* New York: Grove Press, 1977.

Hernández, Luisa Josefina. *Los frutos caídos* (1957). In *Teatro mexicano contemporáneo, Antología,* Fernando de Ita (coord.). México: Fondo de Cultura Económica, 1991, 703–808.

Sor Juana Inés de la Cruz. *Los empeños de una casa* (1683). In *Clásicos del teatro hispanoamericano,* vol. I, Gerardo Luzuriaga and Richard Reeve (comp.). México: Fondo de Cultura Económica, 1994, 155–250.

López, Josefina. *Real Women Have Curves.* Woodstock, Ill: Dramatic Publishing, 1986.

Marichal, Teresa. *Paseo al atardecer* (1984). In *Revista Intermedio de Puerto Rico, Revista de Teatro Puertorriqueño* 2(1) (enero–marzo 1986): 21–39.

Prida. Dolores. *Botánica* (1990). In *Beautiful Señoritas and Other Plays.* Houston: Arte Público Press, 1991.

Raznovich, Diana. *Casa matriz* (1980). Buenos Aires: Ediciones Croquiñol, 1988.

Torres Molina, Susana. *. . .y a otra cosa mariposa* (1981). Buenos Aires: Ed. Búsqueda, 1988.

Secondary Sources

Andrade, Elba, and Hilde Cramsie. "Estudio preliminar." Madrid: Verbum, 1991, 15–24.

Cohen, Deb. "Defining and Defying 'Woman' in Four Plays by Luisa Josefina Hernández." *Latin American Theatre Review* 30(2) (Spring 1997): 89–102.

Cypess, Sandra M. "Los géneros re/velados en *Los empeños de una casa* de Sor Juana Inés de la Cruz." *Hispamérica* 22(64–65) (1993): 177–85.

Feliciano, Wilma. "Language and Identity in Three Plays by Dolores Prida." *Latin American Theatre Review* 28(1) (Fall 1994): 125–38.

Feliciano, Wilma. "Myrna Casas: La mujer y el juego metadrámatico." *Revista del Ateneo Puertorriqueño* IV (10–12) (1994): 147–54.

Larson, Catherine. "Lope de Vega and Elena Garro: The Doubling of *La dama boba.*" *Hispania* 74(1) (March 1991): 15–25.

Larson, Catherine. "Playwrights of Passage: Women and Game-Playing on the Stage." *Latin American Literary Review* 19(38) (1991): 77–89.

Magnarelli, Sharon. "Authoring the Scene, Playing the Role: Mother and Daughter in Gambaro's *La malasangre.*" *Latin American Theatre Review* 27(2) (Spring 1994): 5–27.

Magnarelli, Sharon. "Tea for Two: Performing History and Desire in Berman's *Entre Villa y una mujer desnuda.*" *Latin American Theatre Review* 30(1) (Fall 1996): 55–74.

Marrero, Teresa. "*Real Women Have Curves*: The Articulation of Fat as a Cultural/Feminist Issue." *Ollantay* 1(1) (January 1993): 61–70.

Nigro, Kirsten. "Rosario Castellanos' Debunking of the *Eternal Feminine.*" *Journal of Spanish Studies, Twentieth Century* 8(1–2) (1980): 89–102.

Seda, Laurietz. "El hábito no hace al monge: Tranvestismo, homosexualidad y lesbianismo en . . . *y a otra cosa mariposa* de Susana Torres Molina." *Latin American Theatre Review* 30(2) (Spring 1997): 103–14.

Vargas, Margarita. "Introduction," in *Women Writing Women*, Teresa Cajiao Salas and Margarita Vargas (eds.). Albany: State University of New York Press, 1997, 1–15.

Optional Readings

Warhol, Robyn H., and Diane Price Herndl. *Feminisms: An Anthology of Literary Theory and Criticism*. New Brunswick, N.J.: Rutgers University Press, 1997.

Calendar of Readings and Requirements

Week 1. Introduction to Course: History of Western Drama: Origins, Genres and Conventions.

Greek-Roman roots, medieval religious, Golden Age, XIX century, and modern drama. Dramatic analysis, feminist drama: discussion questions (see end of syllabus).

Week 2. Hayman, How to Read.

Vargas, "Introduction" to *Women Writing Women;* Andrade and Cramsie, "Estudio preliminary," 15–24.

Week 3. Sor Juana. Empeños. Classic Comedy.

Cypess, "Los géneros."

Week 4. Castellanos, Eterno. Persistent Stereotypes.

Nigro, "Debunking."

Week 5. Hernández, Frutos. Realism and Feminism.

Cohen, "Defining."

Week 6. Garro, Dama. Rewriting Classic Drama.

Larson, "Lope de Vega."

Week 7. Berman, Entre Villa. Mexican Myth, History and Metadrama.

Magnarelli, "Tea for Two"; Jones, "Writing the Body," 370 (In *Feminisms*, optional).

Week 8. Casas, Gran circo. Puerto Rican Identity and Politics.

Feliciano, "El juego"; Kolodny, "Dancing Through," 171 (*Feminisms*).

Week 9. Take-Home Midterm due.

"Women and Society in Three of the Plays Studied: Comparison and Contrast," three pages, typed, d/s, in Spanish.

Marichal. *Paseo.* Deconstructing Motherhood and the Literary Canon.

Week 10. Gambaro, La malasangre. Domestic and Political Violence.

Magnarelli, "Authoring the Scene"; Cixous, "The Laugh," 347 (*Feminisms*).

Week 11. Torres Molina, . . . y a otra cosa . . .: Game-Playing on Stage.
Seda, "El hábito."
Raznovich, *Casa Matriz*. Redefining the Mother-Daughter Relationship.
Also, title of research project due; play not studied in class.

Week 12. Prida. Botánica. Identity, Ethnicity, and Food.
Feliciano, "Identity"; Anzaldúa, "La conciencia," 765 *(Feminisms)*.
Also bibliography due, minimum seven sources after 1985.

Week 13. López. Real Women Have Curves. Beauty and Body Image.
Marrero, "The Articulation of Fat."
One page outline or abstract in narrative form due; to be returned with feedback.

Week 14. Oral Reports.
Present results of research project. Bring handout with outline and bibliography.

Week 15. Term Paper due.

Discussion Questions
Historical Framework
1. What are the similarities and differences between feminine/feminist drama? How does this drama evolve along a temporal-geographic axis that spans decades, countries, and cultures?
2. What socio-aesthetic changes and continuities accompany this spacial-temporal progression?

Thematic Content
3. How does the author present or develop the common stock of customs, myths, and mores that shapes the cultural construction of gender roles and power relationships?
4. How does she construct the individual identity of female characters within that society and culture?
5. What conflicts and contradictions emerge between individual women and society? What encourages or thwarts women's motivations?
6. What personal factors determine the prevailing issues, images, and conflicts women confront?
7. What external socio-historical factors influence the stage portrayal of women?
8. How do relationships with men, family, other women, social groups, and institutions (especially the church or state) advance or inhibit the potential of female characters?
9. How do others treat women who deviate from societal expectations?
10. How do the lives of Latin American/Latina characters compare with those of their North American/Anglo counterparts?

Discourse Analysis of Linguistic Devices
11. How does the author use irony, humor, and parody to construct womanhood and shape situations?

12. How does male-female discourse differ, especially with regard to sexually taboo subjects?
13. How do the dialectics of language and actions express the contradictions between what the play proposes to tell and what a careful reading reveals?

Theatricality
14. How does mental representation allow the reader to "play" with the play and participate in the game on a visceral as well as intellectual level?

BRIDGING THE BORDERS: LATINA AND LATIN AMERICAN WOMEN WRITERS

ISABEL VALIELA

> *There must be another way that's not named Sappho*
> *or Mesalina or Mary of Egypt*
> *or Magdalene or Clémence Isaure.*
> *Another way to be human and free.*
> *Another way to be.*
> —Rosario Castellanos

> *Hay tantísimas fronteras*
> *que dividen a la gente,*
> *pero por cada frontera*
> *existe también un puente.*
> *(There are so many borders dividing people,*
> *but for every border there's also a bridge.)*
> —Gina Valdés

This course is designed to explore the connecting links, as well as the dividing lines, of women's lives on both sides of the U.S.–Latin America border. Latinas in the United States and in Latin America share a common heritage that has evolved into multiple variants as a result of geographical, historical, economic, social, and cultural factors. Our course focuses on the conditions of women resulting from the intersection of these factors. Equally important are the many ways that women resist and transform the circumstances of their lives, depending on their inner and outer resources.

The primary materials used are mostly literary texts, approximately half fiction and half autobiographies. The required material includes articles and films. The works are grouped in sets that will enhance the possibility of connecting similar issues and realities, hence the title: Bridging the Borders.

There are three thematic sequences: "the Mexicana-Chicana connection," "from isolation to solidarity," and "the Puerto Rican experience." The deep historical roots of the Mexicana-Chicana connection and the symbolic richness of the Mexican-American border create a logical beginning for this course. This theme plunges the students directly into the main questions of identity, displacement, and issues of Latina gender, race, and class. The second sequence moves south of the Mexican border to examine the conditions of Latin American

353

women across lines of race and class, exploring those factors that isolate women and those that provide support and empowerment. This unit explores the significance of Latin American women's participation in social movements and revolutions, even under extreme conditions. The final sequence concentrates on the unique circumstances of Puerto Rican women, particularly regarding the impact of Puerto Rico's Commonwealth status. How women of different classes experience migration and life in the diaspora is the main focus of this segment. Although seemingly unrelated, the three sequences provide a broad spectrum of different experiences, at the same time focusing on common themes. These themes include the colonial legacy, patriarchal social structures and attitudes, the impact of U.S. domestic and international policy, the impact of race and class on gender; women's isolation, women's agency and social participation; women's spaces, and so on. As the course progresses, the students increasingly make connections with previous readings and discussions, and are able to build a substantial conceptual framework around these common themes and their variations.

THE MEXICANA-CHICANA CONNECTION

In this first part of the course we read two Chicana writers: Gloria Anzaldúa and Sandra Cisneros. These are followed by two Mexican writers of very different times: Laura Esquivel and Sor Juana Inés de la Cruz. In this set we also include Leonor Villegas de Magnón who, as a "fronteriza," a native of the Mexico–U.S. border, insisted on identifying with both Mexico and the United States. We also read poetry and essays by Rosario Castellanos, the most well known Mexican feminist of the twentieth century.

The Mexico–U.S. border tells many stories. It began as a historical event that marked the deep divisions between Mexico and the United States. These divisions were multiple: political, economic, cultural, racial, ethnic, linguistic, philosophical. The acquisition of Mexican territory with the Treaty of Guadalupe-Hidalgo (1848) was one of the first and highest manifestations of U.S. expansionist philosophy and sense of Manifest Destiny. The 100,000 Mexican citizens who inhabited that territory at the time suddenly became aliens in their own land. But in spite of the confiscation of this land and other violations experienced under U.S. jurisdiction, they continued to maintain their Mexican identity through their connection to their original culture, and through their interpersonal connections with family, friends, and acquaintances of Mexican descent. Mexican Americans are unique in this experience vis-à-vis the United States. This is the only Latino group that can trace its roots to a geographic area that lies within the United States territorial borders. The persistent connections formed by these roots have created a bridge for future Mexican migrations to the United States.

Therefore, when we speak of Mexican Americans, they may be descendants of the original inhabitants of Aztlán, situated in what is now U.S. territory, or they may be first generation Mexican Americans. They could be the offspring of any combination of generations.

By studying the works of Chicana and Mexican writers we are able to explore the historical and cultural legacies shared by women on both sides of the border and analyze the ways in which each one of them perceives and acts on those legacies. As Gloria Anzaldúa indicates, the border is much more than a political line separating two countries, it has much broader human dimensions (Anzaldúa 1987, preface). The border is political, economic, historical, physical, psychological, cultural, linguistic, and racial. Gender intersects within all of these borders.

The syllabus emphasizes *spaces* as tools for analysis, which allows us to see the Chicana, as well as all the other U.S. Latina experiences, as a juxtaposition of one environment, one culture, one mentality, over another. When Gloria Anzaldúa's mother is asked what her identity is, she responds: "*Soy mejicana,*" along with everyone else who is asked this question in her small border town. Anzaldúa responds: "*Soy Raza*" (Anzaldúa 1987, 62). They live in the United States all their lives, but essentially they remain Mexican, closely connected to land, race, and culture. This is possible because of that juxtaposition in which two totally different peoples can coexist within a single space, with different degrees of assimilation to the Anglo mainstream world, depending on many variables in U.S. society.

A woman's experience becomes even more complex when the gender relations in her original culture combine with the relations of gender, race, and class in the United States. In a sense, Chicanas are victims of multiple colonizations. Anzaldúa describes the development of a male-dominated Aztec society, and how this development, combined with the Spanish conquest, produced a strong strain of machismo and patriarchal domination in Mexican society (Anzaldúa 1987, 33). She speaks of her difficult and multiple liberations from the restrictions imposed by her own original traditional Mexican culture, whose rigidity was exacerbated by the rural small town atmosphere in which she grew up. As a lesbian Chicana and a mestiza, Anzaldúa also has had to face homophobia and racism from within the Euro-American mainstream.

The roots that connect the generations of Mexicans and Mexican Americans are not subject to domination. They are the roots of affirmation, the ones that continually erase the official political border. These elements of culture and ethnicity pass from generation to generation: ways of being, ways of thinking, moving, talking, cooking, eating, making music, making love, facing death, and many other behavior patterns and attitudes. Other roots have less to do with affirmation and much more to do with collective experience and remembrance. One of these, which acts as a link among all Chicanas, is the collective historical experience of conquest and subjugation, violation and displacement. To be an indigenous woman in Mexico during the conquest was to experience a double violation: one based on race, the other on gender. It was a collective and individual violation. To be a mestiza Chicana in the United States is to experience the original double violation of her ancestors under the Spanish conquest, as well as the multiple violations that Chicanas face as they encounter the gender, race, and class attitudes and policies of the Euro-American mainstream society. How Chicanas define their identity is largely determined by their degrees of social consciousness, historical hindsight, and their abilities to counteract the negativity of the mainstream culture.

The Mexican and Mexican American readings explore these multiple layers of subjugation and the ways in which women on both sides of the border negotiate within themselves and with their societies to overcome those obstacles that hinder their development as full human beings. Their consciousness and ability to take control of their lives convince us that identity is political as well as personal. In the lives of many of the women we read about, agency takes its shape from circumstance and surroundings. Sandra Cisneros' *The House on Mango Street* is a coming-of-age fictionalized memoir that closely resembles Cisneros' upbringing in a multiethnic minority neighborhood in Chicago. It is clear that, as her individual consciousness grows, so does her social consciousness as a minority woman within the United States. Her identity is forged in the midst of poverty, human misery, and despair. But she is also surrounded by human beings who relate to each other with love and attention, counteracting the negative forces that would otherwise bring her down. They feed the strength that will deliver her from Mango Street into a world of her own making, her own house (space). But as she matures she realizes that, as a writer, she is her own house, her own strength. Her strength is made evident by her decision to return to Mango Street through her literary work, introducing her readers to her world, and at the same time returning for those who could not leave.

In similar fashion, the Mexican writers Sor Juana Inés de la Cruz and Laura Esquivel deal with restricted spaces and make manifest women's ability to expand those limitations through their own creative powers. In their cases, they are restricted to the two concrete spaces most commonly relegated to women: the kitchen and the convent cell. Their historical settings are in the pre–twentieth century, thus reflecting a much more rigid and traditional framework for women. Nevertheless, both Sor Juana and Tita, the protagonist of *Like Water for Chocolate*, are able to use their inner and outer resources to survive in their restricted spaces. Sor Juana uses her intellect and her connections to powerful people inside the Catholic Church and outside. Tita uses her culinary talents and the intuitive connections to her indigenous culture.

Leonor Villegas de Magnón considers herself both a Mexican and an American. This *fronteriza* identity, along with her upper class upbringing and American private school and college education, has allowed her to make the best of both worlds. During the Mexican Revolution she moved about at her own will and was not restricted by traditional concepts of women's place. The Mexican Revolution, the historical setting for Esquivel's and Villegas' works, allowed women to move beyond traditional expectations. In the character of Gertrudis, Tita's sister, for example, one can observe this fact, as well as in many of the women in Villegas' *The Rebel*.

FROM ISOLATION TO SOLIDARITY

After the Chicana/Mexicana set of readings, we explore the works of women from three different Latin American countries: Chile, Nicaragua, and Guatemala. The two works by María Luisa Bombal move our attention to the ways in which middle and upper class women in Latin America are conditioned to be passive, decorative entities to complement their husbands. In the novella, *The Final Mist*, and the short story, "The Tree," we see how two women brought up in a similar manner manage to survive as thinking, feeling, human beings. Gioconda Belli's *The Inhabited Woman* explores the radical transformations that women of all classes experience when they become politically and socially conscious. *The Inhabited Woman* includes numerous female characters representing various sectors of the population, but the protagonist, Lavinia Alarcón, is an upper class professional architect and member of the Nicaraguan elite. Unlike Bombal's female characters, who are presented as isolated human entities, disconnected from the world of social and political reality, Lavinia lives within a context full of social and economic injustice at every turn. She is forced to shed her former complacency by the urgent circumstances of her country. Gioconda Belli, who participated in the Sandinista movement against the Somoza regime, provides the reader with a wealth of issues dealing with gender, race, class, the military, the revolutionary movement, and how people living under these extreme circumstances deal with all these intersecting factors in their personal lives. To complement this reading, the students read Cheryl Johnson-Odim's article, "Common Themes, Different Contexts: Third World Women and Feminism," which describes the issues that divide First and Third World feminists, as well as the complexity of issues faced by women in developing countries.

I, Rigoberta Menchú logically follows *The Inhabited Woman*, because it also deals with the lives of women under extremely critical social conditions. In this case, however, the reader's attention focuses on indigenous women's participation in revolutionary movements. Rigoberta's activism allows for significant comparative analysis, especially with regard to the tools she uses as weapons against oppression: the Bible and the Spanish language. She uses the Bible to convince her people of the justness of their cause, thus giving it moral leverage. Sor Juana uses the Bible in defense of women's right to knowledge and participation in education. Rigoberta learns the Spanish language so that she can communicate to the broader society and act as a liaison and intermediary in the conflict between indigenous peoples and *ladinos* (mestizos). We can compare this coopting of the language in Rigoberta's case with the co-opting of the English language by Rosario Ferré and Esmeralda Santiago. The use of a dominant language that is not of one's own origin for the purposes of communicating one's reality is one of the many avenues of resistance, a way of reaching out to a wider audience with a linguistic bridge.

Rigoberta's tale of the exploitation of indigenous peoples in the coffee plantations also provides a good point of comparison with the factors that contribute to the exploitation of migrant workers in the United States. The 1992 article by Mines, Boccalandro, and Gabbard, "The Latinization of U.S. Farm Labor," contains many similarities: intolerable living conditions, misleading information in the media about farm workers, their inability to organize for change; the linguistic disadvantage that makes them readily exploitable, and so on. These conditions are a reflection of the larger picture of colonial domination that has left its legacy and kept its grip on our continent through the exploitation of minority populations.

THE PUERTO RICAN EXPERIENCE

The final readings are by two Puerto Rican writers, Rosario Ferré and Esmeralda Santiago. After Mexican Americans, Puerto Ricans constitute the second largest group of Latinos in the United States. This group is significant not only because of its numbers, but because it sheds light on the U.S.–Latino connections in multiple ways. Unlike Chicanos, Puerto Ricans do not in any way trace their roots to the United States. As a matter of fact, one of the most salient characteristics of this group is their difficult adjustment to the United States precisely because they are deeply attached to their native habitat and culture. One of the most common motifs in Puerto Rican literature is the sharp contrast between the cold, impoverished, ugly surroundings of life in New York City contrasted with the memories of the warm, tropical environment of the native island. Yet, when Puerto Ricans fly over to the United States, they fly with an American passport. U.S. citizenship puts Puerto Ricans in a unique position as Latinos in this country. It also puts them in a unique situation with regard to their own homeland. Puerto Rico, as an *estado libre asociado,* is not a sovereign nation or a state, but an arrangement that still operates very much as a colony. The pros and cons of this arrangement can be assessed by its impact on the lives of Puerto Rican people on the island and in the diaspora within the U.S. mainland.

Rosario Ferré's *The House on the Lagoon* is a six-generation family saga set in Puerto Rico. As it weaves the family's history, it also traces the history of Puerto Rico. Family history and Puerto Rican–U.S. relations are interconnected. The family in this book is mostly bourgeois upper class, but as the story unfolds we discover the existence of internal miscegenation across boundaries of race and class. An interesting aspect of the narrative is the point-counter-point of wife and husband as each recalls the same events. The novel is constructed as a family narrative written by a young wife, Isabel, whose husband secretly reads her story and adds his version. This format allows for close attention to gender dynamics in the novel.

Esmeralda Santiago's *When I Was Puerto Rican* is also a family saga, but on a smaller scale. It focuses attention on the poverty experienced by Puerto Ricans in the 1950s, at the height of Puerto Rican migration to the United States. This autobiographical memoir brings into focus the everyday reality of Puerto Rican poverty, in the island's rural and urban environments, as well as in New York City. Its coming-of-age narrative stays focused on a young girl as she experiences the shock of her changing circumstances and slow assimilation into American society.

Both of these works by Puerto Rican women emphasize the intergenerational connections of women in the family as one of their main sources of strength. They both integrate the rural-urban experience in Puerto Rico, as well as the island–New York experience. As they weave all these connections they also show the human impact of U.S. intervention in Puerto Rico.

It is significant that both of these books were originally written in English. Esmeralda Santiago has also translated her own work from English to Spanish. As Edna Acosta-Belén indicates in her article "Rosario Ferré's Crossover Writing" (Acosta-Belén 1996, 30–31), writing in English is a way to subvert the traditional expectations of what constitutes Latin American literature. It is a way of taking control of the language in order to take control of one's life, and the life of one's work. These elements are weapons of empowerment and avenues for inclusion of previously unacceptable realities.

Unlike Chicanas, to whom writing in English is not new, Puerto Ricans have experienced a different type of colonization, one in which the English language was never truly able to penetrate the island population. Their experience vis-à-vis the United States is a more classic case of "distance colonization." The world of Puerto Ricans is divided by a significant physical distance, *el charco,* the puddle, as they ironically call the large body of water they must cross to come to the United States. In spite of the continuous diasporic-island interaction, it is still not the same experience as the Chicano experience, whose land of origin has remained continuously under their feet. Mexican Americans also have a longer history of contact with U.S. society and its English language. Puerto Ricans went from Spanish control to U.S. control without respite. Yet their literature is connected to the

Spanish and Latin American literary tradition. The works of Puerto Rican literary masters are written in Spanish and read in Spanish-American literature classes. Therefore, the act of writing a literary work in English is a new stance and a definite indicator, whether conscious or unconscious, that the colonized subject has mastered the master's instruments and will now write as an equal in the same arena. The works of Ferré and Santiago render concrete reality to U.S. colonialism and intervention. Written in English, by citizens of the United States, they demand a place in the American canon. The fact that both of these authors have translated their own works from Spanish to English and vice-versa opens the spaces of academic studies, as well as popularizes a reality that was once considered remote and unimportant.

PEDAGOGICAL ISSUES

The articles that accompany these texts range in disciplines from literature, to feminist theory, to Latino and Latin American studies. We also show films to further enhance the students' understanding of the material. To do justice to all of these materials we must find the most effective analytical tools and deliver a considerable amount of background in all of these areas. Finding the pedagogical techniques to effectively teach the interdisciplinary aspects of this course is a challenge because it must be kept at an accessible and understandable level for undergraduate students. This difficulty does not necessarily mean that the course is taught on a superficial level. In fact, the broad range of focus with which we approach each work facilitates the students' task of developing their analytical capacities. As they read the material and participate in the class discussions, students experience an increasing awareness of the various factors that influence the lives of Latinas in the United States and Latin America. The interdisciplinary aspect of the course provides depth to their understanding.

Most of the students have had an introductory women's studies course or none at all. Their basic knowledge of Latin America and the U.S. Latino population is minimal. They need to learn the various contexts in which gender issues are shaped in different cultures and different countries so that they can broaden their perspective. An awareness of how gender, race, class, and the colonial experience contribute to the Latina experience is also one of the main factors in understanding these contexts. It was interesting to note how, at the beginning of the course, the students operated on the assumption that they could judge Latina women's experiences from the perspective of their own experiences as young white middle class American women. Certain aspects of Latin American and U.S. Latino cultures were, in their heads, stereotyped and generalized. For example, the concept of *machismo* was generalized as being specifically Latino, not connected to its roots in patriarchal hierarchies of various cultures. It was clearly necessary to emphasize the differences, as well as the commonalities, that exist in such a broad human category as Latinas/os and the concepts that are often associated with them. Dismantling stereotypes was an important task in our class.

Another important task, closely related to the dismantling of stereotypes, was shifting the focus from First World to Third World perspective. This was one of the most vital transformations that occurred during the course. The positive outcome was partly the result of the selection of readings, partly the result of pedagogy, and partly the result of student receptivity. In fact, the course was planned and formatted to facilitate this transformation, hoping to bring forth a consciousness of the factors that divide these two worlds.

With the premise that bridges are points of connection (spaces where differences are negotiated so that a passage may occur) and borders are points of separation (spaces where differences come face to face, where there is proximity without contact) we have directed this course toward an analysis of transgression: a crossing of boundaries. The entire course is organized in a transgressive way. It does not adhere to standard categories and formats. It is not a chronological survey of literature; it is multidisciplinary; it focuses on women's lives and women's actions or agency: the different degrees to which their common heritage, in the United States and in Latin America, has shaped them and led them to seek different ways of coping with and transforming that reality. Students study jointly U.S. Latino and Latin American realities, topics that have not been studied sufficiently as a connected unit in the past. I assign texts that often mix genre categories. The course could be defined as a women's studies course, a Latin American, or a Latino studies course. It is transgressive not for the sake of transgression, but for the sake of exploring other bridges, other connecting links that have been previously ignored.

The use of the borders-bridges motif lends itself to an analysis of spaces on many levels: psychological, geographical, political, social, and so on. The format and analytical devices of the course point toward a new approach that focuses on Latinas on both sides of the border as they struggle to create spaces where they can live full lives, negotiating between submission and transgression on multiple fronts. The border-bridges motif also leads us to the interstices that defy traditional or conventional boundaries of national, racial, class, and gender relations. Often, these interstices are the spaces where the marginalized negotiate their survival. To understand the power dynamics involved in the relationship between colonial power and colonial subjects, state violence and the victims of state violence, the United States and Latinos, the United States and Latin America, men and women, rich and poor, Euro-Americans and Americans of color, Anglos and Hispanics, it is necessary to focus on the interstices where reality is not defined by the established order. They are democratic spaces where power does not determine the reality of an individual or collective life. Here the disempowered fight back with their own resources to create the bridge to a better life.

CHANGING INSTITUTIONAL STRUCTURES

The works of U.S. Latinos/as written in English, or mostly English with some Spanish, are new additions to American literature. They expose the reality of a long-held American secret: its history of colonization and intervention in the Americas. To write is to make evident a reality, and the language with which we write is part of the evidence. If these works are not included in the American menu of any curriculum, then we must ask why there is no place for them in academic departments. They can no longer be relegated to a crack between English and Spanish departments. As long as there is no space for the study of the Latino experience in English, history, and Latin American studies departments, there will be a need to create a separate Latino enclave in academia. I was able to teach this course as a core course in women's studies at Gettysburg College that fulfills a humanities requirement. In this case, the women's studies program provided a space for a course that reflected its interest in the study of women's global issues. But where would this course have been accepted if it had not been restricted to women writers? Logically, it would have been eligible for inclusion in a Latin American studies program, providing that the program included Latinos in the United States as part of the Latin American realm. The issue of introducing previously excluded areas of study is being raised on campuses all over the nation. Much of the controversy is a manifestation of the larger society's inability to assimilate the growing changes that challenge the fixed national, economic, racial, gender, and class boundaries that have been in place uncontested for a long time. When space remains restricted because of exclusionary policies, then there is a need for a proliferation of separate spaces that will accommodate those who are excluded. Social reality has a way of shifting regularly, and entities structured around fixed categories reflecting that reality tend to need periodic self-evaluation and restructuring. The academic curriculum must follow, not define, the realities that it strives to study and teach.

SELECTED REFERENCES

Acosta-Belén, Edna, ed. 1986. *The Puerto Rican Woman: Perspectives on Culture, History, and Society.* New York: Praeger.

———. 1996. "Rosario Ferré's Crossover Writing." *The Latino Review of Books* 2 (2): 30–31.

Acosta-Belén, Edna, and Christine E. Bose, eds. 1993. *Researching Women in Latin America and the Caribbean.* Boulder: Westview Press.

Acosta-Belén, Edna, and Carlos Santiago. 1995. "Merging the Borders: The Remapping of America." *The Latino Review of Books* 1 (1): 2–12.

Anzaldúa, Gloria. 1987. *Borderlands/La Frontera: The New Mestiza.* San Francisco: Aunt Lute Books.

Belli, Gioconda. 1994. *The Inhabited Woman,* Willimantic, Conn.: Curbstone Press.

Bombal, María Luisa. 1988. *New Islands and Other Stories.* Ithaca, N.Y.: Cornell University Press.

Brittin, Alice A. 1995. "Close Encounters of the Third World Kind: Rigoberta Menchú and Elisabeth Burgos's *Me llamo Rigoberta Menchú.*" *Latin American Perspectives* 22 (4) (Fall): 100–114.

Castellanos, Rosario. 1988a. "Once Again Sor Juana." In M. Ahern, ed., *A Rosario Castellanos Reader,* 222–225. Austin: University of Texas Press.

———. 1988b. "Self-Sacrifice Is a Mad Virtue." In M. Ahern, ed., *A Rosario Castellanos Reader,* 259–263. Austin: University of Texas Press.

Cisneros, Sandra. 1991. *The House on Mango Street.* New York: Vintage Books.

Cruz, Sor Juana Inés de la. 1987. *A Woman of Genius: The Intellectual Autobiography of Sor Juana Inés de la Cruz,* trans. and introduction by Margaret Sayers Peden. Second edition. Salisbury, Conn.: Limestone Press.

Esquivel, Laura. 1992. *Like Water for Chocolate.* New York: Doubleday.

Ferré, Rosario. 1995. *The House on the Lagoon.* New York: Plume.

Glenn, Kathleen M. 1994. "Postmodern Parody and Culinary-Narrative Art in Laura Esquivel's *Como agua para chocolate.*" *Chasqui: Revista de literatura latinoamericana,* Swarthmore, Pa.

Jaquette, Jane, ed. 1989. *The Women's Movement in Latin America.* Boston: Unwin Hyman.

Jehenson, Myriam Yvonne. 1995. *Latin-American Women Writers: Class, Race, and Gender.* Albany: State University of New York Press.

Johnson-Odim, Cheryl. 1991. "Common Themes, Different Contexts: Third World Women and Feminism." In Chandra Mohanty, Ann Russo, and Lourdes Torres, eds., *Third World Women and the Politics of Feminism,* 314–327. Bloomington: Indiana University Press.

Menchú, Rigoberta. 1984. *I, Rigoberta Menchú, an Indian Woman in Guatemala,* ed. Elisabeth Burgos-Debray. New York: Verso.

Mines, Richard, Beatriz Boccalandro, and Susan Gabbard. 1992. "The Latinization of U.S. Farm Labor." *NACLA Report on the Americas: Immigration* 26(1) (July): 42–46.

Paz, Octavio. 1988. "Prologue" of *The Traps of Faith,* trans. Margaret Sayers Peden. Cambridge, Mass.: Belknap Press.

Peterson, V. Spike, and Anne Sisson Runyan. 1993. *Global Gender Issues.* Boulder: Westview Press.

Safa, Helen I. 1993. "The New Women Workers: Does Money Equal Power?" *NACLA Report on the Americas* 27 (1) (July–August): 24–29.

Santiago, Esmeralda. 1993. *When I Was Puerto Rican.* New York: Vintage Press.

Stoltz Chinchilla, Norma. 1993. "Gender and National Politics: Issues and Trends in Women's Participation in Latin American Movements." In Edna Acosta-Belén and Christine E. Bose, eds., *Researching Women in Latin America and the Caribbean,* 37–54. Boulder: Westview Press.

Villegas de Magnón, Leonor. 1994. *The Rebel.* Houston: Arte Público Press.

Books Required

Gloria Anzaldúa. 1987. *Borderlands/La Frontera: The New Mestiza.* San Francisco: Aunt Lute Books.

Gioconda Belli. 1994. *The Inhabited Woman.* Willimantic, Conn.: Curbstone Press.

María Luisa Bombal. 1988. *New Islands and Other Stories.* Ithaca, N.Y.: Cornell University Press.

Sandra Cisneros. 1991. *The House on Mango Street.* New York: Vintage Books.

Sor Juana Inés de la Cruz. 1987. *A Woman of Genius: The Intellectual Autobiography of Sor Juana Inés de la Cruz,* second edition. Margaret Sayers Peden, trans. and introduction. Salisbury, Conn.: Limestone Press.

Laura Esquivel. 1992. *Like Water for Chocolate.* New York: Doubleday.

Rosario Ferré. 1995. *The House on the Lagoon.* New York: Plume.

Rigoberta Menchú. 1984. *I, Rigoberta Menchú, an Indian Woman in Guatemala.* Elisabeth Burgos-Debray, ed. New York: Verso.

Esmeralda Santiago. 1993. *When I Was Puerto Rican.* New York: Vintage Press.

Leonor Villegas de Magnón. 1994. *The Rebel.* Houston: Arte Público Press.

Articles Required

Edna Acosta-Belén and Carlos Santiago. 1995. "Merging the Borders: The Remapping of America." *The Latino Review of Books* 1(1): 2–12.

Alice A. Brittin. 1995. "Close Encounters of the Third World Kind: Rigoberta Menchú and Elisabeth Butgos's *Me llamo Rigoberta Menchú.*" *Latin American Perspectives* 22(4) (Fall): 100–114.

Rosario Castellanos. 1988. "Once Again Sor Juana," in M. Ahern, ed., *A Rosario Castellanos Reader,* 222–25. Austin: University of Texas Press.

Rosario Castellanos. 1988. "Self-Sacrifice Is a Mad Virtue," in M. Ahern, ed., *A Rosario Castellanos Reader,* 259–63. Austin: University of Texas Press.

Katherine M. Glenn. 1994. "Postmodern Parody and Culinary-Narrative Art in Laura Esquivel's *Como agua para chocolate.*" *Chasqui: Revista de literatura latinoamericana,* Swarthmore, Pa.

Cheryl Johnson-Odim. 1991. "Common Themes, Different Contexts: Third World Women and Feminism," in Chandra Mohanty, Ann Russo, and Lourdes Torres, eds., *Third World Women and the Politics of Feminism.* Bloomington: Indiana University Press.

Richard Mines, Beatriz Boccalandro, and Susan Gabbard. 1992. "The Latinization of U.S. Farm Labor." *NACLA Report on the Americas: Immigration* 26(1) (July): 42–46.

Octavio Paz. 1988. "Prologue" of *The Traps of Faith.* Margaret Sayers Peden, trans. Cambridge, Mass.: Belknap Press.

Helen I. Safa. 1993. "The New Women Workers: Does Money Equal Power?" *NACLA Report on the Americas* 27(1)(July/Aug.): 24–29.

Norma Stoltz Chinchilla. 1993. "Gender and National Politics: Issues and Trends in Women's Participation in Latin American Movements," in Edna Acosta-Belén and Christine E. Bose, eds., *Researching Women in Latin America and the Caribbean,* 37–54. Boulder: Westview Press.

Book Recommended
A Spanish-English dictionary.

Course Description
This is an interdisciplinary course deriving its primary material from the field of literature. It is centered on the study of selected works by U.S. Latina writers and Latin American women writers to explore the connecting links, as well as the dividing lines, of women's lives on both sides of the U.S.–Latin America border. These women share a common heritage that has evolved into multiple variants as a result of geographical, historical, economic, and social factors. The focus of our study is on the conditions of women resulting from these multiple intersections. The issues acquire an even greater interest as we study the many ways in which women react to these conditions and develop different forms of agency.

The world in which women move determines the characteristics and quality of their lives. Given this premise, and the need to organize the course around a concept that will include multiple aspects, we will organize our study around the concept of spaces. Spaces can be analyzed on many levels: geographical, social, political, psychological, etc. They affect people's lives in the sense of limiting or expanding their possibilities. Spaces are also a reflection of the creative power of human beings. In Spanish we have the expression: *"No hay callejón sin salida"* (There are no dead end streets). This is an example of how a particular space (street) is used to express a human situation (street as the freedom to move—dead end street as a restriction of movement). We will find, in the course of our readings, many approaches to certain common themes using the concept of spaces as an analytical tool.

Borders and bridges are two very important spaces that provide the main theme and structure of the course. Borders may be seen as points of separation as well as points of proximity. Bridges, on the other hand, are connecting points. We will use these concepts as tools for comparative analysis, and also explore them as they are expressed in our readings.

Course Objectives
1. To introduce students to the main issues facing Latinas in the U.S. and in Latin America through the reading of literary works by some of the most outstanding writers representing the two groups. Complementary activities include reading articles of scholars in related fields (Women's Studies, Latin American Studies, Latino Studies), viewing films, and engaging in a research project.
2. To exercise comparative analysis at many levels.
3. To explore the intersection of gender, race, and class factors as they appear within each historical and/or geographic context.
4. To acquire an appreciation for the complexity of global interconnections.
5. To inspire creativity through the discovery of these authors and the world they depict. The act of creating spaces where before there were none is something we can all identify as a personal goal.

Class Procedures and Requirements
The class will be conducted as a seminar. There will be short background or preparatory lectures followed by discussion. The class discussion will revolve

around preassigned questions on each text. Students are expected to be prepared to lead the discussion on any of the questions.

Every student will write a three- to four-page response paper at the completion of each reading. A response paper is the student's individual reaction to a book, taking into account the relevant aspects discussed in class. The response paper must be typed double spaced and handed in on the assigned day.

During the course of the semester we will be viewing three films: *Like Water for Chocolate; I, the Worst of All;* and *Salt of the Earth.*

There will be articles to read to complement the required texts. Some of these articles expand on particular aspects of women's issues, others give deeper insights into a particular work or aspect of a work. There will be a discussion of each article read and how it applies to the work(s) we are reading.

At the end of the semester each student is required to present a final project, which could be the result of field or bibliographical research. It must be first handed in as a written paper of approximately eight to twelve pages, double spaced. Each student will be assigned a day in which to orally present the project to the class.

There will be a final exam.

PART 3

Curricular Resources: Strategies
for Change

WHAT COUNTS? CRITICAL ANALYSIS OF STATISTICAL INDICATORS

Janice Monk

Progress has been made in developing statistical indicators to reflect women's life experiences and status internationally, most notably with the creation of the Gender Development Index by the U.N. Development Program (1995). But widely used data sources and indicators, such as censuses of population, censuses of agriculture, the U.N. System of National Accounts, gross national product, and gross domestic product, remain inadequate in accounting for what women do. Concepts such as household head, household income, employment and unemployment, and part-time and full-time work mask the nature of women's lives, their work in informal and unpaid sectors, or the unequal division of resources in the household. By introducing students to critical evaluation of statistical measures, we can help them to see the values and assumptions inherent in "objective" measures that shape national and international policies and programs such as the World Bank's and the International Monetary Fund's. Several sources provide good introductions to feminist critiques of statistical measures, including Lourdes Benería's (1982) analysis of the measures of women's work and Marilyn Waring's (1988) critique of the U.N. System of Accounts and other measures. Numerous articles that document women's daily use of time also can serve as valuable background information to complement the exercise that follows.[1] This exercise challenges students to evaluate a census classification of occupations in the light of data collected in interviews with women about their work.

THE EXERCISE

Table 1 lists categories of work identified in a 1982 field study of 105 households on the Caribbean island of Margarita, a tourist resort and free port that is part of Venezuela (Monk and Alexander 1986). Table 2 is an English translation of employment categories used in the 1970 Venezuelan census, the classification system that had been published at the time the field data were collected.

Housework	Housework; seamstress (makes clothes)	Sells clothing on street in nearby town
Cleaner (in government offices) shoe	Laundress (operates from home)	Housework; works in small family store; makes parts of
Weaves hammocks; seamstress (repairs clothes)	Teacher	Sells shoes
Street drink-stand operator	Sells clothing in store	Housework; sells rabbits
Housework; sells corn	Clothing store operator	Shoemaker in home
School cook	Maid	Housework; makes and sells corn bread
Housework; operates small general store in home	Revendedora: retails clothing and housewares (purchased duty free) in streets and to private customers on the island and the mainland	Chambermaid
Housework; rents space in home for small general store	Housework; crochets portions of hammocks for small manufacturer	Raises chickens and sells direct to consumer
Housework; sells soft drinks from home	Housework; operates small fruit and vegetable store	Local government official
Housework; takes in male boarder	Housework; weaves hammocks	Housework; baby sitting

Source: Monk and Alexander 1986.

Professional; technical workers	Transport and communication workers
Agents, administrators, directors	Artisans and factory workers
Office employees and kindred workers	Service workers
Salespersons and kindred workers	Others, not identifiable
Agricultural, livestock, fisheries, hunting, according forestry, etc., workers	Unemployed (identified to categories above)

INSTRUCTIONS

Give students copies of tables 1 and 2 and ask them to assign each of the women represented by the information in table 1 to one of the categories provided in table 2. Then ask them to answer the following questions.

1. Which kinds of work are easy to assign?

2. Which kinds of work present problems in assignment?

3. How useful is the census list of categories for describing women's work?

4. How would you modify the census classifications to give a better description of women's work?

IMPLEMENTING THE EXERCISE

This exercise has been used many times with a variety of groups—undergraduate and graduate students, K–12 teachers, and development practitioners. It has also been adapted or reprinted by other authors. It is easy to implement but challenging. If students work in groups of two or three, I allow fifteen to twenty minutes to assign the categories and answer the questions. Debriefing can be adapted to the situation and time available.

As a follow-up, students may be asked to provide information on their own or their parents' work (paid and unpaid, part-time and full-time). Then ask them to examine the categories of their own national census and see which of the forms of work they have identified would be included and how they would be classified. How many hours of "part-time" employment are required before this work is recorded? What are the possibilities for classifying a person who holds more than one job? Discussion of the readings noted here, or screening of segments of the video *Who's Counting? Marilyn Waring on Sex, Lies, and Global Economics,* may also stimulate critical thinking and awareness of the biases in many taken-for-granted indicators.[2]

NOTES

An earlier version of this exercise was published in Monk (1988). It is reproduced with permission of the publisher.

1. Examples of time use data that reveal complexities of contextual and temporal patterns are included in several chapters in Janet Momsen and Vivian Kinnaird (1993). Vidyamali Samarasinghe (1997) focuses on ways of measuring household work in the global South. Janice Monk and Maria Dolors García-Ramon (1996)

consider issues of geographic scale and varying national definitions in describing European women's work.

2. The video connected with Marilyn Waring's analysis provides important case studies of the implications of current systems of measurement for women, the environment, and peace. Produced by the National Film Board of Canada, it is distributed by Bullfrog Films (see videography, this volume, for contact information).

WORKS CITED

Benería, Lourdes. 1982. "Accounting for Women's Work." In Lourdes Benería, ed., *Women and Development: The Sexual Division of Labor in Rural Societies*, 119–147. New York: Praeger.

Momsen, Janet Henshall, and Vivian Kinnaird. 1993. *Different Places, Different Voices: Gender and Development in Africa, Asia, and Latin America*. London: Routledge.

Monk, Janice. 1988. "Engendering a New Geographic Vision." In John Fien and Rod Gerber, eds., *Teaching Geography for a Better World*, 91–103, 194–195. Edinburgh: Oliver and Boyd.

Monk, Janice, and Charles Alexander. 1986. "Free Port Fallout: Gender, Employment, and Migration on Margarita Island, Venezuela." *Annals of Tourism Research* 13: 393–413.

Monk, Janice, and Maria Dolors García-Ramon. 1996. "Placing Women of the European Union." In Maria Dolors García-Ramon and Janice Monk, eds., *Women of the European Union: The Politics of Work and Daily Life*, 1–30. London: Routledge.

Samarasinghe, Vidyamali. 1997. "Counting Women's Work: Intersections of Time and Space." In John Paul Jones III, Heidi Nast, and Susan M. Roberts, eds., *Thresholds in Feminist Geography*, 129–144. Lanham, Md.: Rowman and Littlefield.

United Nations Development Program. 1995. *Human Development Report 1995*. New York: Oxford University Press.

Waring, Marilyn. 1988. *If Women Counted: A New Feminist Economics*. San Francisco: Harper and Row.

SENSITIZING STUDENTS TO PROBLEMS IN SURVEY RESEARCH: WORK IN RURAL CHAD

HELEN HENDERSON

This teaching exercise is designed to give undergraduate and graduate students in anthropology, geography, and other social science courses experience in working with primary survey research data, formulating questions and hypotheses about variations in data, and displaying findings relevant to a particular research issue. It simulates research efforts of applied development specialists, who are hired by international and national agencies to gather and analyze data in order to recommend policies and design programs for internationally funded agricultural development agencies. The specialists include citizens of the country being studied as well as non-nationals. In the case presented here, the research agenda called for identifying labor allocations in different types of households in rural Chad. The exercise can be used as an introduction to understanding differing ways that people construct work within households and to sensitize students to the problems inherent in survey research. It presents a selection of field data in the form in which many development practitioners first record them.

BACKGROUND FOR THE INSTRUCTOR

The major focus of the research on Chad, presented here in brief, was to collect quantitative and qualitative data on farmers and their agricultural strategies in order to design a food security project to be funded by the International Fund for Agricultural Development (IFAD). In the Sahelian climate, where rain-fed agriculture is often precarious, how family units obtain and use resources is of major interest to persons advising international development funding agencies on ways to address food shortages. As one of these agencies, IFAD was particularly interested in identifying the activities of women in agricultural production and household maintenance activities in order to be able to involve women actively in projects.

The field research for the project was carried out in 1991 near Mongo in Guera Prefecture, a predominantly Muslim area of Chad. Some Christians were probably among the interviewees. Beer-brewing as an income-generating activity indicates that household members were affiliated with Christian or traditional non-Muslim religious groups. The subjects of the survey were sedentary farmers with some livestock and transhumant pastoralists who did some farming. Both groups frequently connected with one another through reciprocal economic exchange relationships. The exercise provides nine questionnaires drawn from responses from actual households in which interviews were conducted. Overall, the team surveyed sixteen villages and conducted interviews in 223 households, which in total represented 1,168 individuals (Henderson, et al. 1997, 130). One or more members of the University of Arizona/IFAD team (myself included) were present at each interview, working with a Chadian researcher.

The people who responded to the survey live in the Sahelian climatic zone where household labor is critical for survival. In this context, polygyny can be viewed as a strategy of economic expansion, increasing labor supplies in order to open new agricultural lands. Most households hold agricultural plots that are allocated to individuals by the household head, as well as plots retained by the household as a unit (and managed by the head). The individual plots are managed by individual wives, siblings, or parents. Within many households subunits consisting of individual women and their children, siblings, or older parents who engage in farming or other subsistence-level activities. Recently, researchers have been analyzing the management strategies of the mostly female-headed subunits or "hearthholds" within larger households.

The households we surveyed in Chad were largely patrilineal; that is, descent was traced through males and kinship groupings were organized along patrilineal lines, males usually receiving land rights through their fathers. Residence was virilocal; that is, the wife moved to the village and compound of the husband.

When working with this exercise, there are two somewhat different definitions of household that students may want to explore: The households can be defined as "particularly dense centers in a field of exchange relationships" (Guyer 1991) or as "a domestic group of kin with a corporate character and an identity that is recognized in the use of terms like family, house, hearth or those who eat from a common pot" (Netting 1993, 58). The household can be looked at as potentially one group—all sharing resources together—or as several groups or hearthholds—each a unit of production and consumption, "demographically made up of a woman and all her dependents whose food security she is either fully or partially responsible for" (Ekejiuba 1995, 51).

THE EXERCISE

Students will address the following research question: How is labor allocated in different types of households? They should consider both interhousehold and intrahousehold variations, and also learn to recognize the existence of "hearthholds."

Students will be involved in

1. a preliminary analysis of survey data to become familiar with the material;

2. development of a system for categorizing and displaying data in order to answer a research question;

3. formulating preliminary "hunches" that would answer the research question; and

4. evaluating the survey instrument as a methodological approach for answering the research question.

Materials for the exercise consist of

1. procedural suggestions for conducting the assignment in the classroom;

2. handout with background information on Chad (see box 1);

3. a map of Chad;

4. a sample table (see box 2); and

5. exercise instructions for students.

HANDOUT FOR STUDENTS   BOX 1

CHAD: BACKGROUND INFORMATION

Geographical remoteness, climate, a poor resource endowment, and lack of infrastructure make Chad one of the most economically underdeveloped countries in the world (see *The World Factbook* on Chad). Northern Chad is arid; southern Chad is tropical rainforest. The total population in 1990 was estimated at 5,688,000. In 1996, life expectancy at birth for males was forty-five years and for females fifty years. The total fertility rate in 1996 was estimated at 5.84 children born per woman. The population density is low in the north and higher in the south. Chad is ethnically divided: In the north and center people are predominantly Muslim, in the south the majority is non-Muslim. French and Arabic are the official languages, but there are more than 100 different languages and dialects used in the country.

The total literate population (defined as persons aged fifteen and over who can read and write in French and Arabic) is 48.1 percent (male: 62.1 percent; female: 34.7 percent). Literacy rates are considerably higher in the south than in the north. Chad has suffered from political upheavals and armed conflict between warring factions from the 1970s to the 1990s.

The majority of the population are small-scale farmers. Agriculture accounts for approximately half of the gross domestic product and employs 80 percent of

---

the workforce. Principal crops are sorghum, millet, and peanuts. Cotton is an export crop. Drought is endemic in the north and central areas, with the result that there are recurrent food shortages.

STUDY AREA

Guera Prefecture is in a semiarid zone with grassy parkland vegetation and is characterized by dry-land farming, and the raising of goats, cattle, and some camels. In polygynous households, each wife usually has a separate house (hearthhold) for herself and her minor children. Farming areas consist of "communal" (household) plots and individual subunit plots. Produce is often sold to "Arab" merchants by the household head. During the dry season, young men often migrate to find work, especially to the capital or to neighboring countries. Many men have also been in the military. A few development projects in the area have provided agricultural technology loans, stimulating the development of small group credit associations.

For more information about the history and environment of Chad, refer to various sources such as the *Encyclopaedia Britannica* (in hard cover or on the World Wide Web) or the *The World Factbook* country listing on Chad at: http://www.odci.gov/cia/publications/factbook/. The data in these sources are regularly updated.

EXERCISE INSTRUCTIONS

TASK I: PRELIMINARY DATA ANALYSIS

You will be divided into pairs and asked to examine three questionnaires that report data from a survey related to household production and consumption in Guera Prefecture in Chad.[1] With your partner, generate one or more research questions that you could answer using the categories of data recorded on the questionnaire.

TASK II: CATEGORIZING AND DISPLAYING DATA

Create a table (similar to the sample table provided by your instructor) that would help you to answer the research question you have posed.

TASK III: FORMING AND ASSESSING PRELIMINARY HYPOTHESES FROM THE CATEGORIZED DATA

Using the table you have constructed and the data on your questionnaires, formulate a preliminary answer to the research question you have posed. Write a short paragraph summarizing your answer.

In a class discussion, evaluate the survey instrument as a methodological approach. What problems did interpretation of the data present? What material would you have liked to collect that is not there?

SAMPLE TABLE   BOX 2

Table 1. Land Use Patterns by Type of Household and Hearthhold.				
Percent (%) of Farmland in:	Male Head of Household (%)	Female Head of Household (%)	Subunit Wives (%)	Total Sample (%)
All cereals	88	84	59	75
Millet	33	52	32	35
Sorghum	43	28	23	32
Berbere	12	4	4	8
All sauce crops	12	16	42	26
Peanuts	6	5	23	13
Sesame	3	7	12	8
Vegetables	3	4	7	5

Source: Chad Survey, 1991, in Henderson, et al. 1997.

NOTE
1. The results of the survey are reported in Henderson, et al. 1997.

SELECTED REFERENCES

Ekejiuba, Felicia I. 1995. "Down to Fundamentals: Women-Centered Hearth-Holds in Rural West Africa." In Deborah Fay Bryceson, ed., *Women Wielding the Hoe,* 47–61. Oxford: Berg.

Guyer, Jane I. 1980. 1991. "Female Farming in Anthropology and African History." In Michaela di Leonardo, ed., *Gender at the Crossroads: Feminist Anthropology in the Postmodern Era,* 257–277. Berkeley: University of California Press.

Henderson, Helen K., Timothy J. Finan, and Mark Langworthy. 1997. "Hearthhold and Household: Gendered Resource Allocation in Chad." *Culture and Agriculture* 19 (3): 130–137.

Netting, Robert. 1993. *Smallholders, Householders: Farm Families and the Ecology of Sustainable Agriculture.* Stanford, Calif.: Stanford University Press.

PROCEDURAL SUGGESTIONS FOR CONDUCTING THE ASSIGNMENT

I recommend a class period of fifty minutes as appropriate for this assignment, with the instructor providing some introductory remarks about Chad and survey work and leaving at least fifteen minutes for class discussion and comparison of results among the teams after they have worked with the survey data. Instructors may want to follow up on this assignment with further discussion the following class period.

In my class of eleven graduate students, participants divided themselves into three groups containing three, four, and four students each. Each group received different sets of questionnaire results. The students took about thirty minutes to complete the assignment in a rough form, but wished that more time had been allotted.

Step One: Distribute Questionnaire Results
The exercise uses nine tables that record data on agricultural production, labor allocation, and consumption. (The questionnaire results can be found at the end of this chapter.) The data are organized by households. Divide the class into pairs and provide each pair of students with three completed questionnaires. Hand out the questionnaire results so that pair A receives Households 1, 2, and 3; pair B, Households 4, 5, and 6; pair C, Households 7, 8, and 9; pair D, Households 1, 2, and 3; and so on. If the class has at least eighteen students, this distribution will assure that each set of three households is examined by more than one pair of students. In a larger class, distributing the same questionnaires to different pairs of students raises the possibility that different interpreters will draw different conclusions from the primary data. This result can then become a point of class discussion.

Step Two: Review How the Data Are Entered on the Questionnaire Results
Data have been entered under the subject heading "Distribution of Labor in the Family" with subcategories for listings of "Agricultural Labor," "Nonagricultural Labor," and "Distribution of Agricultural Production." At the top of the left column of the questionnaire the name of the person identified (often self-identified) as the household head (HH) has been recorded; on the lines below are the names of other members of the household. Children of each woman are listed under her name; persons listed directly under the household head's name may be (and usually are) his or her other relatives. They might include parents, siblings, or children of a wife who is no longer resident in the household. The second column identifies their position in the household, the third, each individual's age and sex (*m* or *f*). An *x* in the remaining columns indicates that the persons listed in the first column worked in a particular type of field (i.e., the field of the household head or in a field belonging to that individual), or she participated in reciprocal exchange groups, was engaged in salaried agricultural work, and/or took care of livestock. Xs in various columns also indicate whether their nonagricultural work included domestic tasks, artisan tasks, salaried work (not in agriculture), commerce (selling goods), or other nonagricultural work. The final columns, at the right sides of the questionnaires, are labeled "Distribution of Agricultural Production." They record whether the named person consumed, sold, or exchanged the agricultural products that she or he produced. When the interviewer had sufficient information, the quantity of goods consumed, sold, or exchanged

was recorded, for example, "50 grain" or "40 peanut." (The unit of measure is a container that holds approximately 2 pounds.)

Step Three: Make a Preliminary Analysis of the Data

Ask pairs of students to make preliminary descriptions and interpretations of the raw survey data. Ask them to suggest the types of issues they can identify in the data, for example, the range of household types, the participation of household members in various production activities, and whether household members contributed labor to their own subunit only or across subunits. Ask each pair to reach a consensus about what their data set indicates with respect to these issues, then have the pair present this consensus to the full class, noting areas where differences in interpretations arose.

Step Four: Categorize and Display the Data

To begin, provide students with a sample table showing how researchers have organized data drawn from this survey research project to answer a question about labor allocation strategies (note that the sample table provided was designed to answer a different question than the one that has been posed to the students). Then, ask students to use the sample table to design their own table or matrix using the survey data to answer a research question.

Students in the graduate seminar that I taught at the University of Arizona developed tables showing similarities and differences in participation in agricultural labor and nonagricultural labor by adult male, adult female, and children under fifteen. Even if a single person performed multiple tasks, this approach should give a rough estimate of labor by gender and age.

Step Five: Form and Assess Preliminary Hypotheses from the Categorized Data

Working in their original pairs, ask students to use the matrix they have designed, in conjunction with their earlier discussions, to formulate preliminary hypotheses to address a research question. These responses should be submitted in written form.

In my class, taking a hypothesis that men are more likely to be paid for their labor than women, students created tables to reveal the type of work—agricultural, salaried agricultural, nonagricultural, salaried nonagricultural—performed by adult males, adult females, and children under the age of fifteen. Students then compared the incidence of paid and nonpaid work by gender.

There are a number of alternative hypotheses that could be examined using the data presented, including the following.

1. Using the hypothesis that female-headed households have fewer workers than male-headed, students could compare overall numbers of workers in the two types of households.

2. Taking the category of "own personal field," students could test the hypothesis that senior wives sold more agricultural produce than did junior wives.
3. Students could test the hypothesis that there is a positive correlation between household size and number of agricultural and nonagricultural activities by creating and interpreting a scattergram that has household size on one axis and number of activities on the other.

Conclude the Activity
The instructor will review the written responses to the hypothesis-assessment task and lead a class discussion on the range of answers presented. In groups of four or five, students can discuss problems they found with the questionnaire, list additional data they would like to have collected, explore alternative methodologies to questionnaire surveys for answering the research questions, and define the advantages and disadvantages of such alternatives. Possible alternative and supplemental approaches include focus groups, participant observation, and in-depth interviews.

STUDENT RESPONSE

The graduate students in my class Gender and International Development had already read the article by Ekejiuba and other articles dealing with power relations within households, especially polygynous households. They were enthusiastic about getting a hands-on exercise, were creative in their constructions of hypotheses, and remarked that they wished they had more time to expand on their hypotheses and to compare findings with other teams.

ADDITIONAL REFERENCES
Bruce, Judith, and Daisy Dwyer, eds. 1988. *A Home Divided.* Stanford, Calif.: Stanford University Press.
Bryceson, Deborah Fahy, ed. 1995. *Women Wielding the Hoe.* Oxford: Berg.
Due, Jean. 1991. "Policies to Overcome the Negative Effects of Structural Adjustment Programs on African Female-Headed Households." In C. H. Gladwin, ed., *Structural Adjustment and African Women Farmers,* 103–127. Gainesville: University of Florida Press.
Guyer, Jane I. 1998. *Household Budgets and Women's Incomes.* Working Paper No. 28. Boston, Mass.: Boston University African Studies Center, Working Papers.
Sen, Amartya K. 1990. "Gender and Cooperative Conflicts." In Irene Tinker, ed., *Persistent Inequalities: Women and World Development,* 123–149. New York: Oxford University Press.

QUESTIONNAIRE RESULTS

Personal Data		Agricultural Labor					
Name	**Family Position**	**Age/ Sex**	**Personal Field**	**Field of Head of Household (HH)**	**Exchange/ Group**	**Salaried Work**	**Livestock**
Moket	HH[1]	60 yr/M	X				X
Mamboui	First Wife	50 yr/F	X				
Mantodji	Child	16 yr/F	X				X
Dimanche	Child	6 yr/M					X
Gody	Child	4 yr/M					
Mankourtou	Second Wife	40 yr/F	X				X
Boto	Child	17 yr/F	X				X
Mantai	Child	10 yr/F					X
Djiman	Child	6 yr/F					
Gaiboa	Child	2 yr/M					
Nagargue	Third Wife	30 yr/F	X				X
Ratou	Child	3 yr/F					
Manyede	Child	1 yr/M					

Note 1.

Each adult (and some children) has a field of heror his own and the children also help their father and mother.

Personal Data			Nonagricultural Labor					Distribution of Agricultural Production		
Name	Family Position	Age/ Sex	Domestic Tasks	Artisan Tasks	Salaried Work	Commerce	Other	Consume	Sell	Exchange
Moket	HH	60 yr/M		X			Gathering	50 Grain 5 Peanut	20 Peanut	
Mamboui	First Wife	50 yr/F	X					10 Grain		
Mantodji	Child	16 yr/F	X					10 Okra	10 Okra	
Dimanche	Child	6 yr/M								
Gody	Child	4 yr/M								
Mankourtou	Second Wife	40 yr/F	X				Gathering	15 Grain		
Boto	Child	17 yr/F	X					5 Okra	2 Okra	
Mantai	Child	10 yr/F	X							
Djiman	Child	6 yr/F								
Gaiboa	Child	2 yr/M								
Nagargue	Third Wife	30 yr/F	X				Gathering	7 Peanut	10 Peanut	
Ratou	Child	3 yr/F								
Manyede	Child	1 yr/M								

Note

The unit of measure referred to here is a container that holds approximately 2 pounds (e.g., 7
peanut = approximately 14 pounds of peanuts).

DISTRIBUTION OF LABOR IN THE FAMILY: HOUSEHOLD 2.

Personal Data			Agricultural Labor				
Name	Family Position	Age/ Sex	Personal Field	Field of Head of Household (HH)	Exchange/ Group	Salaried Work	Livestock
Raterlan	HH	39 yr/M		X	X	X	X
Mumkosia	First Wife	39 yr/F	X	X			
Bani	Child	19 yr/M	X		X	X	X
Abdullah	Child	17 yr/M	X		X	X	X
Gerdji	Child	13 yr/F	X		X	X	X
Tchere	Child	3 yr/M					
Toma	Second Wife	31 yr/F	X		X	X	
Sadia	Child	15 yr/F	X		X	X	
Fatime	Child	13 yr/F	X		X	X	
Kaltouma	Child	6 yr/F					

Personal Data			Nonagricultural Labor					Distribution of Agricultural Production		
Name	Family Position	Age/ Sex	Domestic Tasks	Artisan Tasks	Salaried Work	Commerce	Other	Consume	Sell	Exchange
Raterlan	HH	39 yr/M	X	X				Grain		
Mumkosia	First Wife	39 yr/F						4 Grain		30 Grain[2]
Bani	Child	19 yr/M	X	X						
Abdullah	Child	17 yr/M	X	X					4 Grain	
Gerdji	Child	13 yr/F	X						6 Grain	
Tchere	Child	3 yr/M					X[1]			
Toma	Second Wife	31 yr/F	X		X			X		
Sadia	Child	15 yr/F							12 Grain	
Fatime	Child	13 yr/F								
Kaltouma	Child	6 yr/F								

Notes

The unit of measure referred to here is a container that holds approximately 2 pounds (e.g., 7 peanut = approximately 14 pounds of peanuts).

1. She leads animals to grazing and carries goods to the market.

2. She sends it to her son in school to pay fees.

Personal Data			Agricultural Labor				
Name	Family Position	Age/ Sex	Personal Field	Field of Head of Household (HH)	Exchange/ Group	Salaried Work	Livestock
Hassan	HH	30 yr/M	X	X	X		X
Haline	First Wife	27 yr/F	X	X			
Hissein	Child	7 yr/M					X
Safie	Child	4 yr/F					
Seid	Child	1 yr/M					
Radie	Widow - mother of HH	60 yr/F		X	X		3 Cows
Hapsita	Grandchild	8 yr		X	X		X

Personal Data			Agricultural Labor				
Name	Family Position	Age/ Sex	Personal Field	Field of Head of Household (HH)	Exchange/ Group	Salaried Work	Livestock
Malia	HH[1]	30 yr/F		X			
Yaumon	Child	12 yr/M		X	X		
Kaltouma	Child	8 yr/F		X			
Amamia	Mother of HH	45yr/F	X	X	X		

Note

1. Head of household is a divorcee.

Personal Data			Nonagricultural Labor					Distribution of Agricultural Production		
Name	Family Position	Age/ Sex	Domestic Tasks	Artisan Tasks	Salaried Work	Commerce	Other	Consume	Sell	Exchange
Hassan	HH	30 yr/M	X	X				X		
Haline	First Wife	27 yr/F	X					X	X	
Hissein	Child	7 yr/M								
Safie	Child	4 yr/F								
Seid	Child	1 yr/M								
Radie	Widow— mother of HH	60 yr/F	X				60 Grain			
Hapsita	Grandchild	8 yr	X					Sesame40 40Peanut		

Note

The unit of measure referred to here is a container that holds approximately 2 pounds (e.g., 7 peanut = approximately 14 pounds of peanuts).

Personal Data			Nonagricultural Labor					Distribution of Agricultural Production		
Name	Family Position	Age/ Sex	Domestic Tasks	Artisan Tasks	Salaried Work	Commerce	Other	Consume	Sell	Exchange
Malia	HH	30 yr/F	X	X				X		
Yaumon	Child	12 yr/M	X	X	X	X		X		
Kaltouma	Child	8 yr/F	X	X	X	X				
Amamia	Mother of HH	45 yr/F	X	X				X[1]		

Notes

The unit of measure referred to here is a container that holds approximately 2 pounds (e.g., 7 peanut = approximately 14 pounds of peanuts).

1. Production lost to crickets.

Personal Data			Agricultural Labor				
Name	Family Position	Age/ Sex	Personal Field	Field of Head of Household (HH)	Exchange/ Group	Salaried Work	Livestock
Anour	HH	50 yr/M		X	X		X
Tahira	Mother of HH	65 yr/F	X	X			
Djnlase	Wife	50 yr/F	X	X	X		
Hanra	Child[1]	22 yr/F					
Dboussa	Child	15 yr/M		X		X	X
Achata	Child	12 yr/F	X	X		X	X
Idriss	Child	10 yr/M		X			X
Haroun	Child	8 yr/M					X
Sadia	Child	6 yr/F					

Note

1. Newly married, but still residing in natal home.

Socioeconomic Inquiry in the Regions of Chad: Distribution of Labor in the Family: Household 5.

Table 5b

Personal Data			Nonagricultural Labor					Distribution of Agricultural Production		
Name	Family Position	Age/ Sex	Domestic Tasks	Artisan Tasks	Salaried Work	Commerce	Other	Consume	Sell	Exchange
Anour	HH	50 yr/M	X	X				Grain	Grain	
Tahira	Mother of HH	65 yr/F		X					Peanut	
Djnlase	Wife	50 yr/F	X					Grain	Peanut	
Hanra	Child	22 yr/F							Peanut	
Dboussa	Child	15 yr/M	X	X		X		X		
Achata	Child	12 yr/F	X	X		X		X		
Idriss	Child	10 yr/M		X				X		
Haroun	Child	8 yr/M								
Sadia	Child	6 yr/F								

Note

The unit of measure referred to here is a container that holds approximately 2 pounds (e.g., 7 peanuts = approximately 14 pounds of peanuts).

Personal Data				Agricultural Labor				
Name	Family Position	Age/ Sex	Personal Field	Field of Head of Household (HH)	Exchange/ Group	Salaried Work	Livestock
Debtor	HH	60 yr/M	X	X				
Katche	First Wife	50 yr/F	X	X				
Ambita[1]	Child	20 yr/F	X					
Habiba	Child	11 yr/F						
Karis	Child	9 yr/M						
Kouoni	Child	5 yr/M						
Nayora	Second Wife	35 yr/F	X	X				
Baba	Child	20 yr/M	X	X				
Kourani	Child	18 yr/F						
Manboubou	Child	16 yr/F						X
Mankatch	Child	4 yr/F						

Note

1. Married, husband in military.

Socioeconomic Inquiry in the Regions of Chad:
Distribution of Labor in the Family: Household 6.

Table 6b

Personal Data			Nonagricultural Labor					Distribution of Agricultural Production		
Name	Family Position	Age/ Sex	Domestic Tasks	Artisan Tasks	Salaried Work	Commerce	Other	Consume	Sell	Exchange
Debtor	HH	60 yr/M		X						
Katche	First Wife	50 yr/F	X							
Ambita	Child	20 yr/F	X						12 Peanut[1]	
Habiba	Child	11yr/F	X							
Karis	Child	9 yr/M								
Kouoni	Child	5 yr/M								
Nayora	Second Wife	35 yr/F	X							
Baba	Child	20 yr/M	X						10 Peanut	
Kourani	Child	18 yr/F	X							
Manboubou	Child	16 yr/F								
Mankatch	Child	4 yr/F								

Notes

The unit of measure referred to here is a container that holds approximately 2 pounds (e.g., 7 peanut = approximately 14 pounds of peanuts).

1. Sold peanuts to buy grain.

Personal Data			Agricultural Labor				
Name	Family Position	Age/ Sex	Personal Field	Field of Head of Household (HH)	Exchange/ Group	Salaried Work	Livestock
Idris	HH[1]	50 yr/F		X		X	

Note

1. This non-Muslim woman works alone. She is divorced. At harvest time in a good year she makes beer and invites neighbors to help her in the harvest and get beer in exchange for their work.

Personal Data			Agricultural Labor				
Name	Family Position	Age/ Sex	Personal Field	Field of Head of Household (HH)	Exchange/ Group	Salaried Work	Livestock
Aman	HH	55 yr/M		X	X	X	X
Hawa[1]		25 yr/F	X		X		
Chibo[2]		2 yr/M					
Salom	First Wife	45 yr/F	X	X	X		X
Hassan	Child	16 yr/M	X		X		X
Abakar	Child	7 yr/M	X	X	X		X
Amkala	Second Wife	40 yr/F	X	X	X		X

Notes

1. Wife of first son, Hassan.

2. Male child of first wife's son (son of Hawa and Hassan).

Personal Data			Nonagricultural Labor					Distribution of Agricultural Production		
Name	Family Position	Age/ Sex	Domestic Tasks	Artisan Tasks	Salaried Work	Commerce	Other	Consume	Sell	Exchange
Idris	HH	50 yr/F	X			Makes beer		2 Grain	30 Peanut	3 Peanut[1]

Notes

The unit of measure referred to here is a container that holds approximately 2 pounds (e.g., 7 peanut = approximately 14 pounds of peanuts).

1. She gave three baskets of peanuts to a relative in the village.

Personal Data			Nonagricultural Labor					Distribution of Agricultural Production		
Name	Family Position	Age/ Sex	Domestic Tasks	Artisan Tasks	Salaried Work	Commerce	Other	Consume	Sell	Exchange
Aman	HH	55 yr/M		X				100	X	
Hawa		25 yr/F	X	X				40		
Chibo		2 yr/M								
Salom	First Wife	50 yr/F	X	X				40		
Hassan	Child	16 yr/M		X						
Abakar	Child	7 yr/M								
Amkala	Second Wife	40 yr/F	X	X				20	15	

Note

The unit of measure referred to here is a container that holds approximately 2 pounds (e.g., 7 peanut = approximately 14 pounds of peanuts)

393

SOCIOECONOMIC INQUIRY IN THE REGIONS OF CHAD:
DISTRIBUTION OF LABOR IN THE FAMILY: HOUSEHOLD 9.

TABLE 9A

| **Personal Data** | | | **Agricultural Labor** | | | | |
Name	Family Position	Age/ Sex	Personal Field	Field of Head of Household (HH)	Exchange/ Group	Salaried Work	Livestock
Assane	HH	30 yr/M		X	X		X
Halime	First Wife	27 yr/F		X			
Hissene	Child	6 yr/M					
Safiha	Child	3 yr/F					
Seid	Child	1 yr/M					
Hassane[1]	Father of HH	52 yr/M					

Note

1. Nonresident; he sends money to his son from the capital where he lives.

Personal Data			Nonagricultural Labor					Distribution of Agricultural Production		
Name	Family Position	Age/ Sex	Domestic Tasks	Artisan Tasks	Salaried Work	Commerce	Other	Consume	Sell	Exchange
Assane	HH	30 yr/M						100 Sorghum 20 Peanut		
Halime	First Wife	27 yr/F	X	X				7 Sesame		
Hissene	Child	6 yr/M								
Safiha	Child	3 yr/F								
Seid	Child	1 yr/M								
Hassane	Father of HH	52 yr/M		X						

Note

The unit of measure referred to here is a container that holds approximately 2 pounds (e.g., 7 peanut = approximately 14 pounds of peanuts).

INVESTIGATING THE TRANSNATIONAL DIMENSIONS OF CLASS, RACE, GENDER, AND SEXUAL IDENTITY: ENGAGING STUDENTS IN RESEARCH

LINDA PERSHING

Classism, Sexism, Racism: Issues is a popular course offered each semester by the department of women's studies at the State University of New York at Albany. The course introduces students to analytical perspectives on class bias, racism, sexism, and, in recent years, heterosexism; the connections among them; their mutually reinforcing nature; and the tensions arising from their interrelations. One of the goals of the course is to help students develop an understanding of structural inequality and group oppression from multiple perspectives. Cross-listed in the departments of Africana studies, Latin American and Caribbean studies, and women's studies, this introductory course has an enrollment of sixty to two hundred students per semester, depending on the instructor and her or his teaching style. Students from across the campus take the course because of its reputation for lively classroom discussions and because it fulfills one of the general education requirements (Human Diversity) for graduation.

Prior to 1997, the course focused on class, race, and gender within the context of the United States. I wanted to broaden the curriculum to create a more global approach, making connections and contrasts between the constructions of "difference" in the United States and other societies around the world. One of the texts I used in this course (Bouvard 1995) describes women's efforts to combat oppressive conditions in many cultural contexts. I also amended the content and title of the course to include an additional focus on sexual identity, renaming the course Classism, Racism, Sexism, *and Heterosexism:* Issues.

Rather than a lecture format, I reworked the course to emphasize active, participatory, and empowering ways of learning based on short presentations by members of the teaching team, class discussion and exercises, and student research, presentations, and writing projects. It was not a course in which students listened to lectures and repeated their content back on exams. Instead, I focused on the importance of peer learning, writing and critical thinking skills, active participation, and the open exchange of ideas. I attempted to assist students with the difficult tasks of integrating theory and practice, analysis and experience. The course required that students write, revise, and submit two substantive essays (six to eight pages each); complete several shorter homework assignments; read and give feedback on short papers written by other students; and work collaboratively in global research groups. In this paper, I focus on the organization and focus of these groups.

THE GLOBAL RESEARCH PROJECT

The Global Research Project is designed as a collaborative learning experience that will help students apply ideas they have encountered in their reading and in class discussions to world events. It also helps students see the links between conditions in the United States and other parts of the globe. This project requires that each student conduct in-depth research about an area of the world in which class, race, ethnicity, gender, and/or sexual identity have been pivotal aspects of contemporary social and political turmoil (see box 1 for specific topics; these can be modified by each instructor). The students' job is to investigate how these factors have shaped recent regional, national, or global conflicts in a particular region of the world and under particular historical circumstances. How did these events come about, and what specific cultural, ideological, and historical forces created them? I ask students to research these recent events and conflicts within the context of the history of the region, and to consider the roles that race, culture, ethnicity, class, gender, religion, and sexual identity have played in this conflict.

GLOBAL RESEARCH TOPICS (FOR GROUPS OF TEN TO TWELVE STUDENTS)   BOX 1.

HAWAI'I

Many people in the United States are aware of the treatment that Native Americans have received since Europeans first colonized the Americas, but fewer know that Native Hawaiians are also fighting for their rights to govern themselves and control their own lands and resources. Learn all you can about Hawaiian sovereignty movements, including the history of foreign activity in Hawai'i and how this has affected life in the islands. Place contemporary efforts for Hawaiian self-rule in the context of these historical events, and discuss the impact of economic investment and tourism on Hawai'i. What kinds of grievances have been articulated by Native Hawaiians in recent decades, and what social and political movements have emerged? Who have been the leaders of these movements? Have they been men or women? How has the U.S. government been involved in the conflict? How do issues of economic class, imperialism, and self-determination affect this situation? Examine how tourism and

---

U.S. militarization have shaped life in Hawai'i and how sovereignty movements have responded to these forces. Be sure to look at the issue from all sides and consider the effects and interactions of race, culture, ethnicity, class, gender, and sexual identity in this conflict.

JAPAN

Since World War II, the Japanese have been struggling to come to terms with the use of comfort women (women who provided sexual services to Japanese military men), foreigners, and migrant workers. What controversies have developed, and what efforts have been made to address them? What are the historical conditions that allowed and perpetuated these practices? Find out all you can about Japanese treatment of these groups and the problems they have faced. Place your discussion of comfort women within the larger context of the trafficking of women and the global sex industry. How do the problems faced by certain migrant groups and foreigners in Japan compare to those faced by immigrants to other nations? What has been the response of the Japanese government to protests by these groups? Be sure to look at the issue from all sides and consider the effects and interactions of race, culture, ethnicity, class, gender, and sexual identity in this conflict.

RWANDA

In the 1990s, Rwanda and the surrounding region have been the site of massacres and attacks on civilians, causing massive death and destruction. Half a million Tutsi and thousands of Hutu moderates have been killed since 1994. Learn all you can about the history and social circumstances that have shaped this conflict. How have ethnic or tribal identities been defined among these groups? How, in particular, have women been affected? Has the United Nations been involved, and to what degree? What are some of the reasons that the United Nations and national governments have resisted involvement? Why do so few people in the United States have knowledge about what has occurred in Rwanda? Be sure to look at the issue from all sides and consider the effects and interactions of race, culture, ethnicity, class, gender, and sexual identity in this conflict.

GUATEMALA

In Guatemala, Mexico, and other Central American countries, Mayan Indians have experienced oppression and abuse from the military and the ruling elite. Who are the Maya and what is their cultural history? How were they involved in and affected by the thirty-five-year civil war in Guatemala? What economic, social, and political forces have defined the Maya as an indigenous people? Learn all you can about this situation, comparing it to the lives and histories of native people in the United States. How, in particular, have women been affected? Has the United

States been involved in the conflict, and if so, how? What are some of the reasons that we have heard so little about this conflict in the U.S. popular news media? Have institutional religions, particularly the Catholic Church, responded to this situation, and if so, in what ways? Be sure to look at the issue from all sides and consider the effects and interactions of race, culture, ethnicity, class, gender, and sexual identity in this conflict.

INDIA

The practice of aborting female fetuses has become widespread in segments of Indian society where there are strong cultural preferences for male children. Learn all you can about the cultural and historical circumstances surrounding this phenomenon. How have gender roles and ideas about the significance of men and women, infant mortality rates of boys and girls, the dowry system, economic circumstances, the caste system, religious ideologies, and cultural traditions influenced the practice of aborting female fetuses? How widespread is this practice today and among what groups of people? Is it more common in certain economic groups or regions of the country? What efforts have been taken to address this problem? Be sure to look at the issue from all sides and to consider the effects and interactions of race, culture, ethnicity, class, gender, and sexual identity in this conflict.

The goal of the assignment is for the students in each global research group to educate themselves about their topic and to present their findings to the rest of the class in a joint, oral presentation. Their group has forty-five minutes to present what they have learned. One of the ground rules is that *everyone in the group must have an active role in the oral presentation.* I tell students in advance that they should practice their speaking and time themselves, because I am strict about the forty-five-minute time-limit (e.g., in a group of ten students, if everyone speaks about the same amount of time, each person should speak about four minutes). This is a joint venture, and each member of the group receives the same grade for the oral presentation, so they have to work together to make their presentation effective and hold one another accountable for doing their part. One member of the teaching team is assigned to each group as a liaison and resource person. She or he assists the group in developing their ideas, locating information, and in working on group dynamics. It is the students' job to keep their liaison advised about how she or he can assist them and about the times and places of their group meetings outside of class.

If there are members of the group who are not attending meetings or contributing to the process, I tell students that they need to advise their liaison about this, and group members need to speak directly to that person about her or his lack of participation, because it will affect their joint performance and grade. They have to learn to operate collectively and to divide up the work. I schedule one group presentation on each of the last five class sessions of the semester. This arrangement allows students more time to come to terms with their topic, seek out information, and formulate a presentation that will be educational and engaging. Many students, particularly women, are nervous about speaking in front of the class. I talk with them about the ways in which race, class, gender, and sexual identity affect public speaking and presentational styles, and I encourage them to be creative, take risks, and build their own skills as communicators.

I also offer students the following guidelines, both verbally and in a written handout:

> Lectures and presentations that are read or recited can be extremely boring. When you are speaking to the class, do not read from a piece of paper. You will bore your listeners. It is much more effective to speak from notes or an outline. Be creative and try to find interesting methods to communicate your information. Think of engaging ways to present the material—use visuals, maps, slides, short clips of videos, news clips, handouts, questions and answers, or anything else that will help make the presentation come alive. In past semesters, groups have used role-playing, skits, they have made their own videos, and they used the format of a television game show to convey their information.

In addition, each student is instructed to specialize in a particular aspect of the topic and write an eight-page (double-spaced, including a bibliography) analytical report in conjunction with the group presentation. The written reports are graded individually. I suggest that students summarize the specific topic they are covering, being careful to cite their sources in a footnote or endnote each time they use information that came from any source other than their own knowledge. Each essay should include *at least five outside sources,* and these should be listed in a bibliography. Encyclopedias do not count as one of their five sources, and at least four must be books or articles (not websites) of substance (not short articles from the newspaper or popular magazines like *Newsweek*). Students may also want to use sources from the World Wide Web, but these must be in addition to four written sources. In preparation for the assignment, students receive a style sheet to help them with citation formats. The research paper is due on the day that the group gives their oral presentation.

The global research groups worked fairly well in a class of fifty to sixty students, but the success of the assignment was due in large part to the efforts of the teaching team I developed: one graduate teaching assistant and two undergraduate students (who had taken the course with me before). One student teaching-team member worked with each group. Their personal interaction with the global research groups and their ability to keep me informed about each group's progress were essential. They helped the groups get organized, set up meeting times outside of class to work on the projects, and assisted group members with problems they encountered in developing their presentations. Their participation helped to decenter my role as the instructor and distribute leadership and teaching responsibilities in the classroom. Their involvement also aided me in meeting my goals for the course as a whole: to develop active learning, student writing skills, and lots of discussion in the classroom. Student members of the teaching team had central parts in leading and facilitating classroom discussion, fostering student participation, and encouraging students to take responsibility for the educational process.

EVALUATING THE SUCCESSES AND PROBLEMATIC ASPECTS OF THE PROJECT

SUCCESSES I EXPERIENCED

In general, peer and interactive learning strategies work well in this project. Students tend to become more invested in learning when an assignment is structured so that they immerse themselves in the material and take responsibility for sharing their learning with other members of the class. They begin to take responsibility for their own education—a new concept to many students—and soon realize that no one will do the work for them or keep after them to complete the project. With a little encouragement and guidance, many of the global research groups offered substantive and very creative presentations. Students know what it means to be bored in the classroom, and they often find exciting and interactive ways of presenting material that will keep other students interested. The group presentations can generate tremendous energy in the classroom. Students who have learned about a new topic are often eager to share their knowledge with others, and this can be an empowering learning experience.

One of the goals of the course is to help students develop their abilities to identify underlying assumptions about human diversity and the societal and political consequences of these assumptions. The global research project helps students deepen their understanding of *difference*—how it is conceptualized and the consequences of these conceptualizations—both on an interpersonal and on larger analytical and theoretical levels. Working together in small groups and communicating frequently and informally with other students, they often begin to question their own and one another's assumptions and socialization, what they are reading, how issues are portrayed by the media, and other related issues. When they see how class, race, gender, and sexual identity have operated in other societies to marginalize some groups of people and privilege others, they may begin to recognize these forms of difference as social structures, rather than merely as interpersonal dynamics between individuals.

Through their work on the global research projects, many students begin to realize how ethnocentric their education has been and how little they know about the rest of the world. After each presentation, I ask the class how many of them were aware of the problem that the presenters had just described, and invariably very few students respond affirmatively. Before they conduct their research, most students cannot identify on a map the locations relating to the global research projects. They know little about the cultural practices and next to nothing about the histories of the people affected by these conflicts. They begin to question the limits of their education and to ask why they know so little about the rest of the world. This can lead to very useful discussions about the biases in research; need for feminist and alternative scholarship; ethnocentrism and Eurocentric curricula; the biases of the news media; the ways in which class, race, gender, and sexual identity shape various societies in different and complex ways; and many other issues.

PROBLEMS AND DIFFICULTIES THAT AROSE

The global research project is time consuming and labor intensive, both for students and for the instructor or members of a teaching team. Getting groups organized, helping them get started in their work, building in adequate class time so groups can meet together, and structuring presentations into the course schedule all require significant amounts of time and energy. I would not try to do this without student assistants.

Class size is a pivotal issue in ensuring the success of this project. If there are too many students, it becomes cumbersome to organize them into groups or to structure time for group presentations. The smaller the enrollment, the easier this project is to manage.

Although many students rise to the occasion and take responsibility for their collaborative work, there are always a few students who are not responsible and expect other students to do the work for them. Moreover, it can be difficult to build in enough class time for groups to accomplish all they need to do in order to prepare their presentations, and finding a meeting time outside of class that is suitable for all group members can be problematic. It helps to set up an e-mail list for each group so that they can communicate on-line. I also suggest that they exchange phone numbers (a voluntary option).

The university library at SUNY–Albany had limited resources about some of the research topics, making it necessary for students to use the interlibrary loan service (which is slow) or to seek out materials from other libraries in the area. It is important to check in advance of setting the group topics to be sure that there are adequate resources available about each topic and to talk with students who want to do their research solely via the World Wide Web about the limitations of Internet resources.

As a part of the continual discussion of ethnocentrism that occurs in courses of this kind, I repeatedly address the biases that emerge when students think and talk about the cultural and political practices of other people. There is a tendency for many students to assume that class bias, racism, sexism, and heterosexism occur in other countries or cultures because "those people" are "less educated, more primitive, less liberated," and so on, than people in the United States or Europe. For example, in Global Research Group No. 5 (India) students may try to explain female infanticide or bride burning by claiming that these occur because India is a "backward" society. It is crucial to make students aware of the impact of cultural bias, Eurocentrism, and other forms of prejudice when they are conducting research about groups of people they may see as Other.

Another effective strategy in combating ethnocentrism is to contrast and compare the history and social practices of the United States with those of other societies. In this example, it is effective to discuss the high level of violence against women in the United States when examining female infanticide or bride burning in India. It is essential to avoid an us-versus-them approach to the study of class bias, racism, sexism, and heterosexism in other cultures.

WORK CITED

Bouvard, Marguerite Guzmán. 1995. *Women Reshaping Human Rights: How Extraordinary Activists Are Changing the World*. Wilmington, Del.: SR Books.

WRITING ACROSS BORDERS: AN EXERCISE FOR INTERNATIONALIZING THE WOMEN'S STUDIES CLASSROOM

Julie K. Daniels

Encouraging students to engage with the material we teach continues to be a rewarding challenge for teachers who consider themselves feminists. For me, helping students engage means that I, too, have to engage with the material and with them as I teach in an intellectually reflective way. bell hooks (1994, 86) describes this practice of *engaged pedagogy* as one that emphasizes a commitment to "a process of self-actualization that promotes [the teacher's] own well-being." I think that my own well-being increases as my understanding of feminism expands to encompass global concerns, and I try to pass this idea on to my students. For example, I encourage my students to see that U.S. perspectives are not the only worthwhile perspectives, or even the best vantage point for viewing many issues that concern the majority of the world's people. It is not passé to remind my students that other people in the world worry about hunger, clean water, sturdy housing, access to education, and participating in business. They have much to teach U.S. students.

A rich resource of such people is the pool of international students who enroll in U.S. colleges and universities. I have taught international students who worry about family members that they have left behind so that they could attend school in the United States. Others worry about working the night shift at a frozen food plant so that they can earn the money for school. Another worries about sleeping on a friend's couch instead of getting his own apartment so that he can save money to send home to his mother and three sisters. Their real, lived experiences—and their willingness to share it with me and with their classmates—results in a more inclusive feminist classroom for all of us, students and teacher alike. By providing the educational occasion for this exchange, I am using what Aronowitz and Giroux (1991, 130) call a *border pedagogy,* a practice that they describe as an "opportunit[y] for teachers to deepen their own understanding of the discourse of various others." Making the most of this opportunity is what the following essay attempts to convey.

I like this metaphor of the border, and as we continue to make our courses meaningful for our students and ourselves, we must remember that meaningfulness requires us to help students see across many borders. One border consists of their own physical bodies, which they must see out of in order to understand that their own lived experience is a beginning place but not an end in itself. Identity groups are also borders that need to be crossed in order to understand that the social groups in which they participate exist in both positive and negative relationship to other social groups (Hardiman and Jackson 1997). Students must also see across the border of the country in which they are being educated in order to understand in a significant and serious way the complexity of the international arena and the United States' role in that complexity (Lustig and Koester 1996). We must help them find and articulate an understanding of the global connections between peoples and ideas, whether we teach English or engineering, philosophy or finance, health or horticulture. It is with this spirit of education and inclusion that many of us strive to internationalize our curricula.

But the clichés of the *global village* and the *global marketplace* are difficult to enact, to bring forth from sound bite to sound pedagogical praxis.[1] I would like to offer a classroom activity that I have found useful for getting students in an intermediate-level writing–women's studies course to think across their own borders and to imagine the complexities of learning in an international setting, an exercise that could be carried productively into other women's studies classrooms. Here I explain the exercise as I first experienced it and then modified it, describe the unexpected outcome that led me to see its value in the women's studies classroom, and provide a sample set of instructions for carrying it out in such a classroom.

THE ORIGINAL EXERCISE

I have adapted this exercise from one created by Robin Murie, a colleague at the University of Minnesota who is a specialist in English as a Second Language (ESL) and coordinator of the Commanding English Program at the university's General College.[2] I first experienced this activity myself when Murie used it at a workshop on ESL issues for writing teachers and tutors. At the time, I was teaching at an open-admissions state university that had (and still has) a significant population of ESL students: Many had come to the United States as refugees, primarily the Hmong from Southeast Asia, and many were international students.[3]

Murie began the workshop on writing issues by asking us to write a paragraph in our second most fluent language. The paragraph could be about anything, she said, "But I'd like you to write it in the language you feel most comfortable with after your first or native language. You have ten minutes." I panicked because the language I had studied in college, over a decade before, had been Latin, and I remembered almost nothing. For this assignment, however, I was able to write a few phrases in Spanish about *un perro y un gato, un pato amarillo*, and *mi casa es su casa*, which I had learned from my children, who attend a Spanish-immersion elementary school. I could list a few colors and a few nouns, but I could put no real sentences on the page, nothing that reflected any thought. Frustrated, I began writing about this experience in English, frightening my neighbor across the table who saw my pen moving furiously, covering half a page in the time allotted. "Wow, you wrote a lot," she smiled. Sheepishly, I admitted, "It's all in English; I don't know any other languages." Suddenly, my table-mate's half-dozen lines in German looked pretty impressive, and she smiled again as we turned our attention to the professor.

The point of the assignment, of course, was to let us teachers and tutors feel something of the panic that our ESL students feel when they come into a writing class and we ask them to write on the spot. Those workshop members who were able to get something on paper in a language other than English talked about their experiences: the limitation of writing in the present tense (the tense they remembered best), the frustration of not being able to express complex or abstract ideas in another language, and the embarrassment of presenting a self on the page that sounds stupid or immature. We discussed how facility with language can influence not only our ability to get along in the world, but also our ability to convey a real message, to express ourselves to an audience, and, thus, to affect what others think about us; in other words, a writer's language facility significantly controls her ethos. The exercise we had just experienced made palpable these familiar rhetorical principles.

In addition, the exercise reminded me that the work of adapting to a multicultural or international classroom is my responsibility. I have much to do to make sure that my limited language proficiency does not limit my ability to engage fully with others whose experience is different from my own, nor should it restrict me to simply "importing" international texts into the classroom. I must be purposeful when I address issues of language and diversity. hooks (1994, 173) points out that "[r]ecent discussions of diversity and multiculturalism tend to downplay or ignore the questions of language." If this is indeed true, I have a responsibility to acknowledge my own experience (or lack of it) as I strive to educate myself as I educate my students.

MY ADAPTATION IN THE WRITING–WOMEN'S STUDIES CLASSROOM

Because of the powerful experience I had had, I decided to try this exercise with my own students at that same open-admissions university. I used it in a course called Gender and Writing, an intermediate-level writing course cross-listed with women's studies, in which students read and wrote about the issues around women and language. My initial goals for having students write in their second language were to get them to think about the ways that language not only liberates them (they had heard my "writing is power" speech earlier in the quarter), but also limits them, depending upon their circumstances (one of those circumstances is gender, as our class readings explained), and could, therefore, restrict other people's ability to understand them. My primary goal was for students to think about the relationships among writer, language, and audience, but the assignment had another, unexpected outcome, which is why I consider it also a strategy for internationalizing the women's studies classroom.

After discussing many of the same frustrations that I had heard as a workshop participant, my students (mostly white, mostly female, mostly native English speakers) began talking about the way English is a privileged language around the world, a discussion that raised a number of points related to internationalizing the curriculum. Some students acknowledged that as U.S. citizens, they do not have to know another language to be successful in the world, and, in fact, they are not really expected to have fluency in a second language, even though many high schools and most colleges require a second language.[4] This monolinguism was a luxury in one sense, some students realized, because it allowed them to maintain the fiction of the United States' global superiority ("I mean, we all know that English is the language of business around the world," said one student). But other students pointed out that the lack of another language was a limitation because it made them, as one student said, "Uncomfortable when we travel in other countries. We sound like stuck-up Americans if we can't speak their language." This student's idea of "their language" called up the dichotomous idea of "our language," a dichotomy that points out the need for more education across borders so that students can see across the us-them split. Although being able to communicate in a second language does not guarantee that students will know about the culture out of which that language emerges, it opens up the possibility of such an understanding. hooks (1994, 171) talks about the power of language to create such a possibility for new knowledge when she points out that the nonstandard English used by formerly enslaved people not only "enables resistance to white supremacy, but . . . it forges a space for alternative cultural production and alternative epistemologies—differing ways of thinking and knowing." The classroom can be one such space for discussions of alternative epistemologies.

Perhaps more important still was the moment when a student from Cameroon, whom I will call Liza, pointed out that English was her third language. Her first was the ethnic language of her childhood, her second the French of her grade school and high school days, and her third English, the language of her higher education. Although Liza's presence in the classroom may have "internationalized" the space, in this space she was writing in her third language. The U.S. students' difficulty with writing in any second language led them to consider the lives of international students at the university. Some students expressed admiration, especially for the refugee students, many of whom had had no formal schooling because they had lived in refugee camps. Others mentioned students who had had no written language until recently (the Hmong, for example). Further, the opportunity to talk about Liza's three languages led to questions about her home country. Rather than "exoticizing" this international student the students' discussion became an exchange among peers who were all struggling with language as a means of conveying ideas that arose out of different cultural experiences.[5] I think that the exercise's focus on languages rather than individuals—it was Liza's third language, not Liza herself, that provided the starting point for the discussion—allowed for a better way into the discussion of internationalizing the curriculum.

AN IMPLICATION AND SOME OPPORTUNITIES

One important point in the discussion was not addressed, yet it is central to any internationalizing effort. That is, our readings for the class were predominantly from American writers, with a few from British and New Zealand writers—all writers whose primary language was English.[6] It is difficult to find essays in English about gender and language that do not focus on the English language, but some surely do exist.[7] As responsible teachers and practitioners of a *border* or *engaged* pedagogy committed to our own "self-actualization" (hooks 1994, 86), we must find and bring such texts into the women's studies classroom.

This exercise, which began as a way for students to experience the complexities of communicating with audiences, expanded into an international education encounter. In addition to the issues mentioned, the discussion also highlighted the following:

* access to education—for example, students described the struggle to learn English in a refugee camp before coming to the United States or in an American community college before coming to the university;
* differing expectations of literacy around the world—for example, are the expectations of U.S. schools really that high when compared with the international student who experienced school in three languages?
* the function of language in international relations—for example, why has English come to be the language of worldwide commerce, and what are the implications of this?

The discussion provided a specific illustration and experience of the way language shapes both how others see us (where are you from? how smart are you?) and what we are able to show them. Subtleties of thought cannot be expressed without the appropriate vocabulary, and we have the potential for more information, more knowledge, if we have access to a second language. Communicating in our second-best language forces us into a powerless position, perhaps costing privilege, and we can no longer take communication for granted. This awareness can open the space for examining our own ethnocentrism and internationalizing our classrooms.

USING THE EXERCISE IN THE WOMEN'S STUDIES CLASSROOM

This awareness does not happen by itself, however, and when I use this exercise again, I will structure it somewhat differently, and with new questions specifically aimed to encourage thinking beyond borders:

> Writing Exercise. On your own paper, please write a paragraph in your second most fluent language. Choose your own topic. Your classmates are your audience. You can write a story or explain something or describe something. You have ten minutes.

Giving some direction about audience and purpose for the writing itself helps students choose where to begin. I would deliberately direct students toward the genres of narration, exposition, and description because these, in my experience, encourage specific expression—such as memories, physical objects, people—more often than does the genre of argument, which may be a more familiar form in academic writing and thus lead students to write abstractly. I would also deliberately leave out the "real" purpose of the exercise—a way of beginning a discussion of international experiences—because I want students to focus on what they already know rather than what they do not yet know. This pedagogical move is risky and could be seen as a way of misleading students. It seems, however, that if students knew I wanted to discuss international issues and experiences, then they would write specifically about those instead of what comes most easily for them in their second language.

Questions should direct the discussion toward the kinds of issues that emerged unbidden when I first used this exercise. They should move students toward an exploration of the relationship between language and culture. They should also locate the beginnings of internationalizing the curriculum right within the students themselves, rather than simply importing texts about international issues that are external to many of the students' own experiences.

1. In what languages were we able to write? How many were non-Western languages? What does that tell us about the nature of education in the United States?
2. How much do we know about the culture(s) associated with our second language? How do we know about that culture(s)?
3. What changes in how we express ourselves when we use another language? What causes those changes? How does the language itself influence how you express yourself? What does this say about the culture(s)?
4. What would be gained by learning a non-Western language? What kinds of advantages do people who know a non-Western language have? Why?
5. Does this experience make anyone want to learn another language? Why or why not?
6. What does this experience tell us about people who have facility in more than one language? What does it tell us about people whose first language is not English?

CONCLUSION

So why do I advocate using this exercise with a second language in the women's studies classroom? Because with attention to the issues that the exercise raises, it can lead to an internationalizing of the students' thinking. By engaging (or not) with their second language, U.S.–born students who are native speakers of English have to think about the experiences of others in other countries. The exercise of trying to express ourselves in a second language can humble us and provide what social justice theorists Hardiman and Jackson call an acceptance of our "agent's status" or the understanding that we have power over others. This awareness can move us toward a social consciousness where we internalize our own power and agency as way of working for social change (Hardiman and Jackson 1997, 23).

Although I used this assignment in a women's studies class that was cross-listed with the writing department and was primarily a writing course, I think the exercise could easily and successfully be used in other women's studies courses. Adrienne Rich (1984, 82) reminds us that writing is a way of knowing, not simply a way of recording what we already know, when she writes that "only where there is language is there world." An important step in internationalizing the women's studies classroom is to help students realize that their knowledge of another language can help them know other worlds.

Also, such knowledge could help students know about other modes of expression used by people in other cultures. Persuasion happens in many different ways in many different cultures; what works in the United States does not work in Kenya or Taiwan or Brazil. Women in those countries speak to those in power in their countries differently than U.S. women speak to those in power in this country. As contradictory as it may sound, I believe that an awareness of an appreciation for these *differences* is the beginning of an understanding of the *commonalities* that unite women in their struggle for justice around the world. Aronowitz and Giroux (1991, 127–128) reinforce this idea with their notion of a border pedagogy "in which difference becomes a basis for solidarity and unity rather than for hierarchy, denigration, competition, and discrimination." Feminist epistemologist Meena Dhanda (1994, 256) characterizes this awareness of difference as "acknowledgment" or "a code of personal conduct . . . designed to address the concrete ideas of others . . . with whom we share only a little 'social space.'" Through this exercise of writing in their second-best language and subsequent substantial discussion about the implications of that experience, students are able to enter that social space and learn across their own borders by experiencing what it is like to have one's language use restrict those borders. This experience is a first step toward internationalizing the classroom because it makes real the relationship between language and culture. This specific experience, in turn, provides a basis for a major purpose of internationalizing the classroom—to help students realize the value of other cultural perspectives.

NOTES

1. Here I invoke Paulo Freire's definition of praxis in *Pedagogy of the Oppressed* (1970), which demands serious reflection on a situation as a means to action and the concomitant critical reflection upon that action.

2. One of nineteen colleges at the Twin Cities campus at the University of Minnesota, General College (GC) serves as a transfer college for "students who require special preparation because of personal circumstances or previous education." Thus, "GC plays a special role in the University's realization of the egalitarian principles that sustain its vitality as an urban, land grant, research institution." I would like to thank Professor Murie for granting me permission to adapt her assignment.

3. In my three years at this university, I taught students from Belize, Cameroon, China, Eritria, Iran, Israel, Kenya, Korea, Poland, Russia, Sweden, Taiwan, and Vietnam, among other countries.

4. Another point raised was that the languages taught in school were mostly Western languages, hardly global in scope.

5. Surely this exoticizing is the primary pitfall of such a discussion, and teachers must be careful not to encourage it unwittingly, as Vivian Zamel (1995) articulates in "Strangers to Academia: The Experiences of Faculty and ESL Students Across the Curriculum." In particular, Zamel discusses the problems of such exoticization of ESL students.

6. Although our text, Schaum and Flanagan (1992), had readings from a variety of feminist (and nonfeminist) perspectives, the only essays with an explicit

international focus were Marilyn Waring's "A Woman's Reckoning: An Introduction to the International Economic System" and Wendy Chapkis's "Skin Deep," which focused on the impact of Western advertising on non-Western countries.

7. In our class's textbook, the essay "Becoming Members of Society: Learning the Social Meaning of Gender" by Holly Devor does acknowledge other culture's conceptions of gender, but it focuses on gender in North America, as constructed via social definitions.

WORKS CITED

Aronowitz, Stanley, and Henry A. Giroux. 1991. *Postmodern Education: Politics, Culture, and Social Criticism.* Minneapolis: University of Minnesota Press.

Dhanda, Meena. 1994. "Openness, Identity and Acknowledgement of Persons." In Kathleen Lennon and Margaret Whitford, eds., *Knowing the Difference: Feminist Perspectives in Epistemology*, 249–264. London: Routledge.

Freire, Paolo. 1970. *Pedagogy of the Oppressed.* New York: Herder and Herder.

Hardiman, Rita, and Bailey W. Jackson. 1997. "Conceptual Foundations for Social Justice Courses." In Maurianne Adams, Lee Anne Bell, and Pat Griffin, eds., *Teaching for Diversity and Social Justice*, 16–29. New York: Routledge.

hooks, bell. 1994. *Teaching to Transgress: Education as the Practice of Freedom.* New York: Routledge.

Lustig, Myron W., and Jolene Koester. 1996. *Intercultural Competence: Interpersonal Communication Across Cultures.* New York: HarperCollins.

Rich, Adrienne. 1984. "The Demon Lover." In *The Fact of a Doorframe*, 82. New York: Norton.

Schaum, Melita, and Connie Flanagan. 1992. *Gender Images: Readings for Composition.* Boston: Houghton Mifflin.

Zamel, Vivian. 1995. "Strangers to Academia: The Experiences of Faculty and ESL Students Across the Curriculum." *College Composition and Communication* 46 (4): 506–552.

SIMULATING CULTURAL DISSONANCE: A ROLE-PLAYING EXERCISE

MARTHA E. GEORES AND JOSEPH M. CIRRINCIONE

In low income countries, the process of economic development brings with it more than economic change. Culturally, development is a fluid concept because it involves a gradual adoption of Western ways of doing things, valuing new ways over the customs and traditions that formerly regulated life. Gender roles and ethnicity undergo the most significant change and are the focal point of tensions within developing countries as the society becomes increasingly bifurcated into a tribal or traditional culture and a westernized or "modern" culture.[1] Individuals are often torn by cultural dissonance caused by the tension between their own cultural roots and the lure of a new way of life.

New course content alone is insufficient to convey to students this cultural dissonance and the dilemmas it presents individuals and groups. Experiential learning is necessary to teach effectively about gender and ethnicity in the international context. Studies have shown the effectiveness of active, reflective learning especially when unfamiliar and potentially controversial perspectives and concepts are being introduced. Merryfield and Remy (1995, 8) set forth methods of reflective learning for the internationalized curriculum. According to them, teaching methods in international matters should (1) examine multiple perspectives; (2) teach students how to find, evaluate, and use conflicting sources of information; (3) have students identify and analyze values and attitudes; and (4) have students use knowledge and skills through authentic applications. These methods, though not linked explicitly to feminist pedagogy, are compatible with the way feminist scholars might approach international gender issues in the classroom (Monk, et al. 1991). This paper presents a role-playing exercise that addresses the complex issues of ethnicity and gender from a non–U.S. perspective, using the process of reflective learning. The exercise gives students a chance to analyze a situation from different perspectives of culture, ethnicity, gender, and class.

"BURYING OTIENO": THE EXERCISE[2]

The "Burying Otieno" exercise takes a jurisprudential approach; that is, it calls on students to consider both empirical information and belief systems to confront and take a position concerning a specific conflict (Newmann 1970). The case study allows students to look at significant issues with serious consequences for individuals, groups, and society at large, much as judges apply the law based on the facts of one case. It is not enough for students to identify issues; they must focus on the disjunctures and consider the consequences of solutions to the problem.

The "Burying Otieno" exercise is based on an article by Patricia Stamp (1991) about a controversy in Kenya embodied in the collision of traditional ethnic values with the desire to build a new Kenya by de-emphasizing ethnic group loyalties and following more westernized ways of doing things. The article illuminates or describes a situation where ethnic and gender roles are in conflict based on the differences between ethnic customs and modern ways of doing things. The facts in the case are relatively uncomplicated, but the issues are extremely complex.

Otieno was born into the Umira Kager clan of the Luo ethnic group in Kenya. He left his village early in life and became a prominent attorney in Nairobi. His wife, Wambui, was born into the Kikuyu ethnic group and she also had left her village and pursued a career. They were married in both a civil and a church ceremony, but their marriage was never recognized by either the Luo or Kikuyu. Neither of them maintained close ties with their villages; in fact, they did not even keep a village house as many other modern Kenyans did. Together they raised fifteen children in their Nairobi home. They ascribed to the national goal of helping Kenya become a modern nation. They were both prominent, politically active citizens in postindependence Kenya. Wambui was also especially active in the international women's movement. Otieno died intestate, without a will. The article suggests that he had intentionally decided not to have a will because under common (statutory) law his estate would belong to his wife, Wambui, and that was what he desired. The dispute arose when Wambui sought to retrieve Otieno's body from the mortuary in order to bury him in Nairobi. Otieno's family also claimed rights to bury his body, but in his birthplace. In addition, his brothers claimed traditional rights to inherit his estate, and the obligation to take care of Wambui. A court proceeding developed from the dispute. The issues included determining who had the right to the body, and how his estate would be distributed.

This exercise presents not only issues of gender roles in a changing society, but also the clear conflict between traditional and modern cultures. Students must consider both the modern and traditional cultures existing in Kenya. Gender roles have become subject to increasing questioning and contestation as Kenya undergoes the difficult processes of culture change. The explanation of the exercise follows Merryfield and Remy's (1995) criteria for active learning.

Patricia Stamp's article "Burying Otieno" is required reading for this class exercise, which includes a lecture followed by the role-playing activity in discussion section groups. The article presents multiple perspectives through the stories of the people involved in the dispute. Because roles are not assigned until the discussion section, students become familiar with all of the characters. The lecture is used to introduce some of the principle dilemmas facing the characters in the exercise. The instructor describes the development process and gives the students information on both traditional and modern cultures in Kenya, emphasizing the continued existence of both cultures, especially the existence of two legal systems. Cultural interactions and conflicts are posed for each of the characters. The goal of the lecture is to set the stage for consideration of the various positions on ethnicity and gender roles. Students are expected to define the problems presented by the exercise while discussing the exercise in their discussion groups.

STEP 2. FINDING, EVALUATING, AND USING CONFLICTING INFORMATION

In the discussion sections students are first randomly assigned to one of five character roles. They use the article to obtain information about their character, and to start thinking about conflicting roles. At this time they are also given more detailed information about their character and the character's role in the exercise. The following information is given to the character groups.

Wambui and Her Representatives
Wambui Waiyaki and Silvanus Otieno met in the early 1950s and were married in August 1963. Wambui received a diploma in leadership and community development from a college in Tanganyika (now known as Tanzania), and was quite active in the Kenyan nationalist movement against colonial rule. After Kenyan independence, she continued to be a leader and an activist, especially in two of the major Kenyan women's groups, Maendeleo ya Wanawake and the National Council of Women of Kenya. She was a Kenyan delegate to the 1975 United Nations World Conference on Women, and served as treasurer to the Secretariat of Forum '85, the closing conference of the United Nations' Decade for Women, which was held in Nairobi.

Wambui's marriage to Otieno was controversial and symbolic. They were married at the time of closest alliance between the Kikuyu and the Luo, and for many Kenyans their marriage stood as a symbol for aspirations to a national, rather than an ethnic, identity. Their marriage and professional lives in Nairobi were modern in every sense, and their ties to their clans and ethnic groups were marginal. Their marriage, while an affront to clan traditions, was entirely legal under the colonial Marriage Act. Wambui's rights to Otieno's body were defined in the Kenyan Common Law under the Succession Act, which states that the surviving spouse has administrative authority over the body and the estate of the deceased.

The Umira Kager Clan of the Luo Ethnic Group

The Umira Kager Clan never formally recognized the marriage between Otieno and Wambui, and his death marked an opportunity to return him to his clan to be buried according to clan tradition and customary law in his natal village of Nyamila. Clan members had the power of ethnic clan politics and traditional patrilineage on their side. Nairobi may have been Otieno's house but not his home. In the continuous struggle for scarce monetary and political resources, the Umira Kager clan stood to gain by claiming victory in the case. According to Luo "customary law," the clan had rights to Otieno's body, estate, and lineage. Wambui was considered an upstart "destructive villain" bent on selfish gain at the expense of tradition.

The Kikuyu Tribe

The Kikuyu were torn between supporting fellow tribal member Wambui and supporting the case for stronger ethnic clan tradition and authority through "customary law" as presented by the Luo. On the one hand, the Kikuyu did not want to see the Luo gain power and prominence in the interethnic group power struggle, and they also felt that they should support their fellow clan-member in her hour of need. On the other hand, the Kikuyu would have liked to help strengthen the patriarchal traditional role of clans and ethnic groups, and Wambui may have been a threat to that goal.

The Kenyan Women's Movement and Western Advisors

Members of the Kenyan women's movement were fully aware of Western modern notions of women's rights and gender roles, but were reticent about taking a stand. They were caught between modernity and tradition. This reticence was a product of personal identity as well as the social standing of the women's husbands and families. For the most part, members of the women's movement were an elite group of affluent women with international ties and education, but they were also the wives and daughters of high ranking government officials who were attempting to please a diverse and potentially volatile constituency, which consisted primarily of clan members. The clan members might have been offended if the women's movement supported Wambui.

The women's movement members were coached by representatives from several Western feminist and women's groups who watched the case unfold. These Western women urged the Kenyan women to take a stand on Wambui's behalf, and on behalf of a modern, equitable Kenya.

The Court as an Arm of the Government of President Daniel arap Moi

The court had several questions to consider while going through the evidence in the article and hearing the testimony. Should the burial of Otieno have been subject to customary or common law? Was there any precedent either way? What was the court's position with regard to ethnic politics? Should it have been more concerned with tradition and the status quo than with setting a precedent that may have had a positive effect on women's issues in Kenya, and perhaps cast Kenya as a modernizing nation in the eyes of the world? What was the court's relationship to President Moi's administration? How might this have affected the court's decision?

STEP 3. IDENTIFY AND ANALYZE VALUES AND ATTITUDES

The students meet in character groups to consider not only the information given to them about their character, but also their own beliefs about the character and the situation. They explore strategies for how their character would have approached the court hearing. They think about how they would have played the roles and how a person actually in that situation might have acted. Here the students discuss cultural similarities and differences. Occasionally there will be students from Africa in the course, and their perspectives can be used extensively to demonstrate the reality of the issues under discussion. Students from the United States gain a new perspective when they realize that different cultural values and practices create a dilemma for some of their classmates. After the consultation in character groups, the students are redivided into five groups with one person from each of the character roles in each group, giving each student a chance to present her case.

STEP 4. USE KNOWLEDGE AND SKILLS THROUGH AUTHENTIC APPLICATION

This class exercise presents students with an authentic application. Court hearings actually took place based on the situation presented. Students replicate these real events. Although the article tells them that the actual outcome from the court hearing in Kenya was to give the body to the Umira Kager Clan and the estate to Wambui, they are encouraged to vigorously pursue other outcomes through their advocacy. It is the reasoning for their positions that is most important in this exercise, so even if they come to the same conclusion as the actual court, they must defend that position. In the class, the court hearings are held simultaneously in different parts of the classroom, or in separate rooms depending on space availability. Each character is given time to present her or his testimony and arguments to the court. Wambui and the Umira Kager Clan are each allowed rebuttal time. After hearing the testimony and arguments, the court renders a decision. An alternative way of handling this step would be to with-hold the court's decision from the class by cutting it out of the article, conduct the hearings, reach an outcome, and compare that outcome with the court's.

The discussion section reconvenes and each group reports the out-come of their hearing. The reasoning behind the decision is of more importance than the outcome. The remainder of the class period is spent discussing how and why people presented their characters as they did. The teaching assistant reports the outcome and process to the instructor, who then gives a report on the exercise to the class as a whole during the next lecture period. By introducing the exercise and giving the outcomes in a lecture section, the connection between lecture and discussion is strengthened. Reporting back to the class gives continuity to the exercise and also lets the students know that even though all dis-cussion groups used the same material, the outcomes varied.

CONCLUSION

Feedback from students indicates that this exercise is an effective way to encourage them to develop an appreciation of cultural perspectives other than their own. Dealing with gender inequities in the context of the struggle between traditional and westernized values focuses atten-tion on the multiplicity of conflicts confronting men and women in the development process. Students have expressed surprise that a problem that they initially defined as a cut-and- dried women's rights issue is really quite complex. They are impressed by the dilemmas that face people in developing countries as the cultures change. Many of the students expressed the idea that Wambui was responsible for this conflict. If she had let the tribe have the body, the court proceeding could have been avoided. Through examination of that feeling stu-dents were able to appreciate the complexity of the emotions as well as the legal rights involved in the situation.

By experiencing the conflict, the disjuncture between the way things are and the way students think they should be, students can see the consequences of solutions to problems, a hallmark of reflective learning. Through this exercise they are able to better appreciate the complex mosaic called an international, gendered perspective.

NOTES
1. We recognize the difficulties involved in placing cultures into dualistic cate-gories of *traditional* and *modern*, but these seem the most appropriate terms to use in dealing with the issues raised by this case study.

2. This exercise was designed for use in a freshman level geography course (GEOG 130) on developing countries. The course has 150 students and consists of a large lecture twice a week, and small discussion groups (25 students) that meet once a week. It is in the discussion groups that most of the active reflective learning takes place.

WORKS CITED

Merryfield, Merry M., and Richard C. Remy. 1995. *Teaching About International Conflict and Peace.* Albany: State University of New York Press.

Monk, Janice, Anne Betteridge, and Amy Newhall. 1991. "Introduction: Reaching for Global Feminism in the Curriculum." *Women's Studies International Forum* 14 (4): 238–247.

Newmann, Fred M. 1970. *Clarifying Public Controversy.* Boston: Little, Brown. 1970.

Stamp, Patricia. 1991. "Burying Otieno: The Politics of Gender and Ethnicity in Kenya." *Signs: Journal of Women in Culture and Society* 16 (4): 808–845.

WAYS OF READING: A FACULTY DEVELOPMENT PROJECT AT THE UNIVERSITY OF MINNESOTA

Mary M. Lay

The Ways of Reading project at the University of Minnesota gathered faculty to work in groups on individual courses and on a core course in women's studies, international studies, or area studies. Over a three-year period, different groups met over an entire academic year. The faculty participants volunteered after receiving general announcements on campus and specific notices to department chairs. Those interested in participating in the project were asked to submit a short proposal in the spring prior to the meetings of the working groups. The proposal identified how their work on the project would improve a course for which they had primary responsibility and what knowledge and skills they might bring to revision of the core course. Four faculty and staff members from the Center for Advanced Feminist Studies, who administered the project, and from the department of women's studies and the Institute for International Studies read the proposals and selected faculty members to constitute the working groups for each year. Because participants had to make a year-long commitment to the project, only a few faculty needed to be turned away or put on a waiting list. This chapter describes the work done during the second year of the project, 1996–97, as it was typical of all three years.

One working group, consisting of six faculty from Spanish and Portuguese, women's studies, geography, philosophy, and art, revised a core course entitled "Introduction to Women's Studies." The other working group, consisting of five faculty members from women's studies, French and Italian, philosophy, classical and Near Eastern studies, and German, Scandinavian, and Dutch, developed a new theory course for upper-level undergraduates, entitled International Feminist Theory. Members of both faculty working groups also revised and developed courses within their own curricula. Both groups aimed to integrate concerns of international and area studies into women's studies courses and to integrate concerns of women's studies into international and area studies courses.

The groups met weekly throughout the year, and each faculty member's department was given funding to hire a teaching assistant or instructor to replace the faculty in one course during one quarter that year. A graduate student was also hired to serve as an administrative fellow and research assistant for each group—setting up meetings, arranging for visiting scholars, compiling bibliographies to inform the core courses and individual faculty member's course, and administering the budget.

At the beginning of the project, each group identified goals for revising the core course. For example, the group working on the Introduction to Women's Studies course listed their goals as follows:

1. Create a course inclusive of many perspectives, yet avoid too many voices.

2. Integrate topics about Third World women into the course with due attention to the diversity within this category.

3. Present material in a way that avoids exoticizing Third World women.

4. Give students an understanding of places with which they do not have direct experience.

5. Allay instructors' potential fears of teaching outside their own expertise.

6. Make the course technology rich.

After setting their goals, both groups then identified a set of key intellectual issues that stimulated and guided their work throughout the year. For example, the group working on the "Introduction to Women's Studies" course discussed the following key issues:

1. the process of curriculum integration, specifically that of introducing Third World women into an existing course;

2. the timing of presenting international material at different points within the syllabus;

3. the definitions of complex terms associated with internationalizing a women's studies course;

4. the necessity of choosing to define internationalizing to mean more than integration of material on Third World women specifically;

5. the avoidance of stereotypes; and

6. the importance of making the point that women around the world are not simply victims of oppression.

In the first of the weekly meetings, the group working on Introduction to Women's Studies examined and reviewed the existing course syllabi and scheduled meetings with the chair of the women's studies department, who had primary responsibility for the course, and with the graduate and undergraduate teaching assistants who assisted in the course. Faculty participants read a range of articles addressing feminist pedagogy and describing similar attempts to internationalize women's studies courses at other U.S. institutions. With the help of the graduate student teaching assistant, the group began to develop a working bibliography on internationalizing women's studies curricula, feminist pedagogy, and pedagogical approaches to multicultural and international courses. This bibliography also suggested readings and films for instructors and students. This group took as its starting point the fall quarter 1996 women's studies syllabus, a successful and well-developed course focused on the United States. In order to integrate the international perspectives theoretically and through exploration of particular themes, each group member took primary responsibility for one theme and brought back to the group a series of questions that informed the theme, suggested readings, and recommended pedagogical approaches. Finally, in the fall of 1997, the group presented their suggestions and revised syllabus to University of Minnesota women's studies members and students during a Ways of Reading public seminar.

During the 1996–97 academic year, group members also worked on their individual courses, presenting the current model of the course during the first meetings of the project, and then presenting the revised course at the end of the year. Group members discussed these individual syllabi, offering suggestions on course organization, presentation, and pedagogy. Day-long retreats outside of the Twin Cities area for both working groups offered large, uninterrupted blocks of time for the groups to consider major questions and, at the end of the year, to complete final drafts of syllabi. Finally, meetings with both University of Minnesota personnel and visiting scholars offered excellent opportunities for the faculty working groups to receive feedback on their individual courses and on the core course revisions.

During the 1996–97 academic year, the two working groups invited visiting scholars to spend a few hours or one or two days with them as individuals and collectively, and in some cases give a public presentation. Visiting scholars for the year included Barbara Harlow, Janice Monk, Natalie Kampen, and Ruth Behar, respectively representing the fields of comparative literature, geography, history, and anthropology. Before they arrived on campus, visiting scholars were presented with a series of questions that were currently challenging the working groups and were invited to assign readings to the working groups. When the Ways of Reading project asked other units on campus to cosponsor the visiting scholars, they reached new departments and programs that had not previously collaborated with the Ways of Reading project. For example, the School of Architecture and the departments of art history and cultural studies and comparative literature cosponsored Janice Monk's two-day visit.

Clearly, the success of the Ways of Reading effort at the University of Minnesota reflected the fact that faculty were given time and support to read, discuss, and work on curricular revision. Their work, moreover, also made an impression on the center or unit administering the project, since the graduate student assistants reported weekly to the director of the Center for Advanced Feminist Studies, and at the end of the year, each member of the working groups publicly assessed the value of his or her experience and gathered suggestions for the next year of the project.

INTERNATIONALIZING AND "ENGENDERING" THE CURRICULUM AT THE UNIVERSITY OF MARYLAND

DEBORAH S. ROSENFELT WITH A. LYNN BOLLES

Women and Gender in an Era of Global Change: Internationalizing and "Engendering" the Curriculum was a three-year project housed in the women's studies department and the Curriculum Transformation Project at the University of Maryland, College Park, and cosponsored by the office of international affairs. The project's mission was twofold: to enhance understanding in the university community of the international processes and differing national contexts that structure gender, and to explore women's responses to globalization in their daily lives, forms of activism, and cultural contributions. The project was designed to encourage faculty in a variety of fields at both the College Park campus and other campuses in the University of Maryland system to incorporate into their courses new scholarship and theory about women and gender, with an emphasis on women's experiences in such international processes as economic globalization, the proliferation of new electronic technologies, the rise of religious fundamentalisms, and the spread of ideologies linking democracy and free market capitalism. The project also wanted to look at the movements of women themselves across borders—as immigrants, refugees, scholars, artists, and activists.

The Women and Gender in an Era of Global Change project grew out of the Curriculum Transformation Project's mandate to provide resources for faculty development in feminist and ethnic studies scholarship and pedagogy. The Curriculum Transformation Project, funded by the central administration and housed in women's studies, has offered summer institutes for faculty since 1989, focusing especially on the intersections of gender and race. In the early nineties, the campus began a systematic effort to internationalize its curriculum and extend and strengthen its links with a range of programs abroad. An advisory group to the project recommended that we make efforts to secure external funds to internationalize women's studies and to bring questions of gender into courses and campus initiatives on international issues. We created a board specifically oriented to international issues, and also surveyed faculty throughout the Maryland system to ascertain interest in and secure support for such a project. We received about seventy enthusiastic letters from interested faculty, many appending outlines for courses they wished to transform. The campus does not have specific area studies programs, with the exception of the Center for Latin American Studies, linked to the Spanish and Portuguese department. Because economics, government and politics, history, and sociology do have strong emphases on international issues, these were the departments we most hoped to engage. As it turned out, many of the faculty interested in the project came from departments in the humanities. Already teaching about women and gender, they were eager to discuss issues of international import, particularly processes of globalization.

PROJECT DESIGN

As it evolved, the project supported four basic kinds of activities: (1) a monthlong summer institute; (2) "polyseminars" during the academic year; (3) small developmental stipends for faculty; and (4) a concluding conference. The first two activities built upon successful programs already conducted by the Curriculum Transformation Project and the women's studies program.

THE SUMMER INSTITUTE: THINKING ABOUT WOMEN AND GENDER IN CONTEMPORARY INTERNATIONAL CONTEXTS

Each year we organized an intensive monthlong summer institute for twelve to thirteen faculty from College Park and other Maryland state campuses. We were also able to select two advanced, foreign graduate students each summer whose interests—projects on women's and gender issues in their countries of origin—could enhance and ideally be enhanced by our discussions. The topics shifted from summer to summer depending on the participants' interests, but some remained constant: women and economic development; gender, religion, nation, and the construction of identity; women's rights, reproductive rights, and human rights; local and global feminisms; and sessions on pedagogy and syllabus revision. The institutes were codirected each summer by an anthropologist with specific area expertise: A. Lynn Bolles, on the Caribbean; Seung-kyung Kim, on Korea and the Asian Pacific. Their rich knowledge of local women's lives enabled us to explore the complex relations among local and global, affording examples of and departures from generalizations about the impact of globalization. Several consultants contributed to the seminar in successive summers, among them Janice Monk on pedagogies and on gender and geography; Mark Blackden, head of the gender division of the World Bank's sub-Saharan Africa section; Amrita Basu, on the relation of local feminisms to global gender issues; and Anika Rahman, staff attorney for the Center for Reproductive Law and Policy's international division on women's rights/human rights.

THE POLYSEMINARS

During the regular academic year, faculty explored specific aspects of women's lives and gender issues internationally in polyseminars. A faculty study group and the students in an upper-division women's studies course attended a public lecture and then met with the visiting lecturers for more intensive discussion the following day. Participants in the faculty study group received release time for weekly sessions devoted to both scholarly and pedagogical concerns. Polyseminar themes included Women/Policy/Activism in an Era of Global Change; Globalization, Gender, and Culture; and The World's Women: Agenda for Change. Ten faculty from across the College Park campus participated in each of the annual study groups.

FACULTY DEVELOPMENT GRANTS

Individual stipends in the amount of five hundred dollars were awarded to ten faculty from College Park and other system campuses, for research, travel, or resources related to curriculum development on the themes covered by the grant. Awards were given for projects ranging from the purchase of books or films for university or department libraries to stipends for individuals seeking to document for classroom use their research on women's art, literature, and activism in various countries.

THE CONCLUDING CONFERENCE

A two-day concluding conference, "Transforming Knowledge for a Changing World: Internationalizing Gender, 'Engendering' the International," was designed both to disseminate and extend the work of the previous three years. A plenary session, "Connecting Local and Global Feminisms," featured talks by Amrita Basu, Pamela Sparr, Valentine M. Moghadam, and Reena Bernards, who addressed, respectively, the need for careful attention to local histories and cultures while conceptualizing the emergence of global feminist practice; the current and potential links among poor women in the North and the South as they work for economic change; the priorities and class divisions in the women's movement in the Middle East and North Africa; and the often invisible contributions of women as peacemakers in regional conflicts. Chandra Mohanty's keynote address, "Race, Gender, and Globalization: Pedagogical and Curricular Challenges for Transnational Studies," analyzed critical intersections and assessed challenges. Another keynote, by Sonia Picado, then the Costa Rican ambassador to the United States, raised questions of women's leadership and women's rights. Other panels at the conference featured participants in the project, who discussed dilemmas and progress in teaching international women's studies. The conference attracted over one hundred registrants from throughout and beyond the mid-Atlantic region.

STRENGTHS, WEAKNESSES, AND CHALLENGES

The project revealed the strengths and weaknesses of a multidisciplinary endeavor with a broad set of intellectual commitments. Evaluations—on the whole very positive—reiterated constantly that the opportunity to talk with colleagues across disciplinary lines (and also across national and racial lines, since participants were selected to provide as much diversity as possible) was the greatest strength of the institute, but some also said that the project tried to cover too much and overwhelmed participants with too many readings on too many issues.

Conceptually, the multidisciplinarity of the project proved both difficult and fruitful. Faculty found themselves confronted with research methodologies and ways of reading far different from their own, and not always sympathetic to their own inclinations. Empirically oriented faculty sometimes found the theoretical discussions from interpretive fields influenced by postmodernism to be abstruse and insufficiently grounded in data. Faculty from interpretive fields like literature and film studies sometimes found empirical, data-driven work and even policy documents like the Beijing Platform for Action inadequately theorized. Some faculty ultimately realized that their disciplinary cultures were as powerful in shaping their consciousness and values as other cultural affiliations, and this realization sometimes opened up possibilities for discussing the power of cultural difference in other arenas, for example, in constructing gender identities.

Over the term of the grant we came to realize that these epistemological tensions are related also to tensions between an emphasis on the "local" and an emphasis on the "global." Throughout the grant, we struggled to acknowledge the complex histories, geographies, and cultures of local and regional sites of inquiry even as we concerned ourselves with processes that operated transnationally, like those named above. In one of our institutes we focused especially on sub-Saharan Africa and the Caribbean as a way to give some depth to our explorations of the intersections of global processes with specific regions and cultures. In retrospect, we may have reified a certain North American ethnocentrism by conflating *Third World* with *local*; certainly the project ultimately focused more on the Third World and countries of the South than on those of Europe and the North. We never successfully resolved these tensions, but as time went on, we came to articulate them better and to strategize about how to integrate them more effectively into the curriculum. One of our insights was that certain disciplines—those that manipulate data sets, that do large empirically oriented research projects, that investigate world economic systems, and that look to nation-states and their interactions—claim and in some ways offer more understanding of the "global," whereas others—those that examine local cultures, religious practices, literary and artistic production—claim more methodological affinities with the "local," the specific experiences and expressions of specific peoples. But such an observation also reifies a division between the material and the cultural that much contemporary scholarship in many fields, certainly in cultural studies, works to deconstruct. Such contradictory insights helped us to rearticulate the necessity for interdisciplinary scholarship to gain a full understanding of women's issues (indeed, of all issues) and strategies for change. Ultimately, this sense of collaborative possibilities among the disciplines helped to defuse, if not resolve, the tensions among different disciplinary cultures.

A more intractable dilemma revealed itself gradually: the extent to which our basic understanding of what it might mean to "internationalize" women's studies inevitably was rooted in and shaped by our experience as women's studies practitioners in the United States. Those of us who had focused on women's issues and experiences mostly in the United States learned how local, how "situated," our own knowledge base was, even in areas—for example, differences among women—that had generated a great deal of sophisticated scholarship. Many of our best moments consisted of thoughtful and sometimes heated exchanges among scholars—sometimes participants, sometimes consultants—from different national backgrounds, about the underlying value of specific bodies of research and theory for the women in their countries. Questions about knowledge and power permeated our seminars. We found ourselves longing for more sustained exchanges with women's studies scholars in other locales, conversations in which we could explore more fully the differences and similarities among us, among our research and teaching priorities. This longing inspired a new proposal that will fund such sustained interactions.

IMPACT OF THE PROJECT

The project was very successful in meeting its original goals, though perhaps (in quantitative terms) more successful in assisting women's studies faculty—that is, faculty in various departments already interested in women's and gender issues—to "internationalize" than in inspiring a new interest in women and gender among faculty in international and area studies. Forty faculty of the fifty-six funded participants submitted fifty revised or new course outlines (several submitted outlines for more than one course).[1] Several participants in the project have published essays about their work,[2] and a new reader in feminist theory, inspired by the project, will soon be available, coedited by Seung-kyung Kim at College Park and participant Carol McCann at the University of Maryland, Baltimore County. About a third of the participants gave presentations about or growing from their work on the project to various campus and professional groups. Less tangible, but equally important, the project helped develop and strengthen networks of faculty throughout the Maryland state system who are concerned with the regional, national, and international contexts in which women live their lives. One of our participants thanked us in an informal note for "the most exciting intellectual experience of my life." We concur.

NOTES

1. Twenty-six of the courses were from College Park; the rest from other campuses in the system. Substantially revised courses at College Park included Women in the Media; Family Violence; a group of courses for an undergraduate honors program, College Park Scholars in International Studies; Healing Women (a dramatically reconceptualized Women and Psychoanalysis); Commercial Spanish; and Contemporary Political Fiction by Women (previously Contemporary Writing by Women). Courses extensively revised at other campuses include Women in Perspective (an introduction to women's studies); Feminist Theory; Cultural Anthropology; Women's Rights and Social Policy; Cross-Cultural Perspectives in Nursing; Media Criticism; and World Civilization since 1500. New courses developed in conjunction with the project include Gender, the State and Social Policy in Cross-National Perspective (sociology, University of Maryland, Baltimore County); Globalization, Gender, and Culture (women's studies, University of Maryland, College Park [hereafter UM]); Geography of Women (geography, Towson University [hereafter TU]); International Perspectives on Women (women's studies, TU); Women in Global Perspective: Sisterhood in Europe, West Africa, and the Caribbean (team taught and offered jointly in history at Coppin State, a historically Black college, and the University of Baltimore); Lesbian Communities: Lesbians in Multinational Reception (women's studies, UM); and Women and Comparative Politics (government and politics, UM). This latter course was developed not by a funded participant but by a professor who drew extensively on our resources to create a pioneering course in a large department with very few courses on women, a happy example of the ripple effect of our work.
2. See especially *Women's Studies Quarterly* 26, nos. 3 and 4 (Fall–Winter 1998).

PRODUCTIVE TENSIONS: GLOBAL PROCESSES, LOCAL LIVES AT THE UNIVERSITY OF ARIZONA

KIMBERLY JONES

In 1984, with support from the U.S. Department of Education, scholars at the University of Arizona's Southwest Institute for Research on Women (SIROW) began addressing issues of internationalizing women's studies and integrating gender into international area studies. Three projects followed. The first encouraged faculty teaching internationally oriented courses to integrate topics about women into their courses. The second turned to women's studies courses with the goal of bringing in new scholarship on women from around the world. The third, a collaboration with the Center for Middle Eastern Studies, had multiple goals—introducing gender into courses on the Middle East, bringing topics of Middle Eastern women into women's studies courses, and fostering the inclusion of gender-related material on the Middle East in courses such as world history, comparative politics, and development studies, which had bypassed the Middle East and women. We made considerable gains in the course of these projects, but also identified an array of new conceptual and pedagogical issues that needed to be addressed. With each project, we modified the model we adopted for fostering curriculum and faculty development.

When the opportunity arose to participate in the Women's Studies, Area and International Studies (WSAIS) project, we formulated a model centered on intensive summer institutes. This decision stemmed from the nature of SIROW, a regional consortium that includes more than thirty academic institutions in the southwestern United States and northern Mexico. Because of the great distances in the region, and because each institution has its own calendar, it is impossible to find a time during the academic year when faculty and students from all of the SIROW schools are able to meet. In the first year, we designed an institute for a leadership group of twelve faculty, with the intention that these faculty, several of whom had participated in previous projects, would bring that experience to developing mentoring capacities. Previously we had relied on staff or external consultants for that work. In the second year, we expanded the institute to include thirty-two participants, both faculty and graduate students, who had not previously been involved. This essay emphasizes the work of the second year, but also indicates how that effort allowed us to integrate our previous experiences and what we had learned from the first year's leadership development efforts.

In planning and implementing the institute, we found ourselves considering a number of tensions—between the global and the local, between gender studies and area studies, and between pedagogy and research. First, we wanted to explore the tension between focusing on a single country or geographical region versus carrying out comparative work. How are specific localities influenced by global processes, and, conversely, how does the local level influence the global? How can we strike a balance between the kind of detailed expertise necessary to interpret local events and situations and the broader perspective that is necessary when using a more comparative or global framework?

A second tension was that between gender and area studies. Scholars in gender studies are comfortable dealing with issues concerning gender, but in many cases focus on the United States. Area studies scholars are knowledgeable about their geographical area of interest, but may not be accustomed to considering gender in their work. In either case, it can be difficult to stretch ourselves beyond the work we are accustomed to doing. The question of expertise is crucial: Given the amount of time it takes to become knowledgeable about a new area or a new idiom, how can we learn enough to be competent researchers and teachers in a broader sphere?

Another tension exists between teaching and research, which are often seen as being relatively separate parts of the academic enterprise. Previous SIROW-sponsored institutes had focused on transforming the undergraduate curriculum. For this project, we thought it was important to address both teaching and research, and to consider the connections between them. Therefore, we wanted not only to incorporate discussions of pedagogy and curriculum, but also to consider the ways in which gender and area studies could be combined fruitfully to contribute to interdisciplinary and comparative research—to consider what a combination of area studies and gender studies might offer to teachers and scholars.

Other tensions that the institute incorporated were those between disciplines, always a factor in attempts to teach or do research in an interdisciplinary way, and the tensions between the perspectives of graduate students and faculty members. The existence of these sorts of tensions proved especially beneficial in working on small group projects that were a main focus of the institute, as the groups were able to bring a multitude of perspectives to bear on their tasks. In developing the content of the institute, we spent considerable energy in identifying themes that we thought would enable us to deal productively with these various tensions. Eventually we targeted three themes:

1. development (including political, economic, and environmental change);
2. postcolonial processes and national and ethnic identity formation; and
3. migration, mobility, and human rights.

We also decided to focus on Africa, East Asia, Latin America, and the Middle East because of the presence on campus of faculty members with expertise in these four geographical regions.

CONTRIBUTORS AND PARTICIPANTS

Many people contributed to the project. It was headed by three directors, a sociolinguist from the department of East Asian studies (Kimberly Jones), an art historian who was directing the Center for Middle Eastern Studies (Amy Newhall), and a geographer who is the executive director of SIROW (Janice Monk). They were supported by a half-time associate director (Sandra Shattuck), a specialist in comparative literature. For the second-year institute, these project directors were assisted by four faculty mentors from other SIROW regional institutions, all of whom had attended the first-year leadership development institute. The four participants from that institute who were invited back to serve as mentors in the second year were selected for their expertise in the topics we were considering, their experience in curriculum transformation, and the diverse perspectives they represented (two were humanities scholars and two were social scientists, their research covered a number of different parts of the world, and three of them were originally from outside the United States). Finally, in addition to the directors and mentors, two keynote speakers and six local consultants also contributed, giving talks and leading a variety of sessions during the week of the institute.

Our goal for the institute was to accept thirty participants, a mixture of faculty and graduate students, who would be diverse in terms of their institutions (from small colleges to large research universities), academic disciplines, and geographical regions (both in terms of origin and in terms of areas studied). Because we made substantial efforts to publicize the institute, there were approximately twice as many applicants as there were places, and in the end we had thirty-two participants, half of them faculty and half graduate students, who did indeed reflect the diversity that we had hoped to achieve. Participants were predominantly from the social sciences, with twelve areas of study represented: anthropology, communication, environmental studies, geography, history, international studies, English literature, political science, public health, rangeland management, sociology, and women's studies. Although the teaching and research of a relatively high percentage of the group focused on Latin America, a variety of areas from around the world were represented. Many of the participants either came from another country or had lived abroad. The one way in which the participants were not diverse was sex; all were women (as were all of the applicants who responded by the deadline). Perhaps this composition reflects the burgeoning interest of feminist scholars—the majority of whom are women—in international perspectives, and their consequent willingness to devote time during the summer to an intensive curriculum development program.

GROUP PROJECTS

While previous SIROW institutes had focused on developing syllabi for individual courses, we developed a number of potential projects for the participants to work on. In the first year of the institute, participants had been asked to carry out some sort of project while in attendance. Although we had encouraged group projects at that institute, all of the participants ended up working independently. Because of this, we decided to make collaborative work a requirement at the institute during its second year. Our goal was two-fold: to encourage interdisciplinary and comparative approaches by grouping people with expertise in different areas and to offer a model for some of the pedagogical techniques we planned to discuss. We asked participants to rank the potential projects in order of preference before they arrived at the institute. Then, based on their preferences, we assigned them to small working groups, trying to insure a diversity of participants within each group. There were eight groups, each assisted by one of the eight directors and mentors.

We developed five categories of projects, and within each we tried to give several options for the overall topic a project might address. The five categories included creating

1. a course syllabus that would integrate both global and local perspectives (several potential course titles were suggested);

2. a teaching activity or strategy to foster critical thinking in relation to gender in global or comparative perspectives that would address students' attitudes toward diversity internationally, or engage students in decision-making with respect to an applied problem;

3. a position paper that discussed issues related to the funding and implementation of comparative research and teaching that incorporates gender;

4. a research proposal for a comparative project involving gender; and

5. a curriculum for a program incorporating both global and local perspectives (such as a women's studies major or an area studies graduate program).

At least one group worked on each of these five categories.

INSTITUTE ACTIVITIES

In planning the schedule for the weeklong institute, we included a variety of activities for each day. There was an average of one speaker a day, including our two keynote speakers and a number of local speakers from the University of Arizona. Overall, however, we tried to minimize the amount of time participants would spend listening to speakers, preferring instead to have them grappling more actively with the issues raised by the institute by engaging in discussions; exploring electronic resources, especially the Internet; creating teaching materials; analyzing syllabi, films, and photographic images; brainstorming about how to solve various pedagogical challenges; working on their group projects; and, finally, presenting the results of the group projects to each other.

The first of our two keynote speakers, Deborah Wong, an ethnomusicologist, discussed the connections and tensions between area studies and multicultural studies from the perspective of an Asian studies scholar who has also become interested in Asian American issues. The second keynote speaker, Barbara Thomas-Slayter, a political scientist specializing in international development, reflected on her experiences of working across regional (Asian and African) and disciplinary boundaries. Professors Wong and Thomas-Slayter joined forces to lead a discussion of pedagogy.

Local speakers from the University of Arizona also touched on a variety of issues concerning research and pedagogy. Geographer Sallie Marston discussed how she tries to convey the local relevance of global issues to students, both in class and in an introductory geography textbook she coauthored (Knox and Marston 1998). Anne Betteridge, who teaches Middle Eastern studies and is the executive director of the Middle East Studies Association, discussed current trends in research funding for global, comparative research instead of in-depth studies of specific areas. Political scientist Spike Peterson discussed the interconnection of gender and nationalism and ways of approaching the teaching of international relations. Cass Fey, curator of education at the university's Center for Creative Photography, introduced participants to critical viewing of photographic images.

The institute incorporated a number of hands-on activities to extend participants' skills in using electronic resources, videos, and films, creating teaching activities around prompts such as newspaper articles, illustrations from travel magazines, or (translated) Japanese song lyrics. Three evenings of the week were then set aside for participants to view a variety of films. Several discussions focused on issues such as syllabus design, learning activities, and a set of scenarios presenting pedagogical challenges that might arise in trying to integrate international and comparative perspectives in the courses one teaches.

In addition to the various presentations, workshops, and pedagogy sessions, we also scheduled time for the working groups to meet and discuss their projects. We adopted this full schedule because the participants from the smaller first-year institute, which lasted for ten days, had suggested that the institute was too long and that the unscheduled evenings had been time wasted. Their suggestion was to use evenings for scheduled events and to limit the institute to one week (Sunday night through Saturday night). Not surprisingly, perhaps, many of the second-year participants felt that their institute had been a bit too busy and lamented the lack of free time in the evenings to indulge in less structured interactions with other participants!

REFLECTIONS

Despite some feelings that we had tried to do too much for one week, the level of energy displayed by the participants was extraordinary and contagious. It was clear by the end of the institute that everybody thought they had benefited from the opportunity to converse with a diverse group of faculty and graduate students about the various tensions surrounding the integration of gender and area studies in research and teaching, and especially from the interdisciplinary conversations. The perspectives of graduate students proved to be particularly valuable as the group considered issues of planning courses and curricula. Putting the participants in small working groups to focus on predetermined tasks was also very successful. On the final day of the institute, when the groups presented their projects to each other, it was impressive to see what had been accomplished in such a short time. Some of the groups found it a struggle to adequately incorporate the perspectives of the various disciplines they represented, but they seemed to agree that the struggle was worthwhile. Perhaps the main lesson the institute taught us in the end is that when faced with a specific task to accomplish, the tensions inherent in doing work that is interdisciplinary, comparative, or collaborative, not to mention the tensions that come from trying to incorporate the perspectives of diverse participants, can be effectively channeled into productive dialogue. In the postinstitute period, we provided minigrants to a number of participants to continue collaborative work initiated during the summer programs. The results of their efforts are well represented in this volume.

WORK CITED

Knox, Paul, and Sallie Marston. 1998. *Human Geography: Places and Regions in Global Perspective*. Upper Saddle River, N.J.: Prentice-Hall.

GENDERS, BODIES, BORDERS: A THEME SEMESTER REPORT AT THE UNIVERSITY OF MICHIGAN

ABIGAIL J. STEWART

The fall 1997 theme semester in the University of Michigan's College of Literature, Science, and the Arts, "Genders, Bodies, Borders," was conceived as the culmination of a three-year project entitled "Differences Among Women: International Perspectives." The large project attempted to bring together scholars working in gender studies with those involved in international and area studies in order to enhance the teaching of both through greater understanding and integration across disciplines. During the first two years, the groundwork had been laid in seminars and discussions among faculty and graduate students; during the fall 1997 semester, the work of the past two years was brought together in a broad network of courses and events under the general heading "Genders, Bodies, Borders." A committee of faculty and students planned the overall activities, while the Institute for Research on Women and Gender implemented the theme semester jointly with the women's studies program and the International Institute.

At the University of Michigan, theme semesters are presented during many academic semesters. They are often interdisciplinary efforts, designed to bring together a set of coordinated course offerings on a common theme. They usually involve several public events, open not only to those students in the coordinated courses but to the campus as a whole. Usually they provide some thematic focus within a broad curriculum, as well as extracurricular activities (lectures, films, concerts, exhibitions, etc.). Some theme semesters have focused on the Victorian period, on the theory and practice of evil, on food, and on conflict and community. The seminar participants saw the theme semester as a local "institution" that would provide a suitable vehicle both for curricular innovation (by encouraging faculty to offer courses related to the theme) and as a wider effort at consciousness-raising for the student and faculty communities.

The title, "Genders, Bodies, Borders," was selected after extensive discussion within the seminar. *Genders* signaled both a focus on gender, and recognition of multiple genders. *Bodies* was chosen because in the seminar bodies were often usefully concrete vehicles for the transmission, expression, and performance of both genders and nationhood (e.g., in international conflict). Finally, *borders* reflected our discovery that the metaphor of borderlands was vivid and valuable in highlighting both the national and the global. Bringing the three terms together without specifying the relation among them (by separating them with commas) permitted us to include a wide range of courses that addressed some or all of these three themes in a variety of ways.

The theme semester incorporated four major components: a set of courses and three different series of *enrichment activities*—events open to the general public free of charge. These included a series of public lectures and conferences, a film and video series, and a set of live artistic performances and exhibitions. The range of types of events, combined with their accessibility, made it possible to draw a wide variety of people from both the university and the larger community, thus crossing the border between the academy and the "outside" world. We were able to sponsor an unusually broad array of events, in part because the planning committee was large and diverse, and because our goal was stimulation.

COURSES

The forty-three courses offered represented twenty-six divisions of the university, spanning the College of Literature, Science, and the Arts (LS&A), the Residential College, the School of Art, the School of Social Work, the School of Nursing, and the Medical School. They included thirty-one undergraduate courses (including eight first-year seminars) and twelve graduate courses. Several were developed in a summer seminar that was part of the "Differences Among Women" project. Many were cross-listed with two or more departments or programs. In some cases, the cross-listing linked not only departments but also schools; for example, Women's Health in the World: Issues in Translation and Transnational Perspectives, which was listed with women's studies and history (both LS&A units) and the Medical School's department of obstetrics and gynecology. The total enrollment for all of the courses was 974 students; of these, 787 were undergraduates and 187 were graduate students.

LECTURES AND CONFERENCES

The series of eight public lectures, one panel discussion, and two conferences covered a broad range of topics, several of which dovetailed with various courses. Five lectures concerned international women's health issues, presented by scholars from the social sciences, medicine, and literature. Topics ranged from women's reproductive health to constructions of the body and gender through fashion.

With respect to the larger category of *gender, bodies, borders,* the panel "Borders and Commodities: Gender, Sex and Work in International Perspective," addressed issues ranging from the international prostitutes' rights movement to the exploitation of immigrant Thai workers in Los Angeles. Similarly, a three-day conference, "Rhetorics and Rituals of (Un)Veiling in Early Modern Europe," included workshops, a harp concert at a local church, and a museum exhibition, while a second conference, "Gender, Bodies, Borders," focused on work by almost forty graduate students with two lectures by distinguished scholars.

FILMS

The film series crossed several boundaries, including film and video, American and international films, Hollywood and independent work, male and female directors, fiction and documentary. Ten feature-length films were offered free of charge at the Michigan Theater on Monday evenings. We were also privileged to have filmmaker June Cross on campus to answer questions at a screening of her Emmy-winning documentary *Secret Daughter*, a fascinating examination of her own biracial family.

The weeklong festival of women-made videos included documentaries on such diverse subjects as the history of Barbie, the transsexual liberation movement, Latin American machismo, Serbian war crimes against women, the Chinese Cultural Revolution, and Detroit back-alley abortionists. Also included in this series was a multimedia performance piece by Ann Arbor filmmaker-choreographer Terri Sarris, incorporating dance, video, and the spoken word. Many of the videos were drawn from existing collections at the university and the festival also resulted in additional purchases by the library.

LIVE ARTS EVENTS

The theme semester's international perspective was also particularly evident in the series of performances and exhibitions. The series began with two dance performances and two talk and video presentations on dance by Latina artists. The performances themselves included pieces on "Puerto Rican Barbie," working at the maquiladoras on the U.S.–Mexican border, and the link between Latin women, food, and the erotic in the Western popular imagination. Overlapping some of these performances was an exhibit of paintings, "Little Pieces of Me for Sale: Cuban Geishas," by visiting Cuban artist Rocio Garcia. Garcia's paintings evoke the Japanese image of the Geisha—the masked woman—to portray contemporary Cuban women in an increasingly mercenary society. A second art exhibit was staged by two University of

Michigan anthropologists, Sarah Caldwell and Brian Mooney. Entitled "Crossing Over: Images of Transgender Performance Across Cultures," it presented photographic images of ritual transgender performances in India and the United States and challenged the viewer to confront assumptions about gender identity.

As part of the theme semester, the University Musical Society also featured two distinguished women artists in their concert series and in taped Master of Arts interviews for WUOM radio. In addition, *Womansong*, a collaborative multimedia performance by University of Michigan dance professor Robin Wilson and writer-performer Elise Bryant, celebrated African-American womanhood through dance, video, poetry, and a reading from Bryant's latest play, *The Return of the Gospel Gems.*

The semester concluded with a three-day conference of local women writers from the university and the Ann Arbor community. The program included poetry and fiction readings and a lively and insightful discussion of "Why Women Write," followed by a book-signing and reception at a local bookstore.

ASSESSMENTS

A common thread running through responses to the theme semester was that it provided a lively and stimulating atmosphere—in one professor's words, "a common thematic landscape"—in which questions of gender could be discussed across disciplines. Another faculty member wrote: "I found this the most enjoyable and pedagogically satisfying undergraduate course I've taught for a long time, maybe even for the duration of my 18–19 years at Michigan, and it's clear that the pleasures/satisfactions/successes derive in no small part from the collective intellectual process that originated in the May seminar and the subsequent planning."

The abundance of courses on the theme, spread across the curriculum of a major research university, made it clear that gender has become a major field of academic inquiry. Furthermore, faculty members reported that the enrichment activities provided their classes with an important stimulus for discussions; some required their students to attend a particular event, and some based assignments on theme-semester lectures. Faculty reported that theme-semester events improved students' grasp of course topics that related to gender and national boundaries, giving focus to these concerns in various departments and programs across the curriculum. For example, one faculty member wrote that students who attended the talk by Nahid Toubia had a better grasp than the other students on course materials related to the cross-national comparison of women's situations. At the same time, the events had a reciprocal influence on curricula; faculty sometimes found their classes more enthusiastic than they anticipated. A faculty member reported that she interrupted her syllabus to accommodate a discussion of the Sandra Steingraber lecture because her students were so enthusiastic. She wrote, "We actually spent a whole class period the day of her talk discussing the assigned readings [from Steingraber's book] and half the next class discussing her talk."

Several students in one course commented that "they regretted the theme semester wasn't continuing next term, because they now felt informed/interested/motivated enough (having taken the course) to want to pursue and explore the issues some more."

We believe that the "Genders, Bodies, Borders" theme semester accomplished several of our original objectives—primarily, it stimulated an interdisciplinary discussion of gender and international perspectives that involved not only students, faculty, and staff at the University of Michigan, but also members of the university's wider community. New courses were offered and existing courses redesigned to integrate these interdisciplinary themes. Events were generally well attended. For example, over 300 people participated in the graduate student conference, films drew audiences ranging from 58 to 268, and literary readings 50 to 70 people. Finally, although theme semesters are normally programs within Michigan's undergraduate liberal arts college, "Genders, Bodies, Borders" crossed college boundaries through the participation of the schools of Art, Medicine, Nursing, Social Work, and the Residential College. This broad, cross-college interest suggests that even wider interdisciplinary collaboration may be achieved by operating theme semesters at the university level.

A FINAL NOTE ON FUNDING

The total direct cost of the theme semester events was approximately $60,000. This cost does not include any presemester planning, but does include about $14,000 for support staff hired specifically to manage theme semester activities. It also does not reflect additional costs of events for which the theme semester funds provided only partial funding. For example, the Medical School paid the entire travel and event costs for three speakers and the Interdisciplinary Project on Feminist Practice paid all the costs of one lecture; theme semester funds paid only for publicizing and audio-taping these lectures. Multiple units across campus contributed funds, in addition to the funds provided by the Ford Foundation grant. The Institute for Research on Women and Gender and the women's studies program contributed staff support for planning and management in kind. Thus, the cost of this staff support is not reflected in the total.

DIFFERENCES AMONG WOMEN— INTERNATIONAL PERSPECTIVES: DISCUSSION POINTS FROM A FACULTY SEMINAR

DAVID WILLIAM COHEN AND ABIGAIL J. STEWART

In May 1996 nine faculty (two of whom were facilitators) and five graduate students (one of whom was a coordinator) from seven academic departments at the University of Michigan participated in a seminar designed to provide support for faculty and graduate students who were developing or revising gender-inclusive international and area studies courses, or who were bringing international and area studies attention to gender and women's studies courses. The participants also worked collectively to plan a theme semester of focused courses and activities for the fall of 1997.

The following represents an inventory of some of the discussion points raised in the course of the seminar. Because the purpose of the seminar was to support and encourage faculty efforts toward new inclusion, no effort was made to achieve consensus on any of the issues raised. For that reason, we decided that the best form for this report was to enumerate the questions asked and observations made. We hope that this compilation will serve not only as a record of our seminar, but as an aid for colleagues considering similar curricular revisions. We think that the kinds of issues that emerged in our conversation are likely to emerge whenever faculty attempt to bring these two domains of interest (gender and women's studies, and international or area studies) together. We have grouped the observations and questions under a few broad headings, in the hope that this organization might help those considering similar efforts to identify the issues most pertinent to their interests or anxieties.

A. BRINGING A FOCUS ON WOMEN AND GENDER INTO COURSES

1. Many general issues arise whenever content on women and gender is introduced into courses for the first time.

2. It is important to differentiate the notions of women, gender, and feminism, though these are often collapsed in students' minds.

3. The teacher interested in introducing gender into a course faces a challenge: distinguishing issues that may be readily analyzed or taught through a framework of gender from those issues for which this may not be straightforward.

4. To the extent that all social phenomena may be arguably gendered, how does one then grasp—and then teach about—the specifics of the play of gender on social phenomena?

5. It may be tempting, but it is really problematic, to imagine a standard gendered account, or a woman's viewpoint. Gender is a *transgressive* term or concept, potentially invading every analytical approach.

6. How does one avoid, or move beyond, the additive—beyond attempting to teach about gender only by adding a section, a segment, or a chapter?

7. Part of the value of recent work on gender draws from new questions that emerge when women are put at the center of an analysis.

8. There is an opportunity to raise attention to *men as gender,* as a means of avoiding conceiving of gender entirely in terms of women.

9. One may also help students recognize the topographies of men's and women's approaches to, and within, different fields of political activity; some approaches may be more gendered than others.

10. Gender may be only one of the analytic categories being examined in a course.

11. One can use gender as an analytic category to identify and understand the workings of other issues of structural power relations (e.g., race, colonialism, sexuality, etc.). The reverse is equally true.

12. Women of color may find or locate a doubled vexation in theoretical works, not only in the obliteration of practical concerns and practical interests but also in the reproduction of naturalized languages of analysis associated with older and continuing forms of subjection.

13. How do you introduce unfamiliar concepts of sexuality and sexual and gender identity, for which students may have no starting points?

14. In the final analysis, what does gender mean?

15. Often, courses that incorporate attention to gender also must address issues of theory, especially feminist theory.

16. Feminist critiques have shaken confidence in a number of interpretative frameworks once consensual and conventional in twentieth-century social and cultural history.

17. Gender theory and feminist critique have now moved from partisan, oppositional discourse into general currency.

18. Feminist theories differ widely, and very different feminisms coexist within a single time and place.

19. It is important to link and to differentiate feminist theories and feminist political movements.

B. BRINGING A FOCUS ON INTERNATIONAL OR AREA STUDIES INTO COURSES

1. There are some important theoretical challenges in this kind of teaching, because it is not obvious how to define and work with notions of *the global.*

2. The *international* needs to be theorized, both in the world and in the study of and teaching about the world.

3. Some social scientists use *international* to underline the constructedness of phenomena, while others use the term to assess the universality of phenomena.

4. How do we avoid generalization of an entire people or nation from an individual, powerful testimony (in writing, in film, etc.)?

5. One could lose sight of significant issues relating to race and gender in the United States while seeking to bring attention to international issues and processes.

6. Moving teaching from a focus on the United States toward international perspectives and examples may too easily invite subjective appraisals of situations or circumstances as "better" or "worse" than U.S. standards.

7. The move to comparative and international teaching, with the incorporation of relatively unfamiliar cases and examples, may

lead to essentializing and romanticizing, rather than to critique and analysis.

8. One notes that certain international phenomena—examples, cases, perspectives—are actually peculiar to specific world areas, for example South Asia; going to them does not necessarily produce a more international picture.

9. Some theoretical frameworks that appear to arise within, and to facilitate, an international framework—for example development theory and modernization theory—have themselves arisen within the politics of specific national and transnational contexts and moments.

10. The attention, within the United States, to America's own cultural diversity as a route to the international introduces additional challenges to the teaching of international studies.

11. Migration and immigration policies and processes may produce their own politics, their own internal hegemonies.

12. In the search for comparative gleanings, one may miss the global and transnational interconnections and linkages among processes, programs, and phenomena.

13. The inclusion of other (non-U.S., non–Western, etc.) settings in teaching opens opportunities to see how the West is and has been imagined, at the same time complicating and illuminating notions of the West.

14. In working on an international, transnational, or global plane, the outcomes for both theoretical and practical work may be obverse, paradoxical, and uncomfortable.

15. A complicating feature of teaching about the world through an international framework is that sovereignty—the meanings of nationhood—is itself changing, and may be increasingly interrupted through international practice.

16. Is it possible to stand outside the dialectics of western–non-Western to grasp and teach the international in a more pluralistic manner?

17. Some topics seem especially well-suited to an international, global, or comparative treatment. The study of children—and teaching on children—for example, allows one to see the ways in which international and transnational categories are reproduced.

18. International fora—congresses, conferences—provide opportunities for viewing programs of representation, but they are also political activities in which certain persons or constituencies gain voice and visibility.

19. The study of migration and immigration from and to the United States permits a revising of American imperialism as a subject for study.

20. Literatures of migration constitute not a single voice, but rather a register of multiple and diverse readings of experience, permitting a teacher to complicate a student's propensity to read toward the monotonic or monolithic representation of experience, productively complicating notions of the authentic or essential.

21. One may take the opportunity to draw attention to the economies and sociologies underlying the production and reproduction of representations through which the international is perceived or understood by our students.

22. The challenges of managing international, cross-national, comparative, and also interdisciplinary teaching may invite, indeed demand, team-teaching.

23. There are problems in comparative work, in making comparisons; some provocative and evocative materials illuminating so-called everyday life (film, autobiography, novels, etc.) may complicate any possibility of useful comparisons, while at the same time exciting students' own comparative propensities.

24. At the same time, students may observe that particular things don't work here, underlining their essential approach as an us–them dialogic.

C. THE INTERSECTION OF WOMEN'S AND GENDER STUDIES AND INTERNATIONAL OR AREA STUDIES

1. There is a problem in locating and situating the feminist theorist in the international setting where the epistemological and pedagogical ground may not be stable.

2. One may fall into a view that Western feminism is foundational, and all other feminisms reactive to it. This can be avoided by placing non-Western feminist texts at the beginning, and using texts that are not particularly in dialogue with Western feminism.

3. Much feminist work represented as authentic and, essentially, oppositional can be understood as being in a close dialectical relationship with the work, ideas, power, and method, it critiques.

How does one find the Other outside of these dialogics?

4. One can ask not only how feminisms outside the West were influenced by Western feminisms, but also how Western feminism actually has developed in relation to other feminisms.

5. The examination of gender may be key to getting at the constructedness of nationalism, through the workings of the commonplace.

6. There is opportunity to bring attention to the ways in which ideas, images, identities, and voices have been or are being in certain ways commodified; this may help students understand the ways in which ideas about culture and about women have been commodified in late capitalist society.

7. The gendered child—the adolescent girl, the young male—is a site of control nationally and internationally.

8. How does one measure, map, and understand the gendered dimensions of ethnic conflict?

9. As in the workings of gender, the labor of constructing nationhood is never completed.

10. Among significant theoretical and epistemological issues, one may ask: What underlies European and American scholars' interest in knowing more about the status and condition of women elsewhere? Why are "we" or "they" interested?

11. It is always problematic to attempt to deploy present questions, such as those developing within gender studies, transhistorically; in contrast, historical issues are often foregrounded in international or area studies courses.

12. Among important pedagogical issues, it may be constructive to recognize that a great deal of this material may be uncomfortable for students.

13. With regard to difficult topics such as excision or female genital mutilation (and excision debates globally), it may be productive for students to voice their discomfort as they try to come to terms with the complexities of sensibility and with the complex grounds of "universal" moral standards.

14. It may be valuable to examine multiple accounts/perspectives on a single event (e.g., a war, disaster, movement, conflict), without serving as judge of the best or correct account. Accounts can be selected to permit recognition of the gendered dimensions of a phenomenon.

D. THE METAPHOR OF BORDERLANDS

1. The metaphor of the border, and the lands on both sides of borders, seemed particularly useful for bringing notions of women-gender and nations-areas together.

2. Attention to borders and margins, with respect both to gender and international migration and transnational contact and exchanges, allows unique views of unsettled as well as reified identities.

3. Likewise, attention to borders and margins produces fresh views of the nation and the state.

4. The idea of borderland entered general currency because it undermines certainties and identities, and problematized ways of writing about the state and nation.

5. There may be an irony lurking in the concept of the borderlands: not only are those peoples of the borderlands working simultaneously in multiple settings (for example, the *maquiladora*, Mexico, and the United States), but the borderlands subjects are made to do still further service within scholarly and policy arenas in the analysis and reconceptualization of concerns such as state, nation, and capital.

6. In managing constructions such as the borderlands it is important to distinguish levels of analysis and to differentiate material from metaphorical references.

7. What are the material and epistemological grounds for asserting a superior interpretative or surveillant position on the boundary? How do borderlands studies permit views of the mutual gaze— for example in the construction of distinctions between socialist and capitalist societies in the German setting?

E. CONSUMPTION IS ANOTHER GENERATIVE THEME OR METAPHOR

1. Consumption is a construct in which the gender dimension is unusually prominent and in which regional, national, and international analysis seems particularly appropriate.

2. Arenas of consumption provide opportunities to observe what men and women actually do—together and separately—and how men and women are represented.

3. Within the workings of consumption it is possible to see how gender is given additional valences, or values.

4. Representations of experience, of group, may be constituted in materialist processes as well as in ways other than the material.

5. Within teaching of gender and the international, there is an opportunity to examine representational practices in speaking, writing, performing; and there is an opportunity to examine the workings of audiences, where negotiations of the meaning and authority of representations may occur.

F. TEACHING PRACTICES

1. It is difficult to conceive how a teacher would or could bring together within a single course all the elements and trajectories tabled for discussion in the seminar.

2. In developing courses, how do we move among different and competing and also monolithic paradigms?

3. Does this kind of teaching require more than destabilizing existing conceptual frameworks and constructions?

4. Is it advantageous to cycle back and forth among different moments of history and is it possible to avoid teleologies in doing so?

5. Some pedagogical challenges relate to teaching within traditional disciplines: given that disciplines are generally resistant to new dimensions, spaces, and paradigms, such as those proposed within this seminar, to what extent is it possible to remap, or reconstruct, the introductory courses that have stood as bedrock elements within the consensual programs of disciplinary instruction and training?

6. Different kinds of theories need to be introduced within courses that map gender and the international in some association: how much background do students need in order to begin engaging new constructions and working with theory in this fresh conjuncture?

7. Theories have histories, geographies, sociologies, and politics; there are opportunities to teach theory and at the same time interrogate the working, purpose and power of theory. Such opportunities may be enriched, as well as made more complex, in the juncture of gender and the international.

8. What do we do when students may treat theory as better or worse in terms of "how far it may help us practically?"

9. How does the teacher bring students' attention to the shifting authority of subjectivities over time, while helping them to understand the workings of subjectivities in their own time?

10. How does one attend to the central issue of "getting it right" (positivist work) amid interpretative and epistemological as well as political diversity?

11. How can one address issues of expertise in particular historical and contemporary contexts?

12. How does one reframe the issue of faculty expertise to encourage risk-taking and experimentation even if this would undermine one's authority as a teacher?

13. The possibilities of doubt may be mobilized by the faculty member: through refusing to take an authoritative or final position; in giving privileged stress to questions as opposed to answers; and in sharing authority with students in certain topical domains or through special projects.

14. What are the more or less obvious contingencies in designing courses for undergraduate and graduate students? One may ask what theory does a graduate student need to know to move forward through the literatures and through the development of research. For the undergraduate student, the issue may be what will facilitate the asking of questions.

15. One approach to the expertise issue is to use case studies, individual or group projects, or other approaches, to develop knowledge within the course, then encourage students to make some of the more general, theoretical, or abstract connections.

16. It may be useful to design ways to help students recognize themselves in relation to key concepts (e.g., how their own national identity is constructed in concrete, everyday experiences).

17. Issues and protocols of standards work differently at different levels or in different spheres of the faculty member's responsibilities. An anthology of diverse and competing views may work well, or even be recognized as essential, in teaching but such eclecticism could obscure the critical focus and authority expected in the review of graduate research proposals or in the promotion and tenure reviews of faculty.

18. Certain ways of structuring the course material may be especially well-suited to courses with this complex agenda: contests and debates may reveal alternative visions, perspectives, interpretations, and theories regarding political interests and programs.

19. Debates have their sociologies and economies, and offer opportunities to bring out the framing contests that are substantially beyond the reach, or behind the backs, of the actors or participants.

20. In the presentation of history, it may be necessary or productive to break up the "plodding chronology," to shake up the "embodiment of progress" (e.g., by proceeding from the present backward in time, or by avoiding linear accounts in either direction).

21. Instruction might move among philosophy, theory, and practice, by simply attending to some of the practical issues that do intervene in theoretical and philosophical work.

22. Some opportunity may lie in mixing or interspersing different types of texts, refusing simplistic comparative treatment, and resisting the essentializing capacities of particular media.

23. In working within and through the theory-practice nexus, one may wish to move students past the "why" questions toward the "how" questions; the so-called foundational texts may privilege the "why" questions and obscure the "how" questions.

24. Classroom practices may need to be adapted to the special issues that arise in these courses: how does the teacher work with the understanding or anticipation that, for students, it does matter where a teacher stands on sensitive issues?

25. How can one work with multiple locations, "stages," to help students understand the workings of particular locations, including their own, on their sensibilities?

26. Does one disarm a view or idea by historicizing it? What are the moral and ethical issues in undermining or questioning students' sensibilities?

27. How does one draw students beyond evaluations based on right or wrong and correct or incorrect?

28. What issues of censorship and self-censorship lie between teacher and students in the inclusion within and exclusion from the classroom or course of certain material, films, etc.?

29. How does one teach about sexual violence? What can be incorporated, what cannot?

30. In teaching, it may be valuable to foreground "translation" across different experiences, to identify distinctions among deep differences, family resemblances, and incommensurate experiences.

31. How does one help undergraduates develop, early on, an interpretative, critical competence and confidence that goes beyond their own sensibilities?

32. How does one assist students to move critique beyond the authority to speak: who gets to speak, who can speak for others, etc.?

33. One of the challenges of teaching undergraduates is the communication of indeterminacy, of the force of uncertainty, of the often never completed quality of processes.

34. How do you move students back and forth between understanding myth as history and history as myth?

35. What kinds of starting points are strategic for drawing students toward a critical awareness of conventions and standard narratives even where they may be unfamiliar with these privileged frames of knowledge? How do you work with students in the development of critical tools when they have not yet met some of the ideas and models for which critique might be well served?

36. In team-teaching, how does one work with someone in productive complementarity?

37. In planning new courses—or revising existing ones—the scale of the course may matter as much as the level; some things can only be achieved in a small setting, but even large classes may be broken up into small groups in which certain discussions are possible that would not be possible otherwise.

SUGGESTIONS FOR TEACHERS UNDERTAKING CURRICULUM TRANSFORMATION

WENDY KOLMAR, DEBORAH S. ROSENFELT, AND JANICE MONK

These suggestions originally appeared in the form of a handout prepared by Wendy Kolmar for the New Jersey Project. Deborah Rosenfelt revised and expanded them for the Curriculum Transformation Project at the University of Maryland, and Janice Monk added suggestions on internationalization. They are very general and obviously depend for implementation on institutional context, the level and size of a class, its placement and status in the departmental and university curriculum, and preferred teaching styles.

COURSE CONTENT

- Define and analyze terminology, language, and basic disciplinary concepts; allow new material to challenge basic concepts and to suggest different ways to approach all material in course.

- Make explicit the epistemological tensions between a focus on (comm)unity and one on diversity, a focus on the global and a focus on the regional or local, the need to generalize and the mandate to avoid facile generalizations and attend to the particular.

- Ask new questions about all material. Do not consider gender only for women, race and ethnicity only for people of color, national identity only for recent immigrants and foreign nationals, sexuality only for gays and lesbians, or class only for working class people.

- Do not implicitly identify one kind of experience, one culture, one nation, one body of art and literature as normative, as central, relegating others to the margins or to the categories of variations and deviations. Think about destabilizing such assumptions of centrality when deciding how to begin your course, make assignments, and so on.

- Mark inclusions and exclusions: not, "a top priority for women is pay equity at work," but an identification of which women (white, middle class women in the United States?); not "the family" but an

452

identification of what kind of family and where (e.g., heterosexual nuclear families in modern Western countries). Marking usually unmarked categories can remind students that there are other groups, forms, and social contexts with a legitimacy of their own.

- Create opportunities in papers and presentations—any work that involves additional reading and research—for students to explore diverse materials beyond the assigned readings for the course.

- Consider making a discussion of structures and processes palpable through the use of materials speaking to personal or individual experiences, for example, in films, fiction, autobiography, poetry. Conversely, avoid presenting the stories of individual lives as wholly representative of a culture; contextualize with broader data.

- Avoid representing groups or individuals as victims or as exoticized Others. Aim for empathy and realism, not sympathy and paternalism (Robinson 1988). Balance discussions of oppression with discussions of agency. Avoid taking "culturally challenging practices" like clitoridectomy, foot binding, sati, etc., out of context; locate them in the histories and cultures of which they are a part, and draw analogies between them and practices and issues that will (or should) be more familiar to Western students (e.g., radical cosmetic surgeries, the history of clitoridectomy and hysterectomy in Victorian England and the United States). To critique such practices, cite the words and organizing efforts of activists from the regions in question.

SYLLABUS STRUCTURE

- Integrate material on gender, race-ethnicity, class, sexuality, national identity, etc., throughout the course. Do not confine it to a single section of your syllabus.

- Reexamine the overall structure of your syllabus. For chronological structures, consider what events, activities, etc., are emphasized and honored by the periodization of the syllabus. For thematic syllabi, consider whose experience the themes reflect and/or exclude. For developmental syllabi, consider what developmental model is being imposed on the information and knowledge, and whether or not that model is exclusive.

- In engendering, diversifying, and internationalizing courses, thematic or topical organizations may work better than chronological ones. In most instances, *less is more.* For international courses, consider focusing on a few carefully selected themes or issues across two to four regions. Don't try to cover the whole world. Include diversity *within* regions and countries.

ASSIGNMENTS

- Create assignments that, ideally, encourage students to include materials on gender, race or ethnicity, class, sexuality, and/or region, country, rural-urban axis, and so on in their work—or at least assignments that can be completed equally well using such material and perspectives.

- Make assignments methodologically and epistemologically diverse. They should push students to ask inclusive questions, to use different approaches, and to think in a variety of ways.

- Consider assignments that teach students to explore nontraditional sources of information: that is, their own and their families' experiences, the histories and experiences of other students, popular culture and mass media, and so on.

GRADING

- Make evaluation criteria clear for each assignment and for the course as a whole. Write them out; students with learning disabilities will especially appreciate this, but all students will benefit from it.

- Combine several kinds of evaluation: by the instructor, by peers, by the student him- or herself.

- Give students some control over the evaluation process through elements of contract grading, revision processes, and so on.

- Give early feedback.

CLASSROOM PROCESS

- Consider a model in which instructor and students are coinquirers. Such a model makes it easier to introduce material on which an instructor is not an expert.

- Make students significant sources of knowledge for each other, not only by drawing on their experiences where appropriate but also by creating structures in which they share the knowledge gained from their research with their classmates.

- Vary classroom processes so that you use a range of approaches, some of which may favor some students who may also enjoy different learning styles. Try lectures, rotating chair, panels, discussions, share and pair, games, and so on.

- Be aware of who speaks, whose ideas the instructor and other students pay special attention to, who sits where in the classroom. Use various strategies—small groups, brief written exercises to open the class, going around a circle, changing room arrangements—to disrupt patterns that have developed and to create more ways to include more students.

- Ask students to share responsibility for the inclusivity of the classroom process.

- Use conferences with students to help them develop their interests. Do not advise students about what work to pursue on the basis of your assumptions about which group they belong to. Do not assume that the student with a Spanish accent will want to do a project on Mexican or Mexican American women, that women students will not want to do quantitative work, etc.

- If differences in accent, race, nationality, ability, or sexuality emerge as teaching issues in a class, try to avoid either shoving them under the rug or letting them lead to an explosion.

- Listen openly to special needs and to sides; encourage students to learn from one another, decide judiciously when it is time to move on. If appropriate, seek advice or help from relevant campus offices (e.g., disabled student services, human resources, English as a Second Language institutes, etc.).

- Pay attention to your own and students' comments before and after class. Be aware of which students you interact with on which issues. Remember, the informal curriculum matters too.

WORK CITED

Robinson, Roger. 1988. "Development Issues: Sympathy and Paternalism, Empathy and Realism." In Rod Gerber and John Lidstone, eds., *Developing Skills in Geographical Education*, 152–155. Brisbane: International Geographical Union Commission on Geographical Education with the Jacaranda Press.

CULTURALLY CHALLENGING PRACTICES AND PEDAGOGICAL STRATEGIES

Deborah S. Rosenfelt

In the Women's Studies, Area and International Studies (WSAIS) projects generally, and certainly in our project at the University of Maryland, one question that arose again and again was how to negotiate between the shoals of cultural relativism on the one hand and ethnocentrism on the other, especially in our teaching. This was a particularly vexed question with regard to "culturally challenging practices" like veiling, arranged marriage, clitoridectomy, or sati. How does one teach about practices that appear disturbing or oppressive without either apologizing for them on the basis of their supposed embedment in traditions and local culture, or rejecting them with an outrage grounded in a conviction of the righteousness of Western feminist sensibilities? We found particularly helpful an essay by Isabelle R. Gunning (1992), from which I draw the term "culturally challenging practices." Gunning's rich essay focuses on how to bring multicultural, as well as feminist, perspectives to bear in conceptualizing appropriate stances for human rights work on issues like clitoridectomy. To "arrogant perception"—the perception that reacts to culturally challenging practices simply with horror—Gunning opposes the perspective of the traveler who observes, learns, encounters, reflects, engages with others, who remains open to what others have to teach her; and who takes part in sustained conversations with local activists about how to work for social change. We inferred a set of pedagogical mandates from Gunning's essay, which we named the four Cs:

1. *Contextualize* culturally challenging practices, or indeed any experiences of "the Other" in historical, social, economic, and cultural circumstances. Providing specific contexts helps to avoid representing any practice as timeless, static, unchanging, and undifferentiated from region to region. There are, for example, different forms of female genital surgeries in different regions, some more devastating than others. Some historians have argued that such practices spread during decolonization as a way of resisting Western imperialism, a point made about circumcision in the film *Rites*.[1] Access to healthy food, safe water, and education are issues of equal or greater concern to women and girls in many parts of Africa. An appropriate marriage is often necessary

for survival in the social order of specific regions, and in some areas, such a marriage is not possible unless genital surgery has taken place. As devastating as female genital surgery has been to the health of many women, it does not sum up the life experience of any woman. The horror of Western women at female circumcision sometimes reduces those who have been circumcised to the victims of this one act.

2. *Compare* culturally challenging practices with analogous practices in Western culture. Female circumcision was practiced in England and the United States until the early twentieth century, as a way of addressing an ostensibly disordered female sexuality. Cultural imperatives in the West today dictate that women have thin bodies, large breasts, and smooth youthful faces. Cosmetic surgery and breast enhancement surgery are interventions that alter women's bodies to meet dominant norms of beauty, and eating disorders affect many Western women's health. Obviously, such comparisons should not be carried too far or made too facile. Young feminist students in the West are perhaps too prone already to envisage an undifferentiated patriarchal violence as the source of all women's oppression. Pervasive cultural pressure from mass media to conform to narrow standards of beauty is both similar to and different from the expectations of one's ethnic group that women's genitals should be modified to conform to concepts of cleanliness and sexual order. Students in one of our classes viewed and discussed Alice Walker and Pratibha Parmar's *Warrior Marks,* a passionate film about female circumcision in Africa. Most of us felt that Walker's comparison of female circumcision to her "patriarchal wound," an eye blinded by her brother's BB gun, obscured more than it clarified. In one of our classes, we thought about whether female genital surgeries were analogous to the circumcision of Jewish boys. Ultimately, we concluded that this comparison was not apt, since circumcising infant boys does not, in most instances, have a negative effect on their health or their sense of well-being. But we learned something about "arrogant perception" and its impact on the perceived; the Jewish members of the class felt profoundly uncomfortable when the practice was held up to scrutiny and critique from "outsiders"—and when we (speaking here as a Jewish teacher) realized how difficult the practice was to explain or legitimate in terms an "outsider" could understand.

3. *Critique* the culturally challenging practices of other societies if such practices are indeed oppressive and damaging to women, but with certain provisos. It is important to recognize that not all culturally challenging practices are equally oppressive, and some—arranged marriages and veiling, for example—may well offer substantial advantages to women in particular circumstances. If possible, draw on the critical work of women who are immediately affected by the practices in question. For example, there are many local, national, and regional

groups in Africa and the Middle East working to eliminate female genital surgeries. Students can be asked to use the Internet, as well as the library, to research their contributions.

4. Encourage interested students to explore the possibilities for building *coalitions* to work for social change, or at least for researching those that exist. How are women activists building links and ties across national borders or borders of class, race, ethnicity, religion? What impact have they had? What obstacles have they encountered? Are there possibilities for linking local work in the students' own purview with related work by activists in other regions of the world? Students in my class were moved and empowered by the film *The Vienna Tribunal,* which demonstrates transnational grassroots organizing on women's human rights and against "gender-based violence"; the latter term, coined by feminist activists, according to the Platform for Action includes "female genital mutilation and other traditional practices harmful to women," along with many other forms of violence (*Beijing Declaration* 1996, 74). In addition to displacing an emphasis on victimhood, this emphasis on agency and action also offers students opportunities for implementing their knowledge and expressing their legitimate anger at women's oppression.

This admittedly simplistic catalogue will not resolve every pedagogical dilemma, but it did offer some comfort as we struggled to find a way to appreciate other cultures without glossing over practices deleterious to women, and to critique such practices as feminists without ethnocentric arrogance.

NOTE
1. For full citations for films mentioned here, consult the annotated videography "Women Around the World," also in this volume.

WORKS CITED

The Beijing Declaration and the Platform for Action. 1996. New York: United Nations Department of Public Information.
Gunning, Isabelle R. 1992. "Arrogant Perception, World-Travelling and Multicultural Feminism: The Case of Female Genital Surgeries." *Columbia Human Rights Law Review* 23(2) (Summer): 18–48.

COLLECTIVE BRAINSTORMING: USING SCENARIOS TO ADDRESS CONTENTIOUS ISSUES IN CURRICULUM CHANGE

SANDRA D. SHATTUCK, KIMBERLY JONES, JANICE MONK, AND AMY NEWHALL

Those of us who seek to internationalize women's studies and to introduce gender analysis into area and international studies face a variety of challenges and contentious issues within our various disciplines, institutions, and classrooms. One method of identifying these concerns and beginning to find solutions involves the creation of a particular scenario that illuminates a problem. Small groups then can discuss the specific challengé and collectively formulate possible solutions. Scenarios offer participants in the small groups opportunities to shuttle between practice and theory, to make abstractions more material. The collaborative work involved relies on a variety of experiences, so that, while some members of the group may never have encountered the scenario discussed, others will already have grappled with the issue in their work. Collective brainstorming also allows participants to see that even the most complex and difficult challenges can be addressed in helpful and productive ways.

The scenarios offered here were collaboratively designed for an intensive faculty development seminar, but using scenarios for discussion and problem-solving can also be an effective pedagogical strategy for the classroom.[1] The design of a scenario includes: (1) identifying a concern or problem, (2) constructing a situation that illustrates the problem, and (3) asking for a specific solution. The narrative of the scenario needs to engage the members of the small discussion group by inviting participants to imagine themselves in a clearly delineated situation that presents a meaningful problem.

To design our scenarios, we drew on experiences in past projects that revealed contentious and challenging issues facing our institute participants. When women's studies teachers and scholars begin to internationalize their courses and research, and when international and area studies teachers and scholars begin to incorporate issues of gender, they risk stepping out of their comfortable disciplinary boundaries. Problems regarding faculty expertise thus constitute one of the most difficult aspects of expanding one's teaching and research. The first and second examples provided here address this problem.

The third scenario addresses the issue of departmental resistance to curricular change. Finally, concerns about students' linguistic capacities present a variety of challenges, and we designed the fourth and fifth scenarios to address such problems.

In order to implement this exercise at the institute, we divided our group of thirty-five participants into five groups of seven members and assigned a facilitator to each group. We scheduled approximately fifty minutes out of the ninety-minute session for small-group discussion, after which a member from each group presented the proposed solutions to the larger group. We then asked the groups to post a written summary of solutions on the institute listserv. The list postings allowed all participants to benefit from each group's discussions and obviated some of the restrictions that limited time imposed. This session using scenarios was one of the most popular and lively ones of the institute, partly reflecting the wide range of nationalities, cross-cultural experience, and linguistic abilities of our participants. In the remainder of this essay we provide the five scenarios together with responses to three of them in order to illustrate the range and utility of ideas that can emerge from such an exercise.

SCENARIO 1: FACULTY CONFIDENCE

You are attending an institute designed to introduce international perspectives into teaching and research about women when you overhear a conversation among two of your coparticipants. One admits that she is nervous about introducing material she is unfamiliar with.

She says, "I learned so much from that talk on African women's writing. But while I was taking notes, I realized that not only did I lack expertise in this field, I couldn't even spell some of the writers' names! How can I ever hope to incorporate African women's writing into my literature course, when I know so little? What I don't understand is that I teach about women from the past whose experience I don't share. Why does that seem so much easier? Why doesn't that make me nervous?"

The other responds, "You can teach about women in the past because they are probably white women like you. But as an Anglo woman from the United States, you can't presume to teach about Black women from the United States or from Africa."

As an eavesdropper on this conversation, you can't resist joining in. What do you say?

COLLABORATIVE RESPONSE

The group addressed two aspects of the problem—first, doing justice to new, unfamiliar material, and second, the "right" or ability to teach about people with whom the instructor has no personal-cultural-racial identity or "background."

"I couldn't even spell the [African] women's names. . . . How can I ever teach their writing?" A positive element of this first response (if genuine and not an excuse) is the concern for doing justice to the new material—not just plunging in and doing haphazard work for the sake of complying with requirements to internationalize. This can, however, easily devolve into a cop-out position and be used as an excuse not to do one's homework.

Suggestions:

• Acknowledge and recognize one's limitations in terms of expertise.

• Begin somewhere. Refuse to be paralyzed or confined to only the safe, familiar spaces for engagement.

• Shift pedagogical stance from cocksureness of an expert (with centralized location of authority) to acknowledging ignorance. It is okay not to know everything, to begin somewhere with an eye to being able to share a narrative of one's own learning (students have much to learn from one's attitude of eagerness or openness to learn and venture into something new).

• Bring in other resources by way of augmenting your own. For example, invite colleagues who have done work in the area to come in and share, invite students if they have anything from their respective backgrounds and experiences.

• The last point means willingness to share power and invite collaborative learning.

"I teach about women from the past whose experience I don't share. Why doesn't that make me nervous?" *"You can teach about them because they are white women like you, but as a white American woman, you can't presume to teach about Black women, from the U.S. or from Africa."* The latter comment conflates the right or authority to speak with having personal experience—an argument that rests on certain essentialist notions of the constitution of identities. Question, analyze, and evaluate this assumption: It limits access to knowledge only to group members presumed to have inherent (common) characteristics or experiences not shared by others. Automatically privileging insiders' perspectives overlooks the fact that cultural outsiders can make sensitive and insightful readings—for example, Renato Rosaldo's (1989) account of the Ilongot practice of headhunting in northern Philippines. Alternatively, work by insiders may be more representative of a colonialist view (i.e., having

internalized the colonial gaze) than work done by outsiders (e.g., much of the work in the social sciences by Filipino scholars trained in Western perspectives prior to the indigenization movement in the academy beginning in the late 1970s).

Introducing students to certain conceptual and contextualizing tools of analysis from nonhegemonic, nonethnocentric perspectives is helpful in this regard. Training them in critical thinking and helping them to become aware of the politics of knowledge and knowledge production (e.g., the differing consequences of variable readings or interpretations of certain texts) will enable them to engage critically with new material beyond those presented in class.

SCENARIO 2: THE POLITICS OF FACULTY EXPERTISE

For a number of years as a faculty member in Middle Eastern studies, you have taught a historical course called Mediterranean Cities, which deals with concepts of space and gender in Cairo, Florence, Venice, and Istanbul. At the suggestion of a colleague in East Asian studies, you decide to broaden the scope by changing the list of cities to Cairo, Istanbul, Florence, Kano, Beijing, and Lima, and the name of the course to Gender, Space, and the City: Comparative Perspectives. Your course is approved by your department curriculum committee but is rejected by the college curriculum committee. You find out that the course was rejected because another East Asian studies colleague objected, protesting that you had no expertise in Chinese studies, and that some of the material in the course is likely to overlap with the material covered in the Chinese civilization course that she teaches. The curriculum committee encourages you to resubmit your proposal after considering this faculty member's objections. How will you respond to the curriculum committee's rejection of your course proposal and encouragement to resubmit?

SCENARIO 3: NEGOTIATING PERSPECTIVES ON DIFFERENCE IN WOMEN'S STUDIES

You have attended an institute devoted to integrating international perspectives on women and gender into the curriculum. You return to your home university eager to incorporate what you have learned into the women's studies program where you teach. In a faculty meeting you raise the issue of revising both the introductory women's studies course and the entire women's studies curriculum to reflect international perspectives. Your colleagues argue strongly against your position. They think that women's studies should be centered on students' lives—focusing on experiential learning and addressing diversity in U.S. society with an emphasis on race, ethnicity, class, and sexual orientation.

What can you say to bring them to your point of view? How do you think their perspectives, as well as yours, could be accommodated?

SCENARIO 4: LANGUAGE BARRIERS FOR INTERNATIONAL STUDENTS

You are teaching a course in which several of your students are non-native speakers of English. Two of these non-native speakers come to you and say that they are having trouble understanding your lectures. They are also worried about how you will grade their papers, because English is their second language. Another problem you notice is that when non-native speakers talk in class, some of the native and/or fluent speakers tune out. You presume that these students have difficulty understanding the accented English of some of the non-native speakers. What do you do?

COLLABORATIVE RESPONSE

The main issues the group tried to solve were (1) what to do when international students have a hard time understanding lectures and class discussion, (2) how to grade international students' papers, and (3) how to deal with other students' tuning out when international students speak in class. One person pointed out that international students can be considered resources who contribute to a richer classroom. In addition, we recognized that some international students may be fluent in English, but speak with accents that are difficult for U.S. students to understand, whereas others may have limited competency in written and spoken English.

First, to deal with students' difficulties in understanding what's going on in class, the following ideas were suggested (most of these ideas would probably benefit all of our students):

- Encourage students who are having trouble to tape classes so they can listen to them again.

- Slow down your speech.

- Focus on showing the organization of the specific class period (by giving students an outline of a lecture, for example).

- Incorporate a visual component (by using transparencies, handouts, blackboard, etc.).

- Be aware of your vocabulary, sentence structure, idioms, etc., and consider simplifying when possible.

- Rephrase often ("another way to say this is . . .").

- Help students develop partnerships (they might share notes, read, and comment on each others' papers, each be responsible for explaining a reading from their own language, etc.).

Second, in regard to grading papers (and before the grading phase), the following suggestions were made :

- Recommend that international students have a native speaker go over their papers with them.

- Recommend writing centers, tutoring programs, and other campus resources they may not be aware of.

- Do not water down expectations for our international students but do consider the challenges a newcomer and non-native speaker of English faces.

- Become aware of research that has been done on rhetorical styles in different cultures (ESL instructors on your campus might be able to help).[2]

- Review with your students the rhetorical styles and organizational structures that are acceptable in your discipline.

- For in-class written exams allow dictionaries, consider allowing more time, give out essay questions in advance of the test.

Third, we recognized that students often tune out when their peers speak and that language problems may be only one source of this problem. Suggestions for dealing with it were

- Do small group work and collaborative learning exercises early in the course to build community and to encourage students to identify with each other, to develop interpersonal relationships, and to get used to each other's accents and ways of speaking.

- Encourage other students to recognize areas in which an international student has expertise (while deftly avoiding tokenism, of course).

- Rearticulate students' comments when they seem unclear: "Is this what you're saying?" (not "So what you're saying is . . .").

- Pretend not to understand native speakers of American English (easier to pull off if you are not a speaker of American English).

- Address this sort of issue explicitly. Discuss the need to be considerate of each other; talk about how discussion is more difficult for some than for others (e.g., the problems shy people have expressing themselves, how hard it is for non-native speakers to time an insertion into a discussion, etc.), and explain that discussion may be difficult for everyone at one point or another, depending on the topic. Manipulate your own eye gaze to encourage students to look at each other instead of at you and explain what you are doing and why.

SCENARIO 5: INTRODUCING FOREIGN LANGUAGE TEXTS

You are teaching an upper division women's studies course called Gender, Identity, and Difference: Global and Local Visions. In a unit on women's grassroots environmental activism, you include a reading selected from a Spanish-language newspaper reporting on a women's demonstration against toxic wastes. A number of students complain that this is unfair, because they can not read Spanish. Another student protests that including only one piece in Spanish constitutes tokenism. Still another points out that the imbalance of using English-language materials that are primarily academic and theoretical while including one Spanish selection from a popular source is a clear example of ethnocentrism. How do you respond?

COLLABORATIVE RESPONSE

In addressing this dilemma, the group focused on locating language within society and the classroom, proposing solutions that involved individual and collective strategies. These solutions included the following:

- Use the experience to foster collaborative work. Have Spanish-speaking students translate the article (presuming there are Spanish-speaking students in the class). This would, it is hoped, foster respect for those students' skills. Be careful about assumptions regarding the skills and level of expertise of the translators.

- Have students seek out resources on campus. Students could go to an appropriate student association for help with the translation. They could also go to the university learning center or the Spanish language department to get help. It would be wise to work with all organizations, groups, etc., beforehand so they are aware that students will be approaching them for possible assistance.

- Students themselves could be asked to provide a solution to the situation. Encouraging students to come up with their own solutions allows them to broaden their own perspectives about all students who have special skills and also special needs within the classroom setting. Use this exercise at the beginning of class so that students may be contemplating possible solutions during the course; students may also become presensitized to differences and identities. Students may write about the experience of exposure to the Spanish article and reflect on the impact it had on their learning experience.

- In regard to the popular versus theoretical issue, the instructor could offer a theoretical piece in Spanish but could also include a popular article in English. The point would be that representation of intellectual ability in all cultures is recognized and valued. The instructor could also discuss the value of popular articles for presenting an important picture of the real world and an image of events.

- Power relations are a dominant theme in this scenario. An activity could be developed to address reciprocity in power relations. For example, students could do an exercise to trace their own genealogy and examine the languages associated with their own identities. Along with this, they could examine possible struggles associated with language issues that their own families may have experienced.

- Gender issues of language could also be addressed. One example suggested in the group was that among Koreans who come to the United States, it is often the women who are first to learn English because, as mothers, they must interact with their childrens' teachers and generally be able to provide essential care for their children, which requires expertise in the dominant language.

NOTES

1. Scenarios 1, 2, 3, and 5 were developed collaboratively by Kimberly Jones, Janice Monk, Amy Newhall, and Sandra Shattuck of the University of Arizona. Comments in scenario 1 were adapted from Lensink (1991). Scenario 4 was adapted from material provided by Deborah Rosenfelt, University of Maryland. The group response to scenario 1 was compiled by Lily Mendoza. Kimberly Jones compiled the group response to scenario 4 and Helen Ruth Aspaas the response to scenario 5. We appreciate their contributions.
2. A helpful article that carefully articulates issues of radically differing rhetorical styles and methods can be found in Shen (1994).

WORKS CITED

Lensink, Judy Nolte. 1991. "Strategies for Integrating International Material in the Introductory Women's Studies Course." *Women's Studies International Forum* 14 (4): 277–285.

Rosaldo, Renato. 1989. *Culture and Truth: The Remaking of Social Analysis.* Boston: Beacon Press.

Shen, Fan. 1994. "The Classroom and the Wider Culture: Identity as a Key to Learning English Composition." In Sonia Maasik and Jack Solomon, eds., *Signs of Life in the U.S.A.: Readings on Popular Culture for Writers,* 485–494. Boston: St. Martin's Press.

ELECTRONIC RESOURCES FOR GLOBAL-LOCAL TEACHING AND RESEARCH

RUTH DICKSTEIN

Using electronic resources in teaching and research is now a given, but it is a challenge to separate good, useful, and reliable electronic provenances from the plethora of mediocre to bad sources. This chapter addresses a series of issues related to electronic resources including what products exist, how to keep up with changes and new resources as they become available, and how one can learn to use and evaluate them. Although teachers and scholars may be most familiar with the World Wide Web, there are many other types of electronic resources, such as CD-ROMs, web-accessible indexes, shared cataloging information, discussion groups, electronic journals, and electronic texts. The sources listed in this chapter are selected for quality, scope, and academic focus. All provide information about women internationally or various ethnic groups in the United States.

GUIDES FOR USING INTERNET RESOURCES

1. "Getting Around Online: How, Where, Why?" 1997. Elisabeth Binder. *Feminist Collections* 19 (1) (Fall): 19–21.

    This article reviews a number of guides to searching the Internet and is an excellent source for identifying other helpful guidebooks. The on line version can be found at   : http://www.library.wisc.edu/libraries/WomensStudies/fc/fcbind.htm.

2. *Internet Resources on Women: Using Electronic Media in Curriculum Transformation.* 1997. Joan Korenman. Baltimore: National Center for Curriculum Transformation Resources on Women, Towson State University.

    This is the best and most lucidly written guide to the Internet. It is very clear, well-structured, logical, and written in an absolutely readable style. It includes an extensive list of websites that have been relatively stable over the years and are excellent starting points for further explorations. See item no. 7 about updates.

3. *The Women's Guide to the Wired World: A User-Friendly Handbook and Resource Directory.* 1997. Shana Penn. New York: Feminist Press.

This text is not for beginners. It is quite technical and fails to define basic concepts. It does offer valuable practical advice on organizing women on-line (see the chapter on e-mail meetings).

4. *WOW Women on the Web: A Guide to Gender-Related Resources on the Internet.* 1997. Helen Fallon. Dublin: The Women's Education Research and Resource Centre, University College, Dublin.

The introductory chapters on gender in science and technology in general and the Internet, in particular, are very well written. This book has a limited amount of information about electronic discussion lists, organizations, bibliographies, electronic texts, and library catalogues accessible on the Internet.

FAQS

5. FAQs are a vital source of information about websites. FAQs are files of answers to "frequently asked questions." Look for them when you first select a new website and want to learn about its contents and any tips for using that page.

SOURCES FOR ONGOING INFORMATION

6. *Feminist Collections.* 1980 to present. Madison: Women's Studies Librarian, University of Wisconsin System.

Feminist Collections is a quarterly review of new books in women's studies, with a particular emphasis on reference titles, journals, and media. "Computer Talk," an ongoing section in each issue published since fall 1995, contains descriptions of new websites, information about new listservs, electronic journals, and articles about the use of the Internet in teaching and research. Web versions of this column are available on their website at:
http://www.library.wisc.edu:80/libraries/WomensStudies/fcmain.htm.

7. *Internet Resources on Women: Using Electronic Media in Curriculum Transformation: Additions and Changes.* Compiled by Joan Korenman. At
http://umbc7.umbc.edu/~korenman/wmst/updates.html.

This website is continuously updated, thereby providing the most current information about changes that have occurred since the publication of Korenman's guide (item no. 2). Changes are listed in reverse chronological order and contain descriptive information about new, changed, or defunct discussion groups, websites, electronic journals, and other related sources. The site is also arranged according to the book chapter order.

8. *The Internet Scout Project,* at http://scout.cs.wisc.edu/index.html.

Sponsored by the National Science Foundation, *The Internet Scout Project* provides daily and weekly updates via e-mail of Internet information for educators from kindergarten through university level faculty and students. This project produces two publications. *The Internet Scout Report* is a weekly guide to new Internet resources. Many users subscribe to weekly updates organized in three subject areas: science and engineering, business and economics, and social sciences. *Net Happenings* is a daily update to Internet announcements. Both publications are searchable by Library of Congress subject headings and call numbers at their website. A search for "women AND international" pulled up forty entries. Many were sites that had "international" as part of their focus, but not necessarily the primary focus. Users can either search the website archives or sign on to receive the weekly or daily *Scout Report* or *Net Happenings*.

9. *NetFirst.* Dublin, Ohio: OCLC Online Computer Library Center.

NetFirst is one of the many databases offered by OCLC as part of the *FirstSearch* package. (OCLC is involved in traditional cataloging of books, journals, videos, etc.) *NetFirst* is an attempt to provide the same standards of cataloging to websites, that is, to provide descriptive information for a very different kind of resource than that found on library shelves. Records contain location information and description of contents and are searchable by Library of Congress subject headings or keywords in summaries, names, descriptors, or geographic areas. The sites are selected for quality and stability. Try *NetSearch* rather than a search engine such as *Lycos* or *Alta Vista* to sort out useful websites. For a description of *FirstSearch* and ordering information, visit their website: http://www.oclc.org/oclc/fs/order.htm.

WOMEN AND THE WORLD WIDE WEB

10. *About.com,* at
   http://women3rdworld.about.com/culture/women3rdworld/.

A guide to women's issues in the Third World, this site is a news-alert website focusing on events in women's lives. It includes links to regions and women's topics, such as women and religion, and women refugees. This site is updated frequently.

11. *African Women Global Network (AWOGNet),* at http://www.osu.edu/org/awognet/.

   AWOG is an organization "whose activities are targeted toward the improvement of the living conditions of women and children in Africa." Their page, "African Links," is well organized and contains a number of connections to materials about African women.

12. *The Alan Guttmacher Institute,* at http://www.agi-usa.org.

   This excellent site provides the latest research findings and policy analysis on reproductive health and rights in the United States and internationally. Includes articles from their publications, policy papers, fact sheets, and a table maker for creating data tables from AGI's data. This data includes worldwide information about population, economic development, education, health, marriage and sexuality, childbirth, and contraception.

13. *Aviva,* at http://www.aviva.org/.

   Aviva is a website maintained in London that presents up-to-date news about women around the world. Click on the "site plan" and you can select any region. Choices for information for each area include news, events, groups, resources, courses, and classified advertisements. The site also includes "action alerts" for those wishing to take action on a specific issue.

14. *CLNet Diversity Page,* at http://clnet.ucr.edu/diversity1.html.

   Developed by a number of California librarians and maintained at UCLA, this site contains guides to electronic resources on the Internet under the headings African American, Asian American, Latinos, Native American, multicultural, women's, and gay and lesbian studies. The CLNet home page also connects to a long list of electronic journals and newsletters, research reports, information about jobs, museum collections, and statistics.

15. *Core Lists in Women's Studies,* at http://www.library.wisc.edu:80/libraries/WomensStudies/core/coremain.htm.

Developed and maintained by women's studies librarians from across the United States, this site contains a listing of materials currently in print that should be basic to a good women's studies collection. Currently, thirty lists are available including some on international women and women of color.

16. *IGC Institute for Global Communications: WomensNet,* at http://www.igc.org/igc/gateway/wnindex.html.

Based in San Francisco, California, this site contains international news summaries about women. In 1990 the oldest IGC network, *PeaceNet,* joined with similar networks outside the United States to create the worldwide Association for Progressive Communication (APC). The APC now consists of twenty-one international member networks. It also serves as the primary telecommunications provider at U.N. conferences such as the 1995 World Conference on Women in Beijing. *WomensNet* was founded in 1995 to support feminist work, encourage women's use of the Internet, and prepare for the Women's Conference in Beijing. It provided the Internet infrastructure for emerging documents at the Beijing conference.

17. *International Labour Organization (ILO): All Women Are Working Women,* at http://www.ilo.org/public/english/bureau/inf/pkits/women1.htm.

This web address connects to three papers about women and work and the feminization of poverty as well as to the ILO conventions and recommendations about the lives of women. It includes information on the feminization of poverty, survival strategies, and prospects for women heads of families.

18. *Social Science Information Gateway,* at http://www.sosig.ac.uk/welcome.html.

The Social Science Information Gateway is a British online cataloging project of quality and relevant social science websites. At the home page, select browse, then women's studies. There are links to ecofeminism, women in Islam, the National Organization for Women, and more. The women's studies section is maintained by the Fawcett Library, the largest single women's collection in England.

19. *Women's International News Gathering Service—Wings,* at http://www.wings.org/audio.html.

Wings provides live broadcasts of news. It is available via Real Audio (downloadable free of charge) for those with sound cards and speakers. It does not date the descriptions of when the news was recorded, which is an unfortunate omission.

20. *Women's Studies/Women's Issues Resource Sites.* Compiled by Joan Korenman. At http://research.umbc.edu/~korenman/wmst/links.html.

This website is constantly updated. The section "International Women" has more than seventy-five links to women's groups world-wide. The "Women of Color" section contains about forty links. Many connections are to African American women sites, but there are also links to Asian American and Native American women as well as to women of color in other American ethnic groups.

21. *WIDNET,* at http://www.focusintl.com/widnet.htm.

This bilingual database (French and English) is a network for women in development maintained by the Canadian International Development Agency. It contains full text documents, statistics from WISTAT (see item no. 33), links to numerous international organizations, and the 1995 Beijing Conference.

22. *Women of Color Web*, at http://www.hsph.harvard.edu/grhf/WoC/index.html.

"The Women of Color Web is dedicated to providing access to writings by and about women of color in the U.S." The focus is on issues related to feminisms, sexualities, and reproductive health and rights. The site provides links to organizations, discussion lists, and teaching tools related to women of color.

23. *Women's Studies Information Sources,* at http://www.york.ac.uk/services/library/subjects/womenint.htm.

A well-constructed website developed at the University of York. It includes good connections to websites for women in develop-ment, international organizations, and sites organized by region, for example, Africa, Europe, Asia, and the Americas.

24. *WSSLinks.* Women's Studies Section of the Association of College and Research Libraries (ACRL). At   http://libraries.mit.edu/humani-ties/WomensStudies/wscd.html.

Librarians who are members of the Women's Studies Section of the Association of College and Research Libraries have created this site to provide researchers with links to sites reviewed by librarians. It includes links to bibliographies, electronic discussion forums, newsletters and journals, and organizations. Of special interest is the international page maintained by Katia Roberto.

DISCUSSION GROUPS OR LISTSERVS

Discussion groups, or listservs, are essentially communal mailing lists. Individuals with common interests join a listserv and messages from one are received by all members of the discussion group. In the academic community there are thousands of electronic discussion groups, whose members share information about syllabi, teaching experiences, job postings, conferences, calls for papers and articles, and e-mail discussions about issues of concern to listserv members. Discussion groups for women have been created in just about every academic discipline. Some listservs are moderated and postings carefully monitored, others are more open but with a moderator standing by to remind discussion participants about the focus of that listserv's discussions. For some, membership is restricted; others are open to all who wish to join.

The commands for joining a listserv are virtually the same for all listservs. One sends a message to the listserv sign-on address, leaves the subject line blank, and in the body of the message simply types: subscribe listserv name your name. For example, to subscribe to the major women's studies listserv, WMST-L,

1. send a message to: listserv@listserv.umdd.umd.edu, and

2. in the body of the message type: subscribe wmst-l your name.

For more information about using listservs and their archives, see Korenman's, *Internet Resources on Women*, Chapter X (item no. 2), or the chapter, "Virtual Conversations: Usenet Newsgroups, Conferences, Mailing Lists, Internet Relay Chat," by Victoria Vrana, in *The Women's Guide to the Wired World* (item no. 3).

For the most up-to-date comprehensive listing of women's studies discussion groups consult

25. *The Directory of Scholarly and Professional E-Conferences.* Compiled by Diane K. Kovacs and The Directory Team. At http://n2h2.com/KOVACS/.

Previously titled *Directory of Scholarly E-Conferences,* the site "evaluates and organizes discussion lists, newsgroups, MUDs, MOOs, MUCKs, Mushes, mailing lists, interactive web chat groups" (e-conferences), and so on regarding "topics of interest to scholars and professionals for use in their scholarly, pedagogical, and professional activities. One can search by keyword and retrieve up to forty listserv titles per search. An annual print version is published by the Association of Research Libraries. Contact pubs@cni.org for information.

26. *Gender-Related Electronic Forums,* at
http://research.umbc.edu/~korenman/wmst/forums.html.

Maintained by Joan Korenman from the Center for Women & Information Technology, University of Maryland, Baltimore County, this is the best annotated listing of women's studies listservs. The section titled "Women-Related E-Mail Lists Focused Outside the U.S. and Canada" contains over fifty discussion groups about women from a non–U.S./Canadian perspective, and the "Women of Color E-Mail Lists" enumerates over twenty electronic forums.

27. *Liszt, The Mailing List Directory,* at http://www.liszt.com/.

This is a web list of over 89,000 mailing lists, organized by broad category (religion, health, politics). It also contains a search box allowing users to search by keyword. Included are lists of mailing lists, newsgroups, as well as IRC Chat and directions for creating mailing lists.

ELECTRONIC INDEXES: CD-ROMS AND THE WEB

An index in electronic format can store a warehouse of knowledge on a variety of subjects and issues. These indexes identify books, articles in journals, newspapers, videos, and research reports. The following is a list of electronic databases that include bibliographic citations and abstracts, and in some cases the full text documents on women's studies issues. Electronic indexes exist in CD-ROM format or are accessible via web and in some cases are available both ways.

28. *Anthropological Literature.* 1984–present. New York: Macmillan, Simon and Schuster, G. K. Hall. Availability: CD-ROM from Macmillan, web access through RLG.

This index has approximately one thousand journals and two hundred other titles dealing with anthropology and other related disciplines with articles and essays in anthropology and archaeology, from works published in English and other European languages.

29. *Contemporary Women's Issues Database* (CWI). Beachwood, Ohio: Responsive Database Services, Inc. Availability: CD-ROM and the web.

Most entries in this index contain the full text of the article or report. It includes over 1,500 full text records from more than 600 sources. Source publications include journals, newsletters, reports, fact sheets, guides, newspapers, and pamphlets. The United Nations, Human Rights Watch, World Health Organization, and many NGOs are some of the publishers whose works are included.

30. *Ethnic Newswatch*. 1991–present. Stamford, Conn.: Softline Information, Inc. Availability: CD-ROM and the web.

Ethnic Newswatch includes complete texts of over 250,000 articles, editorials, and reviews published in the United States from approximately 180 ethnic and minority journals, magazines, and newspapers.

31. *GenderWatch* (formerly *Women 'R'*). 1978–present. Stamford, Conn.: Softline Information, Inc. Availability: CD-ROM and the web.

A full-text database that contains primarily ongoing periodicals focusing on women and women's issues in academic and scholarly journals, magazines and newspapers. This database provides information on "the full range of women's subjects as they specifically impact and reflect ethnic and minority women and women of color" and some coverage of international and local issues.

32. *Sociofile*. 1974–present. San Diego: Sociological Abstracts, Inc. Availability: CD-ROM from Silver Platter, web from Ebsco, FirstSearch, Dialog@Carl.

The *Sociofile* includes indexes and abstracts to articles and conference proceedings covering the world's literature on sociology. Includes indexing of more than two thousand journals in thirty different languages in such fields as anthropology, sociolinguistics, education, medicine, community development, philosophy, demography, political science, and social psychology. The CD-ROM is very international in focus.

33. *WISTAT: Women's Indicators and Statistics Database*, version 4. 1999. New York: United Nations Statistical Division. Availability: CD-ROM.

A CD-ROM product that provides searchable statistics on a wide range of conditions in the lives of women and men, such as population, education, economic activity, marital status, health, housing and human settlements, public affairs, political participation, crime, and national production. Data cover 206 countries or areas from 1970 to 1997 with projections to 2025. Data can be printed in chart form, spreadsheets, or downloaded.

34. *Women's Resources International* (WRI). 1972. Baltimore: National Infor-mation Services Corporation (NISC). Availability: CD-ROM and the web.

This index is the largest electronic source available for research in women's studies. It is a global information source combining over 116,000 records from essential women's studies databases such as Women's Studies Abstracts, The University of Toronto's Women's Studies Databases, Women of Color and Southern Women: A Bibliography of Social Science Research, publications from the University of Wisconsin Women's Studies Librarian's office, and more. Materials indexed include journal articles, media, reviews, research reports, editorials, speeches, and interviews.

35. *Women's Studies on Disc.* 1944–present. Old Tappan, N.J.: Simon and Schuster, G. K. Hall. Availability: CD-ROM.

This index to more than 100 magazines and journals with 45,000 citations related to women's studies includes information on women's studies, gender issues, and popular culture. Some coverage of international women, good coverage of ethnic minority women in the United States.

ELECTRONIC JOURNALS

On-line or electronic journals provide direct access to the full text of journal articles via the Internet. See items no. 8 and 9 for finding information on new electronic journal titles. Following is a list of titles available. Most do not charge for access, but a few are now requiring payment for subscriptions.

36. *Advancing Women in Leadership,* at
http://www.advancingwomen.com/awl.html.

The first "on-line professional, refereed journal for women in leadership" that focuses on women's issues.

37. *Feminist Collections: A Quarterly of Women's Studies Resources,* at http://www.library.wisc.edu/libraries/WomensStudies/fcmain.htm.

Discussed in item no. 6.

38. *Feminist Studies in Aotearoa Electronic Journal (FMST)*, at
    http://www.massey.ac.nz/~NZSRDA/nzssreps/journals/fmst.htm.

    This is produced by and for those interested in feminist theory,
    feminist perspectives in philosophy, and contemporary feminist
    debates, publications, and research. FMST operates from a server
    at Otago University, Dunedin, New Zealand. It is moderated from
    Massey University Women Studies, Palmerston North, New
    Zealand.

39. *Gender, Place, and Culture: A Journal of Feminist Geography*, at
    http//www.tandf.co.uk/journals/carfax/0966369X.html.

    A respected journal for feminist geographers, this publication is
    concerned with geography and related disciplines and gender
    issues. Subscription is required.

40. *Journal of South Asian Women Studies*, at
    http://www.asiatica.org/publications/jsaws/.

    The journal is "meant to disseminate works which address theo-
    retical and practical issues of interest to scholars of South Asia
    and to women from South Asia."

41. *Magazines and Newsletters on the Web (Women-Focused)*, at
    http://www.library.wisc.edu/libraries/WomensStudies/mags.htm;
    and
    Women-Related Online Periodicals, at
    http://umbc7.umbc.edu/~korenman/wmst/links_per.html.

    These two meta sites have numerous connections to on-line jour-
    nals and text publications. There is some overlap in coverage, but
    both provide links to useful electronic materials.

42. *Womanist Theory and Research (WTR)*, at
    http://www.uga.edu/~womanist.

    A "biannual, peer-edited, interdisciplinary, intercultural, interna-
    tional journal on women of color. WTR provides a forum for
    exchanging feminist research, theory and ideas among women-of-
    color scholars and students." It is published by the Women's Study
    Consortium at the University of Georgia.

43. *Women and Politics,* at http://www.american.edu/oconnor/wandp/.

The website contains only abstracts to this title, which is a quarterly journal of research and policy studies. "Articles are focused on explaining and enhancing women's place in politics including the areas of political philosophy, international relations, American politics, and comparative politics." Abstracts are posted from 1995 through the present.

44. *Women in Judaism: A Multidisciplinary Journal*
http://www.utoronto.ca/wjudaism/.

This journal is published exclusively on the Internet. Its purpose is to be a forum for scholarly debate on gender-related issues in Judaism.

45. *Women's History Review,* at
http://www.triangle.co.uk/whr/index.htm.

The main goal of this refereed, major international journal is to provide a forum for the publication of new scholarly articles in the rapidly expanding field of women's history. Articles are contributed "from a range of disciplines that further feminist knowledge and debate about women and/or gender relations in history."

46. Women's International Net *(WIN) Magazine,* at
http://winmagazine.org.

WIN is a magazine about women, by women, for women all over the world. *WIN* is a worldwide source for and about women of all nationalities, age groups, beliefs, and backgrounds. Each issue features reports on international issues of concern to women from Africa, Asia, the Pacific, the Middle East, Europe, and the Americas.

EVALUATING WEBSITES AND TEACHING WITH THE WEB

Lately, student research has been criticized for relying so heavily upon items found on the World Wide Web. Using the web is fast, easy, and convenient and has become the major source of information for many. The web can be used as a tool to teach students how to examine information, question validity and authority, and think critically about material they read and hear about. The major criteria for evaluating websites parallel criteria for evaluating print materials: authority, balance, objectivity, currency, audience, references and source of information, and research quality. In addition to these, a global perspective would ask about regional coverage and whether the viewpoint reflects a foreign or native voice.

Valuable resources for approaches to teaching with the Web include

47. *Evaluating Web Resources.* Jan Alexander and Marsha Tate. Chester, Pa.: Wolfgram Memorial Library, Widener University. At http://www2.widener.edu/Wolfgram-Memorial-Library/webevaluation/webeval.htm.

This is a website developed for students at Widener University to teach them about using the web for research. Evaluating Web Resources is one part of an eight-session class. All of the exercises and background information for teaching each class are available at this site. The authors reported on how to use these materials in an article, "Teaching Critical Evaluation Skills for World Wide Web Resources," *Computers in Libraries* (November–December 1996): 49–55.

48. "Listserv Lemmings and Fly-brarians on the Wall: A Librarian-Instructor Team Taming the Cyberbeast in the Large Classroom." 1998. Kari Boyd McBride and Ruth Dickstein. *College and Research Libraries* 59(1) (1998): 10–17.

This article provides explicit techniques used by the authors in their teaching collaboration. It describes how the assignment to evaluate websites was used for the evaluation of all the sources students used and became a more beneficial exercise for the students.

49. "The Web Demands Critical Reading by Students." Kari Boyd McBride and Ruth Dickstein. *Chronicle of Higher Education* 44 (29) (March 20, 1998): B6.

Written by the same authors as the article listed in item no. 48, this article discusses how to incorporate electronic resources in the classroom and ways in which teaching faculty and librarians can forge a successful partnership in the teaching enterprise.

OTHER SITES LISTING EVALUATING CRITERIA

50. *Evaluating Information Found on the Internet.* Latest update, May 2001. Elizabeth Kirk. Milton S. Eisenhower Library, Johns Hopkins University. At http://milton.mse.jhu.edu:8001/research/education/net.html.

This website contains a well-written list of evaluation criteria with clear definitions of each criterion.

51. *Thinking Critically About Discipline-Based World Wide Web Resources.* Esther Grassian. UCLA College Library. At http://www.library.ucla.edu/libraries/college/help/critical/discipline.htm.

This site contains a slightly different list of criteria focusing on the research value of a website.

52. "World Wide Web Review: The Elusive Quality of Web Quality." 1997. Susan Barribeau. *Feminist Collections* 19 (1) (Fall): 17–18. At http://www.library.wisc.edu:80/libraries/WomensStudies/fc/fcbarr.htm

This short model shows how one applies web evaluation criteria and recommends websites with good examples of such criteria.

ACKNOWLEDGMENTS

Valuable assistance for the project was given by Carol Leatherwood and Xan Cloudtree.

INTERNATIONAL SOURCES FOR STATISTICS ON WOMEN

DENISE MOGGE

Arab Women in ESCWA Member States: Statistics, Indicators and Trends. 1994. United Nations Economic and Social Commission for West Asia. New York: United Nations. ISBN 9211281482 (301 pages).

A bilingual publication in Arabic and English, the book contains data in tabular form. Data from 1960 to 1990 are gathered into six chapters plus a section explaining symbols, technical terms, and abbreviations. This book includes bibliographies at the end of each chapter. Data are provided on population, families and households, education and training, health and childbearing, housing, human settlements and environment, women's work and economic activity, and public life and leadership.

Atlas of American Women. 1986. Barbara Gimla Shortridge. New York: Macmillan. ISBN 0029291208 (164 pages).

For a retrospective look at women, this book provides statistical data in the form of color maps and some tables from 1986. An index, list of data sources, and bibliography are included. Textual content supplements maps and tables. Each of the eleven chapters begins with an introduction. Topics include demographics, migration, religion, foreign-born women, labor force, child care, earnings and income, wealthy women, occupations, male-dominated occupations, women in the arts, education, sports (high school, college, and Olympians), relationships, pregnancy, teenage pregnancy, abortion, health, crime, politics, voting, government, League of Women Voters, and ERA. This is not an exhaustive list of all the maps.

The Atlas of Women and Men in India. 1999. Saraswati Raju, Peter J. Atkins, Naresh Kumar, and Janet G. Towsend. New Delhi: Kali for Women. ISBN 8185107947 (131 pages).

This atlas contains statistical data presented in eighty-four colored maps and twenty-four tables on women (and some data on men) in India. Appendices include references, bibliography, state level employment data, district level data, and a technical section. Maps and textual content include the following: India at work, work on the land, crafts and manufacturing, services, education, marriage, life and death, from daughter to mother, power, environment for living, cooking and cleaning, and the future. Data are from the 1980s through the early 1990s.

Compendium of Statistics and Indicators on the Situation of Women 1986 or *Recueil de statistiques et d'indicateurs sur la situation des femmes 1986.* c. 1988. New York: United Nations. ISBN 9210611 (592 pages).

This is a bilingual publication (French and English) that includes 33statistical tables and spreadsheets on the situation of women in 178 countries or areas of the world. Also included is a bibliography of statistical sources consulted. Topics include population, composition, distribution and change, households and families, marital status, fertility, economic participation and population not economically active, national and household income and expenditure, education and literacy, health and health services, disabled persons, housing conditions and human settlements, public affairs and political participation, and criminal justice.

Historical Statistics of Black America. 1995. Jessie Carney Smith and Carrell Horton. New York: Gale Research. ISBN 0810393913 (vol. 1) and 0810393921 (vol. 2) (2, 244 pages).

This extensive work comes in two volumes. The years covered are 1619 to 1990. This work includes reference sources and two indexes, which are organized by year and subject. Statistics on women, as well as some comparative data on women and men, are intermixed with the general statistical data on Black America. These books contain mostly tabular data. Topics of interest include business and economics, crime, law enforcement and legal justice, education, the family, health, disabilities and health care, housing, income, spending and wealth, labor and employment, media, population, the professions, slavery and the slave trade, and vital statistics.

Human Development Report 1995. 1995. U.N. Development Programme. New York: Oxford University Press. ISBN 0195199239 (230 pages).

This U.N. publication presents country rankings according to the human development index (a measure that includes data on life expectancy, educational attainment, and income). It also ranks countries according to a separate gender development index, which takes the same measures but examines them for gender disparities. In addition to extensive statistical tables and explanations of the concepts and measures, it includes numerous graphs, charts, and bulleted highlights focusing on such themes as valuing women's work, women's political positions, and approaches to reducing inequality. A bibliography, glossary of definitions, a chart of abbreviations, and regional "balance sheets" showing "progress" and "deprivation" are included.

The State of Women in the World Atlas, 2nd edition. 1997. Joni Seager. London and New York: Penguin. ISBN 0140513644 (128 pages).

This imaginative, multicolored atlas provides an update on the first edition, which was published in 1986 (Joni Seager and Ann Olson, *Women in the World: An International Atlas*, New York: Simon and Schuster). It focuses primarily on women, and has limited comparative data on men. Data presented in map, graphic, and tabular forms are gathered from a wide array of sources with an emphasis on U.N. publications. Major areas of interest covered are women in the world (including information on ratification of the Convention to Eliminate Discrimination Against Women), families, birthrights, body politics, work, to have and have not (literacy, property rights, credit rights, effects of structural adjustment programs), and power (education, politics).

Statistical Handbook on U.S. Hispanics. 1991. Frank Leopold Schick and Renee Schick. Phoenix: Oryx Press. ISBN 089774554X (225 pages).

This book utilizes graphs, tables, and charts with minimal supplementary text on U.S. Hispanics. It includes a glossary, bibliography, and index. Topics covered are demographics (Hispanic population, geographic distribution and mobility, and age and sex distribution); immigration and naturalization (legal immigration and naturalization, illegal immigration, and apprehensions and expulsions); social characteristics (families, households, living arrangements, and social issues); education (school enrollment and dropouts, and educational attainment); health (births and deaths, health status, and health insurance); politics (voting and voter registration, and elected Hispanic officials); labor force (labor force participation, occupations, agricultural work force, and unemployment); and economic conditions (income and earnings, assets and wealth, and poverty-support programs).

Statistical Handbook on Women in America. 1996. Cynthia Murray Taeuber. Phoenix: Oryx Press. ISBN 1573560057 (354 pages).

Part of a series of Oryx Press publications, this handbook contains tables, charts, and graphs with limited supplementary text regarding women in the United States. Included are an index, guide to information sources, and glossary of terms. Areas covered are demographic events and characteristics, employment and economic status, health characteristics, and social characteristics. A previous edition of *Statistical Handbook on Women in America* is also available for 1991.

Statistical Record of Women Worldwide. 1995. Linda Shmittroth. New York: Gale Research. ISBN 0810388723 (1,047 pages).

This publication contains data presented through tables and graphs, with limited supplementary text. This work also includes an extensive subject and geographic index and bibliography. Topics include attitudes and opinions, business and economics, crime, law enforcement and legal justice, domestic life, education, health and medical care, income, spending and wealth, labor, employment and occupations, the military, population and vital statistics, public life, religion, sexuality, and sports and recreation.

Statistics and Indicators on Women in Africa, 1986 (Statistiques et indicateurs sur les femmes in Afrique, 1986). 1989. United Nations Statistical Office. New York: United Nations. ISBN 9210611330 (225 pages).

Statistical data and indicators extracted from the *Compendium of Statistics and Indicators on the Situation of Women* are presented in tabular form in this book. Statistical data are from 1986, and provide a retrospective look at African women from the 1980s. Written in French and English, topics include population composition, distribution and change, households and families, marital status, fertility, economic participation and population not economically active, national and household income and expenditure, education and literacy, health and health services, disabled persons, housing conditions and human settlements, public affairs and political participation, criminal justice, and population statistics programs. Comparative data on men and women are limited. A detailed bibliography on statistical sources is included.

United Nations Women's Indicators and Statistics Databases (WISTAT). 1994–present. New York: United Nations. CD-ROM.

This database contains economic and social time-series data with population and demographic series projections. Included are detailed statistics on a variety of topics, with comparative information on women and men when available, for 180 countries and areas around the world. All data is in spreadsheet form. All data cover 1970 to 1992, with projections up to 2025. The *WISTAT: Users Guide & Reference Manual* is recommended when using this database. Topics covered are population (composition, distribution), learning and educational series, economic activity, household conditions, human settlements, health, health services, disabled persons, public affairs, political participation, crime and criminal justice, national products, and expenditure. The CD-ROM format allows printing in various chart forms or downloading data for later manipulation.

WIDNET, (Women in Development Network), at http://www.focus-intl.com/statangl.html.

This website includes statistics gathered from the United Nations, *The World's Women 1995: Trends and Statistics* publications. This bilingual site in French and English contains statistics regarding population, family, households, health, education, training, labor, and power from Africa, Asia, Oceania, the Americas, and Europe.

WISTAT Women's Indicators and Statistics Spreadsheet Database for Microcomputers (Version 2): Users Guide and Reference Manual Series K, no. 10. 1992. New York: United Nations. ISBN 9211091233 (239 pages).

This guidebook and reference manual for, *WISTAT* CD-ROM contains spreadsheet data tables that are aids to using the CD-ROM, plus additional information regarding data compilation. *WISTAT* CD-ROM Version 3 can be used with this particular manual (Version 2).

Women and Men in the European Union: A Statistical Portrait. 1995. Statistical Office of the European Communities. Luxembourg: Office for Official Publications of the European Communities. ISBN 9282696197 (206 pages).

This publication includes statistics on women and men gathered from the twelve member states of the European Union in the early 1990s. This work presents data using color charts, graphs and tables with supplementary text, and bulleted formats for quick reference. It is broken down into four parts: population, family life, working life, and participation in decision-making. There are notes and references at the end of each section. Data include demographics, health, family issues, education, economics, and employment statistics.

Women, a World Survey. 1995. Ruth Leger Sivard and Arlette Brauer. Washington, D.C.: World Priorities. ISBN 0918281105 (48 pages).

This work has multicolored graphs, maps, charts, and tables with supplementary text covering information on various aspects of women's lives. Throughout the text, bulleted "highlights" help make this a ready-reference type of resource. Topics covered are perspectives, women's work, women's education, women's health, and legal rights and political power. In addition, information about "women at the top" is provided, as well as a limited glossary of terms and bibliography.

Women in Canada: A Statistical Report, 3d edition. 1995. Statistics Canada Target Group Data Bases. Ottawa: Statistics Canada. ISBN 0660155664 (180 pages). Aso issued in French under the title *Portrait statistiques des femmes au Canada.*

The focus in this reference is on women, although statistics concerning men are also available. A bulleted highlights section is convenient for quick reference. This book contains supplementary text with each chapter and a bibliography at the end of the book. Data are presented through tables and graphs. The twelve chapters include the following topics: women in the population, family status, housing and household facilities, health, education, labor force characteristics, income and earnings, women and the criminal justice system, immigrant women, women in a visible minority, Aboriginal women in Canada, and women with disabilities.

Women of the World: Asia and the Pacific. 1985. Nasra M. Shah. Washington, D.C.: U.S. Dept. of Commerce, Bureau of the Census. For sale by Data User Services Division, Customer Services (Publications), Bureau of the Census. Government Document #C3.2:W 84/8 (141 pages).

This book contains graphs and tables with supplementary text on Asian and Pacific women. The appendixes include information on references, sources of data, tables on Women in Development Databases, and population by age, sex, and rural or urban residence. Topics include population distribution change, literacy and education, women in economic activity, marital status and living arrangements, and fertility and mortality.

Women of the World: Near East and North Africa. 1985. Mary Chamie. Washington, D.C.: U.S. Dept. of Commerce, Bureau of the Census. Government Document #C3.2:W 84/6 (191 pages).

This book contains graphs and tables with supplementary text on Near East and North African women. The appendices include information on references, sources of data, tables on Women in Development Databases, population by age, sex, and rural or urban residence, and abbreviations used. Topics include the following: population distribution change, literacy and education, women in economic activity, marital status and living arrangements, and fertility and mortality.

The Women's Atlas of the United States. 1995. Timothy Fast and Cathy Carroll Fast. New York: Facts on File. ISBN 0816029709 (246 pages).

This multicolored atlas contains maps and statistical data on women and comparative data on women and men from 1995. This work contains limited textual content and includes an index, bibliography, and suggested further readings. Topics covered include demographics, education, employment, family, health, crime, and politics. The data are presented in a straightforward, easy-to-understand manner, which makes good use of colored maps. All statistics are at a state level. A previous edition of *The Women's Atlas of the United States* is also available from 1986.

The World's Women, 1970–1990: Trends and Statistics. 1991. United Nations Statistical Office. New York: United Nations. ISBN 9211613132 (120 pages).

This statistical work presents data through the use of graphs, charts, and tables, with supplementary text and bulleted highlights in each chapter. In addition, information is presented on the Nairobi Forward-Looking Strategies for the Advancement of Women, the Convention on the Elimination of All Forms of Discrimination Against Women, and geographical groupings of countries and areas. Subjects covered are women, families, households, public life, leadership, education and training, health, childbearing, housing, human settlements and the environment, women's work, and the economy.

The World's Women, 1995: Trends and Statistics. 1995. United Nations. New York: United Nations. ISBN 9211613728 (188 pages).

This book presents statistical information through graphs, tables, and charts in addition to supplementary text. In addition, statistical sources, countries, areas and geographical groupings, and technical notes on the tables are provided in the annexes. Also included is a list of abbreviations and acronyms. Contents covered are population, households, families, population growth, distribution, the environment, health, education, work, power, and influence.

The World's Women, 2000: Trends and Statistics. 2000. United Nations. New York: United Nations. ISBN 9211614287 (180 pages).

This book presents statistical information through graphs, tables, and charts plus supplementary text. Contents include population, women and men in families, health, education and communication, work, human rights, and political decision making.

FROM COURSE REVISION TO CURRICULUM TRANSFORMATION IN GRADUATE EDUCATION

Amy Newhall and Diane Riskedahl

Much of the published work in curriculum transformation has been concerned with the revision and creation of individual courses rather than the examination of undergraduate major requirements or the design of graduate degree programs. In this chapter, we offer an exercise designed to stimulate thinking at the curricular level. It was originally presented as an optional task in the SIROW project "Global Processes, Local Lives." A small working group chose to address the challenge of designing a hypothetical graduate program. Their efforts reflect a short but intensive investment of time, not the results of lengthy deliberations that would normally be invested in curriculum construction. They do, however, highlight the range of issues to be confronted in creating a program that is sensitive to the locally grounded knowledges and skills required of area studies specialists, with the theoretical and conceptual understandings of global, transnational, and feminist work.

CURRICULUM DEVELOPMENT EXERCISE

INSTRUCTIONS

Draft a preliminary outline that implements global-local perspectives:

1. for a women's studies major or minor;

2. for a master's program in women's studies; or

3. for a gender sensitive, comparative area studies in a disciplinary or inter-disciplinary-based graduate program.

The outline should include

    a.   assumptions made about students who will pursue the curriculum;

    b.   the rationale for the curriculum design;

c. arguments that could be used to justify the curriculum to colleagues;

d. problems or roadblocks anticipated in implementing the curriculum; and

e. desired student outcomes from the curriculum.

You may wish to comment on the extent to which the group addressed these instructions and on what could be accomplished in the time allowed. This will give some context to the product of the enterprise.

IMPLEMENTING THE EXERCISE

The working group in the SIROW project chose to focus on task 3 of the options offered.[1] We purposely included graduate students in the working group in order to provide their perspectives on program ideas proposed by specialized faculty that might seem to be too arcane or ambitious. We also thought students might be less territorial and more open to methods from outside their disciplines. Many graduate students are keenly aware of the need to acquire integrative interdisciplinary skills in addition to focused area expertise; these days junior faculty positions often hinge upon one's ability to fulfill multiple academic roles spanning disciplinary boundaries. Few academic programs provide such preparation in a systematic, integrated way.

From the outset, it was understood that university structures present a number of barriers to a cross-disciplinary curriculum. One major challenge would be to assure interdepartmental cooperation and funding for interdisciplinary courses. The working group was instructed not to focus on such impediments but to begin with a collaborative orientation toward an idealized curriculum that reflected intellectual priorities. Exploration of the politics of implementation were to be discussed as a later step. The goals were to negotiate the connections between the social sciences and the humanities, determine the ties among the different disciplines within these larger categories, and define the links between the global and the local while keeping the interests of students at the center.

PRELIMINARY REFLECTIONS

The group began by recognizing the limitations of traditional disciplinary degree programs. From this point it sought insight into ways of expanding interdisciplinary coherence beyond the level of individual courses toward a more programmatic synthesis. As the world history movement has highlighted, the links and interdependencies knitting together the regions of the world have always existed, but it is only recently that Western academia has begun to pose global questions. This new direction has been stimulated, perhaps, by modern technologies, multinational economic investments, and new patterns of migration from the Third to the First World. All of these factors have increased awareness of global processes. For some scholars, area studies approaches have failed to address adequately the complexities of either historical or contemporary interconnections. In a recent evaluation of the status of area studies, it was noted that "[t]he fluidity and porousness of borders; the unprecedented mobility of people, ideas, information, and capital; the end of the Cold War, the dissolution of old states, and the rise of new identities and new expressions of nationalism—all have forced a radical questioning of conventional ways of viewing the world and of the rationale for area studies" (Volkman 1998, 28).

The working group agreed that contemporary global changes require some changes in university curricula. Students need to be trained to understand how global and local problems are related, to assess microscopic and macroscopic perspectives, and to analyze and solve problems. The challenge for curriculum designers lies in fostering a broad-based understanding without losing the specialized expertise, for example, the detailed linguistic and cultural knowledge, that has been the strength of traditional area studies programs. Integrating the contributions of the international scholarly community of area and global specialists into courses is a first step. Engaging these colleagues in research and publication is a desirable second step.

In the section that follows, we first present the model curriculum that the working group designed, including a description of the courses and a sample program for a hypothetical student. We then present brief integrative comments that highlight specific concerns that arose in the group's discussion during their work on the exercise.

THE PROPOSED CURRICULUM—GLOBALIZATION, TRANSNATIONALISM, AND CULTURE OR AREA STUDIES: COMPARATIVE AND RELATIONAL APPROACHES

PROGRAM RATIONALE

It is assumed that this program will attract students from diverse backgrounds who are interested in integrating interdisciplinary, cross-cultural, and women's studies. Global, area, and women's studies traditionally have remained in separate academic spheres. In the contemporary political and cultural context, the processes of globalization have necessitated the implementation of a more integrative approach, which strives to avoid historical, cultural, and theoretical homogenization. Counter to this, the continuation of narrowly focused traditional area studies and separate women's studies programs may lead to academic isolation and fails to address the intersection of global and local processes.

STUDENT OUTCOMES

Students will be prepared to understand global and local perspectives and to analyze and problem solve at an integrative level.

PROGRAM DESCRIPTION

This program is designed to provide students with a broad interdisciplinary understanding of global, transnational, and cross-cultural issues, as well as an in-depth disciplinary understanding of a particular culture or area. The program is divided into two tiers and includes M.A. and Ph.D. tracks.

Tier I

Tier I includes eighteen credits required of all students. It is composed of a two-semester course in theoretical and methodological approaches to interdisciplinary and cross-cultural studies, and six reading colloquia that focus on the comparative study of currently important global issues. All courses in Tier I, which present theoretical and empirical models, are intensive and team-taught. Each course is attentive to interdisciplinary, comparative, and relational perspectives as well as to issues of gender, race or ethnicity, and class. The theory and methods course is required, and students may select four out of the six thematic colloquia.

When Tier I is completed, students are required to write a program statement in which they select a discipline and culture or area of interest. They will also select two global themes that they intend to pursue in their area and discipline course work, at least one of which will frame their applied project, M.A. thesis, or Ph.D. dissertation topic.

Tier II

Tier II is for master's and doctoral candidates. The tier consists of an additional eighteen-credit M.A. program or an additional thirty-six-credit course toward the Ph.D. program. Master's candidates focus their studies on either a discipline or a culture or area and may also have the option of selecting an applied program or a thesis-bearing program. Courses are arranged into overlapping disciplinary, thematic, and cognate blocks and include important gender components.

Tier I Course Descriptions
Theory and Research Methods
This is a two-semester course intended to provide students with a broad understanding of theoretical and methodological approaches to historical, interdisciplinary, cross-cultural, and gender analysis. The first semester will introduce students to structural models such as world-systems, class analysis, liberalism, modernization theory, and Gramscian hegemony. The second semester will explore feminism, postmodernism, and praxis theory. Some of the topics that will come under discussion are difference, subaltern studies, discourse analysis, and issues of representation and sociocultural construction.

Problems of Development and Modernity
This course provides an introduction to the historical evolution and contemporary issues of development. Theoretical approaches will include classical and neoclassical economic approaches, dependency theory, gender and development perspectives, cultural perspectives, and other critiques from non-Western works. The course will examine such topics as structural adjustment policies, sustainable development, and development induced cultural transformations. Readings address the relationship and tensions between local and global processes and will underscore the significance of gender, race, and class analyses.

Human Rights and the State
This course is an introduction to the theories and concepts of global human rights. It examines the major debates in human rights (individual and collective rights) as they relate to Western and non-Western conceptions of human rights. Students will explore such topics as gender, development, and political participation. The course will analyze the difficulties of implementing human rights in the state system as well as discuss the growing role of NGOs in monitoring and implementing human rights today.

Race, Class, and Gender in Cross-Cultural Perspective
The objectives of this course are (1) to conceptualize through cross-cultural and theoretical resources the relevance of race and class relations to the issue of gender, and (2) to evaluate the appropriateness of essentialist and differentiated visions of the concept of *women* through the essentialism versus epistemology debate. The first section will be dedicated to the theoretical framework on this issue and its relevance to feminism. The second section will explore women's differences and similarities in terms of class, race, and gender issues. Moreover, these issues will be examine, cross-culturally in connection to more concrete issues such as work, development, reproductive rights, political organization, and sexuality.

Colonialism, Postcolonialism, and Nationalism
This course will present a comparative study of the global and local processes of colonization, colonialism, decolonization, and both Western and anticolonial nationalism. Some of the issues that will be explored include the formation and maintenance of a global, capitalist system; hierarchies of gender, race, and class in colonial and postcolonial societies; cultural representation; political mobilization and other forms of resistance; minority-majority issues; and current debates surrounding nationalism.

Human Space, Ecology, and the Environment
Students will explore issues of resource management, environmental justice, and activism at both the global and local levels. There will be a focus on the impact of contemporary environmental development and technology on the sociocultural geography of human space in terms of a gendered landscape.

Arts and Communication in Cross-Cultural Perspective
Interdisciplinary theoretical and methodological approaches to the cross-cultural study of arts and communication, through the lens of gender, will be utilized to discuss sociocultural phenomena in the contemporary global system. Attention will be given to popular culture, aesthetics, the visual and performing arts, literature, and the media.

INTERPRETING THE CURRICULUM

METHODOLOGICAL AND THEORETICAL CONCERNS

In designing the curriculum, the group members recognized that they wanted to do two things simultaneously: first they needed to decide which subjects might be studied and then they needed to determine how those subjects related to one other. And, they needed to address both aspects on two levels, the theoretical and methodological. Kenneth Prewitt (1997, 8) describes such an effort as "accommodating changing intellectual priorities, notably cross-regional, transnational, processual and thematically focused inquiries. This shift involves replacing a series of vertical structures organized along geographical lines with a horizontal integration of area expertise throughout the various international programs."

As a first step in creating an integrative curriculum, the group focused on ways of preparing students to conceptualize relationally. They decided that such a course of study must prepare students to document social interactions and cultural production empirically at a local level while framing these data within the larger political-economic context of globalization. It needs to work toward collapsing the dichotomy between structure and process, as well as the analytical designations of subject and object. But it must be framed carefully in language that avoids the isolating tendencies of particular disciplinary vocabularies, both theoretical and technical. At the same time, the curriculum must be attentive to the issues of power and diversity within, for example, societies and their interrelations, class, race or ethnicity, and religion.

CURRICULUM DESIGN

In order to avoid the isolating effects of disciplinary training, the group proposed a required full-year course on interdisciplinary theory and methodology that would emphasize cross-cultural and integrative approaches. Students would, in addition, take two accompanying thematic colloquia each semester. These colloquia would explore specific applications of the approaches presented in the year-long theory and methodology course, thereby incorporating the dual structure-process aspects of an interdisciplinary approach. Each colloquium section would be organized in overlapping disciplinary, thematic, and cognate blocks to expose students to a wide spectrum of the analytical methods and languages of the social sciences and humanities.

Choosing the overarching thematic topics for the colloquia required intense discussion and negotiation. Each member of the task group came from a different discipline and each felt the keen challenge of trying to forge connections without surrendering rigor. Ultimately, they recognized that the choice of topics would be predicated upon the composition of the faculty coalition creating and implementing the curriculum. Furthermore, it became clear that such a curriculum would necessarily be a team-taught effort. In this way, broad-based topics would be illuminated by various disciplinary perspectives.

The second tier of courses and the research and writing phase would be directed by the student's particular regional and topical interests, but it would build on the basic organization developed in Tier I. For example, a student with an interest in the Middle East and women and development issues would have been given grounding in various approaches to development in the "Problems of Development and Modernity" colloquium. Her second year of course work would be directed by the approaches she found most relevant to her topic. It might include taking courses in such fields as Near Eastern studies, anthropology, economics, and women's studies.

This second year could have either a research or applied focus. Because an increasing number of graduate students are finding positions outside of academia upon graduation, a key component of the curriculum is to provide students with the opportunity to develop applied skills. Thus, students are given two options: they can prepare an applied project or a master's thesis, depending on their interests.

The working group did not fully develop the Ph.D. track of the curriculum. It was thought that the program's strength was in providing an interdisciplinary bridge that would lead either to certain kinds of employment or to more traditional doctoral and professional degree programs.

In the sample program we describe next, the student has Middle East regional interests coupled with an interest in development. She can choose a number of options. For example, instead of preparing a traditional master's thesis, she might decide to participate in a women and development project by designing and implementing an ethnographic survey and then writing up the whole project report. Or, she might choose to write a grant proposal for a major project. Either of these options would better prepare the student for employment in a development agency. If her interests were more oriented toward academia and research, she might choose the traditional thesis option.

SAMPLE PROGRAM

TIER I

Semester 1: theory and research methods; problems of development and modernity; colonialism, postcolonialism, and nationalism

Semester 2: theory and research methods; race, class, and gender; human space, ecology, and environment

Total credits, Tier I = 18

TIER II

Applied Track
Semester 3: women in international development (anthropology); population and development in the Middle East (Near Eastern studies); structural adjustment policy (political science)

Semester 4: globalization and world systems (economics); participatory development methods (anthropology); women and work (women's studies)

Research Track
Semester 3: Third World feminist theory (women's studies); contemporary politics of the Middle East (Near Eastern studies); theories of mass communication (communication)

Semester 4: population and development in the Middle East (Near Eastern studies); issues in contemporary Middle Eastern literature (literature); political economy and globalization (anthropology)

Final Project Options: (a) grant write-up for development project; (b) work on local project concluding with final project write-up; (c) traditional thesis

Total credits, Tier II = 18

In addition, relevant area language study would be integrated into this program of study.

The sample program laid out here should not be viewed as prescriptive. Our group was interested in serving the needs of nontraditional students who may have difficulty attending a program full-time. Necessarily, their program would be more drawn out, and attention would have to be paid to ensure continuity and linkages. It would require both students and faculty to be flexible and inventive, but many universities regard such commitments as an important step in maintaining a diverse student body. Our design also does not go into detail in addressing several important issues that would need to be resolved for implementation including incorporation of language study, overcoming the rigidity of existing structures in disciplinary and area studies programs, effective team teaching in Tier I, and shifts in thematic interests.

Although the structure of the program we have outlined may seem idealistic, it is an initial step toward formulating a more comprehensive approach to looking at transregional and transcultural issues. Its purpose is to identify and analyze links, while countering the tendency toward historical, cultural, and theoretical homogenization. At the same time the program represents a political undertaking that will link previously isolated scholars and departments. "The core curriculum not only anchors a field of study; it also helps to determine who gets published, who gets read, how resources are distributed, and how power relations are reproduced and challenged within the university" (McDermott 1998, 92).

CONCLUSION

The exercise of developing a curriculum that integrates global, transnational, and area studies provided our group with the opportunity to explore the difficulties of negotiating across disciplines. The time for group discussions during the institute was limited, but totaled about eight hours spread over the week. Some tasks were assumed by individuals, but the bulk of the work was done collectively, highlighting not only the institute's commitment to modeling collaborative learning, but also to interdisciplinary dialogue and to crossing the boundaries of the geographical regions represented by area studies programs. Through emphasizing commonalities of goals, the group was able to transcend the methodological and theoretical differences. All participants were struck by the potential benefits of establishing interdisciplinary links in terms of a programmatic format like a curriculum. Unlike theoretical musing about interdisciplinary connections, each decision made was qualified by departmental and institutional constraints, which required group members to develop innovative ways of achieving the project's goals.

NOTE

1. Members of the SIROW working group included Anna Bergareche, graduate student in sociology at the Universidad Autonoma Ciudad Juárez; Linda Butenhoff, faculty in political science at the University of Northern Colorado; Karen Powers, faculty in history at Northern Arizona University; Diane Riskedahl, graduate student in anthropology at the University of Arizona; and facilitator Amy Newhall, faculty in Near Eastern studies at the University of Arizona.

WORKS CITED

McDermott, Patrice. 1998. "Internationalizing the Core Curriculum." *Women's Studies Quarterly* 3–4 (Fall–Winter): 88–92.

Prewitt, Kenneth. 1997. "(Re)made in the USA: Middle East Studies in the Global Era." *Middle East Report #205* 27 (4): 2–9.

Volkman, Toby Alice. 1998. "Crossing Borders: The Case for Area Studies." *Ford Foundation Report* (Winter): 28.

WOMEN AROUND THE WORLD: A VIDEOGRAPHY

COMPILED BY JACQUELYN E. DAVOLI, JANICE MONK,
SUJATA MOORTI, DEBORAH S. ROSENFELT, AND JOSEPH
CHRISTOPHER SCHAUB

This videography includes documentaries and some feature films that portray women in different cultural contexts around the world, both in the present and the past. The videos are listed alphabetically, with all pertinent information—year of release, principal filmmaker, running time, distributor, and format—followed by an annotation. Most of the annotations were taken in part or directly from the catalogues of major distributors such as Women Make Movies. These short annotations do not include our judgments of the possible uses of the videos, or our critiques. The video list is in no way comprehensive, but rather is intended to provide a sampling—admittedly and inevitably arbitrary—of some high quality films and videos that are especially useful in the classroom, sometimes for the information they provide, sometimes for the discussions they might provoke. Many of the films and videos have won awards, though that was not the basis for their selection. We have seen many of the items ourselves, and have found them useful in our classrooms in the women's studies and international and area studies projects at the University of Maryland and at the University of Arizona. Other films and videos were recommended by project directors or participants in other WSAIS projects. For more information, please contact the distributors; a complete listing with contact information for each distributor can be found at the end of the citations.

VIDEOGRAPHY

Abortion Stories from North and South. 1984. Gail Singer. 55 minutes. National Film Board of Canada. Color, videocassette.

Filmed in Ireland, Peru, Thailand, Japan, and Colombia, this documentary explores policies and practices related to abortion. The video emphasizes the struggles of women to receive abortions, the consequences of illegal abortions, and diverse discourses around women's rights to abortion.

Algeria: Women at War. 1992. Parminder Vir. 52 minutes. Women

Make Movies. Color, French with English subtitles, videocassette. This documentary offers insights into the key role Algerian women played in their country's liberation struggle from the French in the 1950s and 1960s and their equally important place in today's politics. It uses a combination of interviews and archival footage to ponder the position of women in Algeria in the light of thirty years of single party rule, the rise of Islam, and increasing political violence. It questions the balancing act between women's and national liberation struggles.

Arab Women at Work. 1990. Maureen Ali. 26 minutes. United Nations Development Program. Color, videocassette.

Based on papers given at a conference in Cairo on women and development, this video features Arab women academics and political figures plus a voice-over narration of images of women working in diverse settings: fields, factories, clinics, markets, offices, and laboratories. It aims to show the extent of women's contributions to the labor force and to emphasize the need to attend to women's work in development planning.

Asante Market Women. 1982. Claudia Milne. 52 minutes. Filmakers Library. Color, videocassette.

This film examines the matrilineal and polygamous Asante society of Ghana through interviews with women, who exercise complete authority in the wholesale produce market and over their husbands and children. The interviewees reveal the advantages and tribulations of their relationships, the practical problems they confront, and the various solutions they embrace.

To Be a Woman in Burkina Faso. 1992. Maurice Kabore. 14 minutes. Films for the Humanities and Sciences. Color, videocassette.

This video documents the workload of rural and urban women in Burkina Faso. It portrays their agricultural and factory labor, as well as their child care, home care, and cooking, all done without adequate recompense. This film advocates education, equal job opportunities with men, and reasonable sources of income for women as essential for improving women's well-being.

Becoming a Woman in Okrika. 1990. Judith Gleason and Elisa Mereghetti Tesser. 27 minutes. Filmakers Library. Color, videocassette.

Five women, fifteen to seventeen years old, undergo a traditional rite of passage in Okrika. This sequence of events takes place in the village of Ogbogbo, which is part of the Okrika community of Ijo-speaking people who populate the Niger Delta in Rivers State, Nigeria.

Beyond Beijing. 1996. Shirini Heerah and Enrique Beerios. 42 minutes. Women Make Movies. Color, videocassette.

The 1995 United Nations Fourth World Conference on Women and the parallel forum (NGO) that took place in Beijing assembled the largest global gathering of women in recorded history. *Beyond Beijing,* a personal document of the epoch-making events, captures their spirit and shows the strength of the worldwide movement to improve the status of women. Moving back and forth from NGO workshops convened by grassroots activists to ceremonies commemorating women's arts and achievements, the film also includes informal cross-cultural get togethers, compelling North-South exchanges, and candid interviews with individual participants. The video can usefully be combined with *The Beijing Declaration and The Platform for Action: Fourth World Conference on Women, Beijing, China* (New York: United Nations Department of Public Information, 1996) in class discussions and assignments.

Black Kites. 1996. Jo Andres. 26 minutes. Women Make Movies. Color, 35-mm, 16-mm, or videocassette.

Based on 1992 journals of Bosnian visual artist Alma Hajric, who was forced into a basement shelter to survive the siege of Sarajevo, this film is the outcome of a chance encounter between Hajric and filmmaker-choreographer Andres. Focusing on Hajric's inner landscape, the film merges reality-based content with interpretive visual material to reveal the simple truth of her existence. Features sensitive performances by Steve Buscemi and Mimi Goese, with Mira Furlan, a prominent actress from the former Yugoslavia, as narrator.

Black Mother, Black Daughter. 1989. Sylvia Hamilton. 29 minutes. National Film Board of Canada. Color, videocassette.

This film is the first formal record of the history and life experiences of Black women in Nova Scotia. Women from several Black communities speak candidly about their lives and the discrimination they have endured.

The Body Beautiful. 1991. Ngozi Onwurah. 23 minutes. Women Make Movies. Color, 16-mm and videocassette.

This powerful exploration of the relationship between a white mother who has undergone a radical mastectomy and her Black daughter who embarks on a modeling career reveals the profound effects of body image and the strain of racial and sexual identity on their charged, loving bond. Onwurah's excursion into her mother's scorned sexuality interweaves memory and fantasy in provocative ways.

Brincando El Charco: Portrait of a Puerto Rican. 1994. Frances Negron-Muntaner. 55 minutes. Women Make Movies. Color and black and white, Spanish and English subtitles, 16-mm and video-cassette.

Sophisticated in both form and content, *Brincando El Charco* contemplates the notion of identity. Mixing fiction, archival footage, processed interviews, and soap opera drama, the film tells the story of Claudia Marin, a middle class light-skinned photographer and videographer who is attempting to construct a sense of community in the United States.

Calling the Ghosts: A Story About Rape, War, and Women. 1996. Mandy Jacobson and Karmen Jelinsic. 63 minutes. Women Make Movies. Color, 16-mm and videocassette.

Calling the Ghosts is the first-person account of two women caught in a war where rape was used as an everyday weapon. Jadranka Cigeli and Nusreta Sivac, childhood friends and lawyers, enjoyed the lives of "ordinary modern women" in Bosnia-Herzegovina until ethnic conflict made neighbors into enemies. Taken to a Serb concentration camp, the two women, like other Muslim and Croat women interned there, were systematically tortured and humiliated by their captors. Once released, they became effective human rights activists successfully lobbying the U.N. tribunal to include rape as a war crime.

Camp Arirang. 1995. Diana S. Lee and Grace Yoonkyung Lee. 28 minutes. Third World Newsreel. Color with black and white sequences, videocassette.

This video presents a disconcerting look at prostitution and sexual exploitation around U.S. army bases in Korea. The film contains devastating sequences on the consequences for mixed-race children of their parents' liaisons. The connections between furthering U.S. military and economic interests, political corruption, and the quality of local women's lives are powerfully explored.

Carmen Miranda: Bananas Is My Business. 1994. Helena Solberg. 92 minutes. Fox/Lorber Home Video. Color, 35-mm or videocassette.

A filmmaker's journey into the cross-cultural life and career of one of the most successful Latin American performers of all time, Carmen Miranda. For her, professional distortion and personal damage came along with enormous wealth and fame as a Latin American icon fabricated in the image factories of Hollywood. The film seeks to reveal the person behind the elaborate mask.

Carry Greenham Home. 1983. Beeban Kidron and Amanda Richardson. 66 minutes. Women Make Movies. Color, videocassette.

This film focuses on a group of women protesting at a cruise missile base in Greenham Common, England, which became a permanent protest to the British government's escalating nuclear policy and an inspiration to the peace movement internationally.

Carved in Silence. 1987. Felicia Lowe and Charlie Pearson. 45 minutes. CrossCurrent Media, NAATA. Color with black and white sequences, videocassette.

By using historical footage plus dramatized reenactments, this video looks at Chinese immigration to the United States, emphasizing the experience on Angel Island, California, during the Exclusion Era of 1882 to 1943. The video predominantly reports male experiences but includes some women, though it is not a gender analysis.

Columbus Didn't Discover Us. 1992. Felix Antencio-Gonzales and Robbie Leppzer. 24 minutes. Facets Multimedia. Color, voice-over, videocassette.

Using interviews with women and men activists at the First Continental Confer-ence of Indigenous Peoples, which was held in 1990, two years before the 500-year anniversary of Columbus' "discovery" of the American continents, this film offers an alternative view of Columbus' place in history. Speakers discuss the impact the Columbus legacy has had on the lives of indigenous people.

Conjure Women. 1995. Demetria Royals. 85 minutes. Women Make Movies. Color with black and white sequences, videocassette.

African American women artists—choreographer and dancer Anita Gonzalez, performance artist Robbie McCauley, photographer Carrie Mae Weems, and musician Cassandra Wilson—discuss their philosophy of art. The video includes excerpts from the artists' works.

Dadi's Family. 1981. Michael Camerini and Rina Gill. 60 minutes. PBS Home Video. Color, videocassette.

Originally part of a series of films on South Asia made under the over-all direction of Joseph Elder (University of Wisconsin), this portrait of a farming family in India focuses largely on Dadi, the grandmother, who heads a large household of sons, daughters-in-law, and grandchildren. Her ability to maintain the family unit is threatened not only by social and economic change, but by internal pressures within the family itself.

Daughters of Allah. 1998. Sigrun Slapguard. 49 minutes. Filmakers Library. Color, videocassette.

Filmed on the West Bank and in Gaza, the film explores the challenges Palestinian women face as they are trapped between a stalled peace process and an increasingly strong Islamic movement. It includes interviews with militant activists who have chosen to wear the veil for ideological and symbolic reasons. Through narratives of women who have rebelled against the Islamic movement, the film also reveals the conflicts women encounter when they have to adhere to a strict religious code.

Daughters of the Nile. 1993. Hillie Molenaar and Joop van Wijk. 46 minutes. Filmakers Library. Color, Arabic with English subtitles, videocassette.

This video presents mostly rural women speaking about the traditions that control their marriages and marital relations, childbearing, and practices such as circumcision and the limitations on women's mobility and education. In contrast, religious teachers and community men present their viewpoints on normative expectations. The women speak not only of their acceptance of cultural norms, but also of their efforts to gain greater control over their own lives by attending literacy classes. Visually beautiful, but at times presenting confusing images, the representation moves between exoticizing the women and showing them as human beings with individual personalities.

Defending Our Lives. 1993. Margaret Lazarus, Renner Wunderlich, and Stacey Kabat. Cambridge Documentary Films. 41 minutes. Color, videocassette.

This film shows the magnitude and severity of domestic violence in the United States. This video features four women imprisoned for killing their batterers and their terrifying personal testimonies. Each of these women tells her own horrific tale of beatings, rape, and torture at the hands of her husband or boyfriend.

The Desert Is No Lady. 1995. Shelley Williams and Susan Palmer. 45 minutes. Women Make Movies. Color, videocassette.

This film features nine contemporary southwestern U.S. women writers and artists (American Indian, Mexican American, and Anglo) who discuss their senses of personal and cultural identity in relation to their senses of the Southwest as a place. Themes include the meanings of living on the border with Mexico, the cultural conjunctions in the region in the past and present, the importance of language and cultural traditions, and the sensuousness of the land.

Los dos mundos de Angelita. 1983. Jane Morrison. 72 minutes. First Run/Icarus Films. Color, videocassette.

This film tells the story of a nine-year-old girl who moved from her home in Puerto Rico to New York City and finds fitting into a new school overwhelming.

Dreams, Desires and Lunacies (Suenos, deseos, locuras). 1994. Catharine Russo. 80 minutes. Women Make Movies. Color, Spanish with English subtitles, videocassette.

This video documents the landmark Sixth Latin American Feminists' Conference that took place in El Salvador in 1993. It observes both process and practice, capturing the breadth and scope of issues facing feminist movements in Latin America, including participants' efforts to prioritize problems facing women in their countries when developing progressive strategies, and to grapple with potentially diverse issues of race and class. Above all, it gives audiences a clear sense of the strength and vibrancy of feminist movements throughout Latin America.

Early Summer. 1951. Yasujiro Ozu. 135 minutes. Facets Multimedia. Black and white, Japanese with English subtitles, videocassette.

A drama, this film chronicles family tensions in post–World War II Japan caused by newly independent women rebelling against the social conventions they are expected to fulfill. It focuses on Noriko, a young woman who refuses to give up her job to get married just because of her age; rather, she wants a man of means who will respect her intelligence.

Echoes of Dissent. 1997. Peter L. Atipetty and James Mukalel. 30 minutes. Filmakers Library. Color, videocassette.

Contemporary Indian women face challenges and obstacles as traditional and modern values and practices compete. The daily life of an Indian woman is riddled with paradoxes arising from gender differences, marriage and family, and societal roles. Shot in Kerala, India, this film includes interviews with prominent personalities in education, psychology, and the arts who discuss the realities of Indian women and the voices of change that are beginning to be heard.

Family Ties. 1985. Colin Luke. 58 minutes. Landmark Films. Color, Arabic with English subtitles, videocassette.

Nadia Hajib, a Jordanian journalist working in London, interviews urban women in Jordan, Egypt, and Tunisia about their changing family and work relationships. The video highlights generational themes and the persistence of and work relationships. The video highlights generational themes and the persistence of family ties, focusing especially on an extended family in Amman. This film is part of the series *The Arabs: A Living History.*

Femmes aux Yeux Ouverts (*Women with Open Eyes*). 1994. Anne-Laure Folly. 51 minutes. California Newsreel. Color, videocassette.

This film profiles contemporary women in four West African countries: Burkina Faso, Mali, Senegal, and Benin. We meet a woman active in the movement against female genital mutilation, a health care worker educating women about sexually transmitted diseases, and business women who describe how they have set up an association to share expertise and provide mutual assistance.

Fire Eyes. 1994. Soraya Mire and Wendy Matolibla. 57 minutes. Filmakers Library. Color with black and white sequences, videocassette.

Also called *Female Circumcision,* this video explores the socioeconomic, psychological, and medical consequences of the ancient custom of female circumcision, which affects more than eighty million women worldwide. Bringing the director's insider perspective to these issues, this is one of the best documentaries on this controversial subject.

Gabriela. 1988. Trix Betlam. 67 minutes. Women Make Movies. Color, Tagalog with English subtitles, videocassette.

This documentary looks at the work of Gabriela, a mass organization of diverse women's groups in the Philippines. Founded in 1984 in honor of Gabriela Silans, a Filipina nationalist who fought against the Spanish occupation, it brought nuns, students, farm and factory workers, prostitutes, and housewives together to gain a voice in national politics. This voice was particularly important in the overthrow of the Marcos regime. An empowering documentary on the contemporary role and history of women in the Philippines as well as strategies for global feminism.

Gay Cuba. 1995. Sonja de Vries. 57 minutes. Frameline. Color, Spanish with English subtitles, videocassette.

This video features gay women and men in Cuba discussing their personal identities, family relationships, and the gradual liberalization of Cuban policies and attitudes toward homosexuality. It includes segments on HIV/AIDS (including the isolation of people diagnosed with the virus); the relationships between homosexuality, politics, and religion; and gay performances (especially drag artists).

The Global Assembly Line. 1986. Lorraine Gray. 65 minutes. New Day Films. Color, 16-mm and videocassette.

Although more than a decade old, the conditions documented by this powerful film still persist. The film examines the experiences of women in export processing zones along the Mexican border and in the Philippines, taking into account the economic benefits for women of work in the zones, but painfully representing the oppressive nature of much of the work.

Goldwidows: Women in Lesotho. 1991. Don Edkins, Ute Hall, and Mike Schlomer. 52 minutes. First Run/Icarus Films. Color, videocassette.

This film focuses on four Basotho women of Lesotho, a small mountainous country in southern Africa. Although most Basotho men, often up to 60 percent at one time, have worked as migrant laborers in South Africa's gold mines, apartheid laws forbade Lesotho women or children from entering South Africa. Living as practical widows, each tells of her life, coping alone, caught in the inhumane web of South Africa's oppressive system in the pre-Mandela era.

Half the Sky. 1998. Canadian Broadcasting Corporation. 27 minutes. Film-akers Library. Color, videocassette.

Fifty years ago the Chinese Communist revolution promised women equality, but has it reversed the tradition of tyranny toward women? As this film shows, today's Chinese women have little more control over their lives than their ancestors did. Their concerns are neglected while their burdens increase. The film takes us to remote villages and urban factories as it underscores the cultural biases that prevail against women. It outlines women's abilities to receive an education, their devalued status in the arena of paid labor, and the cultural factors that maintain their subordination. It also reveals women's accomplishments.

Half the Sky: The Women of the Jiang Family. 1995. Sun Shuyun. 50 minutes. Bullfrog Films. Color, videocassette.

"Women are half the sky, and they are absolutely the equal of men," declared Mao Zedong. Built around a series of interviews, images of daily life, special family occasions, and archival film, this video explores changes within the lives of four generations of the Jiang family over the last fifty years in China, ranging from the regimentation of women and denial of their needs to contemporary efforts by women to make their demands known.

The Heart of the Matter. 1994. Gini Reticker and Amber Hollibaugh. 54 minutes. First Run/Icarus Films. Color, videocassette.

This film focuses on the inspiring story of Janice Jirau, an HIV-positive African American woman, who deals with the knowledge that she has AIDS. A chorus of other HIV-positive women underscores the far-reaching nature of the problems Janice confronted and draws attention to the alarming growth of the epidemic among women.

Hidden Faces. 1990. Claire Hunt and Kim Longinetto. 52 minutes. Women Make Movies. Color, 16-mm and videocassette.

A complex, interesting film that explores the ambiguous experiences of women in Muslim society through the changing perceptions of a young Egyptian woman. Living in Paris at the beginning of the film, she returns to interview Nawal El Sadaawi, feminist writer, doctor, and activist, developing unanticipated reservations in the process.

History and Memory: For Akiko and Takashige. 1991. Rea Tajiri. 32 minutes. Women Make Movies. Color with black and white sequences, videocassette.

This exploration of personal and cultural memory juxtaposes Hollywood images of Japanese Americans and World War II propaganda with stories from the videomaker's family. Ruminating on the difficult nature of representing the past, the artist blends interviews, memorabilia, a pilgrimage to the camp where her mother was interned, and the story of her father, who had been drafted before Pearl Harbor and returned to find his family's house removed from its site. A haunting testament to the Japanese American experience.

Holding Our Ground. 1987. National Film Board of Canada. 51 minutes. International Film Bureau. Color, videocassette.

This film documents the efforts of a group of Filipino women who have organized to pressure the government for land reform, shelters for street children, and their own money-lending system.

Home Is Struggle. 1991. Marta Bautis. 37 minutes. Women Make Movies. Color, Spanish with English subtitles, videocassette.

Using interviews, photographs, and theatrical vignettes, this film explores the lives of women who have come to the United States from different Latin American countries: Nicaragua, Chile, Argentina, and the Dominican Republic, all for very different economic and political reasons. With each woman presenting individual stories about her past and present and her views on issues such as sexism and political repression, this film presents an absorbing picture of the construction of "Latina" identity and the immigrant experience.

Hopi, Songs of the Fourth World. 1983. Pat Ferrero and Mollie Gregory. 58 minutes. Ferrero Films and New Day Films. Color, 16-mm and videocassette.

This film provides a luminous, slow-paced exploration of the meaning of the Hopi way, a philosophy of living in balance with nature. It describes the Hopi philosophy of life, death, and renewal as revealed in the interweaving life cycle of humans and corn plants. Hopi women are featured in various roles, including those as breadmakers and artists.

Increase and Multiply? 1987. Robert Richter. 55 minutes. Filmakers Library. Color, videocassette.

Filmed in Kenya, Mexico, China, and Zimbabwe, this documentary presents the perspectives of international family planning agencies. It highlights policies and action programs in the four countries as well as the implications of cuts in U.S. funding for family planning that have been prompted by pressure from Christian fundamentalists.

Influences of the Invisible. 1997. Peter L. Attipetty and James Mukalel. 29 minutes. Advanced Media Productions. Color, video-cassette.

Shot in South India, this film plumbs the collective psyche to reveal the power that mythology and tradition wield over women in India today. Interwoven with casual interviews and candid observations, it provides a cultural perspective on women and their issues and context in modern India.

Iraqi Women: Voices from Exile. 1994. Maysoon Pachachi. 54 minutes. Women Make Movies. Color, Arabic with English subtitles, videocassette.

This documentary provides a look at the recent history of Iraq through the eyes and experiences of Iraqi women living in exile in Great Britain. Featuring interviews with the women, it is organized in three parts. The first deals with Iraq in the 1950s to 1970s, emphasizing women's feminist efforts. The second part shows women as political victims and refugees of the Iran-Iraq War. The third part incorporates the Gulf War and its effects on Baghdad, concluding with the women's reflections on their exile in London.

Islam and Feminism. 1991. Nighat Said Khan. 26 minutes. First Run/Icarus Films. Color, videocassette.

This film examines the inequities in Pakistan's laws, which do not distinguish among rape, adultery, and fornication. Under these laws, the testimony of two women is valued as equal to that of one man. A rape victim can be charged with having extramarital sex under Islamic law. In examining these contradictions in the law, the film introduces women's movements such as the Women's Action Forum and the Sindihani Tareeq, organizations that are attempting to battle the severe discrimination facing Pakistani women.

Japan. 1987. Peter Spry-Leverton. Four parts, 60 minutes each. MPI Home Video. Color, videocassette.

This four-part series explores the interplay of traditional cultural values and contemporary, high technology on Japanese society. Part 1, The Electronic Tribe, contrasts the ritualistic family and home life with present-day life in the factory setting, discussing traditional ceremonies. Part 2, The Sword and the Chrysanthemum, discusses the Samurai warriors' influence on the past and current Japanese culture. Part 3, The Legacy of the Shogun, looks at the ways in which the Shogun philosophy of hard work, discipline, and hierarchy still affect Japanese culture in terms of the crime rate, child-rearing practices, industrial acceleration, and office culture. Part 4, A Proper Place in the World, explores changes within Japan during the twentieth century, including the country's ventures in colonialism into Manchuria, its role in World War II, the military occupation by the United States, the beginning of modern industrial development, and the role of women and their economic power.

Japanese American Women: A Sense of Place. 1992. Rosanna Yamagiwa Alfaro and Leita Hagemann Luchetti. 28 minutes. Women Make Movies. Color, videocassette.

The stereotype of the polite, docile, exotic Asian woman is challenged in this documentary in which a dozen women speak about their experiences as the "model minority." The video explores the ambivalent feelings the women have toward both Japan and the United States. The underlying theme is the burden of being different, of being brought up "one of a kind" as opposed to growing up part of an ethnic community. An uneasy feeling prevails of being neither Japanese nor American, and the documentary ultimately becomes the story of Japanese American women and their search for a sense of place.

Kababaihan: Filipina Portraits. 1989. Marie Boti and Malcome Guy. 40 minutes. The Cinema Guild. Color, videocassette.

This film profiles the women activists in the Philippines who were instrumental in the overthrow of the Marcos regime. Included are interviews with women from varying backgrounds and political ideologies, from grassroots community organizers to the heads of the national women's association, Gabriela.

Kamala and Raji: A Film About Two of India's Working Women. 1991. Michael Camerini and Shari Robertson. 46 minutes. Documentary Educational Resources. Color, 16-mm and videocassette.

Kamala and Raji, two working women carving out a place for themselves in contemporary India, tell their own stories without the aid of external narration. Kamala is an organizer for the Self-Employed Women's Association (SEWA), unhappily married to an irresponsible and often abusive husband. Raji, happily married, is a vegetable seller who doubles as a SEWA representative. The two women come to the organization from very different experiences, but with the same sense of determination and fervor. In telling their stories, the women discuss marriage, women's rights, justice, and their personal failures and successes. In the process India comes alive for the viewer, and the experiences of Kamala and Raji become a mirror for the ongoing transformation of Indian cultures.

Khush. 1991. Prathiba Parmar. 24 minutes. Women Make Movies. Color, 16-mm and videocassette.

Khush means "ecstatic pleasure" in Urdu. For South Asian lesbians and gay men in Britain, North America, and India (where homosexuality is still illegal) the term captures the intricacies of being queer and of color. Inspiring testimonies bridge geographical differences to locate shared experiences of isolation and exoticization but also the unremitting joys and solidarity of being khush.

Kim Phuc. 1985. Manus van de Kamp. 26 minutes. First Run/Icarus Films. Color, videocassette.

This video focuses on Kim Phuc, who, as a small girl in 1972, became a symbol of wartime barbarity when her fleeing, napalm-seared figure was caught on newsreel camera. She returns to her village to reconstruct her story of youthful suffering and its aftermath.

Knowing Her Place. 1990. Indu Krishnan. 39 minutes. Women Make Movies. Color, videocassette.

A moving investigation of the cultural schizophrenia experienced by Vasu, an Indian woman who has spent most of her life in the United States. Vasu's relationships with family members in India and New

York reveal profound conflicts between her traditional upbringing and personal aspirations. The tape fuses photographs, verite sequences, and experimental techniques, and is useful for courses on immigration, sex roles, and the study of documentary form.

Laura the Taxi Driver (Benin). 1992. Michele Badarou, Jeanne Falade, and Noelle Laloupo. 13 minutes. Films for the Humanities and Sciences. Color, videocassette.

Laura is a pioneer in an exclusively male profession in Benin. She is a mother and taxi driver, and through her story the attitudes towards working women in Benin are presented.

Leila. 1999. Dariush Mehrjui. 102 minutes. First Run/Icarus. Color, videocassette.

This film explores the relationship between men and women in contemporary Iran. Leila, a woman from an affluent background, discovers at the start of her marriage that she cannot have children. While her husband believes they can be happy without children, his mother is less willing to accept the situation. The film traces the pressures Leila faces to convince her husband to take another wife. It portrays the clash between tradition and modern marriage, between manipulation and the power of love.

Love, Women, and Flowers. 1988. Marta Rodriguez and Jorge Silva. 58 minutes. Women Make Movies. Color, Spanish with English subtitles, videocassette.

Flowers are Colombia's third largest export. But behind the beauty of the carnations and chrysanthemums sold in the United States and Europe lies a story of hazardous labor conditions for the 60,000 women who work in the flower industry. The use of pesticides and fungicides, some banned in the developed countries that export them, has drastic health and environmental consequences. The filmmakers evoke the testimonies of the women workers and document their efforts to organize with intimacy and urgency.

Las Madres: The Mothers of Plaza de Mayo. 1985. Susana Muñoz and Lourdes Portillo. 64 minutes. Women Make Movies. Color, subtitled, 16-mm and videocassette.

This Academy Award–nominated documentary about the Argentinian mothers' movement to demand to know the fate of 30,000 "disappeared" sons and daughters remains as powerful as when it was first released. As well as giving an understanding of Argentinian history in the 1970s and 1980s, *Las Madres* shows the empowerment of women in a society where women are expected to be silent, and an important moment in the development of women's voices in the international movement for human rights.

Maids and Madams. 1985. Mira Hamermesh and Christian Wangler. 52 minutes. Filmakers Library. Color, videocassette.

A painful but excellent exploration of the relationship between Black domestic workers and white employers in South Africa during the apartheid era. Although some of the features of that relationship were shaped specifically by apartheid, the film remains relevant, and can be used in conjunction with texts like Mary Romero's *Maid in the USA* (New York: Routledge, 1992) and Judith Rollins' *Between Women: Domestics and their Employers* (Philidelphia: Temple University Press, 1985).

The Makioka Sisters. 1983. Kon Ichikawa. 140 minutes. Facets Multimedia and Tapeworm Video Distributors. Color, Japanese with English subtitles, videocassette.

This drama centers around the lives of four Japanese sisters who are daughters of an old merchant family that is unknowingly facing the end of a gentler way of life in 1938 Osaka, Japan. The sisters are heiresses to the declining family fortune and must marry well to proper husbands. The efforts of the older sisters to make matches for their younger siblings are entwined with a gradual realization on the part of the elders that the quiet way of life they love and experienced in their formative years is drawing to a close with the advent of World War II.

Mama Benz: An African Market Woman. 1995. Produced by SFINX FILM/TV. 48 minutes. Filmakers Library. Color, videocassette.

The markets of Africa are often run by strong older women who control prices and determine who can buy their goods. Thanks to their business acumen, they have amassed a great deal of wealth. These women are affectionately referred to as Mama Benz, because each one has as her trademark a prized possession, a chauffeured Mercedes Benz. This film focuses on one woman who presides over the cloth market in Lomé, Togo.

As the Mirror Burns. 1990. Di Bretherton and Cristina Pozzan. 58 minutes. Women Make Movies. Color, videocassette.

Most representations of the Viet Nam War show women as innocent bystanders who sometimes became caught up in the conflict but were otherwise uninvolved. This video is designed to redress this misconception. It is estimated that over 70 percent of the guerrilla forces in the war were women not victims but who were active participants in the struggle against foreign domination. The video also shows how the war still shapes Vietnamese women's lives as they continue their work in the fields and factories, on the roads, and in their homes.

Mitsuye and Nellie: Asian American Poets. 1981. Allie Light and Irving Saraf. 58 minutes. Women Make Movies. Color, 16-mm and videocassette.

This documentary examines the lives of Asian Americans through the inspirational poetry of Mitsuye Yamada and Nellie Wong. Interviews, rare archival footage, intimate family scenes, and a lively dialogue between these fascinating women underscore different histories of Chinese and Japanese Americans, but also their shared experiences of biculturalism and generational differences.

Modern Heroes, Modern Slaves. 1998. Production Multi-Monde. 45 minutes. Filmakers Library. Color, videocassette.

Exploring the lives of Filipina women who have been recruited in over-seas domestic work, the film reveals the human costs of this organized labor trade. It underscores the government's role in recruiting women to an industry that sustains the Philippine economy, and points out the government's refusal to prevent the abuse and exploitation. The film also outlines the shifts in gender roles and family organization result-ing from women's efforts to redress the situation.

Monday's Girls. 1993. Ngozi Onwurah. 50 minutes. Women Make Movies. Color, French with English subtitles, videocassette.

Monday's Girls explores the conflict between modern individualism and traditional communities in today's Nigeria through the eyes of two young Waikiriki women from the Niger Delta. Although both come from leading families in the same large island town, Florence looks at the women's initiation ceremony as an honor, while Azikiwe, who has lived in the city for ten years, sees it as an indignity. Director Ngozi Onwurah, herself an Anglo-Nigerian, turns a wry but sympa-thetic eye on the cross-cultural confusions.

In My Country: An International Perspective on Gender. 1993. Ron J. Hammond. 88 minutes. Insight Media. Color, videocassette.

Contents: part 1—daily life; part 2—social issues. Respondents from thirteen different countries offer a personal perspective on life in their cultures with regard to gender. Countries represented include Sweden, Taiwan, Mexico, Fiji, India, St. Vincent (Caribbean), Israel, Lebanon, Zaire, England, China, El Salvador, and Japan. Available with a study guide.

My Home, My Prison. 1992. Erica Marcus and Susana Blaustein Muñoz. 66 minutes. Women Make Movies. Color, Arabic with English subtitles, 16-mm and videocassette.

This film is an uplifting and inspirational documentary based on the autobiography of Palestinian peace activist and journalist Raymonds Hawa Tawil. Set against the backdrop of the last fifty years of Israeli-Palestinian conflict, the film provides a deep understanding of some of the challenges to be faced to bring peace to the Middle East.

Naked Spaces: Living Is Round. 1985. Trinh T. Minh-ha and Jean-Paul Bourdier. 135 minutes. Women Make Movies. Color, 16-mm and videocassette.

This film explores the rhythm and ritual of life in the rural environments of six West African countries (Mauritania, Mali, Burkina Faso, Togo, Benin, and Senegal). The nonlinear structure of the film challenges the traditions of ethnographic filmmaking, while sensuous sights and sounds lead the viewer on a poetic journey to remote locations and show the private interaction of people in their living space.

In the Name of God: Changing Attitudes Towards Mutilation. 1995. Cadmos Film. 29 minutes. Filmakers Library. Color, videocassette.

The film centers on the Fistula Hospital in Addis Ababa, Ethiopia, one of the few places giving medical care to victims of infibulation. It explores the hospital's attempts to train patients to assist doctors in repairing the damages to other women. Overall, it provides a view of Ethiopian women who have started to protest the tradition by their activism, which includes handing out information in schools.

New View/New Eyes. 1993. Gitanjali (aka Gita Saxena). 50 minutes (20-minute version also available). Women Make Movies. Color, 16-mm and videocassette.

An inventive twist on the travelogue, this poetic essay engages the viewer intellectually, aesthetically, and emotionally to reflect on home, migration, and the function of art making. The director takes her aunt and uncle on a trip to Honest Ed's Department Store in Toronto, and herself on a trip to India to meet her father's family. Although India is in no simple way her "home," neither can she hide behind the tourist's camera.

Nice Colored Girls. 1987. Tracey Moffatt. 16 minutes. Women Make Movies. Color, 16-mm and videocassette.

This film explores the history of exploitation between white men and Aboriginal women in Australia, juxtaposing the "first encounter" between colonizers and native women with the attempts of modern urban Aboriginal women to reverse their fortunes.

Night Cries: A Rural Tragedy. 1990. Tracey Moffatt. 19 minutes. Women Make Movies. Color, 35-mm, 16-mm, and videocassette.

On an isolated, surreal Australian homestead, a middle-aged Aboriginal woman nurses her dying white mother. The adopted daughter's attentive gestures mask an almost palpable hostility. Their story alludes to the assimilation policy that forced Aboriginal children to be raised in white families. This stark drama unfolds without dialogue against vivid painted sets as the crooning of an Aboriginal Christian singer provides ironic counterpoint.

No Longer Silent. 1986. Laurette Deschamps. 57 minutes. National Film Board of Canada. Color, videocassette.

This award-winning documentary focuses on feminists in India who are leading the struggle against injustices in their society: bride burning and dowry abuse, abortion of females, and second-rate health care and nutrition, contrasting them with media ads featuring well-dressed, successful women. It also includes a profile of an Indian activist working for the United Nations in the area of rural development.

Not the Numbers Game Series. 1996. Produced by Emily Marlow and Jenny Richards for TVE and BBC. Six 10-minute segments, one edited 44-minute film. Bullfrog Films. Color, videocassette.

The series explores issues that were raised by the 1994 United Nations Cairo Conference on Population and Development. Made by women filmmakers from different countries, the series covers women in India who are demanding the basic services they need for a dignified life, women in Uganda who are calling a halt to the practice of female genital mutilation, women of Bosnia who are struggling to rebuild their lives after the civil war, and features on teenage pregnancy in Peru, industrial employment in Indonesia, and the status of women in postwar Cambodia.

Once This Land Was Ours. 1991. Shikha Jhingan. 19 minutes. Women Make Movies. Color, with English subtitles, videocassette.

This poetic documentary depicts women agriculture workers in India and their struggle to provide for their families. Although they work to produce food for others, they have increasing difficulties feeding their own children. Through moving testimonies and images of the women at work, the tape explores the feminization of poverty in rural India. Particularly useful for discussions about Third World development and women's labor.

Palenque: Un canto. 1992. Maria Raquel Bozzi. 48 minutes. New Day Films. Color, videocassette.

Also called *African Heritage of a Colombian Village.* This film examines the daily life of the villagers of San Basilio de Palenque, Colombia, where the descendants of rebel African slaves still live by, and cherish, their African traditions.

Perhaps Women Are More Economical. 1987. Southeast Asia Collection. 30 minutes. Cornell University. Color, videocassette.

This documentary provides a look at women batik workers in Java and their working conditions, examining both environment and pay. The film asks the question if it is fair to pay women lower wages simply because they are women, even though their work is of the same caliber as men's.

A Place of Rage. 1991. Pratibha Parmar. 52 minutes. Women Make Movies. Color, 16-mm and videocassette.

This celebration of African American women and their achievements features interviews with Angela Davis, June Jordan, and Alice Walker. Within the context of civil rights, Black power, and the feminist movements, the trio reassess how women such as Rosa Parks and Fannie Lou Hamer revolutionized American society.

Pull Ourselves up or Die out: A Field Report. 1985. John Marshall and Claire Ritchie. 26 minutes. Documentary Educational Resources. Color, videocassette.

This film is a field report on the !Kung San people in Namibia between 1980 and 1984, and their experiences of culture shock as they adapt to a cash-based economy, herd-based work, and clash with other groups over water rights.

Quartier Mozart. 1992. Jean-Pierre Bekolo. 80 minutes. Kino on Video. Color, French with English subtitles, videocassette.

This movie is a sexual farce using traditional Cameroonian folk beliefs to explore the sexual politics of an urban neighborhood in Yaounde, Cameroon's capital. Presenting the assimilation of African American pop culture into African traditions, it portrays forty-eight hours in the education of a young schoolgirl. A local sorceress uses witchcraft to give her a first-hand look at sexual politics by having the girl, still proud like a woman who has never known a man, enter the body of a boy struggling to find his place in the male hierarchy established by neighborhood Casanovas.

Que bom te ver viva (*How Nice to See You Alive*). 1989. Lucia Murat. 99 minutes. Women Make Movies. Color, Portuguese with English subtitles, videocassette.

Interviews with women who survived torture and imprisonment for political offenses following the Brazilian military coup of 1968; interspersed with a fictional dramatization of the life of such a survivor.

A Question of Rights Series. 1988. Produced by Emily Marlow, a Television Trust for the Environment Series. 72 minutes, 10 short films. Bullfrog Films. Color, videocassette.

The series of ten works by women filmmakers explores what governments, communities, NGOs, and individuals around the world are doing to recognize and ensure women's rights. Introduced by Bella Abzug, who traces the international agreements on women's rights, the series includes five short films made by women filmmakers. Topics of the films are the sex industry in Latvia, prostitution in Fiji, sexual violence in the Caribbean, and the prevalence of child marriage in different regions.

Rate It X. 1986. Lucy Winer, Lynn Campbell, Claudette Charbonneau, and Paula De Koenigsberg. 93 minutes. Women Make Movies. Color, 16-mm and videocassette.

What do men really think of women? This provocative, highly acclaimed documentary confronts sexism in the United States. A series of disturbing, though sometimes amusing, portraits uncover obvious culprits such as advertising firms and porn shops as well as often overlooked pockets of sexist imagery that promote gender stereotyping and reinforce negative conceptions of women and sexuality. With humor and compassion, the film reveals men's deeply imbedded attitudes, showing how sexism becomes rationalized through commerce, religion, and social values. Controversial upon its release, this film is a challenging, invaluable piece of work that illuminates crucial elements of censorship, advertising, pornography, and violence against women.

Reassemblage. 1982. Trinh T. Minh-ha. 40 minutes. Women Make Movies. Color, 16-mm and videocassette.
Women are the focus but not the object of Trinh T. Minh-ha's influential first film, a complex visual study of the women of rural Senegal. Through a complicity of interaction between film and spectator, this work reflects on documentary filmmaking and the ethnographic representation of cultures.

Rights of Passage. 1999. Diane Best. 30 minutes. Filmakers Library. Color, videocassette.

Through the stories of four young women coming of age in different parts of the world, the film explores how puberty affects individual women's lives. Filmed in Nicaragua, India, Jamaica, and Burkina Faso, it allows adolescent girls to speak for themselves and reveals the vulnerability of young women in societies where their horizons are limited to physical labor and child bearing.

Rising Above: Women of Vietnam. 1995. Heiny Srour. 50 minutes. Bullfrog Films. Color, videocassette.

In the long years of war against France and the United States, Vietnamese women attained some equality as they fought alongside men. But twenty years after the signing of the peace agreement, the revival of Confucianism and the spread of market forces are conspiring to relegate women to the role of second class citizens. This film looks at what has happened since the war to five women who became prominent for their efforts on behalf of their country during the war.

Rites. 1991. Penny Dedman, Debra Michaels, and Nawal El Saadawi. 52 minutes. Filmakers Library. Color, videocassette.

This video strives to give a balanced exploration of female circumcision historically and today, both in Western cultures and in Africa and the Middle East. It examines the cosmetic, punitive, and ritual contexts for this practice, as well as its current construction in fierce attacks by Western observers and in responses that view such attacks as examples of cultural imperialism.

Sa-I-Gu. 1993. Dai Sil Kim-Gibson. 41 minutes. National Asian American Telecommunications Association. Color, videocassette.

This movie explores the embittering effect of the Rodney King verdict and riot of April 29, 1992, on Korean American women shopkeepers, who suffered more than half of the material losses in the conflict. Interviews conducted three months after the riots with several Korean American women shopkeepers illustrate their experiences and feelings about the rioting and their relations with African Americans.

Scraps of Life. 1992. Gayla Jamison. 28 minutes. Filmakers Library. Color, videocassette.

Two thousand people were murdered in Chile during the Pinochet years, according to official government statistics. Although the dictatorship finally came to an end, it left a legacy of bereavement. Surviving women came together to demand truth and justice from the new government. Sewing murals out of scraps of fabrics, called arpilleras, they established a new art form that has recorded Chile's history of oppression and memorialized those who were disappeared.

Samsara: Death and Rebirth in Cambodia. 1989. Ellen Bruno. 28 minutes. (Samsara) Film Library 22-D. Color, videocassette.

Using prophecies, Buddhist teachings, folklore, and dreams to describe Cambodians' worldviews, this film documents the suffering, loss, and rebirth of the Cambodian people in the aftermath of the takeover of their country by Pol Pot and the Khmer Rouge revolutionary forces and the subsequent invasion of Cambodia by Viet Nam. Although not focusing centrally on women, numerous scenes present women's experiences.

Senso Daughters: Daughters of War. 1990. Noriko Sekiguchi. 54 minutes. First Run/Icarus Films. Color, videocassette.

This film tells the story of Japanese and Korean women brought to Papua New Guinea by Japan as "military commodities" during the Japanese campaign in World War II from 1942 to 1945.

Shoot for the Contents. 1991. Trinh T. Minh-ha and Jean-Paul Bourdier. 101 minutes. Women Make Movies. Color, 16-mm and videocassette.

This film is a unique excursion into the maze of allegorical naming and storytelling in China. The film ponders questions of power and change, politics and culture, as refracted by the 1989 events in Tiananmen Square. At the same time, it offers an inquiry into the creative process of filmmaking, intricately layering Chinese popular songs and classical music, the sayings of Mao and Confucius, women's voices, and the words of artists, philosophers and other cultural workers. Exploring color, rhythm, and the changing relationship between ear and eye, this documentary realizes on the screen the shifts of interpretation in contemporary Chinese culture and politics.

Sin City Diary. 1992. Rachel Rivera. 29 minutes. Women Make Movies. Color, Tagalog with English subtitles, videocassette.

This powerful film explores the lives of women who work as prostitutes around the U.S. Navy base at Subic Bay in the Philippines. The program takes the form of a diary to incorporate Rachel Rivera's own experience as a Filipina American. It raises important questions about America's responsibility to its former colony, and the complex relationship between women, prostitutes, militarism, international relations, and the economy.

Sisters in the Struggle. 1991. Dionne Brand. 50 minutes. National Film Board of Canada. Color, videocassette.

This film explores the diversity, vision, and impetus of the contemporary Black women's movement in Canada. The film articulates the struggles of Black women resisting the cultural, economic, and legislative practices that subordinate them.

> *The Sky: A Silent Witness.* 1995. Midge Mackenzie. 27 minutes. Women Make Movies. Color with black and white sequences, 16-mm or videocassette; available in Spanish.

Produced in association with Amnesty International, this documentary about human rights follows a journey to reclaim the remains of 180 massacre victims. Intercut throughout the telling of this story is black and white footage of women from around the globe, including a Tibetan Buddhist nun, a Tiananmen Square demonstrator, and an African American civil rights worker, testifying about human rights abuses in their own countries.

> *Slaying the Dragon.* 1988. Deborah Gee. 58 minutes. Women Make Movies. Color with black and white sequences, videocassette.

This film describes racial and gender stereotyping of Asian women in U.S. motion pictures, television programs, commercials, newsreels, and news broadcasts. It includes interviews with Asian historians, sociologists, actors, and broadcasters.

> *Small Happiness: Women of a Chinese Village.* 1984. Carma Hinton and Richard Gordon. 59 minutes. New Day Films. Color, videocassette.

This Long Bow Group production explores the conditions of life for Chinese women in the village of Long Bow. A richly detailed portrayal of their lives, recording their frank reflections on the legacy of foot binding, the new birth control policy, work, love, and marriage.

> *A Song of Ceylon.* 1985. Laleen Jayamanne. 51 minutes. Women Make Movies. Color, 16-mm and videocassette.

A *Song of Ceylon* is a formally rigorous, visually stunning study of colonialism, gender, and the body. The title echoes the classic British documentary and evokes a country erased from the world map. The soundtrack enacts a Sri Lankan anthropological text observing a woman's ritual exorcism. Visually, the film brings together theatrical conventions and recreations of classic film stills, presenting the body in striking tableaux. This remarkable film is a provocative treatise on hybridity, hysteria, and performance.

> *And Still I Rise.* 1993. Ngozi Onwurah. 30 minutes. Women Make Movies. Color, videocassette.

This video uses images from popular culture to reveal the way the media represents Black women's sexuality. The filmmaker asserts that a combination of fear and fascination produces a stereotypical representation, which in turn impacts the real lives of women. The video intercuts historical and media images with contemporary views of African heritage as women struggle to create new and empowered perspectives.

Sugar Cane Alley. 1995. Eughon Paley. 107 minutes. Facets Multimedia, Inc. and New Yorker Video. Color, French with English subtitles, videocassette.

This feature film, set in 1930s Martinique, tells the story of a young boy from a poor community of caneworkers and his grandfather's determination to secure his education. The story raises issues of race and class relations and of cross-generational ties. For a complementary gender analysis of cross-generational ties, see Lydia Pulsipher's "He Won't Let She Stretch She Foot," in Cindi Katz and Janice Monk, eds., *Full Circles: Geographies of Women Over the Life Course* (London: Routledge, 1993).

From Sunup. 1988. Flora M'mbugu. 28 minutes. Facets Multimedia and Maryknoll World Productions. Color, videocassette.

Shot in Tanzania, this film is a candid, authentic picture of the dawn-to-dusk, life-sustaining efforts of Africans to survive and prosper. It portrays the woman's multiple roles of provider, mother, water-carrier, wood-gatherer, cook, and entrepreneur, demonstrating that each woman has to work constantly to squeeze out a meager living.

Surname Viet, Given Name Nam. 1989. Trinh T. Minh-ha. 108 minutes. Women Make Movies. Color with black and white sequences, 16-mm and videocassette.

This film explores the role of Vietnamese women historically and in contemporary society using dance, printed texts, folk poetry, and the words and experiences of Vietnamese women in Viet Nam (both North and South) and in the United States. Trinh Minh-ha's experimental, postmodern style is difficult for some, but her films repay careful study.

Susana. 1980. Susana Muñoz. 25 minutes. Women Make Movies. Black and white, 16-mm and videocassette.

This film is an autobiographical portrait of a woman who leaves Argentina to get away from the strictures of Latin American cultural and family pressures. It addresses the junctures of racism, sexism, and homophobia both in the United States and Latin America.

The Tenth Dancer. 1993. Sally Ingleton. 52 minutes. Women Make Movies. Color, French with English subtitles, 16-mm and videocassette.

This film provides a window on women's lives in Cambodia, a country under cultural and political reconstruction following the brutal Pol Pot regime. Under Pol Pot over 90 percent of Cambodia's artists were killed, including most of the classical dancers of the Royal Court Ballet. This poignant portrait is the story of one of the 10 percent who survived and her relationship with her pupil. It is a tale of human dignity and a testament to the critical role culture plays in rebuilding society in Cambodia.

Three Generations of Javanese Women. 1984. Martha Stuart Productions. 29 minutes. Communication for Change. Color, 3/4 inch U-matic cassette or 2-inch quadraplex open reel.

In this film, rural Javanese women openly discuss their sex roles, family lives, village society, and how the use of contraception has changed their lives by giving both wife and husband a feeling of liberation.

Times of Darkness. 1997. Karoline Frogner. 90 minutes. Women Make Movies. Color, Norwegian with English subtitles, 35-mm or videocassette.

This film tells the rarely heard story of women's survival and resistance in German-occupied countries during World War II. While testimony and dramatic reenactments combine in a detailed evocation of the past, candid scenes of the film's construction break the narrative to question present-day representations of this history. In interviews, ten Norwegian Jewish and gentile women share their experiences of deportation to concentration camps for their political activities. Recalling how smuggling false papers, aiding underground radio groups, and distributing illegal newspapers led to their imprisonment, they impart the fear of having been caught and the pride of having acted. As these women describe enduring interrogations and torture while pregnant and giving birth in prison, they convey the incredible hardships faced specifically by women in the camps.

Touki-Bouki: The Journey of the Hyena. 1973. Djibril Diop Mambety, Christophe Colombe, and Moustaphe Toure. 85 minutes. Kino on Video. Color, Wolof with English subtitles, videocassette.

This feature film tells the story of two outlaw women who feel alienated from their African society, who decide to seek freedom in the flashy consumerism of European culture and embark on a quest to meet happiness in Paris. This is a Bonnie and Clyde–like story about Africans confronting the Western materialism that is sweeping aside their traditional ties and values.

The Veiled Hope: Women of Palestine. 1994. Norma Marcos. 55 minutes. Women Make Movies. Color, with English subtitles, videocassette.

This film explores the personal and political challenges facing Palestinian women through a series of portraits of women living in Gaza and the West Bank. The women explain how, in their daily lives as doctors, schoolteachers, and activists, they are working to rebuild Palestinian cultural identity. They also provide insight into the complex feelings many women have about the emergence of political Islamic movements. *The Veiled Hope* gives an in-depth analysis of the position of Palestinian women as they juggle women's and national liberation struggles.

A Veiled Revolution. 1982. Marilyn Gaunt and Elizabeth Warnock Fernea. 26 minutes. First Run/Icarus Films. Color, videocassette.

By discussing the modern Egyptian woman's decision of whether or not to wear modest dress and the veil as opposed to Western dress, this documentary deals with the changing lives of women in the Arab world by looking at the early feminists of Egypt in the 1920s who removed the veil and those who are returning to traditional Islamic dress, sometimes with full face veil and gloves. This film also discusses the proper role of women in a modern Islamic society, with specific attention to the practice of women entering mosques to hold study meetings. It considers the struggle for women's rights in Egypt within the framework of local Islamic traditions.

The Vienna Tribunal. 1994. Gerry Rogers. 48 minutes. Women Make Movies. Color, videocassette.

Highlights of moving personal testimonies at the Global Tribunal on Violations of Women's Rights—held in conjunction with the U.N. World Conference on Human Rights in Vienna in 1993—reveal why women's rights need to be seen as human rights. Made in conjunction with the Center for Women's Global Leadership at Rutgers University, *The Vienna Tribunal* is not simply a video documenting events of the past, but a thought-provoking analysis of the abuses women suffer all over the world. More extensive material from the tribunals and a more elaborate analysis is contained in the related book, *Demanding Accountability: The Global Campaign and Vienna Tribunal for Women's Human Rights* by Charlotte Bunch and Niamh Reilly (New Brunswick, N.J.: Rutgers University, Center for Women's Global Leadership, 1994).

Voices of Change. 1996. Lyn Wright and Barbara Doran. Five parts at 92 minutes total. Women Make Movies. Color, videocassette.

A wide-ranging examination both of individual activism and issues facing women worldwide, this five-part documentary offers insights into the realities of international feminism. As women discuss their work for indigenous people's and worker's rights, educational equity, and the search for free expression, they connect their activism to past and future familial and cultural traditions. Part 1, *In Australia,* is about Barbara Cummings, who grew up in a state-run mission as part of a social policy of forced assimilation. After attending the college where she had worked as a cleaning lady, she has become a leader in the Aboriginal rights movement. Part 2, *In Guatemala,* is a film about Sandra Gonzalez, who risked her life by demonstrating to bring a union to the clothing factory where she works. In part 3, *In Latvia,* Mara Kimele endures blacklisting and constant funding struggles to direct theater that nourishes the souls of her people. In part 4, *In Pakistan,* renowned lawyer and human rights activist Asthma Jahangir braves death threats to fight for the rights of rape victims, bonded laborers, and accused blasphemers. Finally, in part 5, *In Canada,* Hong Kong immigrant Tam Goosen's work as a community organizer culminates in her election as the first nonwhite school trustee in the school system attended by her sixteen-year-old daughter. Celebrating the strength and commitment of these diverse women and showing their work as part of their everyday lives, this series of films offers a uniquely detailed look at the power and diversity of international feminisms.

Voices of the Morning. 1992. Meena Nanji. 15 minutes. Women Make Movies. Color, videocassette.

Inspired by *The Hidden Face of Eve: Women in the Arab World* by Nawal El Sadaawi (London: Zed Press, 1980), *Voices of the Morning* is a poetic exploration of Muslim women's lives. It follows the socialization process of a young woman living under Orthodox Islamic law. Resisting traditional definitions of a woman's role in society as only a dutiful daughter or wife, she struggles to find a space for her existence amidst the web of conditions imposed upon her by restrictive familial and societal conventions.

Warrior Marks. 1993. Pratibha Parmar. 57 minutes. Women Make Movies. Color, video.

This controversial film about female genital mutilation in Africa records the perceptions of African American author Alice Walker and includes interviews with circumcised women, activists against female circumcision, and circumcisers. Reaction to the film among African and African American women has been very divided; many viewers have critiqued its equation of female circumcision with Walker's personal "patriarchal wound," her injured eye, and the use of a dancer motif to represent the experience of circumcised girls. Still, the film provokes important questions about how activists from different cultures can form coalitions to intervene ethically to address culturally specific practices that have harmed women.

When Shirley Met Florence. 1994. Ronit Bezalel. 28 minutes. Carousel Film & Video. Color, videocassette.

"When I first saw Shirley, I fell in love with her," exclaims Florence in describing a rich friendship that she believes "was made in heaven." Now, after a lifetime, the two Canadian women continue to cherish the ties that have bound them together for fifty-five years, and to celebrate their passion for music, which first drew them to each other.

Who's Counting? Marilyn Waring on Sex, Lies & Global Economics. 1995. Terre Nash. 94 minutes. National Film Board of Canada. Color, videocassette.

This film is based on the book *If Women Counted: A New Feminist Economics* by Marilyn Waring (San Francisco: Harper & Row, 1988). It is closed-captioned for the hearing impaired. Divided thematically into fifteen chapters, the program is an entertaining primer for anyone who suffers from what Waring refers to as "economics anxiety."

With These Hands: How Women Feed Africa. 1987. Chris Sheppard and Claude Sauvageot. 33 minutes. Filmakers Library. Color, videocassette.

Three women tell stories of the difficult lives in the farmlands of Burkina Faso, Kenya, and Zimbabwe.

Woman Being. 1997. Wen-Jie Qin. 20 minutes. Women Make Movies. Color, Chinese with English subtitles, videocassette.

In a critical examination of changing concepts of beauty in modern China, this film illustrates how a flood of Western pop culture is adversely affecting women's expectations and self-worth. Revisiting her hometown after a long absence, the videomaker traces the impact of a newly booming beauty industry in a country where thirty years ago women were beat up for wearing make-up. Combining interviews and footage from glamour photo studios and television, this film explores the rise of a new super-feminine, highly sexualized ideal for women in China.

Women, HIV and AIDS: Speaking Out in the U.K. 1992. Jayne Chard. 52 minutes. Filmakers Library. Color, videocassette.

This hard-hitting documentary grapples with the special problems of women in the AIDS epidemic, discussing a wide range of subjects such as safe sex, health care for HIV-positive women, and advocacy efforts. By filming a broad cross-section of women, the social and political implications of this disease are raised.

Women in Nicaragua: The Second Revolution. 1982. Jackie Reiter. 28 minutes. First Run/Icarus Films. Color, Spanish with English subtitles, videocassette.

This film includes interviews with Nicaraguan women in which they discuss their role in the Sandanista revolution and their continued fight against the Contras. Nicaraguan women have struggled for years to gain equality with men, and this film explores their efforts to do so and to combat machismo after the triumph of the Sandanista-led revolution in 1979. The film features an interview with Gladys Baez, the first woman to join the Sandanista guerrilla forces in the early 1960s.

Women in the Third World. 1987. Jaime Martin-Escobal. 30 minutes. PBS Home Video. Color, videocassette.

This documentary is part 4 of the film series *Global Links: Women in the Third World.* This specific installment focuses on the economic impact of women in developing countries and efforts to bring rural and urban women together in decision-making processes. This series was filmed on location in Africa, Asia, and Latin America.

The Women Next Door. 1992. Michal Aviad. 80 minutes. Women Make Movies. Color, with English subtitles, 16-mm and videocassette.

A thoughtful documentary about women in the Palestinian-Israeli conflict. Israeli director Michal Aviad was living in the United States when the Intifada broke out in the West Bank and Gaza. Filled with questions about how the occupation affected women on both sides of the conflict, she set off on a journey through Israel and the Occupied Territories with a Palestinian codirector. Their experiences suggest the consequences of living in a militarized society and the roadblocks on the path to peace, but the film also implies the potential power of alliances between women in regional conflict.

Women of Kerala. 1988. Dayal Mathur. 29 minutes. Films Incorporated Video. Color, videocassette.

This film describes a program in Kerala, a densely populated state in southern India, where in the late 1970s women instituted a combined program of contraception, voluntary sterilization, the extension of health care to impoverished areas, and increased education, which resulted in a lowered rate of infant mortality and a 40 percent drop in the birth rate.

Women of Latin America. 1998. Carmen Sarmiento García. 13 part series, 58 minutes per video. Films for the Humanities. Color, videocassette.

This series examines life in thirteen Latin American nations through the eyes of its women. We witness the women transport drugs across borders, fight in rebel armies, bear children in poverty, search for sons and daughters who have vanished during political pogroms, and generally bear the burden of living a harsh, Third-World existence. Other women—teachers, engineers, and politicians—also contribute their stories. Collectively, these diverse women paint a disturbing portrait of people struggling against all odds to survive racial and class discrimination, revolution, political injustice, and chronic economic instability.

Women of Manga (Niger). 1992. Films for the Humanities and Sciences. 12 minutes. Films for the Humanities and Sciences. Color, videocassette.

This film shows the life of the people and women of a warrior tribe whose origin is unknown and which lives today in eastern Niger. By focusing on the traditions according to which the women live, behave, and make themselves beautiful—the complicated body painting, the even more complicated hairstyles and their meanings, and the role of facial scars and jewelry, the video suggests possibilities for discussions of female aesthetics, both among these people and here in the United States, where we tattoo, pierce, and use plastic surgery.

Women of Niger. 1993. Anne Laure Folly. 26 minutes. Women Make Movies. Color, French with English subtitles, videocassette.

Niger is an Islamic country where Muslim fundamentalism clashes with the country's struggle for democracy. Women who speak out about their rights have been physically attacked and excommunicated by the ayatollahs. Working together, women are the most ardent defenders of democracy, which offers the best hope of winning the equal rights that are still denied them. This film is critical viewing for those interested in women's human rights and the impact of fundamentalism.

Women of the Earth: Australian Aborigines. 1999. 56 minutes. Films for the Humanities. Color, videocassette.

Through the eyes of Aboriginal women, this documentary addresses struggles for land rights, and the even greater struggle to retain traditional lifestyles and customs in a world that is fast disappearing. As the stories are told, ancient myths and legends including that of the Dreamtime (creation) are illuminated, and their importance in Aboriginal culture as a source of identity is stressed.

The Women Outside. 1995. J. T. Takagi and Hope Jung Park. 52 minutes. Third World Newsreel. Color, videocassette.

This documentary examines the relationship between Korean women and U.S. military men in the sex trade in Korea and in marriages. It highlights the lack of military accountability, Korean government complicity, the stigma faced by the women and their children in Korean society, issues of violence against the women, and the women's aspirations for better lives for themselves and their children.

As Women See It. 1983. 5 films, each 30 minutes. Women Make Movies. Color, 16-mm and videocassette.

This is a unique collection of films by women about women in Third World countries. *Sudesha* (by Deepa Dhanraj) tells the story of one woman involved in the Chipko environmental movement in India. *Selbe* (by Safi Faye) is a revealing documentary about daily life for women in Senegal. Combining historic newsreel footage with contemporary interviews, *Bread and Dignity* (*Pan y dignidad*) (by María José Alvarez) reviews the role of women in political struggles in Nicaragua. In *Women of El Planeta* (by Maria Barea) two women inspire the women of El Planeta in Peru to take action to solve their own community's problems. *Permissible Dreams* (by Ateyyat El-Abnoudy) is an unforgettable look at life for Egyptian women.

In Women's Hands: The Changing Roles of Women. 1992. Rachel Field and Juan Mandelbaum. 60 minutes. Annenberg/CPB Collection. Color, videocassette.

One of ten programs in the Americas series, this video, despite the broad title, focuses on Chilean politics and economics, examining women's political activism and the effects of changing political-economic regimes on women's lives. It covers the period leading up to the election of Allende's Socialist regime, the military dictatorship of Pinochet, and the early post-dictatorship years. The stories of individual women are highlighted across class and political lines, including rural and urban women, the mothers of the "disappeared," women who were tortured, organizers of community kitchens, and some of the few women who have held political office.

Women Under Siege. 1982. Marilyn Gaunt and Elizabeth Warnock Fernea. 28 minutes. First Run/Icarus Films. Color, videocassette.

Using historical footage and interviews, this film explores the lives of six Palestinian women in the town of Rashadiyah as they coped with the PLO revolution and living in refugee camps in Lebanon, including one that was bombed in June 1982.

USEFUL REFERENCE BOOKS

Women of Color: A Filmography of Minority and Third World Women. 1985. Maryann Oshana. New York: Garland.

Although over a decade old, this book provides a very thorough listing of English-language films whose characters include women of color, or white women passing for women of color. It excludes silent films, but is an excellent resource for any study of minority women's roles in Hollywood cinema.

The Women's Companion to International Film. 1990. Annette Kuhn and Susannah Redstone. Berkeley: University of California Press.

This book contains over six hundred entries by seventy-nine contributors, and ranges over a broad spectrum, both historically and geographically, to include personalities, film movements, concepts in film theory, and technical terms, all written from a feminist perspective. Entries are arranged alphabetically. The work makes an excellent reference book.

DISTRIBUTORS
Advanced Media Productions
8217 113th Street North
Seminole, Fla. 33772
Tel: (813) 319–8661
Fax: (813) 319–9386
E-mail: advmedia@gte.net

Ambrose Video Publishing, Inc.
28 West 44th Street, Suite 2100
New York, N.Y. 10036
Tel: (212) 768–7373
Toll Free: (800) 526–4663
Fax: (212) 768–9282
Home page: http://www.ambrosevideo.com

Annenberg/CPB Collection
P.O. Box 2345
South Burlington, Vt. 05407–2345
Toll Free: (800) LEARNER
Fax: (802) 864–9846

Bullfrog Films
P.O. Box 149
Oley, Pa. 19547
Tel: (610) 779–8226
Toll Free: (800) 543–3764
Fax: (610) 370–1978
E-mail: bullfrog@igc.apc.org; catalog@bullfrogfilms.com
Home page: http://www.bullfrogfilms.com

California Newsreel
149 Ninth Street
San Francisco, Calif. 94103
Tel: (415) 621–6196
Fax: (415) 621–6522
E-mail: newsreel@ix.netcom
Home page: http://www.newsreel.org

Cambridge Documentary Films, Inc.
P.O. Box 390385
Cambridge, Mass. 02139–0004
Tel: (617) 484–3993
Fax: (617) 484–0754

Carousel Film and Video
260 5th Avenue, Room 905
New York, N.Y. 10001
Tel: (212) 683–1660
Toll Free: (800) 683–1660
Fax: (212) 693–1662

The Cinema Guild
1697 Broadway, Suite 506
New York, N.Y. 10019
Tel: (212) 246–5522
Fax: (212) 246–5525
E-mail: thecinema@aol.com
Home page: http://www.cinemaguild.com

Communication for Change
147 West 22nd Street
New York, N.Y. 10011
Tel: (212) 255–2091
Fax: (212) 645–1165

Cornell University
Audio Visual Resource Center
8 Business and Technology Park
Ithaca, N.Y. 14850
Tel: (607) 255–2091
Fax: (607) 255–9946

CrossCurrent Media, NAATA
246 Ninth Street, Second Floor
San Francisco, Calif. 94103
Tel: (415) 552–9550
Fax: (415) 863–0814

Documentary Educational Resources
101 Morse Street
Watertown, Mass. 02172
Tel: (617) 926–0491
Toll Free: (800) 569–6621
Fax: (617) 936–9519
E-mail: docued@der.org
Home page: http://der.org/docued

Facets Multimedia, Inc.
1617 West Fullerton Avenue
Chicago, Ill. 60614
Tel: (312) 281–9075
Toll Free: (800) 331–6197
Fax: (312) 929–5437

Ferrero Films
908 Rhode Island Street
San Francisco, Calif. 94107

Filmakers Library, Inc.
124 East 40th Street
New York, N.Y. 10016
Tel: (212) 808–4980
Toll Free: (800) 555–9815
Fax: (212) 808–4983
E-mail: info@filmakers.com

Films for the Humanities and Sciences
P.O. Box 2053
Princeton, N.J. 08453–2053
Tel: (609) 275–1400
Toll Free: (800) 257–5126
Fax: (609) 275–3767
Home page: http://www.films.com

Films Incorporated Video
5547 North Ravenswood Avenue
Chicago, Ill. 60640–1199
Tel: (312) 878–2600
Toll Free: (800) 323–4222
Fax: (312) 878–0416

First Run/Icarus Films
153 Waverly Place
New York, N.Y. 10014
Tel: (212) 727–1711
Toll Free: (800) 876–1710
Fax: (212) 989–7649
E-mail: frif@echonyc.com

Fox/Lorber Home Video
419 Park Avenue South, 20th Floor
New York, N.Y. 10016
Tel: (212) 686–6777
Fax: (212) 685–2625
Frameline
346 Ninth Street
San Francisco, Calif. 94103
Tel: (415) 703–8650
Fax: (415) 861–1404
E-mail: frameline@aol.com

Insight Media
2162 Broadway
New York, N.Y. 10024–6642
Tel: (212) 721–6316
Fax: (212) 799–5309

International Film Bureau, Inc.
332 South Michigan Avenue
Chicago, Ill. 60604–4382
Tel: (312) 427–4545
Fax: (312) 427–4550

Women Make Movies
Distribution Department
462 Broadway, Suite 500WI
New York, N.Y. 10013
Tel: (212) 925–0606 ext. 360
Fax: (212) 925–2052
E-mail: info@wmm.com
Home page: http://www.wmm.com

ACKNOWLEDGMENTS
Sandra Shattuck, Jennifer Tersigni, and Roberta Moore contributed to earlier versions of this videography.

BIOGRAPHICAL NOTES

EDNA ACOSTA-BÉLEN is Distinguished Service Professor at the State University of New York at Albany. She is also director of the Center for Latino, Latin American, and Caribbean Studies (CELAC). Some of her publications include *Women in the Latin American Development Process* and *Researching Women in Latin America and the Caribbean*, both with C. E. Bose, and *The Puerto Rican Woman: Perspectives on Culture, History, and Society*.

HELEN RUTH ASPAAS is assistant professor of geography in the department of urban studies and planning at Virginia Commonwealth University. She first taught the course Women and the Environment at Utah State University in 1998. Her research addresses rural African women's economic roles and contributions to household survival through participation in the informal sector, as well as the multicultural dimensions of rural women's small-scale and home-based businesses in the Four Corners of the U.S. Southwest.

KATHERINE ELAINE BLISS is assistant professor of Latin American history at the University of Massachusetts, Amherst. She has published essays on gender, health, sexuality, and reformism in Mexico in *Hispanic American Historical Review, Journal of Family History,* and *Latin American Research Review.* Her book *Compromised Positions: Prostitution, Public Health, and Gender Politics in Revolutionary Mexico City* was published by Pennsylvania State University Press in 2001. She is currently researching the cultural and political history of the family planning movement in mid–twentieth-century Mexico.

A. LYNN BOLLES is professor of women's studies and affiliate faculty in anthropology at the University of Maryland. She is the author or coauthor of three books and numerous essays on women and work in Jamaica, Caribbean women's studies, African American and Afro-Caribbean women's contributions to anthropology, and gender and tourism.

MÁRIA BREWER is faculty in the department of French and Italian at the University of Minnesota. Her teaching and research interests are in modern literature, theater and performance, and literary and cultural theory. She is the author of *Claude Simon: Narrativities Without Narrative* (University of Nebraska Press, 1995).

BARBARA BURTON is a cultural anthropologist currently working as a gender and development consultant based in Washington, D.C. Her

538

research interests include migration and refugee issues, human rights, reproductive health, and violence against women. Recently she worked at the International Center for Research on Women (ICRW) as a technical analyst for a large research project on domestic violence in India and as the director of a project to apply a human rights perspective to development research.

GEETA CHOWDHRY is associate professor in the department of political science at Northern Arizona University. She has taught several graduate and undergraduate seminars, including Gender and Development, the Political Economy of Development, and the Political Economy of Hunger.

JOSEPH M. CIRRINCIONE is associate chair and associate professor in the geography department at the University of Maryland, College Park, with a joint appointment in the department of curriculum and instruction. He teaches large introductory lecture courses in geography and is responsible for undergraduate and graduate courses in social studies education. He has coauthored several articles (with Richard Farrell) on the topic of curriculum development within geography, including "The Content of the Geography Curriculum: A Teacher's Perspective" (*Social Education* 53 (2), 1989) and "Teacher Response to Competency Testing on the Maryland Test for Citizenship Skills" (*Social Education* 56 (2), 1992).

DAVID WILLIAM COHEN is professor of anthropology and history at the University of Michigan. He was formerly director of the International Institute. His teaching fields include methodology of oral history, African political culture, precolonial eastern and central Africa, history of South Africa, twentieth-century Africa, the Third World, the production of history, and the politics and sociology of research and scholarship. Recent and forthcoming publications include *The Combing of History; Burying SM: The Politics of Knowledge and the Sociology of Power in Africa* and *Exceptional Spaces: Essays in Performance and History,* both with E. S. Atieno Odhiambo; and "Reading the Minister's Remains: Investigations into the Death of the Honourable Minister John Robert Ouko in Kenya, February 1990."

JULIE K. DANIELS is a faculty member in the Century College English department in White Bear Lake, Minnesota. Her research interests include international technical communication, rhetorical theory, and feminist rhetorical practices and pedagogies.

JACQUELYN E. DAVOLI received her master of arts in women's studies from the University of Arizona. Her research interests include popular culture, the creation and maintenance of social values and norms, formation of law, and the social and legal issues of rape. Her plans for the future include pursuing a law degree and joining the world of politics.

HEATHER S. DELL is assistant professor at the University of Illinois at Springfield. Her work focuses on gender, race, and class in colonial and postcolonial India. She writes about class-based feminist interventions in prostitution and the sex workers' rights movement in Bengal.

RUTH DICKSTEIN is a social sciences librarian who specializes in women's studies at the University of Arizona. She has published two reference books and many articles relating to research in women's studies, including *Women in LC's Terms* and *An Index to Anthologies in Women's Studies: Research Across the Disci-plines, 1980–1984 and 1985–1989*. She has worked for almost twenty years with faculty participating in curriculum transformation programs. She was assisted in the preparation of this chapter by Carole Leatherwood and Xan Cloudtree, both of whom received their master's degrees in information resources and library sciences at the University of Arizona.

CAESAR FARAH is professor of Arabic and Islamic culture at the University of Minnesota and has published broadly on Islam and the history of the Near East. His interest in women's studies derives from his research and writings about women in the Arab and Islamic world, from his work to integrate gender in studies of the medieval historical legacy of Islam, and from his numerous reviews of works on gender with special reference to leaders of feminist movements in Egypt and the Syrian region.

WILMA FELICIANO, Ph.D., is associate professor of Spanish and Latin American studies at the State University of New York, New Paltz. Her research centers on drama and religious syncretism. She has published *El teatro mítico de Carlos Solórzano* (UNAM, 1995), and articles, interviews, and book reviews on Latin American and Latino dramatists. *El Apu Inca de Sapallanga,* her documentary film about a Peruvian conquest play that dates from the early 1600s, was awarded the LASA2000 Award of Merit in Film.

SUSANNA F. FERLITO is associate professor of Italian studies in the department of French and Italian at the University of Minnesota. In 2000 she published *Topographies of Desire: Manzoni, Cultural Practices and Colonial Scars* (with Peter Lang) and is currently working on a book focused on gender, race, ethnicity, and migration in the "new" Italy.

DORIS FRIEDENSOHN was professor of women's studies at New Jersey City University (formerly Jersey City State College) until her retirement in July 1998. A frequent traveler, she has lectured and consulted on program development in American studies and women's studies in Turkey, Mozambique, Austria, the Czech Republic, Nepal, Japan, Argentina, Portugal, and Guinea. She has written about interdisciplinarity, feminist pedagogy, multiculturalism, transnational American studies, and food as a yardstick of identity. She is currently at work on a food memoir, *Delicious Acts of Defiance: Tales of Eating and Everyday Life.*

MARTHA E. GEORES, an associate professor, is director of graduate studies in the geography department at the University of Maryland. She teaches courses on human dimensions of global change and a large introductory course on developing countries. She is the author of *Common Ground: The Struggle for Ownership of the Black Hills National Forest* (Rowman & Littlefield, 1996); "Surviving on a Metaphor: How 'Health Hot Springs' Created and Sustained a Town," in *Place and Health: Making Connections in Geographic Research* (Syracuse University Press, 1999); "The Historic Role of the Forest Community in Sustaining the Black Hills National Forest as a Common-Pool Resource" *(Mountain Research and Development* 18 (1), 1999), and coauthor of several chapters in books on population and environment interactions.

BEVERLY GUY-SHEFTALL is founding director of the Women's Research and Resource Center and Anna Julia Cooper Professor of Women's Studies at Spelman College. She is also founding coeditor of *SAGE: A Scholarly Journal on Black Women.* Her most recent publication is *Words of Fire: An Anthology of African American Feminist Thought* (New Press, 1995).

HELEN HENDERSON is an associate research anthropologist in the bureau of applied research in anthropology at the University of Arizona. She has conducted research on gender issues in agriculture in Niger, Burkina Faso, Mauritania, Chad, and Egypt, and on women and religion in Nigeria. She edited *Gender and Agricultural Development* (University of Arizona Press, 1995), and has published on women in agricultural education, female-headed households, applied research with female farmers, and political and cultural issues among the Onitsha Igbo of Nigeria. Currently she is writing a book on women's everyday lives in Onitsha.

NOURAY IBRYAMOVA is a Ph.D. candidate in international studies at the University of Miami. She has coauthored articles for several journals and edited books on democratization processes in Central and Eastern Europe. Her current research interests are in the fields of international relations and comparative studies, with a focus on European integration, identity, and foreign policy.

HELEN JOHNSON holds degrees from Monash University in Melbourne, Australia. There she lectured in anthropology and women's studies and was graduate coordinator of women's studies. In 2002, she began a new position as senior lecturer at the University of Queensland, Brisbane, Australia, in the faculty for social and behavioral sciences. She has received visiting scholarships at the French University of the Pacific in New Caledonia and at the University of British Columbia, Canada. Her articles have appeared in *Les Nouvelles-Calédoniennes, The Australian Journal of Anthropology, A Reader's Guide to Women's Studies,* and in a U.S. political studies work that examines changing feminist pedagogies. She is fascinated by the epistemological issues of feminist anthropology and finds her work with her women's studies colleagues stimulating in this regard.

KIMBERLY JONES is associate professor of East Asian studies at the University of Arizona, where she teaches Japanese language, linguistics, and culture. Her current research projects include a sociolinguistic investigation of how Japanese women speak in the workplace. She codirected the Global Processes, Local Lives: Comparative Approaches in Women's and Area Studies project at the University of Arizona.

LISETTE JOSEPHIDES teaches in the school of anthropological studies at Queen's University, Belfast. Previously she taught at the Universities of Papua New Guinea and Minnesota, and the London School of Economics. She earned a Ph.D. at the University of London that was based on fieldwork in the Papua New Guinea Highlands and published as *The Production of Inequality.* Recent publications on gender themes include "Disengagement and Desire: The Tactics of Everyday Life (*American Ethnologist*). Currently she is engaged in research on ethics, morality, and human rights.

AMY KAMINSKY is professor of women's studies and associate director of the Interdisciplinary Center for the Study of Global Change at the University of Minnesota. Her books include *Reading the Body Politic: Latin American Women Writers and Feminist Criticism* (1993), *Waterlilies/Flores del agua: An Anthology of Spanish Women Writers from the Fifteenth to the Nineteenth Century* (1996), and *After Exile: Writing the Latin American Diaspora* (1998).

RANJANA KHANNA is assistant professor of English at Duke University. She teaches and works on anglo- and francophone postcolonial theory and literature, psychoanalysis, and feminist theory. She has published articles on transnational feminism, psychoanalysis, autobiography, postcolonial agency, multiculturalism in an international context, postcolonial Joyce, and Algerian film. Currently she is working on two book projects: *Dark Continents: Psychoanalysis and Colonialism* and *Algeria Cuts: Women and Representation, 1830 to the Present.*

KATIE KING is associate professor of women's studies at the University of Maryland, College Park, where she teaches courses in feminist theory, art activism, lesbian and gay global formations, and cultural studies. She is the author of *Theory in Its Feminist Travels: Conversations in U.S. Women's Movements* and is currently working on a book called *Feminism and Writing Technologies.*

AMY KOERBER is a graduate student in scientific and technical communication in the rhetoric department at the University of Minnesota. Her research interests include feminist theory, rhetorical theory, and feminist critiques of science and technology.

WENDY KOLMAR is director of women's studies and associate professor of English at Drew University. She has directed curriculum transformation projects on her own campus and served as a consultant to projects on many other campuses and to the New Jersey Project on Inclusive Curriculum. With Ellen Friedman, Paula Rothenberg, and Charlie Flint, she coedited *Creating an Inclusive College Curriculum* (New York: Teachers College Press, 1996). Recently she coedited an undergraduate feminist theory reader with Fran Bartkowski and guest-edited an issue of *Women's Studies Quarterly* on women and film. She teaches the core interdisciplinary courses in Drew's undergraduate and graduate women's studies programs, as well as Victorian literature, women's literature, and Gothic and supernatural fiction.

ANDRÉ LARDINOIS is professor of ancient Greek language and literature at the Katholieke Universiteit Nijmegen in the Netherlands. He is coauthor (with T. C. Oudemans) of *Tragic Ambiguity: Anthropology, Philosophy, and Sophocles' Antigone* (Leiden, 1987). He also has published articles on Sappho, Homer, and Greek tragedy, and coedited, with Laura McClure, a collection of essays, *Making Silence Speak: Women's Voices in Greek Literature and Society* (Princeton University Press, 2001).

MARY M. LAY is professor of rhetoric and past director of the Center for Advanced Feminist Studies at the University of Minnesota. A former president of the Association of Teachers of Technical Writing, in 1994 she was named an ATTW fellow for her contributions to the association and to the discipline of technical communication. Her publications include *The Rhetoric of Midwifery* (2000), several articles on gender and scientific and technical communication in *Journal of Advanced Composition, Quarterly Journal of Speech,* and *Journal of Business and Technical Communication.* She is coeditor of *Collaborative Writing in Industry: Investigations in Theory and Practice* (1991), *Technical Communication* (1995), and *Body Talk: Rhetoric, Technology, Reproduction* (2000).

HELGA LEITNER received her Ph.D. in geography and in urban and regional planning from the University of Vienna. Currently professor of geography at the University of Minnesota, she has held visiting lectureships at the University College London, the University of Vienna, and the University of Indonesia. She has published widely on international migration, the politics of immigration and citizenship, immigrant incorporation and identities, the political economy of urban development, and political ideologies and landscapes.

DYAN ELLEN MAZURANA, Ph.D., is research scholar and faculty in women's studies at the University of Montana, Missoula. She has authored numerous publications on women, peace, and armed conflict, including, with Susan McKay, *Women and Peacebuilding* (1999) and *Raising Women's Voices for Peace* (2001). With Jane Parpart and Angela Raven-Roberts, she is coediting an international collection on gender, armed conflict, and peacekeeping. Currently, she is conducting research on girls in armed forces and armed opposition groups in Africa.

JUDITH MCDANIEL is a writer and activist who teaches at the University of Arizona. Her book, *Sanctuary: A Journey* (Firebrand Books, 1986), connects activism, theory, and art in a mixed nonfiction essay and poetry format. She is currently writing the biography of lesbian-feminist activist Barbara Deming.

S. LILY MENDOZA is assistant professor in the School of Communication at the University of Denver, where she also teaches critical intercultural communication at the Women's College. She is the author of *Between the Homeland and the Diaspora: The Politics of Theorizing Filipino and Filipino American Identities* (2001). Her current work is on the translocal narratives of Filipino women in intercultural relationships.

CECILIA MENJÍVAR, a sociologist, is associate professor in the school of justice studies at Arizona State University. She teaches courses on gender and international development, urbanization and development, international migration, and refugee studies. She has published articles on gender relations, social networks, family, and second generation immigrants; she is also the author of *Frag-mented Ties: Salvadoran Immigrant Social Networks in America* (University of California Press, 2000).

KRIS MISAGE has moved on from the political science program at the University of Minnesota to pursue an editing career in the Washington, D.C., area.

WILLIAM MISHLER is associate professor in the department of German and Scandianavian/Dutch at the University of Minnesota. He is also a faculty member in the liberal studies program, where he served as director of graduate studies. He participated in the Ways of Reading project in 1995–96.

DENISE MOGGE has a master's degree in library sciences and is affiliated with the school of information resources and library science at the University of Arizona. This is her first contribution to the field of women's studies, although she has a background in sociology that emphasized women's studies and deaf studies. She has worked as a systems librarian for the past year and is now employed as a research associate for a private company.

VALENTINE M. MOGHADAM is director of women's studies and associate professor of sociology at Illinois State University. Born in Tehran, Iran, she attended college in Canada, earned a Ph.D. in the United States, and worked as a senior researcher for the United Nations University. Her interests and publications are in gender and development, social change in the Middle East and North Africa, social movements, globalization, and transnational feminist networks. In 2001 she was awarded a fellowship at the Woodrow Wilson International Center for Scholars in Washington, D.C.

JANICE MONK is executive director of the Southwest Institute for Research on Women (SIROW) and adjunct professor of geography at the University of Arizona. Her work in curriculum transformation has focused on bringing together international and gender studies since the mid–1980s. She is active internationally within geography as coeditor of the series *International Studies of Women and Place* for Routledge (London) and through the International Geographical Union Commission on Gender and Geography.

SUJATA MOORTI is assistant professor of women's studies at Old Dominion University in Norfolk, Virginia. She is completing a book manuscript on the public sphere and television rape narratives. Her publications include "Cathartic Confessions or Emancipatory Texts: Rape Narratives on the Oprah Winfrey Show," *Social Text* 57, Winter 1998.

AMY NEWHALL was a codirector of the SIROW project Global Processes, Local Lives and director of the Center for Middle Eastern Studies. Currently she is assistant professor of Near Eastern studies at the University of Arizona. She has helped organize a number of other SIROW projects directed at internationalizing women's studies and integrating Middle Eastern studies into the undergraduate curriculum. An Islamic art historian, Newhall is interested in the social, political, and economic purposes of state patronage in the premodern Middle East.

LINDA PERSHING is director of the women's studies program at California State University, San Marcos. She earned her Ph.D. at the University of Texas at Austin in 1990. A folklore scholar and feminist theorist, she is the author of *The Ribbon Around the Pentagon: Peace by Piecemakers* (University of Tennessee Press, 1996). Her research focuses on the politics of cultural and artistic expression.

ANGELITA REYES earned her Ph.D. in comparative literature from the University of Iowa. Her areas of teaching and research are women and gender in literary studies, African cultures, and the African diaspora. In addition to numerous national fellowships and international research grants, she received a Fulbright award to the Republic of Bénin in 1997, where she taught American civilization and literature at the National University of Bénin. As a Fulbright professor, Reyes was also involved with the United States Information Agency (USIA) lecture and conference series in the Republic of Bénin, Senegal, Cote d'Ivoire, and Nigeria. Her archival research on Margaret Garner, the fugitive slave woman who inspired Toni Morrison's novel *Beloved,* appears in *Teaching the Novels of Toni Morrison.* Her publications include *Global Voices: Literatures of the Non-Western World* and *African Research in Its Political and Social Dimensions,* the forthcoming *Mothering Across Cultures: Postcolonial Representations* (University of Minnesota Press), and a number of journal articles published in the United States, Europe, and Africa.

DIANE RISKEDAHL is a graduate student in anthropology at the University of Arizona. She is interested in linguistic anthropology and the way language is used by minority groups in the Middle East and among diaspora populations residing in the United States. She holds a master's degree from the University of Colorado, Boulder, and has worked and studied in Kuwait and Lebanon. She is currently a visiting research associate at the American University of Beirut, where she is conducting dissertation research on intertextuality and oral traditions in the postwar reconstruction era in Lebanon.

DEBORAH S. ROSENFELT is professor of women's studies and director of the Curriculum Transformation Project at the University of Maryland, College Park. She writes about women's studies and curricular change in higher education, North American women's literature and culture, and the processes of social change. She directed the WSAIS project Women and Gender in an Era of Global Change: Internationalizing and "Engendering" the Curriculum (1995–97).

BARBARA RUBIN is professor emerita of women's studies at New Jersey City University. She is also cofounder and former director of the university's Speicher-Rubin Women's Center, which was named in her and cofounder Kathryn Speicher's honor. Her articles and essays on women's movements in Israel, Italy, the Netherlands, Bulgaria, and the People's Republic of China have appeared in a variety of journals and magazines including *Women's Studies Quarterly* and *Response: An Intellectual Jewish Review.* She has also published in the field of intergenerational studies, having coauthored *Children and Sex: The Parents Speak* (Facts on File). Throughout her career, she has lectured extensively in the United States and abroad on contemporary U.S. women's issues.

JOSEPH CHRISTOPHER SCHAUB is assistant professor of media studies at Fort Lewis College in Durango, Colorado. Previous publications include "Presenting the Cyborg's Futurist Past" for *Postmodern Culture;* "Microcinemania: The Mansion Theater and Underground Movie Making in Baltimore, Maryland, USA"; and "Generation Feminine: The Evolution of Women's Roles in Two Films by Masayuki Suo" in a special issue of *Post Script.*

NAOMI B. SCHEMAN is professor of philosophy and women's studies and an associate dean in the graduate school at the University of Minnesota. A collection of her essays in feminist epistemology, *Engenderings: Constructions of Knowledge, Authority, and Privilege,* was published by Routledge in 1993. She teaches and writes about the ways in which selves—especially as knowers—are constructed in relation to systems of privilege and through liberatory struggle.

SANDRA D. SHATTUCK is associate director of the Center for Women and Inform-ation Technology (www.umbc.edu/cwit) at the University of Maryland, Baltimore County. Her research interests include the ways in which theories of multiculturalism, postcolonial studies, and feminist literary criticism intersect. Her practice as a teacher includes experimental, critical, and feminist pedagogies, as well as investigations into the various uses of information technology and its efficacy in the classroom.

ERIC SHEPPARD is professor of geography at the University of Minnesota. He has published *The Capitalist Space Economy* (with T. J. Barnes, 1990); *A World of Difference* (with P. W. Porter, 1998); *A Companion to Economic Geography* (with T. J. Barnes, 2000); and over sixty refereed articles and book chapters. He has held visiting appointments at the International Institute for Applied Systems Analysis (Austria), University College London, the University of Indonesia, the University of Melbourne, and the University of Vienna. He has served as editor of *Antipode* and *Environment and Planning,* and he has worked for the U.S. National Science Foundation, the National Council of Geographic Education, and the National Research Council. He has conducted fieldwork in Indonesia, Europe, Latin America, Africa, the Middle East, and East Asia.

EILEEN B. SIVERT is associate professor of French at the University of Minnesota. Her teaching and research interests include nineteenth-century French literature and Quebec women writers. She has published articles on such authors as Honore de Balzac, Prosper Mérimée, Jules Barbey d'Aurevilly, and George Sand, as well as Marie-Claire Blais, Josette Marchessault, and Ying Chen. She is currently working on a book about women novelists of Quebec.

FILOMINA CHIOMA STEADY received her Ph.D. in social anthropology from Oxford University. She is currently professor and chair of Africana studies at Wellesley College and fellow at the Institute for Environmental Studies, University of Wisconsin–Madison. She has taught at Yale University, Boston University, Wesleyan University, of Sierra Leone, and was also chair of women's studies at California State University in Sacramento. She was the Special Advisor on Women, the Environment and Development to the United Nations for the 1992 Earth Summit and has served as consultant to several United Nations Agencies. She has published widely on women in the African diaspora, gender and development, women and the environment. Her publications include *Women and Children First: Environment, Poverty and Sustainable Development* and *Women and the Amistad Connection: Sierra Leone Krio Society.*

ABIGAIL J. STEWART is professor of psychology and women's studies at the University of Michigan; and formerly director of the Institute for Research on Women and Gender. With degrees from Wesleyan University, the London School of Economics, and Harvard University, she has published over ninety scholarly articles and several books, focusing on the psychology of women's lives, personality, and adaptation to change, and the intersection of individual development and social history. She has recently coedited several interdisciplinary volumes, including *Theorizing Feminism: Parallel Trends in the Humanities and Social Sciences* (with Anne Herrmann); *Women Creating Lives: Identities, Resilience, and Resistance* (with Carol E. Franz); and *Feminisms in the Academy* (with Domna C. Stanton). Most recently she published *Separating Together,* a study of the process of family transformation after divorce. Her current research focuses on comparative analyses of longitudinal studies of educated women's lives and personalities.

CONSTANCE A. SULLIVAN is associate professor of Spanish literature and culture at the University of Minnesota. Her research and teaching focuses on cultural discourses of Spain from the eighteenth to the twentieth century, with special emphasis on feminist criticism and women writers. Her most recent project is a biography of the Enlightenment feminist essayist Josefa Amar y Borbón.

ISABEL VALIELA is assistant professor of Spanish at Gettysburg College and also teaches on a rotating basis in the women's studies program. Her areas of research in women's studies include Latin America, the Caribbean, and their diaspora in the United States. Most recently, she co-coordinated and participated in a workshop on feminist theory in Haiti at the invitation of ENFOFANM, one of the most active women's organizations in Port-au-Prince.

MARGARET WADE is a struggling artist and writer in Portland, Oregon, where she is also a program coordinator for the statewide community-building nonprofit organization SOLV.

CYNTHIA A. WOOD is associate professor of interdisciplinary studies at Appalachian State University. She received her Ph.D. in economics from the University of Texas at Austin. Her work has appeared in *Feminist Economics,* and her research interests include gender and development, Latin American economics, and postcolonial feminist theory.

JACQUELYN N. ZITA is former chair of the women's studies department at University of Minnesota. She is also cochair of the National Women's Studies Association (NWSA) Program Administration and Development Committee, and was site-coordinator chair for NWSA 2001. Her research areas include feminist theory and philosophy, biology and the body, and ecology. Currently she is working on a book entitled *Women's Studies as Interdiscipline.*

INDEX

hooks, bell (*continued*)
alternative epistemologies, 407;
on multiculturalism, 288; on
"womanist," 77 n.12
households, 375
House on Mango Street, The
(Cisneros), 356
House on the Lagoon, The
(Ferré), 359
Hudson-Weems, Clenora, 76–77
n.11
Human Geography (course), 8,
203–9; syllabus, 209–14

I, Rigoberta Menchú (Menchú),
302, 304, 357–58
identity, 3, 5, 289; U. S. categories
of, 73–74
Identity Politics and Women
(Moghadam), 170, 173, 219
Igbo women, 69. *See also* lesbians
immigrant, defined, 63 n.1
immigration *(see also* migration);
and area studies, 61; Gender and
Development (course), 145–46;
Latino(a), 46; public debates
about, 61–62
India, 399; dowry violence in, 8,
273, 274–78, 283; reproductive
policies in, 293; Uniform Civil
Code in, 141, 142
Industrial Revolution, 52
infanticide. *See* female infanticide
information technologies, 52, 85
Inhabited Woman, The (Belli), 357
*In Search of Our Mothers' Gardens:
Womanist Prose* (Walker), 74
Institute for Research on Women
(IROW), 64 n.7
Institute for Research on Women
and Gender, 440
International Feminist Theory
(course), 245–50; syllabus,
251–64
International Fund for Agricultural
Development (IFAD), 374
International Interdisciplinary Con-
ferences in Women's Studies, 2
Internationalizing Feminist
Pedagogies (course): elements of,
311–12; mastery, 313; reinscribing

colonial relationships, 312;
syllabus, 314–21
international studies: in curriculum,
443–45; feminist approach,
153–61; provincialization of,
21–23; theory, 6, 7; women's
or gender studies, 445–47
International Women's Year
Conference, 54
Internet. *See* World Wide Web
Introduction to Women's Studies
(course), 420, 421–22; Third
World women, 421
Italian Diaspora (course), 180–83;
syllabus, 183–88

Jackson, Bailey W., 409
Jane Collective, Chicago, 266
Japan, 398
Johnson, Helen, 9
Johnson-Odim, Cheryl, 357
Jonas, Suzanne, 50
Jones, Kimberly, 11, 12, 432
Joshi, Rama, 273, 274
Judaic studies, 32–33
jute mills, 83–84

Kabeer, Naila, 138
Kaminsky, Amy, 9
Kampen, Natalie, 247–48,
336, 422
Kaplan, Caren, 170, 171
Keller, Evelyn Fox, 82
Kendall, K. Limakatso, 72
Kenya, 15, 414
Kikuyu ethnic group, 414, 415, 416
Kim, Seung-kyung, 425, 429
Kincaid, Jamaica, 169
King, Katie, 5
Kinzer, Stephen, 326
Kirby, Vicki, 288
Kishwar, Madhu, 274
knowledge: multicultural cross-
overs, 57–58, 64 n.5; restructuring,
53–54
Koerber, Amy, 5
Kolmar, Wendy, 12, 452
Kumar, Radha, 277

labor: and environment, 227–29;
gendered division, 226

resource mobilization theory, 216
resources, electronic, 13; discussion groups or listservs, 474–75; electronic indexes, 475–77; electronic journals, 477–79; evaluating websites, 479–81; FAQS, 469; guides for using, 468–69; sources for ongoing information, 469–70; women and the World Wide Web, 470–74
resources, film, 500–537
Return of the Gospel Gems, The (Bryant), 439
Rich, Adrienne, 409
Richlin, Amy, 338
Rio Earth Summit, 229
Riskedahl, Diane, 14
Rites, 456
Robins, Kevin, 103, 107, 109, 114, 118
Rockefeller Foundation, 27
Rosaldo, Renato, 461
"Rosario Ferré's Crossover Writing" (Acosta-Belén), 359
Rosenfelt, Deborah S., 7, 11, 12, 14, 452
Rosenmeyer, Patricia, 338
Rosewood, 280
Rubin, Barbara, 9
Russian Institute, 27
Russian Research Center, 27
Rwanda, 398

Sachs, Carolyn, 144
SAGE: A Scholarly Journal on Black Women, 67
Said, Edward, 23, 139
Sandoval, Chela, 118
Sanger, Margaret, 126
Santiago, Esmeralda, 58, 358, 359, 360
Santiago, Petra, 95
Sapir, Edward, 26
Sappho, 337–38
Sarris, Terri, 438
sati, 290, 291, 453, 456
Scattered Hegemonies (Grewal and Kaplan), 170
Schaub, Joseph Christopher, 14
Scheman, Naomi B., 8, 245
Schenker, Alexander, 37
science and technology, 4, 226; feminist standpoint theory, 93; and production and processing, 87–88;

reproductive technologies, 81, 86–87; Western philosophy, 90–91; and women's lives, 5, 81–84, 89, 96; workplace and home, 84–85
Scientific Revolution, 90–91
Scott, Joan, 96
Second Wave, The (Nicholson), 236–37
Secret Daughter, 438
self-reflexivity, 246, 248–49
Sen, Gita, 302
separatism, 266–67
sexism, 8–9; and racism, 272, 280–81, 282–83 *(see also* racialized misogyny)
sexual abuse, black women and, 281, 282
sexual harassment, 279, 281
sexuality: gender research, 69–73; relative and relational, 109–10
"Sexual Politics of Black Womanhood, The" (Collins), 280
Seydoux, Nicolas, 105, 110, 114
Shattuck, Sandra D., 12, 14, 432
Sheppard, Eric, 8
Shiva, Vandana, 88–89
Shohat, Ella, 171, 172
Shrewsbury, Carolyn, 288
Sim, Cecilia Ng Choon, 85
Singapore, 293
Sisters of the Earth (Anderson), 162, 163
Sistren, 172–73
Skeggs, Beverley, 293
slash, 111–12
Small Happiness, 292
Small Place, A (Kincaid), 169
Smelser, Neil, 216, 221
social movements, 8; *(see also* activism); cross-border, 51, 52–53; defined, 215, 221; fundamentalist, 219; research, 215–16; theories, 216–17, 221; women and gender issues, 215; women's movements, 217–18
social reform, 192–94; Latin America, 7–8, 189–91, 193–94
Social Science Research Council (SSRC), 25, 29–30; Committee on World Regions, 25
social sciences, 26–27